Sourcebook of the Structures and Styles in John 1–10

Sourcebook of the Structures and Styles in John 1–10

The Johannine Parallelisms and Chiasms

Sang-Hoon Kim

WIPF & STOCK · Eugene, Oregon

SOURCEBOOK OF THE STRUCTURES AND STYLES IN JOHN 1–10
The Johannine Parallelisms and Chiasms

Copyright © 2014 Sang-Hoon Kim. All rights reserved. Except for brief quotations in critical publications or reviews, no part of this book may be reproduced in any manner without prior written permission from the publisher. Write: Permissions, Wipf and Stock Publishers, 199 W. 8th Ave., Suite 3, Eugene, OR 97401.

Wipf & Stock
An Imprint of Wipf and Stock Publishers
199 W. 8th Ave., Suite 3
Eugene, OR 97401

www.wipfandstock.com

ISBN 13: 978-1-62564-492-3

Manufactured in the U.S.A.

Contents

Preface: A Journey in John   *vii*

Acknowledgments   *xi*

Abbreviations   *xiii*

Introduction   1

The Structure of John   21

1. The Prologue and the Early Testimonies   37
2. The Cana Miracle and the Cleansing of the Temple   74
3. Two Dialogues with Discourses   88
4. The Samaritans and a Royal Official   111
5. The First Sabbath Healing and the Discourse of Jesus   138
6. "I Am the Bread of Life"   169
7. Who Is He and Where Is He From?   207
8. "I Am the Light of the World," I   233
9. "I Am the Light of the World," II   269
10. The Shepherd and the Sheep   292

Bibliography   317

Preface

A Journey in John

In 1982, I graduated from university and entered a theological seminary. Two experiences to that point would prove essential to my future Johannine studies. First, I had developed a deep concern about syntax theory (one among a number of subjects within my English literature and linguistics major at the university) because this theory, based on Noam Chomsky, was so logical and even mathematical to me. Second, I had devoted myself to Christian youth ministry, IVCF, where I had learned and practiced inductive Bible study, which became my strong point after entering the seminary and during the following years. It was not known to me then that these two tools would come to have such significant value with regard to my future career.

During my seminary years, I had many opportunities to teach students how to study the Bible inductively, as well as to preach expository sermons. After graduating from seminary, I served as a staff member of IVCF for a few years and then joined a Bible teaching movement, with some professors, which became the Seoul Bible Institute. In this institute, I served as the person in charge of administration and also gave a few lectures, such as inductive Bible study and expository preaching, as well as inductive study–related lectures on various books in the New Testament. Around 1987, the books of Kaiser, Stuart, and Fee, which were based on syntactic theory and its analysis, were first introduced to me, and I felt surprised for two reasons: first, I was so acquainted with their linguistic methods that I easily recognized them; second, I found that those methods would be effective if I applied them to my inductive way of Bible study. I applied the syntactic method of analysis to inductive study, specifically the Korean Bible, not adopting those methods directly, rather reorganizing and applying them according to the Korean syntactic system. It was a success in terms of its efficiency and the practicality of the method because I realized that the inductive method was somewhat more accurate, making the contents comprehensible, easy to grasp, even visualizable. That was in 1988.

The second opportunity at that time was given to me when I got to use the Apple II, an 8-bit computer with an external 5 1/4-inch breakable, floppy disk drive. That was 1987. Since then, it can be said that I came to recognize the interactivity between the user and the computer, and also between the components of the computer, which are interconnected. Whenever I needed to upgrade it, I had to buy the parts and put them into the computer by myself to reduce the cost. In the event of any trouble, whether of software or hardware, it meant that it demanded a lot of patience to fix or to resettle (including booting and resetting) it. Without proper knowledge of how the computer works and how the components are interrelated, trouble in the machine would never have been resolved.

In 1992, I opened my class on the inductive study of 1 John for church ministers, helping them to study the text and create their own expository sermons. It was an intensive course with some practice. Those who participated in the course showed satisfactory responses, but I was not happy, because three questions arose from the study of 1 John and remained in my head: First, what is the structure of 1 John? Second, why does 1 John have two key verses in 1:3 (fellowship) and 5:13 (eternal life), and which one is more significant? Third, what is the relation between 1 John and John? Every Johannine scholar has their own ideas, but they differ from each other. I was not sure about any of the ideas.

My advanced study in Stellenbosch stimulated me to examine the text with various perspectives and in more depth. At the time of writing my doctoral dissertation, I became used to my newly invented tool for analyzing the text, named Relational Reading, which is oriented and organized around two text-based approaches: linguistic and rhetorical. Five steps of reading were suggested: style relation; logical relation; thematic relation; interpersonal relation; relational goals. This relational way of reading drove me to read the text with the interrelated nature of its syntactic components in mind: logical-semantic networks; thematic flows; interpersonal dynamics; and finally, rhetorical goals. It was a special experience in that I realized I had finally found some significant, complex parallels ways of the Johannine style-structure in 1 John that had hardly been detected by other Johannine scholars. In addition, I recognized the structure of 1 John, as well as the reason why the author used the two key verses of 1:3 and 5:13. But one issue—the relationship between 1 John and John—was still left unsolved.

In 2002, after three years teaching as a full-time lecturer, during which time I enjoyed teaching various subjects, I obtained an assistant professorship at the seminary from which I had graduated seventeen years before. At the Chongshin Seminary, where around fifteen hundred seminary students are enrolled per semester, a mandatory subject, the Johannine writings, was assigned to me. For ten years, I had taught this same subject to four classes (each class has around seventy students) every semester, twice a year, with enough time for repeating, revising, improving, and confirming. My Johannine class mainly focused on the structure-styles of the Johannine writings and their macro-micro meanings.

Discerning the structures and styles of the Johannine writings became my interest and specialty. From my earlier study of 1 John, my studies had extended to the rest of the Johannine writings, such as John and Revelation, as well as to other books in the NT, such as Matthew, Ephesians, and Romans, among others. Eventually, I became sure that the relation between 1 John and John was at last disclosed to me regarding their structure-style system. Based on my research on John, 1 John, and Romans, my papers have regularly been presented at SBL and ETS meetings since then. These opportunities to present my papers at international meetings has sharpened my perspective.

In 2012, it was time to write two books regarding the structure-styles of John and of 1 John. Thankfully, I had a precious sabbatical, being away from my normal busy life, primarily focusing on writing my books. In the midst of my teaching career, I was desperate to take a pause to write what I had studied and discovered, expecting to make a small contribution to Johannine scholarship because, I believe, my research was distinctive for a few reasons.

At first, I started to write two books simultaneously, one on John 1–10 and one on 1 John. But it was not long before I realized that all I could do was to finish one of them during my sabbatical. Most parts of this book (on John 1–10) were newly written. Some of it was revised and updated from previous articles, and rewritten according to the harmony of the book. These have become parts of chapters 1 (vv. 1–18),[1] chapter 5 (vv. 19–30),[2] and chapter 9 (vv. 18–34),[3] including the structure of John[4] and issues of the structures and styles in John 6.[5] It has been my pleasure to write this book regarding John, re-scrutinizing John 1–10 carefully and confirming its Johannine style-structure chapter by chapter. It was hard work but a blissful experience. Two-thirds of the second book (on 1 John), thankfully, have been written, but it has not yet been completed.

1. Kim, "Comparative Study."
2. Kim, "Study on the Chiastic Structure."
3. Kim, "Johannine Complex Structures."
4. Kim and Go, "New Approach."
5. Kim, "Discussion of the Structure."

Acknowledgments

There are so many persons to whom I am indebted, but I will mention a few of them here. Professor H. J. Bernard Combrink, who was my doctoral promoter, helped me sharpen my understanding of how to appreciate and evaluate diverse interpretive theories properly and to academic standards. Professor Johannes P. Louw, who was a co-promoter, scrutinized my dissertation and was highly supportive and encouraged my relational method and its analyses. The insights drawn from his articles and books were invaluable at that time.

It has been a privilege to have taught my students at Chongshin Theological Seminary—their questions and responses have fed back into my research. I am deeply grateful to the board of governors and my fellow professors at Chongshin University and Seminary (CUS) for allowing me a precious sabbatical.

It was advantageous for me to have my research year at Calvin College, in Grand Rapids. The Henry Meeter Center and Dr. Karin Maag provided me with a suitable room in the Center, with computer and phone accommodations to easily access the library system and with scenic views through my windows. Paul Fields and Ryan Noppen helped me a great deal whenever I needed their help.

Dr. Byung-Chan Go and Kyu Seop Kim were helpful colleagues of mine in the studies of structure-style. I am grateful to Rev. Michael Harris, who helped me with proofreading and polishing my phrasing. Hyungmin Oh assisted me in many ways. I want to deeply thank the Wipf & Stock team for their help.

Last, my deepest appreciation goes to my wife, Eunsim, who has kept me company all the time in my long journey. Jusung and Jueun, my loving children, are steadfast supporters of their father. The warm encouragements from my parents and father-in-law have also helped my journey in John, a journey of blessing that never ends, until the day of calling from above.

Sang-Hoon Kim

Abbreviations

ATR	*Anglican Theological Review*
BETS	*Bulletin of the Evangelical Theological Society*
BM	*Beth Miqra*
BSac	*Bibliotheca Sacra*
BTB	*Biblical Theology Bulletin*
CBQ	*Catholic Biblical Quarterly*
CTJ	*Chongshin Theological Journal*
CTR	*Criswell Theological Review*
HeyJ	*Heythrop Journal*
Int	*Interpretation*
JAF	*Journal of American Folklore*
JBL	*Journal of Biblical Literature*
JR	*Journal of Religion*
JSNT	*Journal for the Study of the New Testament*
JSNTSS	*JSNT Supplement Series*
JSOT	*Journal for the Study of the Old Testament*
JSOTSS	*JSOT Supplement Series*
KENTS	*Korean Evangelical New Testament Studies*
LB	*Linguistica Biblica*
NABPRS	*National Association of Baptist Professors of Religion Series*
NAC	*The New American Commentary*

Abbreviations

NCBC	New Century Bible Commentary
NovT	*Novum Testamentum*
NovTSS	NovT Supplement Series
NRSV	*New Revised Standard Version*
NTS	*New Testament Studies*
RB	*Revue Biblique*
RE	*Review and Expositor*
SBL	Society of Biblical Literature
SBLDS	SBL Dissertation Series
SCJ	*Stone-Campbell Journal*
SJT	*Southwestern Journal of Theology*
SNTSMS	Society for New Testament Studies Monograph Series
SVTQ	*St. Vladimir's Theological Quarterly*
TB	*Tyndale Bulletin*
W&W	*Word & World*
ZNW	*Zeitschrift für die neutestamentliche Wissenschaft*

Introduction

"Since modernism has dominated the academy throughout much of the twentieth century, for most Johannine scholars plausible work on this Gospel has always been rooted in modernist assumptions. It is an understatement, however, to say that modernism has not always enamored everyone. Like any other way of viewing the world, modernism too has had the baggage of its own peculiar discontents."[1]

"We must be sure that our desire for attractive or attention-drawing analyses of the Gospel does not detract from the emphases that the Evangelist himself makes in his Gospel."[2]

Johannine Complexity in Writing

John is written with plain expressions and easier vocabulary than other sacred writings in the New Testament. For this reason, John, as well as 1 John, has been primarily used by beginner-level students when they continue studying the Greek text of the NT after finishing the beginner grammar of NT Greek.[3]

However, no other book in the NT compares to John in its complexity. It is difficult to grasp its styles and structures. Many factors confuse Johannine scholars, such as the complexity of styles, repetition, duplication, and seemingly distracting structures that are difficult to discern. Vocabulary seems to be easy, but structures are not. It seems to be written in a plain style, but is complex in its composition.

There are a number of reasons related to inconsistencies in the writing why John may appear to be written by more than one author. For example, if there is just one author, why is the composition seemingly tough and uneven? And although we ignore

---

1. Rohrbaugh, "Gospel of John," 257.
2. Beasley-Murray, *John*, xci.
3. According to Culpepper, "The Gospel uses a relatively limited vocabulary, only 1,011 different words, 112 of which occur only once in the New Testament. Since there are 15,416 words in the Gospel, the vocabulary is only 6.5 percent of the total words, which is almost the lowest in the New Testament." Culpepper, introduction to *Johannine Literature*, 17.

so many repetitive expressions in John, what about constructions that appear to be illogical in sequence and that contain many leaps in logic? How are we to regard these?

Many Johannine scholars have paid attention to problems such as riddles that have "aporias." Fortna explains that the aporias in John show "many inconsistencies, disjunctures and hard connections, even contradictions, which the text shows, notably in the narrative portions, and which cannot be accounted for by textual criticism."[4] According to van Belle, "Naturally the literary aporias and inconsistencies in the gospel text play an important role, too. In this regard, Bultmann counts the additions which interpret the text wrongly or differently, pointing to the narratives which are broken or altered, the lack of clarity in construction, and the lack of inner coherence."[5]

Thus, John has long been the primary material used by source-redactional criticism, which assumes that John was written and redacted by not a few authors or redactors through many generations. This seems to have been the sole option for solving the problem of the complexity of John's structure and composition. However, if these things are not actually true about John, why does it display these seemingly complicated and illogical traits?

It may mean that anyone who has been interested in solving the problematic aporias could not help but choose the historical-critical method over the years. In this regard, Ashton explains that "anyone who is convinced (a) that the awkward transitions in the Gospel require some explanation and (b) that the displacement theory is unsatisfactory must choose between two alternatives: either the evangelist has produced different editions of the Gospel (Brown, Martyn, Lindars) or somebody else, an editor or redactor, has made substantial additions to his work (Schnackenburg, Becker). These two hypotheses are not mutually exclusive, since a final redaction may have been made after extensive revisions on the part of the evangelist himself."[6]

Aporias

Aporias have been regarded as the definitive proof of many editions or literary strata in John. Fortna, for example, claims that "the unevenness of the text of John is due rather to *redaction*, so that the aporias are indications—direct or indirect—of *editorial seams*."[7]

---

4. Fortna, *Gospel of Signs*, 2.

5. Van Belle, *Signs Source*, 29.

6. Ashton, *Understanding the Fourth Gospel*, 199; Ashton, "Second Thoughts," 1–18. Howard-Brook even overrates the value of this sort of approach, saying that "source-oriented methods are a reflection of an Enlightenment mentality in which reason was deemed the divinely given means to reach knowledge." Howard-Brook, *Becoming Children of God*, 13. Regarding the influence of Bultmann, who led and promoted the historical-critical method, particularly source-redactional theory, see the two books Smith, *Composition and Order*, and van Belle, *Signs Source*.

7. Fortna, *Gospel of Signs*, 3. According to him, aporias are categorized by three criteria: ideological, stylistic, and contextual. Fortna, *Gospel of Signs*, 15; Fortna, *Fourth Gospel*, 6; see also de Jonge,

Culpepper elucidates how the historical-critical approach has earned its superiority in the studies of John, highlighting its foci.

> In the majority of studies the gospel has been used as a source for evidence of the process by which it was composed, the theology of the evangelist, or the character and circumstances of the Johannine community. Relying on the standard critical methods, Johannine scholars have generally approached the text looking for tensions, inconsistencies, or "*aporias*" which suggest that separate strains or layers of material are present in the text. The next step is usually to place the "layers" in some sequence by noting the way they are embedded in the gospel and the probable direction of theological development. On the basis of this stratification, the history of the material, the process by which the gospel was composed, and developments within the Johannine community can all be studied. The gospel is seen as preserving evidence of various stages of its origin and various, at times sharply different, theological emphases. The model of research is that of a "tell" in which archaeologists can unearth strata which derive from different historical periods. This model depends on the dissection and differentiation of elements within the gospel. Consequently, little attention has been given to the integrity of the whole, the way its component parts interrelate, its effects upon the reader, or the way it achieves its effects.[8]

As Culpepper points out, this historical approach has disregarded the literary integrity of the text, putting priority on extracting aporias regarding how the text reflects various strata by multiple editors. Is it true that aporias warrant a distinction among the strata, or even give proof of many editions?[9] According to Fortna, the aporias group themselves into recurring patterns.[10] He asserts that these recurring patterns are the product of multiple literary stages—that is, the transition from one literary form to another. Is he correct that so many repetitions or repetitive variations in John are due to various literary stages or strata?[11]

From Window to Mirror

Objecting to the "dissection and differentiation of elements" of the historical-critical approach, which focuses on the "window" of the text, new literary approaches have appeared as alternatives that highlight the "mirror" of the text. This phenomenon of

---

"Gospel and the Epistles," 127–44, particularly 130 in his reference to Martyn. For three types of riddle (literary, historical, and theological), see Anderson, "From One Dialogue to Another," 96–106.

8. Culpepper, *Anatomy of the Fourth Gospel*, 3.

9. Ruckstuhl strongly denies this. Ruckstuhl, "Johannine Language and Style," 128; Quoted by van Belle, *Signs Source*, 304.

10. Fortna, *Gospel of Signs*, 3.

11. Keener, *Gospel of John*, 47–48. Cf. van Belle et al., *Repetitions and Variations*.

literary approach is a kind of paradigm shift from a historical perspective to a literary one.[12]

We may list at least four major approaches in this literary field, as Borchert suggests, "(1) structuralism, which involves an analysis of the implied structures of meaning (such as deep structures at the root of human realities) inherent in a story; (2) rhetorical criticism, which involves the canons of rhetoric or the effectiveness of communication, the study of which goes back to Aristotle and Quintillian; (3) reader-response criticism, which concentrates primarily on reception or meaning from the subjective point of the reader; and (4) narrative analysis, which is the focus of the present segment of this introduction."[13] Borchert regards narrative analysis as the principal way of dealing with John because it focuses on "the story, 'the formal content element,' which involves the dimensions of plot, characters, setting, and point of view," assuming the unity of the work.[14]

But the scholars who have still kept to the historical-critical point of view in studies of John raise the question of the integrity of the method. Howard-Brook asks,

> (1) Hasn't the editing and transmission process hopelessly corrupted the possibility of finding a coherent interpretation of a complete gospel? (2) Doesn't the subjectivity of reading the Bible as "literature" destroy the notion of finding the "correct" meaning of the text? (3) If so, are the interpretations of discourse-oriented critics any more than opinions not unlike those of many film and book reviewers? (4) Furthermore, doesn't the tendency of some discourse-oriented readers to "bracket" historical questions falsely isolate the gospel from what form critics call its *Sitz im Leben* (life situation)? (5) Is it fair to leap two thousand years or more to read a biblical text as if it were a modern novel or film?[15]

Among them, questions (2), (3), and (5) are related to the integrity of the literary methods which regard John as a literary-independent document separate from the author(s). Questions (1) and (4) involve more or less the presuppositions of the historical-critical critics who presume aporias as the conclusive proof of literary editions.

---

12. In the literary-linguistic studies of John, major writings of promoters are regarded as follows: Olsson, *Structure and Meaning in the Fourth Gospel*; Culpepper, *Anatomy of the Fourth Gospel*; Mlakuzhyil, *Christocentric Literary Structure of the Fourth Gospel*; Staley, *Print's First Kiss*; Segovia, *Farewell of the Word*; Stibbe, *John as Storyteller*; Talbert, *Reading John*; Moloney, *Gospel of John*. For this paradigm shift in John, see Segovia, "Toward a New Direction," 1–22; see also George, *Reading the Tapestry*, 3–6; Stibbe, *John as Storyteller*, 5–13. Regarding the contradictory ideas of the terms, "window" and "mirror," see Geller, "Through Windows and Mirrors," 3–40. For the Scandinavian contributions to the literary approach, see Nissen and Pedersen, *New Readings in John*.

13. Borchert, *John 1–11*, 50–51. It is now said that literary criticism has opened various literary approaches based on various literary theories. Conway, "There and Back Again," 78–81.

14. Borchert, *John 1–11*, 51.

15. Howard-Brook, *Becoming Children of God*, 12. Similarly, see Jensen, *John's Gospel as Witness*, 9. He asserts that "the Bible is not a nineteenth century novel, but a collection of ancient literature."

Introduction

In these questions, historical-critical critics raise their voices against the literary critics regarding how to escape from the issue of problematic aporias without using their historical methods.

Aporias vs. Literary Unity

It is said that all the issues are more or less related to the issue of literary consistencies in John, whether there is literary unity and consistency or whether there are literary gaps with historical strata as in aporias.[16]

Ruckstuhl asserts that "throughout the Johannine narrative material the language shows some identical coinage that is different from the Synoptic coinage, and this identity of style suggests that all the Johannine narratives have passed through the medium of one personality who has somehow rethought and recast the traditional material at his disposal."[17] Therefore, the priority of this type of literary approach is how John is constructed—its literary design—and how it is presented in a meaningful system.

Tovey lists three significant benefits to this literary approach: First, literary readings are holistic approaches to the text that do not atomize it into dissected material; second, such readings lay stress on the overall coherence of the narrative and they regard meaning in terms of the relationship of the parts to the whole; third, they understand aporias such as gaps, lacunae, and fissures as sorts of literary strategies or textual signals for the readers. In this sense, he believes that the literary text becomes "a dynamic system of gap."[18]

Nonetheless, historical-critical scholars such as Fortna and de Boer would not agree with the opinions supported by the literary point of view. They have continuously suspected that literary readings disregard the aporias obvious in John in order to reach conclusions of coherence and unity.[19] De Boer has never withdrawn

---

16. Stibbe points out how the historical-critical survey has a bad influence by not concentrating on the literary studies of John: "How could scholars appreciate the artistry of a gospel whose final form had been so violently dislocated? How could those who were concerned with what lies before our eyes, function openly in a context where what now mattered was what lies behind the text?" Stibbe, *Gospel of John as Literature*, 6–7. Regarding "the eclipse of Johannine narrative," see Thatcher, "Anatomies of the Fourth Gospel," 2–8. Regarding the ideology of historical criticism, see Reinhartz, "Building Skyscrapers on Toothpicks," 65–69.

17. Ruckstuhl, "Johannine Language and Style," 145; quoted by van Belle, *Signs Source*, 306. See also Ridderbos, "Structure and Scope," 49–50. Regarding the discovery of the stylistic unit in John, Ridderbos highly values Ruckstuhl's *Die literarische Einheit des Johannesevangeliums*.

18. Tovey, *Narrative Art and Act*, 21.

19. Fortna says, "The redaction-critical method has recently been discounted as antiquarian, seeking to impose on the Gospel an academic and anachronistic concern. For what in the end does it matter—it is argued—how the aporias arose? Are we not simply to come to terms with the text before us, its relevance to us here and now?" Fortna, *Fourth Gospel*, 8. De Boer insists that "coherence or unity, no more than incoherence or fragmentation, cannot be a methodological presupposition that stands beyond critical testing in the public arena and empirical validation from the text itself, whatever method is used." De Boer, "Narrative Criticism, Historical Criticism," 102.

from his position: "A strong case has often been made that the Fourth Gospel is not conceptually coherent nor narratively cohesive, even if it is stylistically uniform. The literary discrepancies and disjunctions which historical critics are wont to label 'aporias', have been deemed too numerous and pervasive to be explained (away) simply in terms of a narrative purpose."[20]

Which idea is right and proper? Are aporias caused by literary-designed strategies (Tovey)[21] or by different strata of multi-editions (Fortna and de Boer)?[22] We may think of another alternative to this issue.[23] Those aporias can mostly be regarded as aporias when we do not understand the Johannine system of arrangement. First, there are aporias if we do not perceive the Johannine arrangement of structures (e.g., the location of the temple cleansing in ch. 2; the relation between two healing events in chs. 5 and 9); second, there are aporias if we ignore literary devices in style such as parallelism or chiasm (e.g., the complexity of the bread discourse in ch. 6; so many repetitions and variations everywhere); third, there are aporias if we fail to read the Johannine writing according to the way it is presented (e.g., dual mode in ch. 1, including the prologue; the existence of ch. 21). We are not, of course, denying that some of these aporias were designed as a literary strategy to get readers to pay closer attention to the text because of its puzzling nature, a characteristic intended to create literary curiosity. However, we still need to maintain the position that more than a few aporias occur when we do not interpret the text according to John's way, for we have found that the text is presented quite consistently and coherently, whether in a macro or micro way.

---

20. De Boer, "Narrative Criticism, Historical Criticism," 102.

21. See van Belle, "Theory of Repetitions and Variations," 22–26; Van der Watt, "Repetition and Functionality," 99–105; Van der Watt, "Riddles, Repetitions," 357–77. See also the Morris concept of variations as a feature of Johannine style. Morris, *Studies in the Fourth Gospel*, 293–319.

22. Regarding the problems of the historical-critical methods in OT studies, Radday points out, "In addition, biblical scholarship in the nineteenth century, and until quite recently, concentrated either on Lower Criticism, i.e. reconstructing an allegedly corrupt Massoretic text, or on Higher Criticism, i.e. differentiating the sources from which the Massoretic text was thought to be composed. Lower Criticism, as it would be, finds little need to attend to matters of structure, while Higher Criticism, which takes any repetition in the flow of a narrative as evidence of separate source materials, is by definition bound to overlook the very essence of chiasm, namely the fact that such repetitions may have been employed in a given composition as an intentional stylistic device. The result, in the final analysis, is that both approaches, and indeed the somewhat myopic scholarly fixation on detailed and minute analysis generally, can combine to preclude even the most dedicated scholar from perceiving the overall structure of many compositions which reveals the presence of chiasm in longer passages and entire books." Radday, "Chiasmus in Hebrew Biblical Narrative," 50.

23. The Leuven School insists that their Leuven hypothesis attempts to maintain a balance between two points of views. See six points of their assertions. Van Belle, "Tradition, Exegetical Formation, and the Leuven Hypothesis," 333–36. For another attempt at a synthetic view between the historical and literary ones, see Beutler, "In Search of a New Synthesis," 23–34; cf. de Boer, "Narrative Criticism, Historical Criticism," 301–14.

Seeing Styles-Structures

The issue of aporias is, therefore, related to authorship. If there are multiple authors or editors, the aporias are definitely due, for the most part, to their existence and consecutive work. If not, many may think that it will be difficult to solve the aporias issue. Yes, it is. However, there is a way to find the proper answers to the Johannine riddles. This issue is related to that of style and structure, which identify a way of writing as unique as a fingerprint. Multiple authors cannot maintain consistency in style and structure throughout the text, either in the macro realm or the micro.

Thus, it is significant to detect its consistency in style and structure. If there is consistency throughout the text, we may conclude that it is by one author. If there is no consistency at all, it may mean that there is more than one author. What about John, in regards to its complex structure?

For this reason, we have to renew our focus on the issue of the styles and structures of John. Styles and structures demonstrate a certain linguistic, literary matrix on which the author has based his or her ways of writing. An author cannot change his or her linguistic, literary context, specific language area, and conventional way of communication of his or her days. Grounded on these factors, the author has his or her own ways of writing, creating literary styles and structures.

The linguistic-literary traits of the author permeate the styles and structures of any literary text. Our task is to find these traits properly and correctly. This task is related to the following questions: (1) What are the traits of styles and structures that we who live in modern days can see?[24] We may see and observe what the text looks like according to our ways of reading. This question leads to the next: (2) To what extent or degree are our ways of reading affected by our modern education and its concepts of logic?

Reading according to John's Way

My assertion is that we have to understand John's way of writing as we read. If it is not a book that many authors or redactors have written and mixed throughout history without any consideration of literary unity, it cannot help but show certain literary consistency. If we can identify John's way of writing as a unique style or composition of structures, and if we can recognize them correctly, we may solve many of the

---

24. Regarding the difference between the modern style and the ancient one in writing, Welch suggests, "It should be apparent that ancient rhetoric and modern prose do not strive to achieve the same ideals. Modern style demands, for example, that an author write more or less linearly, following a line of syllogistic or dialectic reasoning, or developing a continuous flow of ideas. Circuitousness and repetitiveness are shunned in most circumstances. In many ancient contexts, however, repetition and even redundancy appear to represent the rule rather than the exception, parallelism thrived." Welch, preface to *Chiasmus in Antiquity*, 12. See also Dorsey, *Literary Structure of the Old Testament*, 9, 15–16. For a different type of concept against the modern Western critical way, refer to Martyn, "Johannine Community," 183–90.

difficulties in reading John. Those we cannot easily understand due to logical gaps, unnatural contexts, and perplexing repetitions or variations could be derived from the different logic or types of arrangement in writing in our modern way. Do we have to pay proper attention to its own ways of writing such as the styles-structures of John sufficiently to find them as they were meant to be designed?

For a long time, John's styles have been misunderstood by those who read them in a modern way. They cannot have noticed them, for John's styles and structures are not logical when viewed from the modern perspective. If his ways of writing create repetitive, parallel styles and structures, including chiasms, it is understandable why modern-educated scholars have regarded John as a complex book without consistency in writing.

Thus, our first task is to admit that John's way of writing differs from any of today's styles and structures. The primary thing is to make an attempt to see into the styles in the text. What kind of methods does the author use in his arrangement of the micro-macro units? Is there certain literary-linguistic consistency in the way of writing? How do the micro ways of writing affect the macro way of producing the system of structures? Namely, what is the relation between styles and structures?

Structure-Style and Meanings

There are deep connections between styles-structures and produced meanings.[25] We may interpret the text even though we do not recognize it. However, the style is the external form creating its internal meaning. The meaning varies depending on how one writes or how one speaks. In the late twentieth century, pragmatics in linguistics and socio-linguistics began to emerge regarding "language performance" compared to "language competence." By this time, stylistics in literary studies becomes focused as a new concept, "new stylistics." In the biblical interpretation field, a new concern about classical rhetorical theories such as rhetorical criticism began to be highlighted. This approach is more or less related to the pragmatic concept of reading in terms of pursuing the rhetorical impact in communication.

It is reasonable to consider how an understanding of classical frames of dialogue and styles of writing can aid in reading the Greek Bible, an ancient text—that knowing the literary traits in the text may seriously affect the process of reading. Structures and

---

25. According to Geller, "Meaning in language lies in relationship, primarily in that between form and concept, sound and sense." Geller, "Through Windows and Mirrors," 27–28. Radday asserts that "Chiastic structure, it will be seen, is more than an artificial or artistic device. If it were nothing else, it would hardly warrant more than a passing illustration of a few exemplary passages. It is rather, and most remarkably so, a key to meaning. Not paying sufficient attention to it may result in failure to grasp the true theme." Radday, "Chiasmus in Hebrew Biblical Narrative," 51. Regarding the inseparable relation between structure and meaning, see also Dorsey, *Literary Structure of the Old Testament*, 36–41. See also Lee, *Symbolic Narratives of the Fourth Gospel*, 27–35; Man, "Value of Chiasm," 146–54; Derickson, "Matthew's Chiastic Structure," 423–25.

styles are significant in interpreting the text. Styles contain meanings, and meanings are divulged through styles. We cannot separate stylistic expressions from internal meanings. The form, or style, is inseparable from its content, or meaning.[26]

Macro structures are built up by a combination of thought units or paragraphs, in a particular, unique way for communication to the readers. The structure is the frame of the house; the text shows how ideas flow over. A good work cannot be produced without a frame.

Therefore, what we discern in the text's styles and structures is itself the interpreting process. (The issue is whether or not we can find the very authorial styles and structures that he or she imprinted in it.) If we fail to pay attention to those styles and structures as they are, we miss the point(s) of the author, which were carefully intended to be made through those devices. In other words, if someone who has a bias due to an existing prejudice or who does not have any deep concern about the style and structure of a given text, and who therefore does not look carefully into that text, he or she may not properly understand the authorial meanings delivered by style-structures.

Let us look at some expressions. In $[A + B - C + D]$, the value of this expression is always the same, although the sequential order is changed, even if their signs, plus and minus, are not changed. Then, how about $[A + B \times C - D]$ or $[(A+B) \times C - D]$ or $[A + B \times (C - D)]$? These expressions are not the same in value because of the changes in their relationships.

In some cases, as in the first above expression, meanings may not be switched in spite of the changes or rearrangement of style-structures. But in most cases, as in the second expressions, there becomes a considerable difference if there is a change regarding style-structures. Even though the text is arranged in order like [A-B-B'-A'] + [B-C-B'-C'] according to parallelism that was generally used at the time of John, if we read them differently, like [A-B-B'] + [A'-B-C-B'-C'], it will cause a problem in interpretation. The text may become illogical, and the reader cannot recognize the relationships, both in and between [A-B-B'-A'] and [B-C-B'-C'].

The best structure is the one that the author intended to create. Seeing the variety of suggestions about the chiastic structure, why do they differ from each other? Does John have no intended structure? Are there errors or differences caused by their methods or processes? What is the right process to find the structure intended by the author rather than one framed by the interpreter?

---

26. In the past, it has been observed that parallelisms and chiasms as literary devices were used for two purposes: easier memorization and the avoidance of monotony. Cf. Greenstein, "How Does Parallelism Mean?," 42.

Method: Relational Reading (Analysis)

This method of research is based on DA (discourse analysis) from the synchronic perspective.[27] Due to its primary focus on interactive relations between phrases, sentences, or paragraphs, it may be called "relational reading" (or relational analysis).[28]

The purpose of this method of reading is to grasp how the author formulates his or her literary styles through phrasal combinations, and by this means presents ideas and meanings, and to identify the stylistic relations implanted by the author in the text. It approaches a macro understanding of the structures from the results of the data of micro analyses of styles. The way of networking the phrasal or sentential relations would become the way of constructing the structures into larger units, for styles are related to structures.

Generally, authorial ways of constructing styles and structures are maintained consistently throughout the text. If John is written by one author, this consistency should be kept. In this sense, we have to study the text beyond one paragraph or one chapter when we disclose John's ways of constructing structures.

The relational reading means reading to analyze the connectivity between phrases, sentences, paragraphs, or even larger units, in terms of how they are related to each other, producing the textual meanings. Connectivity, cohesion in expression, and detachment in meaning are carefully considered. The unit showing its own strong connectivity among the subunits provides its cohesiveness. The integral parts gather to become a larger unit such as a paragraph or a chapter. If we find how they are arranged, we may interpret the meaning of its structures.

Its methodology is different from the historical-exegetical way of reading and any linguistic-literary method at large today. This method is not adopted from existing methods, rather it is created by its own unique frame of research. There has not been introduced any specific frame of analysis, seeing styles-structures in the relational perspective, particularly combining the macro and micro ways of reading.

The foci of this method are as follows. First, this reading attempts to find the Johannine styles-structures as they were arranged. Second, this reading highlights the interrelational connectivity between the literary constituents, such as words, phrases, sentences, paragraphs, and even beyond. Third, the reading pays attention to the interactive relations between macro and micro units—namely, considering both zoom-in

---

27. The primary concern of DA is to demonstrate the internal coherence and unity of the specific text. See Louw, *Semantics of New Testament Greek*; Nida, *Signs, Sense, Translation*; Porter, *Verbal Aspect in the Greek of the New Testament*; Black, *Linguistics and New Testament Interpretation*; Johanson, *To All the Brethren*.

28. This relational reading does not directly apply the five-fold method of the "relational reading" (stylistic relations, logical relations, thematic relations, interpersonal relations, and relational goals) in the author's dissertation as they were invented and instead its relational perspective is adopted to examine the literary networks of the text. Kim, *Interaction between Koinonia and Zoe in 1 John*. The concept of this relational reading differs from the term of Harner, as he uses "relation analysis," referring to the reader-response theory. Harner, *Relation Analysis of the Fourth Gospel*.

(micro-relations) and zoom-out (macro-relations) regarding literary-linguistic strategies used by the author, complementarily and integratedly.

In the process, two kinds of roles (or functions) among constituents need to be considered: relational roles as well as grammatical-functional ones. Grammatical functions are initially important in terms of the syntactical-semantic dimension. However, interactive relations among constituents and units are no less significant because they create styles-structures in arrangement (or allocation of linguistic resources) of writing in terms of the semantic-pragmatic dimension.[29] We will put the priority on the latter instead of the former, which is initially grounded.

The Procedure of Relational Reading

Its procedure of searching for the interactive relations has been as follows. First, the Greek text is diagrammatically arranged in syntax such as "phrasing" or "diagramming."[30] The syntactic manner of phrasal arrangements, and its analysis, help us to focus on each phrase or sentence in terms of its connectivity to its consecutive phrase-sentences.[31]

Second, the relations among constituents within a sentence (phrasal and sentential relations) and beyond (relations among larger units) are examined in terms of styles-structures regarding how their interaction or interrelatedness such as similarity, difference, or complexity are produced in phrasal-sentential arrangement, logical-thematic development, character presentation, even spatial-temporal matter. It is specifically focused on how they are designed and arranged in the text. Thus, we are searching for what are interrelated in arrangement as far as possible.

Third, the interactive relations in John, whether in style or structure, are mostly seen as patterns of chiasm, parallelism, combined chiasm, combined parallelism, dual, or triple. (The logic or system in writing is not like ours.) The key to the style in John exists in the pairedness of each related constituent within those patterns. Thus, it is essential to find the pairs, in each relation, which are implanted in the text.[32] If

---

29. Studies on style-structure cannot be delimited in the syntactic realm but rather should be extended its scope to semantic and pragmatic ones. This is different from Greenstein who delimits the notion of parallelism as an essentially syntactic device, Geller includes the semantic domain as well as synthetic relation regarding the category of parallelism. See Geller, *Parallelism in Early Hebrew Poetry*, 16; Greenstein, "How Does Parallelism Mean?," 44.

30. This type of syntactical phrasing has been applied in exegetical studies by Kaiser, Stuart, Fee, and others. Kaiser, *Toward An Exegetical Theology*; Stuart, *Old Testament Exegesis*; Fee, *New Testament Exegesis*; Cotterell and Turner, *Linguistics and Biblical Interpretation*; Mounce, *Graded Reader of Biblical Greek*; Guthrie and Duvall, *Biblical Greek Exegesis*.

31. In this book, we are not describing the method of this syntactic arrangement and any example of its analysis in detail, though. We are instead focusing solely on our style-structure matter. For their details, see my article "New Way of Analytic Methods."

32. Avishur uses the term "word pair" as follows: "The term 'word pairs' as used in this study, will be defined as pairs of synonymous, antonymous, or heteronymous words, whose components are

we choose the wrong pairs, the literary puzzle is not solved. If we find the right ones, there is no puzzle any longer. Rather, a literary style, in its original design, emerges from hiding.

Fourth, when interactive relations, particularly in the form of style-structure, are found, they are in priority of significance. There are macro relations (structures) and micro ones (styles). There are manifest ones and obscure ones. There are simple ones and complex ones. Macro relations will be treated first and then micro ones will follow. Apparent ones are emphasized in bold type, indicating their significance over the obscure ones, which are treated in normal type. The relations that are regarded as more essential in each unit (or subunit) will be marked for emphasis with 10 percent shading in the box.

Fifth, we have also to consider the complexity of relations. We think very often in John that there are complex relations, whether they combine more than one relation such as chiasm or parallelism within a limited area, or they are made simultaneously in more than two ways. We may call the first ones (combined relations) "combined chiasm" (an overall chiasm, with an additional parallelism/chiasm added within it) or "combined parallelism" (a dominant parallelism, with an additional chiasm/parallelism added within it).

When more than two relations are designed altogether, we may call it "complex parallelism," disregarding whether or not a chiasm is more dominant than a parallelism. There are at least two interactive relations put together for multiple foci. In other cases, more than two relations may share overlapping spaces as in chain-linking relations. This means that before the first relation ends, the second one starts, overlapping with any part of the first. It seems complex, looking like $[acx^2 + (bc+ad)x + bd]$. This quadratic equation would be not easy to solve if we think solely of the dimension of a linear equation. This complex equation is constructed by multiplication of two linear equations, $(ax + b)$ and $(cx + d)$. Therefore, two equations (or formulas) need to be found separately from each other, such as factoring.

The difficulty in discerning the Johannine styles-structures lies in this type of complex construction of no less than one interactive relation. However, there are ways to solve them, because they are designed consistently and similarly throughout John, if we pay careful attention to them multi-dimensionally.

Interaction between Macro-Structure and Micro-Style

It is natural that the system of writing, if there is one author, reflects its consistency, whether in the macro realm or the micro, whether in structure or in style. If we can see the details in the micro units, such as styles or patterns, in terms of how the text

---

found in tandem as a result of mutual affinity." Avishur, *Stylistic Studies of Word-Pairs*, 1. However, we are not dealing here only with word-pairs, but also the other pairs beyond the word level.

is arranged and located, and moreover find those ways of networks in writing, it becomes possible to grasp the macro way of building up the body of John more easily and properly.[33] Macro and micro are relative terms. One is macro to the other which is micro to the former.

To see the macro structure is similar to seeing a block of apartments. An apartment is a sample that reflects what other similar apartments look like. We have to consider also that there is more than one type of apartment in that block. We may say that even among those various types, there are certain similarities, because they are designed in one mono scheme. It would be also interesting to examine what and how they are different, as well as similar. There is connectivity between them.

A small unit is connected to other neighboring small units and at the same time to the larger ones that comprise it. Regarding this connectivity, we may find similarities among expressions in styles (form) and/or in contents (meaning). We can presume that there are so many similarities in patterns or types throughout John if the text is designed deliberately by one author, although they are seen in complexity. Complexity regarding how to use ways of style-structure itself can indicate the uniqueness of a certain author, like DNA that differentiates one person from others.

Parallelisms and Chiasms

John is Semitic. The arrangement and presentation of ideas are similar to those of the OT, which is full of various parallelisms and chiasms.[34] It employs a Hebraistic mode of thinking.[35] A rabbinic scholar, Israel Abrahams, an orthodox Jew, once addressed his rabbinic evaluation of John at Cambridge in 1924: "To us Jews, the Fourth Gospel is the most Jewish of the four."[36] Networked usage of parallelisms and chiasms

---

33. See Radday, "Chiasmus in Hebrew Biblical Narrative," 111; Dorsey, *Literary Structure of the Old Testament*, 36–38; Thomson, *Chiasmus in the Pauline Letters*, 27–33.

34. E.g., refer to Watson, *Traditional Techniques in Classical Hebrew Verse*, 313–19; Breck, "Chiasmus as a Key," 249–67; Ellis, "Inclusion, Chiasm," 269–338; Stramara, "Chiastic Key," 5–27.

35. According to Godet, "In the language of John, the clothing only is Greek, the body is Hebrew . . . though Greek in its forms, the style is nevertheless, Hebrew in its substance." Godet, *Commentary on John's Gospel*, 138. See also Davies, *Rhetoric and Reference in the Fourth Gospel*, 267–74 (cf. Temple, *Core of the Fourth Gospel*, 5–9, 22–24); Davies, "Reflections on Aspects of the Jewish Background," 43–64; Charlesworth, "Dead Sea Scrolls," 65–97; Lewis, "Semitic Background of the Gospel of John," 97–110. Refer also to several articles in Coloe and Thatcher, *John, Qumran, and the Dead Sea Scrolls*.

36. Neil, *Interpretation of the New Testament*, 338; quoted by Burge, *Interpreting the Gospel of John*, 20. According to Avishur, "In early Semitic literature, word pairs are not marginal in the stylistic patterns; rather, they are foundation stones in the construction of verse cola, characterizing the parallelistic phenomenon. Though the phenomenon of word pairs is dominant in Ancient Semitic poetic verse, it is not absent in the prose." Avishur, *Stylistic Studies of Word-Pairs*, 1. Lund asserts that chiasm is "a cultural heritage from the Semites, the gift of the East to the West." Lund, *Chiasmus in the New Testament*, xxiv.

throughout the text is the Johannine style of writing.[37] Dual (or sometimes triple) presentation of the contents is also the Johannine style of arrangement. These ways of constructing expressions are typical of John and are presented consistently and without exception, regardless of format, whether in poem or in prose and whether in discourse or in narrative.

Brown introduced four types of parallelism in John:[38] synonymous parallelism (the second line repeats the idea of the first: 3:11; 4:36; 6:35, 55; 7:34; 13:16); antithetical parallelism (the second line offers a contrast with the first: 3:18; 8:35; 9:39); synthetic parallelism (the sense flows on from one line to another: 8:44); and staircase parallelism (one line picks up the last principal word of the preceding line: the prologue; 6:37; 8:32; 13:20; 14:21). Besides these, he introduced inverted parallelism (chiasm): "In two units which share a number of parallel features, the first verse of I corresponds to the last verse of II, the second verse of I corresponds to the next to the last verse of II, etc.," examples of which are in 9:36–40 and in the organization of the trial before Pilate (18:28—21:16).[39]

However, Brown determined that the presence of parallelisms is not the dominant characteristic of the discourse,[40] and asserted, "We do not believe that one can consistently find rhyme, strict parallelism, or exact stress patterns. If the prose is solemn, it is far from lyrical. The language of the discourses achieves a monotonous grandeur by repetition of simple words and not by the use of highly literary vocabulary."[41]

First, it is his prejudice that only the poetry shows the parallel feature in it. Prose or discourse can be written with characteristics of parallel features as in John.[42] Second, my claim is that Brown found just small portions of parallelism in John; there are plenty of parallelisms which are networked throughout John, whether they are strict or loose, whether they are parallel, chiastic, or mixed, whether they are in macro structure or in micro style. Third, John is not made up by "a monotonous grandeur by repetition of simple words" but rather by a well-designed, most artistic grandeur by deliberately webbed parallel combinations of simple words.[43]

---

37. According to Welch, chiasm itself was one of the primary literary devices in the ancient Near Eastern languages and is also found in ancient Greek and Latin literature, although its use was not pervasive and it is secondary in its role. Welch, "Chiasmus in Ancient Greek," 250, 264. We can see an aesthetic, chiastic model of Hebrew structure from a Psalm-menorah (Psalm 67) in Meynet, *Rhetorical Analysis*, 62–64.

38. Brown, *Gospel According to John I–XII*, cxxxii. Cf. van Belle, "Repetitions and Variations," 54–56, 59–60.

39. Brown, *Gospel According to John I–XII*, cxxxv.

40. Ibid., cxxxii.

41. Ibid., cxxxv.

42. See Radday, "Chiasmus in Hebrew Biblical Narrative," 50; Welch, preface to *Chiasmus in Antiquity*, 11.

43. Regarding the orality of the first-century literary environments, Harvey presents that repetitions and their related parallelisms as designed "for aesthetic or referential reasons rather than for ease in verse-making." Harvey, *Listening to the Text*, 42–46, esp., 43. Cf. Gray, "Repetition in Oral

Introduction

In this book, we classify all the parallel features simply and in groups, as follows: parallelism (ab-a'b'), chiasm (ab-ba or ab-x-b'a'),[44] combined parallelism (such as a-b1b2-a'-b'2b'1), combined chiasm (such as a-b1b2-b'1b'2-a'), dual (a-a'), and triple (a-a'-a"). We simplify the classification of parallel features for the purpose of paying attention to even varied patterns or complex ones, more flexibly and escaping jargonization. The fixed categorization may interrupt the findings of flexible structures-styles in the text.

Studies of Parallelism and Chiasm in the Bible (in Brief)

Regarding studies of chiasm and parallelism, Hebrew OT scholars have advanced beyond NT Greek scholars. In 1753, Robert Lowth set out to find the stylistic phenomena of parallelism (*parallelismus membrorum*) between phrases in the Hebrew text in Isaiah.[45] In 1823, Thomas Boys applied its perspective to find the larger structure of parallelism.[46] After them, having passed through G. B. Gray, D. H. Müller, E. W. Bullinger, Yehuda Radday, and others, this type of study became a significant part of OT studies.[47]

At the SBL Conference in 1968, James Muilenburg advocated emphasis on literary and rhetorical approaches to the Bible beyond historical criticism ("Form Criticism and Beyond") based on his research into literary features of the Hebrew OT Bible.[48] Since then, these types of literary studies have increased, especially among OT

Literature," 293; Niditch, *Oral World and Written Word*, 13–14. Compare with Thatcher's oral concept that is based on form criticism, categorizing the Johannine riddles. Thatcher, *Riddles of Jesus in John*.

44. Chiasms here include concentric or symmetric patterns, and parallelisms include synonymous, antithetical, synthetic, or staircase parallelisms. Harvey introduces other names of chiasm: introverted parallelism, inverted parallelism, envelope structure, concentric symmetry, concentric structure, circular construction, and pedimental symmetry. Harvey, *Listening to the Text*, 96. See also the terms of Welch: *epanodos*, introverted parallelism, extended introversion, concentrism, the chiform, *palistrophe*, envelope construction, the delta-form, and recursion, as well as simple, compound, and complex chiasmus. Welch, preface to *Chiasmus in Antiquity*, 10.

45. Lowth, *Lectures on the Sacred Poetry of the Hebrews*; Lowth, *Isaiah*.

46. Boys, *Tactia Sacra*. According to Dorsey, Boys carried out the first modern structural analyses of entire biblical books, including some of the NT. Dorsey, *Literary Structure of the Old Testament*, 19.

47. Gray, *Forms of Hebrew Poetry*; Müller, *Die Propheten in ihrer ursprünglichen Form*; Bullinger, *Companion Bible*; Radday, "On Chiasm in Biblical Narrative," 48–72. Bullinger included NT books in his analyses, which seems to be mostly based on the English versions of the Bible, while Radday dealt with Hebrew texts in a Hebrew concept. In his book in 1991, *Literary Structure of the Old Testament*, Dorsey, as an OT scholar, wrote that "the field of research is still in its infancy." See also Berlin, *Dynamics of Biblical Parallelism*.

48. Muilenburg, "For Criticism and Beyond," 1–18. Also see his article, "Study in Hebrew Rhetoric," 97–111.

scholars. D. W. Gooding, H. Parunak, William Shea, Stephen Geller, Yitzhak Avishur, David Dorsey, and others have all contributed to this field of studies.[49]

Probably influenced by the previous studies regarding the parallel features in the OT, NT studies have proceeded slowly but steadily with similar parallel or chiastic phenomena in the texts of NT.

In the NT studies, Nils Lund is a significant pioneer who recognized chiasm as a primary literary device to construct the structures of the NT texts.[50] Culpepper regarded him as "the father of modern studies of chiastic structures."[51] After him, J. Jeremias, David Clark, K. Wolfe, John Welch, Craig Blomberg, Ian Thomson, Luter and Lee, Porter and Reed, and others have followed.[52] Particularly for the Johannine studies, but solely with chiastic orientation, John Gerhard, Peter Ellis, John Breck, Charles Talbert, and Wayne Brouwer have contributed to this field.[53]

Beyond Dichotomies

This reading aims at an integration of some interrelational perspectives regarding style-structure without excluding any points of view, if necessary, because it adopts a relational orientation as its prime foundation. However, this does not mean that all the related views are to be unconditionally applied and put together. It does instead mean that two wings of emphatic views regarding network of descriptions, how expressions or ideas are interrelated to each other, are treated interactively and integratedly.

First, this reading is indebted to both diachronic and synchronic approaches. It is diachronic in that the reading is searching for the specific ancient Johannine ways of writing in parallel constructions and networks in meaning. It is synchronic in that the reading is primarily searching for relations among the textual constituents or units. We are not integrating the traditional historical-critical way of reading with our literary-linguistic one, however, because of its incompatibility either in the interpretation of aporias or regarding the results of analyses.

---

49. See Gooding, "Composition of the Book of Judges," 70–79; Parunak, *Structural Studies in Ezekiel*; Shea, "Qinah Structure of the Book of Lamentations," 103–7; Geller, *Parallelism in Early Biblical Poetry*; Avishur, *Stylistic Studies of Word-Pairs*; Dorsey, *Literary Structure of the Old Testament*.

50. Lund, "Presence of Chiasmus," 74–93; Lund, "Influence of Chiasmus upon the Structure of the Gospels," 27–48; Lund, "Influence of Chiasmus upon the Structure of the Gospel according to Matthew," 405–33; Lund, "Literary Structure of Paul's Hymn to Love," 266–76.

51. Culpepper, "Pivot of John's Prologue," 1–31.

52. Jeremias, "Chiasmus in den Paulusbriefen," 145–56; Clark, "Criteria for Identifying Chiasm," 63–72; Wolfe, "Chiastic Structure of Luke-Acts," 60–71; Welch, "Chiasmus in the New Testament," 211–49; Blomberg, "Structure of 2 Corinthians 1–7," 3–20; Thomson, *Chiasmus in the Pauline Letters*; Luter and Lee, "Philippians as Chiasmus," 89–101; Porter and Reed, "Philippians as a Macro-Chiasm," 213–31. See also Scott, "Chiastic Structure," 17–26; Staley, "Structure of John's Prologue," 241–64.

53. Gerhard, "Literary Unity and Compositional Methods"; Ellis, *Genius of John*; Talbert, *Reading John*; Breck, *Shape of Biblical Language*; Brouwer, *Literary Development of John 13–17*.

Introduction

Second, macro structure and micro style, although the terms, macro and micro, are relative in concept, they are treated together and interactively. The macro understanding in structure becomes the solid ground of observing micro relations, among phrasal-sentential components, that also support the larger frame of units. Neither of the two can be disregarded.

Third, specific and overall analyses are made together. All the parallel relations that occur among constituents, whether at word level or beyond it, whether manifestly or obscurely, whether primarily in function or secondly, are scrutinized to find as much as we can. In this process, any verse of the text is not disregarded, and all the units, if possible, are significantly considered in terms of interrelatedness.

Fourth, grammatical and relational considerations are put together. Grammatical relations among constituents are our primary concern, but they are not all that matters. Relational considerations regarding parallel features are to complement the grammatical sense of reading. It means that both relations need to complement each other. Parallel features created in the text are often beyond grammatical relations.

Fifth, in this reading, syntactic, semantic, and pragmatic relations are considered altogether.[54] The relations among constituents are constructed not only by syntactic disposition but also by semantic consideration in arrangement and its related pragmatic usage in effect. Thus, these three factors need to be considered together, whenever any relational analysis is attempted.

Sixth, both parallelisms and chiasms, including their variations, are examined, whether in macro structure or in micro style, without excluding either. John never sticks to the usage of one of the two excluding the other, but instead uses both with his own literary discretion. One must not delimit his ways of writing. It means that we have to examine the text, considering the Johannine ways primarily, not determining a certain way hastily (whether of parallelism or of chiasm).

Seventh, all the types of parallelisms and chiasms are to be examined, whether they are simple or complex. Simple parallelisms or chiasms are easily discerned and manifest, but complex ones are relatively difficult to find due to their complexity in form. Most of them are complex because two or even three are created at the same time in specific areas. Some of them are designed deliberately and with a specific goal, particularly in John, but some of them would be made from the subconscious activity of the mind of the author, whose literary matrix is of the world of parallelism-chiasm in writing.[55]

---

54. Cf. Berlin considers parallelism in terms of the grammatical linguistic sense such as phonology, morphology, syntax and semantics. Berlin, *Dynamics of Biblical Parallelism*.

55. Lund once referred to this phenomenon: "Any conclusion along these lines must therefore be reached only on the basis of inherent probabilities. I have reached the conclusion that much of these symmetries was altogether subconscious, and that it was felt rather than seen. This is merely another way of saying that the writers had learned their forms so thoroughly that they had forgotten them as forms." Lund, *Chiasmus*, xxv.

Eighth, ancient and modern ways in writing-reading processes complement each other. Parallel styles in writing are ancient—different from our days. Thus, we have to read them with maximum consideration of their own ways of style as far as possible. Nevertheless, we are not free from our modern ways of reading with which we have analyzed the text in detail. We need to attempt our modern ways to scrutinize the Greek text, considering, to the hilt, its own way of writing.

Ninth, Western and Eastern perspectives become complementary to each other. For a long time, the theological heritages, including hermeneutical fields, have belonged to Western theologians. It has not been so long since Asian churches and their scholars have increased in number. Not a few Asian scholars have studied in Western societies and returned to their home countries, teaching subjects at school and writing articles mostly in their own languages. They have rarely had opportunities to share their ideas and academic results with the world. However, there is plenty of potential, equipped with both an Eastern perspective and Western academism. It cannot be denied that this book reflects more or less the Eastern viewpoint, under the influence of a modern Western heritage in academism, attempting to see the world in an integrated way and without sacrificing the other side.[56]

Tenth, the Greek text and its English version (by the author) are interactively used. All the relational analyses are firmly based on the Greek text of John (NA27). But, in their explications and related notes, Greek phrases are used limitedly, only if necessary and frequently with English translations, for the general readers.

Eleventh, analysis and discussion need to complement each other. In most chapters of this book, the relational analysis that searches for the parallel features in its own way is done first. And then discussions with other scholars are provided, limitedly and with some points at issue. The primary focus is put on the relational analysis itself in terms of what and how various relations, particularly parallel features, are created and designed throughout the text. The second focus is to compare its analytical results with other scholars from its own critical point of view.

How to Read the Diagrams in This Book

There are two types of diagram presented in this book. The first is the diagram demonstrating the structural relations that are either sequential or parallel (including chiastic), often both. This diagram is usually used to show clearly how the macro units are related to each other. For example:

---

56. For example, Asians are relatively much more relational compared to Westerners. Their ways of making relationship with others are so much more complex, appearing in the system of language-use. Western languages like English hardly have many ways of expressing something depending on whom we are talking to as Koreans do. Hangul, the Korean language, provides at least sixty-four modes of expression, according to whom one is speaking. "Hara, Hasipsio, Hasijio, Haneunja?, Halrae?, Hasigestheumika?, etc." Not only verbal phrases but also nouns and particles can vary depending on the person whom we meet and speak to. It is said that Hangul is very delicate and complex in describing human relationships.

I.	The gate-shepherd discourse (10:1-16)		A
II.	Two linkers (10:17-21)		
	IIA.	The Father's commandment: Jesus' laying down his life (10:17-18)	B
	IIA'.	Two contradicted responses to Jesus (10:19-21)	B'
III.	At the Feast of Dedication (10:22-42)		A'

It often suggests more than one structure: linear (sequential) and/or parallel (interactive). In the above diagram, a linear structure is named: I, II (IIA and IIA'), III, etc. And a parallel one demonstrates its interactive relation such as: A, B, B', and A'. The first structure is usually more primary than the second. But, in this diagram, it is alleged that the chiastic structure (AB-B'A') has priority over the linear one (I, II, and III).

The second type of diagram, a table type, is more or less complicated to read. This one displays the micro network of phrasal-sentential relations in terms of how they are interrelated and build their own system of syntactic-semantic connections regarding unit-demarcation. See the diagram on p. 20.

First, the title is presented with a mark of division such as IIA1 (the first subunit of IIA, the first one of two [or three] units of II, the second part of the chapter). The verses indicated here, such as "1:19–28," are the part or unit that is about to be dealt with and analyzed in detail.

Second, **II2**, a mark, indicates that this parallel belongs to the second part of the chapter (II) and is the second one named and examined. Its bold type character means that its parallel feature is very manifest, compared with a normal type of character such as II3.

The next phrase, "Combined chiastic," specifies what type of parallel relation it is and now shows that two types (a chiasm, AB-B'A', and a parallelism, $B_1B_2B_3$-$B'_1B'_2B'_3$) are united together, thereby producing a combined chiasm: in this case, the chiasm is larger than the parallelism.

Third, the relations of this parallel are now explicated and articulated, considering their interrelatedness among the constituents, primarily regarding their parallel pairs.

Fourth, a table of relations is drawn for the purpose of demonstrating the network of stylistic relations within a specific unit. "V" stands for verse.

Fifth, the bold typed number **2** means that this is the second parallel and manifest to be examined. And its 10 percent shading columns in the box indicates that this relation is principal, building the system of relations for the unit (or subunit). It is significantly used as we consider the division of the verses, because this primal relation plays a major role in indicating certain inseparable clusters. The plain-type numbers, such as 3 and 5, designate that they are relatively more obscure in parallel than others, such as **2**, **4**, and **6**, which are bold-typed.

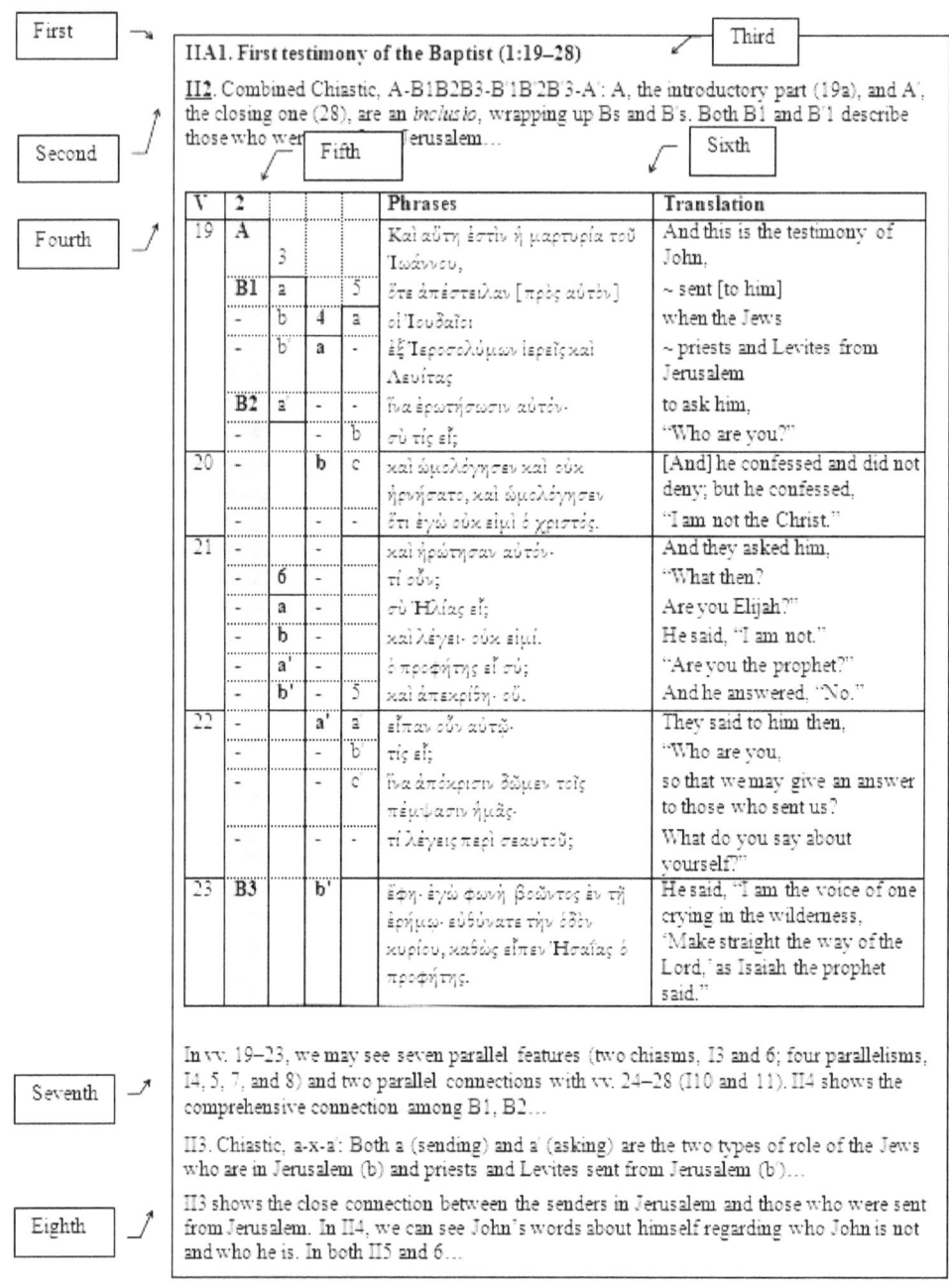

Sixth, the second-to-last columns are presented in the Greek text (NA[27]) and divided according to their parallel features, while the last columns are my own literal translations into English for easier understanding by the readers, who can compare it with the Greek text.

Seventh, an explanation, which sometimes appears before the table, is to explicate how many and what types of parallels are within a unit and how they are interrelated, briefly.

Eighth, the goal of this part is to summarize each parallel relation with a sentence disclosing its key focus.

The Structure of John

Among the more generally accepted is that of considering 1:1–18 as a Prologue, 1:19—12:50 as the Book of Signs, 13:1—20:31 as the Book of Glory, and 21:1–25 as a later addition to the text.[1]

AT MY CLASS OF Johannine Literature, whenever the topic of the structure of John is presented, my students are asked, "How many units does it consist of?" They are encouraged to answer, "Two!"

THE BOOK OF WITNESS

John is the Book of Witness. Of course, it bears witness to Jesus Christ as the Son of God, as the three Synoptic Gospels do. Why, then, should it be called the Book of Witness?[2]

The verb form of witness (*martureo*) and its noun one (*marturia*) are used most in John among the Gospels:[3] eighteen and thirty-five times, respectively, accentuating the significance of witness to Jesus in John. All the episodes in John represent testimonies about Jesus by his witnesses. For example, see the episodes of the meeting between Jesus and his early disciples in ch. 1. What is the difference from the episodes in Synoptics? The primary focus in John is the witness to Jesus by the characters, including the early disciples who do not appear as witnesses at this stage in the three other Gospels. See their testimonies on Jesus (41, Messiah; 45, "Him of whom Moses in the Law and also the prophets wrote"; 49, the Son of God and the King of Israel).

The witness motif is predominant in John, to such an extent as to be utilized in ways of writing, including arranging episodes. Jesus indicates the Father as the main witness to him (5:32, 37). Moreover, Jesus himself is the witness to himself. Thus, there are a total of two main witnesses who bear witness to Jesus: the Father and the

---

1. Bondi, "John 8:39–47," 477.

2. Borchert names it "Testimony about Jesus." Borchert, *John 1–11*, 31. See also O'Grady, *According to John*; Painter, *John: Witness & Theologian*.

3. In all the Johannine literature, including Revelation, *marturia* appears thirty times, and it is used thirty-seven times total in the New Testament. The verb *martureo* appears forty-seven times in Johannine documents, while it is seventy times in the New Testament.

Son himself (8:18). The words of Jesus in 8:17, "Even in your law it is written that the testimony of 'two' men is true" is probably quoted from Deut 19:15 and 17:6, where "two or three" witnesses are focused. Why does the focus shift: from "two or three" to "two"?

There are only the two witnesses who are authentically able to bear their witness to the Son: the Father and the Son himself. There is no one else who compares with them, although there are not a few human witnesses who earnestly bear witness to Jesus in John. The two divine witnesses are the quintessential figures who work together and harmoniously in John, from whom other testimonies such as those of human beings are initiated and originated.

The usage of two witnesses also appears like that of the double testimonies in John regarding reliability and authenticity in testimony. Even the dual description of an event is not only simply sustained but also strongly promoted throughout the Gospel. We may name it a "dual mode," a twofold description or arrangement in writing. This dual mode occurs throughout John, whether in the macro structure or in the micro style, whether it comes just for double emphasis or appears as the Johannine pattern of repetition/variation.

Thus, the dual mode of reading is the key to interpreting the Johannine structure in John, paying attention to John in terms of how they are arranged in dual mode.

The Chiastic Structure of John

There are five parts in John. Chapter 1 is the introductory chapter, while chs. 20–21 are the closing chapters. Both are used as an *inclusio*, opening and closing the witness to Jesus Christ: prologue and first early witnesses (ch. 1); final witnesses to Jesus Christ, particularly his resurrection, and concluding remarks of witness (chs. 20–21).

There are two main bodies: chs. 2–10 and 13–17. Each body consists of two groups of sections. Chapters 2–10 are categorized into two: 2–4 and 5–10; while chs. 13–17 also fall into two: 13–17 and 18–19. In this way, the dual mode of arrangement is still sustained. Two groups in chs. 2–10 are the Cana cycle (chs. 2–4) and the Festival cycle (chs. 5–10). Two groups in chs. 13–19 are classified as the Farewell discourse (chs. 13–17) and the Passion narrative (chs. 18–19).

There remain chs. 11–12, which are the link between the two bodies: chs. 2–10 and 13–19. As a whole, John presents a typical chiastic structure: AB-X-B'A', in which X is not the center of significance but instead the link in the middle that connects the previous chapters with the following ones. A and A' as well as B (B1B2) and B' (B'1B'2) are balanced in symmetry.[4]

---

4. Among those scholars who highlight the overall chiastic structure of John, Deeks is so radical that he categorizes John roughly into four: A (1:1–18); B (1:19—4:54); C (B', 5:1—12:50); D (A', 13:1—20:31), regarding ch. 21 as a later appendix. Deeks, "Structure of the Fourth Gospel," 80. Scott provides another chiastic structure: A1 (ch. 1); B1 (chs. 2–4); C1 (ch. 5); D (ch. 6); C2 (chs. 7–10);

The Structure of John

A.	1:1-51. Introductory part; Dual	
	B1.	2:1-4:54. Cana Cycle
	B2.	5:1-10:42. Festival Cycle
		X.	11:1-12:50. Linker; Dual
	B'1.	13:1-17:26. Farewell Discourse
	B'2.	18:1-19:42. Passion Narrative
A'.	20:1-21:25. Concluding part; Dual	

A. The Introductory Witness (Ch. 1)

Chapter 1 consists of two sections in dual mode: vv. 1–18 and 19–51. The prologue provides a combined chiastic structure (A-B1-C-B2-X-B'2-C-B'1-A'). It means that not only A (1–2) and A' (18), B1 (3–5) and B'1 (16–17), C (6–8) and C' (15), and B2 (9–11) and B'2 (14) are interrelated, centering X (12–13), but also B1 and B2, B'2 and B'1 are deeply related to each other. This type of structure arises when two combined parallels such as ABCD-X-D'C'B'A' and BD-D'B' are intermixed. It is created to proclaim two kinds of testimonies interrelationally and systematically: "our" testimony (1–5, 9–14, and 16–18; the author group, "we") and that of the Baptist (6–8 and 15).[5]

The second section, vv. 19–51, is divided into two: vv. 19–34 and 35–51. Also see two episodes of the Baptist: vv. 19–28 and 29–34. There are also two units in vv. 35–51: 35–42 and 43–51, both of which are again divided into two subunits: vv. 35–37 and 40–42; 43–46 and 47–51.[6] All of them are arranged in dual mode, implying that this chapter is itself an entity, separated from the rest of John. We can see two kinds of witnesses throughout this chapter: the testimonies of disciples and that of the Baptist.[7]

B1. The Cana Cycle (Chs. 2–4)

Throughout chs. 2–4, there are two episodes in each chapter which are interrelated, mainly in theme. Chapter 2 combined the first Cana miracle and the temple cleansing.

B2 (chs. 11–19); A2 (chs. 20–21). Scott, "Chapter Six as the Center of John." Also compare the chiastic structure of Gerhard-Ellis: A (Witness and Discipleship, 1:19—4:3); B (Response: Positive and negative, 4:4—6:15); X (New Exodus, 6:16–21); B' (Response: Positive and Negative, 6:22—12:11); A' (Witness and Discipleship, 12:12—21:25). Ellis, *Genius of John*, 13–15; Ellis, "Understanding the Concentric Structure," 148–49.

5. Cf. O'Day, "Word Become Flesh," 67–71.

6. Mlakuzhyil finds some of this type of two-fold presentation in ch. 1 (19–28 and 29–34; 35–42 and 43–51) and calls it "discovery-diptych." Mlakuzhyil, *Christocentric Literary Structure*, 117.

7. For the diagram of the structure of ch. 1, see the note of ch. 1.

In ch. 3, there are the Nicodemus episode and the Baptist one. In ch. 4, the Samaritan episode and that of a royal official are arranged together.[8]

The first Cana miracle and the temple cleansing episode in ch. 1 share two motifs: renovation (or revival) and replacement (or transformation), both of which are the main issues throughout John.[9] As Jesus revives the wedding banquet by creating new wine, so he reforms the temple system by removing its corruption and proclaiming the temple as the house of the Father. As the Jewish liturgical water is replaced with the new wine which may symbolize a new system established by Jesus, so the second temple, the body of Christ, is highlighted, in the temple episode, and implied to replace the first, old temple. Two episodes are arranged in dual mode, so as to proclaim two similar issues: renovation and replacement, or from old to new.

In ch. 3, the dialogue of Jesus with Nicodemus and the episode of the Baptist are interrelated in that they share significant motifs: the man from heaven; love of God; salvation and condemnation; belief vs. disbelief. Both episodes contain the commentary parts (16–21 and 31–36), which are presumed as having been done by the evangelist who is concerned with comparisons among the characters: Jesus and Nicodemus; Jesus and the Baptist.

Chapter 4 provides two episodes: the Samaritans and a royal official. Two episodes share certain similarity in that there is salvation by Jesus and their belief in him as a group or a family. At the same time, two episodes are in contrast because the Samaritans are lower in racial status at that time, while the official is higher in rank in his society. Nevertheless, both need salvations from Jesus because the Jewish system of religion could not save either of them. Jesus alone grants it to them.

The Cana cycle, from Cana to Cana, also creates a chiastic structure: ABC-C'B'A'. The first Cana miracle (A) is definitely related to the second Cana one (A').[10] The temple episode (B) is more or less related to the Samaritan one (B') in terms of wor-

---

8. Borchert sees the Cana cycle as five events (2:1–11, 13–22; 3:1–36; 4:1–42, 43–54) and two transitional parts (2:12, 23–25). Borchert, *John 1–11*, 151. He regards 4:1–42 as the discourse on Nicodemus and salvation because he probably thinks that it would be difficult to segregate 3:22–36 (the Baptist episode) from 3:1–36, disregarding the dual mode in John. It happens similarly in Carson, *Gospel according to John*, 166–67. Godet and Talbert put 2:1–11 in the category of 1:19—2:11. Godet, *Commentary on John's Gospel*, vi–vii, 299–300, 355. Talbert, *Reading John*, 85–86; Talbert, "Artistry and Theology," 342–45. Stibbe also presents a chiastic structure: A (the first Cana sign, 2:1–11); B (transitional passage, 2:12); C (Jesus and Nicodemus, 3:1–15); D (transitional passage, 3:22); E (Jesus and John the Baptist, 3:23–30); D' (transitional passage, 4:1–3); C' (Jesus and the Samaritan woman, 4:4–42); B' (transitional passage, 4:43–45); A' (the second Cana sign, 4:46–54). Stibbe, "Magnificent but Flawed," 151.

9. See more detail in the note in ch. 2 regarding the structure of ch. 2.

10. Culpepper introduces a sevenfold pattern in similarity between the first Cana sign and the second one: (1) A supplicant presents Jesus with a request (2:3; 4:47); (2) Jesus rebuffs the request (2:4; 4:48); (3) The supplicant persists (2:5; 4:49); (4) Jesus gives instructions that will grant the request (2:7–8; 4:50); (5) The other person complies with Jesus' order, and the sign is accomplished (2:8–9; 4:50); (6) The sign is verified by a third party (2:10; 4:51–53); (7) There is a response of faith (2:11; 4:54). Culpepper, "John 5:1–18," 198–99. According to Culpepper, this sevenfold pattern originated from David Buttrick's classes. See also Borchert, *John 1–11*, 96–98.

ship motif for the new era. The Nicodemus episode (C) and the Baptist one (C') are inseparable, as introduced previously.

It means that two ways of arrangement, the dual mode and chiastic one,[11] are simultaneously designed to classify chs. 2–4 as a group of interrelated sections.[12]

A	The first Cana sign, 2:1-12		A	
A'	The Temple episode, 2:13-25		B	
	B	The dialogue of Jesus with Nicodemus, 3:1-21		C
	B'	The last witness of the Baptist, 3:22-36		C'
		C	The Samaritans episode, 4:1-45	B'
		C'	The second Cana sign, 4:46-54	A'

B2. The Festival Cycle of Jesus (Chs. 5–10)

Six chapters (chs. 5–10), the Festival cycle,[13] each contain an event (or sign) and its related discourse (or dialogue), somehow differing from the previous chapters (2–4) regarding the way that two episodes are arranged in dual mode in each chapter.

All six chapters can be grouped into three: 5–6, 7–8, and 9–10. Each two chapters share similar themes between them. Chapters 5–6 have the life-giver (including the judge) issue in common as the primary motif.[14] Chapters 7–8 share the issue of

---

11. The Cana cycle is deliberately designed by the evangelist. There are, in all six episodes, arranged in dual mode and simultaneously in chiasm, proclamations of Jesus as the reviver, as well as the replacer, of the old system of religion, Judaism, with his own system of religion, Jesus Christ himself. Specifically, the wine miracle at Cana is placed there not only to be matched with the temple episode, but also to create the Cana cycle which is closed by the second Cana miracle (healing the son of a royal official). Thus, the second miracle at Cana cannot be regarded as the second miracle by Jesus in his ministry because it is just the second one at Cana.

12. Ridderbos comments that John theologically provides the sequential, geographical meaning of the Cana cycle that are regarded as "the contours of all the great themes that dominate this entire Gospel." Ridderbos, *Gospel according to John*, 97–99. See also Borchert, *John 1–11*, 145–46. "His order of events is crucial, not our later logic. His order is directed to his purpose for organizing the sections the way they are put together." However, it is not like the structure of Coloe, who provides the narrative one of 1:19—3:36: A. 1:19–34, John (witness); B. 1:35–51, Disciples of John/Jesus; C. 2:1–12, Wedding; X. 2:13–25, My Father's house; C'. 3:1–21, Birth; B'. 3:22–24, Disciples of John/Jesus; A'. 3:25–36, John (friend of the bridegroom). Coloe, "Witness and Friend," 330.

13. We can see the name "Festival Cycle" in Stephen Kim, "Significance of Jesus' Healing," 308 (esp. n. 5), 318.

14. In chs. 5 and 6, the geographical factor (Jerusalem in ch. 5 and Galilee in ch. 6) is not the matter, but rather the thematic issue is concerned. In this sense, Ashton and Lindars are right in that ch. 6 "affords such a good illustration of the concluding assertion of ch. 5, Jesus' claim that Moses 'wrote of me' (5:46)." The reference to Moses continues in ch. 6. Ashton, *Understanding the Fourth Gospel*, 200–201. However, their later insertion theory of ch. 6 is suspicious. Regarding the comparison between chs. 5 and 9, refer to Staley's interesting chapter "Stumbling in the Dark," in his *Reading with a Passion*, 27–54.

whence Jesus came and where he is going to. Chapters 9–10 again contain the life-giver (including the judge) issue as one of its primary themes.

Chapters 5–6 are related to the day of Sabbath (ch. 5) and the season of Passover (ch. 6). Similar to them, chs. 9–10 are related to the day of Sabbath (ch. 9) and the season of Dedication (ch. 10). In this sense, we may name them Sabbath-Passover episodes (chs. 5–6) and Sabbath-Dedication ones (chs. 9–10). In between them, there are chs. 7–8, which focus on the Feast of Tabernacles.

Chs. 5 and 9 are interrelated in terms of the healing episodes on the Sabbath, both of which share the idea that Jesus is the life/light-giver as well as the judge.[15] The two men who are healed by Jesus are contrasted to each other: accuser (ch. 5) and testifier (ch. 9). Chapters 6 and 10 are also related to each other, for they share the motif that Jesus is the shepherd who takes care of his sheep in feeding them and providing abundant life as well as sacrificing himself for them. In this sense, two chapters (5–6) are in a pair with another two chapters (9–10).[16]

Chapters 7–8 are located in the middle of chs. 5–10, focusing on the issue of the origin of Jesus as well as regarding where he is going to. The relation to the Feast of Tabernacles, the light issue (ch. 7) and the water one (ch. 8) are highlighted.[17] Chapters 5–6, 7–8, and 9–10 are paired chapters sharing themes, we can see the chiastic structure within them: A-X-A'. A and A' are mutually connected, while X functions as a center.

However, each two chapters are not totally separated from the other paired chapters. Chapter 6 is linked to the next chapter, ch. 7, in that both share the origin of Jesus issue (6:33, 38, 42, 50–51, 58; 7:27–29, 41–42, and 52) and the Moses motif

---

15. For parallel features between chs. 5 and 9, refer to Malina and Rohrbaugh, *Social-Science Commentary*, 109.

16. Regarding the relation between chs. 9 and 10, see Du Rand, "Syntactical and Narratological," 94–115. However, there are some disagreements with him in detail, particularly the structures of each chapter.

17. Regarding water and light at the Tabernacles, see Talbert, *Reading John*, 148–49, 152–53. The chiastic structure of Coloe regarding the relation of chs. 7–8 is plausible: A (7:1–13). "He could not go about in Judea because the Jews sought to kill him" The Feast of Tabernacles; B (7:14–24). Moses—the issue of origins; C (7:25–36). Who is Jesus?—his origins and destiny; D (7:37–39). Jesus' first reply—Living Water; X (7:40–52). Jesus' identity—*Schisma*, reason—his origins in Galilee; D' (8:12). Jesus' second reply—Light of the world; C' (8:13–30); Who is Jesus?—his origin and destiny; B' (8:31–58). Abraham (8:31–58)—the issue of origins; A' (8:59)—"They took up stones to throw at him; he went out of the temple." Coloe, *God Dwells with Us*, 116–19. Her structure is impressive and seems to be convincing. However, there are a few troubles which remain to be solved. First, there are problems of division. 7:1–15 needs to be divided into vv. 1–9 and 10–15 (see I1 and 2). 8:12–36 is an entity, and thus we need to divide it into 8:12–36 and 37–58. But we may say that these are not a big issue here. Second, here introduction (7:1–13) and conclusion (8:59) are not matched in balance of size, even though they share an issue (their attempts to kill Jesus: 7:1 and 8:59), thereby they seem to be unnatural as a pair. Third, the *schisma* does not occur in 7:40–52, but there are not a few passages of *schisma* in ch. 7, such as vv. 10–15, 25–27, 30–32, and 35–36. It is interesting that we can find hardly any *schisma* in ch. 8. It may mean that *schisma* is the primary issue in ch. 7 but not in ch. 8. Then, how can we say that 7:40–52 are in the center of the structure of chs. 7–8?

(6:32; 7:22–23). Chapters 8 and 9 are also connected to each other because they share the light of the world issue, but with different meanings: regarding light-darkness (or freedom by truth and slavery in sin, ch. 8) and seeing-blinding (ch. 9).

It means that all the chapters from ch. 5 to ch. 10 are connected to each other, both sequentially (chapter by chapter) and interactively (in chiastic relation). Interestingly, *ego eimi*, an emphatic expression regarding the identity of Jesus, appears only in the latter chapters of each paired ones, chs. 6 (the bread of life from heaven), 8 (the light of the world[18] and others), and 10 (the gate of sheep; the good shepherd). There is no *ego eimi* in chs. 5, 7, and 9 regarding the identity of Jesus.[19]

A.	(Ch. 5) Sign (healing) + Discourse (life-giver; judge)	Sabbath	
	(Ch. 6) Sign (feeding/at sea) + Discourse (bread of life)	Passover	*ego eimi*
X.	(Ch. 7) Event (brothers) + Discourse (whence and whereto)	Tabernacle	
	(Ch. 8) Event (adultery) + Discourse (whence and whereto; light/sin)		*ego eimi*
A'.	(Ch. 9) Sign (healing) + Discourse (opening/blinding; judge)	Sabbath	
	(Ch. 10) Discourse (gate/shepherd) + Argument (Son of God; life-giver)	Dedication	*ego eimi*

X. The Linker (Chs. 11–12)

Chapters 11–12 are not regarded as a part either of the previous group of chapters or of the following ones, for they play a role of stepping stone that connects two sides of chapters in the middle of John. These two chapters are not like the previous chapters which are arranged in paired chapters and are instead unique in their formats and contents. Chapters 11–12 are divided into two: 11:1—12:19 and 12:20–50.

In the first part, 11:1—12:19, there are three episodes of Jesus that are all accompanied by the responses of the Jews to Jesus' actions (11:45–57; 12:9–12; 12:17–19). The first episode (resuscitation of Lazarus) is the largest among the three, larger than the size of the two other episodes put together. The last two episodes are arranged in a pair, similar in pattern (an event and the response of the Jews, both of which indicate the Lazarus issue) and in size. As a whole, we can classify the structure of 11:1—12:19 as a trifold parallel, AB-A'B'-A"B" (an event and its related response of the Jews) or as a dual (A-A'[ab-a'b'], the Lazarus episode and its two related episodes which are arranged in ab-a'b').

The second part, 12:20–50, can be categorized into two: vv. 20–36 and 37–50 (twofold narratives). Verses 20–36 that are initiated by a small report on the meeting between a few Greeks and his disciples, Philip and Andrew (20–22), contain three

---

18. In 9:5, the other light of the world verse, *ego* is omitted.

19. Compare with the chiastic structure of Mlakuzhyil: B (5:1–47); C (6:1–71); D (7:1—8:59); D' (9:1–41); C' (10–21); B' (10:22–42). Mlakuzhyil, *Christocentric Literary Structure*, 214–15, 239.

consecutive discourses which are all related to the death motif: 23-26 (a grain of wheat falling into the earth and dying), 27-30 (prayer at Gethsemane), and 31-36 (final condemnation and his death of the cross). Verses 37-50 consist of two: one is the comment of the evangelist on the signs of Jesus and the unbelief in him which are already referred in chs. 2-10; the other is the discourse of Jesus which probably summarizes all the contents of chs. 2-10, proclaiming himself as the judge and the savior who deserves their faith.

Verses 20-36 that contain the issue of Jesus' suffering are related mainly to the following chapters (chs. 13-19) and vv. 37-50 are to the previous chapters (chs. 2-10).[20] 11:1-12:19 where the three episodes are related in terms of the Lazarus issue playing their role of linker, for these episodes reveal the divine identity of Jesus as in chs. 2-10 and also they are all grouped with a mono theme (preparing for the death and resurrection of Jesus) which culminates in the following chapters, 13-19.

A.	a.	The resuscitation of Lazarus, 11:1-44
	b.	The response of the Jews, 11:45-47
	a'.	Mary and ointment, 12:1-8
	b'.	The response of the Jews, 12:9-11
	a".	The final coming of Jesus to Jerusalem, 12:12-17
	b".	The response of the Jews, 12:18-19
A'	a.	Triple discourses regarding Jesus' sufferings, 12:30-36
	a'.	A commentary and a discourse regarding belief, 12:37-50

B'1. The Farewell Discourse (Chs. 13-17)

The first group of chapters in the second main body is chs. 13-17, called the Farewell Discourse. This discourse also contains a few narratives in between but mainly consists of the long discourse of Jesus before his sufferings. Chapters 13-17 demonstrate a typical, chiastic structure: AB-X-B'A': A. 13:1-36, the opening (washing the feet of his disciples, dialogue on departure and love-betrayal); B. 14:1-31, the discourse on departure, love, and *paracletos*; X. 15:1-17, the vine parable and its explanation; B'. 15:18—16:33, the discourse on departure, love, and *paracletos*; A'. 17:1-26, the closing (the prayer of Jesus regarding his departure and unity of disciples). In B and B', not a few issues are duplicated for double, intensified emphases. In A, we can see the opening narrative and, in A', we find the closing prayer. And the themes, in A and A', are shared such as the love of Jesus; loving each other (unity); the departure of Jesus; teaching them with his words; the betrayer (Judas). In the center (X), the

20. See Talbert, *Reading John*, 179-80.

The Structure of John

essential parable describes the inseparable relationship between Jesus (the Vine) and his disciples (its branches) and that among them (for bearing much fruit by loving each other.)[21]

A.	Washing the feet of his disciples (Departure; Love), 13:1-38		
	B.	Departure; Holy Spirit, 14:1-31	
		X.	The Vine parable (Love in unity), 15:1-17
	B'.	Departure; Holy Spirit, 15:18-16:33	
A'.	The last prayer of Jesus (Departure; Unity), 17:1-26		

B'2. The Passion Narrative (Chs. 18–19)

Chapters 18–19, the Passion Narrative, consists of four sections: 18:1–12 (arresting Jesus); 18:13–27 (interrogation of Jesus by the Jewish authorities); 18:28—19:15 (interrogation of Jesus by Pilate); 19:16–42 (his death on the cross). In the middle, there are two kinds of interrogation: by the Jewish authorities and by Pilate, happening in a pair (B and B'). Thus, the first section, the scene of arresting Jesus, and the last one, the scene of his death on the cross, are arranged in a pair (A and A'), embracing the Passion Narrative as the beginning and the closing scenes.

It is so interesting to observe that the scenes of the denial of Peter do not appear consecutively but instead in a dual (18:15–18 and 25–27) that differs from those in the Synoptic Gospels where the denial of Peter is described without any break in between. Accordingly, the scene of interrogation by the Jewish authorities is divided into two (18:13–14 and 19–24). There are in all two occasions when Pilate is questioning Jesus (18:33–38a and 19:9–11) and Pilate is arguing with the Jews regarding the innocence of Jesus (18:38b–40 and 19:4–8). Besides them, Pilate wishes to release Jesus twice (18:39; 19:12) and the Jews cry out to crucify Jesus twice (19:6 and 15). There are two events of "delivery": the Jews hand over Jesus to Pilate (18:30); Pilate delivers him to the soldiers (19:16). The scene of the death of Jesus on the cross is described in a dual

---

21. Compare the chiastic structure of Ellis: A (13:1–32); B (13:33—14:31); C (15:1–25); B' (15:26—16:33); A' (17:1–26). Ellis, *Genius of John*, 210–11. See also the model of Brouwer: A. Gathering scene, 13:1–35; B. Prediction of the disciple's denial, 13:36–38; C. Jesus' departure tempered by the assurance of the father's power, 14:1–14; D. the promise of the *paracletos*, 14:15–26; E. Troubling encounter with the world, 14:27–31. F. The vine and branches teaching, producing a community of mutual love, 15:1–17; E1. Troubling encounter with the world, 15:18–16:4a; D1. The promise of the *paracletos*, 16:4b–15; C1. Jesus' departure tempered by the assurance of the father's power, 16:16–28; B1. Prediction of the disciples' denial, 16;29–33; A1. Departing prayer, 17:1–26. Brouwer, *Literary Development of John 13–17*, 9–10. There are questionable divisions between 14:15–26 and 14:27–31 and between 16:4b–15 and 16:16–28. See also the structure of Moloney: A (13:1–38); B (14:1–31); C (15:1–11); X (15:12–17); C' (15:18–16:3); B' (16:4–33); A' (17:1–26). Moloney, "Function of John 13–17," 66.

mode: 19:16–30 and 31–42, each of which contain two quotations from the OT to be accomplished (19:24, 28 and 19:36–37).[22]

A.	Arrest of Jesus, 18:1-12	
	B.	First interrogation: Jewish authorities, 18:13-27
	B'.	Second interrogation: Pilate, 18:28-19:15
A'.	Death of Jesus, 19:16-42	

A'. The Concluding Part, Final Witnesses (Chs. 20–21)

The resurrection episodes are presented in dual mode: first in Jerusalem (ch. 20) and second at the sea of Tiberias (ch. 21).[23] In Jerusalem, the resurrected Jesus appears to two sorts of people: Mary at the tomb (20:1–18) and his disciples at the door-locked place (20:19–29). There are two scenes in the Mary episodes: the empty tomb (1–10) and meeting Jesus who is risen (11–29). The disciples of Jesus have seen him twice: in the absence of Thomas (19–23) and in the presence of Thomas (24–29). Then, there is the first concluding statement in vv. 30–31.[24]

At the Sea of Tiberias (ch. 21), two scenes are presented in dual mode, too: Jesus and the seven disciples at sea (1–14); Jesus and Peter in dialogue (15–23). Then, there is the second, last concluding statement in vv. 24–25. It is so amazing to examine that the two concluding statements, 20:30–31 and 21:24–25, become a chiastic structure if they are put together: A (20:30, many other signs that are not written); B (20:31, the purpose of this writing); B' (21:24, the truthfulness of this writing); A' (20:25, many other things that are not written).

There are two kinds of witnesses in the introductory part (ch. 1): the Baptist and the early disciples. Similarly, there are two kinds of witnesses to the resurrection of Jesus in the concluding part (chs. 20–21): Mary and the disciples. There are his disciples who appear at both sides of the episodes as significant witnesses for Jesus. The role of the Baptist as the witness to Jesus is replayed by Mary in the latter part of John. It may mean that Mary is the significant figure, at the time of resurrection, who is compared with the Baptist.

---

22. For the apologetic and soteriological meanings of the four quotations, see Garland, "Fulfillment Quotations," 230–50. Cf. Schuchard, *Scripture within Scripture*, 133–49. And compare the structure of Moloney: A (18:1–11); B (18:12–27); C (18:28–19:16); B' (19:17–37); A' (19:38–42). Moloney, "Into Narrative and Beyond," 207.

23. It is absolutely right that Gaventa suggests that John has two endings just as it has two beginnings. Gaventa, "Archive of Excess," 240–52.

24. Although Mlakuzhyil found "resurrection-diptychs" (20:1–10 and 20:11–18; 20:19–23 and 20:24–29), unfortunately, he could not extend this phenomenon to ch. 21 and ignored the double-conclusion. Mlakuzhyil, *Christocentric Literary Structure*, 117.

A.	Resurrected Jesus I (Jerusalem), 20:1-29		
	a.	1.	Mary and the empty tomb (1-10)
		2.	Mary and the risen Jesus (11-18)
	a'.	1.	Jesus and his disciples without Thomas (19-23)
		2.	Jesus and his disciples with Thomas (24-29)
	B.	Purpose of John, 20:30-31	
A'.	Resurrected Jesus II (Sea of Tiberias), 21:1-23		
	a.		Jesus and seven disciples at sea (1-14)
	a'.		Jesus and Peter in dialogue (15-23)
	B'.	Truthfulness in John, 21:24-25	

ISSUES REGARDING THE STRUCTURE OF JOHN[25]

1. *The Overall Structure*[26]

It is the traditional way to divide John into the Book of Signs (1:19—12:50) and the Book of Glory (13:1—20:31), as Dodd and Brown did.[27] It is seen that the end of ch. 12 and the beginning of ch. 13 mark a break in the narrative, and 12:44-50 are regarded as the last words of Jesus in public, while the discourse of chs. 13-17 are for his disciples only. They thought that 1:19—12:50 mainly consist of Jesus' miracles, "signs," and his discourses which interpret the signs.[28] And 13:1—20:31 primarily concerns the theme of Jesus' return to his Father, namely the glorification of Jesus which culminates in the event of resurrection.

R. Brown divided 1:19—12:50 (Book of Signs) into four parts:[29] part one, the opening days of the revelation of Jesus (1:19-51); part two, from Cana to Cana—various

---

25. We may add other issues such as the delimitation of the introductory part; the location of the temple episode. These issues are going to be dealt with in the notes on chs. 1 and 2.

26. For the diverse structure models more than twenty-four types, see Mlakuzhyil, *Christocentric Literary Structure*, 17-85.

27. Dodd, *Interpretation of the Fourth Gospel*, x; he called the latter the Book of the Passion; Brown, *Gospel according to John I-XII*, cxxxviii. Moloney also follows this category: I. The Prologue (1:1-18); II. The Book of Signs (1:19—12:50); III. The Book of Glory (13:1—20:31); IV. The Conclusion to the Gospel (20:30-31); V. Epilogue (21:1-25). Moloney, *Gospel of John*, 23-24. Similarly, Mlakuzhyil suggests his structure: I (1:1—2:11) Introduction; II (chs. 2-12) The Book of Jesus' Signs; III (chs. 13-20) The Book of Jesus' Hour; IV (20:30-31) Conclusion; V (ch. 21) Appendix. Mlakuzhyil, *Christocentric Literary Structure*, xii. The structure of Burge is similar. Burge, *Interpreting the Gospel of John*, 76-82. Another similar division is found in Barrett: I. Prologue (1:1-18); II. Narratives, conversations, and discourses (1:19—12:50); III. Jesus alone with his disciples (13:1—17:26); IV. The passion and resurrection (18:1—20:31); V. An appendix (21:1-25). See also Barrett, *Gospel according to St. John*, 11.

28. Brown, *Gospel according to John I-XII*, cxxxix.

29. Ibid., cxl-cxli. Cf. Brodie, who divides John according to his presumed time development:

responses to Jesus' ministry in the different sections of Palestine (chs. 2–4); part three, Jesus and the principal feasts of the Jews (chs. 5–10); part four, Jesus moves toward the hour of death and glory (chs. 11–12). And he divided 13:1—20:31 (Book of Glory) into three parts and conclusion:[30] part one, the Last Supper (13:1—17:26); part two, the Passion Narrative (18:1—19:42); part three, the risen Jesus (20:1–29); Conclusion to the Book of Glory (20:30-31).

Specifically, Dodd divides Book One into seven episodes:[31] (1) The new beginning (2:1—4:42); (2) The life-giving Word (4:46—5:47); (3) The Bread of life (ch. 6); (4) Light and life (chs. 7–8); (5) Judgement by the Light (9:1—10:21) and Appendix (10:22–39); (6) The victory of life over death (11:1-53); (7) Life through death (12:1–36).[32]

According to Beasley-Murray, John can be divided as follows:[33] I. 1:1–18 (The Prologue); II. 1:19—12:50 (The public ministry of Jesus): A. 1:19–51 (Testimonies to Jesus); B. 2:1—4:42 (The revelation of the new order in Jesus); C. 4:43—5:47 (Jesus the Mediator of life and judgment); D. 6:1–71 (Jesus the Bread of Life); E. 7:1—8:59 (Jesus the Water and Light of Life); F. 9:1—10:42 (Jesus the Light and Shepherd of humankind); G. 11:1–54 (Jesus the Resurrection of the Life); H. 11:55—12:50 (Jesus the King, triumphant through death); III. 13:1—20:31 (The passion and resurrection of Jesus): A. 13:1—17:26 (The ministry of Jesus to the disciples in the upper room); B. 18:1—20:31 (The death and resurrection of Jesus); IV. 21:1-25 (Epilogue: The mission of the church and its chief apostles).

First, regarding the title "Book of Signs," Beasley-Murray pointed out the problem that the whole work in John is viewed as a book of signs according to 20:30-31,

---

Part 1, the first year (1:1—2:22); Part 2, the second year (2:23—ch. 6); Part 3A, the third year (chs. 7–12); Part 3B (chs. 13–21). Brodie, *Gospel according to John*, 41–45.

30. Brown, *Gospel according to John XIII–XXI*, ix–x.

31. Dodd, *Fourth Gospel*, x, 384–89. Cf. Temple, *Core of the Fourth Gospel*, 40–41; Grassi, "Role of Jesus' Mother," 68–71.

32. Compare the relations between the seven signs and discourses of Morris, who suggested those pairs as follows: 1. Water into wine (2:1–11) and the new birth (3:1–21); 2. Healing the nobleman's son (4:46–54) and the water of life (4:1–42); 3. Healing the lame man (5:1–18) and the divine Son (5:19–47); 4. Feeding the multitude (6:1–15) and the bread of life (6:22–65); 5. Walking on the water (6:16–22) and the life-giving Spirit (7:1–52); 6. Sight to the man born blind (9:1–41) and the light of the world (8:12–59); 7. Raising of Lazarus (11:1–57) and the good shepherd (10:1–42). Morris, *Jesus Is the Christ*, 23; Morris, *Gospel according to John*, viii–x; See also Köstenberger, *John*, 52, 89–90. Carson adds the passion and resurrection of Jesus (chs. 18–20) which corresponds to chs. 14–17. It seems to be probable but less convincing because some of them are not deeply related, as Carson pointed out. See Carson, *Gospel according to John*, 274. It is interesting that Grassi explains the Cana miracle of wine (2:1–11) in regard to the Pentecostal coming of Holy Spirit. *Grassi*, "Wedding at Cana," 131–36. Grigsby relates the miracle at Siloam ch. 9 to the living water motif in ch. 4. Grigsby, "Washing in the Pool of Siloam," 254–58.

33. Beasley-Murray, *John*, xci–xcii.

The Structure of John

for the resurrection of Jesus is the ultimate sign of the Christ for man.³⁴ Moreover, the fulfilment of the feast of the Jews is another prime theme in chs. 2–12.

Second, Dodd's seven divisions are criticized by Brown: "Chapters 2–4 are composed of at least five different stories set in different locales; ch. 11 consists substantially of one well-knit narrative. Has not Dodd too been hypnotized by a desire to find a pattern of seven in the Gospel?"³⁵

Third, we have to consider the cohesiveness of chs. 2–4, 5–10, 13–17, and 18–19 as a group of chapters which demonstrate certain parallel or chiastic structure of networks in themselves, as discussed before. We may say that four key concepts of what Jesus is like are presented: the replacer (chs. 2–4, the replacer of Judaism); the revealer (chs. 5–10, the revealer to the world); the lover (chs. 13–17, the lover of his disciples); the sacrificer (chs. 18–19, the sacrificer for his people). These four concepts are interrelated and are also bound two by two: the replacer and the revealer (chs. 2–10); the lover and sacrificer (chs. 13–19).

In the middle of John, there is the sign of the resuscitation of Lazarus (ch. 11): (1) which is described in much more detail than other signs in chs. 2–10; (2) which foretells the resurrection of Jesus; (3) which demonstrates Jesus as the Resurrection and the Life.³⁶ There are also its related two events (ch. 11) and some discourses which are interrelated both to the previous and the following chapters in theme.

2. The Linker

Talbert divides 11:55—12:50 into an introduction (11:55–57), two days (12:1–11 and 12–36), and two conclusions (12:37–43 and 44–50), regarding their function as a conclusion to what has come before (so 12:37–50 to 2:13—11:54) and as an introduction to what follows (so 11:55—12:36 to chs. 13–17).³⁷

First, ch. 11 cannot be included in the group of the previous chapters (2–10 or 5–10), for the pattern, an episode and its following responses of the Jews regarding the Lazarus issue, still continue in the next two episodes (Mary's anointing of his feet; Jesus' final coming to Jerusalem). It means that 11:1—12:19 are bound into a group of episodes.

Second, these three consecutive episodes reflect mainly the sufferings of Jesus as well as his glory regarding resurrection. These themes are not shown primarily in the previous chapters, although they are partially indicated somewhere. Rather, it shows that they are connected to the following chapters in theme.

---

34. Ibid., *John,* xc.

35. Brown, *Gospel according to John I–XII,* cxlii.

36. Hitchcock is probably the first scholar who examined the centering role of the Lazarus episode from a dramatic point of view, perceiving its perfect harmony with all that has preceded and all that is to follow in John. Hitchcock, "Is the Fourth Gospel a Drama?," 20.

37. Talbert, *Reading John,* 179.

Third, moreover, it is sure that ch. 11 should remain as the linker, namely, for chs. 5–10 is a group of chapters that is well-designed in chiastic structure as a whole.[38] There is no way for ch. 11 to be included here.

3. The Farewell Discourse

R. Brown pointed out at least four problems which are not easily solved regarding this issue:[39] First, the first conversation ends in 14:31 as "Let's go" is spoken and may not continue further. Second, there are repetitions and duplications between 13:31—14:31 and 15:4b-33. Third, the vine parable in 15:1-6 is not relevant to the theme of Jesus' departure. Fourth, the various theological themes seem not to have been delivered at the same time.

Due to these problems, scholars such as Stagg have negative views on grasping the consistent structure of the Farewell Discourse, determining that there is not any organized structure and designed arrangement to be found.[40] Moloney also asserts that it is difficult to see John 13-17 as a literary unit, believing there are many strata and a mixture of various contents.[41] He insists that any attempt to categorize each stratum according to style has not been successful. Nonetheless, he regards that it is necessary that John 13-16 may be considered as a literary discourse separate from John 17.

Bultmann, who saw such varied sources which had been mixed and not presented in consistency throughout periods, attempted to rearrange the order of the discourse: 17:1-26; 13:3-35; 15:1-27; 16:1-33; 13:1-30; 13:36-38; 14:1-31.[42] Brown, who supported his stand, also criticized the hypothesis of Bultmann, questioning the final redactor placed 14:30-31 in the middle of the discourse without noticing its problem.[43] Painter, regarding 13:31—16:33 as three strata, insists that three different bundles of contents are combined:[44] the first before the conflict with the synagogue (13:31—14:31); the second during the rejection by the synagogue (15:1—16:4a) and

---

38. Carson regards chs. 11-12 as "Transition: Life and death, king and suffering servant," for he sees that "the final verses of ch. 10 close a giant *inclusio*: Jesus' public ministry begins and ends with the witness of the Baptist (1:19-10:42)." Carson, *Gospel according to John*, 403.

39. Brown, *Gospel according to John XIII-XXI*, 582-83; Cf. Teeple, *Literary Origin of the Gospel of John*, 1; Segovia, "Structure, Tendenz, and Sitz im Leben," 471, 488.

40. Stagg, "Farewell Discourses," 459-60.

41. Moloney, *Gospel of John*, 370-71; cf. Moloney, "Into Narrative and Beyond," 206-7; Moloney, "Function of John 13-17," 43-45.

42. Bultmann, *Gospel of John*, 457-61.

43. Brown, *Gospel according to John XIII-XXI*, 584.

44. Painter, *Quest for the Messiah*, 417-34. Also see the four divisions of Tolmie: The Footwashing and Exposure of the Traitor (13:1-30); The Farewell Discourses: Phase one (13:31—14:31); The Farewell Discourses: Phase two (15:1—16:33); The Prayer of Farewell (17:1-26). Tolmie, *Jesus' Farewell to the Disciples*, 28-32.

the third (16:4b–33) in opposition to the synagogue. Boyd suggests an alternative to solve the discrepancy between 13–14 and 15–17 caused by the problem of 14:30–31 and also the issue of duplication between John 14 and 16.[45] He regards John 14–17 as a conversation after his resurrection.[46]

First, O'Day observes a certain trait of the literary construction in John 13–17, acknowledging the Johannine literary way of writing using the repetitions between 14:1–31 and 16:4–33.[47] Segovia simply insists that at least in John 14–16, there is a deliberate, intended, and artistic design in unity and in consistency.[48]

Second, without ch. 17, the systematic structure of chs. 13–17, the chiastic one, cannot be retained, for they are a group of related chapters in unity: AB-X-B'A'.

Third, it is surely not the evangelist's concern that this discourse is treated by the readers as a one-time speech of Jesus (or event) at one sitting of the last supper, although this discourse was presented probably during the last week of Jesus before his sufferings. Thus, it was unnecessary for him to skip the following verse, "Rise, let us go from here" (14:31), and instead he put it there in the role of a pause that prepares the key discourse (the Vine parable) which is located in the center of the whole Farewell Discourse. Centering on that vine speech (15:1–17), 15:18—16:33 complements as well as duplicates the ideas of 14:1–31 for dual (or twofold) emphatic effect. The prayer of Jesus in ch. 17 closes the Farewell Discourse by reorganizing the ideas which are initiated in ch. 13 and repeatedly explicated in chs. 14–16.

4. The Appendix

According to Bultmann, ch. 21 is a postscript, for John reaches its conclusion with 20:30–31. He asserted, "The only question is from whom this postscript was derived. That the Evangelist himself added it, and put it after his first conclusion, then to append yet a second concluding statement (21:24–25), is extraordinarily improbable."[49] Brown regarded ch. 21 as an epilogue, an added account of post-resurrectional appearances in Galilee.[50]

---

45. Regarding the relation between chs. 14 and 16, refer to Reese, "Literary Structure," 321–31.

46. Boyd, "Ascension according to St John," 208.

47. Borchert regards chs. 13–17 as the Farewell cycle because of its literary unity, including the paired chapters (chs. 13 and 17). For more detail, see Borchert, "Passover and the Narrative Cycles," 312–13.

48. Segovia, *Farewell of the Word*, 34.

49. Bultmann, *Gospel of John,* xii, 700.

50. Godet regarded it as a supplement, dividing John into eight parts (I. 1:1–18; II. 1:19—4:54; III. 5:1—12:50; IV. 13:1—17:26; V. 18:1—19:42; VI. 20:1–29; VII. 20:30–31; VIII. 21:1–25), saying, "The entire book, thus, is composed of eight parts, of which five form the body of the story, or the narrative properly so called; one forms the preamble: one the conclusion: the eighth is a supplement." Godet, *Commentary on John's Gospel*, 64–65. Ashton asserts that the great majority of scholars regard it as an appendix. Ashton, *Understanding the Fourth Gospel*, 199.

Beasley-Murray suggests the theory that ch. 21 was written after the death of the author of chs. 1–20, insisting, "It is not merely the unsuitability of ch. 21 following on 20:30–31 that has to be faced: it is rather that the twentieth chapter in its form, structure, and purpose is conceived as a complete presentation of Jesus in the resurrection. It needs no complementation.... The most compelling ground could have been the death of the Beloved Disciple after the writing of chs. 1–20, and the consequent dismay that it caused among the Johannine churches"[51]

First, ch. 21 is not the appendix to John but instead one of the quintessential sections in the concluding part of John.[52] The appendix theory comes about due to a misreading of the Johannine dual mode, particularly in the concluding part of John.

Second, it is so natural in John to have two kinds of concluding statements (20:30–31 and 21:24–25), which are made up as a chiastic structure as the two are placed in parallel. In other words, without the last statement (21:24–25), the first concluding one is not complete by itself.

Third, while the key verses (1:12–13) in the prologue are presented in the center of the chiastic structure, in the concluding part, they appear in a dual (twofold) way of presentation. These two types of key verses are surrounded by many testimonial reports or episodes regarding Jesus Christ.

A.	Many other signs that are not written, 20:30	
	B.	The purpose of this writing, 20:31
	B'	The truthfulness of this writing, 21:24
A'.	Many other things that are not written, 20:25	

---

51. Beasley-Murray, *John*, 395–96. Although Culpepper seems to still maintain the appendix theory regarding ch. 21, he demonstrates two kinds of authenticity of ch. 21 regarding its role in John, both in the completion of themes that have been raised unsolved in chs. 1–20 and in the literary unity of chs. 1–21. Culpepper, "Design for the Church," 369–70. For similar positions, see George, *Reading the Tapestry*, 1–6, 32–41; see also Cassidy, *John's Gospel in New Perspective*, 69–79; George, *Reading Tapestry*, 23–34; Spencer, "Narrative Echoes in John 21," 64–68.

52. The scholarly support for the value and authenticity of ch. 21 have increased. See Moloney, *Glory Not Dishonor*, 182–92, particularly n. 8; Moloney, "John 21 and the Johannine Story," 237–51. Regarding the interesting analysis of the literary relation between chs. 20–21 based on the speech-act theory, see Tovey, *Narrative Art and Act*, 84–97, 109–15.

1 The Prologue and the Early Testimonies

"No passage in the New Testament compels more interest than the prologue of John's Gospel. It is considered by some to be the gospel in miniature and by others to be an awkwardly connected passage that can be eliminated without loss to the message of John. Exactly what is the prologue?"[1]

DUAL MODE IN STRUCTURE

JOHN 1 CAN BE divided into two groups of passages: vv. 1–18 (I, prologue) and vv. 19–51 (II, early testimonies). Again, vv. 19–51 are categorized into two passages: vv. 19–34 (testimony of John the Baptist) and vv. 35–51 (testimonies of his early disciples).

The testimonies of John the Baptist (19–28) consist of two episodes: vv. 19–28 (first testimony) and vv. 29–34 (second testimony). Similarly, the testimonies of early disciples (35–51) are arranged in two parts: vv. 35–42 (first meeting-witness of the disciples); 43–51 (second meeting-witness of the disciples).

I.	Prologue, 1:1-18		
II.	Early testimonies, 1:19-51		
	IIA	Testimonies of the Baptist, 1:19-34	
		IIA1	First testimony of the Baptist, 1:29-34
		IIA2	Second testimony of the Baptist, 1:35-51
	IIB	Testimonies of early disciples, 1:35-51	
		IIB1	First meeting-witness of the disciples, 1:35-42
		IIB2	Second meeting-witness of the disciples, 1:43-51

1. Brown, "Prologue of the Gospel of John," 429.

Besides the prologue (1–18), all the passages in John 1 are made in double mode, enforcing the repetitive effect for the certainty of the identity of Christ. We may say that even the prologue contains two types of testimonies: of the author group ("we": 1–5, 9–14, 16–18; specifically 14 and 16) and of the Baptist (John: 6–8 and 15).

I. The Prologue (1:1–18)

Combined Chiastic, I1 (A-B1-C-B2-X-B'2-C'-B'1-A')

The structure of vv. 1–18 is a complex, chiastic structure, centering v. 12–13: A-B1-C-B2-X-B'2-C'-B'1-A' (or, if oversimplified, ABCD-X-D'C'B'A'). It means that its structure is basically classified as a chiastic one but with some specific, unique relations among its constituents.

A.				1-2, Deity of the Logos 1: God being with God	A
	B1.			3-5, Relationship with the world 1: Creation, life-light, and non-understanding	B
		C.		6-8, Witness of the Baptist 1	C
			B2.	9-11, Relationship with the world 2: Light, creation, and refusal	D
			X.	12-13, Believers, children of God	X
			B'2.	14, Relationship with the believers 1: Incarnation, experience, and full of grace and truth	D'
		C'.		15, Witness of the Baptist 2	C'
	B'1.			16-17, Relationship with the believers 2: Full of grace of truth; reception	B'
A'.				18, Deity of the Logos 2: Appearing God	A'

This diagram tells us that there are at least four pairs of interrelation: A-A', B1-B'1, C-C', and B2-B'2. Additionally, there are two more, inter-connected pairs such as B1 and B2; B'2 and B'1. As seen in its structure, this unit is designed to deliberately create a chiastic effect as well as having an interactive, repetitive impact on the readers in relation to witnessing the Logos.

How to Discern the Complex, Chiastic Structure of vv. 1–18

1. If we consider the cohesive, parallel (or interactive) features among phrases and sentences, we can say that this unit is made up of nine subunits: vv. 1–2, 3–5, 6–8, 9–11, 12–13, 14, 15, 16–17, and 18. Each subunit contains its own cohesiveness in itself, except vv. 3–5 that seem not to have any connected parallel in themselves, but rather show a certain relationship with other verses such as 9a, 10, 11b, and 17b.

2. Primarily, we can find that there are two seemingly, heterogeneous subunits: vv. 6–8 and v. 15, both describing the Baptist and his testimonies. These differ from other verses that are all witnessed directly by "us" about the Son.

3. We may say that vv. 1–5 are in parallel with vv. 16–18. There seem some common ideas shared between them. But if vv. 3–5 are also related to vv. 9–11, it would be better to distinguish vv. 1–2 from vv. 3–5. So with the case of vv. 16–17 from v. 18.

4. After that, we can see that both vv. 1–2 and v. 18 focus on the deity of the Son, Jesus Christ, demonstrating who he is in relationship with God the Father. The name "God" is repeated: three times in vv. 1–2 and twice in v. 18. We may call them A and A'.

5. Verses 3–5 and vv. 16–17 are in common, telling of his relationship toward the world or "us." In vv. 3–5, "life" and "light" occur twice each, while in vv. 16–17, "grace" appears three times and "truth" once. These terms are related to each other in terms of what kind of benefits could be given by the Son to the people: the world and "us."

Besides, there is a parallel between them: All things (a) through him (b) were made (ἐγένετο, c) in v. 3; grace and truth (a') through Jesus Christ (b') came (ἐγένετο, c') in v. 17. We may call vv. 3–5 and vv. 16–17 as B and B'.

6. As mentioned earlier, vv. 6–8 and v. 15 are in a pair. We may call them C and C'. It is observed that v. 15 does not fit in the middle of v. 14 and vv. 16–17, disrupting the flow of the literary context. See how the ideas smoothly flow from v. 14 to vv. 16–17: "(14) And the Word became flesh and dwelt among us, and we have seen his glory, the glory as of the only begotten from the Father, full of grace and truth. (16–17) And from his fullness we all received grace upon grace. For the law through Moses was given; grace and truth through Jesus Christ came." This phenomenon supports v. 15 (C) as being designed to be there purposefully for being paired with vv. 6–8 (C').

7. Both vv. 9–11 and v. 14 focus on his coming into the world, but the responses toward him who came are in contrast: negative as refusal (9–11) and positive as acceptance (14). We may call them D and D'.

8. In vv. 12–13, we can see a kind of pivotal verses inviting the readers to receive the Son. Thus, we may call it X.

9. We can see a manifest, chiastic structure: A (1–2) and A' (18), B (3–5) and B' (16–17), C (6–8) and C' (15), D (9–11) and D' (14) that are definitely in pairs, centering X (12–13).

10. However, there are some which we cannot ignore such as the connections of vv. 3–5 and 9–11; vv. 14 and 16–17. Verses 3–5 are deeply connected to vv. 9–11 in contents: his creatorship (3, 10b); life and light (4, 9a); his coming but being not received (5, 9b, 10b, 11), though the order of appearance is not the same.

	Creatorship	Life and light	Coming but not being received
3-5	3. All things through him were made, and without him was made not one thing that was made.	4. In him life was, and the life was the light of men.	5. And the light shines in the darkness, and the darkness did not comprehend it.
9-11	10b. and the world was made through him	9a. There was the true light that enlightens every man,	9b. coming into the world. 10b. but the world did not know him. 11. He came to what was his own, but his own people did not receive him.

11. Thus, vv. 3–5 which are paired with vv. 16–17 are simultaneously related to vv. 9–11, so in the case of v. 14 with vv. 16–17, as presented earlier, for v. 14 is regarded as a former part of vv. 16–17.

12. It means that this chiastic structure is not simple, but complex in character. We may call them: A-B1-C-B2-X-B'2-C'-B'1-A', carefully including the relationships of vv. 3–5 and 9–11; vv. 14 and 16–17. A and A', B1 and B'1, C and C', B2 and B'2, including B1 and B2, B'2 and B'1, are interrelated. But B1 and B'2, B2 and B'1 are not related in the same way as the other related pairs.

13. We can find a chiastic connection between v. 14 and vv. 16–18 (see I47), excluding v. 15. We have to divide them into three subunits: vv. 14 (B'2), 16–17 (B'1), and 18 (A'). It is, of course, manifest that v. 14 and vv. 16–17 are divided because of the interruption of v. 15. The reason why we segregate vv. 16–17 from v. 18 is as follows:

First, each of these verses needs to be paired with vv. 1–2 and 3–5, respectively. Second, vv. 1–2 and 3–5 cannot be grouped together, because only vv. 3–5 (B1) are deeply connected to vv. 9–11 (B2) as well as to vv. 16–17. Third, vv. 3–5 (B1) along with vv. 9–11 (B2) deal with the negative response of the world toward the Logos, and vv. 16–17 (B'1) along with v. 14 (B'2) describe the positive response of believers towards the Son, while vv. 1–2 (A) and v. 18 (A') highlight the deity of the Word, the Son of God.

A. Deity of the Logos 1 (1:1–2)

In vv. 1–2, we can see four complex, parallel features. Apart from I3, of parallelism, the others are chiastic. It is extremely artistic that I2 and 3 as well as I4 and 5 are made, together and at the same time. I2 and 3 overlap in themselves. I4 and 5 are parts of I2 or I3. These parallels demonstrate how vv. 1–2 are written, artistically and deliberately.

The Prologue and the Early Testimonies

V	2	3	4	Phrases	Translation
1	a	a	a	Ἐν ἀρχῇ	In the beginning
	b	-	b	ἦν	was
	c	-	c	ὁ λόγος,	the Word
	d	b	c'	καὶ ὁ λόγος	and the Word
	e	-	b'	ἦν	was
	f	-	a' 5	πρὸς τὸν θεόν,	with God
	f'	a'	a	καὶ θεὸς	and ~ God
	e'	-	b	ἦν	was
	d'	-	c	ὁ λόγος.	the Word ~
2	c'	b'	c'	οὗτος	This
	b'	-	b'	ἦν	was
	a'	-	a'	ἐν ἀρχῇ πρὸς τὸν θεόν.	in the beginning with God.

I2.[2] Parallel, abcdef-f'e'd'c'b'a':[3] Each of a-a', b-b', c-c', d-d', e-e', f-f' has its pair that consists of almost the same phrases or words. See particularly the location of four appearances of the verb ἦν: how they are in symmetry. I3. Parallel, ab-a'b':[4] The pair a-a' demonstrates that the Word was the God who preexisted as God. The pair b-b' repeats that the Word was with God (the Father) in the beginning.

I4. Chiastic, abc-c'b'a':[5] The phrases a-a' indicate that the Word was in the beginning (a) with God (a'). His being as the Word is focused in b-b'. In c-c', the term, "the Word," is repeated. I5. Chiastic, abc-c'b'a': Showing that the Word himself (c-c') was God (the Son, a) who was with God (the Father) in the beginning (a'). The final phrase "in the beginning with God" (a' of I5) is the combination of "In the beginning" (a of I4) and "with God" (a' of I4).

These verses describe three points in perfect, poetic design: (1) the preexistence of the Word; (2) His identity as the Word; (3) the Word's identity as God.

B1. Relationship with the World 1 (1:3–5)

Verses 3–5 contain six parallel features within them: See I6–7 in v. 3; I8–9 in v. 4; I10–11 in v. 5. Each verse has two parallels: one chiasm and one parallelism, one of

---

2. In the diagrams, numbers (1, 2, 3, etc.) indicate parallelisms and chiasms; thus, number 1 needs to be called I1, and so on. Among them, the bold numbers indicate the parallels that are relatively more certain or much more probable than the plain type of numbers. Regarding the imperfect style of chiasm, see Lund, *Chiasmus in the New Testament*, xix–xx.

3. Originally, Lund, "Influence of Chiasmus," 42; See also Culpepper, "Pivot of John's Prologue," 9–10; Köstenberger, *John*, 20; Von Wahlde, *Gospel and Letters of John*, 19.

4. Of the two in Staley's complex structure, it is the second one. Staley, *Print's First Kiss*, 51.

5. I4 and I5 are discovered by Bailey, *Poet and Peasant*, 59; cited by Keener, *Gospel of John*, 365.

which embraces the other. And there seems to be no inter-connection of verse-to-verse among vv. 3–5.

V	6					48			41	Phrases	Translation
3	a	7			a			a		πάντα	All things
	b	a			b				-	δι' αὐτοῦ	through him
	-	b			c				-	ἐγένετο,	were made,
	b'	a'							-	καὶ χωρὶς αὐτοῦ	and without him
	-	b'							-	ἐγένετο	was made
	a'								-	οὐδὲ ἕν.	not one thing
	-		8						-	ὃ γέγονεν	that was made.
4		a	9			42				ἐν αὐτῷ	In him
		b	a					a		ζωὴ	life
		-	b					-		ἦν,	was,
		b'	a'					-		καὶ ἡ ζωὴ	and the life
		-	b'					-		ἦν	was
		a'	10	11		43				τὸ φῶς τῶν ἀνθρώπων·	the light of men
5			a	a		a				καὶ τὸ φῶς	And the light
			b	b		-				ἐν τῇ σκοτίᾳ	in the darkness
			c		44	-				φαίνει,	shines,
			a'	b'		a				καὶ ἡ σκοτία	and the darkness
			b'	a'		-				αὐτὸ	it
			c'			-				οὐ κατέλαβεν.	did not comprehend.

I6. Chiastic, ab-b'a':[6] The phrases a ("All things") and a' ("not one thing that was made"), b (δι' αὐτοῦ ἐγένετο, through him were made) and b' (καὶ χωρὶς αὐτοῦ ἐγένετο, and without him was made) are contrasted to each other, but the concept of a-b is in fact repeated in a'-b'. **I7.** Parallel, ab-a'b': The phrases in I7 are part of I6 and show a parallel arrangement with contrastive meaning, a-a' (δι' αὐτοῦ and καὶ χωρὶς αὐτοῦ) and b-b' (ἐγένετο).

I8. Chiastic, ab-b'a': Indicating that in him (a) was life (b) but he himself is the life (b') as well as the light of men (a'). In b-b', the life is repeated, while a-a' shows that where the life is and what is meant to be. **I9.** Parallel, ab-a'b': I9 belongs to I8 and shows a simple, parallel arrangement for repetition: ζωὴ (a) and καὶ ἡ ζωὴ (a'); ἦν (b-b').

I10. Parallel, abc-a'b'c':[7] Each a-b-c is in contrast to each counterpart, a'-b'-c': a ("And the light") and a' ("and the darkness"); b ("in the darkness") and b' ("it"); c ("shines") and c' ("did not comprehend"). Indicating that the light shines in the darkness but the darkness did not respond to it. **I11.** Chiastic, ab-b'a': The light (a-a') is repeatedly contrasted to the darkness (b-b').

6. Von Wahlde, *Commentary on the Gospel of John*, 20.
7. Ibid., 20.

The Prologue and the Early Testimonies

In I6–7, the creatorship of Christ is repeatedly emphasized. In I8–9, it is stated that the life is in him and is the light of men. In I10–11, there is the contrast between the light (representing Christ) that shines in the darkness and the darkness (representing the world) that did not comprehend it.

C. *Witness of the Baptist (1:6–8)*

Verses 6–8 contain five parallel features. I12 and 14 are chiastic, while I13, 15, and 16 are parallel. I12 and 14 are relatively apparent, and others seem to be obscure. We can comprehend the internal cohesiveness of vv. 6–8 only if we consider I12 and 14 as parallels. I12 and 13 show the connection between v. 6 and v. 7, and I14 and 15 does that between v. 7 and v. 8, while I16 does that between v. 6 and v. 8, respectively.

V	12			16		Phrases	Translation
6	a	13		a		Ἐγένετο	There was
	b	a		b		ἄνθρωπος,	a man
	c	b		c		ἀπεσταλμένος παρὰ θεοῦ,	sent from God;
	c'		14	15	46	ὄνομα αὐτῷ Ἰωάννης·	his name *was* John.
7	b'	a'	a	a		οὗτος	This man
	a'	b'	-	-		ἦλθεν	came
		-	-	-		εἰς μαρτυρίαν	for testimony,
		-	b	-		ἵνα μαρτυρήσῃ περὶ τοῦ φωτός,	to bear witness to the light,
			x			ἵνα πάντες πιστεύσωσιν	so that all might believe
			-			δι' αὐτοῦ.	through him.
8		a'	a'	a'		οὐκ ἦν	was not
		-	-	b'		ἐκεῖνος	He
		-	-	c'	46	τὸ φῶς,	the light,
		-	b'	a'		ἀλλ' ἵνα μαρτυρήσῃ περὶ τοῦ φωτός.	but *came* to bear witness to the light.

I12. Chiastic, abc-c'b'a': The phrases a (Ἐγένετο, there was) and a' (ἦλθεν, came) are similar both in content and quality and so do b (ἄνθρωπος, a man) and b' (οὗτος, this man), while c (ἀπεσταλμένος παρὰ θεοῦ, sent from God) and c' (ὄνομα αὐτῷ Ἰωάννης, his name was John) clarify who John is. Each syllable of c and c' are eight in number. **I13.** Parallel, ab-a'b': The phrases b and b' describe John's origin (b, by whom he was sent) and his goal of coming (b', the reason why he was sent), while a-a' indicate him directly.

I14. Chiastic, a-x-a': The central x emphasizes the purpose of John's testimony to the light (namely, belief through him). The indications regarding the testimony of John are repeated in a and a': "This man came for a testimony, to bear witness to the light" (a) and "He was not the light but came to bear witness to the light" (a'). **I15.** Parallel, ab-a'b': Explaining that John was not the light but just came for a testimony to it. The syllables of a (οὗτος ἦλθεν εἰς μαρτυρίαν) are eight in number, while a' (οὐκ ἦν ἐκεῖνος τὸ φῶς) are 7. I16. Parallel, abc-a'b'c': The phrases a ("There was") and a' ("was not") are contrasted to each other and so do c ("sent from God") and c' ("the light"), while b ("a man") and b' ("He") indicate John the Baptist. It means that there are two distinguished facts regarding John the Baptist: who he is (abc) versus who he is not (a'b'c').

I12 describe who John is, and I13 draws John as a testifier from God, and I14 focuses on the purpose of his testimony toward the Son, and I15 and 16 emphasize that John is not the light.

B2. Relationship with the World 2 (1:9-11)

In vv. 9-11, there are eight parallels: six parallelisms (I18, 20, 21, 22, 23, 24) and two chiasms (I17 and 19), being in gear one after the other: I17 and 18; I18 and 19; I19 and 20; I20 and 21; I21 and I23. It means that vv. 9-11 cannot be separated from each other, attaching them together. Besides these parallels, I41-45 are observed, which are deeply related to either vv. 3-5 or v. 14.

V	17						42		**Phrases**	**Translation**
9	a						43	a'	Ἦν	There was
	b							a'	-	τὸ φῶς τὸ ἀληθινόν,	the true light
	b'	18						-	ὅ	that
	a'	a						-	φωτίζει	gives light
		b	19			45		-	πάντα ἄνθρωπον,	to every man,
		a'	a			a			ἐρχόμενον	coming
		b'	b	20				-	εἰς τὸν κόσμον.	into the world.
10			b'	a					ἐν τῷ κόσμῳ	in the world
			a'	b	21	24		41	ἦν,	He was,
				a'	a	a		a'	καὶ ὁ κόσμος	and the world
				b'	b	-		-	δι' αὐτοῦ	through him
				-	c	23	-	44	-	ἐγένετο,	was made,
					a'	a	b	a'	καὶ ὁ κόσμος	but the world
					b'	b	-	-	αὐτὸν	him
				22	c'	c	-	45	-	οὐκ ἔγνω.	did not know.
11	a				a'	a'			εἰς τὰ ἴδια	to what was his own
	b				-	-	44		ἦλθεν,	He came,
	a'				a'	b'	a"		καὶ οἱ ἴδιοι	but his own people
	b'				b'	-	-		αὐτὸν	him
	-				c'	-	-		οὐ παρέλαβον.	did not receive.

The Prologue and the Early Testimonies

I17. Chiastic, ab-b'a': Simultaneously demonstrating both the existence of the light (a-b) and its role (enlightening, a'-b'). The pair a and a' is verbs: Ἦν (a, "There was") and φωτίζει (a', "gives light to"), while the pair b and b' points out the same subject: τὸ φῶς τὸ ἀληθινόν (b, "the true light") and ὅ (b', "that [which]"). **I18**. Parallel, ab-a'b': The verbs a and a' are similar in meaning, his approaching the people (b and b'). The number of syllables of a-b and a'-b' are both eight.

I19. Chiastic, ab-b'a': The a-b shows his approach to the world, while the a'-b' demonstrates his existence in the world. The pair a and a' is the role of the true light: "gives light" (a) and "coming" (a'), while the pair b and b' is related in terms of the objects: "to every man" (b) and "into the world" (b'). I20. Parallel, ab-a'b': The function of this sentence is similar to I19, indicating his relationship with the world in two ways (his existence and his creatorship). The pair b and b' is related to him, while the b-b' is to the world: He was (b) in the world (a) and the world (a') was made through him (b'). **I21**. Parallel, abc-a'b'c': The phrases a-a' refer to the world (a, "and the world" and a', "but the world"), while b-b' refer to him (b, "through him" and b', "him"), but c-c' consist of verb phrases (c, "was made" and c', "did not know"). The a-b-c is contrasted to the a'-b'-c' in meaning.

I22. Parallel, ab-a'b': The phrases a (τὰ ἴδια, his own) and a' (οἱ ἴδιοι, his own people) are related to each other, but his positive action towards them (b, "He came") is in contrast to their negative response to him (b', "[they] did not receive him"). **I23**. Parallel, abc-a'b'c': There is a similar pattern of expression, with the same meaning, with a-b-c repeatedly appears in a'-b'-c'. **I24**. Parallel, ab-a'b': The a (καὶ ὁ κόσμος, but the world) and a' (καὶ οἱ ἴδιοι, but his own people) duplicate his relationship with the world (his creatorship and his approach), while the world showed its negative response towards him (b and b') twice: not knowing (c) and not receiving (c').

Each of these parallels focuses on its own point: there is the true light that shines every man (I17); he came into the world (I18); he who came is the one who was in (I19); he who was in is the creator (I20); the world did not know him (I21); he came to his own people but they did not welcome him (I22); the world neither knows him nor receives him (I23); the world rejected him who deserved to be welcomed by it (I24).

X. Believers, Children of God (1:12–13)

Verses 12–13 contain five parallel features: the first three are parallel (I25, 26, 27); the next two are chiastic (I28 and 29); the last one is triple (I30). All the relations exhibit the connection between v. 12 and v. 13.

V	25	26				Phrases	Translation
12	a	a				ὅσοι δὲ	But to all who
	-	-				ἔλαβον	received
	-	-		29		αὐτόν,	him,
	b				a	ἔδωκεν	he gave
	-				b	αὐτοῖς	them
	-		27	28	x	ἐξουσίαν	power
	-	b	a	a	b'	τέκνα θεοῦ	children of God
	-	-	b	-	a'	γενέσθαι,	to become,
	a'			b		τοῖς πιστεύουσιν	to those who believed
	-				30	εἰς τὸ ὄνομα αὐτοῦ,	in his name,
13		a'		b'	a	οἳ οὐκ ἐξ αἱμάτων	who ~ not of blood
		-		-	a'	οὐδὲ ἐκ θελήματος σαρκὸς	nor of the will of the flesh
		-		-	a"	οὐδὲ ἐκ θελήματος ἀνδρὸς	nor of the will of man,
	b'	b'	a'	a'		ἀλλ' ἐκ θεοῦ	but of God
	-	-	b'	-		ἐγεννήθησαν.	were born.

I25. Parallel, ab-a'b': Receiving (a) and believing (a') are similar in meaning, so is becoming children of God (b) and being born of God (b'). I26. Parallel, ab-a'b': vv. 12–13 seem to be made of two possible parallel pairs (I25 and I26). In a-a', receiving him (a) is neither of blood nor of the will of the flesh nor of the will of man (a'). But in b-b', we can see two phrases with similar meaning: "to become children of God" (b); "but were born of God" (b'). It is highlighted that receiving him is not done in a human manner.

I27. Parallel, ab-a'b': The a-b (becoming children of God) and a'-b' (being born of God) are similar both in content and in form: τέκνα θεοῦ (a, "children of God") and ἀλλ' ἐκ θεοῦ (a', "but of God"); γενέσθαι (b, "to become") and ἐγεννήθησαν (b', "were born"). I28. Chiastic, ab-b'a': The act of b (believing in his name) is contrasted to b' (human ways of acting) in relation to which one is the proper means to becoming children of God (a) and being born of God (a') or not. I29. Chiastic, ab-x-b'a': Indicate that he gave (a) something and thus they become (a') someone, centering on "power" (x), while b and b' indicate the believers, children of God. I30. Triple, a-a'-a": All the three phrases consist of an ἐκ -phrase with the negative adverb οὐκ (or negative conjunction, οὐδέ).

It is emphasized in I25 that receivers become children born of God. I26 contrasts "receiving him" to other human ways: blood, the will of the flesh, and the will of man. I27 shows that children of God are those who are born of God. I28, similarly to I26, contrasts "believing" to other human ways. In I29, the focus is on the "power" given by God to become children of God. I30 focuses on three negative things that are not concerned with the children of God.

B'2. Relationship with the Believers 1 (1:14)

Three partial, chiastic parallels seem to be shown in v. 14, although none of them comprise the whole verse. Rather, v. 14 has its connectivity with other verses such as vv. 9, 11 (I45) and v. 16 (I49).

V	31			45	49	Phrases	Translation
14	a	32		a"	a	Καὶ ὁ λόγος	And the Word
	b	a		-	-	σὰρξ	flesh
	-	b		-	-	ἐγένετο	became
	-	b'		-	-	καὶ ἐσκήνωσεν	and dwelt
	-	a'	33	47	-	ἐν ἡμῖν,	among us,
	b'		a	a	b	καὶ ἐθεασάμεθα	and we have seen
	a'		b	-	-	τὴν δόξαν αὐτοῦ,	his glory,
	-		b'	-	-	δόξαν ὡς μονογενοῦς παρὰ πατρός,	the glory as of the only begotten from the Father,
	-		a'	b	-	πλήρης χάριτος καὶ ἀληθείας.	full of grace and truth.

I31. Chiastic, ab-b'a': The event of a-b made the act of a'-b' possible. The phrases a ("And the Word") and a' ("his glory, the glory as of the only begotten...") are related regarding him, while b ("became flesh and dwelt among us") and b' ("and we have seen") show the connection between his deed (b) and "our" experience of it (b'). I32. Chiastic, ab-b'a': The act of a-b is the cause of a'-b'. The phrases b (ἐγένετο, became) and b' (καὶ ἐσκήνωσεν, and dwelt) are verbs, describing two actions of the Word. I33. In b-b', whose glory is emphasized: "his glory" (b); "the glory as of the only begotten from the Father" (b'). The b is explicated in detail in b'. In a-a', two traits of "his glory" are described: that "we have seen" (a); that are "full of grace and truth" (a').

In I31, the action of the Word (incarnation and dwelling) and the responsive experience of "we" (seeing his glory) are focused on. I32, a part of I31, highlights two deeds of the Word in relation to "we." In I33, whose glory and the kinds of it are emphasized.

C'. Witness of the Baptist (1:15)

Verse 15 holds three parallels (I34, 35, 36). I34 appears in the former part of the verse, focusing on the point that John bears witness to him, while I35 and 36 in its latter part highlight the contents of his testimony.

V			46	Phrases	Translation
15	34		a"	Ἰωάννης	John
	a		-	μαρτυρεῖ	bears witness
	b		-	περὶ αὐτοῦ	to him
	a'			καὶ κέκραγεν λέγων·	and cries out, saying,
	b'	35		οὗτος ἦν ὃν εἶπον·	this was he of whom I said,
		a		ὁ ὀπίσω μου	He who ~ after me
		b	36	ἐρχόμενος	comes
		a'	a	ἔμπροσθέν μου	before me
		b'	b	γέγονεν,	ranks,
			a'	ὅτι πρῶτός μου	for ~ before me
			b'	ἦν.	was.

I34. Parallel, ab-a'b': The phrases a ("bears witness") and a' ("and cries out, saying") are similar in meaning, while both b ("to him") and b' ("this was he of whom I said") point him out. In ab and a'b', the testimony of John is duplicated.

I35. Parallel, ab-a'b': In a-a', ὁ ὀπίσω μου (after me, in a) and ἔμπροσθέν μου (before [higher than] me, a') are contrasted, while b (ἐρχόμενος, comes [coming]) and b' (γέγονεν, ranks [has become]) are in a pair of verbs. **I36.** Parallel, ab-a'b': It is similar to I33 in form but different in meaning. In a-a', there is similarity: ἔμπροσθέν μου (before [higher than] me, a) and ὅτι πρῶτός μου (for ~ before me, a'), while b (γέγονεν, ranks [has become]) and b' (ἦν, was) are also similar. Then a'-b' is the foundation of a-b.

In I34, the act of John's testimony to him is repeated. I35 focuses on the fact that he who came later than John is higher than him, while, in I36, his superiority and existence prior to John are portrayed.

B'1. Relationship with the Believers 2 (1:16–17)

Verses 16–17 have two parallel features: I37 is chiastic and I38 is parallel, and these two verses are coherent with each other. Apart from this, these verses show their connectivity with other verses such as v. 3 (I48) and v. 14 (II47 and 49).

The Prologue and the Early Testimonies

V			47	49	Phrases	Translation
16	37		b'	b'	ὅτι ἐκ τοῦ πληρώματος αὐτοῦ	And from his fullness
	a		a'	-	ἡμεῖς πάντες ἐλάβομεν	we all received
	b	38	-	-	καὶ χάριν ἀντὶ χάριτος·	grace upon grace.
17		a		-	ὅτι ὁ νόμος	For the law
		b		-	διὰ Μωϋσέως	through Moses
		c	48	-	ἐδόθη,	was given;
	b'	a'	a'	-	ἡ χάρις καὶ ἡ ἀλήθεια	grace and truth
	a'	b'	b'	-	διὰ Ἰησοῦ Χριστοῦ	through Jesus Christ
	-	c'	c'	-	ἐγένετο.	came.

I37. Chiastic, ab-b'a': The act of a ("we all received") is realized by the event of a' ("came through Jesus Christ"). The phrases b ("grace upon grace") and b' ("grace and truth") repeat the term "grace" in a similar but different way. **I38.** Parallel, abc-a'b'c':[8] Contrasts between a (the law) and a' (grace and truth), b (Moses) and b' (Jesus Christ) are emphasized, respectively, except for c ("was given") and c' ("came") which are parallel verbs.

In I37, it is highlighted that all things regarding the grace we received came through Jesus Christ. I38 focuses on the contrast between Jesus and Moses regarding grace and law.

A'. Deity of the Logos (1:18)

In v. 18, there is one parallel, I39, and one chiasm, I40, which are complex, binding the verse into one.

V	39	40	49	Phrases	Translation
18	a	a	a'	Θεὸν	God
	b	-	-	οὐδεὶς	no one
	c	-	-	ἑώρακεν πώποτε·	has ever seen;
	a'	b	-	μονογενὴς θεὸς	God the only Son
	-	b'	-	ὁ ὢν εἰς τὸν κόλπον τοῦ πατρός	who is in the bosom of the Father,
	b'	a'	-	ἐκεῖνος	he
	c'	-	-	ἐξηγήσατο.	has declared himself.

I39. Parallel, abc-a'b'c': The first part (a-b-c) is in contrast to its latter part (a'-b'-c'). It indicates that a and a' refer to God (a) or the Son (a', "God the only Son who is in the bosom of the Father"). The phrases b ("no one") and b' ("he") are contrasted in the

---

8. Von Wahlde, *Commentary on the Gospel of John*, 23.

pronouns, while c ("has ever seen") and c' ("has declared himself") are verb phrases that are related in contrastive meaning. **I40.** In b-b', the divinity of the Son of God in relation to the Father is duplicated and accentuated. In a-a', we can see the cause ("no one has ever seen God") and the result (he has declared himself). Because of a', the problem of a is solved. In I39–40, the focus is that no one has ever seen God, but God himself appears, thus we were able to see him who is the Son of God.

The Others

The interrelations between the phrases are observed beyond the verses that are sequentially attached to each other. Verses 3–5 are related to vv. 9–11 as in I41–44, demonstrating how they have common of ideas. However, their order of appearance differs: I41, 42, 43, 44 in vv. 3–5; I42, 43, 41, 44 in vv. 9–11. I45 divulges the connection between vv. 9–11 and v. 14. Unquestionably, vv. 6–8 and v. 15 are interrelated as seen in I46, while I47 reveals the connection between v. 14 and vv. 16–17, and I48 is a phenomenon of the interrelatedness between v. 3 and v. 17. In particular, I49 shows how v. 14 is deeply connected to vv. 16–17 and v. 18, beyond the interruption of v. 15 that is located in between.

I41. Dual, a-a': Emphasizing three times that all things were created by him (3, 10a), repeating δι' αὐτοῦ ἐγένετο (through him was made). **I42.** Dual, a-a': Demonstrating the certain existence of the life, the light: a, "life was, and the life was the light of men" (4); a', "There was the true light" (9a). **I43.** Dual, a-a': Both a and a' repeat the issue of light-shining: a, "And the light shines in the darkness" (5a); a', "the true light that gives light to every man" (9a). **I44.** Triple, a-a'-a": Indicating that the world did not respond to him properly, emphasizing this fact three times: a, "and the darkness did not comprehend it" (5b); a', "but the world did not know him" (10b); a", "but his own people did not receive him" (11b).

I45. Triple, a-a'-a": All three indicate the incarnation of the Son: a, "coming into the world" (9b); a', "He came to what was his own" (11a); a", "And the Word became flesh and dwelt among us" (14a). **I46.** Triple, a-a'-a": All the three focus on John's testimony to him: a, "This man came for testimony, to bear witness to the light" (7a); a', "but *came* to bear witness to the light" (8b); a", "John bears witness to him" (15a).

I47. Chiastic, ab-b'a': The a (14b, "and we have seen his glory…") and a' (16b, "we all received grace upon grace") show what and how we have experienced regarding him, while b ("full of grace and truth") and b' ("And from his fullness") are related in terms of "full" or "fullness" (14, 16). **I48.** Parallel, abc-a'b'c': Both (3a and 17b) syntactic patterns are identical: All things (a) and grace and truth (a'); through him (b) and through Jesus Christ (b'); were made (c) and came (c'). It indicates that all things including grace and truth came through him. It shows also that he who created the world was the One who provided us grace and truth.

I49. Chiastic, ab-b'a': If we exclude v. 15 (regarding John the Baptist), v. 14 and vv. 16–18 may become a chiastic combination: a (14a, incarnation of the Logos)—b (14b, seeing his glory, full of grace and truth)—b' (16–17, receiving full of grace and truth)—a' (18, no one seeing him and appearance of God the only Son). This chiasm indicates that vv. 14–18 are adhesive among themselves except for v. 15.

I41–44 express four related issues regarding the Son: creatorship (I41), life and light (I42), light-shining (I43), and rejection of him (I44). The focus of I45 is on his coming into the world, the so called incarnation, while in I46, John's testimony is highlighted. I47 and 48 accentuate the seeing-receiving of him (I47) and experiential reception of grace from him (I48). In I49, it is stated that the invisible God appeared, so "we" could see him and receive from him.

II. Early Testimonies (1:19–51)

Dual Structure, II1 (A-A')

First, this section consists of two parts: testimonies of the Baptist (19–34, IIA) and testimonies of the early disciples (35–51, IIB). As indicated earlier, we may say that each of them is again divided into two passages: two testimonies of the Baptist (19–28, IIA1; 29–34, IIA2); testimonies of the early disciples (35–42, IIB1; 43–51, IIB2). Again, we see two sub-parts in vv. 35–42: two disciples of the Baptist meet Jesus (35–39) and the meeting-witnessing of Andrew and Peter (40–42). Likewise, vv. 43–49 are divided into two: the meeting-witnessing of Philip and Nathanael (43–46) and the dialogue between Jesus and Nathanael (47–51).

II.	Early testimonies, 1:19-51			
	IIA	Testimonies of the Baptist, 1:19-34		
		IIA1	First testimony of the Baptist, 1:19-28	
		IIA2	Second testimony of the Baptist, 1:29-34	
	IIB	Testimonies of early disciples, 1:35-51		
		IIB1	First meeting-witnessing of early disciples (1:35-42)	
			IIB1a	The Baptist and his two disciples with Jesus (1:35-39)
			IIB1b	Andrew and Peter with Jesus (1:40-42)
		IIB2	Second meeting-witnessing of early disciples (1:43-51)	
			IIB2a	Philip and Nathanael with Jesus (1:43-46)
			IIB2b	Dialogue between Jesus and Nathanael (1:47-51)

Second, it is here considered that the key words of the testimonies of the Baptist introduced in v. 29 ("the Lamb of God") and v. 34 ("the Son of God") are reiterated both in the first part of vv. 35–51 and in the last part: in v. 36 ("the Lamb of God") by the Baptist and in v. 49 ("the Son of God") by Nathanael, that seemingly enclose IIB (35–51, the testimonies of the early disciples).

IIA. Testimonies of the Baptist (1:19–34)

There are two units of the Baptist's testimonies in vv. 19–34: First testimony (19–28, IIA1) and second testimony (29–34, IIA2).

IIA1. First Testimony of the Baptist (1:19–28)

II2. Combined chiastic, A-B1B2B3-B'1B'2B'3-A': A, the introductory part (19a), and A', the closing one (28), are an *inclusio*, wrapping up Bs and B's. Both B1 and B'1 describe those who were sent from Jerusalem, while, in B2 and B'2, they asked the Baptist two types of questions: who are you? (B2) and why do you baptize? (B'2), both regard the Christ-Elijah-the prophet issue sequentially. Then, in B3 and B'3, we read John's answers to them, particularly from the viewpoint of the John-Jesus relationship. John is a loyal servant to him, preparing his way (B3) and staying lower than him (B'3).

The structure is easily discerned, because the parallel phenomena of Bs and B's are much clearer: appearances of those who are sent and their questions on John (B1 and B'1); the triple denials regarding John's identity (B2 and B'2); John's answers regarding who he is (B3 and B'3). The rest of the unit is v. 19a and v. 28, which are supposed to be an introductory part (A) and a closing one (A').

In vv. 19–23, we may see seven parallel features (two chiasms, I3 and 6; four parallelisms, I4, 5, 7, and 8) and two parallel connections with vv. 24–28 (I10 and 11). II4 shows the comprehensive connection between B1, B2, and B3 and others which are spread out in vv. 19–23. They all exhibit their cohesiveness.

II3. Chiastic, ab-b'a': Both a (sending) and a' (asking) are the two types of the role of the Jews who are in Jerusalem (b) and the priests and Levites sent from Jerusalem (b'). They sent them who asked him. **II4.** Parallel, ab-a'b': In both a and a', they asked John who he is at least twice directly: "who are you?" And John replied three times negatively, "I am not . . ." (b), and once positively, "I am the voice . . ." (b').

II5. Parallel, abc-a'b'c': In a-a', they asked John, while the question, "Who are you?," is repeated in b-b'. In c, John confessed that he was not the Christ, while, in c', they continued to ask John regarding his ministry. II6. Chiastic, ab-b'a': In b-b', the question, "who are you?" is repeated, while a-a' are related in terms of the relationship between those who send and those who are sent. It means that those who asked John about his identity are always concerned about those who sent them.

The Prologue and the Early Testimonies

V	2									Phrases	Translation
19	A	3		6						Καὶ αὕτη ἐστὶν ἡ μαρτυρία τοῦ Ἰωάννου,	And this is the testimony of John,
	B1	a		5	a					ὅτε ἀπέστειλαν [πρὸς αὐτὸν]	~ sent [to him]
	-	b	4	a	-					οἱ Ἰουδαῖοι	when the Jews
	-	b'	a	-	-		8		10	ἐξ Ἱεροσολύμων ἱερεῖς καὶ Λευίτας	~ priests and Levites from Jerusalem
	B2	a'	-	-	b	a		a		ἵνα ἐρωτήσωσιν αὐτόν·	to ask him,
	-	-	-	b	-	b		b		σὺ τίς εἶ;	"Who are you?"
20	-	-	b	c					11	καὶ ὡμολόγησεν καὶ οὐκ ἠρνήσατο, καὶ ὡμολόγησεν	[And] he confessed and did not deny; but he confessed,
	-	-	-	-					a	ὅτι ἐγὼ οὐκ εἰμὶ ὁ χριστός.	"I am not the Christ."
21	-	-	-	-	a'					καὶ ἠρώτησαν αὐτόν·	And they asked him,
	-	7	-	-	b'					τί οὖν;	"What then?
	-	a	-							σὺ Ἠλίας εἶ;	Are you Elijah?"
	-	b	-					b		καὶ λέγει· οὐκ εἰμί.	He said, "I am not."
	-	a'	-							ὁ προφήτης εἶ σύ;	"Are you the prophet?"
	-	b'	-	5	6		9	c		καὶ ἀπεκρίθη· οὔ.	And he answered, "No."
22	-	-	a'	a'	b'	a''	a			εἶπαν οὖν αὐτῷ·	They said to him then,
	-	-	-	b'	-	b''	-			τίς εἶ;	"Who are you,
	-	-	-	c'	a'		b			ἵνα ἀπόκρισιν δῶμεν τοῖς πέμψασιν ἡμᾶς·	so that we may give an answer to those who sent us?
	-	-	-	-	-		a'			τί λέγεις περὶ σεαυτοῦ;	What do you say about yourself?"
23	B3	b'			b'					ἔφη· ἐγὼ φωνὴ βοῶντος ἐν τῇ ἐρήμῳ· εὐθύνατε τὴν ὁδὸν κυρίου, καθὼς εἶπεν Ἠσαΐας ὁ προφήτης.	He said, "I am the voice of one crying in the wilderness, 'Make straight the way of the Lord,' as Isaiah the prophet said."

II7. Parallel, ab-a'b': Two questions appear similarly in pattern for emphasis, denying himself regarding who he is not: "Are you Elijah?" (a) and "Are you the prophet?" (a'); "... I am not" (b) and "... No" (b'). II8. Parallel, ab-a'b'-a''b'': Three times, questions regarding who John is recur: σὺ τίς εἶ; (b, who are you?), τί οὖν; (b', what then?), and τίς εἶ; (b'', who are you?). II9. Parallel, ab-a'b': In a-a', the question of the identity of John is repeated: "Who are you" (a) and "what do you say about yourself?" (a'). While, in b' ("I am the voice ..."), the identity of John is disclosed as an answer to those who sent them, in b ("... we may give an answer to those who sent us?").

II3 shows the close connection between the senders in Jerusalem and those who were sent from Jerusalem. In II4 and 9, we can see John's words about himself regarding who John is not and who he is. In both II5 and 6, the questions about the identity of John are repeatedly emphasized. But the focus of II5 is on their suspicion of John regarding his answer, "I am not the Christ," while that of II6 is their concern with those who sent them. II7 focuses on a continuing dialogue, their questions and John's denials regarding his identity, and II8 introduces how those questions are repeated.

V	2				Phrases	Translation
24	B'1			10	Καὶ ἀπεσταλμένοι ἦσαν ἐκ τῶν Φαρισαίων.	Now they had been sent from Pharisees.
		12				
25	B'2	a		a'	καὶ ἠρώτησαν	They asked
-		b		-	αὐτὸν	him
-		a'		-	καὶ εἶπαν	and said to
-		b'		-	αὐτῷ·	him,
-				b'	11 τί οὖν βαπτίζεις	"Why then do you baptize
-				a'	εἰ σὺ οὐκ εἶ ὁ χριστὸς	if you are not the Christ,
-				b'	οὐδὲ Ἠλίας	nor Elijah,
-				c'	οὐδὲ ὁ προφήτης;	nor the prophet?"
26	B'3		13	14	ἀπεκρίθη αὐτοῖς ὁ Ἰωάννης λέγων·	John answered them,
-			a	a	ἐγὼ	"I
-			b	-	βαπτίζω ἐν ὕδατι·	baptize with water,
-			b'	b	μέσος ὑμῶν ἕστηκεν	but among you stands one
-			a'	-	ὃν ὑμεῖς οὐκ οἴδατε,	whom you do not know.
27	-			b'	ὁ ὀπίσω μου ἐρχόμενος,	He is the one who comes after me,
-				a'	οὗ οὐκ εἰμὶ [ἐγὼ] ἄξιος ἵνα λύσω αὐτοῦ τὸν ἱμάντα τοῦ ὑποδήματος.	the thong of whose sandal I am not worthy to untie."
28	A'				ταῦτα ἐν Βηθανίᾳ ἐγένετο πέραν τοῦ Ἰορδάνου, ὅπου ἦν ὁ Ἰωάννης βαπτίζων.	These things happened in Bethany beyond the Jordan, where John was baptizing.

Verses 24–28 contain simply one parallelism (II12) and two chiasms (II13, 14) in them besides two connected parallels with previous verses (II10 and 11). II12 belongs to v. 25 (B'2 of II2) and II13 and 14 belong to vv. 26–27 (B'3 of II2).

II10. Parallel, ab-a'b': Two types of questions are described in ab, "Who are you?," and in a'b', "Why then do you baptize…" II11. Parallel, abc-a'b'c': Triple denials, in abc, regarding who John is: the Christ, Elijah, and the prophet recur in a'b'c'. II12. Parallel, ab-a'b': Asking him (ab) and saying to him (a'b') are related for repetitive emphasis. II13. Chiastic, ab-b'a': "I" (a) and "the one whom you do not know" (a') are contrasted, while the activity of John, baptizing (b), and his standing (b') are compared.

II14. Chiastic, ab-b'a': In a and a', John declares that he is the one who baptizes in water (a, his relationship with the people) but also the one who is even unworthy to untie his sandal (a', his relationship with the Christ), if compared with him in status. Both b and b' describe some facts regarding Jesus: "among you stands one whom you do not know" (b) and "He is the one who comes after me" (b').

II10 produces two key questions regarding John. In II11, three issues are raised regarding John's identity. II12 focuses on the dialogue itself between John and those who were sent by the Pharisees. II13 and 14 are both related to the contrasts between John and Jesus.

IIA2. Second Testimony of the Baptist, 1:29–34

II15. Chiastic, ABC-C'B'A':[9] Both A and A' regard in common John's testimonies to Jesus, sharing similar patterns: (1) John's seeing-saying (A) and his seeing-testifying (A'); two designations of Jesus' identities, "the Lamb of God" (A) and "the Son of God" (A'). In B and B', John's testimonies to Jesus continue, starting with the same phrase, οὗτός ἐστιν (this is). In B, Jesus is testified to as the one who preexists, while, in B', the relation between Jesus and the Spirit is described. C and C' share a few of the same expressions and ideas such as κἀγὼ οὐκ ᾔδειν αὐτόν (and I did not recognize him), in each first part, John's baptism in water, and the Spirit descending upon Jesus.

First, the testimonies of the Baptist in A ("the Lamb of God") and A' ("the Son of God") are an *inclusio* that encloses the unit. Second, in C-C', we can detect a threefold parallel (abc-a'b'c', II21) that is not easily missed. Third, the relation between B and B' is manifest in terms that John's testimonies here differ from other passages such as A-A' focusing on the designations of Christ and C-C' that highlight the baptism of Jesus and the Spirit on him. In B-B', John bears witness to Jesus' divinity: his preexistence and his authority in baptizing with the Holy Spirit.

Except for II15, an overall chiasm of vv. 29–34, there are ten parallel features: two chiasms (I16 and 19), two combined chiasm (I20 and 25), four parallelisms (I17, 21, 22, and 24), and two dual parallels (I18 and 23). II16 is the first part of II15 (ABC) and II24 is the last one (C'B'A'). It means that the organization of this passage is so well-designed, chiastically and also in parallel. As II17 and 18 belong to A of II15 and a of II16, so II19 and 20 are in B of II15 and b of II16. It is observed that II23 is limited to v. 32. But II21 and 22 tighten the connectivity between C and C' of II15. The last parallel II25 is for the B'-A' connection.

II16. Chiastic, ab-b'a': In a and a', John sees Jesus and expressively testifies about him regarding his divinity, while in b and b', the Son is introduced mostly in relation to John himself: "higher than me . . . before me" (b); ". . . He might be manifested . . . I came . . ." (b'). II17. Parallel, ab-b'a': In a-a', John sees (a) and says (a'), regarding Jesus who is coming to him (b) and who is the Lamb of God (b'). II18. Dual, a-a': In a' (who takes away the sin of the world), his first designation, "the Lamb of God" (a) is explicated.

---

9. Talbert, *Reading John*, 81.

V	15	16	17			Phrases	Translation
29	A	a	a			Τῇ ἐπαύριον βλέπει	The next day he saw
-	-	-	b			τὸν Ἰησοῦν ἐρχόμενον πρὸς αὐτὸν	Jesus coming to him
-	-	-	a	18		καὶ λέγει· ἴδε	and said, "Look,
-	-	-	b'	a		ὁ ἀμνὸς τοῦ θεοῦ	the Lamb of God,
-	-	-	-	a'	19	ὁ αἴρων τὴν ἁμαρτίαν τοῦ κόσμου.	who takes away the sin of the world!
30	B	b		a	20	οὗτός ἐστιν ὑπὲρ οὗ ἐγὼ εἶπον·	This is He of whom I said,
-	-	-		b	a1	ὀπίσω μου	'After me
-	-	-		-	a2	ἔρχεται	comes
-	-	-		-	b	ἀνὴρ	a Man
-	-	-		b'	b'	ὃς	who
-	-	-		-	a'1	ἔμπροσθέν μου	~ higher than me
-	-	-		-	a'2	γέγονεν,	has been ~
-	-	-		-	a'	ὅτι πρῶτός μου	because ~ before me.'
-	-	-	21	-		ἦν.	~ he was
31	C	b'		a		κἀγὼ οὐκ ᾔδειν αὐτόν,	And I did not recognize him,
-	-	-		b		ἀλλ' ἵνα φανερωθῇ τῷ Ἰσραὴλ διὰ τοῦτο ἦλθον ἐγὼ ἐν ὕδατι βαπτίζων.	but in order that He might be manifested to Israel, I came baptizing in water."
32	-	a'		c	22	Καὶ ἐμαρτύρησεν Ἰωάννης λέγων	And John testified,
-	-	-		-	a	23	ὅτι τεθέαμαι τὸ πνεῦμα	"I saw the Spirit
-	-	-		-	b	a	καταβαῖνον ὡς περιστερὰν ἐξ οὐρανοῦ	descend as a dove from heaven,
-	-	24		-	c	a'	καὶ ἔμεινεν ἐπ' αὐτόν.	and it remained on Him.
33	C'	a		a'		κἀγὼ οὐκ ᾔδειν αὐτόν,	And I did not recognize Him,
-	-	-		b'		ἀλλ' ὁ πέμψας με βαπτίζειν ἐν ὕδατι	but He who sent me to baptize in water
-	-	-		c'		ἐκεῖνός μοι εἶπεν·	said to me,
-	-	-		-	a'	ἐφ' ὃν ἂν ἴδῃς τὸ πνεῦμα	'He on whom you see the Spirit
-	-	-		-	b'	καταβαῖνον	descend
-	-	25		-	c'	καὶ μένον ἐπ' αὐτόν,	and remain (on him),
-	B'	b	a1			οὗτός ἐστιν	this is
-	-	-	a2			ὁ βαπτίζων ἐν πνεύματι ἁγίῳ.	He who baptizes with the Holy Spirit.'
34	A'	a'	x			κἀγὼ ἑώρακα καὶ μεμαρτύρηκα	I have seen and have testified
-	-	b'	a'1			ὅτι οὗτός ἐστιν	that this is
-	-	-	a'2			ὁ υἱὸς τοῦ θεοῦ.	the Son of God."

II19. Chiastic, ab-b'a': Externally, ὀπίσω μου (after me) in b and ἔμπροσθέν μου in b' (before me, higher than me) are contrasted in a pair. With this word-play, this man,

in a, is disclosed as the one who preexisted before John, in a'.[10] **II20**. Combined chiastic, a1a2-b-b'-a'1a'2: In b-b' of II19, two clauses (a1a2-b and b'-a'1a'2) are, syntactically and probably in rhyme, interrelated to each other: ὀπίσω μου (a1, 3 syllables; after me) and ἔμπροσθέν μου (a'2, 3 syllables; before me); ἔρχεται (a2, 3 syllables; comes) and γέγονεν (a'2, 3 syllables; has been); and ἀνὴρ (b, 2 syllables; a man) and ὅς (b', one syllable; who).

II21. Parallel, abc-a'b'c': In both a and a', the same expression, κἀγὼ οὐκ ᾔδειν αὐτόν (And I did not recognize him) is repeated, while, in b-b', the issue of baptism in water is shared, while the c-c' pair focuses on the Spirit descending on the Son. **II22**. Parallel, abc-a'b'c': The c-c' part of II21 demonstrates a similar, three-partitioned semantic pattern in parallel: ὅτι τεθέαμαι τὸ πνεῦμα (a, I saw the Spirit) and ἐφ' ὃν ἂν ἴδῃς τὸ πνεῦμα (a', He on whom you see the Spirit); καταβαῖνον (b, descend) and καταβαῖνον (b', descend); καὶ ἔμεινεν ἐπ' αὐτόν (c, and it remained on him) and καὶ μένον ἐπ' αὐτόν (c', and remain on him). II23. Dual, a-a': This pattern shows the dual roles of the Holy Spirit: descending as a dove (a) and remaining on him (a').

II24. Parallel, ab-a'b': In a, John who did not know the Son is told by the Father, regarding how to find him, and in a', John sees the Son as he has been told and comes to testify about him. In b-b', the identities of the Son are introduced in similar pattern: "this is he who baptizes with Holy Spirit" (b) and "this is the Son of God" (b'). **II25**. Combined chiastic, a1a2-x-a'1b'1: Two similar patterns are shown regarding his divine identities: οὗτός ἐστιν (a1 and a'1, this is); "he who baptizes with Holy Spirit" (a2) and "the Son of God" (a'2). The central x displays John as an eyewitness.

II15 comprises all the issues in vv. 29–34, primarily focusing on the two designations: "the Lamb of God" and "the Son of God." In comparison with II16 that relatively emphasizes the relationship with John and Jesus regarding his superiority, II24 emphasizes his relation to the Holy Spirit as the Son of God. II17 and 18 in v. 29; II19 and 20 in v. 30 are related to the issues: his identity as the Lamb of God (v. 29); his superiority to John (v. 30). II23 describes the status of the Spirit regarding Jesus, while II25 finally accentuates the divine identity of Jesus. II21 and 22 disclose how John becomes an eyewitness to the Jesus event.

IIB. Testimonies of Early Disciples (1:35–51)

II26. Dual, A-A': As discussed earlier, it is a dual mode in vv. 35–51: A, first meeting-witnessing of early disciples (35–42); A', second meeting-witnessing of the early disciples (43–51).

II27. Parallel, ABCDEF-A'B'C'D'E'F':[11] As a whole, vv. 35–51 are in dual mode, but, in detail, they are made up of a parallel structure with twelve segmented facets.

---

10. See the parallel between v. 15 and v. 30 where almost the same expression is repeated: ὁ ὀπίσω μου ἐρχόμενος ἔμπροσθέν μου γέγονεν, ὅτι πρῶτός μου ἦν.

11. Compare with the spiral structure of Mlakuzhyil: b (35–37); c (37–39); d (40–42a); e (42); c' (43–44); d' (45–46); e' (47–40); f (51). Mlakuzhyil, *Christocentric Literary Structure*, 133.

Each of the two units (35–42 and 43–51) can be segmented into six facets. Both A and A' describe how they (two disciples of the Baptist; Philip) meet Jesus and how Jesus called them (39, "Come and see"; 43, "Follow me"). In B and B', two specific disciples are introduced by the evangelist: Andrew (B); Philip (B'). In C and C', Andrew introduces Jesus regarding who he is (C) and Philip does similarly (C'); in D and D', they bring their men to Jesus: Peter (D) and Nathanael (D'). In F and F', Jesus speaks to Peter (F) and he does to Nathanael (F').

It is interesting to observe that, in the first unit (35–42), A (35–39, their meeting with Jesus) is longer than A' (43), while, in the second unit (43–51), F' (47–51, Jesus' dialogue with Nathanael) is so much longer than F (42b), thereby the two units keep the balance in symmetry as a whole. A (35–39) is designed as a cohesive, combined chiasm (II28) similar to F' (47–51) which is bound by a chiastic structure (II42).

First, if we compare the two units of the early disciples with those of other writings such as the Synoptic Gospels (focusing mainly on Jesus' calling and their rapid responses), the focus here is on their testimonies toward Jesus. Second, the dual arrangements of the units (II26) are manifest. The similarity of their sequential orders (II27) may accentuate the repetitive impact of their testimonies to Jesus regarding who he is.

IIB1. First Meeting-Witnessing of Early Disciples (1:35–42)

II28. Combined chiastic, A1A2-B-B'-A'1A'2: In A1A2, John testifies about Jesus to his two disciples (A1) and the two follow Jesus after hearing from John (A2). In A'B', Jesus invites the two (A'1) and they stay with him (A'2). In this way, A2 and A2' are related in terms of their actions concerning Jesus, following him, while, in A1 and A'1, they testify to Jesus (A'1) and are invited by Jesus (A'1). Meanwhile, in B and B', there is a dialogue between Jesus (B), regarding the previous issue, "following him" (A2), and them (B'), regarding the next issue, "staying with him" (A'2).

As a whole, in the first scene (35–37), the Baptist testifies about Jesus to his two disciples and they follow Jesus, based on John's testimony. In the second scene (38), the first dialogue between Jesus and them is introduced. The last scene (39) presents the second dialogue between him and them.

First, there seems to be a pattern: saying and doing. As John says about Jesus, they do follow Jesus (35–37). As Jesus says to them, they stay with him (39). Second, in the middle of unit (38), the dialogue between Jesus and them is located. Third, we can name A1 (saying) and A2 (doing). Fourth, as we divide Jesus' part (A1; including John's part, A'1) and two disciples' (A2 and A'2), we name B (their question of Jesus) and B' (his question of them).

The Prologue and the Early Testimonies

V	27	28	29	30		Phrases	Translation
35	A	A1	a	a		Τῇ ἐπαύριον πάλιν εἱστήκει	The next day again ~ was standing
	-	-	b	-	32	ὁ Ἰωάννης καὶ ἐκ τῶν μαθητῶν αὐτοῦ δύο	~ John ~ with two of his disciples,
36	-	-	c	b	a	καὶ ἐμβλέψας	and he looked at Jesus
	-	-	d	-	-	τῷ Ἰησοῦ περιπατοῦντι	as He walked,
	-	-	e	-	b	λέγει·	and said,
	-	-	f	x	31 x	ἴδε ὁ ἀμνὸς τοῦ θεοῦ.	"Look, the Lamb of God!"
37	-	A2	b'	a	b'	καὶ ἤκουσαν οἱ δύο μαθηταὶ αὐτοῦ λαλοῦντος	And the two disciples heard him say this,
	-	-	a'	a'	a'	καὶ ἠκολούθησαν τῷ Ἰησοῦ.	and they followed Jesus.
38	-	B	a'			στραφεὶς δὲ	~ turned,
	-	-	b'			ὁ Ἰησοῦς	Jesus ~
	-	-	c'			καὶ θεασάμενος	and saw
	-	-	d'	33		αὐτοὺς ἀκολουθοῦντας	them following,
	-	-	e'	a		λέγει αὐτοῖς·	and said to them,
	-	-	f'	b	35	τί ζητεῖτε;	"What do you seek?"
	-	B'	a'	a	34	οἱ δὲ εἶπαν αὐτῷ· ῥαββί, ὃ λέγεται μεθερμηνευόμενον διδάσκαλε,	And they said to Him, "Rabbi" (which is translated Teacher),
	-	-	b'	a	-	ποῦ μένεις;	"where do you stay?"
39	-	A'1		b	36	λέγει αὐτοῖς·	He said to them,
	-	-	b	-	a	ἔρχεσθε	"Come
	-	-	-	-	b	καὶ ὄψεσθε.	and see."
	-	A'2	b'	b'	a'	ἦλθαν οὖν	They came therefore
	-	-	-	-	b'	καὶ εἶδαν	and saw
	-	-	a'	-		ποῦ μένει	where he stayed,
	-	-			a'	καὶ παρ' αὐτῷ ἔμειναν τὴν ἡμέραν ἐκείνην· ὥρα ἦν ὡς δεκάτη.	and they stayed with Him that day. It was about the tenth hour.
40	B				37	Ἦν Ἀνδρέας ὁ ἀδελφὸς Σίμωνος Πέτρου εἷς ἐκ τῶν δύο	Andrew, Simon Peter's brother, was one of the two
	-		a			τῶν ἀκουσάντων	who heard
	-		b			παρὰ Ἰωάννου	from John
	-		a'			καὶ ἀκολουθησάντων	and followed
	-		b'			αὐτῷ·	Him.
41	C					εὑρίσκει οὗτος πρῶτον τὸν ἀδελφὸν τὸν ἴδιον Σίμωνα	This man first found his own brother Simon,
	D					καὶ λέγει αὐτῷ· εὑρήκαμεν τὸν Μεσσίαν, ὅ ἐστιν μεθερμηνευόμενον χριστός.	and said to him, "We have found the Messiah" (which is translated Christ).
42	E					ἤγαγεν αὐτὸν πρὸς τὸν Ἰησοῦν.	He brought him to Jesus.
	F				38	ἐμβλέψας αὐτῷ ὁ Ἰησοῦς εἶπεν·	Jesus looked at him, and said,
	-		a			σὺ εἶ Σίμων ὁ υἱὸς Ἰωάννου,	"You are Simon son of John.
	-		a'			σὺ κληθήσῃ Κηφᾶς, ὃ ἑρμηνεύεται Πέτρος.	You will be called Cephas" (which is translated Peter).

II28 covers vv. 35–39 which contain ten additional parallel features: four parallelisms (I29, 33, and 36–37), four chiasms (II30, 32, and 34–35), and two duals (I31 and 38). II31 and 32 show the connection of A1 and A2 of II28 as just as II35 does that of A'1 and A'2; II33 of B and B'. But, II29 and 34 are broader in scope than the others. We can say at least that II29 in the first part, A1A2-B, of II28 and II34–35 in the last one, B'-A'1A'2, demonstrate a certain cohesiveness within themselves. All these parallels are together combined into one body of unit. While, in vv. 40–42, there are only two parallels (II38–39). Even in v. 41–42a, we cannot find any parallel with other verses besides its connection to vv. 45–46 as CDE and C'D'E' of II27.

II29. Parallel, abcdef-a'b'c'd'e'f': Interestingly, two sentences are made of a syntactically similar pattern in order: subjects (John with two disciples and Jesus, b-b'), action 1 (standing and turning, a-a'), action 2 (looking and seeing, c-c'), what 1 (Jesus' walking and their following, d-d'), action 3 (both saying, e-e'), and what 2 ("Look, the Lamb of God" and "What do you seek?," f-f'). **II30.** Chiastic, ab-x-b'a': The two disciples standing with John (a) eventually follows Jesus (a'), for John testifies about Jesus to them (b) and they heard it from him (b'). The content of the testimony of John is revealed in x, "Look, the Lamb of God."

I31. Dual, a-a': The two disciples "heard" about Jesus (a) and then "followed" Jesus (a'). These verbs contain their two actions regarding Jesus. **II32.** Chiastic, ab-x-b'a': John looks at Jesus (a) and the two follow Jesus (a'), while John speaks about him (b) and they hear it (b'). In the center, x, the content of the saying of John, or the hearing of the two, is located.

II33. Parallel, ab-a'b': Jesus says (a) and they say (a'), while the content of Jesus' saying, "What do you seek?" (b) and that of theirs, "where do you stay" (b') are followed. **II34.** Chiastic, ab-b'a': There are similar, syntactical patterns: ποῦ μένεις (a, where do you stay?) and ποῦ μένει (a', where he stayed); ἔρχεσθε καὶ ὄψεσθε (b, come and see) and ἦλθαν οὖν καὶ εἶδαν (b', they came therefore and saw). **II35.** Chiastic, ab-b'a': In b-b', Jesus says to them, "Come and see," (b) and they obey Jesus' word: "They came therefore and saw . . ." (b'). In a, they ask Jesus, "where do you stay?," in a', they stay with him. **II36.** Parallel, ab-a'b':[12] In both a and a', "coming" is focused, while, in b-b', "seeing" appears.

II37. Parallel, ab-a'b': They heard (a) from him (b) and followed (a') him (b'). In a-a', what they did is shown, while, in b-b', two objects for these actions are presented: John (b) and Jesus (b'). **II38.** Dual, a-a': Jesus' twofold sayings describing Peter are presented: "You are Simon son of John" and "You will be called Cephas."

The foci of the parallels are as follows: comparison between John and Jesus (II29); John's testimony and his two disciples in comparison (II30); their two deeds, hearing and following (II31); John's testimony and the two disciples with emphasis on the identity of Jesus (II32); dialogue between Jesus and them (II33); Jesus' invitation and their obedience (II34 and 36); similar to II33 but with the emphasis on their staying

---

12. Mlakuzhyil, *Christocentric Literary Structure*, 122.

The Prologue and the Early Testimonies

with Jesus (II35). In II37, the focus is on their deeds: hearing and following, while, in II38, the twofold references to Simon are spoken by Jesus.

IIB2. Second Meeting-Witnessing of Early Disciples (1:43–51)

There are seven parallels in total: four parallelisms (II39, 41, and 43–44) and three chiasms (II40, 42, and 45). II39–40 are mostly partial in range, while II42 comprises the whole later part of vv. 43–51, namely, vv. 47–51 (F of II27). II41 connects vv. 46 and 48 and II43–46 support the cohesiveness of II42.

II39. Parallel, abc-a'b'c': As Jesus does to Philip, so Philip does to Nathanael: Jesus found Philip (a) and he found Nathanael (a'); Jesus said to him (b), "Follow Me" (c) and he said to Nathanael (b'), letting him follow Jesus (c'). **II40.** Chiastic, a-x-a': Jesus is introduced in two ways: the one written in Moses' law and prophets (a) and Jesus of Nazareth, the son of Joseph (a'). The man of a' is indeed the one in a, whom Philip found (x). II41. Parallel, ab-a'b': In a-a', Nathanael raises questions to Philip (a, "Can anything good come out of Nazareth?") and to Jesus (a', "How do you know me?"). In b-b', we can see Philip's answer (b, "Come and see") and Jesus' answer ("Look . . . in whom is no guile").

II42. Chiastic, ab-x-b'a': In b-b', the issue, "I saw you under the fig tree," is repeated, revealing Jesus' divine omniscience. Jesus' knowing (b) becomes Nathanael's believing (b'). In the center, x, Nathanael's confession of Jesus as the Son of God and the King of Israel is located. In a, there is Jesus' acknowledgement of Nathanael, while, in a', we can find his promise to him to see something great regarding the Son. II43. Parallel, ab-a'b': In this parallel, we may see two kinds of Jesus' knowledge spoken to Nathanael (a-a'), who he is really about (b) and where he was (b').

II44. Parallel, ab-a'b': Two ways of confession about Jesus are presented with the pronoun σὺ (you) emphasis. **II45.** Chiastic, ab-b'a': In the center, x, "Truly, truly, I say to you" is highlighted, while, in both b and b', seeing is focused: ὄψῃ (you will see, b; singular) and ὄψεσθε (you will see; b'; plural). Nathanael is not only going to see but others also will see. We may be told that "greater things than these" (a) what he will see is nothing but "heaven open, and the angels of God ascending and descending on the Son of Man" (a') what they will see. We may recognize that "greater things than these" (a) are namely the divine, mysterious things regarding the Son (a'). The center x could be the emphatic expression of Jesus: "Truly, truly, I said to you."

In II39, Philip follows the example of Jesus who called him first. The focus of II40 is on the fact that "we" have found him for whom we have waited. In II41, two dialogues: between Nathanael and Philip; Nathanael and Jesus are compared, focusing on an inquirer, Nathanael. The function of II42 (F' of II27) seems to be twofold: first, it is for extending the Nathanael episode longer than the Simon one (F of II27); second, it is for highlighting his confession of Jesus as "the Son of God" and "the King of Israel," matching it with the Baptist's confession, "the Lamb of God" in v. 36. As discussed earlier, these two testimonies seem to be an *inclusio* embracing vv. 35–51 as a whole.

Sourcebook of the Structures and Styles in John 1–10

In II43, two sorts of recognition from Jesus regarding Nathanael are arranged. In II44, we can see the repeated, emphatic σὺ (you) regarding who Jesus is. II45 emphasizes "seeing" in future.

V	27			Phrases	Translation
43	A'			Τῇ ἐπαύριον ἠθέλησεν ἐξελθεῖν εἰς τὴν Γαλιλαίαν	The next day He wanted to go out to Galilee,
		39			
-		a		καὶ εὑρίσκει Φίλιππον.	and he found Philip.
-		b		καὶ λέγει αὐτῷ ὁ Ἰησοῦς·	Jesus said to him,
-		c		ἀκολούθει μοι.	"Follow Me."
44	B'			ἦν δὲ ὁ Φίλιππος ἀπὸ Βηθσαϊδά, ἐκ τῆς πόλεως Ἀνδρέου καὶ Πέτρου.	Now Philip was from Bethsaida, the town of Andrew and Peter.
45	C'	a'		εὑρίσκει Φίλιππος τὸν Ναθαναὴλ	Philip found Nathanael
	D'	b'	40	καὶ λέγει αὐτῷ·	and said to him,
-		c'	a	ὃν ἔγραψεν Μωϋσῆς ἐν τῷ νόμῳ καὶ οἱ προφῆται	~ Him of whom Moses in the Law and also the prophets wrote,
-		-	x	εὑρήκαμεν,	"We have found ~
-		-	a'	Ἰησοῦν υἱὸν τοῦ Ἰωσὴφ τὸν ἀπὸ Ναζαρέτ.	Jesus of Nazareth, the son of Joseph."
			41		
46	E'		a	καὶ εἶπεν αὐτῷ Ναθαναήλ· ἐκ Ναζαρὲτ δύναταί τι ἀγαθὸν εἶναι;	Nathanael said to him, "Can anything good come out of Nazareth?"
-			b	λέγει αὐτῷ [ὁ] Φίλιππος· ἔρχου καὶ ἴδε.	Philip said to him "Come and see."
		42			
47	F'	a		Εἶδεν ὁ Ἰησοῦς τὸν Ναθαναὴλ ἐρχόμενον πρὸς αὐτὸν	Jesus saw Nathanael coming to Him,
			43		
-		-	a	καὶ λέγει περὶ αὐτοῦ·	and said of him,
-		-	b	ἴδε ἀληθῶς Ἰσραηλίτης ἐν ᾧ δόλος οὐκ ἔστιν.	"Look, a true Israelite, in whom is no guile!"
48	-	b	a'	λέγει αὐτῷ Ναθαναήλ· πόθεν με γινώσκεις;	Nathanael said to Him, "How do you know me?"
-		a'	b'	ἀπεκρίθη Ἰησοῦς καὶ εἶπεν αὐτῷ·	Jesus answered him,
-		-	b'	πρὸ τοῦ σε Φίλιππον φωνῆσαι ὄντα ὑπὸ τὴν συκῆν εἶδόν σε.	"Before Philip called you, when you were under the fig tree, I saw you."
49	-	x	44	ἀπεκρίθη αὐτῷ Ναθαναήλ· ῥαββί,	Nathanael answered Him, "Rabbi,
-		-	a	σὺ	you
-		-	b	εἶ ὁ υἱὸς τοῦ θεοῦ,	are the Son of God;
-		-	a'	σὺ	you
-		-	b'	βασιλεὺς εἶ τοῦ Ἰσραήλ.	are the King of Israel."
50	-	b'		ἀπεκρίθη Ἰησοῦς καὶ εἶπεν αὐτῷ· ὅτι εἶπόν σοι ὅτι εἶδόν σε ὑποκάτω τῆς συκῆς, πιστεύεις;	Jesus answered him, "Because I said to you, I saw you under the fig tree, do you believe?
			45		
-		a'	a	μείζω τούτων	~ greater things than these."
-		-	b	ὄψῃ.	You will see ~
51	-	-	x	καὶ λέγει αὐτῷ· ἀμὴν ἀμὴν λέγω ὑμῖν,	And He said to him, "Truly, truly, I say to you,
-		-	b'	ὄψεσθε	you will see
-		-	a'	τὸν οὐρανὸν ἀνεῳγότα καὶ τοὺς ἀγγέλους τοῦ θεοῦ ἀναβαίνοντας καὶ καταβαίνοντας ἐπὶ τὸν υἱὸν τοῦ ἀνθρώπου.	heaven open, and the angels of God ascending and descending on the Son of man."

Reading in Style-Structure

1. The divine identification of the Logos is primarily explained both in vv. 1–2 and v. 18. In these verses, he is God the Word who existed with God in the beginning. And he is also called God the only Son who is in the bosom of the Father and finally declared himself to be so. These two concepts, God the Logos and God the Son, are the prioritized terms for Christ here.

2. Considering the connectivity between vv. 3–5 and 9–11, we may say additionally what the Son is and does: First, the Son cooperated with the Father in creation, making all creatures including people. Without him, there is nothing created. Second, life and light are the characteristics of the Son, all being given to deliver the people in darkness. Third, the Son came into the world, the people, which originally belonged to him. Fourth, the people neither recognized nor accepted him, their savior. These ideas are repeated at least twice for emphasis through these verses.

3. In contrast to the pair of vv. 3–5 and 9–11, that of vv. 14 and 16–17 displays the difference in the relationship between the Son and his believers: First, he was incarnated and dwelt among them. Second, they have seen his glory, full of grace and truth. Third, they are given and receive this grace and truth through Jesus Christ.

4. In the center of the structure, unbelievers in the previous verses become true believers in the following verses, by their reception of and belief in him. Belief in Jesus is the key, repositioning the status of darkness in vv. 5, 10–1 to the new one of light in vv. 14, 16–17.

5. The testimonies of the Baptist are located in vv. 6–8 and v. 15 and are arranged in a pair to complete the whole chiastic structure of vv. 1–18. His witnesses are regarded: First, John is the witness from God toward the Son. Second, his purpose of witness is that all may believe in the Son. Third, John is compared to the Son in some aspects: light-testifier; existing rank.

As a whole, there are two kinds of witnesses: the author (or author group, "we") and John the Baptist. Thus, we can hear two combined voices of witness toward the Son: throughout the verses (author) and partially as well (John the Baptist).

6. Regarding his deity, Jesus is testified to in several ways: his preexistence and superiority to the Baptist (26–27, 30); the Lamb of God who takes away the sin of the world (29, 36); he on whom the Spirit descends and remains (32–33); he who baptizes with the Holy Spirit (33); the Son of God (34, 49); Messiah (41); he of whom Moses in the Law and also the prophets wrote (45); Jesus of Nazareth, the son of Joseph (45); the King of Israel (49). Among them, although some are repeated twice, two designations, the Lamb of God and the Son of God, can be regarded as the primarily significant names of the testimonies. These two names appear in vv. 29 and 34 as an *inclusio* of

vv. 29–34 (II15) and reappear in vv. 35 and 49 as another *inclusio* of vv. 35–51 (II27).[13] We can imagine that the two names considerably reflect the main issues in John.

7. Two episodes regarding Andrew-Simon and Philip-Nathanael show that they are arranged for particular purpose to testify to Jesus in a dual mode, for they are in parallel as in II27. When we read them, we need to compare each of the parallels such as A-A', B-B', C-C', D-D', E-E', F-F'. For example, in A-A', Andrew follows Jesus when he heard of him, while Philip is found by Jesus by his initiative.[14]

8. Considering the Johannine style of chiasm, in II45, we can interpret what Jesus said in v. 50 regarding "greater things than these." What you (Nathanael) will see (ὄψῃ, singular) is what you (probably his disciples) will see (ὄψεσθε, plural), namely "the angels of God ascending and descending on the Son of Man" that is an assumed reference to his crucifixion and resurrection.

Issues in Structure-Style

1. The Structure of the Prologue

Moloney divides the prologue into three sections:[15] I. The Word of God becomes the light of the world (vv. 1–5); II. The incarnation of the Word (vv. 6–14); III. The revealer: the only Son turned toward the Father (vv. 15–18). He thinks that there is a recurring statement and restatement of the same message in these sections as follows: (a) The Word is announced or described (1–2 [I], 6–8 [II], 15 [III]); (b) The revelation brought by the Word is coming into the world (3–4 [I], 9 [II]); (c) Mankind responds (5 [I], 10–13 [II], 16 [III]); (d) and the object of belief is described: the only Son of the Father (14 [II], 17–18 [III]).

Excluding some verses (6–8, 9, 12c–13, 15, and 17–18) that he regarded as later additions, Brown classified four strophes:[16] First strophe: vv. 1–2, the Word with God; Second strophe: vv. 3–5, the Word and creation; Third strophe: vv. 10–12b, the Word in the world; Fourth strophe: vv. 14, 16, the community's share in the Word.

Interestingly, Borgen, regarding the prologue as a unit and matching it with three ideas of Genesis 1:1–3, presents three pairs:[17] (a) vv. 1–2 and vv. 14–18: the Logos and God before creation, and the Epiphany with the coming of Jesus; (b) v. 3 and vv. 10–13: the Logos which creates in primordial time, and which claims its posses-

---

13. Here we may regard "the King of Israel" (49) as an additional title to "the Son of God."

14. For the details, see the above note (II27)

15. Moloney, *Gospel of John*, 34. Similarly, Godet shows simplistic divisions: The Logos (1–4); the Logos unrecognized (5–11); the Logos received (12–18). Godet, *John's Gospel*, 242–43.

16. Brown, *Gospel according to John I-XII*, 22. Compare the seven strophes of Gordley, "Johannine Prologue," 786–92.

17. Borgen, "Logos Was the True Light," 110. Cf. Evans, *Word and Glory*, 77–79.

sion by the coming of Jesus; (c) vv. 4–5 and vv. 6–9: Light and nightfall in primordial time, and the coming of Light with Jesus' coming, with the Baptist as a witness. This structure drives us to interpret vv. 1–2 together with vv. 14–18; likewise v. 3 with vv. 10–13; and also vv. 4–5 with vv. 6–9.

Considering the three sections of Moloney, we may indicate some points: First, if we regard vv. 1–2 as an announcement of the deity of the Word (see his "a"), we have to admit that these verses are paired with v. 18 rather than v. 15. Particularly, the format of vv. 1–2 differs from that of either vv. 6–8 or of v. 15. Additionally, there is no Baptist in vv. 1–2. Second, the relation between vv. 3–4 and 9 (see his "b") needs to be explained by that between vv. 3–5 and 9–11 (see B1 and B2 of I1). Thus we cannot see anything related with this point in his third section (15–18). Third, that there is any shared idea between vv. 5 and 10–13 (see his "c") is also explained by the existence of the relation between vv. 3–5 and 9–11. Fourth, there is surely a connection between vv. 14 and 17–18 (see his "d") but also with v. 16 (see B'2 and B'1 of I1; also ab-b'a' of I46). Moreover, we have to ask why that idea (the only Son of the Father) does not appear in his "I."

As far as Brown's strophes are concerned, we may say as follows: First, there is no proper reason that he excluded v. 9 from the third strophe, which is similar in style to vv. 10–11. Verses 9–11 contain the chain-link parallels such as I17–24 which overlap in a few parts, one by one and sequentially. Without v. 9, there is a lack of connectivity between vv. 3–5 and 9–11 (see "10" of the note of I1). Second, the assertion that vv. 12c–13 are added later for the additional explanation of v. 12ab is caused by ignorance of the construction of vv. 12–13 (see I25 and 28–29), which matches in style with the rest of the prologue. Third, vv. 17–18 are not added to v. 16, but vv. 16–17 and 18 are designed to match with vv. 3–5 and 1–2, respectively. And vv. 16–17 (B'1 of I1) are intended to relate with v. 14 (B'2). Thus, the relation between vv. 1–2 and 3–5 is like that between vv. 18 and 16–17 and also the relation between vv. 3–5 and 9–11 is like that between vv. 16–17 and 14. Additionally, as mentioned earlier, vv. 14, 16–17, and 18 are constructed to create a chiasm (I46).

Borgen's three pairs from his comparison of the prologue with Genesis 1:1–3 is insightful but seems to be obscure. First, the relation between light-life (4–5, 9) and grace-truth (14, 16–17), both of which are given from the Son or represented by him, is not explained.[18] Second, the heterogeneous verse regarding the Baptist, v. 15, in the context of vv. 14–18, is not properly explained. Third, the relation between vv. 3 and 10–13 is questionable. The only idea to be shared between them is of the creation,

---

18. It is interesting that Coloe suggests a bipartite structure based on three sensory verb-phrases: have seen, A (3–5) and A' (14); have heard, B (6–8) and B' (15); have experienced, C (9–13) and C' (16–17), putting aside vv. 1–2 as introduction and v. 18 as conclusion. Her structure of the threefold development is hinted at by the sensible expressions in 1 John 1:1–3. Coloe, *God Dwells with Us*, 18–19. We may say that her problems lie in her not being aware of the connected similarities between vv. 3–5 and 9–11 and between vv. 14 and 16–17 and, moreover, in the prologue, there are no manifest sensory expressions as in the preface of 1 John, but rather just implied ones.

which appears in vv. 3 and 10 only and does not appear anywhere in vv. 11–13. In vv. 11–13, the ideas of the coming of the Son and the refusal-acceptance of the people are dominant. These ideas are also scattered in vv. 5, 14, 16–17, and 18.

2. Chiastic Structures of the Prologue

Among the scholars who present their own suggestions on the chiastic structure of the prologue, the model of Staley would be representative. He presents a chiastic structure as follows:[19] A (1–5). The relations with the Logos: a. God; b. creation; c. humankind; B (6–8). The witness of John the Baptist; C (9–11). The coming of the Light/Logos and the refusal; D (12–13). Benefit of belief in the Logos; C' (14). The coming of the Logos and the acceptance; B' (15). The witness of John the Baptist; A' (16–18). The relations with the Logos: c'. mankind; b'. re-creation; a'. God.

Culpepper suggests a scrutinized structure of chiasm, focusing on some common features among the verses:[20] A (1–2, the Word) and A' (18, who has made him known); B (3a, came into being through him . . . not one thing came into being) and B' (17, through Moses . . . came through Jesus Christ); C (3b–5, life . . . light) and C' (16, fullness . . . grace upon grace); D (6–8, John . . . witness to testify to the light) and D' (15, John testified); E (9–10, coming into the world . . . was in the world) and E' (14, Word became flesh and lived among us); F (11, what was his own, and his own people) and F' (13, not of blood or of the will of the flesh or of the will of man); G (12a, who received him) and G' (12c, . . . who believed in his name); H (12b, children of God).

The structure of Staley is clearly seen. First, the relations between vv. 6–8 and 15 and between vv. 9–11 and 14 are properly suggested and the pivotal feature of vv. 12–13 is well explained.

However, second, the relations between vv. 3–5 and 9–11 and between vv. 14 and 16–18 are ignored. We may consider the relation between vv. 1–5 and 16–18 as he does, but in this case we are losing the relation between vv. 3–5 and 9–11 as well as that between vv. 14 and 16–17. Third, it seems to be groundless to regard vv. 1–5 as "God-creation-humankind" and vv. 16–18 as "humankind-recreation-God." We can see "God" in vv. 1–2 and 18. We assume that "creation" is referred to in v. 3 and "recreation" (grace and truth came through Jesus Christ) is in v. 17. If we consider v. 17 in relation to re-creation, how about vv. 12–13 where the regeneration of people is primarily referred to? And the creation issue comes up again in v. 10. Moreover, the closer and more similar verses in the human-related issue to vv. 4–5 are vv. 9–11 than v. 16. (See the relation between vv. 3–5 and 9–11, B1 and B2 of I1.)

The structure of Culpepper is more extended than that of Staley. First, he is right to disclose the relation between vv. 1–2 and 18 as well as that between vv. 6–8 and

---

19. Staley, "Structure of John's Prologues," 241–64; Staley, *Print's First Kiss*, 52–57. Cf. Van der Watt, "Composition of the Prologue," 329–31; Voorwinde, "John's Prologue," 27–43.

20. Culpepper, "Pivot of John's Prologue," 1–31; Cf. Giblin, "Two Complementary Literary," 94.

15.[21] Second, his divisions of ABC-C'B'A' (1–5 and 16–18) are exactly the same as the idea of Staley (God-creation-humankind and humankind-recreation-God). Thus, he is also ignoring the connections between vv. 3–5 and 9–11 and also between vv. 14 and 16–17. Third, he categorizes vv. 9–11 into E (9–10) and F (11), matching with F' (13) and E' (14), so as to split v. 12 into G-H-G'. As a result, his model shows ignorance of the inner cohesiveness in vv. 9–11 as well as vv. 12–13. It is possible that there is a split of v. 12 as a-b-a' (see I25), as he suggests. But v. 12 cannot be segregated from v. 13 because these two verses are strongly combined as in I25–29.

3. The Original Hymn

Bultmann and many scholars who follow him have thought that the origin of the prologue is a Christian hymn. According to Bultmann, in the prologue, each couplet is made up of two short sentences, expressing one thought (9, 12, and 14b).[22] In vv. 1, 4, 14a, and 16, the second couplets develop the first. In v. 3, the two parts of couplet create a parallelism and, in vv. 5, 10, and 11, antitheses are produced. "In each sentence two words normally carry the emphasis, and the second of these stressed words often recurs as the first word emphasized in the next sentence. This is not only the case with the two parts of a couplet; as occasion offers, single verses are also joined together in this way, and the result is a kind of chain-locking of the sentences." He excluded vv. 6–8, 13, and 15 from this category, seeing them as interruptions.[23]

Brown who mainly agreed with the idea of Bultmann pointed out that vv. 1–5, 10–11, and 14 are the original passages of a hymn as is generally agreed.[24]

Von Wahlde suggests how to discern the features of the original hymn in the prologue: (1) the individual clauses are quite short; (2) the clauses contain a rhythmic parallelism; (3) there is a repeated use of a catchword connection (chaining or staircase parallelism). In this way, he proposes that vv. 1–5, 10–12, 14, and 16 sustain the original hymn.[25]

It is not possible to deny any prior existence of the original hymn in the prologue regarding its poetic features such as the couplets of short sentences and the many parallels in style. However, it is possible to distinguish what is plausible from what is spurious in the process of presenting this theory.

21. See also Lamarche, "Prologue of John," 55–57.

22. Bultmann, *Gospel of John*, 13–18; Bultmann, "History of Religions Background," 27–46. Brown thought that only v. 15 as prose does not match the careful poetry of the hymnal trait of the prologue. Brown, *Gospel according to John I–XII*, cxxxiv. But Borgen discards the delimitation between poetry and prose in the prologue. Borgen, "Logos Was the True Light," 108–9.

23. See also Smith, *Composition and Order*, 2. On the contrary, Robinson claimed that vv. 6–9 and 14 were the original beginning. Robinson, "Relation of the Prologue," 124–28; cited by Carter, "Prologue and John's Gospel," 36–37.

24. Brown, *Gospel according to John I–XII*, 21.

25. Von Wahlde, *Commentary on the Gospel of John*, 19, specifically n. 7.

First, the so-called Baptist's "prosaic verses" (6–8 and 15) need to be treated fairly. Verses 6–7a show a similar phenomenon of poetic chiasm (see I12) with the rest of the prologue: Ἐγένετο (a) and ἦλθεν (a'); ἄνθρωπος (b) and οὗτος (b'); ἀπεσταλμένος παρὰ θεοῦ (c) and ὄνομα αὐτῷ Ἰωάννης (c'). Compare abc with c'b'a' both in meaning, form, and even syllable numbers. See also how vv. 7–8 constitute a chiasm (a-x-a', I14). See also three parallelisms in v. 15 (I34–36), particularly the last two (I35 and 36) in terms of how they produce perfect parallelisms. These phenomena cannot be treated as different from the rest of the prologue.

Second, vv. 6–8 and 15 do not break the unity of the prologue but instead become essential constituents of the chiastic structure (C and C' of I1), without which we might have not seen the relations between vv. 3–5 and 16–17 and between vv. 9–11 and 14. For vv. 6–8 exist where they are, vv. 3–5 and 9–11 become regarded as a pair (B1 and B2), far from the misunderstanding that they look as if they are duplicated. The relation between vv. 3–5 (B1) and 9–11 (B2) leads us to pay attention to the connection between vv. 14 (B'2) and 16–17 (B'1), because the former is similar to the latter. Thus, vv. 6–8 cannot be inserted due to an editorial misunderstanding of the concept of the incarnation in v. 5 (*contra* Bultmann).

Third, v. 17 is not an imitation of v. 16 (*contra* von Wahlde). The parallelism in v. 17 (see I38), as he discovers, reflects the typical style in the prologue. Verse 16 does not have its own parallel within itself but constitutes a chiasm (I37) with the help of v. 17.

Fourth, the parallelism is not only found in v. 3 (*contra* Bultmann) but also in many other places, such as vv. 1–2 (I3), 5 (I10), 6–7a (I12), 9 (I18), 10 (I21), 10–11 (I23–24), 12–13 (I25), 15 (I34–36), 17 (I38), even 18 (I39). There are couplets and triplets everywhere in the prologue, which are components for creating various parallels.

Fifth, there is no reason to exclude vv. 15–18 from the original prologue because the completeness in design for chiastic structure is broken without them. Verse 14 is one of the constituents of the latter part (14–18) of the prologue which emphasizes the testimony of "we" (believers) after receiving him as their Savior in comparison with the former part (1–11), which repeats the rejection by the people three times. The emphasis on the divine character of the Son appears in both parts with a balance (1–3, 10; 14, 16, and 18). The incarnation reference occurs frequently in v. 5, 9, 10, 11, 14, 15, and 18.

Sixth, Borgen raises the question whether it is necessary to demarcate the poetry from the prose in the prologue, rejecting the hypothesis of the hymn theory.[26] Rather we may say that the prologue is itself the hymn in perfect design. (1) Its (combined) chiastic structure is creative and beautiful in design. (2) Each sentence is interwoven into more than one parallel, creating a network of rhythms and rhymes as in poetry.

---

26. Borgen, "Logos Was the True Light," 107–9, depending on Elterster, "Der Logos und sein Prophet," 109–34.

4. An Aramaic Original

C. F. Burney, who observed the form of a hymn consisting of eleven couplets after translating the passage into Aramaic, concluded that vv. 1–5, 10–11, 14, and 16–17 preserve an Aramaic version of the hymn.[27] This idea was adopted by Bultmann,[28] but has been rejected by many.[29]

First, against the Aramaic original theory, Beasley-Murray introduces Bernard's critical comments on that idea:[30] the hymn not only has couplets but also triplets (1, 10, and 18) and also single lines (2 and 14e).

Second, most of all, it is sure that any translation only keeps its original pattern or style as it had been written with difficulty. If any text is translated into a different language, its own format is easily damaged, even if the translator pays much attention to keeping the style in the process of translation.

Third, thus it is improbable that the prologue which reflects a cohesive, perfect scheme in style and structure came from the translation of an Aramaic original.

5. The Verses of the Baptist (6–8 and 15)

Not a few scholars have regarded vv. 6–8 and 15 as later additions and interruptions of the prologue. These verses are regarded as heterogeneous to the literary context of the prologue. For example, Bultmann saw a break of continuity because of the existence of v. 15 in using a different subject from the previous verse (14, ἡμεῖς) and from the following one (16, ἡμεῖς). Verses 14 and 16 show the continuity, containing the connecting words, πλήρης and ἐκ τοῦ πληρώματος.[31]

As for vv. 6–8, it has been thought among scholars that these verses were inserted because the evangelist misunderstood v. 5 as containing a description of the incarnation, and thus they inserted the prosaic passage to explain it.[32]

Painter also indicates that the triple introduction of the Baptist (6–8, 15, and 19ff) is strange and the location of vv. 6–8 seems inappropriate because the incarnation is not referred to until v. 14.[33] He thinks that the testimony of the Baptist should have first appeared in v. 15, following v. 14, as an additional note to the proclamation of the incarnation (14).

---

27. Beasley-Murray, *John*, 3. On the contrary, Teeple insists on a gnostic origin. Teeple, *Literary Origin of the Gospel of John*, 126–41.
28. Bultmann, *Gospel of John*, 15.
29. Haenchen, *John 1*, 129.
30. Beasley-Murray, *John*, 3.
31. Bultmann, *Gospel of John*, 12.
32. Haenchen, *John 1*, 13.
33. Painter, *Quest for the Messiah*, 141.

First, vv. 6–8 and 15 are deliberately located where they match each other in the chiastic structure and also help the other verses which consist of pairs. See how vv. 6–8 are located in the middle of vv. 1–11, so that they divide these verses into two groups (1–5 and 9–11). It is the same in v. 15 which divides vv. 14–18 into two groups (14 and 16–18). Without these verses, the chiastic structure could not be constructed. Without vv. 6–8 and its counterpart v. 15 (if we extract them), no one can find the relation between vv. 3–5 and 16–17, (1) because vv. 3–5 and 9–11 are indeed similar in contents and (2) because v. 14 looks not to be detached from vv. 16–17 and so is attachable and inseparable to them.

Second, in this sense, vv. 6–8 are not inserted where they are because the author misunderstood the incarnation in v. 5. (See "First and Second," N.3 for more details.) The prologue does not provide a time difference between the former part (1–11) and the latter one (14–18) such as before or after the incarnation. The former focuses on the rejection by the people, while the latter highlights the acceptance of believers. In the center (12–13), the significance of the acceptance is suggested.

Third, the Baptist testimonies (6–8 and 15) complement the "we" testimonies in the prologue in terms of being dual testimonies (8:17), as 1:19–51 are similarly constituted by the two testimonies of the Baptist and the early disciples of Jesus. The two kinds of (dual) testimonies are interrelated and arranged in design to convince the readers regarding who Jesus is.

6. Some Other Verses That Are Added Later

Brown regarded also vv. 12c–13 and 17–18 as additions: to explain how men become God's children (12c–13) and to explain love in place of love (17–18),[34] strongly depending on Bultmann who had excluded vv. 12c–13 and 17–18 from the original hymn.[35] Bultmann regarded v. 12c (τοῖς πιστεύουσιν . . .) and v. 13 as the exegetical comments on the notion τέκνα θεοῦ (v. 12b) and v. 17 as an exegetical gloss on v. 16 and v. 18 as an addition on stylistic grounds.

Painter extracts v. 3b from the poetic form of vv. 1–5, asserting that v. 3b ("and without him was made not one thing that was made") is an addition because it contains the phenomenon of repetition and has a polemical character, so as to see clearly the "interlocking themes" in vv. 1–5.[36]

First, according to Brown, the elimination of some verses which are regarded as additional is subjective.[37] Bernard eliminated vv. 6–9, 12–13, and 15–17; Bultmann, vv. 6–8, 12c–13, 15, and 17–18; Haenchen, 6–8, 12–13, 15, and 18; Käsemann, 2, 6–9,

---

34. Brown, *Gospel according to John I–XII*, 22.
35. Bultmann, *Gospel of John*, 17.
36. Painter, *Quest for the Messiah*, 139.
37. Brown, *Gospel according to John I–XII*, 22; also Painter, *Quest for the Messiah*, 139.

The Prologue and the Early Testimonies

and 12–18; Schnackenburg, 2, 5–8, 12–13, 15, 17–18. Brown himself removed vv. 6–9, 12c–13, 15, and 17–18 from the original hymn.

Second, we have already argued whether some verses are added.[38] We are going to summarize as follows: (1) v. 9 cannot be removed because of the existence of parallels in vv. 9–11; (2) vv. 12–13 show the coherence of construction; (3) vv. 16–17 and 18 are designed to match with vv. 3–5 and 1–2; (4) v. 17 is not an imitation of v. 16; (5) the parallel features permeate throughout the prologue.

Third, regarding Painter's removal of v. 3b, we can say that v. 3b is an essential part of I6 (ab-b'a'), without which v. 3 does not stand alone. It means that the couplet in v. 3 is broken. All the three verses in vv. 3–5 show the similar pattern of a couplet with two short related sentences each (see I8 in 4; I10 in 5). It is so natural to see the triple appearance of γίνομαι in v. 3 as in the triple uses of the logos in v. 1.[39] If anyone excludes v. 3b, he is arbitrarily ignoring the system in the style as a whole.

7. The Structure of vv. 19–34

Bultmann thought that vv. 19–34 are not an original unit.[40] According to him, vv. 22–24 break the continuity between v. 21 and v. 25, are far from the literary context, and do not have any clear relation to v. 21, because they are a later interpolation, "an ecclesiastical redaction." Additionally, he argued that v. 26 should be followed by v. 31 because they are the answer to the question in v. 25; v. 27 is an additional comment; vv. 28–30 are misplaced; vv. 32–33b are an insertion.

First, it is a dual mode of presentation if vv. 19–28 and 29–34 are put together, similarly to vv. 40–51, where there are twofold passages regarding the testimonies of the early disciples of Jesus. It means that it is unnecessary to combine the two passages into a united one or rearrange them according to the idea of the interpreter.

Second, without vv. 22–24, it may be said that the relation between vv. 21 and 25 seems to be more natural, but we can say that it is not Johannine. Verses 22–24 contain a latter part of B2, B3, and B'1 of II2, which are essential to constitute the combined chiastic system of structure (19–28, II2). Even if we exclude vv. 22–24, we may see a chiastic structure in vv. 19–21 and 25–28: the opening and closing parts (19a and 28) and two questions and two answers (19b–21 and 25–27). But, with the help of vv. 22–24, some Johannine parallels are more observable, particularly as II4 (19b–23, ab-a'b'), II9 (22–23, ab-a'b'), and II11 (20b–21 and 25b, abc-a'b'c'), all of which show in common the recurring pattern of Johannine parallels.

Third, it may be right to indicate that the answer in v. 26 to the question in v. 25 still continues in v. 31. But we have to consider that: (1) v. 27 is properly matched with

---

38. See Brown's strophes in N1 and "Third-Sixth" of N3 for more details.

39. It is unnecessary to remove v. 3b to keep the form of interlocking themes in vv. 1–5 as Painter suggests. Painter, *Quest for the Messiah*, 139–40.

40. Bultmann, *Gospel of John*, 84.

v. 26 (see II14); (2) v. 31 is an essential part to the parallelism of vv. 31–33a (II21), inseparable from vv. 32–33a (see also II15 where vv. 31–33a become the center of the chiasm, C and C'). Thus, vv. 31–32 are not simply repeated in v. 33, but these verses create a beautiful parallelism (II21).

Fourth, the function of v. 28 is to be matched with v. 19a so as to be an *inclusio* (A and A' of II2) and to link the first testimony of the Baptist (19–28) to his second testimony (29–34), where vv. 29 and 34 are constructed as an *inclusio* (A and A' of II15).

Fifth, v. 33b ("this is he who baptizes with Holy Spirit") is paired with v. 30, revealing what the deity of Jesus is about and constructing B and B' of II15. And vv. 33b–34 are designed as a combined chiasm (a1a2-x-a'1a'2, II25).

8. The Seven Days Theory

Moloney presents the seven days theory grounded on the ancient celebration of Pentecost and Exodus 19. According to him, there were four extra days of preparation before the three days of Exodus 19 for the revelation of God and the gift of the Torah. The last day of the four days of distant preparation becomes the first day of the following three days in Exodus 19. On the third day the glory of God is revealed.[41] Moloney insists that this order of the events is compared with the sequential arrangement of John 1:19—2:12, where there are four days of preparation: day one (19–28); day two (29–34); day three (35–42); day four (43–51), and also where there is the third day after the four days (2:1–12), the day when the glory of Jesus is revealed (2:11).

First, this theory is too reasonable to ignore its possibility. John uses "the next day" in vv. 29, 35, and 43, and "the third day" in 2:1. The phrase, "the next day," is used significantly to categorize the previous unit from the following one: 29 (IIA1 and IIA2); 35 (IIA and IIB); 43 (IIB1 and IIB2). It means that this phrase is used here as a demarcation marker.

Second, we can say that the phrase "on the third day" (2:1), as another demarcation marker, plays the role of a division between the previous units in ch. 1 and the new one in ch. 2. It means that "the next day" appears whenever a new unit comes up, vv. 29 (the first phrase of 29–34), 35 (the first phrase of 35–42), and 43 (the first phrase of 43–51).

Third, in this sense, we may basically admit the seven days theory. Nevertheless, it does not mean that it demands us to regard 1:19–51 and 2:1–12 as in the same category such as introductory stories to John. It is certain that the Cana miracle is connected to the previous ones in ch. 1 in terms that, "on the third day," the glory of Jesus is finally revealed. The role of 2:1–12 is a linker (or bridge) between ch. 1 and the following chapters, specifically chs. 2–4, where the glory of Jesus, initiated as a fanfare

---

41. Moloney, *Gospel of John*, 50. Moloney introduces a comment of the *Mekilta* (19:10): "That was the sixth day of the week on which the Torah was given," comparing the *doxa* of God in Ex. 19:16 and the *doxa* of Jesus in John 2:11. See also Moloney, *Belief in the Word*, 57–59.

The Prologue and the Early Testimonies

in 2:11, is gradually revealed. In this sense, this episode needs to be regarded as the first section of chs. 2–4.

9. *Verses 35–51 as the Original Verses*

Based on his edition theory, von Wahlde insists that vv. 35–49 (without 35a, 36b, and 43a) are coherent in narrative sequence and have many features that came from the original edition as follows:[42] (1) the several examples of the translation of Hebrew terms; (2) belief occurs in a chain reaction form; (3) the easy manner in which this belief comes about; (4) the Christology that does not rise above the traditional categories of Jewish expectation; (5) the way Jesus' supernatural knowledge of Peter's name and of Nathanael's previous whereabouts; (6) the awkwardness of Andrew's "first" getting Peter as the relics of an earlier tradition.

First, if we can treat vv. 35–51 as an original, it is necessary to regard other passages such as vv. 19–34 as originals because those verses show similarity in structure and in style as well. Examine the construction of vv. 35–51 (II27). We may also regard smaller parallels shown everywhere. If we consider this phenomenon in style as belonging to the first author or editor, why cannot we do the same to other passages? It is certain that the text could not have been written in a similar style or structure, if there were second and third editors who must have twisted the arrangement of the text without any consideration of structuring any specific scheme of design, whether at macro (paragraph) or micro (sentence and clause) levels.

Second, in the episodes of the meeting between Jesus and his early disciples, the primary difference from the Synoptic Gospels is that all John's episodes are described as the testimonies of his disciples toward Jesus, their master. His disciples become his witnesses to the identity of Jesus. But it is not the case in the Synoptic Gospels. It means that there are two (dual) witness groups: the Baptist and the early disciples of Jesus in this chapter, in a similar way to the prologue (the Baptist and "we").

Third, the reason why the term "first" is used in the case of Andrew (41) seems to be that two episodes in vv. 41 and 45 are considered in the mind of the evangelist. Andrew first takes the action that finds Simon and testifies to him regarding Jesus and then Philip finds Nathanael in a similar way that Andrew has done. In the mind of the author, the cycle, particularly regarding the pair (CD and C'D' of II27), would have been already considered. Thus, we need to regard this term as necessary here for the parallel structure (II27) and not regard the subject of v. 43 as Andrew in terms of his second action.[43]

---

42. Von Wahlde, *Commentary on the Gospel of John*, 67–68.

43. Bultmann dealt with the awkwardness of "first" in v. 41 by replacing the subject of v. 43, who finds Philip, from Jesus to Andrew who found first Peter. Bultmann, *Gospel of John*, 98.

2 The Cana Miracle and the Cleansing of the Temple

"When the temple no longer existed, and Israel's sacrificial cult no longer functioned, the rabbis turned to the law to find in torah a replacement for all they had lost. Around the same time, the Fourth Evangelist presents Jesus, not Torah, as the new temple. But if that were the only transformation, the Christian community would be as desolate in the departure of Jesus as the community of Israel was in the loss of their temple. The gospel narrative doubly transforms the heritage of Israel, transferring the image of the temple to the Christian community that remains in the world, under the guidance of the Spirit-Paraclete."[1]

DUAL MODE IN STRUCTURE

TWO SEEMINGLY UNRELATED EVENTS appear together in John 2: The first sign at Cana (1–11) and the cleansing of the temple (12–25). These two are bound to deliver the specific, significant message: the renewal of Judaism and its replacement.

1. The reason why the two episodes are located here needs to be answered. Does the first sign at Cana have to be grouped into the previous chapter, particularly vv. 19–51? Why does the cleansing of the temple appear after the first Cana sign? Is it the second cleansing of the temple? Is there any probable reason why the author designs to put these two together in ch. 2?

2. The first sign at Cana seems to be unnatural appearing in the first place of Jesus' miracles, just because it was the first sign of Jesus. There are some awkward elements in this episode. First, this sign was not seemingly first intended by Jesus, but Mary insisted that he do it. Second, moreover, he said, "My hour has not yet come." But why did he do that then? Third, of all the miracles of Jesus, just imagine why was the sign

---

1. Coloe, "Temple Imagery in John," 381.

The Cana Miracle and the Cleansing of the Temple

of water-into-wine first? We may ask whether this episode is in fact warranted to be introduced in the first place in spite of all these issues.

3. Why is the cleansing of the temple located here just after the first sign at Cana? Was it the second cleansing caused by Jesus in the temple, different from that written in the last part of the Synoptic Gospels (Matt 21:12–13; Mark 11:15–17; Luke 19:45–46)? It is not consistent that an event in the same circumstances and with the similar process should happen twice. This happening was like dropping a bomb in the temple. It is difficult to think that the hostile Jews would allow Jesus to do the same thing in the temple in their defenseless state. Why then is this episode placed here in ch. 2?

4. The cleansing of the temple in John consists of two parts: cleansing the temple (12–17) and building the temple (18–25). The cleansing of the temple episode is shared with the Synoptic Gospels, but the latter, building the temple, is unique to John. In Matthew and Mark, this building the temple issue is not written in the same situation (see Matt 26:61; Mark 14:58). This issue is manifestly related to his resurrection (John 3:21–22). His resurrected body is the new temple in a new world. The old Herod's temple is replaced by the new temple of Jesus. Replacement is the motif here.[2]

5. It is obvious that the first part, the cleansing of the temple, focuses on the issue of purification regarding the obsolete system of religion, Judaism. As they were corrupt, they needed to be totally cleansed. They needed to be restored, revived, and reformed into the original state of purity.

6. Thus, it is inferred that the cleansing of the temple episode in John is delivered in relation to two issues: restoration and replacement.

7. In the Cana miracle, it is the sense of restoration when water is turned into wine at the banquet. They needed wine at the wedding for their enjoyment. But there is no wine besides the jars of water for ritual purposes. There is still ritual but no more wine at the wedding. The wedding losing wine and good wine are contrasted. However, Jesus restores the vivid scene of wedding celebration, transforming water into wine. It is restoration.

8. The water-into-wine event is not only for restoration but also replacement. Jesus definitely transforms the water of Judaic ritual of purification into the wine of celebration. Replacing water with wine, it goes beyond restoration to the replacement of the enervated, ritual religion, Judaism, into the new system of religion by Jesus. This is the symbolism of the event.

9. In conclusion, two events, the first sign at Cana and the cleansing of the temple, deliver in common the message: restoration and replacement. Ritual and temple were

---

2. Cf. Coloe, "Temple Imagery in John," 381.

predominant issues in the Judaism. The Judaism of ritual and temple should be renewed by Jesus and also replaced by the system of Jesus.³

10. Two episodes are dual in design, both pointing out the similar issues that primarily permeate John.

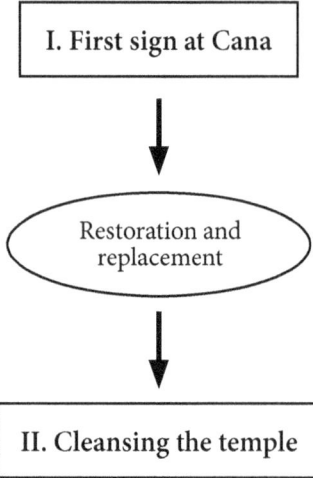

I. The First Sign at Cana (2:1–11)

Chiastic Structure, I1 (ABC-X-C'B'A')

1. In the opening of the story, vv. 1–2, there are the mother of Jesus, Jesus, and his disciples, while in the closing, v. 11, there are Jesus and his disciples. In these parts only, his disciples appear and also the name of Cana in Galilee is described. We may name A and A'. Through the story, the disciples eventually believe in him (A').

2. Besides vv. 1–2 and 11, there are five scenes, including dialogues: Jesus and his mother (3–4); his mother and the servants (5); Jesus and the servants (6–8); the master of the banquet and the servants (9a); the master of banquet and the bridegroom (9b–10).

3. We may locate vv. 6–8 in the center of the unit, X, where the miracle of the wine is disclosed in detail.

4. It needs to be checked whether other pairs might match each other: vv. 3–4 and 9b–10; vv. 5 and 9a.

5. The dialogue between the mother of Jesus and himself (B, 3–4) can be compared with that between the master of banquet and the bridegroom (B', 10), in terms of dialogue between two persons on the issue of wine: from quantity (B) to quality (B').

---

3. In terms of Jesus' messianic acts to his disciples (1–11) and to Israel and its religious leaders (12–22), see Kim, "Significance of Jesus' First Sign-Miracle," 208–14.

The Cana Miracle and the Cleansing of the Temple

6. We may also compare the relation between the mother and the servants (C, 5) with that between the servants and the master of banquet (C', 9a), in each of which the servants appear.

7. Thus, we can see the chiastic structure, I1: ABC-X-C'B'A'.[4]

V	1	2		Phrases	Translation
1	A	a	3	Καὶ τῇ ἡμέρᾳ τῇ τρίτῃ	On the third day
-	-	-	a	γάμος ἐγένετο	there was a wedding.
-	-	b	4	ἐν Κανὰ τῆς Γαλιλαίας,	in Cana in Galilee
-	-	a'	a	καὶ ἦν	~ was
-	a'	-	-	ἡ μήτηρ τοῦ Ἰησοῦ	The mother of Jesus ~
-	-	b'	b	ἐκεῖ·	there,
2	-		a'	ἐκλήθη δὲ καὶ ὁ Ἰησοῦς καὶ οἱ μαθηταὶ αὐτοῦ	~ was invited, and Jesus also ~ and His disciples,
-			b'	εἰς τὸν γάμον.	to the wedding.
3	B			καὶ ὑστερήσαντος οἴνου λέγει ἡ μήτηρ τοῦ Ἰησοῦ πρὸς αὐτόν· οἶνον οὐκ ἔχουσιν.	When the wine ran out, Jesus' mother said to Him, "They have no wine."
4	-		5	[καὶ] λέγει αὐτῇ ὁ Ἰησοῦς· τί ἐμοὶ καὶ σοί, γύναι; οὔπω ἥκει ἡ ὥρα μου.	Jesus said to here, "Woman, what do I have to do with you? My hour has not yet come."
5	C	a	6	λέγει ἡ μήτηρ αὐτοῦ τοῖς διακόνοις·	His mother said to the servants,
-	-	-	a	ὅ τι ἂν λέγῃ ὑμῖν	"whatever he tells you,
-	-	-	b	ποιήσατε.	do it."
6	X	x		ἦσαν δὲ ἐκεῖ λίθιναι ὑδρίαι ἓξ κατὰ τὸν καθαρισμὸν τῶν Ἰουδαίων κείμεναι, χωροῦσαι ἀνὰ μετρητὰς δύο ἢ τρεῖς.	Now there were six stone water jars set there for the Jewish rites of purification, each holding twenty or thirty gallons.
7	-	a'	a'	λέγει αὐτοῖς ὁ Ἰησοῦς· γεμίσατε τὰς ὑδρίας ὕδατος.	Jesus said to them, "Fill the jars with water."
-	-	-	b'	καὶ ἐγέμισαν αὐτὰς ἕως ἄνω.	And they filled them up to the brim.
8	-	-	a''	καὶ λέγει αὐτοῖς· ἀντλήσατε νῦν καὶ φέρετε τῷ ἀρχιτρικλίνῳ·	Then He said to them, "Now draw some out and take it to the master of the banquet."
-	-	-	b''	οἱ δὲ ἤνεγκαν.	And they took it.

In vv. 1–8, there are at least five parallels: three parallelisms (I3, 4, and 6), one chiasm (I5), and one dual (I2). I2–4 exist in vv. 1–2 (A of I1), while I5–6 demonstrate the connection between vv. 5 and 6–8, probably accentuating the significance of the inseparability of listening and obeying. But there seems to be no parallels within vv. 3–4 and beyond the verses except for I1.

I2. Dual, a-a': This sentence indicates that there were two kinds of things: a wedding (a) and the mother of Jesus (a'). I3. Parallel, ab-a'b': There was a wedding (a) and

---

4. Compare the chiasm of Ellis: A (1–2); B (3–5); C (6–8); B' (9–10); A' (11). Ellis, *Genius of John*, 10–11. And also Bulembat, "Head-Waiter and Bridegroom," 56–63.

there was the mother of Jesus (a'). Both b and b' describe the particular place, Cana. I4. Parallel, ab-a'b': Comparably, the mother of Jesus was there (a-b), while Jesus and his disciples were invited (a'-b'). Both b and b' have in common the place of the wedding.

I5. Chiastic, a-x-a': In a, the mother speaks to the servant seriously to follow Jesus' words, and, in a', they follow exactly what Jesus says to them. In the middle, x, the six stone water jars are highlighted as a resource. I6. Parallel, ab-a'b'-a"b": All the a-a'-a" are related in terms of Jesus' commands, while all the b-b'-b" are connected in terms of the servant's obedience to Jesus. This parallel emphasizes that the servants did whatever Jesus told them.

Comparing with I2 that simply focuses on two facts: a wedding and his mother, I3 may be regarded as a rhythmic parallel. In I4, his mother and Jesus are somehow compared. She was there and Jesus and his disciples were invited. I5 highlights two things: hearing-obeying and the ritual water, while I6 focuses only on the issue of hearing-obeying.

V	1	7		Phrases	Translation
9	C'	a		ὡς δὲ ἐγεύσατο	And when ~ tasted ~
-	-	b		ὁ ἀρχιτρίκλινος τὸ ὕδωρ οἶνον γεγενημένον καὶ οὐκ ᾔδει	~ the master of the banquet ~ the water that had become wine, and did not know
-	-	x		πόθεν ἐστίν,	where it came from,
-	-	b'		οἱ δὲ διάκονοι ᾔδεισαν	but the servants ~ knew,
-	-	a'		οἱ ἠντληκότες τὸ ὕδωρ,	who had drawn the water ~
-	B'			φωνεῖ τὸν νυμφίον ὁ ἀρχιτρίκλινος	The master of the banquet called the bridegroom,
10	-		8	9	καὶ λέγει αὐτῷ·	and said to him,
-	-	a	a		πᾶς ἄνθρωπος	"Every man
-	-	-	b1		πρῶτον	~ first,
-	-	b	b2		τὸν καλὸν οἶνον	~ the good wine ~
-	-	-	b3		τίθησιν	brings out ~
-	-	a'			καὶ ὅταν μεθυσθῶσιν	and when they are drunk,
-	-	b'			τὸν ἐλάσσω·	then the poorer wine;
-	-		a'		σὺ	but you
-	-		b'3		τετήρηκας	have kept
-	-		b'2		τὸν καλὸν οἶνον	the good wine
-	10	11	b'1	ἕως ἄρτι.	until now."
11	A'	a	a		Ταύτην ἐποίησεν ἀρχὴν τῶν σημείων	This, the first of his signs, ~ did ~
-	x	-			ὁ Ἰησοῦς ἐν Κανὰ τῆς Γαλιλαίας	Jesus ~ at Cana in Galilee,
-	a'	-			καὶ ἐφανέρωσεν τὴν δόξαν αὐτοῦ,	and manifested His glory,
-	-	a'			καὶ ἐπίστευσαν εἰς αὐτὸν οἱ μαθηταὶ αὐτοῦ.	and His disciples believed in Him.

Verses 9–11 contain five parallels: two chiasms (I7 and 10), one parallelism (I8), one dual (I11), and one combined parallel (I9). I7, 8–9, and 10–11 show the unity of

each verse: v. 9a, v. 10, v. 11, respectively. There is no parallel beyond each verse except for I1, which overarches the unit.

I7. Chiastic, ab-x-b'a': In b and b', the master of the banquet is contrasted with the servants: he does not know what happened (b), while they do know what really happened there (b'). The master of the banquet tasted (a) but the servants did not but had just drawn the water (a'). Nevertheless, they knew all about where the wine came from (x), because they obeyed his words, taking part in the scene of the miracle.

I8. Parallel, ab-a'b': Both a and a' are related in terms of time when the wine is presented. In b and b', the good wine and the bad are contrasted. Two different times of serving the wine are contrasted here. **I9**. Combined parallel, a-b1b2b3-a'-b'1b'2b'3: Both a and a' compare the figures: "Every man" (a) and "you" (a'). The reverse order of arrangement of b1b2b3 appears in b'3b'2b'1: πρῶτον (first, b1) and ἕως ἄρτι (until now, b'1); τὸν καλὸν οἶνον (the good wine, b2) and τὸν καλὸν οἶνον (the good wine, b'2); τίθησιν (brings out, b3) and τετήρηκας (have kept, b'3). Two pairs, b1-b'1 and b3-b'3, contain their own contrasted relations within them, while the pair, b2-b'2, is identical.

I10. Chiastic, a-x-a': In the center, x, Jesus and the place where his sign is performed are presented. In a, he did his first sign and, in a', his glory is manifested. we may say that a is rephrased in a'. **I11**. Dual, a-a': The first part (a, his first sign at Cana) is the cause of the last one (a', the belief of his disciples), the result of the former.

The foci are as follows: the ignorance of the master of the banquet and the knowledge of the servants regarding the source of the wine (I7); the contrast between everyman and the bridegroom in bringing out the good wine (I8); the time of the bringing out of the wine (I9); probably the place where the sign occurred (I10); sign and belief (I11).

II. The Cleansing of the Temple (2:12–25)

Chiastic Structure, II1 (AB-B'A')

1. We may divide the unit into four subunits: vv. 12–13, 14–17, 18–22, and 23–25. Verses 12–13 are an opening scene of the event when Jesus and his disciples went up to Jerusalem when the Passover was near. In the second scene, Jesus cleansed the temple. The third scene is for the dialogue between the Jews and Jesus regarding the temple of his body. It is in the final scene that many believed in him but he did not entrust himself to them.

2. The opening (12–13) and the closing (23–25) can be regarded as a pair: A and A': the time (the Passover) and the place (Jerusalem) are in common.

3. In the middle, two related stories are presented in a pair: cleansing the temple (B) and building the temple (B').

4. Thus, the structure is chiastic: AB-B'A'.

V	1	2				Phrases	Translation
12	A	a				Μετὰ τοῦτο κατέβη εἰς Καφαρναοὺμ αὐτὸς καὶ ἡ μήτηρ αὐτοῦ καὶ οἱ ἀδελφοὶ [αὐτοῦ] καὶ οἱ μαθηταὶ αὐτοῦ	After this He went down to Capernaum, with His mother, and brothers and His disciples,
	-	b				καὶ ἐκεῖ ἔμειναν οὐ πολλὰς ἡμέρας.	and they stayed not many days.
13	-	b'				Καὶ ἐγγὺς ἦν τὸ πάσχα τῶν Ἰουδαίων,	And the Passover of the Jews was at hand,
	-	a'	3		7	καὶ ἀνέβη εἰς Ἱεροσόλυμα ὁ Ἰησοῦς.	and Jesus went up to Jerusalem.
14	B	a		a		Καὶ εὗρεν ἐν τῷ ἱερῷ τοὺς πωλοῦντας βόας καὶ πρόβατα καὶ περιστερὰς καὶ τοὺς κερματιστὰς καθημένους,	And He found in the temple men selling oxen and sheep and doves, and the moneychangers sitting.
		4		5			
15	-	a	b	a		καὶ ποιήσας φραγέλλιον ἐκ σχοινίων	And He made a whip of cords,
	-	-	-	a'	6	πάντας ἐξέβαλεν ἐκ τοῦ ἱεροῦ τά τε πρόβατα καὶ τοὺς βόας,	he drove all out of the temple, with the sheep and the oxen.
	-	a'	-	a		καὶ τῶν κολλυβιστῶν ἐξέχεεν τὸ κέρμα	And He poured out the coins of the moneychangers
	-	-	-	a'		καὶ τὰς τραπέζας ἀνέτρεψεν,	and overturned their tables.
16	-	-	b'			καὶ τοῖς τὰς περιστερὰς πωλοῦσιν εἶπεν·	And to those who sold the pigeons He said,
			8				
	-	-	-	a		ἄρατε ταῦτα ἐντεῦθεν,	"Take these things away;
	-	-	a'	a'		μὴ ποιεῖτε τὸν οἶκον τοῦ πατρός μου οἶκον ἐμπορίου.	Do not make my Father's house a marketplace."
		9					
17	-	a			b	ἐμνήσθησαν οἱ μαθηταὶ αὐτοῦ ὅτι γεγραμμένον ἐστίν· ὁ ζῆλος τοῦ οἴκου σου καταφάγεταί με.	His disciples remembered that it was written, "Zeal for your house will consume me."

There are seven parallels here: four duals (II4, 5, 6, and 8), two chiasms (II2 and 3), and one parallelism (II7). I2 shows the cohesion in vv. 12–13 (A of II1) and I3 does that in vv. 14–17 (B of II1) with the help of II4–6, while II7 and 9 are for connectivity between vv. 14–17 (B of II1) and 18–22 (B' of II1).

II2. Chiastic, ab-b'a': Both b and b' are related in terms of time: how many days they stayed (b); the Passover was near (b'). Meanwhile, Jesus went down (κατέβη) to Capernaum in a and he went up (ἀνέβη) to Jerusalem in a'.

II3. Chiastic, ab-b'a': In b and b', Jesus expels two groups of people but in different ways: driving-out with a whip of cords men selling oxen and sheep and moneychangers (b); just saying to men selling the pigeons, "Take these things away" (b'). Jesus found that the temple had become a marketplace in a, and he was restoring it as he said in a'. II4. Dual, a-a': Jesus acted differently towards two types of men, expelling them from the temple: making a whip of cords and driving-out the merchants (a); pouring-out the coins of the moneychangers and overturning their tables (a'). II5. Dual, a-a': Regarding the merchants, Jesus did two things: making a whip of cords (a) and driving them out (a'). II6. Dual, a-a': Regarding the moneychangers, Jesus did two things: pouring out their coins (a) and overturning their tables (a').

II7. Parallel, ab-a'b': In both b and b', the disciples remember two things: what is written (b) and what Jesus said (b'). In a, the temple cleansing case is first presented, while, in a', the dialogue regarding a new temple, his body, follows. II8. Dual, a-a': Jesus says two sentences in expelling the merchants: "Take these things away" (a) and "Do not make my Father's house a marketplace" (a').

In II2, "went down to Capernaum" and "went up to Jerusalem" are compared. In II3, Jesus' two ways of expelling the two groups are mainly compared. II4–6, 8 show that Jesus acts mostly in two ways. In II7, what is written and what Jesus said are equally highlighted.

V	1		10		7	Phrases	Translation
18	B'		a		a'	Ἀπεκρίθησαν οὖν οἱ Ἰουδαῖοι καὶ εἶπαν αὐτῷ·	The Jews then said to Him,
	-		-		-	τί σημεῖον δεικνύεις ἡμῖν ὅτι ταῦτα ποιεῖς;	"What sign do you show us for doing these things?"
19	-		b	11	-	ἀπεκρίθη Ἰησοῦς καὶ εἶπεν αὐτοῖς·	Jesus answered them, "
	-		-	a	-	λύσατε τὸν ναὸν τοῦτον	Destroy this temple,
	-		-	b	-	καὶ ἐν τρισὶν ἡμέραις ἐγερῶ αὐτόν.	and in three days I will raise it up."
20	-		b'		-	εἶπαν οὖν οἱ Ἰουδαῖοι·	The Jews then said,
	-		-	a'	-	τεσσεράκοντα καὶ ἓξ ἔτεσιν οἰκοδομήθη ὁ ναὸς οὗτος,	"It has taken forty-six years to build this temple,
	-		-	b'	-	καὶ σὺ ἐν τρισὶν ἡμέραις ἐγερεῖς αὐτόν;	and will you raise it up in three days?"
21	-		a'	12		ἐκεῖνος δὲ ἔλεγεν περὶ τοῦ ναοῦ τοῦ σώματος αὐτοῦ.	But He spoke of the temple of His body.
22	-	9		a	b'	ὅτε οὖν ἠγέρθη ἐκ νεκρῶν,	When therefore He was raised from the death,
	-	b		b1	-	ἐμνήσθησαν οἱ μαθηταὶ αὐτοῦ ὅτι τοῦτο ἔλεγεν,	His disciples remembered that he had said this.
	-			b2	-	καὶ ἐπίστευσαν	And they believed
	-	a'		-	-	τῇ γραφῇ	the Scripture
	-	b'		-	-	καὶ τῷ λόγῳ ὃν εἶπεν ὁ Ἰησοῦς.	and the word which Jesus had spoken.
23	A'		13		a'	Ὡς δὲ ἦν ἐν τοῖς Ἱεροσολύμοις ἐν τῷ πάσχα ἐν τῇ ἑορτῇ,	Now when He was in Jerusalem at the feast of Passover,
	-		a		b'2	πολλοὶ ἐπίστευσαν εἰς τὸ ὄνομα αὐτοῦ	many believed in His name
	-		b	14	b'1	θεωροῦντες αὐτοῦ τὰ σημεῖα ἃ ἐποίει·	when they saw His signs which He was doing.
24	-		a'	a		αὐτὸς δὲ Ἰησοῦς οὐκ ἐπίστευεν αὐτὸν αὐτοῖς	But Jesus did not entrust Himself to them,
	-		b'	b		διὰ τὸ αὐτὸν γινώσκειν πάντας	for He knew all men.
25	-		a'			καὶ ὅτι οὐ χρείαν εἶχεν ἵνα τις μαρτυρήσῃ περὶ τοῦ ἀνθρώπου·	And He did not need man's testimony about man,
	-		b'			αὐτὸς γὰρ ἐγίνωσκεν τί ἦν ἐν τῷ ἀνθρώπῳ.	for He knew what was in man.

There are six parallels: four parallelisms (II9, 11, 13, and 14), one chiasm (II10), and one combined parallelism (II12). II10 and 11 strengthen the unity of vv. 18–22, probably with the help of II7 and 9, and II13 and 14 does that of vv. 23–25 (A' of II1). While, II12 is for the connection of vv. 22–23, probably for the purpose of creating continuity between vv. 23–25 and the previous subunit, vv. 18–22.

II9. Parallel, ab-a'b': His disciples remembered, regarding the relation between temple and Jesus, what was written, in a, and what Jesus said, in a'. Finally, they believe both what was written, the Scripture (b), and what he said, his word (b').

II10. Chiastic, ab-b'a': In b and b', Jesus metaphorically speaks about two temples, particularly regarding the new temple, his body (b), but the Jews do not understand anything (b'). The Jews want to see signs from Jesus (a) but Jesus spoke of the most essential sign regarding the temple of his body (a'). **II11**. Parallel, ab-a'b': As Jesus speaks about destroying the temple (a), the Jews speak about its building (a'). Both b and b' focus on raising it up in three days.

II12. Combined parallel, a-b1b2-b'2b'1-a': Both a and a' are related in terms of time: the time after his resurrection (a) and the time of Jesus in Jerusalem at the feast (a'). Both believe in Jesus in b2 and b'2. His disciples remember something (b1), while many saw his signs (b'1). It is said that the people believed in Jesus after seeing signs, but his disciples believed in him because of the word of Jesus as well as the Scripture.

II13. Parallel, ab-a'b': There is the contrast between the many who believed (ἐπίστευσαν) in his name (a) and Jesus who did not entrust (οὐκ ἐπίστευεν) himself to them (a'). They saw signs (b), while Jesus knew all men (b'). They believe after seeing signs, but Jesus does not entrust himself to them because of his knowledge of them. **II14**. Parallel, ab-a'b': Both in b and b', the focus is on Jesus' knowledge about men, while in a-a', there are negative responses of Jesus to them: "Jesus did not entrust himself to them" (a) and "He did not need man's testimony about man" (a').

The foci are: the double emphasis is on what is written and what Jesus said (II9); his body as a new sign regarding the temple (II10); the contrast between the Herod's temple and his body as the temple (II11); two contrastive reasons of beliefs: remembrance versus seeing signs (II12); the contrast between their belief versus Jesus not entrusting himself to them (II13); the double emphasis of the negative responses of Jesus to them (II14).

Reading in Style-Structure

1. Regarding the dual mode in structure, as we have discussed, two episodes, the first sign at Cana (1–11) and the cleansing of the temple (12–25), need to be read concerning their connection in theme: restoration and replacement. It means that reading one episode needs to be complemented by reading the other one.

2. The contrast between the master of banquet and the servants is clear in v. 9 (I7). The possessors of knowledge here are the servants but paradoxically not the master of the banquet.

3. The disciples' remembrance is repeated vv. 17 and 22. The first remembrance is related to what is written, while the second is to what Jesus said to them. These two are the firm ground of their belief in v. 22. (See II9.)

4. The belief of his disciples is in contrast to that of the "many," those who believed Jesus after seeing his signs in Jerusalem in v. 23. His disciples believed in him based on two types of words: the Scripture and the word of Jesus. On the contrary, the people believed in him after seeing something.

5. Thus, not an awkward contrast between their beliefs in him (23) and that Jesus did not entrust himself to them (24) exists (see II13).[5] Jesus knew all that is in man, particularly regarding them. Jesus and his disciples are on the same side, while the people at that time are not.

Issues in Structure-Style

1. The Location of the Cana Miracle and the Cleansing the Temple

Beasley-Murray regards this chapter as a "completeness of its own" where a miraculous deed is conjoined with a non-miraculous act.[6] He agrees not only with Bultmann who called it a "diptych" which forms a prelude to the story of the ministry of Jesus,[7] but also with Dodd who regarded chs. 2–4 "as bound together by a single theme," the replacement of the old purifications.[8]

The reason why Bultmann called ch. 2 a diptych is because he saw that the chapter represents Jesus' ministry symbolically: "the miracle of the wine in vv. 1–11 is expressly designated the ἀρχὴν τῶν σημείων (11), and the cleansing of the temple in vv. 13–22 symbolizes the end—the death and the resurrection of Jesus."[9]

First, it is clearly right that Beasley-Murray and others indicate that the Cana miracle is a half of the diptych of two events (the Cana miracle and the cleansing the

---

5. For the strong contrast that is made between v. 23 and Jesus' response, see Farelly, "John 2:23–25," 43–44.
6. Beasley-Murray, *John*, 31.
7. Bultmann, *Gospel of John*, 112.
8. Dodd also connected this replacement to 1:17. See Dodd, *Fourth Gospel*, 297–99, 303; agreed by Beasley-Murray, *John*, 31.
9. Bultmann, *Gospel of John*, 112.

temple) in ch. 2 and also the first part of chs. 2–4 which embrace a common issue: replacement of the old purifications.[10]

According to Beasley-Murray, "The three chapters together present the replacement of the old purifications by the wine of the kingdom of God, the old temple by the new in the risen Lord, an exposition of new birth for new creation, a contrast between the water of Jacob's well with the living water from Christ, and the worship of Jerusalem and Gerizim with worship in Spirit and in truth."[11]

Second, we may add some titles seemingly missed in his "new" concepts appearing in chs 2–4: ch. 1, new wine and new temple; ch. 2, new birth and new bridegroom (the man from heaven); ch. 3, new water-worship-savior and new life (healing).[12]

Third, chs. 2–4 produce a chiastic system of structure (the Cana cycle) as a whole: The first Cana (A, 2:1–11) and the second Cana (A', 4:43–54);[13] The temple episode (2:12–25, B) and the Samaritans episode regarding worship (4:1–42, B'); The dialogue of Jesus with Nicodemus and his discourse (3:1–21, C) and the Baptist's dialogue and his discourse (3:22–36, C').

Fourth, at the same time, chs. 2–4 consist of a dual arrangement in each chapter: The Cana miracle (2:1–11) and the cleansing the temple (2:12–25) in terms of restoration and replacement with new ones; the dialogue of Jesus with Nicodemus and his discourse (3:1–21) and the Baptist's dialogue and his discourse (3:22–36), where the significant issues such as the love of God, the man from heaven, and belief-and-eternal-life vs. unbelief-and-condemnation are shared; the salvation of the Samaritans (4:1–42) and the salvation of the household of a Jewish, royal official (4:43–54). Two paired episodes or dialogues are bound in each chapter. It is the typical, dual mode of arrangement in design.

But, fifth, one hesitates to agree with the idea of Bultmann, who regarded the Cana miracle as the first sign and thought the cleansing of the temple symbolized the end—the death and the resurrection of Jesus. Although the temple episode is definitely related to the issue of the death and the resurrection of Jesus as described in

---

10. In this sense, we do not support the priority of John that the cleansing the temple episode happened earlier as in the order of John (Weiss, Lagrange, McNeile, Brooke, and Robinson) nor the theory that the cleansing event happened twice by Jesus (Hendricksen and Morris). See Brown, *Gospel according to John I–XII*, 117; Borchert, *John 1–11*, 162n31; Hendricksen, *Exposition of the Gospel according to John*, 120; Morris, *Gospel according to John*, 188–91. The two episodes in John 2 are arranged not in sequential order but in theological priority. See Barrett, *Gospel according to St. John*, 195; Carson, *Gospel according to John*, 177–78; Witherington, *John's Wisdom*, 985–86.

11. Beasley-Murray, *John*, 31; Carson, *Gospel according to John*, 166.

12. Burge treats the dialogue of the Baptist (3:22–35) as an "excursus on the Baptist" without dealing with the proper concern regarding the issue, although he considers the Cana cycle in relation to the replacement issue (purification vessels, 2:1–12; the temple, 2:13–25; a rabbi, 3:1–21; a sacred well, 4:1–42; close of the institutions section, 4:43–54). Burge, *Interpreting the Gospel of John*, 76–77.

13. Painter rightly indicates the function of the two Cana signs as an *inclusio*, which demonstrates two related miracle quest stories initiated by an implicit or explicit request to Jesus. Painter, *Quest for the Messiah*, 188–89.

vv. 19–22, why is the issue described here differently from the Synoptics? Is it just to remind the reader of the significance of the death-resurrection of Jesus the first time in relation to the temple? Even though we should not ignore the significance of the death-resurrection of Jesus, we also have to recognize that this episode is related to the Cana miracle, particularly the restoration (the cleansing the temple) and the replacement (with the new temple, the body of Christ).

In this sense, if Bultmann intended to explain that the Cana episode is the first sign, while the cleansing one is the last in symbolization, thereby the two become a pair in ch. 2,[14] it is not enough to give a reason for the connection between the two episodes. Moreover, his idea seems not to be compatible with the "Cana cycle" that focuses on the first and second events at Cana as a sort of *inclusio* in chs. 2–4.

Sixth, as discussed earlier, the two episodes in ch. 2 share the same purpose of restoration and replacement of the old system (Judaism that lacks vitality and inner purification) by the new one (Jesus Christ as the provider of the new, better one and as the new temple himself).[15]

2. The Function of v. 12

Brown regarded v. 12 as a transitional passage (Jesus goes to Capernaum), categorizing it differently from the previous verses but doubting that this verse plays the role of a connective between vv. 1–11 (at Cana) and 13–25 (at Jerusalem) because the way to Capernaum is a long journey from Jerusalem.[16]

First, we may agree with Brown if we consider only the geographical sense, because the distance between Capernaum and Jerusalem is further than between Cana and Capernaum. It may lead to v. 12 being recommended as a closing part of vv. 1–12. Moloney indicates that vv. 1–2 and 12 share characteristics:[17] who have made a journey (ἐκλήθη, 2) to be "there" (ἐκεῖ, 1) at Cana, move away (κατέβη, 12) to be in another place (ἐκεῖ, 12) at Capernaum.

But, second, there are some reasons why we would rather put v. 12 with the cluster of vv. 13–25: (1) In the vv. 1–11, there is an *inclusio*: vv. 1–2 (A) and 11 (A′ of I1), where the name Cana appears as the opening and closing; (2) There is no parallel between vv. 11 and 12. It may mean that there is no room for v. 12 as the closing; (3) Verses 12 and 13 instead consist of a chiasm (II2, ab-b′a′), showing a connection between them; (4) In this chiasm, there are some impressive, contrasted ideas between them: (a) going down to Capernaum vs. going up to Jerusalem; (b) his mother and

---

14. Bultmann, *Gospel of John*, 112.

15. For this issue in detail, see Dual Mode in Structure. Regarding the replacement of the new temple, refer also to Haenchen, *John 1*, 187.

16. Brown, *Gospel according to John*, 112–13. Also see Painter who regarded it as an appended note. Painter, *Quest for the Messiah*, 192.

17. Moloney, *Gospel of John*, 66.

disciples vs. the Jews; (c) staying not many days (ordinary days) vs. being at hand (the Passover); And (5) we can also see a similar phenomenon of contrast between vv. 12 and 24–25: the people with whom Jesus stayed and felt at ease (including his brothers) vs. the people to whom he did not entrust himself. Consider vv. 12–13 (A) and 23–25 (A') as an *inclusio* of vv. 13–25 (see II1).

Thus, third, we would like to categorize this chapter into vv. 1–11 and 12–25, paying much attention to the function of v. 12: being attached to the following verses in construction as well as linking vv. 1–11 and 13–25.

3. The Structure of the Cana Miracle

Seeing vv. 1–10 as a typical *miracle story*, Bultmann regarded vv. 1–2 as the setting, vv. 3–5 as the preparation of the miracle, vv. 6–8 as the miracle itself, vv. 9–10 as the conclusion and emphasis of the paradox of the miracle.[18]

First, Moloney revises the structure of Bultmann by regarding vv. 6–10 as the main action of the story, and v. 11 as the narrator's comments, and v. 12 as the account of closing paired with vv. 1–2.[19]

Second, as discussed earlier in the note on I1, around the center of the miracle (X, 6–8), the scene where the mother of Jesus spoke to the servants (C, 5) and the scene where the servants and the master of the banquet are contrasted (C', 9a) are paired in terms that the servants are listening to her and they are obeying the order of Jesus.

Third, the dialogue between Jesus and his mother (B, 3–4) can pair with that between the master of the banquet and the bridegroom (B', 9b–10). Both groups discuss the wine: the lack of wine (3–4) and the high quality of the wine (9b–10).

Fourth, it means that there are four scenes, except for the miracle scene (6–8): two scenes before the miracle (3–4 and 5); two scenes after the miracle (9a and 9b–10).

Fifth, vv. 1–2 and 11 are an *inclusio*: opening (A) and closing (A'), where the disciples of Jesus appear in front.

Sixth, as a result, we can see that this Cana miracle is not presented as a linear description like a typical miracle story, but instead as a chiastic structure.

---

18. Bultmann, *Gospel of John*, 115.

19. Moloney, *Gospel of John*, 66. But Moloney does not agree with Bultmann, thinking that the Cana miracle does not show a typical miracle story because there are "problem" (3a); "request" (3b); "reaction" (5); consequence (6–11) instead of the order of the miracle story according to Bultmann such as a problem, a request, the miracle, the successful outcome, and the wonder of all who saw. Moloney, *Gospel of John*, 70; he refers to Bultmann, *History of the Synoptic Tradition*, 318–31.

4. The Structure of the Cleansing of the Temple

Schnackenburg explained vv. 13–25 as "a diptych (a double altarpiece on two leaves hinged together)" as follows:[20] (1) the action of Jesus (14–15); the words of Jesus (16); the "remembering" of disciples (17); (2) the action of the Jews (18); the words of Jesus (19); the misunderstanding of the Jews and the comment of the Evangelist (20–21); the "remembering" of the disciples (22).

First, as far as the concept of diptych is concerned, it is agreeable, but not with regard to Schnackenburg's points of division. How can we regard v. 18 as "the action of the Jews," which is in fact their words (question)? Regarding the misunderstanding of the Jews and the comment of the Evangelist (20–21), how can we explain why these verses are put there but any related verse does not appear in the first part of the diptych? Additionally, does not his model exclude the first part ([12–]13) and also the last part (23–25) of the event?

Second, if we set apart the opening (12–13) and the closing parts (23–25), there are left two scenes (see II1): the scene where Jesus cleansed the temple (14–16) with the comment regarding the memory of the disciples (17); the scene where Jesus and the Jews are in dialogue about the resurrection of his body as the sign of the temple (18–21) with the comment regarding the memory of the disciples (22). It means that vv. 14–22 consist of a parallelism, ab-a'b' (II7), recurring in a similar concept in b (17) and b' (22).

Third, as a whole, if we include the first and last parts, this unit consists of a chiastic structure, AB-B'A' (II1). We have seen that vv. 14–17 and 18–22 are paired (a diptych) as B and B' (or ab and a'b' of II7). Verses 12–13 and 23–25 are in a pair: A and A', because their functions are for opening and closing, sharing the time (the Passover, 13 and 23) and the place (Jerusalem, 13 and 23), as indicated already. We may add that there is the contrast between the people with whom Jesus stays (12) and the people to whom he does not entrust himself (24–25).[21]

Fourth, the reason why vv. 14–16 and 18–21 are not described in the same format is that vv. 14–16 have their own chiasm (II3, ab-b'a') and vv. 18–21 also their own one (II10, ab-b'a') but they do not share any detail between themselves.

Fifth, this type of structure, that is, more than two parallels or chiasms combined together, is a common phenomenon in John. We may say that it is typical of John.

---

20. Schnackenburg, *Gospel according to St. John*, 344; Cited by Beasley-Murray, *John*, 38. Compare Ellis': A (13); B (14–17); C (18–21); B' (22); A' (23–25). Ellis, *Genius of John*, 45–49.

21. In this sense, vv. 23–25 are neither an addition (Wellhausen) nor the introduction to the next chapter (Haenchen and Painter). Wellhausen, *Das Evangelium Johannis*, 16; cited by Haenchen, 191–92. See also Painter, *Quest for the Messiah*, 195–98. See also the connection between vv. 22 and 23 (II12), in terms of how the belief of his disciples and that of "many" are differentiated: the former believe based on the words but the latter after seeing his signs.

3 Two Dialogues with Discourses

"Few of the minor figures in the Gospels have held as much fascination for scholars as John's Nicodemus. The reason for this is not difficult to find: Nicodemus is a puzzling, enigmatic figure. He appears early in the Gospel with a profession of faith on his lips (3:1–21), but he is quickly reduced to confused silence by Jesus' surprisingly acerbic response."[1]

"For the newspaper-type readers the situation in this chapter could be quite confusing not only because it does not seem to fit the sequence here, but also because the discourse at 3:31–36 seems to cover a set of themes similar to those included in the series of discourse related to the earlier Nicodemus event."[2]

Dual Mode in Structure

As a whole, John 3 consists of two units of narrative: the dialogue between Jesus and Nicodemus (1–21) and that between the Baptist and his disciples (22–36). Both episodes contain their own discourse parts that explain further related issues, presumably given by the author: vv. 16–23 and vv. 31–36.

Nevertheless, there is no division of the units to demarcate them regarding the dialogue and the discourse such as vv. 1–15 and 16–23; 24–30 and 31–36, as we might have assumed. The division has to be made according to the cohesiveness of the structure deliberately designed through the text.

It is obvious that John 3 is grouped into two: vv. 1–21 and 22–36. The first unit can be classified into two subunits: vv. 1–11 and 12–21 (see I1, particularly considering I2

---

1. Bassler, "Mixed Signals," 635.
2. Borchert, *John 1–11*, 187–88.

Two Dialogues with Discourses

and I18). And the last unit can also be divided into two subunits: vv. 22–31 and 32–36 (see II1, also considering II2 and II20). It is the typical dual mode in John.

I.		Jesus and Nicodemus (3:1-21)	
	IIA.	Born again (3:1-11)	A
	IIB.	Belief and life (3:12-21)	B
II.		The Baptist's testimony to Jesus (3:22-36)	
	IIA.	The Baptist's testimony and his disciples (3:22-31)	A'
	IIB.	The Father and the Son (3:32-36)	B'

SHARED ISSUES IN I (1–21) AND II (22–36)

The two dialogues in John 3 are deeply connected to each other, sharing more than a few ideas. What we do not know is whether these two units are arranged in sequential order, but what we know is that the two are in common in presenting issues such as the divine character of the Son, the testimony of the Son, belief and unbelief, God's love, etc.

Shared issues	I (1-21)	II (22-36)
1. The one from heaven	He who descended from heaven, the Son of man (13)	He who comes from above (31)
2. Earthly vs. heavenly	Earthly things versus heavenly things (12)	From heaven vs. from the earth; Belonging to the earth vs. being above all (31)
3. Jesus' own testimony	'Our' testimony (11-12)	His testimony (32-33)
4. Belief and unbelief	Belief and eternal life (15, 16); Unbelief and judgment (18-19)	Belief and eternal life (36); Unbelief and wrath (36)
5. God's love	God's love toward the world (16-17)	God's love toward his Son (35)
6. Contrasts among characters	Human teacher, Nicodemus vs. divine teacher, Jesus; etc.	Jesus, the bride, vs. the Baptist, his friend; etc.

Thus, we know that two units (1–21 and 22–36) are in a pair, I and II. It means that these two are designed to emphasize similar issues, particularly "belief in the Son from heaven and salvation as its result."

In this sense, we may clarify a parallel structure: A (1–11); B (12–21); A' (22–31); B' (32–36).

I. Jesus and Nicodemus (3:1–21)

Dual Structure, I1 (A-A')

There are two clusters, connected to each other but shifted in theme. In A (1–11), the theme, "born again [above]," is primary, while, in A' (12–21), the belief and life issue is dominant.

In fact, the dialogue between Jesus and Nicodemus starts at v. 1 and ends probably at v. 15. From v. 16 to v. 21, we may read a supplementary note of the author as a testifier of Jesus. However, the reasons we are not dividing vv. 1–21 into vv. 1–15 and 16–21 but rather into vv. 1–11 and 12–21 are twofold:

First, themes are shifted from vv. 1–11 ("born again") to vv. 12–21 ("belief and life"). It means that vv. 12–15 and 16–21 share the same issue, so they may not be separated. Second, most of all, cohesiveness as a cluster is found in each subunit: vv. 1–11 (see I2) and 12–21 (see I18). We may say that vv. 12–21 cannot be separated within them.

IA. Born Again (3:1–11)

Chiastic Structure, I2 (AB-B'A')

1. The first part of the passage and the last one are so deeply connected. There are some ideas shared between vv. 1–2 and 10–11: First, Nicodemus is introduced as a man of the Pharisees, a ruler of the Jews (1) and Jesus calls him the teacher of Israel (10); Second, Nicodemus said, "we know that..." (2) but Jesus finally said, "you do not know these things"—"we speak what we know" (10–11); Third, Nicodemus focuses on the fact that Jesus came from God and does heavenly signs (2), while Jesus emphasizes his testimony: "we say what we know and we testify what we have seen" (11).

2. Through these connected ideas, the readers discern which person is the one who knows all about the truth, between Nicodemus, the teacher of Israel, and Jesus, the teacher from God. Moreover, a shift in focus occurs: from signs (human focus) to testimony (divine focus). We name these verses A (1–2) and A' (10–11).

3. In between this cluster, vv. 1–11, there are two subunits starting with an emphatic expression of Jesus, "Truly, truly, I say to you" (3 and 5). There are a pair of Jesus-Nicodemus dialogues: Jesus' answer and Nicodemus' asking-back, vv. 3–4 and 5–9. We may name them B (3–4) and B' (5–9). B focuses on "born again," while B' is on "born of the Spirit."

In vv. 1–11, there are eight parallelisms (I6, 8–11, 14, and 16–17), six chiasms (I3, 5, 7, 12–13, and 15), and one triple (I4). I3–5 are related to the cohesion of vv. 1–2 (A of I2) and I6–7 to that of v. 4 (a part of B) and I10–14 to that of vv. 5–8 (a part of B')

Two Dialogues with Discourses

and I15–17 to that of v. 11 (a part of A'). Meanwhile, I8 and 9 show the connection between vv. 3–4 (B of I2) and vv. 5–9 (B'). Verse 9 does not have any parallel except for the connection with v. 4 as for B-B' of I9. Similarly, v. 10 is only related to vv. 1–2 as for A-A' it is of I2.

V	2	3			Phrases	Translation
1	A	a	4		Ἦν δὲ	Now there was
	-	b	a		ἄνθρωπος ἐκ τῶν Φαρισαίων,	a man of the Pharisees,
	-	-	a'		Νικόδημος ὄνομα αὐτῷ,	named Nicodemus,
	-	-	a''		ἄρχων τῶν Ἰουδαίων·	a ruler of the Jews.
2	-	b'			οὗτος	This man
	-	a'			ἦλθεν πρὸς αὐτὸν νυκτὸς	came to Jesus by night
	-				καὶ εἶπεν αὐτῷ·	and said to him,
	-		5		ῥαββί, οἴδαμεν	"Rabbi, we know
	-		a		ὅτι ἀπὸ θεοῦ ἐλήλυθας διδάσκαλος·	that you have come from God as a teacher,
	-		b		οὐδεὶς γὰρ δύναται ταῦτα τὰ σημεῖα ποιεῖν	for no one can do these signs
	-		b'		ἃ σὺ ποιεῖς,	that you do,
	-		a'	8	9	ἐὰν μὴ ᾖ ὁ θεὸς μετ' αὐτοῦ.	unless God is with him."
3	B		a	A	ἀπεκρίθη Ἰησοῦς καὶ εἶπεν αὐτῷ·	Jesus answered him,
	-		b	-	ἀμὴν ἀμὴν λέγω σοι,	"Truly, truly, I say to you,
	-		c	-	ἐὰν μή τις γεννηθῇ ἄνωθεν,	unless one is born again,
	-		d	-	οὐ δύναται ἰδεῖν τὴν βασιλείαν τοῦ θεοῦ.	he cannot see the kingdom of God."
4	-	6		B	Λέγει πρὸς αὐτὸν [ὁ] Νικόδημος·	Nocodemus said to him,
	-	a	7	-	πῶς δύναται ἄνθρωπος	"How can a man
	-	b	a	-	γεννηθῆναι	be born
	-	-	b	-	γέρων ὤν;	when he is old?
	-	a'		-	μὴ δύναται	Can
	-	b'		-	εἰς τὴν κοιλίαν τῆς μητρὸς αὐτοῦ	~ into his mother's womb
	-	-	b'	-	δεύτερον εἰσελθεῖν	he enter a second time ~
	-	-	a'	-	καὶ γεννηθῆναι;	and be born?"

I3. Chiastic, ab-b'a': Both b and b' indicate and describe Nicodemus, while, in a-a', related verbs are shown: "he was" (a); "he came to Jesus" (a'). **I4**. Triple, a-a'-a'': Introduction to Nicodemus is presented in three divisions: ἄνθρωπος ἐκ τῶν Φαρισαίων (a, 9 syllables); Νικόδημος ὄνομα αὐτῷ (a', 9 syllables); ἄρχων τῶν Ἰουδαίων (a'', 7 syllables). **I5**. Chiastic, ab-b'a': In both a and a', Nicodemus relates Jesus with God: a teacher from God (a); the person with whom God is (a'). In b-b', the focus is on what Jesus has done, such as signs.

I6. Parallel, ab-a'b': Nicodemus repeats his sentence twice, paraphrasing his words: "how can a man . . ." (a) means that a man cannot do . . . (a'); "to be born when he is old" (b) is paraphrased as "to enter a second time into his mother's womb and be born" (b'). **I7**. Chiastic, ab-b'a': The infinitive γεννηθῆναι (to be born, a-a') is used twice for emphasis of repetition, while b (when he is old) and b' (he enter a second time) are related to demonstrate the impracticality of humanly being "born again."

I8. Parallel, abcd-a'b'c'd':[3] vv. 3 and 5 (A-A' of I6) share exactly the same pattern of sentences.[4] In this sense, we may grasp that "born again" (c) is namely "born of water and the Spirit" (c'); "he cannot see the kingdom of God" (d) is, in other words, "he cannot enter the kingdom of God" (d'). **I9**. Parallel, AB-A'B': As discussed in I2, Both A and A' of I6 are Jesus' answers initiated with his eminent phrase, "Truly, truly, I say to you," focusing on "born again" (A) or "born of the Spirit" (A'). While, in B-B', Nicodemus responds to Jesus, having totally misinterpreted what he had been told.[5]

Their foci are: the coming of Nicodemus (I3); the triple introduction to Nicodemus (I4); Jesus' signs in relation to God (I5); human inability to be born again (I6); the double emphasis on being born (I7); the relation between born again and born of the Spirit regarding entering heaven (I8); Nicodemus' misunderstanding of born again and the double emphasis on spiritual rebirth (I9).

I10. Parallel, ab-a'b': In a-a', Jesus asserts the truth that a man should be born again to enter the kingdom of God, emphatically (a) and personally (a'). In b-b', Jesus provides two related explanations: the distinction between being born of the flesh and of the Spirit (b); the incomprehensibility of being born of the Spirit (b'). **I11**. Parallel, abcd-a'b'c'd': Two sentences are in a pair of parallels, designed to be contrasted visibly: τὸ γεγεννημένον (what is born, a) and καὶ τὸ γεγεννημένον (and what is born, a'); ἐκ τῆς σαρκὸς (of the flesh, b) and ἐκ τοῦ πνεύματος (of the Spirit, b'); σάρξ (flesh, c) and πνεῦμά (spirit, c'); ἐστιν (is, d) and ἐστιν (is, d'). In a-a' and d-d', there are repetitions, while, in b-b' and c-c', the flesh is contrasted to the Spirit (or spirit).

I12. Chiastic, ab-b'a': In a and a', the wind (πνεῦμα) is compared to the Spirit (πνεῦμα), where an ambiguous word, πνεῦμα, is used. The unpredictability of the wind is explained in b-b': hearing its sound (b), you do not know where it comes from and where it goes (b'). **I13**. Chiastic, ab-b'a': In a-a', the fact that the wind blows where it wishes is repeatedly described, while, in b-b', hearing (b) is compared and connected to not-knowing (b'). **I14**. Parallel, ab-a'b': Two syllables (πόθεν, a, and καὶ ποῦ, a') and three syllables (ἔρχεται, b, and ὑπάγει, b') in rhyme are kept to intensify its quality of parallelism.

---

3. Cf. Mlakuzhyil, *Christocentric Literary Structure*, 122.

4. The double *amen* ("Amen, amen, I say to you") is used twenty-five times in John and is "the most Johannine of expressions." Brown, *Gospel according to John XIII–XXI*, 1106. It may be said that this double emphasis of amen can be regarded not only as the emphatic, solemn declarations of what follows but also as one of the Johannine dual expressions. Cf. Culpepper, "AMEN, AMEN Sayings," 57–58.

5. Cf. O'Day, "Spirituality and Community," 59–60.

Two Dialogues with Discourses

V	2	10		8	9	Phrases	Translation
5	B'	a		a'	A'	ἀπεκρίθη Ἰησοῦς·	Jesus answered,
	-	-		b'	-	ἀμὴν ἀμὴν λέγω σοι,	"Truly, truly, I say to you,
	-	-		c'	-	ἐὰν μή τις γεννηθῇ ἐξ ὕδατος καὶ πνεύματος,	unless one is born of water and the Spirit,
	-	-	11	d'	-	οὐ δύναται εἰσελθεῖν εἰς τὴν βασιλείαν τοῦ θεοῦ.	he cannot enter the kingdom of God.
6	-	b		a	-	τὸ γεγεννημένον	What is born
	-	-		b	-	ἐκ τῆς σαρκὸς	of the flesh
	-	-		c	-	σάρξ	~ flesh,
	-	-		d	-	ἐστιν,	is ~
	-	-		a'	-	καὶ τὸ γεγεννημένον	and what is born
	-	-		b'	-	ἐκ τοῦ πνεύματος	of the Spirit
	-	-		c'	-	πνεῦμά	~spirit.
	-	-		d'	-	ἐστιν.	is ~
7	-	a'	12 13		-	μὴ θαυμάσῃς ὅτι εἶπόν σοι· δεῖ ὑμᾶς γεννηθῆναι ἄνωθεν.	Do not marvel that I said to you, 'You must be born again.'
8	-	b'	a	a	-	τὸ πνεῦμα ὅπου θέλει πνεῖ	The wind blows where it wishes
	-	-	b	b	-	καὶ τὴν φωνὴν αὐτοῦ ἀκούεις,	and you hear the sound of it,
	-	-	b'	b'	14 -	ἀλλ' οὐκ οἶδας	but do not know
	-	-		a'	a -	πόθεν	where ~ from
	-	-		-	b -	ἔρχεται	~ it comes ~
	-	-		a'	a -	καὶ ποῦ	and where
	-	-		b'	b -	ὑπάγει·	it goes.
	-	-	a'		-	οὕτως ἐστὶν πᾶς ὁ γεγεννημένος ἐκ τοῦ πνεύματος.	So it is with everyone born of the Spirit."
9	-				B'	Ἀπεκρίθη Νικόδημος καὶ εἶπεν αὐτῷ· πῶς δύναται ταῦτα γενέσθαι;	Nicodemus answered and said to him, "How can these things happen?"
10	A'		15			ἀπεκρίθη Ἰησοῦς καὶ εἶπεν αὐτῷ· σὺ εἶ ὁ διδάσκαλος τοῦ Ἰσραὴλ καὶ ταῦτα οὐ γινώσκεις;	Jesus answered to him, "You are the teacher of Israel. But do you not know these things?
11	-	a	16			ἀμὴν ἀμὴν λέγω σοι	Truly, truly, I say to you,
	-	b	a			ὅτι ὃ οἴδαμεν	~ what we know,
	-	-	b	17		λαλοῦμεν	we speak ~
	-	b'	a' a			καὶ ὃ ἑωράκαμεν	and ~ to what we have seen,
	-	-	b' b			μαρτυροῦμεν,	~ testify ~
	-	a'	a'			καὶ τὴν μαρτυρίαν ἡμῶν	~ our testimony.
	-	-	b'			οὐ λαμβάνετε.	but you do not receive ~

I15. Chiastic, ab-b'a': In b-b', we can recognize two statements regarding their testimonies: "we speak what we know" (b) and "and we testify to what we have seen" (b'). Thus, this genuine saying of Jesus (a), followed by b-b', should have been accepted by "you" (a'). **I16**. Parallel, ab-a'b': This well-designed parallel increases their qualification as witnesses to the truth: ὅτι ὃ οἴδαμεν (what we know, a) and καὶ ὃ ἑωράκαμεν (and to what we have seen, a'); λαλοῦμεν (we speak, b) and μαρτυροῦμεν (we testify, b'). Knowing (a) and seeing (a') are in a pair, and also speaking (b) and testifying (b') are in a pair. **I17**. Parallel, ab-a'b': "What we have seen" (a) is namely "our testimony" (a'). "Our" role is to testify (b), while "your" role is to receive it but "you" did not (b').

We may see the foci of the parallels: Jesus' double emphasis on born again and his explanations (I10); the contrast between the flesh and the Spirit (I11); the similarity between the wind and the Spirit (I12–13); where the wind comes from and where it goes (I14); the contrast between Jesus' witness and their action in not receiving it (I15); the reliability of Jesus' testimony (I16); testimony and refusal (I17).

IB. Belief and Life (3:12–21)

CHIASTIC STRUCTURE, II18 (A-X-A')

1. The tone of vv. 12–15 is negative, sternly warning against their unbelief, while, on the contrary, vv. 16–17 are positive in tone, highlighting the mercifulness of God who sent his Son for salvation. Although vv. 18–21 reflect both negativity and positivity in tone, the negative tone mostly prevails, in order that the verses may warn the readers regarding the judgment of unbelief. Verses 12–15 and 18–21 can be a pair in terms of the negativity in tone.

2. Moreover, each of vv. 12–15, 16–17, and 18–21 shows its own cohesiveness. I19 (with I20–22), I25 (with I24, 26–27), and I29 (with I30–35) support their cohesive phenomena, respectively. It means that these three subunits are each proven.

3. Thus, we may call vv. 16–17 as X. And vv. 12–15 and 18–21 may be regarded as A and A'. They share the issue of unbelief as their connectivity. In A, Jesus criticizes those who do not believe in him. In A', the judgment resulting on these unbelievers as well as evil-doers is accentuated.

4. At the same time, we observe that there are two links connecting vv. 14–15 to v. 16 (I23) and v. 17 to v. 18 (I28). These links are to keep a certain connectivity with the previous or following verses.

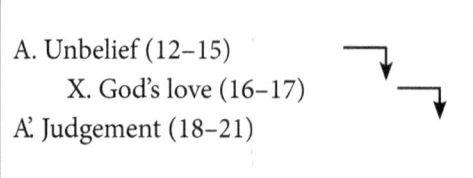

Two Dialogues with Discourses

In vv. 12–21, we may see seventeen parallels (I19–35): eight chiasms (I19, 21–22, 24, 29, 31, 33, and 35), five parallelisms (I20, 23, 30, 32, and 34), two dual (I26–27), one combined parallelism (I25), and one combined chiasm (I28). I19–22 demonstrate the cohesiveness of vv. 12–15 (A of I18), while I29–35 show how vv. 18–21 need to be regarded as a subunit (A') and I24–27 prove that vv. 16–17 are tightened as a subunit (X). But I23 and I28 are for a connection between A and X; X and A'.

V	18	19	20		Phrases	Translation
12	A	a	a		εἰ τὰ ἐπίγεια εἶπον ὑμῖν	[If] I have told you earthly things
	-	-	b		καὶ οὐ πιστεύετε,	and you do not believe,
	-	b	a'		πῶς ἐὰν εἴπω ὑμῖν τὰ ἐπουράνια	how then ~ if I speak of heavenly things?
	-	-	b'	21	πιστεύσετε;	~ will you believe ~
13	-	b'	a		καὶ οὐδεὶς	No one
	-	-	b		ἀναβέβηκεν	has ascended
	-	-	c		εἰς τὸν οὐρανὸν	into heaven
	-	-	c'		εἰ μὴ ὁ ἐκ τοῦ οὐρανοῦ	but he who ~ from heaven,
	-	-	b'		καταβάς,	~ descended ~
	-	22	a'	23	ὁ υἱὸς τοῦ ἀνθρώπου.	the Son of man.
14	-	a'	a	a	Καὶ καθὼς Μωϋσῆς	And as Moses
	-	-	b	-	ὕψωσεν	lifted up
	-	-	c	-	τὸν ὄφιν ἐν τῇ ἐρήμῳ,	the serpent in the wilderness,
	-	-	c'	-	οὕτως	so
	-	-	b'	-	ὑψωθῆναι δεῖ	must ~ be lifted up,
	-	-	a'	-	τὸν υἱὸν τοῦ ἀνθρώπου,	~ the Son of man ~
15	-	-		b	ἵνα πᾶς ὁ πιστεύων ἐν αὐτῷ ἔχῃ ζωὴν αἰώνιον.	that everyone who believes in him may have eternal life.

I19. Chiastic, ab-b'a': If we consider carefully this chiastic arrangement, we may infer what earthly things and heavenly things are. The heavenly things are presented in b-b', namely the ascending and descending acts of the Son of Man. Thus, earthly things could be indicated in a', v. 14: Moses' lifting up of the serpent and likewise the being lifted-up of the Son of Man. The reason that these are earthly things is probably that they have happened on earth as has been seen, in contrast to the Son's ascending-descending, heavenly actions.

I20. Parallel, ab-a'b': In a-a', earthly things (a) are compared with heavenly things (a'), while b-b' focus on the unbelief of the hearer. **I21**. Chiastic, abc-c'b'a':[6] The constituents of the two sentences are inversely in parallel to create a contrast between the two: καὶ οὐδεὶς (no one, a) and ὁ υἱὸς τοῦ ἀνθρώπου (the Son of Man, a'); ἀναβέβηκεν (has ascended, b) and καταβάς (descended, b'); εἰς τὸν οὐρανὸν (into heaven, c) and εἰ μὴ ὁ ἐκ τοῦ οὐρανοῦ (except he who ~ from heaven, c'). **I22**. Chi-

---

6. Cf. Mlakuzhyil, *Christocentric Literary Structure*, 129.

astic, abc-c'b'a': The resurrection of Jesus is described in comparison with the event when Moses lifted up the serpent, probably in inverted order: Καὶ καθὼς Μωϋσῆς (And as Moses, a) and τὸν υἱὸν τοῦ ἀνθρώπου (the Son of Man, a'); ὕψωσεν (lifted up, b) and ὑψωθῆναι δεῖ (must be lifted up, b'); τὸν ὄφιν ἐν τῇ ἐρήμῳ (the serpent in the wilderness, c) and οὕτως (so, c').

I23. Parallel, ab-a'b': In b and b', the issue, believing in him and having eternal life, is duplicated. The Son's being lifted-up (a) is related to God's love in sending his Son (a'); both describe two ways of expressing God's love through the Son.

I19 is comprehensive of vv. 12–15, accentuating "your" unbelief whether it is earthly or heavenly. I20 contrasts earthly things to heavenly things regarding unbelief. In I21, there is a contrast between "no one" versus the Son of Man regarding heaven. I22 compares the event of Moses with that of Jesus. In I23, two foci are maintained: God sent his Son to be lifted up; for the purpose of salvation.

V	18	24		23		Phrases	Translation
16	X	a 25		a'		οὕτως γὰρ ἠγάπησεν ὁ θεὸς τὸν κόσμον,	For God so loved the world
	-	b	a1	-	26	ὥστε τὸν υἱὸν τὸν μονογενῆ ἔδωκεν,	that he gave his only Son,
	-	b'	a2	a	b'	ἵνα πᾶς ὁ πιστεύων εἰς αὐτὸν μὴ ἀπόληται	that everyone who believes in him will not perish
	-	a'	b	a'	- 28	ἀλλ᾽ ἔχῃ ζωὴν αἰώνιον.	but have eternal life.
17	-		a'1 27		a	οὐ γὰρ ἀπέστειλεν ὁ θεὸς τὸν υἱὸν εἰς τὸν κόσμον	For God did not send the Son into the world
	-		a'2	a	b1	ἵνα κρίνῃ τὸν κόσμον,	to judge the world,
	-		b'	a'	b2	ἀλλ᾽ ἵνα σωθῇ ὁ κόσμος δι᾽ αὐτοῦ.	but that the world might be saved through him.

I24. Chiastic, ab-b'a': This sentence provides the idea that God's love (a) is eventually proved by us having eternal life (a'), in two ways: God's giving his Son (b) and our belief in him (b'). I25. Combined parallel, a1a2-b-a'1a'2-b': For emphasis, the three divided parts are arranged in parallel: the contrast between "he gave his only Son" (a1) and "God did not send the Son" (a'1); the similarity between believer who will not perish (a2) and the world not to be judged (a'2); the similarity between having eternal life (b) and being saved through him (b'). I26. Dual, a-a': Not to perish (a) is to have eternal life (a'), a duplicated concept. I27. Dual, a-a': The clause "to judge the world" (a) is contrasted to ". . . the world might be saved through him" (a') for emphasis.

I28. Combined chiastic, a-b1b2-b'2b'1-a': In b1-b'1, "to judge the world" (b1) is similar in expression with ". . . has been judged already" (b'1), while being saved through him (b2) and being not judged (b'2) are related in concept. The Father-Son relationship is in common focused in a and a'.

In I24, God's love initiates having eternal life through the Son. In I25, the contrast between being judged and having eternal life is focused on the Son. In I26, not-perishing is having eternal life and, in I27, judgment and salvation are in contrast. I28 contrasts God's intention not to judge the world with their unbelief which is judged already.

V	18	29	30			28	Phrases	Translation
18	A'	a	a			b'2	ὁ πιστεύων εἰς αὐτὸν	He who believes in him
	-	-	b			-	οὐ κρίνεται·	is not judged,
	-	b	a'			b'1	ὁ δὲ μὴ πιστεύων	but he who does not believe
	-	-	b'			-	ἤδη κέκριται,	has been judged already,
	-	c	31			a'	ὅτι μὴ πεπίστευκεν εἰς τὸ ὄνομα τοῦ μονογενοῦς υἱοῦ τοῦ θεοῦ.	because he has not believed in the name of the only Son of God.
19	-	x	a				αὕτη δέ ἐστιν ἡ κρίσις	And this is the judgment,
	-	c'	b				ὅτι τὸ φῶς ἐλήλυθεν εἰς τὸν κόσμον	that the light has come into the world,
	-	-	b'				καὶ ἠγάπησαν οἱ ἄνθρωποι μᾶλλον τὸ σκότος ἢ τὸ φῶς·	and men loved darkness rather than light,
	-	-	a'	32	33		ἦν γὰρ αὐτῶν πονηρὰ τὰ ἔργα.	because their deeds were evil.
20	-	b'		a	a	34	πᾶς γὰρ ὁ φαῦλα πράσσων	For everyone who does evil
	-	-		b	b	a	μισεῖ	hates
	-	-		-	-	b	τὸ φῶς	the light,
	-	-		-	b'	a'	καὶ οὐκ ἔρχεται	and does not come
	-	-		-	-	b'	πρὸς τὸ φῶς,	to the light,
	-	-		35	c	a'	ἵνα μὴ ἐλεγχθῇ τὰ ἔργα αὐτοῦ·	lest his deeds should be exposed.
21	-	a'	a	a'			ὁ δὲ ποιῶν τὴν ἀλήθειαν	But he who practices the truth
	-	-	b	b'			ἔρχεται πρὸς τὸ φῶς,	comes to the light,
	-	-	b'	c'			ἵνα φανερωθῇ αὐτοῦ τὰ ἔργα	that his deeds may be manifested
	-	-	a'	-			ὅτι ἐν θεῷ ἐστιν εἰργασμένα.	as having been wrought in God."

I29. Chiastic, abc-x-c'b'a': Both a and a' describe the person who has a relationship with God such as a believer who is not judged (a) or a doer of the truth, who comes to the light (a'). In b-b', the non-believer who has been judged (b) and the evil-doer who hates the light (b') are compared. In c-c', the act of non-belief (c) is similarly compared with the act of loving darkness rather than light (c'). In the center, x, the statement, αὕτη δέ ἐστιν ἡ κρίσις (and this is the judgment) is emphatically declared. Besides the pair a-a', the others such as b-b' and c-c' including x are negative in content.

I30. Parallel, ab-a'b':[7] Two contrasted sentences are in parallel: ὁ πιστεύων εἰς αὐτὸν (He who believes in him, a) and ὁ δὲ μὴ πιστεύων (but he who does not believe, a'); οὐ κρίνεται (is not judge, b) and ἤδη κέκριται (has been judged already, b'). I31. Chiastic, ab-b'a': In b-b', the light that has come (b) is contrasted with the darkness

---

7. Cf. Mlakuzhyil, *Christocentric Literary Structure*, 123.

that men love (b'). Their evil deeds (a') resulting from their choice of the darkness (b') seems to be a judgement in itself (a).

I32. Parallel, abc-a'b'c':[8] The evil-doer (a) is contrasted with the practicer of the truth (a'). Their distinguishable deeds are presented in b-b': "hates the light, and does not come to the light" (b) and "comes to the light" (b'). The goals of their actions in relation to the light are shown: "lest his deeds should be exposed" (c) and "that his deeds may be manifested as having been wrought in God" (c'). This antithetical pair of sentences clearly discloses the difference between the evil-doer and the practicer of the truth. **I33**. Chiastic, ab-b'a': The two actions of the evil-doer regarding the light are presented in b-b' (hating the light, b, and not coming to the light, b'), while a-a' show that even the evil-doer (a) does not wish to expose his deeds (a'). **I34**. Parallel, ab-a'b': The relation between the evil-doer and the light is presented in two clauses, duplicated and in parallel: "[he] hates" (a) and "and does not come" (a'); "the light" (b) and "to the light" (b'). **I35**. Chiastic, ab-b'a': In both b and b', the practicer of the truth comes to the light (b) for the purpose of his deeds being disclosed (b'). The relation between a and a' demonstrates the relationship in cooperation between the practicer of the truth and God.

I29 covers vv. 18–21, highlighting the judgment of unbelievers and evil-doers. In I30, the believer and unbeliever are in contrast regarding judgment. I31 focuses on the reasons for being judged. In I32, the evil-doer and the practicer of the truth are in contrast regarding their relationship with God. I33–34 focus on the relation between the evil-doer and the light, while I35, on the contrary, focuses on the relation between the practicer of the truth and the light.

II. THE BAPTIST'S TESTIMONY TO JESUS (3:22–36)

Dual Structure, II1 (A-A')

1. This section can be divided into two parts: (1) The dialogue between the Baptist and his disciples regarding Jesus' baptism; (2) The testimony towards Jesus. But it seems to be obscure to determine how to separate the two. In particular, the problem is the location of v. 31, whether it belongs to the previous part (22–30) or the following part (32–36).

2. Verse 31 belongs to the previous verses, because we find that vv. 22–31 form two subunits: vv. 22–26 and 27–31, both of which are designed in chiasm: A-X-A' (II3 and 9). It means that v. 31 (A' in II9) has a parallel relation with vv. 27–28 (A), where the contrast between Jesus and the Baptist appears. Moreover, v. 31 seems not to have any parallel with the following verses.

---

8. Ibid., 124.

3. Thus, as a whole, it is said that vv. 22–36 need to be divided into two: vv. 22–31 (A) and 32–36 (A'). It is also in a dual mode.

4. A (22–31) deals with the dialogue of the Baptist and his testimony to Jesus, while A' (32–36) is simply a discourse describing the relationship between the Father and the Son.

IIA. *The Baptist's Testimony and His Disciples (3:22–31)*

DUAL STRUCTURE, II2 (A-A')

The issue shifts from the baptism of Jesus (22–26) to the Baptist's testimony to Jesus regarding the divinity of the Son (27–31). Each subunit forms its own chiasm for its structure: II3 (22–26) and II9 (27–31). Thus, we can name them as A (22–26) and A' (27–31) in dual mode.

| A. | The dialogue between the Baptist and his disciples (22-26) | A-X-A' |
| A'. | The testimony of the Baptist (27-31) | A-X-A' |

A. THE DIALOGUE BETWEEN THE BAPTIST AND HIS DISCIPLES (3:22–26)

In vv. 22–26, there are six parallels: one overall chiasm (II3), three parallelisms (II4, 5, and 8), and two duals (II6–7). II4 and 5 may support the cohesion of part A of II3, and II6 does that for X of II3, while II7 and 8 belong to A' of II3. Verses 22–26 seem not to have any connective parallel with the following verses (27–31).

II3. Chiastic, A-X-A': Both in A and A', the baptism of Jesus and that of John are compared, appearing together. In X, two things in relation to John are made plain: (1) he is still free; (2) there is an argument between his disciples and a Jew.

II4. Parallel, ab-a'b': Jesus in a (Jesus went into . . .) and John in a' (John was) are compared, while, both in b-b', what Jesus did and what John did are described, particularly regarding their baptisms. II5. Parallel, ab-a'b': John was there (a) and also there was plenty of water (a'), so he was baptizing (b) and people who came were being baptized (b'). II6. Dual, a-a': Two things are presented in relation to John: his status of not being in prison (a); an argument between his disciples and a Jew.

II7. Dual, a-a': The disciples of John say two things referring to Jesus: who was with John beyond the Jordan (a); about whom John testifies (a'). II8. Parallel, ab-a'b': This parallel is to show the relation between this man (a), who is baptizing (b), and everyone (a'), who comes to him (b'), in terms of how they are deeply involved together.

The foci of the parallels are: the contrast between Jesus' baptism and the Baptist's baptism (II3); what Jesus did and what the Baptist did (II4); what the Baptist did and what people did (II5); two pieces of information about the Baptist (II6); two references to Jesus (II7); what Jesus does and what everyone does (II8).

V	3	4		Phrases	Translation
22	A	a		Μετὰ ταῦτα ἦλθεν ὁ Ἰησοῦς καὶ οἱ μαθηταὶ αὐτοῦ εἰς τὴν Ἰουδαίαν γῆν	After these things Jesus and His disciples went into the land of Judea,
	-	b	5	καὶ ἐκεῖ διέτριβεν μετ' αὐτῶν καὶ ἐβάπτιζεν.	and there he spent time with them and baptized.
23	-	a'	a	Ἦν δὲ καὶ ὁ Ἰωάννης	Now John also was
	-	b'	b	βαπτίζων ἐν Αἰνὼν ἐγγὺς τοῦ Σαλείμ,	baptizing at Aenon near Salim,
	-		a'	ὅτι ὕδατα πολλὰ ἦν ἐκεῖ,	because there was plenty of water,
	-		b'	καὶ παρεγίνοντο καὶ ἐβαπτίζοντο·	and people were coming and were being baptized.
			6		
24	X	a		οὔπω γὰρ ἦν βεβλημένος εἰς τὴν φυλακὴν ὁ Ἰωάννης.	For John had not yet been put in prison.
25	-	a'		Ἐγένετο οὖν ζήτησις ἐκ τῶν μαθητῶν Ἰωάννου μετὰ Ἰουδαίου περὶ καθαρισμοῦ.	Then there arose an argument between John's disciples and a Jew over purification.
26	A'			καὶ ἦλθον πρὸς τὸν Ἰωάννην καὶ εἶπαν αὐτῷ· ῥαββί,	And they came to John and said to him, "Rabbi,
			7		
	-		a	ὃς ἦν μετὰ σοῦ πέραν τοῦ Ἰορδάνου,	he who was with you beyond the Jordan,
	-		a'	ᾧ σὺ μεμαρτύρηκας,	about whom you testifies-
	-	8		ἴδε	see,
	-		a	οὗτος	he
	-		b	βαπτίζει	is baptizing,
	-		a'	καὶ πάντες	and everyone
	-		b'	ἔρχονται πρὸς αὐτόν.	is going to him."

A'. The Testimony of the Baptist (3:27–31)

In vv. 27–31, there are eleven parallels: five parallelisms (II11, 15, and 17–19), four chiasms (II9, 12–13, and 16), and two duals (II10 and 14). II9 is a comprehensive, chiastic structure. II10 and 11 belong to vv. 27–28 (A of II9), while vv. 29–30 (X of II9) show cohesiveness, containing at least four parallels (II12–15). II16–19 support the cohesive character of v. 31 (A' of II9).

II9. Chiastic, A-X-A': Both in A and A', the contrast between John and Jesus is repeated in terms of the divinity of the Son, the Christ: Jesus is the one who receives something from heaven but John is not the Christ (A); Jesus is the man from above, who is above all, but John is from the earth (A'). In the center, X, John describes himself as a friend of the bridegroom, who is just a minor figure in the scene, speaking regarding who is the major figure. In A-A', the divine figure and the human one are in contrast, while, in X, the major vs. the minor is highlighted.

II10. Dual, a-a': For the purpose of emphasis, this duplicated statement is used, implying that Jesus is not a mere man (a) and is given something special from heaven (a'). **II11. Parallel, ab-a'b':** This parallel shows the relationship of John to the Christ in terms of how he differs from the Christ: "I am not" (a) and "but I have been sent" (a'); "the Christ" (b) and "before him" (b'). The Baptist clarifies who he is not and what he has to do.

V	9				Phrases	Translation
27	A	10			Ἀπεκρίθη Ἰωάννης καὶ εἶπεν·	John answered,
-		a			οὐ δύναται ἄνθρωπος λαμβάνειν οὐδὲ ἓν	"A man cannot receive anything
-		a'			ἐὰν μὴ ᾖ δεδομένον αὐτῷ ἐκ τοῦ οὐρανοῦ.	except what is given him from heaven.
28	-		11		αὐτοὶ ὑμεῖς μοι μαρτυρεῖτε ὅτι εἶπον	You yourselves testify that I said,
-	-		a		[ὅτι] οὐκ εἰμὶ ἐγὼ	'I am not
-	-		b		ὁ χριστός,	the Christ,
-	-		a'		ἀλλ᾽ ὅτι ἀπεσταλμένος εἰμὶ	but I have been sent
-	-		b'	12 13	ἔμπροσθεν ἐκείνου.	before him.'
29	X		a	a	ὁ ἔχων τὴν νύμφην	He who has the bride
-			-	b	νυμφίος ἐστίν·	is the bridegroom.
-			-	b'	ὁ δὲ φίλος τοῦ νυμφίου,	The friend of the bridegroom,
-		14	-	a'	ὁ ἑστηκὼς καὶ ἀκούων αὐτοῦ	who stands and hears him,
-		a	x		χαρᾷ χαίρει διὰ τὴν φωνὴν τοῦ νυμφίου.	rejoices greatly at the bridegroom's voice.
-		a'	-	15	αὕτη οὖν ἡ χαρὰ ἡ ἐμὴ πεπλήρωται.	Therefore, this joy of mine has been full.
30	-		a'	a	ἐκεῖνον	He
-	-		-	b	δεῖ αὐξάνειν,	must increase,
-	-		-	a'	ἐμὲ δὲ	but I
-	16	17	-	19 b'	ἐλαττοῦσθαι.	must decrease."
31	A'	a	a	a	Ὁ ἄνωθεν ἐρχόμενος	He who comes from above
-	-	b		b	ἐπάνω πάντων ἐστίν·	is above all,
-	-	x	a' 18		ὁ ὢν ἐκ τῆς γῆς	he who is from the earth
-	-	-	b'	a	ἐκ τῆς γῆς	~ to the earth
-	-	-	-	b	ἐστιν	belongs ~
-	-	-	-	a'	καὶ ἐκ τῆς γῆς	and ~ of the earth.
-	-	-	-	b'	λαλεῖ.	~ speaks ~
-	-	a'		a'	ὁ ἐκ τοῦ οὐρανοῦ ἐρχόμενος	He who comes from heaven
-	-	-		b'	[ἐπάνω πάντων ἐστίν].	is above all.

II12. Chiastic, a-x-a': The contrast between the bridegroom and his friend in a recurs in a', between he who must increase and he who must decrease. While, in the center, x, John declares himself full of joy as a humble friend, being with the Christ and seeing him increase. **II13. Chiastic, ab-b'a':** In b-b', the bridegroom and his friend are compared, while, in a-a', the contrast between the bridegroom who has the bride and the friend who just stands and hears him is made in terms of the main figure. **II14. Dual, a-a':** The expression of great rejoicing (a) or full of joy (a') is duplicated for

emphasis. II15. Parallel, ab-a'b': A typical contrastive, parallelism is presented, for intensified emphasis, keeping a perfect rhyme of syllables: ἐκεῖνον (He, a, 3 syllables) and ἐμὲ δὲ (but I, a', 3 syllables); δεῖ αὐξάνειν (must increase, b, 4 syllables) and ἐλαττοῦσθαι (must decrease, b', 4 syllables).

II16. Chiastic, a-x-a': Both a and a' describe him who comes from above, being above all, while, in the center x, the contrastive figure who is from the earth is depicted. II17. Parallel, ab-a'b': The contrastive difference between Jesus who comes from above (a) and John who is from the earth (a') is demonstrated: "is above all" (b) and "belongs to the earth and speaks of the earth" (b'), highlighting the contrast between the superiority of Jesus and the inferiority of John. II18. Parallel, ab-a'b': This parallel is to disclose the limitations of John as a human being in contrast to Jesus, the Christ, created as a rhymed parallelism: ἐκ τῆς γῆς (of the earth, a, 3 syllables) and καὶ ἐκ τῆς γῆς (and of the earth, a', 4 syallables); ἐστιν (is, b, 2 syllables) and λαλεῖ (speaks, b', 2 syllables). II19. Parallel, ab-a'b': For repetitive emphasis, this parallelism is designed: Ὁ ἄνωθεν ἐρχόμενος (He who comes from above, a) and ὁ ἐκ τοῦ οὐρανοῦ ἐρχόμενος (He who comes from heaven, a'); ἐπάνω πάντων ἐστίν (is above all, b) and ἐπάνω πάντων ἐστίν (is above all, b').

The foci of parallels are: Jesus as the main figure and the Baptist as an assistant (II9); being given from heaven (II10); who the Baptist is not and what he has to do (II11); the Baptist's humble joy because of Jesus (II12); the contrast between the bridegroom and his friend (II13); duplicated status of joy (II14); his increase and my decrease (II15); he who comes from above versus he who is from the earth (II16–17); belonging to the earth and speaking of the earth (II18); a double emphasis of Jesus' position as the one from heaven (II19).

IIB. The Father and the Son (3:32-36)

CHIASTIC STRUCTURE, II20 (AB-B'A')

In B and B', the intimacy between God and the Son is similarly described in two ways of presentation: God sent his Son and gave him the Spirit (B); God loves the Son and has given all things (B'). In A-A', we can see that dual foci regarding the relationship with the Son are provided: he who testifies, the Son, and he who receives his testimony (A); he who believe in the Son, having life, and he who does not obey the Son, not seeing life (A').

In vv. 32–36, nine parallels appear: five chiasms (II20–24), two parallelism (II26 and 27), and two duals (II25 and 28). II20 is the main structure in chiasm. II22 and 23 belong to vv. 32–33 (A of II20), II24–25 to v. 34 (B), II26 to v. 35 (B'), and II27 and 28 to v. 36 (A'), while II21 is for a connection between vv. 32–33 (A) and 34 (B).

Two Dialogues with Discourses

V	20	21	22	23	Phrases	Translation
32	A	a	a	a	ὃ ἑώρακεν καὶ ἤκουσεν τοῦτο	~ to what he has seen and heard,
-	-	-	-	b	μαρτυρεῖ,	He testifies ~
-	-	b	b	b'	καὶ τὴν μαρτυρίαν αὐτοῦ	~ his testimony.
-	-	-	-	a'	οὐδεὶς λαμβάνει.	but no one receives ~
33	-	b'	b'		ὁ λαβὼν αὐτοῦ τὴν μαρτυρίαν	He who receives his testimony
-	-	-	a'	24	ἐσφράγισεν ὅτι ὁ θεὸς ἀληθής ἐστιν.	has certified that God is true.
34	B	a'	a	25	ὃν γὰρ	For he whom
-	-	-	-	a	ἀπέστειλεν ὁ θεὸς	God has sent
-	-	-	x	a'	τὰ ῥήματα τοῦ θεοῦ	~ the words of God,
-	-	-	-	-	λαλεῖ,	speaks ~
-	-	26	a'		οὐ γὰρ ἐκ μέτρου δίδωσιν τὸ πνεῦμα.	for he gives the Spirit without measure.
35	B'	a			ὁ πατὴρ ἀγαπᾷ	The Father loves
-		b			τὸν υἱὸν	the Son
-		a'			καὶ πάντα δέδωκεν	and has given all things
-	27	b'			ἐν τῇ χειρὶ αὐτοῦ.	into his hand.
36	A'	a			ὁ πιστεύων	He who believes
-		b			εἰς τὸν υἱὸν	in the Son
-		c			ἔχει	has
-		d			ζωὴν αἰώνιον·	eternal life,
-		a'			ὁ δὲ ἀπειθῶν	but he who does not obey
-		b'	28		τῷ υἱῷ	the Son
-		c'	a		οὐκ ὄψεται	will not see
-		d'	-		ζωήν,	life,
-		a'			ἀλλ' ἡ ὀργὴ τοῦ θεοῦ μένει ἐπ' αὐτόν.	and God's wrath remains on him.

II21. Chiastic, ab-b'a': Both in a and a', the Son testifies what he has seen and heard [from the Father] (a) and speaks the words of God who sent him (a'). Both a and a' describe the Son's statements relating to the Father. While, in b-b', there are two different responses to the testimony of the Son: negative (b) and positive (b'). II22. Chiastic, ab-b'a': In the middle, b-b', rejecter and receiver are contrasted regarding the Son's testimony. For the Son testifies to what he has seen and heard from the Father, receiving his testimony means proving the truthfulness of God who showed his Son and said to him what he testifies. II23. Chiastic, ab-b'a': In b-b', phrases related to testimony are shown: "He testifies" (b) and "his testimony" (b'). And, in a-a', the Son who has seen and heard (a) is contrasted to "no one," who does not receive it (a').

II24. Chiastic, a-x-a': In a-a', two deeds of God in relation to the Son are introduced: God has sent him (a); he gives the Spirit without measure (a'). While, in x, the action of the Son is highlighted: "he speaks the words of God." II25. Dual, a-a': God has sent the Son (a) and the Son speaks the words of God (a'). The relationship between God and his Son is explained in these two ways. II26. Parallel, ab-a'b': Both b-b' are related to the Son, while both a-a' are described in the relation of the Father to the Son: loving (a) and giving (a').

II27. Parallel, abcd-a'b'c'd':[9] Two sentences are contrasted in parallel, syntactically and semantically: ὁ πιστεύων (He who believes, a) and ὁ δὲ ἀπειθῶν (but he who does not obey, a'); εἰς τὸν υἱόν (in the Son, b) and τῷ υἱῷ (the Son, b'); ἔχει (has, c) and οὐκ ὄψεται (will not see, c'); ζωὴν αἰώνιον (eternal life, d) and ζωήν (life, d'). The contrast occurs between a and a' as well as between c and c', while b-b' and d-d' contain duplicated concepts. II28. Dual, a-a': Two negative results of disobedience to the Son are doubly presented: "he will not see life" (a) and "God's wrath remains on him" (a').

The foci of parallels are: the Father-Son relationship and the demand for belief (II20); the authenticity of his testimony and the necessity of belief (II21); the significance of receiving his testimony (II22); his testimony and their unbelief (II23); God's role and his Son's role (II24–25); God's love for his Son (II26); believer versus unbeliever (II27); seeing no life and God's wrath (II28).

Reading in Structure-Style

1. The contrast between Nicodemus and Jesus is highlighted as seen in I2 (specifically A-A' in pair). Nicodemus is introduced as a man of high rank and a Rabbi (teacher of Israel) in Judaism. Thus, he is qualified to say, "we know that . . ." (2). But Jesus as the divine teacher discloses his ignorance of spiritual matters (10–11). This contrast is a key to understand the episode.

2. Verses 3–9 consists of a cycle (B-B', I2): Jesus' saying and Nicodemus' doubt (3–4 and 5–9). The latter part (5–9) is explanatory of the former one (3–4). For instance, being born again [above] is nothing but being born of water and the Spirit.

3. There are three "Truly, truly, I say to you" (vv. 3, 5, 11), the emphatic expression of Jesus, among which vv. 3 and 5 share a common function, emphasizing the significance of the born again issue. But in v. 11, it is used differently and instead accentuates the authenticity of the testimony.

4. For vv. 12–21 are made up of three subunits (I18): vv. 12–15, 16–17, and 18–21, among which two are negative in tone (12–15 and 18–21), we may say that the tone as a whole is both more or less negative. Nevertheless, the positivity of the center (16–17) strongly lights up the whole passage.

5. What are earthly things and heavenly things (12)? Considering the parallel I19 (12–15), we may say that earthly things are visible to human eyes such as the Moses' event lifting up the serpent and Jesus' crucifixion, and that heavenly things are invisible to human eyes illustrated by the Son's descending from heaven.

---

9. Cf. Mlakuzhyil, *Christocentric Literary Structure*, 123.

6. In Jesus' baptism and the Baptist's baptism (A-A', II3), that there was plenty of water in the Baptist's case and that everyone is going to him in Jesus' case are contrasted.

7. As vv. 16–21 are added to the dialogue between Jesus and Nicodemus, further explaining the previous part of Jesus' words regarding belief and eternal life, vv. 32[31]–36 are similar in function added to the dialogue between the Baptist and his disciples, also explaining the issue, belief and eternal life.

8. It is difficult to determine that v. 31 belongs to the original words of the Baptist as vv. 27–30 do. Even if this verse does not, we can admit that the author intends to bind vv. 27–31 as a cluster (see A', II9) by adding v. 31 after v. 30 to complete a chiastic structure (II9). Referring to vv. 32–36 creates its own chiastic structure, II20.

9. Verses 32–36 are not arranged according to modern logic, in a sequential order. Rather they are intended to create a chiastic structure as in II20. If we rearrange them sequentially, we have to do as follows: First, the Father has given all things to the Son (35); Second, God has sent him who speaks the words of God (34); Third, the Son testifies what he as seen and heard but no one receives his testimony (32–33); Fourth, he who believes in the Son has eternal life but the unbeliever will not see life (36). The author arranges them to highlight human responses to the testimony of Jesus both in front and in the rear and also to put the Father-Son relationship at the center of the structure.

Issues in Structure-Style

1. The Structure of vv. 1–21

Focusing on the themes, Bultmann grouped vv. 1–21 into vv. 1–8 (the coming of the Revealer explained by the necessity of rebirth) and 9–21 (the coming of the Revealer as the κρίσις of the world).[10]

Brown advanced this and provided more detail, by classifying the first section of this chapter as follows:[11] "1. Verses 2–8. Begetting from on high through the Spirit is necessary for entrance into the kingdom of God; natural birth is insufficient. (a) 2–3: First question and answer: the fact of begetting from on high; (b) 4–8: Second question and answer: the how of the begetting—through the Spirit. 2. Verses 9–21. All of this is made possible only when the Son has ascended to the Father, and it is offered only to those who believe in Jesus. 9–10: The third question and answer introduces this whole section. (a) 11–15: The Son must ascend to the Father (in order to give the Spirit); (b) 16–21: Belief in Jesus is necessary in order to profit from this gift."

---

10. Bultmann, *Gospel of John*, 132.

11. Brown, *Gospel according to John I–XII*, 136–37. Similarly, Snodgrass, "That Which Is Born from *PNEUMA*," 185–86.

Beasley-Murray approaches the structure in a different way, seeing the dialogue of Jesus in the second person end in v. 12, thus regarding vv. 13–21 as a monologue in the voice of Christ, which contains the ascent of the Son of Man (13), the crucifixion-resurrection (14–15), a confessional summary of the Gospel (16) and a kerygmatic reflection on the mission of the Son of God with its concomitant of judgment (17–21).[12]

First, it is understandable that Bultmann and Brown divided the first section according to the triple cycle of dialogue between Jesus and Nicodemus such as vv. 2–3 (the first); 4–8 (the second); 9–21 (the last).

Second, the problem lies in that they, specifically Brown, did not pay proper attention to the function of vv. 10–11 in spite of observing the similarity between vv. 2 and 10.[13] Verses 1–2 and 10–11 are an *inclusio*, which belongs to the chiastic structure (I2, AB-B'A' in 1–11). See the difference of relation between vv. 1–2 and 3–8 (continued dialogue) from that between vv. 9–10 and 11–21 (discourse). It means that the function of vv. 9–10 differs from vv. 2–3 unlike Brown's assertion. Rather vv. 1–2 are for opening and vv. 10–11 are for closing, thereby they are in *inclusio*.

Third, if we place vv. 10–11 as a counterpart of vv. 1–2 in pair or *inclusio*, considering the connectivity between them regarding their shared ideas, as discussed in I2, we may also easily grasp the structure of vv. 12–21 (I18, A-X-A').

Fourth, they ignored the similarity between vv. 4 and 9 (the second and third sayings of Nicodemus questioning the rebirth). This similarity is more intense than that with v. 2 (his first saying dealing with who Jesus is). The relation between vv. 4 and 9 is as similar as that between vv. 3 and 5–8 which are the two sayings of Jesus about rebirth.

Fifth, the structure of Brown did not explain how the similarity between vv. 14–15 and 16–21 happens. As discussed earlier in I18, vv. 12–21 are made up of a chiastic structure: A (12–15); X (16–17); A' (18–21). A is related and extended in explanation to X and A'. The discourse of Jesus (12–15) seems to be re-emphasized and interpreted in vv. 16–21. In other words, vv. 16–21 are an additional explanation to vv. 12–15. When the explanatory note was added for emphasis, the structure was maintained as a chiastic one, one of John's typical ways.

Sixth, we presume that vv. 12–15 belong to Jesus himself but the rest seems not to be so. If this is right, we also cannot ignore the relation between vv. 11 and 12–21: the former is for "our" witness, while the latter becomes the contents of this "our" witness. Thus, we may say that vv. 12–21 consist of two kinds ("our") of witnesses: the testimony of Jesus (probably 12–15) plus that of his disciples including the evangelist (16–21), presented for "our testimony."

Seventh, this "our" testimony continues up to the second section (22–36): the testimony of the Baptist (22–30) and that of the evangelist (31–36).[14]

12. Beasley-Murray, *John*, 46.
13. Brown, *Gospel according to John I–XII*, 137.
14. Carson also sees vv. 16–21 and 31–36 as extended comments by the Evangelist or his

Two Dialogues with Discourses

Eighth, against Schnackenburg who saw v. 12 as the last verse of the Jesus discourse, Brown emphasized that there is no change of speaker[15] and there are still a few reasons why vv. 12–21 cannot be attributed to different speakers, such as using a connective (καί) in v. 13 and a connective (γάρ) in v. 16.[16]

Ninth, we may say that connectives such as καί and γάρ are not the primary or decisive factor whether the verses belong to the dialogue of Jesus or are not part of it. On the contrary, the connective γάρ (16) can be regarded as a marker leading the explanatory passage of the evangelist (16–21) to the previous discourse of Jesus, particularly vv. 12–15 (*contra* Brown).

Tenth, it is probable to say that the discourse of Jesus continues up to v. 15. The first person pronoun ("I") is used in v. 12, and the Son of Man and its related third person pronoun ("he") appears in vv. 13–15. Using the name of the Son of Man for himself, Jesus also uses the third person pronoun to refer to himself (13:31; *contra* Beasley-Murray). It seems that this use of the third person pronoun does not continue longer than beyond a few verses. Thus, we can attribute vv. 13–15 as well as v. 12 to the words of Jesus himself.

Eleventh, the name, the only Son (μονογενής) in vv. 16 and 18, one of the titles for Jesus, is not used by Jesus himself. This is the name used in the confession by the evangelist (1:14, 18) who is the witness of Jesus. Although there is no sign of change of speaker, from v. 16 up to v. 21, the explanatory note and the confessional message of the gospel of Jesus, particularly regarding vv. 12–15, are presented by the evangelist. In this way, the discourse of Jesus (12–15) and the comment of the evangelist become "our testimony" as in v. 11.

Twelfth, vv. 12–21, which consists of a chiastic structure (I18, A-X-A') as a whole, provide three subsections (12–15, A; 16–17, X; and 18–21, A'), each of which produces a chiasm (I19, ab-b'a' in 12–15), a combined parallelism (I25, a1a2-b-a'1a'2-b' in 16–17), and a chiasm (I29, abc-x-c'b'a' in 18–21). It means that each of them maintains its own cohesiveness in itself and is connected to each other in a chiastic way as a whole.

Finally, it seems not to be the concern of the evangelist to demarcate the part which belongs originally to the discourse of Jesus from the part which does not. His total concern is to bear his sincere witness to Jesus regarding who Jesus is and why we have to believe in him, by presenting in his own structure-style.

---

explanatory reflections. Carson, *Gospel according to John*, 203–4, 212.

15. Brown, *Gospel according to John I–XII*, 149 According to him, some scholars regard v. 13 as the verse from which the speaker is changed (Tillmann, Belser, Schnackenburg) and others v. 16 (Westcott, Lagrange, Bernard, Van den Bussche, Braun, Lightfoot).

16. Brown, *Gospel according to John I–XII*, 149. The phenomenon that the last clauses of vv. 15 and 16 are the same is caused by the fact that the v. 16 is the explanatory note to similarly repeat and reemphasize the idea of the previous verse, v. 16.

2. The Structure of vv. 22–36 and Its Function to vv. 1–21

Bultmann relocated the sayings in vv. 31–36 just after vv. 1–21, because he treated these verses as those originally belong to the dialogue of Jesus and his discourse both in style and theme.[17] And then he regarded vv. 22–30 (the witness of the Baptist) as an appendix, considering its length and importance as inferior.[18] According to him, the main section falls into three subsections: vv. 1–8, 9–21, and 31–36 (the authoritative witness of the Revealer).[19]

But Dodd criticizes the assumption of Bultmann, pointing out that vv. 31–36 are not an appropriate continuation of vv. 13–21 but rather a recapitulation of the idea because of the thematic discontinuity between vv. 31 and vv. 13–21.[20]

Thyen insists that there is a similarity between 2:23–25 and vv. 22–24 as introductions (or reports) to the dialogue of Jesus (1–12) and that of the Baptist (25–30), respectively. According to him, vv. 13–21 and 31–36 are monologues, giving "the voice of Christ."[21]

Since Bultmann regarded vv. 22–30 as an appendix, some scholars such as Brown have re-valued and relocated them apart from the place where they are. As for Brown, vv. 22–30 reflect phenomena of poor sequence (externally) and unclear logic of the story (internally). Depending on Boismard, he thought that these verses belong to the opening relation between John the Baptist and Jesus, rather than in the sequence where they are now,[22] suggesting that they originally followed shortly after 1:19–34.

Regarding the reason why these verses are transposed to their present place, Brown assumed two things:[23] (1) the editor wrought the theological pattern of the training of the disciples on a series of days in ch. 1, thus displacing vv. 22–30 where they are now; (2) the editor had a desire to bring out the baptismal motif of the Nicodemus story.

First, when Bultmann separated vv. 31–36 from the location after vv. 22–30 and relocated them just after vv. 1–21, he recognized that the chapter falls into two parts of differing length and importance: vv. 1–21 and 22–30. By his relocation of vv. 31–36,

---

17. Bultmann, *Gospel of John*, 131.
18. Burge treats vv. 22–36 totally as an excursus on the Baptist. Burge, *From Biblical Text*, 77.
19. Bultmann, *Gospel of John*, 132.
20. Dodd, *Fourth Gospel*, 309; also Beasley-Murray, *John*, 46.
21. Beasley-Murray basically supports its frame of division but doubts the claim that vv. 13–21 and 31–36 are spoken by Jesus. Beasley-Murray, *John*, 46. Originally, Thyen, "Aus der Literatur zum Johannesevangelium," 112. Compare the division of Talbert, who sees 2:23—3:2 and 3:13–21 as a pair in three points: (a) belief in his name (2:23; 3:16, 18); (b) coming by night (3:1–2a) and loving darkness (3:19–21); coming from God (3:2b, 13–17). Talbert, *Reading John*, 97.
22. Boismard, "Les traditions johanniques," 25–30; cited by Brown, *Gospel according to John I–XII*, 154.
23. Brown, *Gospel according to John I–XII*, 155.

Two Dialogues with Discourses

the balance between vv. 1–21 and 22–36 is broken. Their balance in length and significance can be maintained if we consider the location as it is now.

Second, as discussed earlier (see II1 and 2), vv. 22–36 consist of two subsections (II1, A-A'): the dialogue between the Baptist and his disciples (22–31, A) and its related discourse (32–36, A'). Verses 22–31 are again arranged in dual mode (II2): vv. 22–26 (A) and 27–31 (A').

Third, both vv. 22–26 and 27–31 maintain their own chiasms (A-X-A', II3 and 9) for their own inner cohesiveness. II3 highlights the contrast between the baptism of Jesus (22–23, A) and that of the Baptist (26, A'). II9 focuses on the contrast between the divinity of Jesus and the humanness of the Baptist, both in vv. 27–28 (A) and 31 (A'), while in the middle of the unit (29–30) there is another type of contrast: between the major figure (Jesus) and the minor one (the Baptist).

Fourth, it means that v. 31 belongs to the cluster of vv. 27–31, although it seems to be a part of the commentary by the evangelist, which starts at v. 31 and ends at v. 36. This phenomenon is similar but in the reverse of the discourse of Jesus combined with the commentary of the evangelist in vv. 12–21. For this time, a part of the commentary of the evangelist (31) combines with the discourse of the Baptist (27–30).

Fifth, as a result, vv. 22–31 (mainly the dialogue of the Baptist) can be in a pair with vv. 1–11 (the dialogue of Jesus) the same as vv. 32–36 (the second discourse part) with vv. 12–21 (the first discourse part).[24] In each dialogue, we can see the similarity, such as the contrast between the teacher from heaven and the teacher of Israel (1–11, particularly, focusing on the relation of an *inclusio* between vv. 1–2 and 10–11) and that between the Christ from above and the person who was sent before him (22–31).

Sixth, in the latter parts, shared ideas between vv. 12–21 and 32–36 exist such as belief vs. unbelief, eternal life vs. wrath of God, and love of God (toward the world in 16–17; toward the Son in 35).[25]

Seventh, in vv. 1–21, vv. 12–15, the discourse of Jesus, can be regarded as a linking part that plays a role of stepping stone (or of a hinge) connecting the dialogue of Jesus (1–11) and the commentary of the evangelist (16–21). In vv. 22–36, v. 31, presumably a commentary of the evangelist, plays that role connecting the dialogue of the Baptist (22–30) and the commentary of the evangelist (32–36). Interestingly, these two parts share the idea of the One from heaven as well as the contrast between heaven and earth.

Eighth, it is concluded that vv. 1–21 and 22–36 are in dual mode, each of which similarly consists of two subunits: a dialogue and a discourse (including a commentary). Verses 1–11 are related to vv. 22–31 and vv. 12–21 to vv. 32–36 both in form (a

---

24. Refer to the five parallels of Wilson between vv. 1–21 and 22–36. Wilson, "Integrity of John 3:22–36," 37–38.

25. Cf. Moloney, *Gospel of John*, 89–90. Moloney sees that vv. 1–10 and 22–30 form a diptych, as both contain a narrative and that vv. 11–21 and 31–36 share the claim that Jesus is the unique revealer of the heavenly, and the ideas of salvation or condemnation.

dialogue and a discourse) and in theme (the contrast among the characters and the message of the gospel).

Ninth, thus, vv. 31–36 can neither be attached to the end of vv. 1–21, nor can vv. 22–30 regarded as an appendix to the ch. 3 (*contra* Bultmann). Verses 1–21 and 22–36 are beautifully arranged as a pair, keeping the balance of significance and sharing the themes. We can see the "our" testimony that consists of the testimony of Jesus himself through his dialogue with Nicodemus, that of the Baptist through his dialogue with his disciples, and those (dual testimonies) of the evangelist in a recurring pattern.

Tenth, 2:23–25 are not the introduction to the ch. 3 (*contra* Thyen),[26] because these verses are constructed as an *inclusio* with 2:12–13, as discussed previously. Also the belief of the people (in these verses) who believed in him after seeing the signs is contrasted, within ch. 2, to that of the disciples of Jesus (17 and 22) who believed in him based on the Scripture and the sayings of Jesus. If we remove these verses from the cluster 2:13–25, 2:13–22 would not reflect a typical method of John in its structure by itself but remain incomplete.

Eleventh, additionally, vv. 22–24 cannot be separated as an entity, belonging to the cluster vv. 22–26, because there is II3, a chiasm, that consists of vv. 22–23 (A), 24–25 (X), and 26 (A').[27] Thus, we can say that ch. 3 does not need 2:23–25 for the building of its own structure.

	1-21		Matching points	22-36	
1-11	I. The dialogue of Jesus		The contrasts among the characters: between Jesus and Nicodemus; between Jesus and the Baptist	I. The dialogue of the Baptist	22-30
12-15	II. The discourse of Jesus		The One who came from heaven The contrast between heaven vs. earth	The commentary of the evangelist	31
16-21	The commentary of the evangelist		Belief in the Son The love of God Belief vs. unbelief Eternal life vs. condemnation	II. The commentary of the evangelist (continued)	32-36

---

26. See Topel, "Note on the Methodology," 214–19.

27. Compare also the division of Moloney: vv. 22–24 (Introduction); vv. 25–30 (John the Baptist bears witness); vv. 31–36 (The discourse-commentary of the narrator). Moloney, *Gospel of John*, 104.

4 The Samaritans and a Royal Official

"The story of Jesus' encounter with the Samaritans in John 4 reaches a climax when the people of Sychar acclaim him "the Savior of the world" (4:42). This title appears nowhere else in the Fourth Gospel and was not a typical messianic designation in the first-century in the Greco-Roman world, however, the full title 'Savior of the world' was used for the emperor."[1]

Dual Mode in Structure

JOHN 4 CONTAINS AT least two Jesus events. One is related to the Samaritans, while the other is the healing miracle of Jesus at Cana. It is advisable to divide the chapter into two units such as vv. 1–42 and 43–54. The reasons are as follows:

1. In the beginning of the story at Sychar, there is the introductory note (1–4), explaining why Jesus has to pass through Samaria.

2. From v. 5 to v. 27, the first main body of the story consists of a typical, chiastic structure: ABC-C'B'A' (see I5), where four issues of the dialogue between Jesus and a woman are networked in chiasm: the Giver of eternal water (B) – woman and man (C) – worship and race (C') – Messiah (B').

3. Verses 28–42 show a chiastic structure: AB-B'A' (I35), where the evangelization of the woman (28–30, A) is in a pair with the belief of the Samaritans (39–42, A'), while the dialogue between Jesus and his disciples is the center, containing two sub-parts (31–34, B; 35–38, B').

---

1. Koester, "Savior of the World," 665.

4. In other words, vv. 1–42 can be divided into three parts: vv. 1–4, 5–27, and 28–42. And vv. 5–27 and 28–42 can be regarded as a pair consisting of two main bodies. Where is the counterpart of vv. 1–4?

5. The second episode at Cana (46–54) demonstrates its own chiastic structure: ABCD-D'C'B'A' (see II1). It means that this episode is regarded as a separable entity in itself.

6. It is presumed that the function of vv. 43–45 is like that of vv. 1–4. There are a few similar ideas to be shared. First, both describe the movements of Jesus: Jesus left Judea and departed to Galilee (3); he departed to Galilee and came there (43, 45). Second, there are other characters which do not appear in the following sections such as Pharisees (1) and Galileans (45). Most of all, these two are not included in the chiastic structures, such as I5 and II1, that follow.

7. Thus, we can distinguish them from other main bodies by dividing John 4 into: vv. 1–4, 5–42, 43–45, and 46–54. There are two ways to arrange them: First, [I, A (1–4) – B (5–42)] – [II, A' (43–45) – B' (46–54)]; Second, [I, A (1–4) – X (5–42) – A' (43–45)] and [II (46–54)]. The first case is seeing that John 4 is designed in dual mode: I and II, each of which contains a similar pattern: A and B. The function of A-A' is regarded as introductory to the main episode, B-B', which follows. The second case also sees that there are two stories in dual mode (I and II). But it regards I (1–45) as a comprehensive, chiastic structure, A-X-A' (or AB-B'A'), attaching vv. 43–45 to the previous passage.

8. Which one is proper to an understanding of the structure of John 4? Moreover, which one was originally intended by the author? It would be difficult to answer this. But the first one is preferred, for the function of vv. 43–45 seems to be suitable to an introductory part of the following episode rather than an ending part of the previous section, in terms that the location is Galilee.

In conclusion, we can display the structure as follows:

I.	Jesus and the Samaritans (4:1-42)			
	IA.	Introductory scene (4:1-4)		A
	IB.	Two Samaritan episodes (4:5-42)		B
		IB1.	Dialogue between Jesus and a Samaritan woman (4:5-27)	
		IB2.	Dialogue between Jesus and his disciples and belief of the Samaritans (4:28-42)	
II.	The second sign at Cana (4:43-54)			
	IIA.	Introductory scene (4:43-45)		A'
	IIB.	The second sign at Cana (4:46-54)		B'

How They Are Related: I (1–42) and II (43–54)

1. It is worthy of consideration that these two events may occur subsequently, one after the other. Having left Judea, Jesus went to Sychar to pass through Samaria, and finally he reached Cana, Galilee. Thus, it is highly probable to see that event I happened prior to event II.

2. However, it cannot be the crucial reason why I (the Samarian episode) and II (the Cana episode) are located together in John 4. As we have observed the two episodes are tightened in each chapter such as chs. 2 and 3. There were reasons for that.

3. Here in John 4, two episodes are related as follows: First, two regions share a similarity in that both were isolated areas from Judea at that time.[2] Jesus left Judea because of their leaders, the Pharisees, and went to Galilee via Samaria. The Judeans looked down on the Galileans and they rejected the Samaritans totally. Jesus takes care of both of them.

Second, there is the contrast between the Samaritans including the woman and a royal official of Galilee.[3] Regardless of their social status and racial type, Jesus shows his deep concern for them: whether they are lowly in society or high in rank. Jesus is "the Savior of the world" as the Samaritans confess (42).

I. Jesus and the Samaritans (4:1–42)

IA (A) and IB (B), I1

As discussed earlier, the Samaritan episode consists of the introductory note (A, IA, 1–4) and the main body of the story (B, IB, 5–42), which comprises two main units: vv. 5–27 (IB1, dialogue between Jesus and a woman) and 28–42 (IB2, dialogue between Jesus and his disciples and the belief of the Samaritans).

IA. Introductory Scene (4:1–4)

In vv. 1–4, there are three parallels: two parallelisms (I3 and 4), and a dual (I2). I2 and 3 are limited to vv. 1–3, while I4 that extends to v. 4 also continues its connection in parallel with v. 5.

---

2. In John, the Galileans would be closer to the Samaritans rather than to the Judaeans (cf. chs. 7–8; specifically 7:27, 41, 52 and 8:48). Purvis, "Fourth Gospel and the Samaritans," 157–58.

3. For the contrast between Nicodemus and the Samaritan woman, see Dockery, "Reading John 4:1–15," 128–30. We cannot be sure of Mead's assertion that the βασιλικός (46) was a Gentile officer. Mead, "βασιλικός in John 4:46–53," 69–72.

V	2	3	4	Phrases	Translation
1	a		a	Ὡς οὖν ἔγνω ὁ Ἰησοῦς ὅτι ἤκουσαν οἱ Φαρισαῖοι ὅτι Ἰησοῦς πλείονας μαθητὰς ποιεῖ καὶ βαπτίζει ἢ Ἰωάννης	Now when Jesus knew that the Pharisees had heard that he was making and baptizing more disciples than John,
2	-		-	-καίτοιγε Ἰησοῦς αὐτὸς οὐκ ἐβάπτιζεν ἀλλ' οἱ μαθηταὶ αὐτοῦ-	although Jesus himself did not baptize, but his disciples did,
3	a'	a	b	ἀφῆκεν	he left
-	-	b	-	τὴν Ἰουδαίαν	Judea
-	-	a'	-	καὶ ἀπῆλθεν πάλιν	and departed again
-	-	b'	-	εἰς τὴν Γαλιλαίαν.	to Galilee.
4	-		a'	Ἔδει δὲ αὐτὸν διέρχεσθαι διὰ τῆς Σαμαρείας.	And he had to pass through Samaria.

I2. Dual, a-a': These verses, vv. 1–4, contain two acts of Jesus: knowing about the Pharisees who heard something regarding his baptism (a) and leaving Judea and departing to Galilee, passing through Samaria (a'), which are described in parallel. I3. Parallel, ab-a'b': Jesus' leaving (ἀφῆκεν, a) Judea (τὴν Ἰουδαίαν, b) and departing (καὶ ἀπῆλθεν πάλιν, a') to Galilee (εἰς τὴν Γαλιλαίαν, b') are presented in parallel. I4. Parallel, ab-a'b': Jesus' actions seem to be arranged in parallel: when he knew (a), he left and departed to . . . (b); when he had to pass through (a'), he came to . . . (b'). In a-a', we see the reasons that Jesus has to move, and in b-b', he does move.

In I2, the reason he has to leave Judea and his movement to Galilee via Samaria are explained. And I3 introduces two acts of Jesus to Galilee, while, in I4, we see Jesus who came to Samaria after leaving Judea for Galilee.

IB. Two Samaritan Episodes (4:5–42)

IB1. Dialogue between Jesus and a Samaritan Woman (4:5–27)

Chiastic Structure, I5 (ABC-C'B'A')

1. There are six scenes in vv. 5–27. At the opening scene, Jesus met a woman while his disciples went into the town, and he starts his dialogue with her. There are two key parallels (I6 and 8) supporting this subunit in unity. Verses 5–7a (I6) describes the scene where Jesus and the woman came to the place at that time and vv. 7b–9 (I8) show how their dialogue starts.

2. There are four issues in sequence during the dialogue: living water (10–15); husband (sex, 16–18); worship and race (19–24); Messiah (25–26). Each subunit is made up in a cohesive entity containing its own parallels within (particularly, see II10 and 13 for vv. 10–15; I21 for vv. 16–18; I25 and 29 for vv. 19–24; I33 for vv. 25–26; I35 for v. 27).

3. Among four themes, the first one and the last one could be in a pair, because they both point to the divinity of Jesus as Christ and Savior. And in the second and third ones, we may recognize that they are related in terms of sex (man and woman)[4] and race (Jews and Samaritans), where the identity of Jesus seems not to surface. There is also another comparison in the two scenes, the first and last ones, where the pronoun "I" (ἐγώ) of Jesus appears (14 and 26). Thus, we can regard vv. 10–15 and 25–26; vv. 16–18 and 19–24 as pairs.

4. In v. 27, the closing scene, the disciples went back to Jesus and saw that Jesus was having a dialogue with a woman. This scene is matched in a pair to the first scene where Jesus starts a dialogue with the woman. We can name them A (5–9) and A' (27).

5. Considering the connectivity of the four issues, we can name them B (10–15); C (16–18); C' (19–24); B' (25–26). Here, B + B' are almost equal to C + C' in size of verses. Thus, we may say that the structure is chiastic: ABC-C'B'A'.[5]

A.	Beginning of the dialogue (5-9)		
	B.	Living water (10-15)	
		C.	Woman and man (16-18)
		C'.	Worship and racial issue (19-24)
	B'.	Messiah (25-26)	
A'.	Closing of the dialogue (27)		

A. Beginning of the Dialogue (4:5–9)

In vv. 5–9, we find two chiasms (I6 and 9) and two parallelisms (I7 and 8). I6–7 demonstrate the cohesiveness of vv. 5–7a, and I8 does that of vv. 7b–9, while, in I9, vv. 7b and 9 are connected with vv. 10 and 15. Here, the pillars supporting the unity of vv. 5–9 (A, I5) are I6 and I8.

---

4. Purvis interprets the five husbands as the five pagan gods which the Samaritans had served. Purvis, "Fourth Gospel and the Samaritans," 180–82. But this interpretation seems not to fit the confession of the woman in v. 29.

5. Referring to Bligh and Ellis, Coloe introduces a chiastic structure in vv. 1–45. A (1–6): Jesus leaves Judea for Galilee, travels through Samaria; B (7–15): Jesus asks a woman for a drink. Dialogue on two "water"; C (16–18): Woman told to go and bring her husband; D (19–26): Place and nature of true worship; C' (27–30): Woman goes and brings the villagers; B' (31–38): Disciples ask Jesus to eat. Dialogue on two "foods"; A' (39–45): Jesus in the village then resumes his journey to Galilee. Her structure that puts the "worship" issue in its center is impressive and plausible. However, we have to point out: that there is an ignorance of the close relation between vv. 28–30 (witness of the woman) and 39–42 (its result: belief of the Samaritans); that there are four interrelated issues in the dialogue between Jesus and the woman (Living water, 10–15; Woman and man, 16–18; Worship and race, 19–24; Messiah, 25–26); that there are two related issues in the dialogue between Jesus and his disciples (Food of Jesus, 31–34; Harvest, 35–38). Coloe, *God Dwells with Us*, 86–87; Cf. Bligh, "Jesus in Samaria," 329–31; Ellis, *Genius of John*, 66–76; Eslinger, "Wooing of the Woman," 170.

V	4	6		Phrases	Translation
5	b'	a		Ἔρχεται οὖν εἰς πόλιν τῆς Σαμαρείας λεγομένην Συχὰρ πλησίον τοῦ χωρίου ὃ ἔδωκεν Ἰακὼβ [τῷ] Ἰωσὴφ τῷ υἱῷ αὐτοῦ·	So he came to a town of Samaria, called Sychar, near the field that Jacob gave to his son Joseph.
			7		
6		b	a	ἦν δὲ ἐκεῖ πηγὴ τοῦ Ἰακώβ.	Jacob's well was there,
		x	b	ὁ οὖν Ἰησοῦς κεκοπιακὼς ἐκ τῆς ὁδοιπορίας ἐκαθέζετο οὕτως ἐπὶ τῇ πηγῇ·	and so Jesus, being wearied from his journey, sat down by the well.
		b'	a'	ὥρα ἦν ὡς ἕκτη.	It was about the sixth hour.
7		a'	b'	Ἔρχεται γυνὴ ἐκ τῆς Σαμαρείας ἀντλῆσαι ὕδωρ.	A Samaritan woman came to draw water.
	8	9			
	a	a		λέγει αὐτῇ ὁ Ἰησοῦς·	Jesus said to her,
	b	-		δός μοι πεῖν·	"Give me a drink."
8	c			οἱ γὰρ μαθηταὶ αὐτοῦ ἀπεληλύθεισαν εἰς τὴν πόλιν ἵνα τροφὰς ἀγοράσωσιν.	For his disciples had gone away into the town to buy food.
9	a'	b		λέγει οὖν αὐτῷ ἡ γυνὴ ἡ Σαμαρῖτις·	The Samaritan woman said to him,
	b'	-		πῶς σὺ Ἰουδαῖος ὢν παρ' ἐμοῦ πεῖν αἰτεῖς γυναικὸς Σαμαρίτιδος οὔσης;	"How do you, being a Jew, ask a drink of me, a woman of Samaria?
	c'			οὐ γὰρ συγχρῶνται Ἰουδαῖοι Σαμαρίταις.	For Jews do not associate with Samaritans.

I6. Chiastic, ab-x-b'a': In a, Jesus came to Sychar, while, in a', a Samaritan woman came to draw water. In this way, Jesus and she are going to meet together. In b, the place, Jacob's well, is introduced, while, in b', the time, about the sixth hour, is presented. In the center x, Jesus being wearied sat down by the well. It is expected that he is about to do something there. I7. Parallel, ab-a'b': In b and b', the place and the time are known, while, in a-a', Jesus sat down by the well (a) and the woman came to draw water at the well (a').

I8. Parallel, abc-a'b'c': In a-a', Jesus said to her (a) and she said to him in turn (a'). Jesus told her, "Give me a drink" (b) and she raised a question in reply, "How do you, being a Jew, ask a drink of me, a woman of Samaria?" (b'). In c-c', the readers are informed of a contradiction: his disciples, the Jews, went to the town of Samaritans to buy food (c) but originally Jews did not associate with Samaritans (c'). This pair, c-c', exists here to provide information of the background regarding the dialogue between Jesus and the woman. I9. Chiastic, ab-b'a': When Jesus asks her to give him a drink (a), she does not realize why he asks so (b). His intention is to give her living water (b'). Eventually, she comes round asking for him "this-never-thirsty-water" (a'). Firstly, Jesus asks her (a), but finally she asks him back (a'). In b-b', the purpose of the dialogue is disclosed.

I6–7 provide the information regarding when, where, and how Jesus met a woman. I8 focuses on the point of contact, water, by Jesus to her, explaining its social situation. I9 highlights the shift of her attitude towards Jesus: from suspicious to positive.

B. Giver of Eternal Water (4:10–15)

In vv. 10–15, there are eleven parallels: four chiasms (I10–11, 13, and 15), four parallelisms (I17–20), and three duals (I12, 14, and 16). We may say that I10 and 13 are like pillars leading this subunit into unity and that they are complex in parallel, because they overlap in vv. 11–12. I10–11 and 14–16 are mostly related in vv. 10–12, while I17–20 reflect the cohesion of vv. 13–15. I13 as well as I12 play a role of link between vv. 10–12 and 13–15.

V	9				12	Phrases	Translation
10	b'	10			a	ἀπεκρίθη Ἰησοῦς καὶ εἶπεν αὐτῇ·	Jesus answered her,
-	-	a	11		-	εἰ ᾔδεις	"If you knew
-	-	-	a		-	τὴν δωρεὰν τοῦ θεοῦ	the gift of God,
-	-	-	b		-	καὶ τίς ἐστιν ὁ λέγων σοι·	and who it is that is saying to you,
-	-	b			-	δός μοι πεῖν, σὺ ἂν ᾔτησας αὐτὸν	'Give me a drink,' you would have asked him,
13	-	x			-	καὶ ἔδωκεν ἄν σοι ὕδωρ ζῶν.	and he would have given you living water."
11	a	14	b'		-	Λέγει αὐτῷ [ἡ γυνή]· κύριε,	The woman said to him, "Sir,
-	-	a	-		-	οὔτε ἄντλημα ἔχεις	you have no bucket
-	-	a'	-	15	16	καὶ τὸ φρέαρ ἐστὶν βαθύ·	and the well is deep.
-	-	-	-	a	a	πόθεν οὖν ἔχεις τὸ ὕδωρ τὸ ζῶν;	Where do you get this living water?
12	b	a'	b'	x	a'	μὴ σὺ μείζων εἶ τοῦ πατρὸς ἡμῶν Ἰακώβ,	Are you greater than our father Jacob,
-	-	-	a'	a'	-	ὃς ἔδωκεν ἡμῖν τὸ φρέαρ καὶ αὐτὸς ἐξ αὐτοῦ ἔπιεν καὶ οἱ υἱοὶ αὐτοῦ καὶ τὰ θρέμματα αὐτοῦ;	who gave us the well and drank from it himself, and his sons, and his cattle?"
13	c		18			ἀπεκρίθη Ἰησοῦς καὶ εἶπεν αὐτῇ·	Jesus answered her,
-		a				πᾶς ὁ πίνων	"Everyone who drinks
-		b				ἐκ τοῦ ὕδατος τούτου	of this water
-		c				διψήσει	will be thirsty
-	17	d	19			πάλιν·	again,
14	c'	a	a'	a		ὃς δ' ἂν πίῃ	but whoever drinks.
-	-	b'	-			ἐκ τοῦ ὕδατος οὗ ἐγὼ δώσω αὐτῷ,	of the water that I will give him
-	-	b	c'	b		οὐ μὴ διψήσει	will never thirst
-	-	-	d'	-	20	εἰς τὸν αἰῶνα,	eternally,
b'	a'			a		ἀλλὰ τὸ ὕδωρ ὃ δώσω αὐτῷ	The water I will give him
-	b'			b		γενήσεται ἐν αὐτῷ πηγὴ ὕδατος ἁλλομένου εἰς ζωὴν αἰώνιον.	will become in him a well of water welling up to eternal life."
15	a'	a'			a'	Λέγει πρὸς αὐτὸν ἡ γυνή· κύριε,	The woman said to him, "Sir,
-	-		a'	a'	-	δός μοι τοῦτο τὸ ὕδωρ,	give me this water,
-	-		b'			ἵνα μὴ διψῶ	so that I may not thirst,
-	-		b'		-	μηδὲ διέρχωμαι ἐνθάδε ἀντλεῖν.	nor come here to draw."

I10. Chiastic, ab-x-b'a': In the center x, the issue of the living water Jesus is giving comes up. In b-b', she cannot understand (b') what he said, "you would have asked him" regarding the water (b). In a-a', there are two contrastive issues: (1) the gift of God (a) versus the gift of Jacob (a'); (2) who is greater: he who is saying to her (a) versus the father Jacob who gave the well (a')? **I11.** Chiastic, ab-b'a': Refer to a-a' of I10. **I12.** Dual, a-a': As Jesus promises her living water, if she asks him for it (a), she finally asks for that water (a').

I13. Chiastic, abc-a'b'c': The woman changes from a negative, reluctant response (a) to a positive, progressive response (a'). In b-b', two different wells are contrasted: the well of Jacob (b) versus the well of Jesus, up to eternal life (b'). In c-c', the water from the well of Jacob (c) is contrasted to that of Jesus (c').

I14. Dual, a-a': This dual expression shows her deep doubt about Jesus' word regarding living water: "you have no bucket" (a); "and the well is deep" (a'). **I15.** Chiastic, a-x-a': In a-a', the woman implies a contrast between Jesus who seems not to have any way to get water (a) and Jacob who gave them the well (a'). The essential issue of her statements lies in that which is greater, Jesus or Jacob (x). **I16.** Dual, a-a': Two questions or the doubts of the woman are presented together: "Where do you get . . . ?" (a) and "Are you greater . . ." (a').

I17. Parallel, ab-a'b': In a-a', the focus is on the water that Jesus gives, while b-b' emphasize the eternal outcomes after drinking it. **I18.** Parallel, abcd-a'b'c'd': Two, syntactically similar sentences are created for emphasis of contrast: πᾶς ὁ πίνων (Everyone who drinks, a) and ὃς δ' ἂν πίῃ (but whoever drinks, a'); ἐκ τοῦ ὕδατος τούτου (of this water, b) and ἐκ τοῦ ὕδατος οὗ ἐγὼ δώσω αὐτῷ (of the water that I will give him, b'); διψήσει (will be thirsty, c) and οὐ μὴ διψήσει (will never thirst, c'); πάλιν (d) and εἰς τὸν αἰῶνα (eternally, d'). All the pairs are intentionally contrasted.

I19. Parallel, ab-a'b': In a-a', Jesus says that he will give the water (a), so she asks him to give her this water (a'). In b-b', the focus is on no-thirstiness. **I20.** Parallel, ab-a'b': In a-a', Jesus speaks about the water that he will give (a), so she asks for it (a'). In b-b', the focus is on the well of water continuously welling up. In her statement, she shows her lack of understanding about it: "nor come here to draw" (b').

Their foci are as follows: Jesus who gives living water versus Jacob who gave the well there (I10–11); before she did not know Jesus and afterwards she knows him regarding the living water (I12); living water versus water from the well regarding who Jesus is (I13); two reasons for being unable to get water (I14); who is greater, Jesus or Jacob? (I15–16); the quality of the living water (I17); living water versus water from the well (I18); thirsty versus not-thirsty (II19); misunderstanding of welling up to eternal life (I20).

C. Woman and Man (4:16–18)

Verses 16–18 have four parallels: three chiasms (I21–22 and 24) and one parallelism (I23), among which I21 is the main pillar supported by I22–24.

V	21			Phrases	Translation
16	a	22		λέγει αὐτῇ·	He said to her,
-	-	a		ὕπαγε	"Go,
-	-	x		φώνησον τὸν ἄνδρα σου	call your husband,
-	-	a'	23	καὶ ἐλθὲ ἐνθάδε.	and come here."
17	b		a	ἀπεκρίθη ἡ γυνὴ καὶ εἶπεν αὐτῷ·	The woman answered him,
-	-		b	οὐκ ἔχω ἄνδρα.	"I have no husband."
-	b'	24	a'	λέγει αὐτῇ ὁ Ἰησοῦς·	Jesus said to her,
-	-	a	-	καλῶς εἶπας	"You have well said,
-	-	b	b'	ὅτι ἄνδρα οὐκ ἔχω·	'I have no husband,'
18	a'	x		πέντε γὰρ ἄνδρας ἔσχες	for you have had five husbands,
-	-	b'		καὶ νῦν ὃν ἔχεις οὐκ ἔστιν σου ἀνήρ·	and he whom you now have is not your husband.
-	-	a'		τοῦτο ἀληθὲς εἴρηκας.	This you have said truly."

I21. Chiastic, ab-b'a': In b-b', the sentence "I have no husband" is repeated: once by her and once by Jesus. The reason that Jesus said to her to call her husband in a is disclosed in a' by his words. **I22**. Chiastic, a-x-a': "Go" (a) and "come here" (a') seem to be in a pair, centering on x, "call your husband." **I23**. Parallel, ab-a'b': In a-a', the woman answered (a) and Jesus speaks back to her (a'). In b-b', "I have no husband" are duplicated. **I24**. Chiastic, ab-x-b'a': Both in a-a', Jesus compliments her: "You have well said" (a); "This you have said truly" (a'). In b, the woman says that she has no husband, but, in b', Jesus discloses her current status of marriage. In the center x, the five men in her past are divulged.

In I21, the intention of Jesus in letting her call her husband is disclosed. I22 simply focus on calling her husband by using similar verbs: "go"-"come." In I24, no husband and five husbands are compared.

C'. Worship and the Racial Issue (4:19–24)

In vv. 19–24, there are eight parallels: six parallelisms (I25–29, and 31) and two chiasms (I30 and 32). I25, 29, and 32 are three complex, main parallels throughout this subunit, overlapped in v. 21 (I25 and 29) and again v. 23 (I29 and 32). As I26 belongs to I25 (b and b'), so I30 does I29 (b and b'). I27 supports the connection between I25 and I29.

I25. Parallel, ab-a'b': In a, the woman regards Jesus as a prophet and, in a', Jesus demands her to believe him. Both b and b' focus on the place of worship: this mountain or Jerusalem. She needs to move on from seeing him as a prophet (a) to believing in him as greater than a prophet (a'). It is said that the shift from the controversy about the place of worship (b) to focusing on the worship itself (b') is necessary for the worshiper of God in this new day.

V	25	26	27	28		Phrases	Translation
19	a					Λέγει αὐτῷ ἡ γυνή· κύριε, θεωρῶ ὅτι προφήτης εἶ σύ.	The woman said to him, "Sir, I perceive that you are a prophet.
20	b	a	a	a		οἱ πατέρες ἡμῶν	Our fathers
-	-	-	-	b		ἐν τῷ ὄρει τούτῳ	~ on this mountain,
-	-	-	-	c		προσεκύνησαν·	worshiped ~
-	-	b	b	a'		καὶ ὑμεῖς λέγετε	but your people say
-	-	-	-	b'		ὅτι ἐν Ἱεροσολύμοις	that in Jerusalem
-	-	-	-	c'		ἐστὶν ὁ τόπος ὅπου προσκυνεῖν δεῖ.	is the place where people must worship."
21	a			29		λέγει αὐτῇ ὁ Ἰησοῦς· πίστευέ μοι, γύναι,	Jesus said to her, "Woman, believe me,
	b		a	30		ὅτι ἔρχεται ὥρα	an hour is coming
-	a'		b	a		ὅτε οὔτε ἐν τῷ ὄρει τούτῳ	when neither on this mountain,
-	b'		-	-		οὔτε ἐν Ἱεροσολύμοις	nor in Jerusalem,
-			-	b	31	προσκυνήσετε τῷ πατρί.	will you worship the Father.
22		a'	c	a		ὑμεῖς	You
	-	-	-	b		προσκυνεῖτε	worship
	-	-	-	c		ὃ οὐκ οἴδατε·	what you do not know.
	-	b'	-	a'		ἡμεῖς	We
	-	-	-	b'		προσκυνοῦμεν	worship
	-	-	-	c'		ὃ οἴδαμεν,	what we know,
	-					ὅτι ἡ σωτηρία ἐκ τῶν Ἰουδαίων ἐστίν.	for salvation is from the Jews.
23		a'			32	ἀλλ' ἔρχεται ὥρα καὶ νῦν ἐστιν,	But an hour is coming, and now is,
		b'	b'	a		ὅτε οἱ ἀληθινοὶ προσκυνηταὶ προσκυνήσουσιν τῷ πατρὶ	when the true worshipers will worship the Father
		-	a'	-		ἐν πνεύματι καὶ ἀληθείᾳ·	in spirit and in truth,
		c'		b		καὶ γὰρ ὁ πατὴρ τοιούτους ζητεῖ τοὺς προσκυνοῦντας αὐτόν.	for the Father seeks such worshipers.
24				b'		πνεῦμα ὁ θεός,	God is spirit,
				a'		καὶ τοὺς προσκυνοῦντας αὐτὸν ἐν πνεύματι καὶ ἀληθείᾳ δεῖ προσκυνεῖν.	and his worshipers must worship in spirit and in truth."

I26. Parallel, ab-a'b': Samaritans prefer their mountain (a), but for Jews Jerusalem is the only worship place (b). But in Jesus saying, these places are both denied as places of worship (a' and b'). **I27.** Parallel, ab-a'b': Samaritans worship on this mountain (a). Thus, they worship what they do not know (a'). Jews worship in Jerusalem (b). It says that they worship what they know (b'). It is implied that Jews have worshiped as been indicated since ancient days (a'), while Samaritans have not followed in that way (b'). **I28.** Parallel, abc-a'b'c': Both in a-a', the contrastive subjects are presented in six syllables: οἱ πατέρες ἡμῶν (our fathers) vs. καὶ ὑμεῖς λέγετε (but your people say) and, in b-b', the mountain of Samaritans (Gerizim) is contrasted with Jerusalem. Both c-c' are related to the concept of worship. In this parallelism, the focus seems to be on the fathers of the Samaritans as the people who actually worshiped but the Jews are the ones who speak about the worship place.

I29. Parallel, abc-a'b'c': Both in a-a', the same expression is repeated: "an hour is coming," signaling the connection between a and a'; or between abc, the unit initiated by a, and a'b'c', one by a'. That "when you will worship the Father neither on this mountain, nor in Jerusalem" (b) means "when the true worshipers will worship the Father in spirit and in truth" (b'). Thus, b' complements the contents of b. Without b', b may not be understood fully. In c, there is still a racial discrimination between the Jews and the Samaritans, but in c' we admit that there will be no more difference of race in worshiping God, for the Father seeks only true worshipers regardless of their race or innate privilege.

I30. Chiastic, ab-b'a': In relation to I29, b is duplicated in b' regarding worshiping the Father, while the focus on the place of worship, neither this mountain nor Jerusalem (a) is moved onto the quality of worship, in spirit and in truth (a'). **I31**, Parallel, abc-a'b'c': In a-a', the subjects are contrasted: ὑμεῖς (you) and ἡμεῖς (we). In b-b', the same verb appears but with different persons: the second plural (προσκυνεῖτε, you worship) and the first plural (προσκυνοῦμεν, we worship). And, in c-c', another contrast is presented: ὃ οὐκ οἴδατε (what you do not know) and ὃ οἴδαμεν (what we know). **I32**. Chiastic, ab-b'a': Both in a and a', worshiping in spirit and in truth are doubly expressed for emphasis, while, in b-b', the reason why we have to worship like that is explained: the Father who is spirit (b') seeks such worshipers (b). The pair, b-b', is complementary.

In I25–26, two places of worship are focused on and also the issue of the identity of Jesus is. I27 contrasts the Jews and the Samaritans regarding their religions. In I28, the contrast between Gerizim and Jerusalem appears. In I29–30, regardless of race, religion, and place of worship, it is highlighted that it is the time for the true worshiper to worship God. I31 focuses on the contrast between the Jews who know about worship and the Samaritans who do not. I32 focuses on God seeking those people who worship him in spirit and in truth.

B'. Messiah (4:25–26)

In vv. 25–26, there are two parallels: one parallelism (I33) and one chiasm (I34), showing the cohesiveness of vv. 25–26.

V	33		Phrases	Translation
25	a	34	Λέγει αὐτῷ ἡ γυνή·	The woman said to him,
	b	a	οἶδα	"I know
-		b	ὅτι Μεσσίας ἔρχεται ὁ λεγόμενος χριστός·	that Messiah is coming (he who is called Christ).
-		b'	ὅταν ἔλθῃ ἐκεῖνος,	When he comes,
-		a'	ἀναγγελεῖ ἡμῖν ἅπαντα.	he will declare everything to us."
26	a'		λέγει αὐτῇ ὁ Ἰησοῦς·	Jesus said to her,
	b'		ἐγώ εἰμι, ὁ λαλῶν σοι.	"I who speak to you am he."

I33. Parallel, ab-a'b': The woman said to him (a) and then Jesus said to her (a'), while b-b' are concentrated on the issue of Messiah. I34. Chiastic, ab-b'a': In b-b', the similar contents are duplicated: "that Messiah is coming" (b) and "when he comes" (b'). In a-a', the knowledge concerned is in relation to the coming of the Messiah: "I know" (a) and "he will declare everything to us" (a'). It is implied that all the truth will be declared and they will come to know all about this when Messiah comes. I33 does not focus on Jesus but a Messiah whom she expects to come, while I34, the part of I33 (b), simply focuses on the fact that she knows that Messiah is coming.

A'. Closing of the Dialogue (4:27)

Verse 27 seems to contain two parallels: one parallelism (I33) and a dual (I34). But they are somehow obscure in themselves.

V	35		Phrases	Translation
27	a		Καὶ ἐπὶ τούτῳ ἦλθαν οἱ μαθηταὶ αὐτοῦ καὶ ἐθαύμαζον	Just then his disciples came, and they marveled
	b		ὅτι μετὰ γυναικὸς ἐλάλει·	that he was talking with a woman,
	a'	36	οὐδεὶς μέντοι εἶπεν·	but no one said,
	b'	a	τί ζητεῖς	"What do you seek?"
-		a'	ἢ τί λαλεῖς μετ' αὐτῆς;	or, "Why do you speak with her?"

I35. Parallel, ab-a'b': While both a and a' deal with the actions of his disciples: coming-marvelling (a) and not-saying (a'), b and b' are related to the conversation between Jesus the woman. I36. Dual, a-a': There are two questions by his disciples in themselves, actually of similar meaning: "What do you seek?" (a) and "Why do you speak with her?" (a'). In I35, his disciples marveled but did not comment on Jesus' conversation with the woman. I36 duplicates the questions regarding the reason for the conversation.

IB2. Dialogue between Jesus and His Disciples and the Belief of the Samaritans (4:28–42)

Chiastic Structure, I37 (AB-B'A')

1. There are at least three scenes in vv. 28–42. The first scene is vv. 28–30, where the woman as a new believer went into the town and testified to Jesus publicly.

2. In the middle of the unit there is a dialogue between Jesus and his disciples regarding two issues: food to eat (31–35) and sowing-reaping (36–38). Thus, we may divide this middle scene into two: vv. 31–35 and 36–38.

3. The last scene is vv. 39–42 where, as a result of the woman's evangelism, Samaritans are coming to him, finally believing in him for themselves. This scene is, of course, in a pair with the first scene (28–30).

4. Thus, we can see the chiastic structure: A (28–30) – B (31–35) – B' (36–38) –A' (39–42).

A.	Evangelism of the woman (28-30)
B.	Food of Jesus (31-34)
B'.	Harvest (35-38)
A'.	Belief of the Samaritans (39-42)

A. Evangelism by the Woman (4:28–30)

In vv. 28–30, there are two parallels: one chiasm (I38) and one dual (I39). I38 overarches three verses and I39 is a part of I38 (a).

V	38	39	Phrases	Translation
28	a	a	ἀφῆκεν οὖν τὴν ὑδρίαν αὐτῆς ἡ γυνὴ	So the woman left her water jar,
	-	a'	καὶ ἀπῆλθεν εἰς τὴν πόλιν καὶ λέγει τοῖς ἀνθρώποις·	and went away into the town, and said to the people,
29	b		δεῦτε ἴδετε ἄνθρωπον ὃς εἶπέν μοι πάντα ὅσα ἐποίησα,	"Come, see a man who told me everything I ever did.
	b'		μήτι οὗτός ἐστιν ὁ χριστός;	Is this man the Christ?"
30	a'		ἐξῆλθον ἐκ τῆς πόλεως καὶ ἤρχοντο πρὸς αὐτόν.	They went out of the town and were coming to him.

I38. Chiastic, ab-b'a': In a, the woman went away (from the scene with Jesus) into the town to her people, while, in a', they went out of the town, coming to Jesus. Both b and b' are her dual testimony regarding the identity of Jesus. I39. Dual, a-a': Leaving her jar (a) and going into the town (a') are the dual actions of the woman. I38 compares her act with their act, focusing on her testimony to Christ, while I39 deals with her two acts.

B. Food of Jesus (4:31–34)

In vv. 31–34, there are in all three parallelisms (I40–42). I40 comprises vv. 31–34, while I41 shows the relation of b-b' of I40, and I42 is a part of I41 (b').

V	40			Phrases	Translation
31	a			Ἐν τῷ μεταξὺ ἠρώτων αὐτὸν οἱ μαθηταὶ λέγοντες· ῥαββί, φάγε.	Meanwhile the disciples were requesting him, saying, "Rabbi, eat."
32	b	41		ὁ δὲ εἶπεν αὐτοῖς·	But he said to them,
-		a		ἐγὼ βρῶσιν ἔχω φαγεῖν	"I have food to eat
-		b		ἣν ὑμεῖς οὐκ οἴδατε.	that you do not know about."
33	a'			ἔλεγον οὖν οἱ μαθηταὶ πρὸς ἀλλήλους· μή τις ἤνεγκεν αὐτῷ φαγεῖν;	So the disciples said to one another, "Has anyone brought him food?"
34	b'			λέγει αὐτοῖς ὁ Ἰησοῦς·	Jesus said to them,
-		a'	42	ἐμὸν βρῶμά ἐστιν	"My food is
-		b'	a	ἵνα ποιήσω	to do
-		-	b	τὸ θέλημα τοῦ πέμψαντός με	the will of him who sent me
-		-	a'	καὶ τελειώσω	and to finish
-		-	b'	αὐτοῦ τὸ ἔργον.	his work.

I40. Parallel, ab-a'b': Both a and a' introduce the sayings of his disciples regarding food to eat: spoken to Jesus (a) and spoken to one another (a'). While, in b-b', the sayings of Jesus are presented, explaining what his food is all about: food that you do not know (a); his food is to do the will of the sender and to finish the Father's work (a'). **I41.** Parallel, ab-a'b': Both a and a' are related in terms of his food to eat. The reason that the disciples do not know about the food of Jesus is disclosed in b', for this food is not physical. **I42.** Parallel, ab-a'b': For emphatic purposes, this parallel unit is designed: ἵνα ποιήσω (to do, a) and καὶ τελειώσω (and to finish, a'); τὸ θέλημα τοῦ πέμψαντός με (the will of him who sent me, b) and αὐτοῦ τὸ ἔργον (his work, b'). As a whole, I40 focuses on the food of Jesus, while I41 discloses what kind of food it is. I42 emphasizes the act of Jesus.

B'. Harvest (4:35–38)

In vv. 35–38, there are nine parallels: five parallelisms (I44–45, 47, 49, and 51) and four chiasms (I43, 46, 48, and 50). Among these, I43 and 45 are the main parallels holding the overall subunit. I44 belongs to a part of I43 (a-a'). I46 and 48 are parts of I45 (a), I49 and I51 belong to b and b' of I45, respectively. I50 shows the connection between a' and b' of I45 as I47 does between a and b of I45.

The Samaritans and a Royal Official

I43. Chiastic, ab-b'a': In a-a', the harvest issue is repeated: "... There are yet four months, then comes the harvest?" (a) and "... they are already white for harvest" (a'), while b-b' focus on an attitude of awareness of the time: lifting up of eyes (b); looking at the fields (b'). **I44. Parallel, ab-a'b'**: Similarly, syntactical arrangements are made: ὅτι ἔτι τετράμηνός ἐστιν ([that] there are yet four months, a) and ὅτι λευκαί εἰσιν (that they are ~ white, a'); καὶ ὁ θερισμὸς ἔρχεται; (then comes the harvest?, b) and πρὸς θερισμόν ἤδη (already ~ for harvest, b'). The pair, b and b', is duplicated, but, in a-a', a contrast is made.

V	43				Phrases	Translation
35	a	44			οὐχ ὑμεῖς λέγετε	Do you not say,
	-	a			ὅτι ἔτι τετράμηνός ἐστιν	'There are yet four months,
	-	b			καὶ ὁ θερισμὸς ἔρχεται;	then comes the harvest?'
	b				ἰδοὺ λέγω ὑμῖν, ἐπάρατε τοὺς ὀφθαλμοὺς ὑμῶν	Look, I say to you, lift up your eyes,
	b'				καὶ θεάσασθε τὰς χώρας	and look at the fields,
	a'	a'			ὅτι λευκαί εἰσιν	that they are ~ white
	-	b'	45		πρὸς θερισμόν ἤδη.	~ already ~ for harvest.
36			a	46	ὁ θερίζων	He who reaps
			-	a	μισθὸν	~ wages,
			-	b	λαμβάνει	receives ~
			-	b'	καὶ συνάγει	and gathers
			-	a'	καρπὸν	fruit
	47	48	-		εἰς ζωὴν αἰώνιον,	for eternal life,
	a	a	-		ἵνα ὁ σπείρων	so that the sower
		x	-		ὁμοῦ χαίρῃ	~ may rejoice together.
	b	a'	-		καὶ ὁ θερίζων.	~ and the reaper ~
37			b	49	ἐν γὰρ τούτῳ ὁ λόγος ἐστὶν ἀληθινός	For thus the saying is true,
			-	a	ὅτι ἄλλος ἐστὶν	'One
	a'		-	b	ὁ σπείρων	the sower,
			-	a'	καὶ ἄλλος	and another *is*
	b'		-	b'	50 ὁ θερίζων.	the reaper.'
38		a'	a		ἐγὼ ἀπέστειλα ὑμᾶς θερίζειν	I sent you to reap
		-	b	51	ὃ οὐχ ὑμεῖς κεκοπιάκατε·	what you have not worked for.
		b'	b'	a	ἄλλοι	Others
		-	-	b	κεκοπιάκασιν	have done the hard work,
		-	a'	a'	καὶ ὑμεῖς	and you
		-	-	b'	εἰς τὸν κόπον αὐτῶν εἰσεληλύθατε.	have entered into their labor."

I45. Parallel, ab-a'b': All the four units (a, b, b', and a') consist of two things: sowing and reaping. However, we may categorize them into two groups: (1) a-a', focusing on harvesting itself such as gathering fruit and then sharing the joy (a), sending "you" to reap (a'); (2) b-b', focusing mainly on the two roles of sowing and reaping such as

"One is the sower and another is the reaper" (b), "others, who have done the hard work, and you, who have entered into their labor" (b').

146. Chiastic, ab-b'a': A sort of rhyming chiasm is presented: μισθὸν (wages, a, 2 syllables) and καρπὸν (fruit, a', 2 syllables); λαμβάνει (receives, b, 3 syllables) and καὶ συνάγει (and gathers, b', 3 syllables excluding καί). **147.** Parallel, ab-a'b': In a-a', sowing or sower appears, while, in b-b', reaping or reaper comes up. **148.** Chiastic, a-x-a': In a-a', the sower (a) is contrasted to the reaper (a'), while, in the center x, rejoicing together is highlighted. **149.** Parallel, ab-a'b': Two clauses are compared to one another, syntactically and semantically: ὅτι ἄλλος ἐστὶν ([that] one is, a) and καὶ ἄλλος (another, a'); ὁ σπείρων (the sower, b) and ὁ θερίζων (the reaper, b').

150. Chiastic, ab-b'a': Both b-b' focus on the fact that others, not but "you," have done the hard work, probably sowing, while a-a' focus on the act of "you" in relation to harvest: "I sent you to reap" (a); "and you have entered into their labor," definitely for harvest (a'). **151.** Parallel, ab-a'b': This is also a parallel arrangement, comparing others with "you": ἄλλοι (Others, a) and καὶ ὑμεῖς (and you, a'); κεκοπιάκασιν (have done the hard work, b) and εἰς τὸν κόπον αὐτῶν εἰσεληλύθατε (have entered into their labor, b').

Their foci are as follows: the immediacy of harvest (I43–44); the sower and the reaper (I45, 47, 49); two acts of the reaper (I46); rejoicing of the sower-reaper (I48); "you" are the reapers who have entered into their labor (I50–51).

A'. Belief of the Samaritans (4:39–42)

In vv. 39–42, there are six parallels: two chiasms (I52 and 54), two parallelisms (I53 and 57), and two duals (I55–56). The main pillar is I52 which overarches vv. 39–42. I53 shows the connection between a (39) and a' (41–42) of I52, while I54–56 simply belong to vv. 41–42 (a' of I52). I57 is broader than I52, extending its connection to the following verse, v. 43.

152. Chiastic, ab-b'a': In a and a', we can see paired passages in terms of them coming to believe in him: first because of her testimony (a) and then because of the word of Jesus (a'). In relation to b-b', it may be gathered that they asked Jesus to stay there (b, cause), he stays there two days (b', result). **153.** Parallel, abc-a'b'c': In relation to I52, specifically a-a' of I52, the three divided parts are arranged in parallel: they believe in him (a) and many more believe (a'); "because of the woman's testimony" (b) and "because of his word" (b'); the contents of her testimony (c) and the contents of their belief (c').

The Samaritans and a Royal Official

V	52	53		57	Phrases	Translation
39	a	a		a	Ἐκ δὲ τῆς πόλεως ἐκείνης πολλοὶ ἐπίστευσαν εἰς αὐτὸν τῶν Σαμαριτῶν	Many Samaritans from that town believed in him
	-	b		-	διὰ τὸν λόγον τῆς γυναικὸς μαρτυρούσης	because of the woman's testimony,
	-	c		-	ὅτι εἶπέν μοι πάντα ἃ ἐποίησα.	"He told me everything I ever did."
40	b			b	ὡς οὖν ἦλθον πρὸς αὐτὸν οἱ Σαμαρῖται, ἠρώτων αὐτὸν μεῖναι παρ' αὐτοῖς·	So when the Samaritans came to him, they were asking him to stay with them,
	b'		54	-	καὶ ἔμεινεν ἐκεῖ δύο ἡμέρας.	and he stayed there two days.
41	a'	a'	a	a'	καὶ πολλῷ πλείους ἐπίστευσαν	And many more believed
	-	b'	b	-	διὰ τὸν λόγον αὐτοῦ,	because of his word.
42	-	c'		55	τῇ τε γυναικὶ ἔλεγον	They said to the woman,
	-	-	b'	a	ὅτι οὐκέτι διὰ τὴν σὴν λαλιὰν	"We no longer ~ because of your words,
	-	-	a'	-	πιστεύομεν,	~ believe ~
	-	-	56	a'	αὐτοὶ γὰρ	for ~ for ourselves,
	-	-	a	-	ἀκηκόαμεν	~ we have heard ~
	-	-	a'	-	καὶ οἴδαμεν	and we know
	-	-		-	ὅτι οὗτός ἐστιν ἀληθῶς ὁ σωτὴρ τοῦ κόσμου.	that this one really is the Savior of the world."

I54. Chiastic, ab-b'a': Both in a-a', the verb, to believe, is repeated: ἐπίστευσαν (they believed, a) and πιστεύομεν (we believe, a'), while, in b-b', διὰ τὸν λόγον αὐτοῦ (because of his word, b) and διὰ τὴν σὴν λαλιὰν (because of your words, b') are contrasted. I55. Dual, a-a': The two sentences are arranged dually for double emphasis: we believe not because of your words (a); we have heard, and we know the truth regarding him, the Savior of the world (a'). I56. Dual, a-a': Two verbs are doubly presented: "we have heard" (a) and "we know" (a'). I57. Parallel, ab-a'b': In a, many Samaritans believe in him because of the woman's testimony but, in a', they finally believe in him because of his word itself. In b, they ask Jesus to stay with them two days, and, in b', Jesus left there after two days.

In I52, the focus is on their belief in Jesus during his stay caused by two reasons: the woman's testimony and his own word. I53 highlights the process of how they came to believe in him. In I54, the woman's word is compared with Jesus' own word. In I55, indirect input by hearing the testimony is compared to direct input by experiencing the truth itself. I56 shows two kinds of experience. While, I57 additionally compares that he stayed there with that he departed there.

II. The Second Sign at Cana (4:43–54)

IIA (A') and IIB (B'), II1

As discussed earlier, the second sign at Cana episode consists of the introductory note (A', IIA, 43–45) and the main body of the story (B', IIB, 46–54), which shows its own chiastic structure (II4).

IIA. Introductory Scene (4:43–45)

Verses 43–45 contain two parallels: one parallelism (II2) and on chiasm (II3). II2 comprises vv. 43–45 and II3 belongs to v. 45 only.

V	2		50	Phrases	Translation
43	a		b'	Μετὰ δὲ τὰς δύο ἡμέρας ἐξῆλθεν ἐκεῖθεν εἰς τὴν Γαλιλαίαν·	After the two days he departed to Galilee.
44	b	3		αὐτὸς γὰρ Ἰησοῦς ἐμαρτύρησεν ὅτι προφήτης ἐν τῇ ἰδίᾳ πατρίδι τιμὴν οὐκ ἔχει.	For Jesus himself testified that a prophet has no honor in his own country.
45	a'	a		ὅτε οὖν ἦλθεν εἰς τὴν Γαλιλαίαν,	So when he came to Galilee,
	b'	b		ἐδέξαντο αὐτὸν οἱ Γαλιλαῖοι	the Galileans welcomed him,
	-	b'		πάντα ἑωρακότες ὅσα ἐποίησεν ἐν Ἱεροσολύμοις ἐν τῇ ἑορτῇ,	having seen all that he had done in Jerusalem at the feast,
	-	a'		καὶ αὐτοὶ γὰρ ἦλθον εἰς τὴν ἑορτήν.	for they themselves also went to the feast.

II2. Parallel, ab-a'b': In a, Jesus departed to Galilee and, in a', he came there. It is expected that Jesus is not welcome in his hometown (b), but they welcome him (b'), just as the Samaritans did. II3. Chiastic, ab-b'a': In a-a', the focus seems to be on the verb ἔρχομαι: he came (ἐξῆλθεν) to Galilee (a); they went (came, ἦλθον) to the feast (a'). In b, the Galileans welcome him. The reason for their welcome is suggested in b', namely that they have seen what Jesus had done in Jerusalem.

II2 repeats that Jesus came to Galilee and introduces the unexpected response of the Galileans. II3 focuses simply on the reason that they welcomed him.

IIB. The Second Sign at Cana (4:46–54)

CHIASTIC STRUCTURE, II4 (ABCD-D'C'B'A')

In A (46) and A' (54), two signs performed in Cana are indicated: one that Jesus made the water wine (A); the second that he performs (A'). A is an opening part, while A' is a closing one. The man who came to Jesus and begged him to heal his son (B, 47) finally believes in him with his household (B', 53b). In C (48–49), Jesus refers to signs and wonders, and, in C' (52–53a), the miracle of healing is emphasized. In D (50), Jesus tells him, "Go, your son will live." Believing in him, the man departs. In D' (51), when he goes down, as he was told, he hears that his son lives, as he had been told.

V	4	5					Phrases	Translation
46	A	a					Ἦλθεν οὖν πάλιν εἰς τὴν Κανὰ τῆς Γαλιλαίας, ὅπου ἐποίησεν τὸ ὕδωρ οἶνον.	He came therefore again to Cana in Galilee, where he had made the water wine.
-	-	a'	6	7			Καὶ ἦν τις βασιλικὸς οὗ ὁ υἱὸς ἠσθένει ἐν Καφαρναούμ.	And there was a certain royal official whose son was sick at Capernaum.
47	B	a	a		8	10	οὗτος ἀκούσας ὅτι Ἰησοῦς ἥκει ἐκ τῆς Ἰουδαίας εἰς τὴν Γαλιλαίαν	When this man heard that Jesus had come from Judea to Galilee,
-	-	-	a'	a	-	a	ἀπῆλθεν πρὸς αὐτὸν	he went to him
-	9	b	-	a'	-	-	καὶ ἠρώτα	and begged him
-	a	-	-	-	-	-	ἵνα καταβῇ	to come down
-	a'	-	-	-	-	-	καὶ ἰάσηται αὐτοῦ τὸν υἱόν,	and heal his son,
-	-	-	-	-	-	-	ἤμελλεν γὰρ ἀποθνῄσκειν.	for he was about to die.
48	C		c			b	εἶπεν οὖν ὁ Ἰησοῦς πρὸς αὐτόν· ἐὰν μὴ σημεῖα καὶ τέρατα ἴδητε, οὐ μὴ πιστεύσητε.	Jesus therefore said to him, "Unless you people see signs and wonders you will never believe."
49	-					a'	λέγει πρὸς αὐτὸν ὁ βασιλικός· κύριε,	The official said to him, "Sir,
-	-					-	κατάβηθι	come down
-	-				11	-	πρὶν ἀποθανεῖν τὸ παιδίον μου.	before my child dies."
50	D	-		a	12	b'	λέγει αὐτῷ ὁ Ἰησοῦς·	Jesus said to him,
-	-	-	-	a	-		πορεύου,	"Go,
-	-	-	-	b	-		ὁ υἱός σου ζῇ.	your son will live."
-	-	-	d	b	b'		Ἐπίστευσεν ὁ ἄνθρωπος τῷ λόγῳ ὃν εἶπεν αὐτῷ ὁ Ἰησοῦς	The man believed the word that Jesus spoke to him,
-	-	-	-	-	a'		καὶ ἐπορεύετο.	and he departed.

In vv. 46–50, there are nine parallels: three chiasms (II4, 11–12), two parallelisms (II6 and 10), and four duals (II5, 7–9). II4 is the backbone of the unit (46–54) overarching the whole passage into unity. There is no parallel that embraces vv. 46–50 alone or vv. 51–54 alone. It is interesting that I4 and I6 coexist here without any interruption to each other. Thus, we may say that they are complex in arrangement. II5, 7–9, and 12 support the cohesiveness of each constituent of II4 such as A, B, and D, respectively. II10 seems to exist to combine the first part of II4 (BCD) or II6 (abc). II11 is to connect D and D' of II4.

II5. Dual, a-a': It is doubly expressed. He came to Cana (a), and a certain royal official was there (a'). Jesus who performed the heavenly miracle of the wine in Cana is about to meet a man, a highly ranked figure in Galilee, who was there in Cana. **II6.** Parallel, abcd-a'b'c'd': vv. 47–53 may be regarded as another parallel arrangement. In a, this man heard that Jesus had come and went to him, and, in a', he went down and met his servants. In b, he begged Jesus to heal his son, and, in b', he inquired of his servants the hour his son got better. In c, Jesus referred to signs and wonders, and then said to him that his son would live. In c', his servants told him the exact hour of the healing, so he recognized that the miracle had happened when Jesus had spoken to him. In d, the man believed the word of Jesus, and, in d', he and his household believed in him.

Comparison of II4 and II6

II4	Scenes	II6
A	At Cana (46)	
B	The man goes to meet Jesus (47a).	a
	He begs him to heal his son (47b).	b
C	Jesus refers to signs and wonders, and the man requests to come (48-49).	c
D	Jesus says, "Go, your son will live" (50a)	
	His obedience to go (50b)	d
D'	After going, he meets his servants who told that his son was alive (51)	a'
C'	He inquired the hour of being healed (52)	b'
	At the hour when Jesus said his word (53a)	c'
B'	He and his household believe in Jesus (53b)	d'
A'	The second sign at Cana (54)	

II7. Dual, a-a': The man heard that Jesus had come (a) and so went to him to beg him for something (a'). **II8**. Dual, a-a': His two actions, going to him and begging him are presented in parallel. **II9**. Dual, a-a': His two requests, coming down and healing his son are dual. **II10**. Parallel, ab-a'b': He asks Jesus to come down to help his son twice in a and a'. The word of Jesus regarding signs and wonders is first presented (b) and then his word, "Go, your son will live," follows (b').

II11. Chiastic, ab-b'a': The word of Jesus that his son will live (a) is realized when he met his servants in a'. In b-b', he went down as he was told. **II12**. Chiastic, ab-b'a': As Jesus told him to go (a), he departed (a'). As Jesus told him, "you son will live" (b), he believed the word (b'). They are inversely arranged.

II4 comprises the whole unit (46–54) with multiple foci: his second sign; asking-believing; healing as a sign; obedience. Similarly, II6 contains: two meetings (with Jesus and with his servants); begging Jesus and inquiring of his servants; healing timing; belief of the man and belief of his household. Others are as follows: background information of the event (II5); hearing of his coming and going to ask (II7); going and begging (II8); coming-down and healing (II9); asking and sign (II10); healing of Jesus and obedience of the man (II11); his belief and obedience (II12).

The Samaritans and a Royal Official

V	4	6	11	Phrases	Translation
51	D'	a'	b'	ἤδη δὲ αὐτοῦ καταβαίνοντος	And as he was now going down,
	-	-	a'	οἱ δοῦλοι αὐτοῦ ὑπήντησαν αὐτῷ λέγοντες ὅτι ὁ παῖς αὐτοῦ ζῇ.	his servants met him and told him that this son was alive.
52	C'	13	b'	ἐπύθετο οὖν	So he inquired
	-	a	-	τὴν ὥραν παρ' αὐτῶν	of them the hour
	-	b	-	ἐν ᾗ κομψότερον ἔσχεν·	when he got better,
	-		c'	εἶπαν οὖν αὐτῷ	they said to him,
	-	a'	-	ὅτι ἐχθὲς ὥραν ἑβδόμην	"Yesterday at the seventh hour
	-	b'	-	ἀφῆκεν αὐτὸν ὁ πυρετός.	the fever left him.
53	-		-	ἔγνω οὖν ὁ πατὴρ	Then the father knew
	-	a''	-	ὅτι [ἐν] ἐκείνῃ τῇ ὥρᾳ ἐν ᾗ εἶπεν αὐτῷ ὁ Ἰησοῦς·	that this was the hour when Jesus had said to him,
	-	b''	-	ὁ υἱός σου ζῇ,	"Your son will live."
	B'		d'	καὶ ἐπίστευσεν αὐτὸς καὶ ἡ οἰκία αὐτοῦ ὅλη.	And he himself believed, and his whole household.
54	A'			Τοῦτο [δὲ] πάλιν δεύτερον σημεῖον ἐποίησεν ὁ Ἰησοῦς ἐλθὼν ἐκ τῆς Ἰουδαίας εἰς τὴν Γαλιλαίαν.	This was the second sign that Jesus performed, having come from Judea to Galilee.

In vv. 51–54, there seems to be only one parallel, a triple (II13), which only demonstrates the cohesiveness of vv. 52–53, particularly C' of II4. This phenomenon is that we can scarcely find the parallels within the verses besides II4, 6, and 11 that accentuate the connectivity with the previous verses which may show that these verses exist only as a counterpart of the previous verses (46–50).

II13. Triple: ab-a'b'-a''b'': All the a-a'-a'' are related to each other in terms of "the hour," while, all the b-b'-b'' depict that his son got better. In this way, triple repetitions occur here. It demonstrates that this healing sign did not happen by chance.

Reading in Structure-Style

1. As discussed earlier (I5), there are four issues sequentially appearing in vv. 10–26: living water (10–15, B); husband (sex life, 16–18, C); worship and race (19–24, C'); Messiah (25–26, B'). Among these four, we need to pay attention to their interaction in pairs. The first and last issues, living water and Messiah, are interrelated in terms of who Jesus is including what he gives (living water); what he lets them know (as the Christ). The two issues in the middle refer to two contemporary, human issues such as sex life and race including worship. The woman-man issue is personal to her, while the racial issue is publicly shared by all the Samaritans at that time.

2. Considering the connection between v. 8 and v. 9c (c-c', I8), we may see a contradiction at that time that Jews did not associate with Samaritans, but they did have contact

with them to buy food in case of hunger as his disciples did. Jesus broke up this awkward situation by having a personal dialogue with a Samaritan woman.

3. In vv. 10–12 (see I10–11), two issues are in the forefront: the gift of God and who he is. The former is related to water from the well, while the latter is to Jacob in comparison with Jesus who declares himself as the one who gives her living water (10b, x of I10).

4. Verse 22 seems to declare a contrast between the knowledge of the Jews ("we") and the ignorance of the Samaritans ("you") regarding worship and salvation. However, if we consider its connections with v. 20 (I27) and vv. 21–23 (I29–30), we may realize that Jesus is simply referring to the contemporary, current status of the religions of two races, hardly supporting the side of the Jews. Rather, he mentions that the hour is coming (future), distinct from that time, demolishing their racial discrimination, regarding true worship.

5. Who is "he who reaps receives wages and gathers fruit"? (36) In I45, this verse is in a pair with v. 38a ("I sent you to reap what you have not worked for," a-a'), complementing the former verse in an additional explanation. In v. 38a, "I" indicating Jesus as the reaper who plays a role of harvester and also who sends his servants to participate in his reaping ministry. If Jesus says "you are the reaper(s)" in v. 38a, his disciples would be those who reap in v. 36. In this sense, the reaper in v. 36 is none but Jesus himself and the sower will be God the Father. And "others who have done the hard work" in v. 38b will be those who have sown and taken care of that seed after being sent from God.

6. In the chiastic structure of vv. 46–54 (II4), we can see the connection between v. 46 where Cana is referred to and v. 54 where his second sign is mentioned. Was this the second sign to happen at Cana? Or, did the sign happen secondly after his coming from Judea and Samaria to Galilee in John 4? Or, did this sign happen secondly in his public ministry including at Cana?

It is difficult to conceive that this miracle happened secondly in his total ministry. First, even though we do not regard the miraculous restoration of the Samaritans as one of them, we can read of his other plural signs in 2:23 (αὐτοῦ τὰ σημεῖα ἃ ἐποίει, his signs which he did) before John 4. Second, v. 54 does not only describe the second sign as that which Jesus performed but also adds that it happened after he came from Judea to Galilee. Thus, it is certainly not that this sign is the second one of his public ministry, but that it is the second one at Cana.

Then, why is this second sign at Cana intentionally highlighted here, as we can read in vv. 46 and 54: "Cana in Galilee, where he had made the water wine" (46); "This was the second sign that Jesus performed . . ." (54).

We can presume that this Cana sign needs to be read in connection with the first Cana one in John 2. The two signs at Cana are in a pair as a whole, namely in the group of chs. 2–4. Both signs disclose the identity of Jesus who overpowers the limitation of human ability, represented by Judaism and Judean aristocracy. Additionally, both share one more thing: obedience to Jesus. As the servants obey the words of Jesus, the royal official does what Jesus tells him to do.

Issues in Structure-Style

1. The Structure of the Samaritan Episode

Bultmann divided the Samaritan episode into two scenes and one conclusion to be followed:[6] Scene 1, the dialogue with the Samaritan woman (4–26); Scene 2, the dialogue with the disciples (27–38); The conclusion, the conversion of the townspeople (39–42). According to him, scene 1 consists of two clusters: The living water (6–15; again into 7–10 and 11–15); True worship of the Father (16–26; again into 16–18 and 19–26).[7]

According to Bultmann, this episode falls into two clusters: Jesus' witness to himself (1–30) and the relation of the believer's witness to Jesus' self-witness (31–42).[8]

Moloney observed that the narrative in Sychar is described as linear in time:[9] As the disciples go to buy food (8), Jesus talks with a Samaritan woman. As the disciples come back she returns to the village (28), and her fellow villagers begin to come toward Jesus (30). While they are on their way Jesus speaks to the disciples (31–38). The Samaritans arrive, invite him to stay with them (40), and eventually come to faith in him. After his two days with them he departs to Galilee (43). And then, he categorizes vv. 1–42 into four scenes: vv. 1–15, Jesus and the Samaritan woman I (1–6 and 7–15); vv. 16–30, Jesus and the Samaritan woman II (16–19, 20–26, and 27–30); vv. 31–38, Jesus' comments (31–33, 34, and 35–38); vv. 39–42, Jesus and the Samaritan villagers (39, 40a, 40b, 41, and 42).[10]

First, it has been, as discussed earlier (I5), overlooked that there are four issues in the dialogue of Jesus with the Samaritan woman: Living water (10–15); Woman and man (16–18);[11] Worship and racial issue (19–24); Messiah (25–26). There is a chiastic

---

6. Bultmann, *Gospel of John*, 176–85; See also Sheeley, "Lift up Your Eyes," 82–85.

7. Bultmann, *Gospel of John*, 176–77; Compare the division of Beasley-Murray: 6–18, the living water from Christ, 19–26, the worship that the Father seeks. Beasley-Murray, *John*, 59.

8. Bultmann, *Gospel of John*, 176.

9. Moloney, *Gospel of John*, 113.

10. Ibid., 114–46.

11. In the perspective of speech-act theory, Botha pays proper attention to the abruptness and the sudden nature of the change of topic in v. 16 (the start of the husband issue). However, we may say that this abruptness of shift in topic also occurs in v. 19 (the start of the worship issue) and 25 (the start of the Messiah issue), whenever new topics are introduced. Botha, "John 4.16," 183–84.

relation in theme among them: AB-B'A', that is, the first and last are related to each other in terms of who Jesus is (the Giver of the eternal water and Messiah); the second and third are also related in terms of contemporary issues at that time (sex life and worship including race). At the same time, they reflect a phenomenon in size: AB-A'B, that is, the first and third are larger, while the second and last are smaller.

Second, if we set aside vv. 10–26, there remain vv. 5–9 which are supported by two smaller clusters I6 (5–7a, a chiasm) and I8 (7b–9; a parallelism). These verses describe how Jesus and the woman start their dialogue. If we regard them as the opening, which verse(s) can be the closing ones? Verse 27 or vv. 27–30 can be regarded as these verses. But vv. 28–30 are strongly connected to vv. 39–42 in content[12] and thus we need to focus on the function of v. 27. Verse 27 as the closing scene declares two things that are somehow related to vv. 5–9: where the disciples are back from: the moment of closing the dialogue. In this sense, vv. 5–9 and 27 are in a pair as an *inclusio* (A and A' of I5).

Third, if we can see that vv. 28–30 are regarded as introductory to vv. 28–38 (42), what is the function of vv. 39–42 which are deeply related to the former? Verses 39–42 cannot be regarded as the conclusion to the whole Samaritan episode (like Brown), apart from the inseparable relation to vv. 28–30. These verses, vv. 28–30 and 39–42, are an *inclusio* (A and A' of I37).[13]

Fourth, descriptions of the episode are done in a linear manner but its structure is not, for it is rather much more dynamic in construction. The structure of the Samaritan episode is dual, presenting each part of a chiastic structure.

2. The Relation between vv. 28–30 and 40

Bultmann insisted that the original conclusion is vv. 28–30 and 40, believing that vv. 39 and 40 are not compatible with each other and that v. 39 is impossible after v. 30, for it completely ignores the arrival of the Samaritans already described in v. 30.[14] But he argued that we cannot omit v. 30 in favor of v. 39, because it is demanded by v. 29 and also that v. 39 differs from the style of the evangelist, thereby v. 40 was the original continuation of v. 30.

However, Dodd regarded vv. 27–42 as a dialogue with a dramatic technique in a rudimentary form:[15] "The action takes place on two stages, a front stage and a back stage, as we might put it. The return of the disciples and the departure of the woman (27–8a) divide the *dramatis personae* into two groups. On the front stage Jesus con-

---

12. The possibility cannot be excluded that vv. 28–30 are used as a part of the closing, that is, belonging to vv. 27–30, and also playing a role in the opening of the following unit (28–42).

13. However, it is not like the chiastic structure of Coloe: A (1–6) B (7–15); C (16–18); D (19–26); C' (27–30); B' (31–38); A' (39–45). Coloe, *God Dwells with Us*, 87.

14. Bultmann, *Gospel of John*, 175.

15. Dodd, *Fourth Gospel*, 315.

verses with his disciples (31–38). Meanwhile (Ἐν τῷ μεταξύ) on the back stage the woman converses with her fellow-townsmen and induces them to accompany her to the place where she left Jesus (28b–30, 39). The two groups then converge and move together to the town, where Jesus makes a short stay (40). The scene is thus at an end, but the final sentence uttered by the Samaritans (41–42), like the concluding chorus of a Greek play, sums up the meaning of the whole."

First, as Bultmann argued, the seemingly reverse order in the behavior of the Samaritans between their coming to Jesus (20) and believing in him because of the woman's testimony (39) may cause confusion to the readers. This was the reason he placed v. 40 after v. 30 excluding v. 39.

But, second, it is said that John's way of writing, creating a parallel (or chiastic) system in structure, is certainly overlooked in the interpretation of Bultmann. Verses 28–30 and 39–42 become A and A' in I39 (as an *inclusio*).

Third, in particular, v. 39 belongs to the cluster vv. 39–42, which consists of a chiasm (I52, ab-b'a'), where vv. 39 (a) and 41–42 (a') are in a pair regarding their belief and confession on Jesus. In the middle (40), there is their invitation to Jesus to stay with them and thus he stayed. The function of vv. 39–42 is to close the second part of the Samaritan episode, re-highlighting their belief in Jesus and emphasizing their confession (or testimony) that Jesus is the Savior of the world.

Fourth, vv. 31–38 focus on the harvest of the people, such as the Samaritans, in the dialogue of Jesus with his disciples. In the first part of the Samaritan episode, the dialogue with the woman, the issues are theological (living water and Messiah), social (sex life and race), even liturgical (worship), while in the second one, the dialogue with the disciples, the issue is regarding the ministry of harvest, the work of God.

Fifth, therefore, probably agreeing with Dodd,[16] Talbert is right in seeing an ABA' pattern in vv. 28–42: A. The woman goes from the well and bears witness to the Samaritans: Can this be the Christ (28–30); B. Jesus instructs the disciples about mission (31–38); A'. The Samaritans come to the well and bear witness to the woman: This is indeed the Savior of the world (39–42).[17]

3. The Function of 4:43–45 and Its Relation with 2:23–25

Bultmann emphasized the similarity of 2:23–25 and 4:43–45, asserting that the latter needs to be regarded as the introduction to a new section (4:43—6:59) which consists of the two miracle stories and the discourses or dialogues which follow them: 6:1–59; 5:1–47 (alongside with 7:15–24 and 8:13–20).[18] Thus the feeding miracle (ch. 6) and the healing of the lame man (ch. 5) correspond to the episodes of Nicodemus and

---

16. Also see Beasley-Murray, *John*, 59.
17. Talbert, *Reading John*, 116.
18. Bultmann, *Gospel of John*, 111–12, 203.

the Samaritans. According to him, chs. 3 and 4 show the coming of the Revealer as the κρίσις who brings a new existence and a new form of worship, chs. 6 and 5 reflect the κρίσις of the natural desire for life (ch. 6) and as the κρίσις of religion (ch. 5). In this sense, to him, the significance of the Cana healing episode (46–54) was not clear enough, although he introduced Dodd who suggested the connection between the two stories: 4:46–54 and 5:1–18.[19]

Brown explained the relation between 2:23–25 and 4:43–45 more convincingly:[20] "4:44–45 and 2:23–25 have much in common. These two passages also have a similar function in the outline of John. After the description in 2:23–25 of those in Jerusalem who believed in Jesus because of his signs, one of these "believers," Nicodemus, came to Jesus with his inadequate understanding of Jesus' powers. Jesus had to explain to Nicodemus that he was really the one who had come from above to give eternal life. So also, after the description in 4:44–45 of the Galileans who welcomed Jesus because of his works, a royal official from Galilee comes to Jesus with an inadequate understanding of Jesus' power. Jesus will lead the man to a deeper understanding of his function as the giver of life."

First, the explanation of Brown regarding the relation between 2:23–25 and 4:43–45 is persuasive and acceptable, for it sees the similarity of their functions to the verses that follow them: the Nicodemus episode and the healing ministry at Cana. Additionally, both passages are similar not only in role as a link but also in style (dialogue) and also in contrast such as belief (or welcome) of the multitude (positivity) vs. thought (or testimony) of Jesus (negativity).[21]

But, second, it is difficult to accept the view of Bultmann who saw their function as an introduction to the sections after them: chs. 3–4 and 5–6 each. It is an overestimation of the function of 4:43–45 as well as that of 2:23–25.

Third, we have to say that, in relation to 2:23–25, the role of 4:43–45 is to be examined in terms of content, function, and structure, and also regarding differences as well as similarities.

Fourth, as discussed in ch. 2, 2:23–25 are more attached to the previous verses than to the following ones, for they belong to vv. 12–25 (II1, AB-B'A') in chiasm (see also the connection between vv. 22 and 23, II12, a-b1b2-a'-b'2b'1) and we can see the contrast in issue between the belief of the disciples based on Scripture and the words of Jesus vs. that of the people on the signs in 2:22 (including 17) and 23. Nevertheless, we may admit that these verses play a role of link between the previous chapter and the following one.[22]

---

19. Ibid., 203; Dodd, *Fourth Gospel*, 318. Beasley-Murray also emphasizes that 4:43—5:47 consist of two signs of healing miracles. Beasley-Murray, *John*, 70.

20. Brown, *Gospel according to John I-XII*, 188.

21. In this sense, v. 44 cannot be regarded as a parenthesis (*contra* Bultmann, *Gospel of John*, 204).

22. Beside these two passages, in chs. 2–4, there are similar links: 2:12; 4:1–4; 4:54.

Fifth, moreover, vv. 43–45 and 1–4 are alike in function,[23] as discussed earlier (Dual Mode in Structure), to the following sections, becoming A and A' in a pair in the whole structure (AB-A'B'). Verses 43–45 can be treated as the link that connects the healing ministry and the Samaritan episode as 2:23–25 do in between the temple episode and the Nicodemus one. However, it is observed that the former is closer to the following section (4:46–54), while the latter is closer to the previous one (2:12–22).

Sixth, chs. 3–4 differ from chs. 5–6 both in content and form. Chapters 3–4 are part of the Cana cycle (chs. 2–4), while chs. 5–6 belong to the group of chs. 5–10 (see the introduction on the structure in John). If we treat 2:23–25 as the introduction to chs. 3–4, the Cana cycle ("From Cana to Cana"[24]) would be ruined.[25]

Seventh, the two Cana episodes are similar not only in size but also in style, as Temple points out that the two Cana miracles are the only two signs in John that do not lead immediately into a discourse.[26] Thus, as Moloney suggested regarding vv. 46–54, "this section of the story has come full cycle."[27] See also the chiastic structure of vv. 46–54 (II4, ABCD-D'C'B'A'). In particular see the relation between vv. 46 (A) and 54 (A'), in terms of how the reference to Cana is repeated as a pair.

Eighth, thus, how Bultmann explained the relation between chs. 3–4 and 5–6 is not persuasive: "We find in chs. 3 and 4 a portrayal of the confrontation of the most diverse individuals with the revelation, and in chs. 6 and 5 a portrayal of the conflict of the revelation with the questions of natural life and religion."[28] It is unnatural to connect chs. 3–4 with chs. 5–6 in that way. The reason why he persisted to explain the relation of those chapters is caused by him putting his priority on the relation between 2:23–25 and 4:43–45 because he regarded their function as introductory passages. In short, the function of vv. 43–45 as a link between two episodes and also as a counterpart to vv. 1–4 are essential within the chapter rather than beyond it.

---

23. Brown observed a resemblance between vv. 3b and 43. Brown, *Gospel according to John I–XII*, 186.

24. Ibid., 195.

25. Bultmann and Beasley-Murray do not highlight this Cana cycle because they emphasize more the connection of 4:43–54 to the following chapter(s).

26. Temple, "Two Signs in the Fourth Gospel," 170; cited by Brown, *Gospel according to John I–XII*, 194.

27. Moloney, *Gospel of John*, 114.

28. Bultmann, *Gospel of John*, 112.

5 The First Sabbath Healing and the Discourse of Jesus

"The healing is a sign that the actions of Jesus must be understood as the actions of God himself. As Jesus says in verse 19 'The son can do nothing *by himself.*' He heals a man who believed that God's power was an impersonal force present in the pool. By doing so on the Sabbath he confronts those who assume that Jesus wields God's power independent of God's will. In these circumstances, the healing serves as a sign of the central point of the discourse: that Jesus does only what the Father does."[1]

DUAL MODE IN STRUCTURE

BROADLY SPEAKING, JOHN 5 can be divided into two sections: an event (1–18) and the discourses (19–47) that follow. The healing ministry of Jesus (1–18) is made up of a cohesive entity, while the discourse section consists of two units: the twofold authority of the Son (19–30); the testimony to the Son (31–47). Of the two, the last one can be divided again into two subunits: the testimony from the Father (31–37a) and their unbelief of the testimony (37b–47).

Thus, we may have an outline:

I.	The healing ministry of Jesus (5:1-18)			A
II.	Its related discourses (5:19-47)			
	IIA.	Twofold authority of the Son (5:19-30)		B
	IIB.	The testimony to the Son (5:31-47)		
		IIB1.	The Father's testimony (5:31-37a)	A'
		IIB2.	Their unbelief on the testimony (5:37b-47)	B'

---

1. Bryan, "Power in the Pool," 21, italics in original.

Another Possibility

It is possible to divide John 5 into four units: the healing ministry (1–18), the first discourse, twofold authority of the Son (19–30), the second one, the Father's testimony (31–37a), and the last one, their unbelief concerning the testimony (37b–47).

In this case, we may think of a parallel structure: A (the healing ministry, 1–18); B (the Son as Life-Giver and Judge, 19–30); A' (the testimony of the Father through the works of the Son, 31–37a); B' (belief and unbelief in the Son, 37b–47). In A-A', Jesus' healing ministry as his work is the focus (particularly see 36), while, in B-B', the belief and unbelief issue is shared (cf. 23–34, 38, 40, and 46–47).

Preferred Dual Structure

The first view of structure is to see John 5 as in a dual mode, while the second is to regard the text as a parallel structure. These two views are both based on the fact that all the four clusters (1–18, 19–30, 31–37a, and 37b–47) are cohesive entities more or less independent of each other: ABC-C'B'A' (1–18, I1); A-X-A' (19–30, II1); A-X-A' (31–37a, II31); A-X-A' (37b–47, II42). Thus, it is difficult to determine which of the two (dual or parallel) was originally designed. It seems to be just a matter of the organization of these four units.

Here, the first one is preferred:

First, the connection between vv. 31–37a and 37b–47 seems to be stronger than that between vv. 19–30 and 31–37a. There is surely no link between v. 30 and v. 31 in parallel, while we may see a parallel (II62) between v. 37a and vv. 37b–38.

Second, the testimony issue (31–37a) seems to need the belief-unbelief issue as its supplementary unit, thereby completing the testimony-belief motif. We can already see this motif in vv. 19–30 where Jesus testifies to himself and demands their true belief in him.

Third, if we consider the pattern, first an event (or dialogue of issue) and then its related discourse (with dialogue), as in most cases in John 5–10, the dual structure seems to be suitable here.

Finally, in the matter of size, when we put together vv. 31–37a and 37b–47, the three groups of verses (1–18, 19–30, and 31–47) are almost similar in amount.

I. The Healing Ministry of Jesus (5:1–18)

Chiastic Structure, I1 (ABC-C'B'A')

1. The introductory scene appears in vv. 1–3. There was Bethesda where Jesus and many others are.

2. The first meeting between Jesus and the man who has been sick for thirty eight years is written in vv. 5–8. In comparison with this, there is the second meeting between them, Jesus and the man who is cured, in vv. 13–15. In the first meeting, Jesus cures him, and in the second, he tries to heal his soul, but he is betrayed by being reported to the Jews. These two scenes are in parallel.

3. In the middle of the passage (9–12), we can see that there is a Sabbath controversy among the people. The healing ministry of Jesus on the Sabbath arouses the hostility of the Jews against him. It is observed that vv. 9–12 consist of two parallels: vv. 9–10 (I9) and 11–12 (I10). Thus, we may divide them into two and name them: C (9–10) and C' (11–12).

4. The closing scene (16–18) is that Jesus and the Jews who are seeking to kill him come to the fore. In the first scene (1–3), there is Jesus and many others who are sick and expect to be helped by Jesus, while, in the last one, there is Jesus and the Jews who persecute him because of his healing. We may name them: A (1–3) and A' (16–18).

5. In this way, the second scene (5–8) and the fifth one (13–15) are named: B and B'. Therefore, the structure is chiastic: ABC-C'B'A'.[2]

6. In this structure, Jesus who heals someone in need is in contrast with the Jews who criticize him (A-A'); Jesus who always helps and the man who is helped but betrays him for fear of the Jews are in contrast (B-B'); also a comparison exists between the man who is healed and the Jews who find fault with his healing ministry on the Sabbath (C-C').

A.	Introductory scene: Jesus and a multitude in sickness (1-3)		
	B.	The first meeting of Jesus with the man before healing (5-8)	
		C.	Sabbath controversy 1: the Jews and the man (9-10)
		C'.	Sabbath controversy 2: the Jews and the man (11-12)
	B'.	The second meeting of Jesus with the man after healing (13-15)	
A'.	Closing scene: Jesus and the Jews (16-18)		

ABC. The First Part of the Healing Ministry of Jesus (5:1–10)

In vv. 1–10, there are nine parallels: three chiasms (I6–7, and 9), three parallelisms (I2–3, 8), and two duals (I4–5). I2–3, and 9 are the main pillars supporting A, B, and C (of I1), respectively. They make it possible to be grouped according to their cohesion. I4–5 belong to b of I3, as I6–7 do to a' of I3. But I8 is to connect v. 8 to v. 9.

---

2. Compare the chiastic structure of Ellis: A (1–10); B (11–13); C (14); B' (15); A' (16–18). Ellis, *Genius of John*, 86–87.

The First Sabbath Healing and the Discourse of Jesus

V	1	2				Phrases	Translation
1	A	a				Μετὰ ταῦτα ἦν ἑορτὴ τῶν Ἰουδαίων	After these things there was a feast of the Jews,
-	-	b				καὶ ἀνέβη Ἰησοῦς εἰς Ἱεροσόλυμα.	and Jesus went up to Jerusalem.
2	-	a'				Ἔστιν δὲ ἐν τοῖς Ἱεροσολύμοις ἐπὶ τῇ προβατικῇ κολυμβήθρα ἡ ἐπιλεγομένη Ἑβραϊστὶ Βηθζαθὰ πέντε στοὰς ἔχουσα.	Now there is in Jerusalem by the Sheep Gate a pool, in Hebrew called Bethesda, which has five porticoes.
3	-	b'				ἐν ταύταις κατέκειτο πλῆθος τῶν ἀσθενούντων, τυφλῶν, χωλῶν, ξηρῶν.	In these lay a multitude of those who were sick, blind, lame, and paralyzed.
			3				
5	B	a		4	5	ἦν δέ τις ἄνθρωπος ἐκεῖ τριάκοντα [καὶ] ὀκτὼ ἔτη ἔχων ἐν τῇ ἀσθενείᾳ αὐτοῦ·	One man was there, who had been thirty-eight years in his sickness.
6	-	b	a	a		τοῦτον ἰδὼν ὁ Ἰησοῦς κατακείμενον	When Jesus saw him lying there,
-	-	-	a'	-		καὶ γνοὺς ὅτι πολὺν ἤδη χρόνον ἔχει,	and knew that he had already been a long time *in this condition*,
-	-	-		a'		λέγει αὐτῷ· θέλεις ὑγιὴς γενέσθαι;	he said to him, "Do you want to get well?"
7	-	-	a'	6		ἀπεκρίθη αὐτῷ ὁ ἀσθενῶν· κύριε,	The sick man answered him, "Sir,
-	-	-	-	a		ἄνθρωπον οὐκ ἔχω	I have no man
-	-	-	-	x	7	ἵνα ὅταν ταραχθῇ τὸ ὕδωρ βάλῃ με εἰς τὴν κολυμβήθραν·	to put me into the pool when the water is stirred.
-	-	-	a'	a		ἐν ᾧ δὲ ἔρχομαι	While ~ am coming,
-	-	-	-	b		ἐγώ,	~ I ~
-	-	-	-	b'		ἄλλος	another
-	-	-	-	a'		πρὸ ἐμοῦ καταβαίνει.	goes down ahead of me."
8	-	b'			8	λέγει αὐτῷ ὁ Ἰησοῦς·	Jesus said to him,
-	-	-			a	ἔγειρε	"Rise,
-	-	-			b	ἆρον τὸν κράβαττόν σου	pick up your mat
-	-	-		9	c	καὶ περιπάτει.	and walk."
9	C	a			a'	καὶ εὐθέως ἐγένετο ὑγιὴς ὁ ἄνθρωπος	And at once the man became well,
-	-	-			b'	καὶ ἦρεν τὸν κράβαττον αὐτοῦ	and he picked up his mat
-	-	-			c'	καὶ περιεπάτει.	and walked.
-	-	b				Ἦν δὲ σάββατον ἐν ἐκείνῃ τῇ ἡμέρᾳ.	Now that day was the Sabbath.
10	-	b'				ἔλεγον οὖν οἱ Ἰουδαῖοι τῷ τεθεραπευμένῳ·	So the Jews said to the man who was cured,
-	-	-				σάββατόν ἐστιν,	"It is the Sabbath,
-	-	a'				καὶ οὐκ ἔξεστίν σοι ἆραι τὸν κράβαττόν σου.	and it is not permitted for you to carry your mat."

I2. Parallel, ab-a'b': In a, the time, a feast, is referred, while, in a', the place, Bethesda, is mentioned. In b-b', Jesus went up to Jerusalem (b), and a multitude of sick persons were there (b').

I3. Parallel, ab-a'b': In a and a', the man who is sick is introduced (a) and his wish or complaint is presented (a'). Both a-a' reflect the status of his illness. In b-b', Jesus first approaches him (b) and then heals him (b'). I4. Dual, a-a': Jesus saw him (a) and

141

knew his condition (a'). Two connected clauses regarding Jesus' senses are arranged together. I5. Dual, a-a': His seeing and knowing him (a) is related to his action to heal him (a').

I6. Chiastic, a-x-a': In the center x, the wish of the sick man is presented: putting him in the pool when the water is stirred. While, in a-a', he complains about his situation: "I have no man" (a); "while I am coming" (a'). **I7**. Chiastic, ab-b'a': For the contrast, a rhyming chiasm is presented in this sentence: ἐν ᾧ δὲ ἔρχομαι (While ~ am coming, a, 6 syllables) and πρὸ ἐμοῦ καταβαίνει (goes down ahead of me, a', 7 syllables); ἐγώ (I, b, 2 syllables) and ἄλλος (another, b', 2 syllables).

I8. Parallel, abc-a'b'c': As Jesus commands him, he is healed and follows his order: "Rise" (a) and the man became well (a'); "pick up your mat" (b) and "he picked up his mat" (b'); "walk" (c) and "walked" (c'). **I9**. Chiastic, ab-b'a': Both in b-b', the Sabbath is repeatedly focused, while, both in a-a', the action of carrying the mat appears in the foreground.

In I2, we can see the time, the place, and the characters: Jesus and sick persons. I3 contrasts Jesus who takes the initiative to heal the man who is complaining in misery. I4–5 focus on how Jesus tries to help him. In I6–7, the focus is on the man's complaint. I8 shows how the healing miracle happens, while I9 shows that even the healing process is criticized by the Jews who adhere to their religious tradition.

C'B'A'. The Last Part of the Healing Ministry of Jesus (5:11–18)

In vv. 11–18, there are seven parallels: four parallelisms (I10, 13–14, and 16), two chiasms (I11–12), and one dual (I15). I10–11 and 13 are the main parallels significant to support the C'B'A' structure, demonstrating how each of the subunits shows its own cohesion. I12 belongs to I11, and I14–16 do to I13.

I10. Parallel, abcd-a'b'c'd': The saying of the man who was sick and the question of the Jews are almost perfectly in parallel: ὁ δὲ ἀπεκρίθη αὐτοῖς (But he answered them, a) and ἠρώτησαν αὐτόν (They asked him, a'); ὁ ποιήσας με ὑγιῆ (He who made me well, b) and τίς ἐστιν (Who is, b'); ἐκεῖνός μοι εἶπεν (said to me, c) and ὁ ἄνθρωπος ὁ εἰπών σοι (the man who said to you, c'); ἆρον τὸν κράβαττόν σου καὶ περιπάτει (Pick up your mat and walk, d) and ἆρον καὶ περιπάτει; (Pick up and walk, d'). **I11**. Chiastic, ab-b'a': At first the man did not know who it was (a), but finally when he recognizes Jesus as his healer and reports to the Jews (a'). In b, Jesus had withdrawn. This was the reason why the man did not know who it was. However, in b', Jesus initially re-approaches him to give more help. In short, Jesus who withdrew in b appears to him in b'. The man eventually betrays his Savior (a'). **I12**. Chiastic, a-x-a': Becoming well (a) is related to "nothing worse may happen" (a'). Sin (x) is the key issue here.

The First Sabbath Healing and the Discourse of Jesus

V	1	10			Phrases	Translation
11	C'	a			ὁ δὲ ἀπεκρίθη αὐτοῖς·	But he answered them,
-	-	b			ὁ ποιήσας με ὑγιῆ	"He who made me well
-	-	c			ἐκεῖνός μοι εἶπεν·	said to me,
-	-	d			ἆρον τὸν κράβαττόν σου καὶ περιπάτει.	'Pick up your mat and walk.'"
12	-	a'			ἠρώτησαν αὐτόν·	They asked him,
-	-	b'			τίς ἐστιν	"Who is
-	-	c'			ὁ ἄνθρωπος ὁ εἰπών σοι·	the man who said to you,
-	-	d'	11		ἆρον καὶ περιπάτει;	'Pick up and walk'?"
13	B'	a			ὁ δὲ ἰαθεὶς οὐκ ᾔδει	Now he who was healed did not know
-	-	-			τίς ἐστιν,	who it was,
-	-	b			ὁ γὰρ Ἰησοῦς ἐξένευσεν	for Jesus had withdrawn,
-	-	-			ὄχλου ὄντος ἐν τῷ τόπῳ.	as there was a crowd in the place.
14	-	b'			μετὰ ταῦτα εὑρίσκει αὐτὸν ὁ Ἰησοῦς ἐν τῷ ἱερῷ	After these things Jesus found him in the temple
-	-	-	12		καὶ εἶπεν αὐτῷ·	and said to him,
-	-	-	a		ἴδε ὑγιὴς γέγονας,	"Look, you become well.
-	-	-	x		μηκέτι ἁμάρτανε,	Do not sin anymore,
-	-	-	a'		ἵνα μὴ χεῖρόν σοί τι γένηται.	so that nothing worse may happen to you."
15	-	a'			ἀπῆλθεν ὁ ἄνθρωπος καὶ ἀνήγγειλεν τοῖς Ἰουδαίοις	The man went away and reported to the Jews
-	-	-	13		ὅτι Ἰησοῦς ἐστιν ὁ ποιήσας αὐτὸν ὑγιῆ.	that it was Jesus who had made him well.
16	A'	a			καὶ διὰ τοῦτο ἐδίωκον οἱ Ἰουδαῖοι τὸν Ἰησοῦν,	And for this reason the Jews were persecuting Jesus,
-	-	b			ὅτι ταῦτα ἐποίει ἐν σαββάτῳ.	for he did these things on the Sabbath.
17	-	c	14		Ὁ δὲ [Ἰησοῦς] ἀπεκρίνατο αὐτοῖς·	But Jesus answered them,
-	-	-	a		ὁ πατήρ μου	"My Father
-	-	-	b		ἕως ἄρτι ἐργάζεται	is working until now,
-	-	-	a'		κἀγὼ	and I, too,
-	-	-	b'		ἐργάζομαι·	am working."
18	-	a'	15		διὰ τοῦτο οὖν μᾶλλον ἐζήτουν αὐτὸν οἱ Ἰουδαῖοι ἀποκτεῖναι,	For this reason therefore the Jews were seeking all the more to kill him,
-	-	b'	16	a	ὅτι οὐ μόνον ἔλυεν τὸ σάββατον,	because he not only was breaking the Sabbath
-	-	c'	a	a'	ἀλλὰ καὶ πατέρα ἴδιον	but also ~ his own Father,
-	-	-	b	-	ἔλεγεν	~ was calling
-	-	-	c	-	τὸν θεόν	God ~
-	-	-	a'	-	ἴσον ἑαυτόν	~ himself equal
-	-	-	b'	-	ποιῶν	making ~
-	-	-	c'	-	τῷ θεῷ.	with God.

I13. Parallel, abc-a'b'c': Both in a-a', the Jews are seeking to persecute Jesus. These are related to the Sabbath miracle of healing (b-b'). In c-c', the relationship between the Father and the Son is highlighted by Jesus' word himself (c) and by the charge raised by the Jews (c'). I14. Parallel, ab-a'b': This saying is a sort of parallelism: ὁ πατήρ μου (My Father, a) and κἀγὼ (and I too, a'); ἕως ἄρτι ἐργάζεται (is working until now, b) and ἐργάζομαι (am working, b'). I15. Dual, a-a': Two charges against Jesus are arranged: breaking the Sabbath (a) and calling himself God and making himself equal with God (a'). I16. Parallel, abc-a'b'c': A sort of syntactic parallel appears: ἀλλὰ καὶ πατέρα ἴδιον (but also ~ his own Father, a) and ἴσον ἑαυτὸν (himself equal, a'); ἔλεγεν (was calling, b) and ποιῶν (making, b'); τὸν θεὸν (God, c) and τῷ θεῷ (with God, c').

In I10, the words of the man who is cured and those of the Jews who ask him are compared. In I11, there is the contrast between Jesus who meets him twice and the man who finally reports him to the Jews. I12 focuses on the relation between sickness and sin. I13 and 15 emphasize two reasons why the Jews persecute Jesus. I14 is to compare his work with the Father's. I16 repeats the divine equality of the Son with the Father.

II. Its Related Discourses (5:19–47)

Dual Structure, IIA and IIB

As discussed earlier in Dual Mode in Structure, vv. 19–47 can be grouped into two discourses: the twofold authority of the Son (19–30, IIA); the testimony to the Son (31–47, IIB). The two units are presented dually.

IIA. Twofold Authority of the Son (5:19–30)

Chiastic Structure, II1 (A-X-A')

1. The beginning (19–20) and the last part (30) share a similar pattern of significance (see II65). Both focus on "the Son does nothing by himself." The Son acts after seeing whatever the Father does and shows him regarding his works (19–20), surely as in the case of the previous healing, "life-giving" ministry. In v. 30, he seeks the will of the Father, particularly in judgment.

2. The middle of the section, vv. 21–29, is a comprehensive entity in cohesion, because it is clearly in a combined parallel structure: ABC-D1D2-A'B'C'-D'2D'1 (II8). In this sense, we may divide it into two subunits: ABC-D1D2 (21–25) and A'B'C'-D'2D'1 (26–29). Thus, we can name them: B and B'. However, considering that this unit is indeed an inseparable one, we may regard it simply as X (or X1 and X2).

The First Sabbath Healing and the Discourse of Jesus

3. Verses 19–20 and v. 30 can become A and A', both of which emphasize that the Son does what the Father does. And X emphasizes mainly two facts, the Son's authority given from his Father: giving life and giving judgment. A is related to the issue of giving life, while A' to that of giving judgment.

A.		The Son does what the Father does (19-20)	*Inclusio*
	X1.	Giving-life and judgment of the Son I (21-25)	ABC-D1D2
	X2.	Giving-life and judgment of the Son II (26-29)	A'B'C'-D'2D'1
A'.		The Son does according to the Father's will (30)	*Inclusio*

A. The Son Does What the Father Does (5:19–20)

Verses 19–20 contain an overall, combined chiastic structure (II2), three parallelisms (II6–7), and two chiasms (II3–5). II3 and 4 are found in v. 19, while II5–7 appear in v. 20. The connectivity between v. 19 and v. 20 may be sustained by the structure II2.

V						Phrases	Translations
19						Ἀπεκρίνατο οὖν ὁ Ἰησοῦς καὶ ἔλεγεν αὐτοῖς·	Jesus therefore answered and said to them,
	2			66			
	A	3		65	a	ἀμὴν ἀμὴν λέγω ὑμῖν,	"Truly, truly, I say to you,
	B1	a		a		οὐ δύναται	~ can ~
	-	-		b		ὁ υἱὸς	the Son ~
	-	-		c		ποιεῖν	do
	-	-		d		ἀφ' ἑαυτοῦ	~ by himself,
	-	-	4	e		οὐδὲν	nothing ~
	-	b	a			ἐὰν μή τι βλέπῃ	unless he sees
	-	-	b			τὸν πατέρα ποιοῦντα·	his Father doing,
	B2	b'	b'			ἃ γὰρ ἂν ἐκεῖνος ποιῇ,	for whatever he does,
	-	a'	a'	5		ταῦτα καὶ ὁ υἱὸς ὁμοίως ποιεῖ.	these things also does the Son likewise.
20	X		6	a		ὁ γὰρ πατὴρ	For the Father
	-		a	-		φιλεῖ	loves
	-		7	b	-	τὸν υἱόν,	the Son,
	B'2	a		b		καὶ πάντα	and ~ all ~
	-	b	a'	-		δείκνυσιν	shows
	-	c	b'	-		αὐτῷ	him ~
	-	d		-		ἃ αὐτὸς ποιεῖ,	~ he does;
	B'1	a'	b'			καὶ μείζονα τούτων	and greater ~ than these
	-	b'		-		δείξει	~ will he show
	-	c'		-		αὐτῷ	him,
	-	d'		-		ἔργα,	works ~
	A'			a'		ἵνα ὑμεῖς θαυμάζητε.	that you may marvel.

II2. Combined chiastic, A-B1B2-X-B'2B'1-A': B1 ("the Son can do nothing by himself, unless he sees his Father doing") and B2 ("for whatever he does, these things also does the Son likewise") are the resultant deeds of the Son after the Father's showing deeds to him as in B'2 ("and shows him all he does") and B'1 ("and greater works than these will he show him"). It means that B'2 and B'1 are the sources of the deeds of the Son as in B2 and B1. X ("For the Father loves the Son") is focused as the center of this chiasm, demonstrating why the Father shows the Son all these things. The emphatic sentence of Jesus in A ("Truly, truly, I say to you") is somehow connected to A' ("that you may marvel").

II3. Chiastic, ab-b'a': Both a ("the Son can do nothing by himself") and a' ("these things also does the Son likewise") regard the Son's deeds following his Father's doings that are indicated in b ("unless he sees his Father doing") and b' ("for whatever he does"). A repeated effect of emphasis is successfully made by duplicating the similar contents with variants. II4. Chiastic, ab-b'a': Both b ("his Father doing") and b' ("for whatever he does") are related in terms of the Father's doing, while a ("unless he sees") and a' ("these things also does the Son likewise") are also related in terms of "seeing-doing" after the Father. The Son's seeing of his Father's doing leads to his doing likewise.

II5. Chiastic, ab-b'a': If b ("and shows him all he does") and b' ("and greater works than these will he show") are considered to be in a pair, a ("For the Father loves the Son") is connected to a' ("that you may marvel"). It may mean that a causes a', consequentially or intentionally. II6. Parallel, ab-a'b': Both a ("loves") and a' ("shows") are the act of the Father to the Son, b ("the Son") and b' ("him"). The Father has certain acts, loving and showing, towards his Son. II7. Parallel, abcd-a'b'c'd': The part, abcd, is syntactically, almost identical to its counterpart, a'b'c'd', respectively. The Father shows (b) or will show (b') the Son (c and c') "all he does" (a-d) or "greater works than these" (a'-d'). This parallelism creates the duplicated effect of emphasizing the fact that the Father shows everything the Son has to see.

In II2, two foci appear: the Son does what the Father does; the Father shows the Son what he does. II3 duplicates the idea that the Son does what the Father does. II4 focuses on the seeing-doing of the Son. In II5, it is focused on the Father showing the Son. II6 highlights two deeds of the Father for the Son: loving and showing. In II7, it is emphasized that what the Father shows is and will be.

X. GIVING-LIFE AND JUDGMENT OF THE SON (5:21–29)

II8. Combined parallel, ABC-D1D2-A'B'C'-D'2D'1: Both A ("For as the Father raises the dead and gives them life, so also the Son gives life to whom he wishes") and A' ("For as the Father has life in himself, so he gave to the Son also to have life in himself") show the Father-Son relationship in relation to the "life" issue. The similar pattern ὥσπερ γὰρ (ὁ πατὴρ) - οὕτως καὶ (ὁ υἱὸς or τῷ υἱῷ) appears in common in A and A'. The

The First Sabbath Healing and the Discourse of Jesus

Father has life and then gave the Son to have it in himself (A) and lets him give it to whom he wishes (A'). In B ("For the Father judges no one, but has given all judgment to the Son") and B' ("and he gave him authority to execute judgment"), the "judgment" issue is concentrated on, instead of the "life" one. The judgment is originally the authority of the Father, but he gave the Son authority to exercise all judgment. B is indeed equal to B' in meaning.

The purpose that the Father gives the Son authority both to give life and to execute judgment to anyone he wishes is for people to adequately honor the Son as in C ("that all may honor the Son, just as they honor the Father. He who does not honor the Son does not honor the Father who sent him"). In this sense, C' ("because he is the Son of Man") also needs to be interpreted as the contents, demonstrating the divine identity of the Son regarding who he really is (cf. Dan 7:13–14; cf. John 9:35). The fact that he is the Son of Man (C') leads to the result that people should honor him (C). Thus, C' is prior to C as A' is to A.

Both D1 ("Truly, truly, I say to you, he who hears my word and believes him who sent me has eternal life and does not come into judgment, but has passed from death to life") and D'1 ("and will come forth, those who have done good, to the resurrection of life, and those who have done evil, to the resurrection of judgment") emphasize who the person is, who has eternal life in relation to both "belief" and "act," while in D2 ("Truly, truly, I say to you, the hour is coming and now is, when the dead will hear the voice of the Son of God, and those who hear will live") and D'2 ("Do not marvel at this, for the hour is coming when all who are in the graves will hear his voice"), at least two things are duplicated: "the hour is coming" and "the time when the dead hear the voice of the Son." Believers in the Son and those who do good will receive the resurrection of life at his return. The relation of D1 to D'1 is complementary. D1 focuses on the belief, while D'1 emphasizes the deed. D2 and D'2 are almost similar in meaning.

21	The Father and the Son give life to whom they wish.	A		A'	The Father gave to the Son to have life in himself.	26
22	The Father has given all judgment to the Son.	B		B'	He gave him authority to execute judgment.	27a
23	Honoring the Son is honoring the Father	C		C'	He is the Son of Man.	27b
24	Hearer and believer have eternal life, not coming into judgment.	D1		D'2	The hour is coming; all who are in the graves will hear his voice.	28
25	The hour is coming; the dead will hear the voice of the Son.	D2		D'1	The resurrection of life to the doer of good vs. that of judgment to the evil-doer.	29

X1. Giving-Life and the Judgment of the Son I (5:21–25)

Verses 21–25 are the first part of the overall, combined parallelism (II8), producing five parallelisms (II9–10, 13–15) and also six chiasms (II11, 16–20), one dual (II12), and one complex (II21). Each of vv. 21–25 contains its own internal parallels such as II9–11 in v. 21, II12 in v. 22, II13–15 in v. 23, II16–19 in v. 24, and II20–21 in v. 25. Meanwhile, II63–64 demonstrate the connection between vv. 24–25 (D1-D2, II8) and vv. 28–29 (D'2-D'2, II8).

II9. Parallel, ab-a'b': The Father (a) and the Son (a') do the same thing, "raising the dead and giving life" (b and b'). It focuses on the fact that the Father and the Son share in common the divine authority to give life. **II10.** Parallel, ab-a'b': Both a ("the dead") and a' ("to whom he wishes") refer to the people whom the Father-Son raise, while b ("and gives them life") and b' ("gives life") are their divine acts to "give life" to them. Like II9, this parallel also emphasizes that the Father-Son share in giving life to the dead. **II11.** Chiastic, a-x-a': The word, a ("raises"), is duplicated in a' ("and gives them life"), while the center x ("the dead") is the object to be raised or given life. This chiasm focuses on who will be raised. **II12.** Dual, a-a': Both a ("judges no one") and a' ("but has given all judgment to the Son") are dual acts of the Father regarding judgment. He does not judge anyone and gives all authority of judgment to the Son.

II13. Parallel, ab-a'b': "Honoring the Son" in a is contrasted to "not honoring the Son" in a', just as "honoring the Father" in b is reversed to "not honoring the Father who sent him" in b'. Honoring the Father means honoring the Son, the reverse is also true. **II14.** Parallel, ab-a'b': As a ("that all may honor") is related to b ("the Son"), its object, so a' ("just as they honor") is to b' ("the Father"). It shows that to honor the Son is to honor the Father. **II15.** Parallel, ab-a'b': Both a ("He who does not honor") and a' ("does not honor") are duplicated regarding "not honoring," while b ("the Son") and b' ("the Father who sent him") are closely related to each other. Not to honor the Son is namely not to honor the Father.

II16. Chiastic, ab-b'a': Both b ("he who hears") and b' ("and believes") show the connection between "hearing" and "believing," while a ("my word") and a' ("him who sent me") are objects of these acts, respectively. Hearing "my word" means believing the Father. **II17.** Chiastic, ab-b'a': In this, a ("has") and a' ("does not come") are verbal phrases, while b ("eternal life") and b' ("and ~ into judgment") are contrasted in concept. Having eternal life guarantees not coming into judgment. **II18.** Chiastic, ab-b'a': The issue of a ("and ~ into judgment") and b ("does not come") is duplicated in that of b' ("but has passed") and a' ("from death to life"), but reversed in arrangement. Two similar, but negative-positive types of expressions are shown for the purpose of emphatic repetition. II19. Chiastic, ab-b'a': Both a ("eternal life") and a' ("to life") regard the "life" issue, while both b ("and ~ into judgment") and b' ("from death") regard the "judgment" or "death" issue. Two antithetical words such as life and judgment (or death) are contrasted twice.

The First Sabbath Healing and the Discourse of Jesus

V	8	9					Phrases	Translations
21	A	a		11			ὥσπερ γὰρ ὁ πατὴρ	For as the Father
-	-	b	10	a			ἐγείρει	raises
-	-	-	a	x			τοὺς νεκροὺς	the dead
-	-	-	b	a'			καὶ ζῳοποιεῖ,	and gives them life,
-	-	a'					οὕτως καὶ ὁ υἱὸς	so also the Son
-	-	b'	a'				οὓς θέλει	~ to whom he wishes.
-	-	-	b'				ζῳοποιεῖ.	gives life ~
22	B	12					οὐδὲ γὰρ ὁ πατὴρ	For the Father
-	-	a					κρίνει οὐδένα,	judges no one,
-	-	a'					ἀλλὰ τὴν κρίσιν πᾶσαν δέδωκεν τῷ υἱῷ,	but has given all judgment to the Son,
-	-		13	14				
23	C		a	a			ἵνα πάντες τιμῶσιν	that all may honor
-	-		-	b			τὸν υἱὸν	the Son,
-	-		b	a'			καθὼς τιμῶσιν	just as they honor
-	-	15	-	b'			τὸν πατέρα.	the Father.
-	-	a	a'				ὁ μὴ τιμῶν	He who does not honor
-	-	b	-				τὸν υἱὸν	the Son
-	-	a'	b'				οὐ τιμᾷ	does not honor
-	-	b'	-				τὸν πατέρα	the Father
-	-					66	τὸν πέμψαντα αὐτόν.	who sent him.
24	D1	16				a'	Ἀμὴν ἀμὴν λέγω ὑμῖν	Truly, truly, I say to you,
-	-	a					ὅτι ὁ τὸν λόγον μου	~ my word
-	-	b					ἀκούων	he who hears ~
-	-	b'					καὶ πιστεύων	and believes
-	-	a'	17		64		τῷ πέμψαντί με	him who sent me
-	-		a	19	a		ἔχει	has
-	-	18	b	a	-		ζωὴν αἰώνιον	eternal life
-	-	a	b'	b	b		καὶ εἰς κρίσιν	and ~ into judgment,
-	-	b	a'	-			οὐκ ἔρχεται,	does not come ~
-	-	b'					ἀλλὰ μεταβέβηκεν	but has passed
-	-	a'		b'			ἐκ τοῦ θανάτου	from death
-	-	-		a'		66	εἰς τὴν ζωήν.	to life.
25	D2	20			63	a"	ἀμὴν ἀμὴν λέγω ὑμῖν	Truly, truly, I say to you,
-	-	a		a			ὅτι ἔρχεται	~ is coming
-	-	b		-			ὥρα	the hour ~
-	-	b'		-			καὶ νῦν	and now
-	-	a'	21	-			ἐστιν	is,
-	-		a1	b1			ὅτε οἱ νεκροὶ	when the dead
-	-		a2	b2			ἀκούσουσιν	will hear
-	-		x	b3			τῆς φωνῆς τοῦ υἱοῦ τοῦ θεοῦ	the voice of the Son of God,
-	-		a'2				καὶ οἱ ἀκούσαντες	and those hear
-	-		a'1				ζήσουσιν.	will live.

II20. Chiastic, ab-b'a': The relation of a ("is coming") and b ("the hour") is similar to that of b' ("and now") and a' ("is"), but reversed in order. It is an emphatic expression by repeating similar, related contents. **II21.** Combined chiastic, a1a2-x-a'2a'1: In this, a2 ("will hear") and a'2 ("and those hear") are duplicated, while the dead in a1 ("when the dead") has the result of a'1 ("will live"), while x ("the voice of the Son of God") is emphasized as the center of this complex chiasm. This complex chiasm persuades the readers that the dead will finally live as they hear the voice of the Son. In short, it means that the "hearer will live."

Their foci are: giving life of the Father and the Son (II9); those whom the Father and the Son give life (II10); raising the dead and giving life (II11); dual acts of the Father's judgment (II12); honoring the Son and honoring the Father (II13–15); hearing and believing (II16); eternal life vs. judgment (II17); movement from judgment (II18); life vs. judgment (II19); coming hour and now (II20); those who hear the voice of the Son (II21).

X2. Giving-Life and Judgment of the Son II (5:26–29)

Verses 26–29 belong to the overall, combined parallelism (II8), producing two parallelisms (II25, 27) and also three chiasms (II22, 24, and 26) with one complex one (II23). Then, vv. 26–27 and vv. 28–29 cannot be divided within verses, equally showing a certain close connection between the two verses: II22–25 in vv. 26–27 and II26–27 in vv. 28–29.

While the first part of II8, ABC-D1D2 (21–25), is constituted by relatively clear-cut, grouped verses with their own parallels, the second one of II8, A'B'C'-D'2D'1 (26–29), does not show this phenomenon, rather producing two groups of combined verses: vv. 26–27 and 28–29.

II22. Chiastic, ab-b'a': Both b ("so he gave to the Son also to have life in himself") and b' ("and he gave him authority to execute judgment") deal with the Father's acts to give something to the Son in the Father-Son relationship. And a ("For as the Father has life in himself") focuses on the Father only, particularly regarding what he originally has in himself. Here as a is the reason for b, so is a' that of b', while a' ("because he is the Son of Man") focuses on the Son only, regarding who the Son is.

The First Sabbath Healing and the Discourse of Jesus

V	8	22				Phrases	Translations
26	A'	a	23			ὥσπερ γὰρ ὁ πατὴρ	For as the Father
-	-	-	a1			ἔχει	has
-	-	-	a2			ζωὴν	life
-	-	-	b	24	25	ἐν ἑαυτῷ,	in himself,
-	-	b		a	a	οὕτως καὶ τῷ υἱῷ	so ~ to the Son also
-	-	-		b	-	ἔδωκεν	he gave ~
-	-	-	a'2	c		ζωὴν	~ life
-	-	-	a'1		b	ἔχειν	to have ~
-	-	-	b'		-	ἐν ἑαυτῷ.	in himself;
27	B'	b'		c'	a'	καὶ ἐξουσίαν	and ~ authority
-	-	-		b'	-	ἔδωκεν	he gave
-	-	-		a'	-	αὐτῷ	him ~
-	-	-			b'	κρίσιν	~ judgment,
-	-	-			-	ποιεῖν,	to execute ~
-	C'	a'				ὅτι υἱὸς ἀνθρώπου ἐστίν.	because he is the Son of Man.
28	D'2				63	μὴ θαυμάζετε τοῦτο,	Do not marvel at this,
-	-				a'	ὅτι ἔρχεται	for ~ is coming
-	-	26			-	ὥρα	the hour ~
-	-	a			b'1	ἐν ᾗ πάντες οἱ ἐν τοῖς μνημείοις	when all who are in the graves
-	-	b			b'2	ἀκούσουσιν	will hear
-	-	-			b'3	τῆς φωνῆς αὐτοῦ	his voice,
29	D'1	b'	27			καὶ ἐκπορεύσονται	and will come forth,
-	-	a'	a		64	οἱ τὰ ἀγαθὰ ποιήσαντες	those who have done good,
-	-	-	b		a'	εἰς ἀνάστασιν	to the resurrection
-	-	-	-		-	ζωῆς,	of life,
-	-	-	a'		-	οἱ δὲ τὰ φαῦλα πράξαντες	and those who have done evil,
-	-	-	b'		b'	εἰς ἀνάστασιν	to the resurrection
-	-	-	-		-	κρίσεως.	of judgment.

II23. Combined parallel, a1a2-b-a'2a'1-b': We may say that a1 ("has") and a'1 ("to have") are paired in repetition, as a2 ("life") and a'2 ("life"), b ("in himself") and b' ("in himself") are in a pair. The Father and the Son share common life in themselves. II24. Chiastic, abc-c'b'a': b ("he gave") and b' ("he gave") are identical, describing the Father's act of giving, while c ("life") and c' ("and ~ authority") indicate two things which the Father gave, while a ("so ~ to the Son also") and a' ("him") demonstrate to whom the Father gave them. A similar syntax of sentences is arranged in reverse order. II25. Parallel, ab-a'b': Syntactically, a (οὕτως καὶ τῷ υἱῷ ἔδωκεν ζωὴν) is similar in expression to a' (καὶ ἐξουσίαν ἔδωκεν αὐτῷ), while b (ἔχειν ἐν ἑαυτῷ) is similar in syntax to b' (κρίσιν ποιεῖν). Both clauses indicate what the Father gave his Son: "having life" and "doing judgment."

II26. Chiastic, ab-b'a': Certain phenomena, syntactically and semantically similar but reversed in arrangement, happen between the first clause, a ("when all who are in the graves") and b ("will hear his voice"), and the second, a' ("those who have done good") and b' ("and will come forth"). Both a and a' indicate the dead, while b and b' are their acts of response, hearing and coming forth. **II27.** Parallel, ab-a'b': As a ("those who have done good") is contrasted to a' ("and those who have done evil"), so b ("to the resurrection of life") is contrasted to b' ("to the resurrection of judgment"). The same pattern of syntax with antithetical meaning appears here, demonstrating who are going to have life or judgment at the time of resurrection.

In II22 and 25, two authorities of the Son, giving life and executing judgment, given from the Father, are emphasized. II23 focuses on the fact that the Father and the Son share together regarding life, while II24 focuses on what the Father gives the Son. II26 draws a parallel of phenomenon in resurrection. In II27, two kinds of resurrection are in contrast.

A'. The Son Does according to the Father's Will (5:30)

Verse 30 has one chiasm (II28), one parallelism (II30), and one combined chiasm (II29), representing its own cohesion within the verse, highlighting the issue: the Son's doing-not-anything-alone. It seems not to have any parallel with other verses, besides II65 demonstrating the strong connection between v. 30 (A' of II1) and vv. 19–20 (A of II1).

V	28	29		65	Phrases	Translations
30	A	a1		a'	Οὐ δύναμαι	~ can
	-	-		b'	ἐγὼ	I ~
	-	-		c'	ποιεῖν	do ~
	-	-		d'	ἀπ' ἐμαυτοῦ	~ by myself;
	-	-		e'	οὐδέν·	nothing ~
	B	a2			καθὼς ἀκούω κρίνω,	as I hear, I judge;
	B'	x			καὶ ἡ κρίσις ἡ ἐμὴ δικαία ἐστίν,	my judgment is just,
	A'	a'1	30		ὅτι οὐ ζητῶ	for I do not seek
	-	-	a		τὸ θέλημα	~ will,
	-	-	b		τὸ ἐμὸν	my own ~
	-	a'2	a'		ἀλλὰ τὸ θέλημα	but the will
	-	-	b'		τοῦ πέμψαντός με.	of him who sent me.

II28. Chiastic, AB-B'A': Both B ("as I hear, I judge") and B' ("my judgment is just") focus on the judgment of the Son, while A ("I can do nothing by myself") and A' ("for I do not seek my own will, but the will of him who sent me") are related, both

revealing that the Son does not do anything for himself but acts in total dependence on the Father, particularly regarding the rightful motive of the Son who judges.

II29. Combined chiastic, a1a2-x-a'1a'2: Both a1 ("I can do nothing by myself") and a'1 ("for I do not seek my own will") indicate the Son's will regarding how not to decide by himself, while a2 ("as I hear, I judge") and a'2 ("but the will of him who sent me") demonstrate his dependence totally on his Father. The center, x ("my judgment is just") is highlighted. This combined chiasm creates an emphasis of duplication, showing the deep relationship between the Father and the Son in judgment as well as defending his justice in judgment. **II30.** Parallel, ab-a'b': The word, a ("will"), is repeated in a' ("but the will"), while b ("my own") is contrasted with b' ("of him who sent me"). This parallelism strengthens the contrast between "my own will" and "the will of my Father."

In II28–29, doing-not-anything-alone and seeking-his-will are focused in regard to the judgment of the Son. And in II30, "my" own will and the Father's will are in contrast.

IIB. The Testimony to the Son (5:31–47)

Dual Structure, IIB1 and IIB2

As a whole, vv. 31–37 are divided into two units: vv. 31–37a (IIB1, the Father's testimony) and 37b–47 (IIB2, their unbelief of the testimony). Although there is a continuity between v. 37a and 37b, as seen in II62, the connection within vv. 36–37a (II37) and that within vv. 37b–40 (II43) are much stronger. Thus, it is recommended to divide v. 37a and 37b. Each unit shows its own, comprehensive parallel: II31 (31–37a) and II42 (37b–47).

A.	The Father's testimony (31-37a)	A-X-A'
A'.	Their unbelief of the testimony (37b-47)	A-X-A'

IIB1. The Father's Testimony (5:31–37a)

Chiastic Structure, II31 (A-X-A')

1. Concerning the parallel features, this unit can be divided into three subunits: vv. 31–32, 33–35, and 36–37a. Each of them consists of at least one comprehensive parallel such as II32 (31–32), II35 (33–35), and II37 (36–37a).

2. Verses 31–32 and vv. 36–37a are in a pair, both describing in common another testifier for the Son, whose testimony is true, while the focus of vv. 33–35 is the Baptist, a human testifier. Thus, we may name them: A (31–32), X (33–35), and A' (36–37a), for they are chiastic.

3. Concerning the pair of A-A', the true testifier in v. 32 is not the Baptist, because Jesus says, "I do not receive testimony from man" in v. 34, but rather none other than the Father who sent his Son. For, according to this chiasm, "another who testifies about me" in v. 32 is "the Father who has testified about me" in v. 37. The Son demonstrates here the divine testifier, the Father, in contrast to the human testifier such as JB (X, 33–35).

A.	Another testifier (31-32)	
	X.	A human testifier, the Baptist (33-35)
A'.	The Father as his testifier (36-37a)	

A. Another Testifier (5:31-32)

Verses 31–32 contain two parallelisms (II32–33) and one chiasm (II34). Verses 31–32 (A of II31) are not to be separated because of II32–34, introducing another testifier whose testimony is true.

II32. Parallel, AB-A'B': There are two testifiers, "I" in A ("If I testify about myself") and "another" in A' ("there is another who testifies about me"), and there are two following results regarding the truthfulness of the testimonies in B ("my testimony is not true") and in B' ("and I know that the testimony which he testifies about me is true"). In this way, the Son claims another testifier about him exists beside him.

V	32	33		Phrases	Translations
31	A	a		Ἐὰν ἐγὼ	If I
	-	b		μαρτυρῶ	testify
	-	c	34	περὶ ἐμαυτοῦ,	about myself,
	B	a		ἡ μαρτυρία μου	my testimony
	-	b		οὐκ ἔστιν ἀληθής·	is not true;
32	A'	a'		ἄλλος	there ~ another ~
	-	b'		ἐστὶν ὁ μαρτυρῶν	is ~who testifies
	-	c'		περὶ ἐμοῦ,	about me,
	B'			καὶ οἶδα	and I know
	-	b'		ὅτι ἀληθής ἐστιν	that ~ is true.
	-	a'		ἡ μαρτυρία	the testimony
	-		-	ἣν μαρτυρεῖ περὶ ἐμοῦ.	which he testifies about me ~

II33. Parallel, abc-a'b'c': The syntactic styles of two sentences are similar: a (Ἐὰν ἐγὼ) - b (μαρτυρῶ) - c (περὶ ἐμοῦ) and a' (ἄλλος) - b' (ἐστὶν ὁ μαρτυρῶν) - c' (περὶ ἐμοῦ). Two testifiers about the Son were referred to here. **II34. Chiastic, ab-b'a'**: Both b ("is not true") and b' ("that ~ is true") are related in terms of truthfulness, while both a

The First Sabbath Healing and the Discourse of Jesus

("my testimony") and a' ("the testimony which he testifies about me") indicate two types of testimony regarding the Son which are in common.

In II32, "my" testimony and that of another testifier are in comparison. II33 repeatedly emphasizes the object of the testimony: Jesus (περὶ ἐμοῦ, about me), while II34 compares the truthfulness of "my" testimony alone with that of another testifier.

X. The Baptist, a Human Testifier (5:33–35)

Verses 33–35 seem to have one chiasm (II35) and one parallel (II36), having no connection of parallels with other verses, highlighting the Baptist as a human testifier.

V	35	36	Phrases	Translations
33	A	a	ὑμεῖς ἀπεστάλκατε	You have sent
	-	b	πρὸς Ἰωάννην,	to John,
	B	a'	καὶ μεμαρτύρηκεν	and he has testified
	-	b'	τῇ ἀληθείᾳ·	to the truth.
34	C		ἐγὼ δὲ οὐ παρὰ ἀνθρώπου τὴν μαρτυρίαν λαμβάνω,	But I do not receive testimony from the man,
	C'		ἀλλὰ ταῦτα λέγω ἵνα ὑμεῖς σωθῆτε.	but I say these things that you may be saved.
35	B'		ἐκεῖνος ἦν ὁ λύχνος ὁ καιόμενος καὶ φαίνων,	He was a lamp that burned and gave light,
	A'		ὑμεῖς δὲ ἠθελήσατε ἀγαλλιαθῆναι πρὸς ὥραν ἐν τῷ φωτὶ αὐτοῦ.	and you were willing to rejoice for a while in his light.

II35. Chiastic, ABC-C'B'A': We may say that B ("and he has testified to the truth") refers to the role of John the Baptist and B' ("He was a lamp that burned and gave light") tells us about who John is, regarding his role. Both A ("You have sent to John") and A' ("and you were willing to rejoice for a while in his light") are interrelated, focusing on the relation between "you" and John. Both C ("But I do not receive testimony from the man") and C' ("but I say these things that you may be saved") indicate something the Son ("I") does regarding testimony about him. Although the Son does not want to receive any testimony from a man like John, he is referring to the Baptist simply for them to be saved. **II36.** Parallel, ab-a'b': The deed of "you" in a ("You have sent") and the deed of "John" in a' ("and he has testified") are compared, regarding their references, b ("to John") and b' ("to the truth"), respectively. That they sent someone to the Baptist is what they only did regarding the truth, but that the Baptist did testify to the truth is what he surely did.

II35 focuses on the Baptist's limitations and strength as a human testifier, while II36 compares the Jews and the Baptist regarding their actions.

A'. The Father as His Testifier (5:36–37a)

Verses 36–37a contain one overall chiasm (II37), three parallelisms (II39–41), and one dual (II38), focusing on the Father as his true testifier who testifies to the Son through the works of the Son.

V	37	38			Phrases	Translations
36	A	a			Ἐγὼ δὲ ἔχω τὴν μαρτυρίαν	But I have testimony
-		39	41		μείζω τοῦ Ἰωάννου·	greater than that of John;
-	B	a		a	τὰ γὰρ ἔργα	for the works
-		b		-	ἃ δέδωκέν μοι ὁ πατὴρ	that the Father has given me
-		40	b		ἵνα τελειώσω αὐτά,	to accomplish,
-	B'	a'	a'	a'	αὐτὰ τὰ ἔργα	the very works
-		-	b'	-	ἃ ποιῶ	that I do,
-		-	b	b	μαρτυρεῖ	testify
-		-	c	-	περὶ ἐμοῦ	about me,
-				62	ὅτι ὁ πατήρ με ἀπέσταλκεν.	that the Father has sent me.
37a	A'		a'	a	καὶ ὁ πέμψας με πατὴρ ἐκεῖνος	And the Father who sent me
-			b'	-	μεμαρτύρηκεν	has testified
-			c'	-	περὶ ἐμοῦ.	about me.

II37. Chiastic, AB-B'A': Both B ("for the works that the Father has given me to accomplish") and B' ("the very works that I do, testify about me, that the Father has sent me") deal in common with the works of the Son based on the Father-Son relationship. Thus, the testimony referred in A ("But I have testimony greater than that of John") may indicate the testimony from the Father as in A' ("And the Father who sent me has testified about me. You have neither heard his voice at any time, nor seen his form"). His testimony about his Son was fully revealed through the miraculous works of the Son as in B and B'. In other words, the testimony which is greater than that of John is that of the Father, being demonstrated through the divine works that the Son does.

II38. Parallel, a-a': "The testimony" that "I have" in a is "the very works that I do" which "testify about me" in a'. It means that the testimony of the Father is revealed through the very works that the Son does. II39. Parallel, ab-a'b': Both a ("for the works") and a' ("the very works") describe "the works" that the Father has given the Son to do (b), and that he does (b'), creating the repetitive effect of emphasis in relation to the divine works done by the Son.

II40. Parallel, abc-a'b'c': Both a ("the very works that I do") and a' ("And the Father who sent me") are two subjects, having the same role to "testify" (b) or to "have testified" (b') "about me" (c-c'). Two types of testifier, "the works of the Son" and "the Father," are referred to here by the Son himself. II41. Parallel, ab-a'b': Both a ("for the works that the Father has given me") and a' ("the very works that I do") duplicate in common "the works of the Son," but a focuses on the fact that the Father has given them to the Son, while a' emphasizes that the Son does them. These works of the Son were given to be accomplished (b) and also to "testify about me" (b'). These are two functions of the works of the Son.

In II37, the relation of the Father's testimony to the Son and the works given to him are emphasized. II38 divulges the relation between another testimony and the works of the Son, while II40 discloses the relation between the works of the Son and the Father's testimony. In II39 and 41, the works of the Son are the focus.

IIB2. Their Unbelief of the Testimony (5:37b–47)

Chiastic Structure, II42 (A-X-A')

1. Verses 37b–47 are divided into three subunits: vv. 37b–40, 41–44, and 45–47. Each of them consists at least of one comprehensive parallel such as II43 (37b–40), II51 (41–44), and II55 (45–47).

2. We may say that vv. 37b–40 and vv. 45–47 are paired, containing a similar issue, pointing out their unbelief. Verses 37b–40 indicate their unbelief of the Son or not coming to him and also vv. 45–47 focus on their unbelief of his words causing them to be accused by Moses. In this sense, These subunits are in a pair. We can name them: A (their unbelief and the Scripture) and A' (their unbelief and Moses).

3. Meanwhile, vv. 41–44 highlight the reasons for their unbelief of the Son: having not the love of God and seeking not his glory, constructing its own chiasm: AB-B'A' (II51). We may name this subunit as X (not loving God and seeking their glory).

A.	Their unbelief and the Scripture (37b-40)		ABC-C'B'A'
	X.	Not loving God and seeking their glory (41-44)	AB-B'A'
A'.	Their unbelief and Moses (45-47)		ABC-X-C'B'A'

A. Their Unbelief and the Scripture (5:37b–40)

Verses 37b–40 show one overall chiasm (II43), five parallelisms (II44–46, 49–50), one combined chiasm (II48), and one dual (II47). They demonstrate the necessity of believing in or coming to the Son to have life. Among the parallels, II44–47 are related particularly to the cohesiveness of vv. 37b–38a (A of II43).

V	43	44	45		47	62	Phrases	Translations
37b	A	a	a		a	b	οὔτε φωνὴν αὐτοῦ πώποτε	~ neither ~ his voice at any time,
-		b	b	46	-	-	ἀκηκόατε	You have ~ heard ~
-		a'		a	-	-	οὔτε εἶδος αὐτοῦ	nor ~ his form;
-		b'		b	-	-	ἑωράκατε,	[have] seen ~
38	-		a'	a'	a'	b	καὶ τὸν λόγον αὐτοῦ	and ~ his word
-			b'	b'	-	-	οὐκ ἔχετε	you do not have ~
-		48			-	-	ἐν ὑμῖν μένοντα,	abiding in you,
	B	a1				a'	ὅτι ὃν ἀπέστειλεν ἐκεῖνος, τούτῳ ὑμεῖς οὐ πιστεύετε.	for you do not believe him whom he has sent.
			49	50				
39	C	a2	a	a			ἐραυνᾶτε	You search
-	-	-		b			τὰς γραφάς,	the Scriptures
-	-	-	b	a'			ὅτι ὑμεῖς δοκεῖτε	because you think
-	-	-		b'			ἐν αὐταῖς ζωὴν αἰώνιον ἔχειν·	that in them you have eternal life;
	C'	x					καὶ ἐκεῖναί εἰσιν αἱ μαρτυροῦσαι περὶ ἐμοῦ·	these are testimonies about me.
40	B'	a'1	a'				καὶ οὐ θέλετε ἐλθεῖν πρός με	And you do not want to come to me
	A'	a'2	b'				ἵνα ζωὴν ἔχητε.	that you may have life.

II43. Chiastic, AB-B'A': Both B ("for you do not believe him whom he has sent") and B' ("And you do not want to come to me") focus on their unbelief or on not-coming-attitude to the Son. The pair A ("You have neither heard his voice at any time, nor seen his form; and you do not have his word abiding in you") and A' ("that you may have life") imply that the close relationship with the Father means, in other words, having life. It may be said that to have life is nothing other than to experience God and also to have his word inside them. Both C ("You search the Scriptures because you think that in them you have eternal life") and C' ("these are testimonies about me") are regarding the written Scriptures testifying to him. Although they search the Scriptures to have eternal life, they cannot obtain it, because they cannot contact the Father, physically or actually. Even they do not believe the Son, never coming to him who is testified to by the very writings, thus failing to obtain the life.

II44. Parallel, ab-a'b': A repetitive effect of two related verbs (perfect tense) of perception such as "hearing" in b (ἀκηκόατε) and "seeing" in b' (ἑωράκατε) appears, and these two verbs are negated by a similar pattern of phrases such as a (οὔτε φωνὴν αὐτοῦ πώποτε) and a' (οὔτε εἶδος αὐτοῦ), respectively. It doubly emphasizes that humans cannot physically reach God. **II45.** Parallel, ab-a'b': In this, b ("you have heard") and b' ("you do not have") are verbal phrases (or verbs), while a ("neither ~ his voice at any time") and a' ("and ~ his word") are their related objects, respectively. Both clauses focus in common on the fact that no one can access the Father without the help of the Son.

II46. Parallel, ab-a'b': Similarly with II44, b ("[you have] seen ~") and b' ("you do not have ~ abiding in you") are verbal phrases, while a ("nor ~ his form") and a' ("and ~ his word") are their related objects, respectively, these clauses also emphasizing man's inability to reach the Father. **II47.** Dual, a-a': Two different sentences with similar meanings are presented here with repetitive effect: a ("You have neither heard his voice at any time, nor seen his form") and a' ("and you do not have his word abiding in you").

II48. Combined chiastic, a1a2-x-a'1a'2: Unbelief in a1 ("for you do not believe him whom he has sent") is, in other words, not-coming in a'1 ("And you do not want to come to me"); "you" have the desire to have life as in a2 ("You search the Scriptures because you think that in them you have eternal life") and a'2 ("that you may have life"), while x ("these are testimonies about me") can be the center of this complex chiasm. "You" have the desire to have life, thus searching the Scriptures, namely testimonies about "me," but "you" do not want to come or believe "me," thus failing to obtain life.

II49. Parallel, ab-a'b': Both a ("You search the Scriptures") and a' ("And you do not want to come to me") describe "your" deeds trying to do or not to do, while the goal of their deeds is to have life as in b ("because you think that in them you have eternal life") and b' ("that you may have life"), "you" deeply desire to have life, thus trying to search the Scriptures, while not coming to "me," finally failing to have it. **II50.** Parallel, ab-a'b': "Your" attempts appear in a ("You search") and a' ("because you think") regarding the Scriptures, b ("the Scriptures") and b' ("that in them you have eternal life"). "You" do something regarding the Scriptures, for "you" think there is life in them.

In II43, there are a few foci: the relation between experiencing God and having his word; remaining in his word and having life; their unbelief and not-coming; the Scriptures and belief. II44 focuses on hearing-seeing regarding God. II45 relates hearing his voice to having his word, while II46 relates seeing his form to having his word. II47 equates experiencing God with having his word. II48 focuses on the testimony of the Scriptures and their unbelief. II49 contrasts their attitude toward the Scriptures and their-not-coming-to-him. II50 focuses on their searching-thinking.

X. Not Loving God and Seeking Their Glory (5:41–44)

There are four parallels in vv. 41–44: a comprehensive chiasm (II51) and three parallelisms (II52–54). II52 shows the connectivity between vv. 41–42 (A of II51) and v. 44 (A' of II51), while v. 43 has its own cohesion (B-B' of II51). Verses 41–44 have a purpose to disclose the hidden reasons for their unbelief: not having the love of God and not seeking his glory.

V	51	52		Phrases	Translations
41	A	a		Δόξαν παρὰ ἀνθρώπων οὐ λαμβάνω,	I do not accept glory from men,
42	-	b		ἀλλ' ἔγνωκα ὑμᾶς ὅτι τὴν ἀγάπην τοῦ θεοῦ οὐκ ἔχετε ἐν ἑαυτοῖς.	but I know you, that you do not have the love of God in yourselves.
			53		
43	B		a	ἐγὼ	I
-		b		ἐλήλυθα	have come
-		c		ἐν τῷ ὀνόματι τοῦ πατρός μου,	in my Father's name,
-		d		καὶ οὐ λαμβάνετέ με·	and you do not accept me;
	B'	a'		ἐὰν ἄλλος	if another
-		b'		ἔλθῃ	comes
-		c'		ἐν τῷ ὀνόματι τῷ ἰδίῳ,	in his own name,
-		d'		ἐκεῖνον λήμψεσθε.	you will accept him.
44	A'		54	πῶς δύνασθε ὑμεῖς πιστεῦσαι	How can you believe,
-	a'		a	δόξαν	~ glory
-	-		b	παρὰ ἀλλήλων	from one another
-	-		c	λαμβάνοντες,	who accept ~
-	b'		a'	καὶ τὴν δόξαν	and ~ the glory
-	-		b'	τὴν παρὰ τοῦ μόνου θεοῦ	from the only God?
-	-		c'	οὐ ζητεῖτε;	do not seek ~

II51. Chiastic, AB-B'A': A ("I do not accept glory from men, but I know you, that you do not have the love of God in yourselves") and A' ("How can you believe, who accept glory from one another and do not seek the glory from the only God?") are contrasted, in meaning, in terms of 'accepting glory from whom,' while B ("I have come in my Father's name, and you do not accept me") and B' ("if another comes in his own name, you will accept him") are parallel both in meaning of contrast and in syntax. This chiasm discloses their unbelief and denial of the Son. **II52.** Parallel, ab-a'b': The relation between a ("I do not accept glory from men") and a' ("who accept glory from one another") is antithetical, indicating the contrasted attitude of "I" and "you", respectively, while both b ("but I know you, that you do not have the love of God in yourselves") and b' ("and do not seek the glory from the only God?") focus on "you" who do not have a right attitude towards God regarding either the love of God or the glory from God.

II53. Parallel, abcd-a'b'c'd': Fourfold syntactic-divided parts shown in a ("I") - b ("have come") - c ("in my Father's name") - d ("and you do not accept me") are similarly produced as in a' ("if another") - b' ("comes") - c' ("in his own name") - d' ("you will accept him"), thus creating a well-designed parallelism of contrast, focusing on "your" not-acceptance of "me." **II54.** Parallel, abc-a'b'c': Both a ("~ glory") and a' ("and ~ the glory") focus on "glory" as the objects, while b ("from one another") and b' ("from the only God") are in contrast regarding from whom "you" wish to get the glory, while c ("who accept ~") and c' ("do not seek") focus on their verbal deeds, the accepting and seeking of the glory. This parallelism demonstrates which glory "you" really pursue: from men or from God.

II51 discloses the relation between seeking the glory and believing in the Son. In II52, having the love of God is compared with not-seeking the glory of God. In II53, their double standard of acceptance is pointed out. In II54, seeking their own glory and seeking the glory of God are in contrast.

A'. Their Unbelief and Moses (5:45–47)

In vv. 45–47, there are seven parallels: one comprehensive chiasm (II55), two chiasms (II56 and 60), two combined chiasms (II57–58), and two parallelisms (II59 and 61), focusing his criticism on their unbelief. It is difficult to separate these three verses from each other, because they are mixed with not a few parallels to each other, as seen in II55–61.

V	55					Phrases	Translations
45	A	56	57			Μὴ δοκεῖτε	Do not think
-	-	a	a1			ὅτι ἐγὼ	that I
-	-	-	a2			κατηγορήσω ὑμῶν	will accuse you
-	-	-	x			πρὸς τὸν πατέρα·	before the Father.
-	B	b	a'2			ἔστιν ὁ κατηγορῶν ὑμῶν	your accuser is
-	-	-	a'1			Μωϋσῆς,	Moses,
-	-	-		58	59	εἰς ὃν ὑμεῖς ἠλπίκατε.	on whom you set your hopes.
46	C	b'	a1	a		εἰ γὰρ ἐπιστεύετε	If you believed
-	-	-	-	b		Μωϋσεῖ,	Moses,
-	X	a'	a2	a'		ἐπιστεύετε ἄν	you would believe
-	-	-	-	b'	60	ἐμοί·	me,
-	C'		x		a	περὶ γὰρ ἐμοῦ	for ~ about me.
-	-	-	-		b	61 ἐκεῖνος ἔγραψεν.	he wrote ~
47	B'		a'1	b'	a	εἰ δὲ τοῖς ἐκείνου γράμμασιν	But if ~ his writings,
-	-	-	-	-	b	οὐ πιστεύετε,	you do not believe ~
-	A'		a'2	a'	a'	πῶς τοῖς ἐμοῖς ῥήμασιν	how ~ my words?
-	-	-	-	-	b'	πιστεύσετε;	will you believe ~

II55. Chiastic, ABC-C'B'A': B ("Your accuser is Moses, on whom you set your hopes") and B' ("But if you do not believe his writings") as well as C ("If you believed Moses") and C' ("for he wrote about me") highlight a great biblical character, Moses. In B and B', "you" are negatively criticized because of their unbelief of Moses regarding his writings, while in C and C', two positive facts, regarding their belief in Moses and his writings about "me," are interrelated. The Son tells them that he is not the accuser as in A ("Do not think that I will accuse you before the Father"), even though they do

not believe him as in A' ("how will you believe my words?"). The clause focusing the belief on "me," X ("you would believe me") is regarded as the center of the chiasm.

II56. Chiastic, ab-b'a': Both b ("Your accuser is Moses, on whom you set your hopes") and b' ("If you believed Moses") are related concerning Moses, whom they believed or hoped but who will accuse them, while a ("Do not think that I will accuse you before the Father") and a' ("you would believe me") highlight the Son, whom they have to believe and who will not accuse them. **II57.** Combined chiastic, a1a2-x-a'2a'1: Both a1 ("that I") and a'1 ("Moses") are the compared characters who might accuse "you," while the verbal phrases are located in a2 ("will accuse you") and a'2 ("your accuser is"). This type of accusing will be done "before the Father" (x), which is the center of chiasm.

II58. Combined chiastic, a1a2-x-a'1a'2: in a1 ("If you believed Moses") and a'1 ("but if you do not believe his writings"), belief in Moses is highlighted, while, in a2 ("you would believe me") and a'2 ("how will you believe my words?"), the belief in "me" is rather focused, while x ("for he wrote about me") shows the relationship between Moses and "me." This complex chiasm tells that those who believe Moses or his writings cannot but believe "me" or "my words." **II59.** Parallel, ab-a'b': Syntactically, a ("If you believed") - b ("Moses") is similar, in pattern, with a' ("you would believe") - b' ("me"), while semantically, the latter is the result of the former. Belief in Moses leads to belief in "me."

II60. Chiastic, ab-b'a': Both b ("he wrote ~") and b' ("But if you do not believe his writings") regard "he wrote" or "his writings," while a ("for ~ about me") and a' ("how will you believe my words?") are related regarding "me" or "my words." If "you" do not believe "his writings" that he wrote about "me," you will not believe "my words" that I spoke about "me." **II61.** Parallel, ab-a'b': "His writings" in a ("But if ~ his writings") is compared with "my words" in a' ("how ~ my words"), while b ("you do not believe") and b' ("will you believe") in common focus on "your unbelief."

In II55, Moses, a testifier to the Son, and the Jews who do not believe in him are in contrast. II56 focuses on their unbelief and the accusation of it. In II57, there is a comparison between Jesus and Moses regarding accusation. In II58, two related concepts are emphatic: belief in Moses and belief in Jesus; belief in Moses' writings and belief in "my" words. II59 focuses on the former, while II60–61 do so on the latter.

Extra Parallels

II62. Chiastic, ab-b'a': In vv. 37a–38, both a ("And the Father who sent me has testified about me") and a' ("for you do not believe him whom he has sent") describe in common the Father-Son relationship, particularly regarding the Father's action in sending his Son, while both b ("You have neither heard his voice at any time, nor seen his form") and b' ("and you do not have his word abiding in you") focus on their inaccessibility or unrelatedness to the Father. The chiasm tells that if "you" want to access to the Father who is neither seen nor heard, "you" have to believe him whom the Father has sent.

II63. Combined parallel, a-b1b2b3-a'-b'1b'2b'3: In vv. 25 and 28, the phrases, a ("the hour is coming") - b1 ("when the dead") - b2 ("will hear") - b3 ("the voice of the Son of God") and a' ("for the hour coming") - b'1 ("when all who are in the graves") - b'2 ("will hear") - b'3 ("his voice"), are arranged in parallel, syntactically and symmetrically, both demonstrating the resurrection of the dead responding to the voice of the Son. This parallel supports the connection between D2 and D'2 of II8.

II64. Parallel, ab-a'b': In vv. 24 and 29, both a ("has eternal life") and a' ("to the resurrection of life") focus on eternal life, while both b ("and does not come into judgment") and b' ("to the resurrection of judgment") highlight judgment. The contrasts between life and judgment are duplicated. This parallel sustains the connection between D1 and D'1 of II8.

II65. Parallel, abcde-a'b'c'd'e': In vv. 19 and 30, each part of a ("~ can ~") - b ("the Son ~") - c ("do") - d ("~ by himself") - e ("nothing ~") are repeated in a' ("~ can") - b' ("I ~") - c' ("do ~") - d' ("~ by myself") - e' ("nothing ~"), in exact order of syntax and symmetrically. This parallel demonstrates the connection between A and A' of II1.

I66. Parallel, a-a'-a": In vv. 19, 24–25, a threefold repetition, a-a'-a" ("Truly, truly, I say to you") happens here. Among them, the latter two (a' and a") are much closer to each other, as seen in D1 and D2 of II8, than the former (a).

Reading in Structure-Style

1. In the healing episode, besides the contrast between Jesus who heals and the Jews who are not concerned about healing, it is significant to contrast Jesus, who withdraws due to the crowd but takes the initiative to find the man and lead him to his salvation, and the man, who reports him to the Jews after knowing who healed him (13–15, II11). Jesus loves him but in return he betrays him.

2. Comparing I8 (8–9) and I10 (11–12), the focus shifts: from "rising" (being well) to "picking up the mat and walking." Both foci are sustained in the words of Jesus (8). But as for the Jews, the latter is prioritized, excluding the former.

3. As discussed previously in II31, Jesus refers to the Father as his other testifier (32), who is not the Baptist. Jesus does not entrust himself to any human testifier such as the Baptist (34; cf. 2:24–25). As he refers to "another" (ἄλλος, masculine singular), "the works" (τὰ ἔργα, neutral plural, 36) seem not to be suitable to be referred to. Rather "the Father" (37) is regarded here as the very one who testifies to the Son. In fact, the works of the Son are not separate from the Father. In other words, that the works of the Son testify about him means that the Father testifies to his Son through the works that he gave him to accomplish (36). In this sense, the Father and the Son testify regarding the Son together (8:17–18).

4. It is similar that, considering II43, the testimony of the Scriptures (39) include Moses' testimony may belong to that of the Father to the Son. In II43, the testimony of the Scriptures (A) and that of Moses (A') are in a pair, indicating the same theme. We may assume that the testimony of the Scriptures is also related to that of the Father similarly to that of the works. In vv. 37b–38, experiencing God is, in other words, having his word abiding within (see II47), which is the Scriptures that testify of the Son. It means that accepting the testimony of the Scriptures is related to experiencing God, resulting in having life.

Issues in Structure-Style

1. The Structure of vv. 19–30

Bultmann regarded vv. 27–29 (and 30b) as the work of a later editor "in an attempt to reconcile the dangerous statements in vv. 24f."[3] Based on Bultmann, Haenchen extended the work of the editor up to vv. 22–23.[4] The reason that he thought vv. 22–23 differ from vv. 19–21 is probably because there is seemingly a logical gap between vv. 21 and 22–23. He thought, "In chapter 5 there are thus relatively long insertions in the text of the Evangelist made by the redactor."[5] As for Bultmann, v. 26 is "a new formulation, though related to v. 21" and v. 27 is "another, and indeed unnecessary and clumsy repetition of the statement."[6] Meanwhile, he pointed out that v. 30 "leads back to vv. 19f., completing the circle for the first section of the discourse."[7]

In these verses, Brown observed some parallels:[8] A. The power of life shared by the Father and the Son (26, 21); B. The power of judgment shared by the Father and the Son (27, 22); C. The reaction of surprise (28, 20); D. An hour is coming (and is now here) when the dead hear the voice of the Son (28, 25); E. Those who have done right (have listened) shall live (29, 25); F. The Son does nothing by himself; The Son sees or hears what he must do (30, 19).

First, as discussed much in II1 and 8, the structure of vv. 19–30 is chiastic as a whole (II1): A (19–20) – X (21–29) – A' (30). And the X of II1, vv. 21–29, complex-chiastic in structure: ABC-D1D2-A'B'C'-D'2D'1, a very typical Johannine pattern.[9]

---

3. Bultmann, *Gospel of John*, 261.

4. Haenchen, *John 1*, 251–52. Haenchen regarded vv. 22–23 as a new concept that has nothing to do with either the previous verses (19–21) or the following ones (24–26).

5. Bultmann, *Gospel of John*, 260.

6. Ibid., 260–61.

7. Ibid., 262.

8. Brown, *Gospel according to John I–XII*, 219.

9. Brown criticized Léon-Dufour, who regarded v. 24 as the center of his chiasm and ignored the relation between vv. 25 and 28; cited by Brown, *Gospel according to John I–XII*, 219; Léon-Dufour, "Trois chiasmes johanniques," 253–55; See also Bullinger, *Figures of Speech*, 378; Giblin, "Two Complementary Literary Structures," 96–99, 103. We can see a similar model with Léon-Dufour from

Second, thus, it is so natural to see a certain connectivity between vv. 19–20 and 30 (the relation of A-A' of II1) and between vv. 21 and 26 (that of A-A' of II8) as many scholars including Bultmann have observed.[10]

Third, vv. 22–23, B-C of the first part of II8 (21–29), matching their counterpart, v. 27, B'-C' of the latter section of II8, describe two issues: (1) "doing judgment" given by the Father, as one of the Son's authorities; (2) honoring the Son as a deserving response to him. Consider v. 27, B'-C', in terms of their focus: (1) "doing judgment" given by the Father; (2) his being "the Son of Man" as a deserving title for him (to be honored). It ought to be said that vv. 22–23 are the verses coherent to the whole system of II8, and cannot be arbitrarily separated from the rest of this parallelism (*contra* Haenchen).

Fourth, more specifically, the reason why the Son of Man issue comes out in v. 27b ("because he is the Son of Man," C') is because it is designed to harmonize with its counterpart, v. 23 (C). In other words, the Son should be honored like the Father (C) is literally "because he is the Son of Man" (C').[11] However, it is not denied that v. 27b needs to be interpreted in context as well, in relation to its previous phrase, v. 27a. We may say that the author designed to create certain twofold, interactive connections: a sequential one between v. 27a (B') and 27b (C'); a chiastic one between v. 27b (C') and v. 23 (C).

Fifth, the reasons why we cannot say that v. 26 is "a new formulation" and v. 27 is "another, and indeed unnecessary and clumsy repetition of the statement" are as follows (*contra* Bultmann): (1) vv. 26–27 are neither added nor inserted without any schematic thought by someone like a redactor, rather these are the coherent part of a well-designed, parallel cluster, II8; (2) v. 26 (A') surely matches its counterpart, v. 21 (A), both telling of the Father-Son relationship regarding the "life" issue; (3) v. 27 (particularly 27a) is not merely the "unnecessary and clumsy repetition" of v. 22, but is also persistently created by the overall design of the final author who keeps his consistent writing style throughout the text of John (*contra* Bultmann).

Sixth, similarly, vv. 28–29 are also treated as D'2-D'1, essential parts of II8, matching their counterparts, D1-D2 (24–25). See also II63 and 64. These verses were not

---

Talbert: A. v. 19: Subordination of the Son to the Father; B. v. 20: We will marvel at the greater works of the Son; C. vv. 21–23: Just as the Father, so the son (life and judgment, 21–23); D. v. 24: Truly, truly, I say to you (has life); D'. v. 25: Truly, truly, I say to you (now is – will live); C'. vv. 26–27: Just as the Father, so the Son (life and judgment); B'. vv. 28–29: do not marvel at this, for the greater works of future resurrection and judgment are yet to come; A'. v. 30: Subordination of the Son to the One who sent him. Talbert, *Reading John*, 124. Talbert is right to see the relation between vv. 19 and 30 and between vv. 21–23 and 26–27. But we have to point out his ignorance of the model that: (1) The inseparability of vv. 19–20 (II2–7) matching v. 30, e.g., see specifically the relation between vv. 20 and 30 such as seeing (20) and hearing (30); (2) the pair of vv. 24–25 and 28–29 regarding its similarity both in form and theme.

10. Bultmann, *Gospel of John*, 262; Ridderbos, *Gospel according to John*, 192, 201–2; Beasley-Murray, *John*, 77; Carson, *Gospel according to John*, 259.

11. Brown, *Gospel according to John I–XII*, 219.

created or added "to reconcile the dangerous statements in vv. 24–25," as Bultmann insists. Rather, these are presented to make a perfect match with vv. 24–25 in terms of repetitive emphases of significant issues such as "getting-life" and "receiving-judgment," and also a complementary interaction in content such as "getting life through belief" in vv. 24–25 and "getting life through good deeds" in vv. 28–29.

Seventh, the way of observing parallels by Brown causes a misconception leading to them not being designed in a literary scheme. This is the reason why he regarded vv. 26–30 as "another version of the speech reported in 19–25, coming from a different stage of the Johannine tradition,"[12] because he saw the parallels in his mixed way, not following the right step to recognize the Johannine way of writing.

2. Realized Eschatology and the Final One

Godet suggests that "in a first cycle, the thought of v. 17 has been quite summarily developed (vv. 19, 20). Then the works of the Father which the Son is to accomplish are precisely stated in a second cycle (vv. 21–23); those of *making alive* and *judging*. Finally, in a third cycle (vv. 24–29) the thought makes a final advance, which brings it to its end, in the sense that vv. 24–26 apply to the resurrection and spiritual judgment, and vv. 27–29 to the final judgment and the resurrection of the dead . . . such as Luthardt, Weiss and Keil."[13]

Borchert understands that vv. 25–29 begin with another double *amen* saying regarding the twofold eschatological views, insisting that v. 25 starts a new passage as the NIV and other commentaries such as Morris and thus "the other paragraphing produces a choppy thought pattern."[14]

First, we can presume that "realized eschatology" is referred to in vv. 24–25, while the final judgment appears in vv. 28–29. However, we cannot say that vv. 24–27 apply to the spiritual judgment, while vv. 27–29 to the final judgment, as Godet insists, for at least vv. 26–27 cannot be regarded as part of vv. 24–27, instead they are part of vv. 26–29. We also cannot support the view of Morris seeing vv. 25–29 as "the Son and Judgment" being different from vv. 19–24, "the Father and the Son." These divisions are made without any consideration of the parallel features in vv. 21–29.

Second, if we have to deal with "realized eschatology" and "final eschatology" in these verses, we may admit that vv. 24–25 (instead of 24–26) deal with the former, while vv. 28–29 (instead of 27–29) focus on the latter, on condition that v. 25 is

---

12. In the usages of the Son of Man in John (1:51; 3:13, 14; 6:27, 53, 62; 8:28; 9:35; 12:23, 34; 13:31), its name is always related to the divinity of Jesus such as the Judge of the universe in relation to Dan 7:13–14.

13. Godet, *Commentary on John's Gospel*, 469, 482. Whitacre is also similar, seeing that the two contents (the divinity of Christ and his authority to judge) are repeated in vv. 24–29. Whitacre, *John*, 130–32.

14. Borchert, *John 1–11*, 240–42 Morris names vv. 19–24 as "The Father and the Son" and vv. 25–29 as "The Son and the judgment." Morris, *Gospel according to John*, 311–55.

regarded only as the statement of so-called "spiritual redemption" rather than salvation at his return.

Third, it is more significant to recognize that vv. 24–25 and vv. 28–29 are complementary, presenting a twofold salvation with belief and (or) with good deeds.

3. The Structure of vv. 31–47

Haenchen insists that in v. 37, "in addition to these 'works,' the Father is now also mentioned as witness. That is not suitable to the context. The Father is indeed the sole witness that really must be considered. . . . It is difficult for the interpreter to account for the fact that God is mentioned as a witness alongside the Baptist, the works, and Scripture."[15] Beasley-Murray also maintained this position: "The reference to the Father as the third witness, coming after John the Baptist, is thought to be out of place."[16]

Moreover, based on Bultmann,[17] Haenchen insists "that the entire segment, Verses 31–47, which treat the problem of 'witness' (μαρτυρία) and of 'glory' (δόξα), is a redactional addition."[18] Regarding vv. 45–47, he says "That applies also to verses 45–47. These verses are not really connected with verses 43f., but come closer to verses 39f., without simply being united thematically with them."[19]

First, according to II31, "another testifier" in v. 32, belonging to be A part, is evidently the Father who is mainly dealt with in vv. 36–37a (A'). Although John the Baptist who is the main issue of vv. 33–35 appears subsequent to v. 32, vv. 31–32 (A) are the counterpart of vv. 36–37a in II31, thus leading us to interpret them in relation to vv. 36–37a.

Second, in this way, the reference to the Father in v. 37 cannot be regarded as "not suitable to the context" (*contra* Haenchen): (1) v. 37a with v. 36 (the Father as his testifier, A' of II31) and vv. 31–32 (another testifier, A) match each other and thus are suitable to be located as they are. (2) In particular, see II37 where its A ("But I have testimony greater than that of John") in v. 36a is harmonized with A' ("And the Father who sent me has testified about me") in v. 37a. This pair, A and A', demonstrate the Father as the sole testifier about the Son. (3) The works of the Son appearing in B-B' in 36bc cannot be regarded as another testifier independent from the Father. These works have been given to the Son by the Father, the sole, divine testifier, to accomplish. Thus, the Father does testify through the works of the Son given by the Father. In this way, these works testify about the Son. "The works" cannot be separated from the Father and the Son, demonstrating the firm intimacy of the Father-Son relationship.

---

15. Haenchen, *John 1*, 263; cf. Beasley-Murray, *John*, 72.
16. Beasley-Murray, *John*, 72.
17. Bultmann, *Gospel of John*, 262–72.
18. Haenchen, *John 1*, 266.
19. Haenchen, *John 1*, 265–66.

Third, vv. 31–47 cannot be divided into vv. 31–40 and 41–47.[20] Based on II31–41 (31–37a) and II42–61 (37b–47), these verses are to be categorized into vv. 31–37a and 37b–47. Verses 31–37a focus much on "the testimony about the Son," while vv. 37b–47 highlight "the belief-unbelief" issue. See II31 and 42 for their chiastic structures.

Fourth, vv. 45–47 (A'), are the counterpart of vv. 37b–40 (A), as seen in II42. Thus, these verses can be shown "not to be connected to the previous verses, vv. 43–44," (X). In II42, both A and A' concentrate on their unbelief, while X focuses on the reason for their unbelief. The function of vv. 45–47 is to repeat the idea of "their unbelief," with emphasis, that is first referred in vv. 37b–40.

---

20. Compare the division of Moloney: (a) vv. 31–32: The problem of an acceptable witness to Jesus is raised by Jesus himself; (b) vv. 33–40: A series of witnesses are presented to "the Jews." They are (i) John the Baptist (33–35), (ii) the works of Jesus (36), (iii) the word of the unseen Father (37–40); (c) vv. 41–44: Jesus presents two contrasting understandings of *doxa*; (d) vv. 45–47: "The Jews" are accused by the writings of Moses. Moloney, *Signs and Shadows*, 19–20. Also compare the suggestion of Asiedu-Peprah. Believing that v. 18 is a narrative intrusion, he again divides vv. 17–47 into three: i. Reasons justifying Sabbath activity (17, 19–30); ii. Witnesses Invoked (31–40); iii. Defence transformed into accusations (41–47). Asiedu-Peprah, *Johannine Sabbath Conflicts*, 58.

6 "I Am the Bread of Life"

"The seemingly universal disposition to place food symbolism at the center of celebration, personal and public, and the power of the imagery of sustenance bring John 6 to center stage in the gospel drama. The claim of Rudolf Schnackenburg that this chapter is the climax of the Galilean ministry is not unwarranted."[1]

"As for John 6 and his own repeated efforts to interpret that passage across the decades, Kysar now concludes that the chapter is 'hopelessly ambiguous and no amount of research or study will (or even should) finally resolve that ambiguity.'"[2]

Dual Mode in Structure

JOHN 6 CAN BE divided into two sections: two episodes of Jesus (the feeding miracle, 1–15; the scene at the sea, 16–21); the dialogue of Jesus with those who follow him (22–71). In this sense, the entire structure is in dual mode.[3]

Two episodes of Jesus occur sequentially. The feeding miracle is first presented, closing at v. 15. Secondly, the scene at the sea, when Jesus walked on the sea, follows. These two episodes are also presented in dual mode.

The dialogue section (22–71) is not presented in this pattern, but in a chiastic structure instead. Three units are provided here: the multitude seeking Jesus (22–29, A); the bread of life dialogue (30–58, X); leaving disciples vs. staying ones (59–71, A'). Each of them reflects its own cohesive entity (see II1, II12, and II64).

---

1. Bailey, "John 6," 95–96.
2. Cited by Carson, "Reflections upon a Johannine Pilgrimage," 102; Kysar, *Voyages with John*, 249.
3. Carson suggests the overall structure of ch. 6 as: A (1–15); B (16–21); C (22–26); A (27–58); B (59–71). Carson, *Gospel according to John*, 273. The relation between vv. 16–21 and 59–71 seems not to be convincing.

169

I.	Two episodes of Jesus at Galilee (6:1-21)	
	IA.	The feeding miracle (6:1-15)
	IA'.	The scene at the sea (6:16-21)
II.	The dialogue between Jesus and those who seeking him (6:22-71)	
	IIA.	The multitude seeking Jesus (6:22-29)
	IIX.	The bread of life dialogue (6:30-58)
	IIA.	Leaving disciples vs. staying ones (6:59-71)

I. Two Episodes of Jesus in Galilee (6:1–21)

Dual, I1 (IA-IA')

This section (1–21) consists of two clusters: the feeding miracle (1–15, IA) and the scene at the sea (16–21, IA'). They are sequentially arranged. Both happen at the Sea of Galilee, when the Passover is near.

A.	The feeding miracle (1-15)	AB-B'A'
A'.	The scene at the sea (16-21)	A-X-A'

IA. The Feeding Miracle (6:1–15)

I2. Chiastic, AB-B'A': The cluster is divided into four parts: (1) Jesus and the multitude who follow him (A, 1–4); (2) there is a dialogue between Jesus and his disciples regarding feeding the people (B, 5–9); (3) there is the feeding miracle where Jesus orders and his disciples obey (B', 10–13); (4) there are Jesus and the people who are about to make him their king (A', 14–15). A and A' are in a pair in terms that Jesus and the people come to the fore, so are B and B', where the relationship between Jesus and his disciples is highlighted in relation to the feeding miracle.[4]

In vv. 1–15, there are thirteen parallels: four parallelisms (I4, 6, 9, 11), seven chiasms (I2–3, 5, 7–8, 10, 14), one combined parallelism (I12), and one dual (13). I2 is the main frame comprising the whole unit, each part of which is supported by I3 (A), I5–6 (B), I7 and I10 (B'), and I12 (A'). Except for I5–6 (B), there are more than two complex parallels appearing together. The most complex parallel is seen in vv. 10–13 (B' of I2), where at least five parallels are mixed. Among them, I10–11 are for the connection between vv. 12 and 13.

---

4. Compare the chiastic structure of Ellis: A (1–3); B (4–9); C (10); B' (11–13); A' (14–15). Ellis, *Genius of John*, 100–101.

"I Am the Bread of Life"

V	2	3	4		Phrases	Translation
1	A	a	a		Μετὰ ταῦτα ἀπῆλθεν ὁ Ἰησοῦς πέραν τῆς θαλάσσης τῆς Γαλιλαίας τῆς Τιβεριάδος.	After these things Jesus went away to the other side of the Sea of Galilee, which is the Sea of Tiberias.
2	-	b	b		ἠκολούθει δὲ αὐτῷ ὄχλος πολύς, ὅτι ἐθεώρουν τὰ σημεῖα ἃ ἐποίει ἐπὶ τῶν ἀσθενούντων.	And a multitude followed him, because they saw the signs which he was performed on those who were sick.
3	-	b'	a'		ἀνῆλθεν δὲ εἰς τὸ ὄρος Ἰησοῦς	Jesus went up on the mountain
	-	-	b'		καὶ ἐκεῖ ἐκάθητο μετὰ τῶν μαθητῶν αὐτοῦ.	and sat down there with his disciples.
4	-	a		5	ἦν δὲ ἐγγὺς τὸ πάσχα, ἡ ἑορτὴ τῶν Ἰουδαίων.	Now the Passover, the feast of the Jews was near.
5	B		a		Ἐπάρας οὖν τοὺς ὀφθαλμοὺς ὁ Ἰησοῦς καὶ θεασάμενος ὅτι πολὺς ὄχλος ἔρχεται πρὸς αὐτὸν	Jesus therefore, lifting up his eyes and seeing that a great multitude was coming to him,
	-		b		λέγει πρὸς Φίλιππον· πόθεν ἀγοράσωμεν ἄρτους ἵνα φάγωσιν οὗτοι;	said to Philip, "Where are we to buy bread so that these people may eat?"
6	-		b'		τοῦτο δὲ ἔλεγεν πειράζων αὐτόν·	And he said this to test him,
	-		a'	6	αὐτὸς γὰρ ᾔδει τί ἔμελλεν ποιεῖν.	for he himself knew what he was going to do.
7	-			a	ἀπεκρίθη αὐτῷ [ὁ] Φίλιππος·	Philip answered him,
	-			b	διακοσίων δηναρίων ἄρτοι οὐκ ἀρκοῦσιν αὐτοῖς	"Two hundred denarii worth of bread is not be sufficient for them,
	-			c	ἵνα ἕκαστος βραχύ [τι] λάβῃ.	for each one to receive a little."
8	-			a'	λέγει αὐτῷ εἷς ἐκ τῶν μαθητῶν αὐτοῦ, Ἀνδρέας ὁ ἀδελφὸς Σίμωνος Πέτρου·	One of his disciples, Andrew, Simon Peter's brother, said to him,
9	-			b'	ἔστιν παιδάριον ὧδε ὃς ἔχει πέντε ἄρτους κριθίνους καὶ δύο ὀψάρια·	"There is a boy here who has five barley loaves and two fish.
	-			c'	ἀλλὰ ταῦτα τί ἐστιν εἰς τοσούτους;	But what are they for so many people?"

13. Chiastic, ab-b'a': In a-a', we may see the place (a, the other side of the Sea of Galilee) and the time (a', the Passover being near) in a pair. A multitude follow him because of his signs having been seen by them (b), while, Jesus is with his disciples, sitting down on the mountain (b'). 14. Parallel, ab-a'b': In a-a', Jesus went away (ἀπῆλθεν, a) and went up (ἀνῆλθεν, a'). But, in b-b', the multitude who follow him and Jesus who sits down with his disciples are compared.

15. Chiastic, ab-b'a': When Jesus saw a multitude coming to him (a), he already knew what he was going to do (a'). But he asks Philip a question (b) in order to test him (b'), actually teaching him and letting him know about this, as well as the other disciples with him. 16. Parallel, abc-a'b'c': Philip and Andrew are compared in their actions: Philip, answering him, (a) and Andrew, saying to him, (a'); about two hundred denarii to feed them all (b) and about five barley loaves and two fish that they have (b'); regarding its deficiency (c) and regarding their deficiency (c').

In I3, the place and the time are introduced along with the characters: Jesus and the multitude. In I4, the Jesus' act of sitting with his disciples seems to be the focus. In I5, the knowledge of Jesus and the ignorance of Philip are compared. In I6, Philip and Andrew are compared in their manners.

V	7	8		Phrases	Translation
10	B'	a	a		εἶπεν ὁ Ἰησοῦς· ποιήσατε τοὺς ἀνθρώπους ἀναπεσεῖν.	Jesus said, "Make the people sit down."
-	-	-	x		ἦν δὲ χόρτος πολὺς ἐν τῷ τόπῳ.	Now there was much grass in the place,
-	-	-	a'	9	ἀνέπεσαν οὖν οἱ ἄνδρες τὸν ἀριθμὸν ὡς πεντακισχίλιοι.	so the men sat down, in number about five thousand.
11	-	x		a	ἔλαβεν οὖν τοὺς ἄρτους ὁ Ἰησοῦς	Jesus then took the loaves,
-	-	-		b	καὶ εὐχαριστήσας διέδωκεν τοῖς ἀνακειμένοις	and when he had gave thanks, he distributed to those who were seated,
-	-	-		a'	ὁμοίως καὶ ἐκ τῶν ὀψαρίων	so also the fish,
-	-	-	10	b'	ὅσον ἤθελον.	as much as they wanted.
12	-	a'	a		ὡς δὲ ἐνεπλήσθησαν,	And when they were filled,
-	-	-	b	11	λέγει τοῖς μαθηταῖς αὐτοῦ·	he said to his disciples,
-	-	-	-	a	συναγάγετε τὰ περισσεύσαντα κλάσματα,	"Gather up the leftover pieces
-	-	-	-	b	ἵνα μή τι ἀπόληται.	that nothing may be lost."
13	-		b	a'	συνήγαγον οὖν	So they gathered them up
-	-		-	b'	καὶ ἐγέμισαν δώδεκα κοφίνους κλασμάτων ἐκ τῶν πέντε ἄρτων τῶν κριθίνων	and filled twelve baskets with the pieces of the five barley loaves
-	-	12		a	ἃ ἐπερίσσευσαν τοῖς βεβρωκόσιν.	left over by those who had eaten.
14	A'	a1			Οἱ οὖν ἄνθρωποι ἰδόντες	After therefore the people saw the sign
-	-	a2	13		ὃ ἐποίησεν σημεῖον	that he had performed,
-	-	b	a		ἔλεγον ὅτι οὗτός ἐστιν ἀληθῶς ὁ προφήτης ὁ ἐρχόμενος εἰς τὸν κόσμον.	they said, "This is indeed the prophet who is to come into the world."
-	-	-	14			
15	-	a'1	a		Ἰησοῦς οὖν γνοὺς	Jesus then, knowing
-	-	a'2	x		ὅτι μέλλουσιν ἔρχεσθαι	that they were about to come
-	-	-	a'	-	καὶ ἁρπάζειν αὐτὸν ἵνα ποιήσωσιν βασιλέα,	and take him by force to make him king,
-	-	b'	a'		ἀνεχώρησεν πάλιν εἰς τὸ ὄρος αὐτὸς μόνος.	withdrew again to the mountain by himself.

I7. Chiastic, a-x-a': Two commands of Jesus to his disciples appear twice. Jesus first commands his disciples to make the people sit down (a) and lastly gives a second order to gather up the leftovers (a'). In the center x, Jesus gives thanks and distributes bread and fish. I8. Chiastic, a-x-a': As Jesus commands his disciples to make the people sit down (a), they follow exactly what he says (a'). In the middle, "much grass" is described. I9. Parallel, ab-a'b': In a-a', Jesus took the loaves (a) and so also the fishes (a'). And he gives thanks and distributes the loaves (b) [and fishes (a')] as much as they wanted (b'). The relation between b and b' seems to be complementary.

I10. Chiastic, ab-b'a': In a and a', it is indicated that they are filled (a) and that there are leftovers by those who had eaten (a'). In b-b', Jesus orders the disciples to gather the leftovers up (b), so they gather them up (b'). **I11**. Parallel, ab-a'b': In a-a', as Jesus commands his disciples to gather up the leftovers (a), they follow (a'). According to Jesus' saying that nothing may be lost (b), they gather them all up to fill twelve baskets (b').

I12. Combined parallel, a1a2-b-a'1a'2-b': There are some comparisons: the people saw the sign (a1) that he had performed (a2), while Jesus knew (a'1) what they were about to do regarding him (a'2). They see the surface, but Jesus knows the inside. They say that he is the prophet (b), probably who has to say more, but Jesus simply withdraws himself (b'), not saying a word. I13. Dual, a-a': In a, they say that he is the prophet, and, in a', they are making him their king. I14. Chiastic, a-x-a': When Jesus knows what they want (a), he withdraws to the mountain by himself (a'). In the middle, x, it is seen that they are coming to make him their king.

I7 accentuates the two commands of Jesus regarding the feeding miracle. I8 connects the command of Jesus and the obedience of the disciples. I9 focuses on how much of the loaves and the fish Jesus feeds the people. I10 focuses on how much is left over after they are filled. I11 highlights the second command of Jesus and the obedience of the disciples. I12 contrasts what the people saw and said to what Jesus knew and withdrew himself. I13 reveals what they think of him and try to do to him. I14 focuses on what he did after knowing something.

IA'. The Scene at the Sea (6:16–21)

I15. Chiastic, A-X-A': We may say that A depicts the background of the scene, the pre-scene where the disciples went but Jesus was not there (16–17), while A' is the main scene, where Jesus met his disciples, walking on the sea (19–21), while in X, there is the crisis at sea caused by the strong wind.

In vv. 16–21, there are seven parallels: one overall, chiastic structure (I15) with four chiasms (I17, 19–21), one combined chiasm (I16), and one parallelism (I18). Among them, I16 (A) and I19 (A'), along with I18 overlapping in a few phrases with I16 and I19, are the main supporters to the frame I15, while I17 and 20–21 are partially applied as parallels.

I16. Combined parallel, a1a2-x-a'1a'2: In a1, evening came, and, in a'1, it was already dark. Both a1-a'1 describe a similar situation of time. But, in a2-a'2, the disciples who went down to the sea and Jesus who was not with them are compared. In x, the disciples did something for themselves without their master. I17. Chiastic, a-x-a': In the center x, the focus is on them getting into a boat, while, in a-a', they went down to the sea (a), and started to cross the sea (a').

V	15	16			Phrases	Translation
16	A	a1		17	Ὡς δὲ ὀψία ἐγένετο	Now when evening came,
-		a2		a	κατέβησαν οἱ μαθηταὶ αὐτοῦ ἐπὶ τὴν θάλασσαν	his disciples went down to the sea,
17	-	x		x	καὶ ἐμβάντες εἰς πλοῖον	and after getting into a boat,
-	-		18	a'	ἤρχοντο πέραν τῆς θαλάσσης εἰς Καφαρναούμ.	they started to cross the sea to Capernaum.
-		a'1	a		καὶ σκοτία ἤδη ἐγεγόνει	And it was already dark,
-		a'2	b		καὶ οὔπω ἐληλύθει πρὸς αὐτοὺς ὁ Ἰησοῦς,	and Jesus had not yet come to them.
18	X	a'	19		ἥ τε θάλασσα ἀνέμου μεγάλου πνέοντος διεγείρετο.	And the sea rose because a strong wind was blowing.
19	A'	b'	a		ἐληλακότες οὖν ὡς σταδίους εἴκοσι πέντε ἢ τριάκοντα	When they had rowed about three or four miles,
-			b	a	20 21 θεωροῦσιν τὸν Ἰησοῦν	they saw Jesus
-			-	- b	περιπατοῦντα ἐπὶ τῆς θαλάσσης	walking on the sea
-			-	- b'	καὶ ἐγγὺς τοῦ πλοίου γινόμενον,	and drawing near to the boat.
-			b	a'	καὶ ἐφοβήθησαν.	They were frightened,
20	-		x	b'	ὁ δὲ λέγει αὐτοῖς· ἐγώ εἰμι· μὴ φοβεῖσθε.	but he said to them, "It is I. Do not be afraid."
21	-		b'	a'	ἤθελον οὖν λαβεῖν αὐτὸν εἰς τὸ πλοῖον,	then they were willing therefore to receive him into the boat.
-			a'		καὶ εὐθέως ἐγένετο τὸ πλοῖον ἐπὶ τῆς γῆς εἰς ἣν ὑπῆγον.	And immediately the boat was at the land where they were heading.

I18. Parallel, ab-a'b': In a-a', the time (already dark, in a) and the situation (the sea rose, in a') are connected. In b-b', Jesus who was not with them and his disciples who were without Jesus are compared again. **I19.** Chiastic, abc-c'b'a': The start of the scene, that they still rowed the boat, (a) and its end, the boat arrived suddenly, (a'), are in a pair. We see, in b, that Jesus walks on the sea to meet his disciples and, in b', that they welcome him willingly. In c-c', they are in fear (c) and Jesus says to them not to be afraid because ἐγώ εἰμι (I am) (c').

I20. Chiastic, ab-b'a': In a, they saw Jesus walking on the sea, drawing near to the boat, and eventually they welcomed him into the boat in a'. In the middle of the scene, they are frightened (b) and Jesus told them not to be afraid because "It is I" (b'). **I21.** Chiastic, ab-b'a': When they saw Jesus (a), they were frightened (a'). Jesus was walking on the sea (b) and was drawing near to the boat (b').

I16 focuses on the night situation and also on where Jesus and his disciples are. In I17, the disciples are on a boat crossing the sea. In I18, what Jesus did at sea and what the response of the disciples was are compared. In I19, Jesus walks on the sea and his disciples finally welcomed him in the midst of their fear. I20–21 focus on the first response of his disciples when they saw Jesus on the sea.

II. The Dialogue between Jesus and Those Who Seek Jesus (6:22–71)

Chiastic Structure, II1 (IIA-IIX-IIA')

1. In the first part of the section (22–29), which is in dual mode (II2), the multitude seeks Jesus and are getting on boats (22–24); and then they meet Jesus and ask him two questions and Jesus replies with two answers (25–29; see II7).

2. Although this type of question-answer pattern still flows up to vv. 30–36, the focus of issue slightly shifts from vv. 26–29 (working the work of God) to vv. 30–36 (the bread of life as the sign of belief).

3. Most of all, it is perceived that vv. 30–58 are entirely made up of a well-designed chiastic structure (II12, AB-X-B'A'), repeating the significance of the bread of life issue. We need to separate this unit from the following verses (59–71) as well as the previous ones (22–29).

4. The last part of the section (59–71) which is also in a dual (see II64) is in parallel with the first one (22–29). In the first part, the people actively seek and ask Jesus as if they would become his disciples, but in the last part, there are two differentiated groups of people: who are called "many of his disciples" but finally leave Jesus; who are his disciples confessing him and staying with him. Between the two parts, the contrast in the attitudes of the people toward Jesus is shown.

5. Thus, we may name each of them: A (22–29, those who seek Jesus); X (30–58, the bread of life dialogue); A' (59–71, those who leave vs. those who stay).

A.		The multitude seeking Jesus (22-29)	A-A'
	X.	The bread of life dialogue (30-58)	AB-X-B'A'
A'.		The leaving disciples vs. staying ones (59-71)	A-A'

IIA. The Multitude Seeking Jesus (6:22–29)

II2. Dual, A-A': There are two divisions: the multitude look for Jesus because of his feeding miracle (A, 22–24); there is the dialogue between Jesus and them regarding the food of eternal life and the work of God, namely believing in him (A', 25–29).

A.	The multitude seeking Jesus who feed them (22-24)	ab-a'b'
A'.	The work of God for the food of life (25-29)	ab-a'b'

A. The Multitude Seeking Jesus Who Feeds Them (6:22–24)

In vv. 22–24, there are four parallels: one parallelism (II3), one dual (II5), one combined parallelism (II4), and one chiasm (II6),[5] which is extended to v. 25. In these verses (A of II2), the main parallel is II3, or II4 if we have to exclude v. 23 because of its textual problem.

V	3	4		Phrases	Translation
22	a	a		Τῇ ἐπαύριον ὁ ὄχλος ὁ ἑστηκὼς πέραν τῆς θαλάσσης εἶδον	The next day the multitude that stood on the other side of the sea saw
-	-	b1	5	ὅτι πλοιάριον ἄλλο οὐκ ἦν ἐκεῖ εἰ μὴ ἕν	that there was no other small boat there,
-	-	b2	a	καὶ ὅτι οὐ συνεισῆλθεν τοῖς μαθηταῖς αὐτοῦ ὁ Ἰησοῦς εἰς τὸ πλοῖον	and that Jesus had not entered the boat with his disciples,
-	-	-	a'	ἀλλὰ μόνοι οἱ μαθηταὶ αὐτοῦ ἀπῆλθον·	but that his disciples had gone away alone.
23	b			ἄλλα ἦλθεν πλοιά[ρια] ἐκ Τιβεριάδος ἐγγὺς τοῦ τόπου ὅπου ἔφαγον τὸν ἄρτον	But some boats from Tiberias came near the place where they ate the bread after the
			6	εὐχαριστήσαντος τοῦ κυρίου.	Lord had given thanks.
24	a	a'	a	ὅτε οὖν εἶδεν ὁ ὄχλος	So when the crowd saw
-		b'2	-	ὅτι Ἰησοῦς οὐκ ἔστιν ἐκεῖ οὐδὲ οἱ μαθηταὶ αὐτοῦ,	that Jesus was not there, nor his disciples,
	b	b'1	b	ἐνέβησαν αὐτοὶ εἰς τὰ πλοιάρια καὶ ἦλθον εἰς Καφαρναοὺμ ζητοῦντες τὸν Ἰησοῦν.	they themselves got into the boats and went to Capernaum, seeking Jesus.

II3. Parallel, ab-a'b': In a, the multitude does not recognize where Jesus had gone, but, in a', they realize that Jesus is not there, nor his disciples. When some boats arrive there (b), they get into the boats and go to Capernaum, seeking Jesus (b'). (If there was not v. 23 originally, II3 would not be realized. But considering the Johannine style of creating a parallel, it is expected that v. 23 existed here.) II4. Combined parallel, a-b1b2-a'-b'2b'1: Both a and a' focus in common on what the multitude saw. Both b2 and b'2 describe Jesus and his disciples who were not there. In b1-b'1, at first there were not any boats (b1), but when they got boats they got into them to seek Jesus (b'1).

II5. Dual, a-a': Two sentences (a and a') are similar in meaning and are paraphrased: Jesus had not entered the boat with his disciples (a); thus, his disciples had gone away alone, not with him (a'). II6. Chiastic, ab-b'a': In b, they went to Capernaum, seeking Jesus, while, in b', they found him at last. Both b and b' are related in terms of their actions regarding Jesus. The question in a', "Rabbi, when did you get here?" is for a, that Jesus was not there.

In II3, how the multitude get into the boats, seeking Jesus is explained. In II4, it is repeated what they saw. II5 focuses on where Jesus and his disciples are. II6 focuses on how they meet Jesus.

---

5. The function of II6 is to connect vv. 22–24 and 25–29. If there are not II4 (the relation between vv. 22 and 24) and II7 in vv. 25–29, v. 25 cannot be separated from the cluster of vv. 25–29 because of its connection with the previous verse (24).

"I Am the Bread of Life"

A'. The Work of God for the Food of Life (6:25–29)

In vv. 25–29, there are five parallels: one overarching parallelism (II7), three chiasms (II8–9 and 11), and one dual (II10). II7 is the pillar structure (A' of II2), while II8–10 belong to vv. 26–27 (b of II7) and II11 to vv. 28–29 (a'b' of II7).

V	7			6	Phrases	Translation
25	a			b'	καὶ εὑρόντες αὐτὸν πέραν τῆς θαλάσσης	And when they found him on the other side of the sea,
-				a'	εἶπον αὐτῷ· ῥαββί, πότε ὧδε γέγονας;	they said to him, "Rabbi, when did you get here?"
26	b / 8				Ἀπεκρίθη αὐτοῖς ὁ Ἰησοῦς καὶ εἶπεν· ἀμὴν ἀμὴν λέγω ὑμῖν,	Jesus answered them, "Truly, truly, I say to you,
-	a	9			ζητεῖτέ με	you seek me,
-	b	a			οὐχ ὅτι εἴδετε σημεῖα,	not because you saw signs,
-	-	b			ἀλλ' ὅτι ἐφάγετε ἐκ τῶν ἄρτων καὶ ἐχορτάσθητε.	but because you ate the loaves and were filled.
27	b'	b' / 10			ἐργάζεσθε μὴ τὴν βρῶσιν τὴν ἀπολλυμένην	Do not work for the food which perishes,
-	-	a'	a		ἀλλὰ τὴν βρῶσιν τὴν μένουσαν εἰς ζωὴν αἰώνιον,	but for the food which endures to eternal life,
-	-	-	a'		ἣν ὁ υἱὸς τοῦ ἀνθρώπου ὑμῖν δώσει·	which the Son of man will give to you,
-	a'				τοῦτον γὰρ ὁ πατὴρ ἐσφράγισεν ὁ θεός.	for on him God the Father has set his seal."
28	a'			11	εἶπον οὖν πρὸς αὐτόν·	Then they said to him,
-	-			a	τί ποιῶμεν	"What shall we do,
-	-			b	ἵνα ἐργαζώμεθα τὰ ἔργα τοῦ θεοῦ;	that we may work the works of God?"
29	b'				ἀπεκρίθη [ὁ] Ἰησοῦς καὶ εἶπεν αὐτοῖς·	Jesus answered them,
-	-			b'	τοῦτό ἐστιν τὸ ἔργον τοῦ θεοῦ,	"This is the work of God,
-	-			a'	ἵνα πιστεύητε εἰς ὃν ἀπέστειλεν ἐκεῖνος.	that you believe in him whom he has sent."

II7. Parallel, ab-a'b': In a-a', the Jews ask Jesus twice regarding when he came (a, 25) and what they have to work (a', 28). The words of Jesus are twofold: what the food for eternal life is (b, 26–27) and what the work of God is (b', 29). **II8**. Chiastic, ab-b'a': In b, signs are contrasted to the loaves, while, in b', the perishable food is contrasted to the food to eternal life. In a-a', "you" who seek Jesus (a) and the Father who set his seal on him (a') are contrasted.

II9. Chiastic, ab-b'a': Both b and b' are regarding food, physical and perishable, and, in a-a', signs are focused regarding the food for eternal life. **II10**. Dual, a-a': Similar meaning is duplicated in a and a': the food enduring to eternal life (a); that given by the Son of Man (a').

II11. Chiastic, ab-b'a': Both in b and b', the expression, the work of God, is emphasized, but the works of God (plural) in b and the work of God (singular) in b' are contrasted. In a-a', the question, "What shall we do" (a), and its answer, "you believe in him whom he has sent" (a'), are provided in a pair.

II7 is related to the frame: question (the Jews) and answer (Jesus) and the relation between working for the food of life and the work of God is emphasized. In II8, the contrast between the people who seek Jesus because of the feeding sign and the Father who promotes his plan of eternal life through his Son is highlighted. In II9, the contrast between the perishable food and the non-perishable occurs. II10 explains what the food of life is, while II11 focuses on what the work of God is.

IIX. The Bread of Life Dialogue (6:30–58)

CHIASTIC STRUCTURE, II12 (AB-X-B'A')

1. Verses 30–36 consist of two subunits, each of which contains one question and its answer: vv. 30–33 (the bread of God as the sign of belief) and 34–36 ("I am the bread of life"). Each of them has its chiastic cohesion such as II14 (ab-b'a', 30–33) and II23 (ab-b'a', 34–36). This unit in a dual pattern can be regarded as an entity. We may call it A.

2. In the next passage, we cannot see the bread of life issue until v. 41. This verse belongs to vv. 41–43 that can be considered as an entity, having its own chiasm (II32) containing the same issue, the grumbling of the Jews.

3. In vv. 44–47, the bread of life issue is also not seen, it reappears after v. 48. This unit (44–47) has a combined chiasm (II36) binding the passage into a cluster. Two units, vv. 37–40 and vv. 44–47, need to be considered whether they are in a pair. These two deal with the same issue: those who come to Jesus will not be lost and be raised up at the last day. They are inevitably in a pair.

4. The last cluster, vv. 48–58, deals with the bread of life issue again and repetitively. In the middle of this unit, there is a scene of the argument among the Jews about the flesh of Jesus (52). Centering on this verse, the previous verses (48–51) and the following ones (53–58) are parallel with the same issue, the bread of life, but their foci are slightly shifted: from "I am the bread of life" to "the flesh of the Son to be eaten and his blood to be drunk for eternal life."

5. As a whole, we can see that the bread of life issue occurs both in vv. 30–36 and vv. 48–58. Thus, they need to be named A and A'. Verses 37–40 and vv. 44–47 are named B and B', because they are parallel, centering on vv. 41–43 (X).

6. In this way, we may classify this section as a chiastic structure as follows: A. The bread of God as the sign (30–36); B. I will not lose those who come to me (37–40); X.

The grumbling of the Jews (41–43); B'. I will raise up those who come to me (44–47); A'. The bread of life to make them live (48–57).[6]

A.	The bread of God as the sign (30-36)				
		B.	I will not lose those who come to me by the Father (37-40)		
				X.	The grumbling of the Jews (41-43)
		B'.	I will raise up those who come to me by the Father (44-47)		
A'.	The bread of life to make them live (48-58)				

A. THE BREAD OF GOD AS THE SIGN (6:30–36)

II13. Parallel, AB-A'B': As discussed earlier in II12, vv. 30–36 show twofold scenes (two dialogues between Jesus and the Jews). In the first scene, the Jews ask about the sign of belief (A), while the answer of Jesus is the bread of God as the heavenly sign (B). In the second scene, they ask Jesus to give them the bread of life (A') and Jesus replies that he is the bread of life (B').

In vv. 30–36, there are at least thirteen parallels: eight parallelisms (II13, 15–16, 18, 21–22, and 24), four chiasms (II14, 17, 20, and 23), and one combined chiasm (II19). II25 is extended to the next verse (37). II13 is the overarching structure, while II14 (AB of II14) and 23 (A'B') as the main pillars are supporting it. II16–19 exist to hold vv. 32–33 (B of II13) together, as II24 does to v. 35 (B'). II15 is to connect vv. 30 and 31, as II23 is between vv. 34 and 35–36. II21–22 connect B and B' of II13. In addition, in II25, there seems to be a connection between vv. 35–36 and 37. It is an *inclusio* that the seeing-believing motif occurs both in vv. 30 and 36 (see II59).

---

6. Cf. Maritz and van Belle introduce a chiastic structure centering on v. 35: A (22–27); B (28–29); C (30–33); X (35); C' (34–40); B' (41–51); A' (52–59). Maritz and van Belle, "Imagery of Eating and Drinking," 335–36. Their problems are not difficult to find: (1) vv. 22–29 are not divided as they have done rather into vv. 22–24 (II3) and 25–29 (II7); (2) vv. 30–58 have a perfect chiastic structure, AB-X-B'A' (II12). It means that v. 35 cannot be regarded as a center of the structure; (3) Therefore, they come to ignore those relations between vv. 30–36 and 48–58; between vv. 37–40 and 44–47. We may say that v. 35 is not the center, but vv. 30–36 that contain v. 35 playing the role of the axe with their corresponding passage, vv. 44–58 that also contain the *ego eimi* phrase (48 and 51; cf. 50 and 58, "This is the bread . . ."). Also compare the chiastic structure of Beutler: A (1–15); B (16–21); C (22–27); D (28–29); E (30–33); E' (34–40); D' (41–51); C' (52–59); B' (60–65); A' (66–71). It is difficult to accept his structure besides AB and B'A' for similar reasons as in Maritz and van Belle. Beutler, "Structure of John 6," 115–27.

V	13	14					Phrases	Translations
30	A	a	15				Εἶπον οὖν αὐτῷ·	They said therefore to him.
-	-	a					τί οὖν ποιεῖς σὺ σημεῖον,	What sign then do you do,
-	-	b					ἵνα ἴδωμεν καὶ πιστεύσωμέν σοι;	that we may see and believe you?
-	-	a'	18				τί ἐργάζῃ;	What do you work?
31	-	b	b'	a				οἱ πατέρες ἡμῶν τὸ μάννα ἔφαγον ἐν τῇ ἐρήμῳ,	Our fathers ate the manna in the wilderness;
-	-	-		b			καθώς ἐστιν γεγραμμένον· ἄρτον ἐκ τοῦ οὐρανοῦ ἔδωκεν αὐτοῖς φαγεῖν.	as it is written, "He gave them bread from heaven to eat."
32	B	b'					εἶπεν οὖν αὐτοῖς ὁ Ἰησοῦς·	Jesus therefore said to them.
-	-		16	17			ἀμὴν ἀμὴν λέγω ὑμῖν,	Truly, truly, I say to you.
-	-	a	a	a'			οὐ Μωϋσῆς δέδωκεν ὑμῖν	Moses has not given you
-	-	b	-	-			τὸν ἄρτον ἐκ τοῦ οὐρανοῦ,	the bread from heaven,
-	-	a'	b	b'			ἀλλ᾽ ὁ πατήρ μου δίδωσιν ὑμῖν	but my Father does give you
-	-	b'	-	-	21	22	τὸν ἄρτον ἐκ τοῦ οὐρανοῦ τὸν ἀληθινόν·	the true bread from heaven.
33	-	a'	b'	19	20	a	a	ὁ γὰρ ἄρτος τοῦ θεοῦ ἐστιν	For the bread of God is
-	-	-	a'	a1	a	b	b	ὁ καταβαίνων	he who comes down
-	-	-	-	a2	-	-	-	ἐκ τοῦ οὐρανοῦ	from heaven,
-	-	-	-	x	b	-	-	καὶ ζωὴν	and ~ life
-	-	-	-	a'1	-	-	-	διδοὺς	~ gives ~
-	-	23	-	a'2	-	-	-	τῷ κόσμῳ.	to the world.
34	A'	a						εἶπον οὖν πρὸς αὐτόν· κύριε,	They said therefore to him, Lord,
-	-	-		b'				πάντοτε δὸς ἡμῖν	give us ~ always.
-	-	-	25	a'				τὸν ἄρτον τοῦτον.	this bread ~
35	B'	b	a					εἶπεν αὐτοῖς ὁ Ἰησοῦς·	And Jesus said to them,
-	-	-	-	a'	a'			ἐγώ εἰμι ὁ ἄρτος	I am the bread
-	-	24	-	b'	-			τῆς ζωῆς·	of life.
-	-	b'	a	b		b'		ὁ ἐρχόμενος	He who comes
-	-	-	b	-		-		πρὸς ἐμὲ	to me
-	-	-	c	-		-		οὐ μὴ πεινάσῃ,	will never be hungry,
-	-	-	a'	-		-		καὶ ὁ πιστεύων	and he who believes
-	-	-	b'	-		-		εἰς ἐμὲ	in me
-	-	-	c'	-		-		οὐ μὴ διψήσει πώποτε.	will never be thirsty.
36	-	a'	a'					Ἀλλ᾽ εἶπον ὑμῖν ὅτι καὶ ἑωράκατέ [με] καὶ οὐ πιστεύετε.	But I said to you, that you have seen [me], and you do not believe.

II14. Parallel, ab-a'b': In b-b', the Jews proudly refer to the event of the manna from heaven (b), while Jesus emphasizes the fact that it was not Moses but "my Father" who did it and still does (b'). In a-a', they ask about the sign so that they may believe him (a), while Jesus presents the bread of God as the true sign (a'). **II15.** Parallel,

"I Am the Bread of Life"

ab-a'b': In this, a (what sign) is similarly repeated in a' (what work), because of b', their assertion regarding the manna that their fathers ate, the issue raised by them in b ("that we may see and believe you?") can be known to the listeners regarding what kind of sign they really want to see. In other words, they asked Jesus about some sign like the manna (or the sign of five loaves and two fishes).

II16. Parallel, ab-a'b': "Moses who has not given you" in a is contrasted to "my Father who does give you" in a', while b, "the bread from heaven", similarly recurs in b', "the true bread from heaven". But the present tense "give" reminds us that the bread is not the manna in the wilderness. II17. Chiastic, ab-b'a': The contrast between "Moses who has not given" something in a and "he who comes down from heaven" and "gives" something in a' is shown, while b ("the true bread from heaven" that "my Father does give you") is summarized as b', "the bread of God".

II18. Parallel, ab-a'b': Although their fathers ate the manna (a), but Moses was not the one who gave or has given "the bread from heaven" (a'). Only "my Father" gave (b) and gives (b') the people the bread from heaven. **II19**. Mixed Chiastic, a_1a_2-x-$a'_1a'_2$: "He who comes down" (a_1) is the one who "gives" (a'_1), and "from heaven" in a_2 and "to the world" (a'_2) are in a pair in the aspect of two directions, centering and emphasizing x, "life". II20. Chiastic, ab-b'a': In this, b and b' are parallel by using the same verb, "give", while a' ("this bread") is identified by a ("For the bread of God is he who [*or* the bread that] comes down from heaven"), even though the Jews do not know what the bread is.

II21. Parallel, ab-a'b': Both a and a' indicate his identity as "the bread", while both b and b' show his role as the giver of life. The contents of b ("he who comes down from heaven and gives life to the world") is summarized in b' ("of life"). **II22**. Parallel, ab-a'b': Both a ("the bread of God") and a' ("the bread of life") reveal his identity. And b is Jesus' role as the giver of life ("come down"-"give"), while b' is the role of the receiver of life ("come"-"believe").

II23. Chiastic, ab-b'a': In a-a', the Jews demand Jesus to give them the bread from heaven (a), but Jesus, on the contrary, points out their unbelief in spite of seeing him (a'). Jesus has already provided them the true bread from heaven but they have failed to take it. In b-b', Jesus reveals two things: that he is the bread of life (b) and the related consequence if they come to him (b'). **II24**. Parallel, abc-a'b'c': The same pattern with similar issue in a ("he who comes"), b ("to me"), and c ("will never be hungry") reappears in a' ("he who believes"), b' ("in me"), and c' ("will never be thirsty"). II25. Parallel, ab-a'b': In a-a', Jesus says that he is the bread of life (a), thus they have to believe him after seeing him (a'). Both b-b' demonstrate what happens if they come to believe in him: neither being hungry nor being thirsty (b); he will never cast them out (b').

The foci of parallels are: the bread from heaven as the true sign from God (II14); the manna as a sign (II15); Moses vs. "his" Father (II16); the manna vs. the bread of God (II17); from whom is the heavenly bread (II18); the heavenly being who gives life (II19); the Jews' misunderstanding of the heavenly bread (II20); what the bread of life

181

SOURCEBOOK OF THE STRUCTURES AND STYLES IN JOHN 1–10

is (II21); giving life and its consequence (II22); their request and their unbelief (II23); believing in him and its results (II24).

B. I WILL NOT LOSE THOSE WHO COME TO ME (6:37–40)

In vv. 37–40, there are six parallels: four chiasms (II26–29) and two parallelisms (II30–31). Two parallels, II26 and 30, are the main ones that occur simultaneously, comprising the cluster. II27–28 belong to a part of II26 (a), while II29 shows the connectivity among vv. 38–39. II31 belongs to II30 (b-b'). It means that vv. 37–40 cannot be separated because of their close connection.

V	26	27		25	Phrases	Translations
37	a	a	28	b'	πᾶν ὃ δίδωσίν μοι ὁ πατὴρ	All that the Father gives me
	-	b	a	-	πρὸς ἐμὲ	~ to me,
	-	-	b	-	ἥξει,	will come ~
	-	b'	b'	-	καὶ τὸν ἐρχόμενον	and ~ the one who comes
	-	-	a'	-	πρὸς ἐμὲ	to me
	-	a'		29 -	οὐ μὴ ἐκβάλω ἔξω,	I will never cast out ~.
38	b			a	ὅτι καταβέβηκα ἀπὸ τοῦ οὐρανοῦ	For I have come from heaven
	-		30	b	οὐχ ἵνα ποιῶ τὸ θέλημα τὸ ἐμὸν ἀλλὰ τὸ θέλημα τοῦ πέμψαντός με.	not to do my own will, but the will of him who sent me.
39	b'	a		b'	τοῦτο δέ ἐστιν τὸ θέλημα τοῦ πέμψαντός με,	And this is the will of him who sent me,
	a'	b	31 a	a'	ἵνα πᾶν ὃ δέδωκέν μοι	that of all that he has given me
	-	-	b	-	μὴ ἀπολέσω ἐξ αὐτοῦ,	I should lose nothing,
	-	-	c	-	ἀλλ' ἀναστήσω αὐτὸ [ἐν] τῇ ἐσχάτῃ ἡμέρᾳ.	but raise it [them] up at the last day.
40	a'				τοῦτο γάρ ἐστιν τὸ θέλημα τοῦ πατρός μου,	For this is the will of my Father,
		b'	a'		ἵνα πᾶς ὁ θεωρῶν τὸν υἱὸν	that everyone who sees the Son
		-	-		καὶ πιστεύων εἰς αὐτὸν	and believes in him
		-	b'		ἔχῃ ζωὴν αἰώνιον,	may have eternal life,
		-	c'		καὶ ἀναστήσω αὐτὸν ἐγὼ [ἐν] τῇ ἐσχάτῃ ἡμέρᾳ.	And I will raise him up at the last day.

II26. Chiastic, ab-b'a': In b-b', the will of the Father is repeatedly emphasized: "I have come from heaven . . . but [to do] the will of him who sent me" (b); "And this is the will of him who sent me" (b'). In a-a', the similar promise or guarantee of Jesus toward those who come to him is highlighted: "I will never cast out the one who comes to me" (a); "I should lose nothing, but raise it [them] up at the last day" (a'). **II27.** Chiastic, ab-b'a': In this, b ("will come to me") and b' ("and the who comes") are in a pair, while a ("All that the Father gives me") is complemented by a' ("I will never cast

out"). That is to say, Jesus will not cast out all who his Father gives him. **II28**. Chiastic, ab-b'a': Two phrases ("to me"-"will come") are repeated in chiasm ("and the one who comes"-"to me").

II29. Chiastic, ab-b'a': In this, b and b' are common in referring to "the will of him who sent me", while a' ("not-losing-anyone" and "raising-it[them]-up") is the mission of him "who has come from heaven" in a. **II30**. Parallel, ab-a'b': In this, a and a' are in common in referring to "the will of him who sent me (or of my Father)", while b indicates Jesus' will to protect and raise up the believers and b' focuses on the faith of the believers and its results. **II31**. Parallel, abc-a'b'c': In this, c and c' ("raising-them-up") are duplicated, while a and a' regard in common the people who have been given to Jesus or who believe in him. That the believer "may have eternal life" (b') can be done by Jesus' will, "I should lose nothing" (b).

In II26, what the will of the Father is and the promise of life given to the believer are shown. II27 focuses on that he who comes to Jesus will not be cast out, while II28 repeats coming to Jesus. In II29, it is disclosed that the will of the Father is that Jesus does not lose anyone and raises him/her up eventually. II30–31 compares Jesus' role and the believer's one to fulfill the will of the Father.

X. The Grumbling of the Jews (6:41–43)

Verses 41–43 comprise four-fold complex parallels: two chiasms (II32–33) and two parallelisms (II34–35), showing their tight relationship among themselves. Each of II33–35 belongs to II32, partially.

V	32	33		Phrases	Translations
41	a	a		Ἐγόγγυζον οὖν οἱ Ἰουδαῖοι περὶ αὐτοῦ	The Jews then were grumbling about him,
	b	b	a	ὅτι εἶπεν·	because he said,
	-		b	ἐγώ εἰμι ὁ ἄρτος	"I am the bread
	-		34 -	ὁ καταβὰς ἐκ τοῦ οὐρανοῦ,	that came down from heaven."
42	c		a	καὶ ἔλεγον· οὐχ οὗτός ἐστιν Ἰησοῦς	And they said, "Is this not Jesus,
	-		b	ὁ υἱὸς Ἰωσήφ,	the son of Joseph,
	c'		a'	οὗ ἡμεῖς οἴδαμεν	~ we know?
	-		b'	τὸν πατέρα καὶ τὴν μητέρα;	whose father and mother ~
	b'		a'	πῶς νῦν λέγει	How does he now say,
	-		b'	ὅτι ἐκ τοῦ οὐρανοῦ καταβέβηκα;	"I have come down from heaven."
43	a'	b'		ἀπεκρίθη Ἰησοῦς καὶ εἶπεν αὐτοῖς·	Jesus therefore answered and said to them,
	-	a'		μὴ γογγύζετε μετ' ἀλλήλων.	"Do not grumble among yourselves.

II32. Chiastic, abc-c'b'a': Both a and a' indicate the Jews' grumbling about him, while b and b' tell of his coming down from heaven as the heavenly bread, while c and

c' are related to each other in terms of the Jews' knowledge of some physical information about Jesus. **II33**. Chiastic, ab-b'a': In this, a (they were "grumbling") is related to a' ("Do not grumble"), as b ("because he said") is to b' ("Jesus . . . said to them").

II34. Parallel, ab-a'b': Both a ("And they said 'Is this not Jesus'") and a' ("we know [him]") show the Jews' understanding of Jesus, while b and b' indicate the physical information about him and his parents. II35. Parallel, ab-a'b': Jesus' words in a-b ("because he said"-"I am the bread that came down from heaven") are reflected in the Jews' words in a'-b' ("How does he now say"- "I have come down from heaven").

II32 discloses their reason for grumbling about him in repetition. In II33, they were grumbling and Jesus rebukes them. In II34, their knowledge of him is suggested as twofold. In II35, the word of Jesus regarding the heavenly bread is repeated.

B'. I Will Raise Up Those Who Come to Me (6:44–47)

In vv. 44–47, there is one overarching, combined chiastic structure (II36), another combined chiasm (II37), and a typical chiasm (II38). II37 serves to help the connection between vv. 44–45, while II38 shows the cohesion within v. 46.

V	36	37		Phrases	Translations
44	A1	a1		οὐδεὶς δύναται ἐλθεῖν πρός με	No one can come to me,
	-	a2		ἐὰν μὴ ὁ πατὴρ ὁ πέμψας με ἑλκύσῃ αὐτόν,	unless the Father who sent me draws him;
	A2	x		κἀγὼ ἀναστήσω αὐτὸν ἐν τῇ ἐσχάτῃ ἡμέρᾳ.	and I will raise him up at the last day.
45	X	a'2		ἔστιν γεγραμμένον ἐν τοῖς προφήταις· καὶ ἔσονται πάντες διδακτοὶ θεοῦ·	It is written in the prophets, "And they will all be taught by God.
	-	a'1	38	πᾶς ὁ ἀκούσας παρὰ τοῦ πατρὸς καὶ μαθὼν ἔρχεται πρὸς ἐμέ.	Everyone who has heard to the Father and learned from him comes to me.
46	A'1		a	οὐχ ὅτι τὸν πατέρα	Not that ~ the Father,
	-		b	ἑώρακέν	~ has seen ~
	-		c	τις	any man ~
	-		x	εἰ μὴ ὁ ὢν παρὰ τοῦ θεοῦ,	except the one who is from God;
	-		c'	οὗτος	this one
	-		b'	ἑώρακεν	has seen
	-		a'	τὸν πατέρα.	the Father.
47	A'2			Ἀμὴν ἀμὴν λέγω ὑμῖν, ὁ πιστεύων ἔχει ζωὴν αἰώνιον.	Truly, truly, I say to you, he who believes has eternal life.

II36. Combined chiastic, A1A2-X-A'1A'2: In A1-A'1, the special relationship between the Father and the Son is emphasized: the Father sent the Son and draws the person to him (A1); The Son only can have seen the Father (A'1). In A2-A'2, the similar issue, giving-life, is shown: the Son will raise the person up whom the Father

draws (A2); the believer in the Son has eternal life (A'2). In the center, X, the writing of the prophets is introduced.

II37. Combined chiastic, a1a2-x-a'1a'2: As "their coming" in a1 is done by "the Father's drawing" in a2, so "their coming" in a'2 is accomplished by "their learning" (or "being taught" and "hearing") from God in a'1 and a'2. It means that the men who learn from God will naturally come to Jesus and the men who did not learn from God cannot come to him. X ("raising-him-up") is the center of the chiasm. **II38**. Chiastic, abc-x-c'b'a: This chiasm shows the contrast between a-b-c ("Not that ~ the Father"- "~ has seen ~"- "any man ~") and c'- b'-a' ("this one"- "has seen"- "the Father"), centering x ("except the one who is from God") that is regarding Jesus' identity.

In II36, the intimate relationship between the Father and the Son as well as the believer's eternal life are focused together. II37 focuses on who can come to the Son in relation to the Father and also his promise of resurrection. II38 highlights the uniqueness of the Son who can see the Father.

A'. THE BREAD OF LIFE TO MAKE THEM LIVE (6:48–58)

In vv. 48–58, there is one comprehensive, chiastic structure (II39) with not a few parallels: fourteen parallelisms (II40–44, 46–52, 56, and 58), three chiasms (II54–55 and 57), and two combined chiasms (II45 and 53). We may say that in II39 there are two main pillars: II40 and 45.

Interestingly, so many parallelisms are preferred in this cluster. In vv. 48–52, all the parallels are of parallelisms except for the overarching structure, II39. Among them, II40–43 are related to the cohesion of A of II39, while II44 is for the connection between A and X. II46–47 and 49–50 support the connection of v. 53 to v. 54 (A1-A2 of II45), as II51 and 53–54 does v. 56 to v. 57 (A'2-A'1 of II45). II48 shows the connection between vv. 54 and 56 (A2-A'2 of II45). II55–58 are used for the connection between vv. 57 and 58.

II39. Chiastic, A-X-A': As discussed earlier in II13, these verses are divided into three, creating a chiasm: "I am the bread of life" (A, 48–51); the Jews' argument about the flesh of Jesus (X, 52); the flesh of Jesus is to be eaten and his blood to be drunk for eternal life (A', 53–58). Placing the Jews' argument in the center (X), two similar, connected verses are in parallel (A-A').

V	39	40				Phrases	Translations
48	A	a				Ἐγώ εἰμι ὁ ἄρτος	I am the bread
-		b	41			τῆς ζωῆς.	of life.
49	-	c	a			οἱ πατέρες ὑμῶν	Your fathers
-	-	-	b			ἔφαγον ἐν τῇ ἐρήμῳ τὸ μάννα	ate the manna in the wilderness,
-	-	-	c			καὶ ἀπέθανον·	and they died.
50	-	a'				οὗτός ἐστιν ὁ ἄρτος	This is the bread
-	-	b'	42			ὁ ἐκ τοῦ οὐρανοῦ καταβαίνων,	that comes down from heaven,
-	-	c'	a'	a		ἵνα τις	so that one
-	-	-	b'	b		ἐξ αὐτοῦ φάγῃ	may eat of it
-	-	-	c'	c	43	καὶ μὴ ἀποθάνῃ.	and not die.
51	-	a''		a		ἐγώ εἰμι ὁ ἄρτος	I am the bread,
-	-	b''		-		ὁ ζῶν ὁ ἐκ τοῦ οὐρανοῦ καταβάς·	the living one, that came down from heaven;
-	-	c''	a'	b		ἐάν τις	if anyone
-	-	-	b'	-		φάγῃ ἐκ τούτου τοῦ ἄρτου	eats of this bread,
-	-	-	c'	-	44	ζήσει εἰς τὸν αἰῶνα,	he will live forever;
-	-			a'	a	καὶ ὁ ἄρτος δὲ ὃν ἐγὼ δώσω	and the bread that I will give
-	-			b'	b	ἡ σάρξ μού ἐστιν ὑπὲρ τῆς τοῦ κόσμου ζωῆς.	is my flesh for the life of the world."
52	X					Ἐμάχοντο οὖν πρὸς ἀλλήλους οἱ Ἰουδαῖοι λέγοντες·	The Jews are therefore arguing with one another,
-					a'	πῶς δύναται οὗτος ἡμῖν δοῦναι	"How can this man give us
-					b'	τὴν σάρκα [αὐτοῦ] φαγεῖν;	[his] flesh to eat?"

II40. Parallel, abc-a'b'c'-a"b"c": Triple parallel features are found: a ("I am the bread"), a' ("This is the bread"), and a" ("I am the bread") are repeated; b ("of life"), b' ("that comes down from heaven"), and b" ("the living one, that came down from heaven") all indicate what sort of the bread he is; c ("Your fathers ate . . . and they died"), c' ("so that one may eat of it and not die"), and c" ("if anyone eats of this bread, he will live forever") are all related to the same concepts, "eating" and "dying." Interestingly, ab and a"b" are much more similar than a'b', while c' and c" are closer to each other than to c. II41. Parallel, abc-a'b'c': Phrasal pairs such as a ("your fathers") and a' ("one"), b ("ate the manna") and b' ("may eat of it"), and c ("they died") and c' ("and not die") are observed, but the idea of a-b-c- is reversed in a'-b'-c'.

II42. Parallel, abc-a'b'c': Both the two clauses, with parallel phrases, represent the same connotation: eating and not dying (or living forever). I34 and 35 are quite similar but slightly different in pattern. II43. Parallel, ab-a'b': a and a' indicate "his being the bread" (a) or "giving the bread" (a'), while b ("living forever") and b' ("for the life") are related to the receiver's (or the world's) life, who have it. II44. Parallel, ab-a'b': The statement of Jesus in ab ("giving the bread"- "my flesh for the life") is restated through

"I Am the Bread of Life"

the mouths of the Jews in a'b' ("how can this man give us"- "[his] flesh to eat"). Indeed, a and a', b and b' are in a pair.

II45. Chiastic, A1A2-X-A'2A'1: A1 recurs in A'1 in terms of "eating-drinking" and "living" (or "having life") because of Jesus. In A2 and A'2, exactly the same expression, "He who eats my flesh and drinks my blood" appears, both showing the succeeding results of "eating-drinking." In X, centered in the chiasm, the qualities of his flesh and his blood, are described. **II46**. Parallel, ab-a'b': The phrases, a-b ("unless . . . no life in you"), are negative in expressing the "eating-drinking" motif, while, in a'-b' (". . . has eternal life, and I will raise him up . . ."), this concept is positively stated. **II47**. Parallel, ab-a'b'-a"b": The "eating-drinking" motif simply recurs in triple parallels (one negative and two positives).

II48. Parallel, ab-a'b': In this, a ("He who eats my flesh and drinks my blood") is identical to a', while b ("and I will raise him up at the last day") and b' ("[he] remains in me and I in him") indicate the complementary results of "eating-drinking," namely, having life and mutual remaining, binding these two closely. **II49**. Parallel, ab-a'b': Simple parallel features are made between a-b ("eat"-"the flesh") and a'-b' ("drink"-"his blood"). **II50**. Parallel, ab-a'b': Simple parallel phrases are found between a-b ("eats"-"my flesh") and a'-b' ("drinks"-"my blood").

II51. Parallel, ab-a'b': It is exactly the same pattern of II50. **II52**. Parallel, abc-a'b'c': A simple parallel pattern, a-b-c ("For my flesh"- "is true"- "food") and a'-b'-c' ("and my blood"- "is true"- "drink"), in describing what his flesh and his blood are, is shown. **II53**. Combined chiastic, a1a2-x-a'1a'2: Both a1 ("eating-drinking" and then "mutual remaining") and a'1 ("eating" and then "living") indicate, in common, mutual remaining or living between Jesus and his believer. And a2 ("As the living Father sent me") and a'2 ("and I live because of the Father") describe the relationship between the Father and the Son with their livingness. In x, we can see the Father-Son relationship: living Father and living Son. **II54**. Chiastic, ab-b'a': simple parallelism both in rhyme (5 syllables in Greek) and pattern between a-b ("in me"- "[he] remains") and b'-a' ("in him"- "and I") is created.

II55. Chiastic, ab-b'a': Both a ("so he who eats me also will live because of me") and a' ("he who eats this bread will live forever") connote the same meaning regarding Jesus, the living bread, while, in b ("This is bread that came down from heaven") and b' ("not as the fathers ate"), this heavenly bread and the manna are contrasted. **II56**. Parallel, ab-a'b': The phrases, a ("so he who eats me also") and b ("will live because of me"), are similarly and complementarily expressed in a' ("he who eats this bread") and b' ("will live forever").

II57. Chiastic, a-x-a': Both a ("This is the bread that came down from heaven") and a' ("he who eats this bread will live forever") show Jesus' identity and role as the heavenly bread, while x ("not as the fathers ate") focuses on its dissimilarity with the manna. **II58**. Parallel, ab-a'b': Two pairs, a ("not as the fathers ate") and a' ("he who eats this bread"), b ("and died") and b' ("will live forever"), are contrasted to each other, respectively. A-b reflect the negativity and a'-b' the positivity.

Sourcebook of the Structures and Styles in John 1–10

V	39						Phrases	Translations
53	A'	45					εἶπεν οὖν αὐτοῖς ὁ Ἰησοῦς·	Then Jesus said to them,
-	-	A1					ἀμὴν ἀμὴν	"Truly, truly,
-	-	-	46	47	49		λέγω ὑμῖν,	I say to you,
-	-	-	a	a	a		ἐὰν μὴ φάγητε	unless you eat
-	-	-	-	-	b		τὴν σάρκα τοῦ υἱοῦ τοῦ ἀνθρώπου	the flesh of the Son of man
-	-	-	-	b	a'		καὶ πίητε	and drink
-	-	-	-	-	b'		αὐτοῦ τὸ αἷμα,	his blood,
-	-	-	b	48	50		οὐκ ἔχετε ζωὴν ἐν ἑαυτοῖς.	you have no life in you.
54	-	A2	a'	a'	a		ὁ τρώγων	He who eats
-	-	-	-	-	b		μου τὴν σάρκα	my flesh
-	-	-	-	b'	a'		καὶ πίνων	and drinks
-	-	-	-	-	b'		μου τὸ αἷμα	my blood
-	-	-	b'	b			ἔχει ζωὴν αἰώνιον,	has eternal life,
-	-	-	-	-			κἀγὼ ἀναστήσω αὐτὸν	and I will raise him up
-	-	-	-	-	52		τῇ ἐσχάτῃ ἡμέρᾳ.	at the last day.
55	-	X			a		ἡ γὰρ σάρξ μου	For my flesh
-	-				b		ἀληθής ἐστιν	is true
-	-				c		βρῶσις,	food
-	-				a'		καὶ τὸ αἷμά μου	and my blood
-	-				b'		ἀληθής ἐστιν	is true
-	-			51	c'	53	πόσις.	drink.
56	-	A'2	a''	a'	a	a1	ὁ τρώγων	He who eats
-	-	-	-	-	b	-	μου τὴν σάρκα	my flesh
-	-	-	b''	-	a'	-	καὶ πίνων	and drinks
-	-	-	-	-	b	54	μου τὸ αἷμα	my blood
-	-	-	-	b'	a	a2	ἐν ἐμοὶ	~ in me,
-	-	-	-	-	b	-	μένει	remains ~
-	-	-	-	-	b'	-	κἀγὼ	and I
-	-	-	-	-	a'	-	ἐν αὐτῷ.	in him.
57	-	A'1				x	καθὼς ἀπέστειλέν με ὁ ζῶν πατὴρ	As the living Father sent me,
-	-	-	55	56		-	κἀγὼ ζῶ διὰ τὸν πατέρα,	and I live because of the Father,
-	-	-	a	a		a'1	καὶ ὁ τρώγων με κἀκεῖνος	so he who eats me also
-	-	-	-	b	57	a'2	ζήσει δι' ἐμέ.	will live because of me.
58	-		b	a			οὗτός ἐστιν ὁ ἄρτος	This is the bread
-	-		-	-	58		ὁ ἐξ οὐρανοῦ καταβάς,	that came down from heaven;
-	-		b'	x	a		οὐ καθὼς ἔφαγον οἱ πατέρες	not as the fathers ate,
-	-		-	-	b		καὶ ἀπέθανον·	and died,
-	-		a'	a	a'	a'	ὁ τρώγων τοῦτον τὸν ἄρτον	he who eats this bread
-	-		-	b	-	b'	ζήσει εἰς τὸν αἰῶνα.	will live forever.

The foci of the parallels are: from the emphasis that he is the bread of life to that of his flesh and blood to be taken (II39); three times repetition of the bread of life (II40); eating-dying vs. eating-not-dying (II41); eating-not-dying and eating-living (II42); his being the living bread and his giving the bread (II43); how to give the flesh to eat (II44); eating-drinking him and living as a consequence (II45–46); eating the flesh and drinking the blood (II47, 49–51); having life and living with him (II48); true food and true drink (II52); two relations: the living Father and the living Son as well as the Son and the believer (II53); mutual abode (II54); the manna vs. the heavenly bread (II55); eating-living (II56); eating bread and living forever (II57); eating-dying vs. eating-living (II58).

Extra Parallels in 6:30–58

At least five extra parallels, II59–63, are found elsewhere in vv. 30–58. Three parallelisms with exactly identical sentences as in II60 ("Truly, truly, I say to you"), II61 ("I am the bread"), and II62 ("This is the bread") are presented, while, in II63, similar expressions are repeated four times. But II59 shows a different style of parallelism that consists of "seeing" and "believing" issues.

II59. Parallel, ab-a'b'-a"b"-a'"b'": All a parts (a ["... we may see"], a' ["... you have seen [me]"], a" ["... who sees the Son"], and a'" ["... has seen ... has seen ..."]) are related in terms of "seeing," while all b parts (b ["... believe you?"], b' ["... you do not believe"], b" ["... and believes in him"], and b'" ["he who believes ..."]) are related in terms of "believing." In this II59, a-b is the Jew's request, while a'-b' is Jesus' rebuke to them. But a"-b" and a'"-b'" are related to his promise to them. **II60**. Parallel, ab-a'b'-a"b": Triple repetition ("Truly, truly, I say to you"), occurs. Specifically, we can observe that ab in v. 32 and a"b" in v. 53 have an identical expression, "Jesus therefore said to them" as their previous sentences.

II61. Parallel, ab-a'b'-a"b"-a'"b'": The four-fold "I am the bread" is repetitively used in a, a', a", and a'", while all bs (b ["of life"], b' ["that came down from heaven"], b" ["of life"], and b'" ["the living one, that came down from heaven"]) indicate what kind of bread he is. Here, b is duplicated in b", and b' is similarly repeated in b'". In here, ab in v. 35 and a"b" in v. 48 are identical. **II62**. Parallel, abcd-a'b'c'd': Similarly, a ("This is the bread") and a', and b ("that come down from heaven") and b' are duplicated pairs except one variation of tense from "comes", in b, to "came" ("that came down from heaven"), in b'. And c-d ("so that one may eat of it and not die") is related to c'-d' ("not as the fathers ate, and died"), closely but contrastively in meaning. **II63**. Parallel, ab-a'b'-a"b"-a'"b'": There are four-fold repetitions, "I will raise him (or it) up at the last day," appearing in vv. 39, 40, 44, and 54.

In II59, seeing and believing are the key issue. In II60, the emphatic expression of Jesus is repeated. In II61, the declaration of Jesus to be the bread of life is repeated. In II62, the quality of the bread as a heavenly being is emphasized. In II63, the resurrection by the Son occurs repetitively.

Sourcebook of the Structures and Styles in John 1–10

V	59				Phrases	Translations
30	a				ἵνα ἴδωμεν	that we may see
	b	60			καὶ πιστεύσωμέν σοι;	and believe you?
32		a			ἀμὴν ἀμὴν	Truly, truly,
		b	61		λέγω ὑμῖν,	I say to you.
35			a		ἐγώ εἰμι ὁ ἄρτος	I am the bread
			b		τῆς ζωῆς·	of life.
36	a'				ὅτι καὶ ἑωράκατέ [με]	that you have seen [me],
	b'			63	καὶ οὐ πιστεύετε.	and you do not believe.
39				a	ἀλλ' ἀναστήσω αὐτὸ	but raise it [them] up
				b	[ἐν] τῇ ἐσχάτῃ ἡμέρᾳ.	at the last day.
40	a''				ἵνα πᾶς ὁ θεωρῶν τὸν υἱὸν	that everyone who sees the Son
	b''				καὶ πιστεύων εἰς αὐτὸν	and believes in him
				a'	καὶ ἀναστήσω αὐτὸν ἐγὼ	And I will raise him up
				b'	[ἐν] τῇ ἐσχάτῃ ἡμέρᾳ.	at the last day.
41		a'			ἐγώ εἰμι ὁ ἄρτος	"I am the bread
		b'			ὁ καταβὰς ἐκ τοῦ οὐρανοῦ,	that came down from heaven."
44				a''	κἀγὼ ἀναστήσω αὐτὸν	and I will raise him up
				b''	ἐν τῇ ἐσχάτῃ ἡμέρᾳ.	at the last day.
46	a'''				οὐχ ὅτι τὸν πατέρα ἑώρακέν τις εἰ μὴ ὁ ὢν παρὰ τοῦ θεοῦ, οὗτος ἑώρακεν τὸν πατέρα.	Not that any man has see the Father, except the one who is from God; this one has seen the Father.
47		a'			Ἀμὴν ἀμὴν	Truly, truly,
		b'			λέγω ὑμῖν,	I say to you,
	b'''				ὁ πιστεύων ἔχει	he who believes has
48			a''		Ἐγώ εἰμι ὁ ἄρτος	I am the bread
			b''	62	τῆς ζωῆς.	of life.
50				a	οὗτός ἐστιν ὁ ἄρτος	This is the bread
				b	ὁ ἐκ τοῦ οὐρανοῦ καταβαίνων,	that comes down from heaven,
				c	ἵνα τις ἐξ αὐτοῦ φάγῃ	so that one may eat of it
				d	καὶ μὴ ἀποθάνῃ.	and not die.
51			a'''		ἐγώ εἰμι ὁ ἄρτος	I am the bread,
			b'''		ὁ ζῶν ὁ ἐκ τοῦ οὐρανοῦ καταβάς·	the living one, that came down from heaven;
53		a''			ἀμὴν ἀμὴν	"Truly, truly,
		b''			λέγω ὑμῖν,	I say to you,
54				a'''	κἀγὼ ἀναστήσω αὐτὸν	and I will raise him up
				b'''	τῇ ἐσχάτῃ ἡμέρᾳ.	at the last day.
58				a'	οὗτός ἐστιν ὁ ἄρτος	This is the bread
				b'	ὁ ἐξ οὐρανοῦ καταβάς,	that came down from heaven;
				c'	οὐ καθὼς ἔφαγον οἱ πατέρες	not as the fathers ate,
				d'	καὶ ἀπέθανον·	and died,

"I Am the Bread of Life"

IIA'. The Leaving Disciples vs. Staying Ones (6:59–71)

Dual Structure, II64 (A-A')

This unit consists of two subunits with their own chiastic frames: vv. 59–63 (II65, A-B1B2-B'1B'2-A'); vv. 64–71 (II73, ABC-X-C'B'A'). In this sense, it is in a dual, A and A'. In the former (A), the disciples misunderstand the spiritual words of Jesus, while, in the latter (A'), the unbelieving-leaving disciples are in contrast to the believing-staying ones.

A.	The disciples who misunderstand (59-63)	A-B1B2-B'1B'2-A'
A'.	The unbelieving-leaving disciples vs. the believing-staying ones (64-71)	ABC-X-C'B'A'

A. The Disciples Who Misunderstand (6:59–63)

In vv. 59–63, there are eight parallels: four duals (II66, 69, and 71–72), one chiasm (II70), one parallelism (II68), one combined chiasm (II65), and one combined parallelism (II67). Comparing other units, this unit contains many more dual types of parallels throughout the unit. The essential pillar is II65 maintaining the unit. The other parallels sustain altogether the cohesiveness within each part: II66–71.

V	65	66			Phrases	Translation
59	A	a	67	68	Ταῦτα εἶπεν ἐν συναγωγῇ διδάσκων ἐν Καφαρναούμ.	He said these things in the synagogue, as he taught in Capernaum.
60	B1	a'	a	a	Πολλοὶ οὖν ἀκούσαντες ἐκ τῶν μαθητῶν αὐτοῦ εἶπαν·	Then many of his disciples, when they heard these things, said,
	B2		b1	b	σκληρός ἐστιν ὁ λόγος οὗτος·	"This is a hard teaching.
	-		b2	-	τίς δύναται αὐτοῦ ἀκούειν;	Who can listen to it?"
61	B'1		a'	a'	εἰδὼς δὲ ὁ Ἰησοῦς ἐν ἑαυτῷ	But Jesus, knowing in himself
	-		-	b'	ὅτι γογγύζουσιν περὶ τούτου οἱ μαθηταὶ αὐτοῦ	that his disciples murmured at it,
	-	69	-		εἶπεν αὐτοῖς·	said to them,
	B'2	a	b'2		τοῦτο ὑμᾶς σκανδαλίζει;	"Does this cause you to stumble?
62	-	a'	b'1		ἐὰν οὖν θεωρῆτε τὸν υἱὸν τοῦ ἀνθρώπου	Then what if you see the Son of man
			70	71	ἀναβαίνοντα ὅπου ἦν τὸ πρότερον;	ascending to where he was before?
63	A'		a	a	τὸ πνεῦμά ἐστιν τὸ ζῳοποιοῦν,	It is the Spirit that gives life,
	-	72	x	a'	ἡ σὰρξ οὐκ ὠφελεῖ οὐδέν·	the flesh is of no help.
	-		a	a'	τὰ ῥήματα ἃ ἐγὼ λελάληκα ὑμῖν πνεῦμά ἐστιν	The words I have spoken to you are spirit
	-		a'	-	καὶ ζωή ἐστιν.	and are life.

II65. Combined chiastic, A-B1B2-B'1B'2-A': In v. 60, many of his disciples who heard the words of Jesus (B1), being disturbed because of his hard teaching regarding the bread of life (B2), and, in vv. 61–62, Jesus who knows their murmuring says (B'1), brings up another hard issue regarding his ascending to heaven (B'2), probably harder than the previous one. In A, we read that Jesus says and teaches, while, in A', we may read what his words of teaching are, particularly regarding the Spirit. **II66.** Dual, a-a': Jesus taught (a) and they responded (a'). It is cause (a) and effect (a').

II67. Combined parallel, a-b1b2-a'-b'2b'1: In a-a', many disciples heard and said (a), and Jesus knew and said (a'). Their doubtful question, "Who can listen to it?" (b2) is echoed in Jesus' saying, "Does this cause you to stumble?" (b'2). They said, "This is a hard teaching" (b1), but Jesus presents a harder one, regarding seeing "the Son of Man ascending to where he was before" (b'1). **II68.** Parallel, ab-a'b': They heard and said (a) and Jesus knew (a'), while the content of their saying is b (about hard teaching), and that which Jesus knew is b' (about their murmuring).

II69. Dual, a-a': Two questions in return, a and a', are presented: in this case, a' is the harder teaching to understand than the previous one, that causes them to stumble (a). **II70.** Chiastic, a-x-a': In a, the Spirit is focused as the one who gives life, and, in a', his words are regarded as spirit, that is life. In this sense, the Spirit and his words are deeply interrelated. Thus, the flesh in x is differentiated from a and a'. **II71.** Dual, a-a': The Spirit that gives life (a) is contrasted to the flesh of no help (a'). **II72.** Dual, a-a': His words are regarded as two related terms: spirit (a) and life (a'). It is a double emphasis.

A'. The Unbelieving-Leaving Disciples vs. the Believing-Staying Ones (6:64–71)

In vv. 64–71, there are eight parallels: four duals (II75–77 and 79), three chiasms (II73–74 and 80), and one parallelism (II78). This unit also contains not a few dual types of parallel. The essential pillar is II73 maintaining this unit. The other parallels sustain altogether the cohesiveness within each part: II74–80.

II73. Chiastic, ABC-X-C'B'A': This cluster is a typical chiastic structure. In A, Jesus points out those who do not believe and also the man who finally betrays him, and, in A', he refers to Judas Iscariot who is going to betray him. In B, Jesus says "that no one can come to me unless it has been granted him from the Father," and, in B', he says, "Did I not choose you, the twelve?" We can see the relation between the Father's permission to come to the Son (B) and the Son's choice of the twelve (B'). In C and C', there is a contrast between some disciples who go back, staying with him no longer (C) and other disciples who believe, staying with him (C'). In the center X, Jesus says, "You do not want to leave too, do you?" is highlighted. As a whole, the tone is not bright but rather gloomy, like predicting his coming suffering.

"I Am the Bread of Life"

V	73	74		Phrases	Translation
64	A	a		ἀλλ' εἰσὶν ἐξ ὑμῶν τινες οἳ οὐ πιστεύουσιν.	But there are some of you who do not believe."
	-	x	75	ᾔδει γὰρ ἐξ ἀρχῆς ὁ Ἰησοῦς	For Jesus knew from the beginning
	-	a'	a	τίνες εἰσὶν οἱ μὴ πιστεύοντες	who they were who did not believe,
	-	-	a'	καὶ τίς ἐστιν ὁ παραδώσων αὐτόν.	and who it was that would betray him.
65	B			καὶ ἔλεγεν· διὰ τοῦτο εἴρηκα ὑμῖν	And he said, "For this reason I have said to you,
		76			
	-	a		ὅτι οὐδεὶς δύναται ἐλθεῖν πρός με	that no one can come to me
	-	a'		ἐὰν μὴ ᾖ δεδομένον αὐτῷ ἐκ τοῦ πατρός.	unless it has been granted him from the Father."
		77			
66	C	a		Ἐκ τούτου πολλοὶ [ἐκ] τῶν μαθητῶν αὐτοῦ ἀπῆλθον εἰς τὰ ὀπίσω	As a result of this many of his disciples went back
	-	a'		καὶ οὐκέτι μετ' αὐτοῦ περιεπάτουν.	and were no longer walking with him.
67	X			εἶπεν οὖν ὁ Ἰησοῦς τοῖς δώδεκα· μὴ καὶ ὑμεῖς θέλετε ὑπάγειν;	Jesus said therefore to the twelve, "You do not want to leave too, do you?"
68	C'	78		ἀπεκρίθη αὐτῷ Σίμων Πέτρος·	Simon Peter answered him,
	-	a		κύριε, πρὸς τίνα ἀπελευσόμεθα;	"Lord, to whom shall we go?
	-	b		ῥήματα ζωῆς αἰωνίου ἔχεις,	You have words of eternal life.
69	-	a'	79	καὶ ἡμεῖς	And we
	-	-	a	πεπιστεύκαμεν	have believed
	-	-	a'	καὶ ἐγνώκαμεν	and have come to know
	-	b'		ὅτι σὺ εἶ ὁ ἅγιος τοῦ θεοῦ.	that you are the Holy One of God."
70	B'			ἀπεκρίθη αὐτοῖς ὁ Ἰησοῦς· οὐκ ἐγὼ ὑμᾶς τοὺς δώδεκα ἐξελεξάμην;	Jesus answered them, "Did I not choose you, the twelve?
		80			
	A'	a		καὶ ἐξ ὑμῶν εἷς διάβολός ἐστιν.	Yet one of you is a devil."
71	-	x		ἔλεγεν δὲ τὸν Ἰούδαν Σίμωνος Ἰσκαριώτου·	Now he meant Judas the son of Simon Iscariot,
	-	a'		οὗτος γὰρ ἔμελλεν παραδιδόναι αὐτόν, εἷς ἐκ τῶν δώδεκα.	for he, one of the twelve, was going to betray him.

II74. Chiastic, a-x-a': In a-a', the unbelief issue is accentuated: "there are some of you who do not believe" (a); "who they were who did not believe … would betray him" (a'). But Jesus is the one who knew from the beginning (x). II75. Dual, a-a': Those who did not believe (a) and the man who would betray him (a') are compared in a pair. II76. Dual, a-a': Here, a' (unless it has been granted him from the Father) is the cause of a (no one can come to me). II77. Dual, a-a': Dual expressions are written for emphasis: they went back (a) and they were not walking with him any more (a'), both describing how they left him.

II78. Parallel, ab-a'b': In a and a', Peter decides not to leave Jesus (a) because he believes in him (a'). Both in b and b', there are his confessions of him regarding what Jesus has, words of eternal life, (b) and who he is, the Holy one of God, (b'). II79. Dual, a-a': Belief and knowledge are presented in a pair. **II80**. Chiastic, a-x-a': In the center x, the name of betrayer comes up, Judas the son of Iscariot, while, what kind of person he is (he is a devil, a) and what he is going to do (... to betray him, a') are in a pair.

Their foci are: their murmuring and the Jesus' lesson (II65); Jesus taught and they responded (II66); their responses and Jesus' rebuke (II67); their murmuring and his knowing (II68); a harder teaching (II69); spiritual words of Jesus vs. the flesh (II70); the flesh vs. the Spirit (II71); spirit is life (II72); unbelieving-betraying, calling-choosing, and leaving-vs.-staying (II73); Jesus knows who the unbelievers are (II74); unbeliever-betrayer (II75); calling from the Father and coming to the Son (II76); how they left him (II77); the confession of Peter staying with him (II78); belief and knowledge (II79); the double emphasis on Judas, the betrayer (II80).

Reading in Structure-Style

1. In vv. 1–4, there is the contrast between the multitude who follow Jesus and Jesus who sits down with his disciples as seen in I3–4. There are so many people who follow and applaud him because of the miraculous sign of his healing ministry. Jesus does not ignore them but his priority seems to lie in being with his disciples and taking care of them. For this reason, at the beginning of the feeding miracle, Jesus first starts with the dialogue with his disciples, particularly with Philip and Andrew.

2. Considering I6 in vv. 7–9, Philip and Andrew show the same phenomenon, both having limited concepts regarding what Jesus is going to do, taking care of the hungry multitude. Philip talks about two hundred denarii, while Andrew submits five barley loaves and two fish. Both know those are not sufficient to feed them. Through the dialogue with them, Jesus discloses the human limitations of his disciples, who never recognize the ability of the Son.

3. We may say that there are four clusters containing the bread of life issue: vv. 30–33, 34–36, 48–52, and 53–58. They are not simply repeated in the same issue. There are some relations of purpose.

First, the first cluster (30–33) focuses on the difference between the manna and the heavenly bread, and the second one (34–36) is presented to demonstrate what the bread of life is, Jesus himself.

Second, in the third one (48–52), it is re-highlighted that Jesus is the bread of life (Ἐγώ εἰμι ὁ ἄρτος τῆς ζωῆς). In relation to this, two foci are shown: "I am ..." and "the bread of life." For the first focus, Jesus repeats "I am ..." twice or "This is ..." once, emphasizing that he is the bread of life. For the second one, the living-not-dying issue is emphatically repeated. Another role of this cluster is to link to the last one, introducing the issue of his flesh and blood.

Third, in the last cluster (53–58), the flesh to be eaten and the blood to be drunk are repetitively accented.

Fourth, in this sense, we may say that vv. 34–36 and vv. 48–52 share the idea of "I am the bread of life." It may be also said that vv. 30–33 and vv. 53–58 are in a pair in terms that the former indicates what the bread of life is not like, while the latter describes what the bread of life is like: the flesh and the blood of Jesus.

4. As a pair of II12 (B-B'), vv. 37–40 and 44–47 share significant issues: the believer has eternal life (40 and 47); "I will raise him up at the last day" (39–40 and 44); those who the Father gives me or draws to "me" come to "me" (37 and 44). But the former focuses on the will of the Father, never losing any believer (37, 39), while the latter places its weight on those who come to him being led by the Father (44–45), thereby complementing the former in terms of how they can come to the Son.

5. The function of v. 58 needs to be carefully examined. This verse is not included in the combined chiasm II45 that comprises all the other verses in vv. 53–58. Apart from this verse, II45 is created, although all the verses (53–58) are somehow related to each other in terms of the same issue: the bread of life.

It is found that there are differences between vv. 53–57 and 58: First, vv. 53–57 use the expression of eating the flesh and the blood of the Son (or eating "me"), namely the sacramental issue, while v. 58 goes back to the expression which is shown in the previous verses, particularly vv. 48–51 (and also 33, 35) regarding the heavenly bread not as the fathers ate; Second, the emphatic expression οὗτός ἐστιν ὁ ἄρτος . . . (This is the bread . . .) is not found in vv. 53–57, but in vv. 48–51, specifically v. 50 (see II62). Its similar expression is ἐγώ εἰμι ὁ ἄρτος (I am the bread . . .) appears in vv. 48, 51 (and also 35).

The reason that v. 58 appears in this location is seemingly to create an *inclusio* binding vv. 48–58 as a unit. This verse matches vv. 48–49 where the manna their fathers ate in the wilderness is referred to in contrast to the bread of life.

Comparing the counterpart of II12, A (30–36), where the bread of life issue first comes up, there is a similarity between vv. 30–36 and vv. 48–58, because both use a type of *inclusio*. The seeing-believing issue raised in v. 30 recurs in v. 36, creating an *inclusio* binding vv. 30–36 together (see II59).

6. II73 in vv. 64–71 shows a typical Johannine chiasm. We need to read the text, carefully considering the pair of parallels such as vv. 64 and 70b–71 (A-A'); vv. 65 and 70a (B-B'); vv. 66 and 68–69 (C-C'). A' explains who the betrayer is referred to in A. In A-A', we read that those who do not believe in him and the betrayer, Judas, are likewise treated here. In B-B', those who are granted from the Father come to the Son (B), the believers, are treated likewise with those who are chosen by the Son (B'), the disciples. In C-C', there is the contrast between those who leave Jesus and those who stay with him. In the center, X, there exists the question of Jesus: "how about you?"

Sourcebook of the Structures and Styles in John 1–10

Issues according to the Structure-Style

1. Structure: Outline of Division

Brown divided the chapter into six units, focusing on the issue, Jesus at Passover:[7] The multiplication of the loaves (1–15); Walking on the Sea of Galilee (16–21); The crowd comes to Jesus (22–24); Preface to the discourse on the Bread of Life (25–34); Discourse on the Bread of Life (35–59); Reactions to the discourse on the Bread of Life (60–71).

According to Beasley-Murray,[8] the chapter needs to be categorized into four: Two signs: the feeding of the multitude (1–15) and the walking on the sea (16–21); Two dialogues: a search for Jesus (22–26) and a demand for a sign from heaven (27–31); A discourse on the Bread of Life (32–59); Two more dialogues: defecting disciples (60–65) and the Twelve (66–71).

Talbert simply introduces a three part outline:[9] (1) vv. 1–26, held together by an *inclusio* (the other side of the sea, vv. 1, 25); (2) vv. 27–59, held together by an *inclusio* (Capernaum, vv. 24, 59); (3) vv. 67–71.

Moloney suggests a little more systematic scheme of structure:[10] An introduction: where? when? who? why? (1–4); The miracle of the loaves and fishes (5–15); The miracle on the sea (16–21); A second introduction: where? when? who? why? (22–24); The discourse on the bread from heaven (25–59); The crisis created by the word of Jesus (60–71).

There seems to be no argument about the division of vv. 1–21 into vv. 1–15 and 16–21. The controversial issues are mostly found in vv. 22–71. On which ground can we categorize them?

First, there are three kinds of dialogue in John 6 regarding the characters such as that between Jesus and his disciples who follow him (1–21) and that between Jesus and the Jews who seek him (22–58) and that between Jesus and two opposite types of the disciples: who leave him and who stay with him (59–71). In this way, three sections of division seem to be possible at first.

Second, the reasons that we divide again vv. 22–71 into three units, as discussed earlier, are (1) that vv. 30–58 need to be regarded as an independent entity (see II12); (2) that vv. 22–29 and 59–71 are in a pair in terms of the responses of the people toward Jesus: from seeking Jesus (22–29, before the dialogue) to leaving him or staying with him (59–71, after the dialogue).

Third, vv. 22–29 are again arranged dually, being divided into vv. 22–24 (seeking him) and 25–29 (the works of God), similarly to vv. 59–71 with vv. 59–66 (leaving

---

7. Brown, *Gospel according to John I–XII*, xi; 231–304.
8. Beasley-Murray, *John*, 85–99.
9. Talbert, *Reading John*, 131.
10. Moloney, *Gospel of John*, 193–232; see also Moloney, *Signs and Shadows*, 30–64; Moloney, "Function of Prolepsis," 130–32.

disciples) and 67–71 (remaining disciples).[11] The cohesiveness in parallel among each of vv. 22–24 (see II3–4), 25–29 (see II7), 59–63 (see II65), and 64–71 (see II73) supports that each of them is designed as a unit. These may help to think that vv. 22–29 and 59–71 are in a pair as the opening and the closing of the discourse.

Fourth, vv. 30–58 are beautifully designed as a chiastic structure: AB-X-B'A', as discussed in II12.

Fifth, therefore, we have concluded that the structure of this chapter is in a dual as a whole: vv. 1–21 and 22–71, in which three subsections are presented: vv. 22–29, 30–58, and 59–71.[12]

2. Insertions of vv. 6, 15, and 17b

According to von Wahlde,[13] among vv. 1–21, vv. 6, 15, and 17b are additions from the second or third edition. He insists that vv. 6 and 15 were especially edited by the second editor to make Jesus superior to human events regarding the supernatural knowledge of Jesus, presuming that v. 17b was from the third edition.[14]

First, the edition theory that these verses are inserted by the final editor is difficult to prove as either a fact or a theory. Von Wahlde insists his theory is based on the supernatural power in the knowledge of Jesus appearing in those verses. But we have to say that the feeding miracle is itself caused by the divine power of Jesus.

Second, the more important thing is that these verses are observed as natural elements within their contexts. Without them, the passages may not be Johannine. For example, I5 (5–6, ab-b'a') is built because of v. 6, without which v. 5 may not stand alone, similarly as vv. 1–4 have I3 (ab-b'a') and vv. 7–9 have I6 (abc-a'b'c').

Third, this is same in the case of v. 15, a part of I12 (14–15, a1a2-b-a'1a'2-b'). Without v. 15, v. 14 may not be stabilized alone in a Johannine style. And also, by combining v. 14 and 15, this part (14–15) stands in a match with vv. 1–4 (A of I2).

---

11. Considering the themes in vv. 59–71, we may divide them into vv. 59–66 (leaving disciples) and 67–71 (staying disciples). But considering the parallel system in use, it is better to divide them into vv. 59–63 (II65, a-b1b2-b'1b'2-a') and 64–71 (II73, abc-x-c'b'a'). Cf. Talbert sees vv. 60–71 as a concentric pattern: A. v. 60: Many of Jesus' disciples react negatively; B. vv. 61–63: The words of life; C. vv. 64–65; Betrayal; A'. v. 66: Many of his disciples react by desertion; B'. vv. 67–69: The words of life; C'. vv. 70–71: Betrayal. Talbert, *Reading John*, 135–36.

12. Moloney introduces, "Five interventions from the crowd or 'the Jews' give the following discourse its shape: (a) Verses 25–29: . . . (b) Verses 30–33: . . . (c) Verses 34–40: . . . (d) Verses 41–51; . . . (e) Verse 52–59 . . ." Moloney, *Signs and Shadows*, 42–43. It is said that he ignores the relation between vv. 37–40 and 44–47 as well as the difference between vv. 34–36 and 37–40 and also the difference between vv. 44–47 and 48–51.

13. Von Wahlde, *Commentary on the Gospel of John*, 274–78.

14. Kysar assures that "a growing consensus as to the sources utilized by the fourth evangelist is emerging," particularly in ch. 6. Kysar, "Source Analysis of the Fourth Gospel," 147. Anderson rejects the idea of editorial seams in ch. 6: "Aporias are not necessarily indicative of editorial seams in John 6", although he supports the later insertion of ch. 6 in John. Anderson, "*Sitz im Leben*," 4–5.

Fourth, v. 17b makes I16 (a1a2-x-a'1a'2) possible and, without the verse, I15 (a-x-a') as well as I17 (a-x-a') may not be sustained. In particular, see how v. 17b is combined with v. 16 in a pair of chiasms for I16.

Fifth, we can say that these verses (6, 15, and 17b) are constituents of Johannine style in parallel in the very places where they are. Without them, the text cannot be typical of John because the structure and the style are broken and damaged.

3. The Functions of vv. 22–24 and 25–34

Brown regarded vv. 22–24 as a transitional part to the bread of life discourse,[15] and insisted that vv. 25–34 serve as a preface to this discourse as well as connecting the discourse to the previous verses (1–21). In this case, we may say that he considers v. 35 as the starting verse of the bread of life discourse,[16] which is composed of two distinct parts: "the two themes verses (primary 'sapiential' revelation and secondary the Eucharist, 35–50) and the Eucharist verses (51–58)."[17]

First, it is more appropriate that Moloney regards the function of vv. 22–24 as similar to that of vv. 1–4 in terms of "where? when? who? why?" than Brown regarding vv. 22–24 as the transitional part and vv. 25–34 as the preface to the discourse of the bread of life, for vv. 22–24 have the role of introduction to the discourse that follows, similarly to vv. 1–4 the feeding episode.

Second, but if we consider that vv. 5–15 and 25–59 as well as vv. 15–21 and 60–71 are matched as Moloney seems to imply in his two cycles of three divided sections, we are not persuaded. Instead, we have to pay attention to the phenomenon that vv. 25–71 are arranged in a different pattern from vv. 6–21, although we admit that vv. 1–4 and 22–24 are shared with the introductory function.

Third, moreover, vv. 25–34 should not be regarded as an entity, because vv. 30–34 are a part of vv. 30–58 and vv. 25–29 are separated from the following verses (see II1 and 7).

Fourth, the theme of vv. 25–29 is "the work of God for the food of life," somehow different from that of vv. 30–58, which mainly focuses on "Jesus as the bread of life" and starts from the cluster of vv. 30–36. In this sense, it is not proper to regard vv. 25–34 as a preface to the following discourse.

Fifth, the reason that Brown so insisted is to separate vv. 35–58 from the previous verses for the purpose of emphasizing some common features between vv. 35–50 and 51–58 such as giving the bread (31–32 and 51–52), the Son of Man (27 and 53). He highlighted some repetitions between vv. 35, 38 and 51; 40 and 54; 46 and 53,

---

15. Brown, *Gospel according to John I–XII*, 256.
16. Brown depended on Dodd who saw vv. 26–34 as the beginning part of the discourse and vv. 35–50 as the essence of the bread of life discourse. And he regarded vv. 51–59 as the third part. Dodd, *Fourth Gospel*, 335–40.
17. Brown, *Gospel according to John I–XII*, 272.

57; 49–50 and 58, suggesting that these two passages share in their composition and statement.

Sixth, but we need to pay proper attention to the fact that v. 35 ("I am the bread of life") is not closer in sameness to v. 51 ("I am the bread, the living one, that came down from heaven") but to v. 48 ("I am the bread of life").

Seventh, it is said that vv. 50 and 58 share a similar pattern, not because of the parallel between vv. 35–50 and 51–58 but because of the chiastic parallel in vv. 48–58 (see II39).

Eighth, we cannot ignore the thematic connection between vv. 32–33 and 35, although there seems to be an interruption of v. 34 in the middle. We also need to pay attention to the two-fold expressions in a pair for a parallelism in vv. 30–36 (see II13 where vv. 32–33 and 35–36 are B and B').

Ninth, vv. 30–36 have the structure: two questions by the Jews (30–31 and 34) and two answers by Jesus (32–33 and 35–36), while vv. 48–58 consist of two discourse parts of Jesus (48–51 and 53–58)[18] and one interruption by the Jews in the middle (52). These two sections are connected to each other in terms of the same theme, "the declaration of Jesus on being the bread of life."

4. Verse 27 as the Starting Point of the Dialogue of Bread of Life

Bultmann took v. 27 as his starting-point, presuming it to be the beginning of the dialogue by analogy with 4:14, and thought that v. 34 in the analogy with 4:15 has to follow v. 27.[19] In this way, he rearranged the order of verses: vv. 27, 34, 35, 30–33, 47–51a, 41–46, 36–40, even though he admitted that "the original order cannot be restored with certainty" and "it is perhaps not always possible to distinguish the Evangelist's comments from the editor's glosses."[20]

According to Bultmann, the way v. 26 is related to v. 25 reflects that the transition to the dialogue is artificial and the way vv. 27ff. are related with the previous events is also awkward. And the crowd in vv. 30–31 should not have asked Jesus for a miracle because they had experienced the feeding miracle.[21] In his thought, the dialogue is

---

18. Talbert sees a concentric pattern in vv. 49–58. A. vv. 49–50: Ate . . . died/eat . . . not die; B. v. 51: My flesh/eat . . . live; C. v. 52: How . . . eat; C'. vv. 53–54: Unless . . . eat; B'. vv. 55–57: My flesh/eat . . . live; A'. v. 58: Ate . . . died/eat . . . live. It is said: First, v. 48 which is deeply connected in theme to the following verses is excluded; Second, the relation between vv. 51 (his B) and 55–57 (his B') is weaker than that between vv. 51 ("I am the bread, the living one . . .") and 48 ("I am the bread of life"); Third, the "my flesh" issue does not appear only in vv. 51 (his B) and 55–57 (his B') but also in vv. 53 ("the flesh of the Son of Man"), 54 ("my flesh"). And the "eat and live" issue appears also in vv. 54 and 58; Fourth, the strong connection between vv. 54 and 46 is not considered; Fifth, additionally, the relation between the verses before v. 35 and those after v. 48 is ignored. Talbert, *Reading John*, 135–37.

19. Bultmann, *Gospel of John*, 221.

20. Regarding the Bultmann type of rearrangement, see Smith, *Composition and Order*, 116–212.

21. Bultmann, *Gospel of John*, 218.

mixed and distorted in order. Thus, as for him, v. 27 is not the beginning verse from which the passage is provided sequentially. Rather, the verse is to be placed first as nothing but a starting point for the total rearrangement of the following verses.

First, we may think of the possibility that the characters appearing in vv. 25–27 and those in vv. 30–31 could be different, as Beasley-Murray suggests.[22] But the problem is not having any evidence to prove it. Or, we may assume that the people in v. 30, if they are those who have already experienced the feeding miracle, ask Jesus to perform a continual feeding miracle as the manna was given to their fathers in the desert.

Second, we may also consider the suggestion of von Wahlde who extracts vv. 30–50 from the discourse comparing them with the synagogue homily. However, it is difficult to agree with his idea totally. (See below, number 5.)

Third, as discussed earlier, the distinct issue from the previous verses, "Jesus as the bread of life," starts at v. 30 and continues up to v. 58. (See the note of II12. And also see number 1.)

Fourth, as discussed already, vv. 25–29 are made up of a parallelism (II7), which includes the whole passage in unity: two cycles of question-answer.

Fifth, above all, it is not plausible to rearrange the text as vv. 27, 34, 35, 30–33, 47–51a, 41–46, then 36–40, as Bultmann did due to his presupposition that these verses are arranged illogically and mixed unnaturally. They are not so. Verses 27 and 34 partake in certain designed parallels such as II7–8, and II13 and 23, respectively, in the locations where they are.

Sixth, the pattern in 4:14–15 (Jesus' saying on the living water and her request to be given) is not similar to vv. 27 and 34 but with vv. 33–34 (Jesus' saying on the bread of life and their request to be given) or with vv. 34–35 (their request to be given and Jesus' saying on the bread of life) which is in reverse order.

Seventh, the awkwardness of vv. 25–26 is regarded as one phenomenon in the Johannine pattern of dialogue (for example, see 4:15 and 16; 7:20 and 21; 8:53 and 54; 12:34 and 35–36; 14:22 and 23; 18:35 and 36.). Jesus does not answer them by what they want to know on the surface but does what is really necessary in order to answer them.

---

22. Beasley-Murray, *John*, 259.

"I Am the Bread of Life"

5. Verses 30–50 as the Synagogue Homily

Based on P. Borgen,[23] von Wahlde presents vv. 31–50 according to the Synagogue homily format:[24] a. Quotation of Scripture by the Jews (31); b. Interpretative paraphrase of Scripture (32); c. Exegesis of: "Bread from heaven" (33–36); d. Exegesis of: "The Father gives" (37–40); e. Objection to thesis: Coming down from heaven (41–44); f. Subordinate quotation of Scripture (45–47); g. Exegesis of: "To eat" and concluding paraphrase of the original quotation (49–50).

First, von Wahlde considers vv. 30–50 as a cluster in unity for the Jewish homily which also means that vv. 51–58 are added later to the previous discourse.[25] Based on Borgen, he regards vv. 49–50 as the exegesis of "to eat." However, what is the reason for excluding the following verse, v. 51, which is also related to this theme?

Second, moreover, it is obscure for him to include vv. 33–36 in the exegesis of "Bread from heaven," disregarding vv. 50–51 and 58, where we find the same issue.

Third, as discussed somewhere, vv. 48–58 are designed as one united cluster (see II39). If we have to segregate the sacramental part from these verses, we shall extract vv. 53–57 (see II45) rather than vv. 51–58. In vv. 48–51, there is a deliberate parallel of repetition, II40, binding the verses together.[26]

Fourth, the relation between vv. 48–49 ("I am the bread of life . . .") and 51 ("I am the bread, the living one . . .") and that between v. 50 ("This is the bread that comes down from heaven . . .") and v. 58 ("This is the bread that came down from heaven . . .") are in parallel. (The relation among vv. 48–51 is chiastic, a-x-a', if we consider only those verses, but that becomes a parallelism, ab-a'b', if we include v. 58 in relation to vv. 48–51.)[27] The repetitions in these verses are designed, intentionally and in scheme.

Fifth, the functions of vv. 52 and 53–57 are special. In the middle of vv. 48–58, there is v. 52, a somewhat heterogeneous verse regarding the argument of the Jews. If we see v. 52 as the center of the verses (X), there are three expressions of similar pattern (ἐγώ εἰμι or οὗτός ἐστιν ὁ ἄρτος) on the left side (A, 48–51) and there is just one related to this on the right side (A', 53–58; specifically 58). Then, with only the

---

23. Borgen himself divided the text unlike Von Wahlde. According to him, "the first part of the discourse (vv. 32–48) a midrashic paraphrase of the words of Scripture: "He gave them bread from heaven," while the latter part (vv. 49–58) is a midrashic paraphrase of the words of Scripture: "to eat." Over the latter part of the discourse, a paraphrase of the earlier words ("he gave them bread from heaven") continues, but the paraphrase of the action of eating ("to eat") predominated." Borgen, *Bread from Heaven*, 40–42; cited by Moloney, *Signs and Shadows*, 31–32; also Borgen, "John 6," 279–85. The theory of Borgen is persuasive, but he did not make the connection between vv. 37–40 and 44–47.

24. Von Wahlde, *Commentary on the Gospel of John*, 302.

25. Ibid.

26. The relation among vv. 48–51 is chiastic (a-x-a'): a (48–49, Ἐγώ εἰμι ὁ ἄρτος τῆς ζωῆς . . .); a' (51, ἐγώ εἰμι ὁ ἄρτος ὁ ζῶν . . .); x (50, οὗτός ἐστιν ὁ ἄρτος . . .).

27. If we see the relation among vv. 48–51, it is typically chiastic. But if we include v. 58 with them, its relation is parallel: a (48–49, Ἐγώ εἰμι ὁ ἄρτος τῆς ζωῆς . . .); b (50, οὗτός ἐστιν ὁ ἄρτος . . .); a' (51, ἐγώ εἰμι ὁ ἄρτος ὁ ζῶν . . .); b' (58, οὗτός ἐστιν ὁ ἄρτος . . .).

οὗτός ἐστιν ὁ ἄρτος sentence in v. 58, there is not enough to obtain a balance. The later part of vv. 48–58 needs to have a complementary part like vv. 53–57, a sacramental supplement to the previous, emphatic scheme describing who and how Jesus is the bread of life (48–51). In this way, vv. 48–58 sustain a symmetrical, balanced chiastic structure (II39, A-X-A').

Sixth, in his analysis, von Wahlde names vv. 37–40 as "d. Exegesis of 'The Father gives'" and vv. 44–47 as "f. Subordinate quotation of Scripture." However, the relation between vv. 37–40 and 44–47 is not that of arrangement in a row, as d and f are, but instead of a pair in parallel, as seen in II12 (B and B'), both describing the same theme regarding the declaration of Jesus that he will not lose those who come to him by the Father.

Seventh, we also need to point out that vv. 44–47 do not actually deal with the issue of the bread that the Father gives as implied in his d (Exegesis of "The Father gives," 44–47) but rather with those whom the Father gives. It is the bread which God gave their fathers in v. 31, which is not the people. If anyone refers to the bread that the Father gives, it would be better to mention vv. 32 (the bread from heaven that the Father does give), 33 (the bread of God coming down from heaven), 50–51 (the bread that come down from heaven), or 57 (the Father sent him who is the bread of life).

Eighth, as a conclusion, it is not persuasive to segregate vv. 30–50 from vv. 51–58, whether these verses are similar to the format of the synagogue homily or not.

6. The Repetition in vv. 38–40 as a Ground for a Different Origin

Von Wahlde finds that the wording of vv. 38–39 and that of v. 40 share similarity and concludes that they do not come from the same author.[28] According to him, vv. 39, 40d, 44c which share the similar expression, "I will raise him up on the last day," are considered as additions to the place where they are by many scholars. He determines their presence to be awkward among the verses, regarding them as "bundling."

First, as discussed regarding this issue, the repetition in vv. 38–40 is a phenomenon of Johannine use in parallel style (see II26 and 30). This phenomenon appears also in vv. 48–51 (see II40) and 53–57 (see II45) and is easily found everywhere in John. The repetition is the expression of Johannine emphasis and style in use.

Second, if we suppose that the phenomenon of repetition is caused because of multiple authors, it would be difficult to find any schematic design of style such as parallelism and chiasm. But we know that those verses are made up of a deliberate, parallel network of wording, continually and consistently, such as II26 (ab-b'a') and 30 (ab-a'b') in vv. 37–40.

---

28. Von Wahlhe, *Commentary on the Gospel of John*, 300.

Third, this type of Johannine repetition is not only for rhetorical emphasis but also a way of communication to extend the previous contents for further explanation and their complementation, effectively and naturally.

7. A Chiasm in vv. 36–40

Léon-Dufour introduces the chiasm in vv. 36–40:[29] a. seeing and not believing (36); b. not driving out what the Father has given (37); x. I have come down from heaven (38); b'. losing nothing of what he has given (39); a'. looking and believing (40).

Brown recognized that vv. 36–40 have no close association with the theme of the bread of life, and thus presumed that they have "a history of their own."[30]

First, it is plausible to find a chiasm in vv. 36–40 as Brown and Léon-Dufour introduce, because there are pairs in parallel among the verses. If we compare it with II26 and 30, we know that this chiasm includes v. 36 which our models (II26 and 30) do not. It is sure that v. 36 can be parallel with v. 40, for both focus on the seeing-believing motif. In our analysis, the relation between vv. 36 and 40 is described as II59 which comprises all the related verses such as vv. 30, 36, 40, 46, and 47 with this seeing-believing motif.

Second, the primary issue lies in the function of v. 36. What is the role of v. 36 in the literary context? Is v. 36 designed to be attached to the previous verses (30–35) or the following ones (37–40)? The reasons that this verse is closer in relation to vv. 30–35 than to vv. 37–40 are: (1) Considering the relation of closeness between the verses, the contrast between "he who believes in him" (35) and "you who do not believe" (36) is clearer and more distinct than that between "you who do not believe" (36) and "he who comes to me" (37); (2) The theme of vv. 37–40 (the declaration of Jesus not to lose those who come to him by the Father) differs from that of vv. 30–36 (the bread of God as the sign); (3) The tone of vv. 37–40 is positive in all the verses, while that of vv. 30–36 is mixed: positive and negative, among which v. 36 reflects the negative tone; (4) Considering the related parallels such as II13 (30–36, AB-A'B') and 23 (34–36, ab-b'a'), it is difficult to separate v. 36 from vv. 30–36; (5) Additionally, vv. 30 and 36 consist of an *inclusio*, binding vv. 30–36 altogether and sharing a seeing-believing motif.

Third, we do not deny that there is a certain continuity between vv. 30–36 and 37–40 as seen in II59 that connects vv. 30 and 36 (the relation of *inclusio*), and also vv. 36 and 40 (link between vv. 30–36 and 37–40), and also vv. 40 and 46–47 (link between vv. 37–40 and 44–47).

Fourth, we also do not ignore that vv. 37–40 are matched with vv. 44–47, as vv. 30–36 with vv. 48–58.

---

29. Léon-Dufour, "Le mystère du pain de vie," 481–523; cited by Brown, *Gospel according to John I–XII*, 275–76.

30. Brown, *Gospel according to John I–XII*, 275.

8. The Parallel between vv. 32–35 and 48–51

After separating the two dialogues of vv. 22–26 and 27–31 from the discourse, Beasley-Murray observes that vv. 32–35 and 48–51 are parallel.[31] Based on this parallel, he ramifies the discourse of the bread of life as follows: a. The true meaning of the Scriptures: Jesus the real Bread of Life (32–35); b. The demand for faith (36–40); c. The grumbling of the Jews and the reiterated call for faith (41–47); d. Jesus the Bread of Life from heaven (48–51); e. The life-giving flesh and blood of Jesus (52–59).

First, it is recommendable to search for the parallel between vv. 32–35 and 48–51. The parallel features between those verses definitely exist as we have seen the relation in parallel between vv. 30–37 and 48–58.

Second, however, as discussed, the parallel needs to extend its realm into vv. 30–37 and 48–58 (B and B' of II12). The parallel between vv. 32–35 and 48–51 is just partial to the whole. Observe how the similar, related expressions occur in vv. 30–37 and 48–58: for example, four times each: the bread from heaven (31); the bread from heaven (32); the bread of God (33); the bread of life (35); the bread of life (48); the bread that comes down from heaven (50); the bread, the living one, that came down from heaven (51); the bread that came down from heaven (58).

Third, the arrangement of Beasley-Murray is to stand them in a row just in sequence (a-b-c-d-e), disregarding their interactive relations, although he recognizes certain parallels within them, particularly between a (32–35) and d (48–51). What is the reason for such a parallel?

9. Verses 51–58 as the Later Edition

Bultmann thought that vv. 51–58 are in contrast to the previous verses both in theme (the sacramental meal of the Eucharist) and in terminology regarding ideas, thus maintaining that an ecclesiatical redactor added them to make the discourse more acceptable to the church.[32]

Although Brown criticized Bultmann's theory of redaction in that vv. 51–58 have many features in common with the rest of the chapter, he also admitted that vv. 51–58 had a different origin from the other passages in John 6, regarding that vv. 35–50 are complete and "constitute a well-rounded discourse in themselves."[33] Brown prioritized his finding on the parallel in structure between vv. 35–50 and 51–58, thereby insisting that both passages share not a few Johannine ideas with the same beginning, the same ending, and the same type of interrupting objection, and thus that v. 35 is the beginning point of the discourse.[34]

---

31. Beasley-Murray, *John*, 86.
32. Bultmann, *Gospel of John*, 218; see also Brown, *Gospel according to John I–XII*, 286.
33. Brown, *Gospel according to John I–XII*, 290.
34. Ibid., 293–94.

First, we can say that it is appropriate that Brown paid attention to the similarity in theme between vv. 35–50 and 51–58 such as giving the bread (31–32 and 51–52) and the Son of Man (27 and 53), the concluding vv. 51–58 belonging to the general body of Johannine tradition.

Second, however, he insisted that vv. 51–58 have a different origin from the previous verses and the discourse of vv. 35–50 is complete in itself, but we cannot agree with him. We have already discussed this, particularly in number 3 (see Sixth to Ninth).

Third, above all, his grouping of verses such as vv. 35–50 and 51–58 is problematic, for vv. 30–36 and 48–58 need to be regarded as clusters, as we have discussed (see number 1 and 3). If vv. 51–58 were a part added later to the original text, certain chiastic and parallel features such as II39 (48–58), II40 (48–51), and II45 (53–57) could not exist there as they do. Moreover, we could not see any connection between vv. 30–36 and 48–58 as well as between vv. 37–40 and 44–47.

10. The Function of vv. 59–71

Beasley-Murray says that "It is important to remember that the chapter does not cease at the close of the discourse, but with the narration of its effects: the disciples of Jesus cannot endure it, and forsake him; the Twelve attain the climax of their growing faith, and confess Jesus as the Holy One of God."[35] He describes what these verses are like but does not present why they are needed in this location regarding the structure.

First, if there were not vv. 59–71, the chiastic structure of vv. 22–71 (see the note of II1, A-X-A') could not be built up here. It means that these verses (A') function as a counterpart of the structure, matching vv. 22–29 (A), where those who seek Jesus appear as the characters. In vv. 59–71, there are two types of disciples: leaving ones and staying ones. In the opening scene, they are all seeking Jesus but, in the last scene, they are divided into two opposing groups regarding their responses toward Jesus. It is not critical whether those who seek Jesus in vv. 22–29 are the same persons who are called "his disciples" in vv. 59–71 (specifically in 60–66). In this chiastic structure, the contrast and the comparison among those characters are delivered in scheme.[36]

Second, in this way, ch. 6 was written according to the Johannine format in structure-style, presumably by a single author who designed and arranged the materials of the Gospel in his own way with deliberate purpose, communicative to the people of his day. We cannot imagine that there have been multiple authors or editors for John because of the Johannine style and structure which are presented, consistently

---

35. Beasley-Murray, *John*, 99. Dodd regarded vv. 6–71 as an appendix or epilogue, comparable with: 22–36 and 4:31–42. Dodd, *Fourth Gospel*, 340.

36. Crossan argues the emphasis of the connection between vv. 1–15 (disciples) and 67–71 (Twelve) in the perspective of structuralism. If we can consider this in John 6, there is an *inclusio*. Crossan, "It Is Written," 146.

and interactively, throughout the chapter. If there were multiple editors, we could not recognize any parallel feature and any schematic design in the text. The text was not made by works which were mixed, added, stitched, or mended.

7 Who Is He and Where Is He From?

"The progression of thought in Johannine discourses and dialogues is often tortuous. the discussions between Jesus and his interlocutors seem to move by fits and starts, reintegrating motifs and themes which appear elsewhere. It is thus frequently difficult to find a clear progression in what seems to be pastiche of theological motifs."[1]

Dual Mode in Structure

1. There are many interrelated subunits in John 7 regarding who Jesus really is and where he comes from. We can divide them into two groups of episodes due to at least three factors: characters, places and times. In vv. 1–9, there are Jesus and his brothers at Galilee before the Feast of Tabernacles, while, in vv. 10–52, we can see the interaction between Jesus and the Jews at Jerusalem at the feast. In this sense, the chapter is also dual in mode.

| I. | Jesus and his brothers: who he is and where he is from (7:1-9) | AB-B'A' |
| II. | Jesus and the Jews: who he is and where he is from (7:10-52) | ABCD-X-D'C'B'A' |

2. It is recognizable that vv. 1–9 (Jesus and his brothers) are regarded as an entity with its own cohesive cluster (see I1, AB-B'A').

3. In vv. 10–52, it is unique that there are many scenes of arguments among the Jews regarding Jesus, among which the direct words of Jesus are arranged one after another. If we select all the parts of words of Jesus from vv. 10–52, they are as follows: vv. 16–19, 21–24, 28–29, 33–34, and 37–38. Besides them, there remain vv. 10–15, 20, 25–27, 30–32, 35–36, 39, 40–44, and 45–52.

---

1. Attridge, "Thematic Development," 160.

4. Let us arrange them in order: vv. 10–15 (the act of Jesus and the argument of the Jews); 16–19 (the words of Jesus); 20 (a question by the Jews); 21–24 (the words of Jesus); 25–27 (the argument of the Jews); 28–29 (the words of Jesus); 30–32 (the argument of the Jews); 33–34 (the words of Jesus); 35–36 (the argument of the Jews); 37–38 (the words of Jesus); 39 (authorial explanation); 40–44 (the argument of the Jews); 45–52 (the argument of the Jews).

5. Among them, we may bind some verses together. First, vv. 16–19 (words), 20 (a question), and 21–24 (words) need to be combined into one subunit, because they constitute two sequentially connected parallels (II6 and 9) of unity. Second, we can put vv. 37–38 and 39 together because they are bound with not a few parallelisms (II28 and 31–32) and v. 39 is indeed an explanatory note on the previous verses. Third, vv. 40–44 and 45–52 can be put together, for both are the arguments among the Jews: among the multitude (40–44); between the officers and their leaders and also among the Pharisees (45–52).

6. Thus, we are arranging them as follows: vv. 10–15 (argument), 16–24 (words-question), 25–27 (argument), 28–29 (words), 30–32 (argument), 33–34 (words), 35–36 (argument), 37–39 (words), 40–52 (arguments). There are in all nine subunits.

7. Among the four parts of the words of Jesus, the second (28–29) and the third (33–34) are closely connected to each other, dealing with a similar issue: where he is from and where he is returning to. And the first part (16–24) focuses on the defense and the rebuke of Jesus against the unbelief of the Jews, while the last (37–39) contains the invitation to belief and the promise of Jesus. It means that the second and third are in a pair with a similar issue, and the first and last may be in a pair with the relation of contrast.

8. Among the five parts of the arguments of the Jews, the second (25–27) and the fourth (35–36) are interrelated, exactly as vv. 28–29 and 33–34 are, having a similar issue: where he is from and where he is going. They include two or three questions in them, mostly reflecting a negative response against him. Differently, the first one (10–15) and the last one (40–52) reflect both sides of responses to him: positive and negative. In the first, the controversy is whether he is a good man or a deceiver, while, in the last, the division occurs because of the prophet argument: he is a prophet; it cannot be him because he is from Galilee.

9. The connection of vv. 10–15 with vv. 45–52 as well as vv. 40–44 is sustained because of at least four factors: First, the deceiver motif is found in both subunits (12, 46); Second, the Jews are astonished because of his words: "How did this man get such learning without having studied?" (15); "No one ever spoke like this man" (46). Third, both contain the positive-negative controversy in them as in the case of vv. 40–44. Fourth, vv. 40–44 and 45–52 are inseparable because of their continuity in theme

(where he is from) and style (controversy-conflict). Indeed, vv. 45–52 are complementary to vv. 40–44.

10. Therefore, we may say that, among the arguments of the Jews, the first and last can be in a pair, and the second and fourth can also be in a pair. Then, the third one (30–32) may be the center, mostly introducing the positive response of the believer in him as well as indicating his time that had not yet come.

11. Let us match them according to their corresponding pairs: vv. 10–15 (A) and 40–52 (A'); vv. 16–24 (B) and 37–39 (B'); vv. 25–27 (C) and 35–36 (C') ; vv. 28–29 (D) and 33–34 (D'). The center is vv. 30–32 (X). It is a designed, structure of chiasm.

Connections of sub-units

10-15	[Jews] Positive-negative in argument: where he is; what kind of the person he is; how he knows the letters	A	A'	[Jews] Positive-negative in argument: where Christ is from; how Jesus speaks; who the believers are	40-52
16-24	[**Jesus**] His defence and the rebuke against their unbelief	B	B'	[**Jesus**] His invitation to the belief and the promise of the Spirit	37-39
25-27	[Jews] Negative in response: who he is and where he is from	C	C'	[Jews] Negative in response: where he is going and what he says	35-36
28-29	[**Jesus**] Regarding where I am from and where I am going back	D	D'	[**Jesus**] Regarding where I am from and where I am going back	33-34
30-32	[Jews] Positive-negative in response: who he is	X			

12. There is one thing to be further considered, that is, the balance in size, particularly between the first and last arguments, vv. 10–15 (A) and 40–52 (A'), and between two related discourses, vv. 16–24 (B) and 37–39 (B'). Verses 10–15 are smaller than vv. 40–52 in size similarly to vv. 37–39 being smaller than vv. 16–24. Thus, it is logically inferred that the combination of vv. 10–15 and 16–24 can match in size that of vv. 37–39 and 40–52. It may mean that vv. 10–24 are in a pair with vv. 37–52 in terms of the union of the first section with the last one, both of which consist of one argument passage and one discourse of Jesus, presented together, similar in size.

13. If we do combine these verses together and regard vv. 10–24 and 37–52 as two larger sections. There remain only vv. 25–36 which consist of five subsections: C-D-X-D'-C', which are interrelated and somehow cohesive: three argument passages and two short discourses of Jesus in between; even their sizes are similar to each other. If we count them altogether, their size is similar to either vv. 10–24 or 37–52.

14. It means that we can divide vv. 10–52 into three sections: vv. 10–24, 25–36, and 37–52, which are arranged in balance of size; among which vv. 10–24 and 37–52 are in a pair, while vv. 25–36 are in the middle. Therefore, on a larger scale, we can re-name them: A (10–24); X (25–36); A' (37–52).

15. If we do this, we can find that: (1) The structure of vv. 10–52 becomes seen as simpler than before: three sections (A-X-A') with nine subunits within (ABCD-X-D'C'B'A'); (2) The balance of size is kept well among the three sections; (3) The positive-negative responses to Jesus in the arguments of the Jews appear in all the three sections in balance; (4) The issue of the origin of Jesus also comes up in all the three sections; (5) Each section contains one other issue besides the original one: The Sabbath healing ministry (in A); Where Jesus is going (in X); The promise of the Spirit (in A').

A. 7:10-24	A				The Jews: Where he is and how he knows (7:10-15)
	B				**Jesus**: My teaching and my work (7:16-24)
X. 7:25-36		C			The Jews: We know where he is from (7:25-27)
		D			**Jesus**: I am from Him who sent me (7:28-29)
			X		The Jews: he is the Christ or not (7:30-32)
		D'			**Jesus**: I go to the One who sent me (7:33-34)
		C'			The Jews: Where he is going (7:35-36)
A'. 7:37-52	B'				**Jesus**: Invitation and promise of the Spirit (7:37-39)
	A'				The Jews: The prophet from Galilee? (7:40-52)

I. Jesus and His Brothers: Who He Is and Where He Is From (7:1–9)

The main frame here is I1 (AB-B'A'), a comprehensive, chiastic structure, containing six parallels: three chiasms (I2, 5, and 7), one combined chiasm (I3), and two parallelism (I6 and 8). I2 belongs to A of I1, and I3 to B, and I5–6 to B', while I7–8 do not limit themselves simply within A', but extend to connect the following verse (10).

I1. Chiastic, AB-B'A': In A, Jesus would not go about in Judea and stays in Galilee, and, A', Jesus says he is not going up to Jerusalem and remains in Galilee. In B and B', there is an argument between his brothers, who insist on him going to Judea (B), and Jesus, who talks about his time (B'). **I2.** Chiastic, ab-b'a': In a, the place, Galilee where Jesus goes around, and, in a', the time, the Feast of Tabernacles, are focused. While, b and b' are related in terms that Jesus would not go to Judea (b) and his reason for not wishing to (b'). He wants to stay in Galilee for a while (a), but the Jew's feast is near (a').

Who Is He and Where Is He From?

V	1	2			Phrases	Translation
1	A	a			Καὶ μετὰ ταῦτα περιεπάτει ὁ Ἰησοῦς ἐν τῇ Γαλιλαίᾳ·	And after these things Jesus went around in Galilee,
	-	b			οὐ γὰρ ἤθελεν ἐν τῇ Ἰουδαίᾳ περιπατεῖν,	for he would not go about in Judea,
	-	b'			ὅτι ἐζήτουν αὐτὸν οἱ Ἰουδαῖοι ἀποκτεῖναι.	because the Jews were seeking to kill him.
2	-	a'			Ἦν δὲ ἐγγὺς ἡ ἑορτὴ τῶν Ἰουδαίων ἡ σκηνοπηγία.	Now the Jews' feast, the Feast of Tabernacles was near,
		3				
3	B	a			εἶπον οὖν πρὸς αὐτὸν οἱ ἀδελφοὶ αὐτοῦ· μετάβηθι ἐντεῦθεν καὶ ὕπαγε εἰς τὴν Ἰουδαίαν,	So his brothers said to him, "Depart from here and go to Judea,
	-	b1			ἵνα καὶ οἱ μαθηταί σου θεωρήσουσιν	so that your disciples may see
	-	b2			σοῦ τὰ ἔργα ἃ ποιεῖς·	your works you are doing.
4	-	c			οὐδεὶς γάρ τι ἐν κρυπτῷ ποιεῖ	For no one does anything in secret
	-	c'			καὶ ζητεῖ αὐτὸς ἐν παρρησίᾳ εἶναι.	and seeks to be in public.
	-	b'2			εἰ ταῦτα ποιεῖς,	If you do these things,
	-	b'1			φανέρωσον σεαυτὸν τῷ κόσμῳ.	show yourself to the world."
5	-	a'			οὐδὲ γὰρ οἱ ἀδελφοὶ αὐτοῦ ἐπίστευον εἰς αὐτόν.	For even his brothers did not believe in him.
	4					
6	B'	a	5	6	λέγει οὖν αὐτοῖς ὁ Ἰησοῦς·	Jesus said to them,
	-	-	a	a	ὁ καιρὸς ὁ ἐμὸς	"My time
	-	-	-	b	οὔπω πάρεστιν,	has not been yet present,
	-	-	b	a'	ὁ δὲ καιρὸς ὁ ὑμέτερος	but your time
	-	-	-	b'	πάντοτέ ἐστιν ἕτοιμος.	is always ready.
7	-	x	b'		οὐ δύναται ὁ κόσμος μισεῖν ὑμᾶς,	The world cannot hate you,
	-	-	a'		ἐμὲ δὲ μισεῖ,	but it hates me
	-	-	-		ὅτι ἐγὼ μαρτυρῶ περὶ αὐτοῦ ὅτι τὰ ἔργα αὐτοῦ πονηρά ἐστιν.	because I testify of it that its works are evil.
		7		8		
8	A'	a'	a	a	ὑμεῖς ἀνάβητε εἰς τὴν ἑορτήν·	You go to the feast.
	-	-	b	b	ἐγὼ οὐκ ἀναβαίνω εἰς τὴν ἑορτὴν ταύτην,	I am not going up to this feast,
	-	-	x		ὅτι ὁ ἐμὸς καιρὸς οὔπω πεπλήρωται.	for my time has not yet fully come.
9	-	b'			ταῦτα δὲ εἰπὼν	And having said this,
	-	-			αὐτὸς ἔμεινεν ἐν τῇ Γαλιλαίᾳ.	he remained in Galilee.

I3. Combined chiastic, a-b1b2-c-c'-b'2b'1-a': His brothers stir Jesus up to go to Judea (a), for they do not believe in him (a'). Their excuses for persuading him are similarly provided in b1b2 and b'2b'1: "so that your disciples may see" (b1) and "show yourself to the world" (b'1); "your works you are doing" (b2) and "If you do these things" (b'2). In c-c', we may read their sarcasm about Jesus' public ministry, his brothers, "For no one does anything in secret and seeks to be in public." **I4**. Chiastic, a-x-a': In a-a', two contrasts between him and his brothers come up: "my time" vs. "your time" (a); "you go to the feast" vs. "I am not going up to this feast" (a'). In the center x, two relations, that between the world and "you," and that between Jesus and the world, regarding its hatred, are presented.

I5. Chiastic, ab-b'a': In this chiasm, a and b are contrasted with one another as well as b' and a'. Both a and a' regard Jesus: "my time" (a) and "it hates me" (a'), while both b and b' are related to "you": "your time" (b) and "the world cannot hate you" (b'). **I6**. Parallel, ab-a'b': Two clauses are interrelated in contrast: ὁ καιρὸς ὁ ἐμός (My time, a) and ὁ δὲ καιρὸς ὁ ὑμέτερος (but your time, a'); οὔπω πάρεστιν (has not yet been present, b) and πάντοτέ ἐστιν ἕτοιμος (is always ready, b').

I7. Chiastic, ab-x-b'a': In a, Jesus says to his brothers, "You go to the feast," and, in a', they go to the feast. As he says, "I am not going up to this feast" (b), he remains in Galilee (b'). In the center x, a sentence, "for my time has not yet fully come," is highlighted. I8. Parallel, ab-a'b': As Jesus says to his brothers, "You go to the feast" (a), they go (a'). Then, he says, "I am not going up to this feast" (b), but finally he goes up not in public but in secret (b').

In I1, there is an argument between Jesus and his brothers whether to stay or go. In I2, there are the place, the time, and the reason not to go to Judea. I3 focuses on the unbelief of his brothers. In I4, the word of Jesus that "my time has not yet come" is related to the hatred of the world. I5 contrasts Jesus ("I") to his brothers ("you") regarding the time and hatred of the world. In I6, "your time" and "my time" are in contrast. In I7, Jesus tells his brothers to go, but as for him, he has not yet gone. In I8, Jesus finally went up Jerusalem but in secret.

II. Jesus and the Jews: Who He Is and Where He Is From (7:10–52)

Chiastic Structure, II1 (ABCD-X-D'C'B'A'): See the previous note on the structure of vv. 10–52.

A. The Jews: Where He Is and How He Knows (7:10–15)

In these verses, II2 is the main structure of combined chiasm with three chiasms (II3–5). II3 also shows the cohesiveness in vv. 10–14. II4 reflects the connection of B-B' of I2, and II5 is related to the connection between A'1 and A'2.

II2. Combined chiastic, A1A2-B-B'-A'1A'2: In A1, Jesus went up to Jerusalem in secret and, in A'1, he went up into the temple and taught in public. Both regard where he went and what he did. In A2, the Jews are seeking him and raise a question, while, in A'2, they are amazed and also raise a question. Both show a similar pattern in style.

Who Is He and Where Is He From?

In B, there is whispering regarding the controversy of who Jesus is, and in B', they still keep speaking but not openly.

V	2			7	8	Phrases	Translation
10	A1			a'	a'	Ὡς δὲ ἀνέβησαν οἱ ἀδελφοὶ αὐτοῦ εἰς τὴν ἑορτήν,	But after his brothers had gone up to the feast,
-	-	3	a		b'	τότε καὶ αὐτὸς ἀνέβη οὐ φανερῶς ἀλλ' [ὡς] ἐν κρυπτῷ.	then he also went up, not publicly but in secret.
11	A2	b				οἱ οὖν Ἰουδαῖοι ἐζήτουν αὐτὸν ἐν τῇ ἑορτῇ καὶ ἔλεγον·	Now the Jews were seeking him at the feast, and saying,
-	-	-	4			ποῦ ἐστιν ἐκεῖνος;	"Where is that man?"
12	B	x	a			καὶ γογγυσμὸς περὶ αὐτοῦ ἦν πολὺς ἐν τοῖς ὄχλοις·	And there was much whispering about him among the people.
-	-	-	b			οἱ μὲν ἔλεγον ὅτι ἀγαθός ἐστιν, ἄλλοι [δὲ] ἔλεγον· οὔ,	Some said, "He is a good man." Others said, "No,
-	-	-	b'			ἀλλὰ πλανᾷ τὸν ὄχλον.	he deceives the multitude."
13	B'	b'	a'			οὐδεὶς μέντοι παρρησίᾳ ἐλάλει περὶ αὐτοῦ διὰ τὸν φόβον τῶν Ἰουδαίων.	However, no one was speaking openly of him for fear of the Jews.
				5			
14	A'1	a'	a			Ἤδη δὲ τῆς ἑορτῆς μεσούσης ἀνέβη Ἰησοῦς εἰς τὸ ἱερὸν	About the middle of the feast Jesus went up into the temple
-	-	-	b			καὶ ἐδίδασκεν.	and taught.
15	A'2			b'		ἐθαύμαζον οὖν οἱ Ἰουδαῖοι	The Jews were amazed
-				a'		λέγοντες·	and said,
-						πῶς οὗτος γράμματα οἶδεν μὴ μεμαθηκώς;	"How did this man get such learning without having studied?"

II3. Chiastic, ab-x-b'a': In a, when Jesus goes up, he does so in secret. But in a', in the middle of the feast, he does not stay this way, teaching in public. In b, the Jews are seeking him but, in b', they are not speaking openly of him for fear. In the center x, there is a controversy about who Jesus is: "He is a good man" versus "No, he deceives the multitude." II4. Chiastic, ab-b'a': In b-b', the controversy regarding the identity of Jesus is focused, while, in a-a', "whispering about him" (a) and "not speaking openly" (a') are similarly described. II5. Parallel, ab-a'b': As Jesus went up into the temple (a) and taught (b), the Jews were amazed (a') and said something (b'). One is the cause (ab), and the other is its result (a'b').

In II2, there are two questions raised by the Jews as well as one controversy regarding Jesus. In II3, the teaching of Jesus and the controversy of the Jews are arranged. II4 focuses on the whispering controversy concerning what Jesus is about. II5 draws on what he did and how they responded to it.

B. Jesus: My Teaching and My Work (7:16-24)

V					Phrases	Translation
16	6				ἀπεκρίθη οὖν αὐτοῖς [ὁ] Ἰησοῦς καὶ εἶπεν·	So Jesus answered them,
	a				ἡ ἐμὴ διδαχὴ οὐκ ἔστιν ἐμὴ	"My teaching is not mine,
	b				ἀλλὰ τοῦ πέμψαντός με·	but his who sent me.
17	x				ἐάν τις θέλῃ τὸ θέλημα αὐτοῦ ποιεῖν, γνώσεται περὶ τῆς διδαχῆς	If anyone wants to do God's will, he will know of the teaching,
		7				
	b'	a			πότερον ἐκ τοῦ θεοῦ ἐστιν	whether it is of God
	a'	b	8	9	ἢ ἐγὼ ἀπ' ἐμαυτοῦ λαλῶ.	or whether I speak from myself.
18		b'	a	a	ὁ ἀφ' ἑαυτοῦ λαλῶν	He who speaks from himself
		-	b	-	τὴν δόξαν τὴν ἰδίαν ζητεῖ·	seeks his own glory,
		a'	b'	-	ὁ δὲ ζητῶν τὴν δόξαν τοῦ πέμψαντος αὐτὸν	but he who seeks the glory of the one who sent him
		10				
	a		a'	-	οὗτος ἀληθής ἐστιν	is true,
	a'		-	-	καὶ ἀδικία ἐν αὐτῷ οὐκ ἔστιν.	and there is no unrighteousness in him.
19				b	Οὐ Μωϋσῆς δέδωκεν ὑμῖν τὸν νόμον;	Has not Moses given you the law?
				c	καὶ οὐδεὶς ἐξ ὑμῶν ποιεῖ τὸν νόμον.	Yet none of you keeps the law.
				d	τί με ζητεῖτε ἀποκτεῖναι;	Why do you seek to kill me?"
20				e	ἀπεκρίθη ὁ ὄχλος·	The people answered,
				-	δαιμόνιον ἔχεις·	"You have a demon.
				-	τίς σε ζητεῖ ἀποκτεῖναι;	Who is seeking to kill you?"
21	11			a'	ἀπεκρίθη Ἰησοῦς καὶ εἶπεν αὐτοῖς·	Jesus answered them,
	a1			-	ἓν ἔργον ἐποίησα	"I did one work,
	a2			-	καὶ πάντες θαυμάζετε.	and you are all amazed.
22	b			b'	διὰ τοῦτο Μωϋσῆς δέδωκεν ὑμῖν τὴν περιτομήν-	Because Moses has given you circumcision
	-			-	οὐχ ὅτι ἐκ τοῦ Μωϋσέως ἐστὶν ἀλλ' ἐκ τῶν πατέρων-	(not that it is from Moses, but from the fathers),
	c			c'	καὶ ἐν σαββάτῳ περιτέμνετε ἄνθρωπον.	you circumcise a child on the Sabbath.
23	c'			-	εἰ περιτομὴν λαμβάνει ἄνθρωπος ἐν σαββάτῳ	If a man receives circumcision on the Sabbath,
	b'			-	ἵνα μὴ λυθῇ ὁ νόμος Μωϋσέως,	so that the law of Moses may not be broken,
	a'2			d'	ἐμοὶ χολᾶτε	are you angry with me
	a'1			-	ὅτι ὅλον ἄνθρωπον ὑγιῆ ἐποίησα ἐν σαββάτῳ;	because on the Sabbath I made a man's whole body well?
		12				
24		a		e'	μὴ κρίνετε	Do not judge
		b		-	κατ' ὄψιν,	by appearance,
		b'		-	ἀλλὰ τὴν δικαίαν κρίσιν	but ~ with righteous judgment."
		a'		-	κρίνετε.	~ judge ~

There is no one overarching structure, but II6 and II9 play the role of main pillars sequentially supporting the unity of this subunit. There are seven parallels: four chiasms (II6–8 and 12), one combined chiasm (II11), one parallelism (II9), and one dual (II10). II7 links II6 and II9, while II8 and 10 lie in a of II9. There is no parallel in vv. 19–20 except for the parts of II9 (bcde). II11 reflect the unity of the latter half of II9, while II12 belongs to only e' of II9.

II6. Chiastic, ab-x-b'a': Both in a and a', Jesus insists that his teaching is not from himself, while, both in b and b', the focus is repeatedly on that his teaching is from the Father. In the center x, it is assured that "anyone who wants to do the will of God" comes to know this fact. **II7**. Chiastic, ab-b'a': In a-a', "whether it is of God" (a) is related to "but he who seeks the glory of the one who sent him . . ." (a'). Namely, he who teaches from God or the things of God (a) is the one who seeks the glory of God (a'), in contrast to him who speaks from himself (b and b'), thus seeking his own glory (b').

II8. Chiastic, ab-b'a': Two subjects are contrasted in a pair. Syntactically, ὁ ἀφ' ἑαυτοῦ λαλῶν (He who speaks from himself, a) is compared to ὁ δὲ ζητῶν τὴν δόξαν τοῦ πέμψαντος αὐτὸν (but he who seeks the glory of the one who sent him, b'). But semantically, b and b' are in a pair of contrast: "seeks his own glory" versus ". . . seeks the glory of the one who sent him." Thus, it is said that "he who speaks from himself" (a) is contrasted to the one, who is true and in whom is no unrighteousness (a').

II9. Parallel, abcde-a'b'c'd'e': In a-a', Jesus says that he is true and has no unrighteousness in him, for he seeks the glory of the Father, as he does not speak from himself (a) and that he did one work leading them to be amazed (a'). It means that what he does and says is all true, as long as he seeks the Father's glory. In b-b', Jesus refers to the law of Moses: "Has not Moses given you the law?" (b) and "Moses has given you circumcision" (b'). The circumcision (b') belongs to Moses' law (b). In c-c', Jesus criticizes them for their inconsistency: "Yet none of you keeps the law" (c) and "you circumcise a child on the Sabbath, so that the law of Moses may not be broken" (c'). We need to read c' first and then c, for c and c' are complementary. It means that the Jews circumcise children on the Sabbath, to keep the law of Moses (c'), but they are now accusing Jesus of his healing on the Sabbath, and thus, they are not keepers of the law (c). In d-d', Jesus accuses them of their intention to kill him: "Why do you seek to kill me?" (d) and "are you angry with me because on the Sabbath I made a man's whole body well?" (d'). In d', the reason why they came to kill him as in d comes up. In e-e', they misunderstand what Jesus tells them regarding killing him and rather criticise him for having a demon (e); Jesus rebukes them for judging him, rashly and carelessly (e'), as they do in e. Unless his discourse in vv. 21–23 is fully told, vv. 19–21 may not be interpreted.

II10. Dual, a-a': "This man is true" (a) and "and there is no unrighteousness in him" are double expressions regarding he who speaks of God. **II11**. Combined chiastic, a1a2-bc-c'b'-a'2a'1: That Jesus did heal a man and they responded to it at first with amazement (a1a2), but finally they became angry with him for it (a'2a'1). Here a1-a'1 are related to his healing ministry: "I did one deed" (a1) and "... I made a man's whole body well" (a'1), while a2-a'2 are their responses: "you are all amazed" (a2) and "are you angry with me?" (a'2). Both b and b' are related to the law of Moses: "... Moses has given you circumcision" (b) and "... the law of Moses may not be broken" (b'). In c-c', the circumcision-on-the-Sabbath issue is in common. II12. Chiastic, ab-b'a': Syntactically and semantically, two clauses are arranged in chiasm: μὴ κρίνετε (Do not judge, a) and κρίνετε (judge, a'); κατ' ὄψιν (by appearance, b) and ἀλλὰ τὴν δικαίαν κρίσιν (but ~ with righteous judgment, b').

In II6, Jesus insists that his teaching is from the Father. II7 focuses on whose glory he is seeking. II8, the one who seeks the glory of the Sender is true. In II9, the Jews are told that they are going to kill Jesus by breaking the law in spite of his sincere words and truthful deed. In II10, true and righteous are dually emphasized. In II11, there is the contrast between the positive response to Jesus and the negative one of the Jews. II12 emphasizes righteous judgement.

C. The Jews: We Know Where He Is From (7:25–27)

Among three parallels: two chiasms (II13 and 15) and one parallelism (II14), II13 and 15 are considered weightier ones than II14.

V				Phrases	Translation
25	13			Ἔλεγον οὖν τινες ἐκ τῶν Ἱεροσολυμιτῶν·	Then some of the people of Jerusalem said,
		a		οὐχ οὗτός ἐστιν ὃν ζητοῦσιν ἀποκτεῖναι;	"Is not this the man whom they seek to kill?
26		b		καὶ ἴδε παρρησίᾳ λαλεῖ	And look, he is speaking publicly,
		b'		καὶ οὐδὲν αὐτῷ λέγουσιν.	and they say nothing to him.
		a'	14	μήποτε ἀληθῶς ἔγνωσαν οἱ ἄρχοντες	Have not the rulers really known
		-	a	15	ὅτι οὗτός ἐστιν ὁ χριστός;	that this man is the Christ, have they?
27		b	a	ἀλλὰ τοῦτον οἴδαμεν πόθεν ἐστίν·	But we know where this man is from.
		a'	x	ὁ δὲ χριστὸς ὅταν ἔρχηται	When the Christ comes,
		b'	a'	οὐδεὶς γινώσκει πόθεν ἐστίν.	no one will know where he is from."

II13. Chiastic, ab-b'a': In b-b', b ("he is speaking publicly") is contrasted to b' ("and they say nothing to him"). Both in a-a', they raise two related questions in contradiction: "Is not this the man whom they seek to kill?" (a) and "Have not the rulers really known that this man is the Christ, have they?" (a'). II14. Parallel, ab-a'b': Both a and a' are related in terms of the Christ issue: "this man is the Christ ...?" (a) and "When the Christ comes" (a'). Both b and b' regard where he comes from: "But we know where this man is from" (b) and "no one will know where he is from" (b'). II15. Chiastic, a-x-a': In the center x, the Christ who comes is the issue, while a and a' describe the issue of where he comes from.

Who Is He and Where Is He From?

In II13, there are two negative questions raised by the Jews. In II14–15, it is emphasized that they know where Jesus is from, compared to the true origin of the Christ.

D. Jesus: I Am from Him Who Sent Me (7:28–29)

There are only two parallels: one chiasm (II16) and one combined chiasm (II17), mixed together in complex.

V			Phrases	Translation
28	16		ἔκραξεν οὖν ἐν τῷ ἱερῷ διδάσκων ὁ Ἰησοῦς καὶ λέγων·	So Jesus cried out in the temple, teaching and saying,
	a		κἀμὲ οἴδατε	"You know me,
	b	17	καὶ οἴδατε πόθεν εἰμί·	and you know where I am from.
	b'	a1	καὶ ἀπ' ἐμαυτοῦ οὐκ ἐλήλυθα,	But I have not come of myself,
	a'	a2	ἀλλ' ἔστιν ἀληθινὸς ὁ πέμψας με,	but he who sent me is true,
	-	b	ὃν ὑμεῖς οὐκ οἴδατε·	whom you do not know.
29		b'	ἐγὼ οἶδα αὐτόν,	I know him,
		a'1	ὅτι παρ' αὐτοῦ εἰμι	because I am from him
		a'2	κἀκεῖνός με ἀπέστειλεν.	and he sent me."

II16. Chiastic, ab-b'a': In b-b', Jesus says that "you" think that "you know where I am from" (b) but "you" do not know exactly where I am from, for "I have not come of myself" (b'). In a-a', Jesus says that "you" think that "you know me" (a), but "you" do not know "me" actually, for "you" do not know that "he who sent me is true" (a').
II17. Combined chiastic, a1a2-b-b'-a'1a'2: In a1-a'1, "I have not come of myself" (a1) is complemented by "because I am from him" (a'1). And a2 and a'2 share the idea that the Father sent the Son. In b, they do not know the Father, but on the contrary, in b', Jesus knows him.

In II16, there is a contrast between what "you" know about "me" vs. what "you" do not know about "me." In II17, it is emphasized that they do not know the Father who sent the Son.

X. The Believer: He Is the Christ (7:30–32)

There are four parallels: three chiasms (II18–20) and one parallelism (II21), among which II18 is primarily significant to unify the subunit. The others are partial in their role of connection.

II18. Chiastic, ab-b'a': In a, the Jews were seeking to seize Jesus but could not do that. At last, in a', the leaders of the Jews now send officers to arrest him. In the middle, b and b' are two compared reactions from many of the multitude, believing in him,

(b) and from the Pharisees, hearing that the multitude whisper about him, (b'). **II19**. Chiastic, a-x-a': In the center x, his time that had not yet come is the focus. In a and a', two contrastive responses are provided: those who were seeking to seize him but failing (a); those who believed in him (a').

II20. Chiastic, ab-b'a': Many of the multitude who believed in him (a) and the leaders of the Jews who sent officers to arrest him (a') are in contrast. And believers who say and admit Jesus as Christ (b) and the Pharisees who hear the multitude whispering about him (b') are also contrasted. **II21**. Parallel, ab-a'b': The Pharisees heard (a) and, with the chief priest, sent officers (a'). The multitude whisper about him (b) and the leaders are arresting him (b').

V	18	19		Phrases	Translation
30	a	a		Ἐζήτουν οὖν αὐτὸν πιάσαι,	So they were seeking to seize him,
	-	-		καὶ οὐδεὶς ἐπέβαλεν ἐπ' αὐτὸν τὴν χεῖρα,	but no one laid a hand on him,
	-	x	20	ὅτι οὔπω ἐληλύθει ἡ ὥρα αὐτοῦ.	because his time had not yet come.
31	b	a'	a	Ἐκ τοῦ ὄχλου δὲ πολλοὶ ἐπίστευσαν εἰς αὐτόν	But many of the multitude believed in him.
	-		b	καὶ ἔλεγον· ὁ χριστὸς ὅταν ἔλθῃ	And they said, "When the Christ comes,
	-	-	21	μὴ πλείονα σημεῖα ποιήσει ὧν οὗτος ἐποίησεν;	will he do more signs than this man has done?"
32	b'	b'	a	ἤκουσαν οἱ Φαρισαῖοι	The Pharisees heard
	-	-	b	τοῦ ὄχλου γογγύζοντος περὶ αὐτοῦ ταῦτα,	the multitude whispering such things about him.
	a'	a'	a'	καὶ ἀπέστειλαν οἱ ἀρχιερεῖς καὶ οἱ Φαρισαῖοι ὑπηρέτας	And the chief priest and Pharisees sent officers
	-	-	b'	ἵνα πιάσωσιν αὐτόν.	to arrest him.

In II18, there is the contrast between those who are seizing Jesus vs. the believers. In II19, the contrast between those who seek to seize Jesus and the believers is focused in relation to his time. In II20, there are two sides of the reaction to Jesus. In II21, another contrast between the multitude whispering about Jesus vs. the leaders of the Jews who sent to arrest him is shown.

D'. Jesus: I Go to the One Who Sent Me (7:33-34)

Except for II22 which is connected with vv. 35-36 (C' of II1), there are three parallels: one combined chiasm (II23), one dual (II24), and parallelism (II25). II22 demonstrates the connection between vv. 33-34 (D' of II1) and 35-36 (C'). II25 is also related to this connection. II23 is the parallel that binds these verses into one.

Who Is He and Where Is He From?

V	22			Phrases	Translation
33	a	23		Εἶπεν οὖν ὁ Ἰησοῦς·	Jesus then said,
-	-	a1		ἔτι χρόνον μικρὸν μεθ' ὑμῶν εἰμι	"I am with you for a short time,
-	-	a2	24	25	καὶ ὑπάγω πρὸς τὸν πέμψαντά με.	and then I go to the one who sent me.
34	b	b	a	a	ζητήσετέ με	You will seek me
-	-	b'	-	b	καὶ οὐχ εὑρήσετέ [με],	and you will not find me,
-	-	a'2	a'	c	καὶ ὅπου εἰμὶ ἐγὼ	and where I am,
-	-	a'1	-	d	ὑμεῖς οὐ δύνασθε ἐλθεῖν.	you cannot come."

II22. Parallel, ab-a'b': In b-b', the same contents of Jesus' saying is duplicated: "You will seek me and you will not find me, and where I am, you cannot come." What Jesus says (b) is exactly reiterated by the Jews (b'). In a, Jesus expresses that he is going to the Father. And, in a', they respond with questions: "Where is this man going to . . . ?" and "Is he going to the Dispersion . . . ?"

II23. Combined chiastic, a1a2-b-b'-a'2a'1: Jesus says that he is with them for a short time (a1) but they cannot come to him (a'1). He is going to the Father who sent him (a2), from heaven where the Father is. He will be where the Father is, namely the place "where I am" (a'2). They will seek him (b) but they will not find him (b'), because he will go finally (a1a2) and they cannot come where he is (a'2a'1). II24. Dual, a-a': The similar ideas, "you will not find me"(a) and "you cannot come" (a'), are shared, indicating that they do not know where he is, although they will be seeking him. II25. Parallels, abcd-a'b'c'd': four clauses recur exactly: "You will seek me" (a-a'); "and you will not find me" (b-b'); "and where I am" (c-c'); "you cannot come" (d-d'). As Jesus told them, they repeat it the word by the word.

In II22, it is emphasized that they cannot come where Jesus is going and they do not even know its meaning at all. In II23, the focus is on that they cannot come where he is going. In II24, their inability to go where Jesus is going is doubly emphasized. In II25, the same words of Jesus are reiterated.

C'. The Jews: Where He Is Going (7:35–36)

Verses 35–36 have continuity with the previous verses, vv. 33–34, as seen in II22. II27 is the same parallel as II24. II26 belongs to a' of II22, and II27 to b'.

II26. Chiastic, a-x-a': Both in a-a', "where Jesus is going" is focused and, in the center x, "not to find him" is located. II27. Dual, a-a': See II24. In II26, the misunderstanding of the Jews regarding where Jesus is going is emphasized. In II27, it is repeated that they cannot have access to Jesus, as in II24.

V	22				Phrases	Translation
35	a'	26			εἶπον οὖν οἱ Ἰουδαῖοι πρὸς ἑαυτούς·	The Jews said to one another,
-	-	a			ποῦ οὗτος μέλλει πορεύεσθαι	"Where is this man going to go
-	-	x			ὅτι ἡμεῖς οὐχ εὑρήσομεν αὐτόν;	that we shall not find him?
-	-	a'			μὴ εἰς τὴν διασπορὰν τῶν Ἑλλήνων μέλλει πορεύεσθαι καὶ διδάσκειν τοὺς Ἕλληνας;	Is he going to go to the Dispersion among the Greeks and teach the Greeks?
36	b'		27	25	τίς ἐστιν ὁ λόγος οὗτος	What is this statement
-	-	a		a	ὃν εἶπεν· ζητήσετέ με	that he said, 'You will seek me,
-	-	-		b	καὶ οὐχ εὑρήσετέ [με],	and will not find me,
-	-	a'		c	καὶ ὅπου εἰμὶ ἐγὼ	and where I am,
-	-	-		d	ὑμεῖς οὐ δύνασθε ἐλθεῖν;	you cannot come'?"

B'. Jesus: Invitation and Promise of the Spirit (7:37–39)

There are six parallels: three chiasms (II29, 31, and 33), two parallelisms (II28 and 32), and one dual (II30). Among them, II28 is comprehensive. The others are complex, being webbed with each other.

V						Phrases	Translation
37						Ἐν δὲ τῇ ἐσχάτῃ ἡμέρᾳ τῇ μεγάλῃ τῆς ἑορτῆς εἱστήκει ὁ Ἰησοῦς καὶ ἔκραξεν λέγων·	On the last day, the great day of the feast, Jesus stood and cried out, saying,
	28	29					
	a	a	30			ἐάν τις διψᾷ	"If anyone is thirsty,
-	-	b	a			ἐρχέσθω πρός με	let him come to me
-	-	-	a'	31		καὶ πινέτω.	and drink.
38	b	b'		a	32	ὁ πιστεύων εἰς ἐμέ,	He who believes in me,
-	-	a'		b	a	καθὼς εἶπεν ἡ γραφή, ποταμοὶ ἐκ τῆς κοιλίας αὐτοῦ ῥεύσουσιν ὕδατος ζῶντος.	as the Scripture said, 'Rivers of living water will flow from within him.'"
39	a'		33	b'	b	τοῦτο δὲ εἶπεν	And he said this
-	-		a	-	-	περὶ τοῦ πνεύματος	about the Spirit,
-	-		b	-	a'	ὃ ἔμελλον λαμβάνειν	whom ~ were to receive;
-	-		-	a'	-	οἱ πιστεύσαντες εἰς αὐτόν·	~ those who believed in him ~
-	b'		b'	-	b'	οὔπω γὰρ ἦν πνεῦμα,	for the Spirit was not yet given,
-	-		a'	-	-	ὅτι Ἰησοῦς οὐδέπω ἐδοξάσθη.	because Jesus was not yet glorified.

II28. Parallel, ab-a'b': In a-a', come-and-drink (a) and believe-and-receive (a') are similarly focused. In this way, coming to Jesus means believing in him, and drinking from him is receiving the Spirit. In b-b', the promise of living water is concerning the

future ("will flow," b), when Jesus said this, it was before the Spirit was given (b'). **II29**. Chiastic, ab-b'a':[2] It is assured that, in b-b', coming to Jesus and drinking (b) means, in other words, believing in him (b'). Even if he was thirsty (a), rivers of living water come to flow from within him, eventually (a'). We read that the problem of a is solved in a', by way of b-b'. II30. Dual, a-a': Coming (a) and drinking (a') are two ways of action for believers.

II31. Chiastic, ab-b'a': Both a and a' focus on believers in him, while, b-b', share the idea of the Spirit. The Scripture said (b) and Jesus said (b'), regarding the Spirit: its result (b); receiving it (b'). II32. Parallel, ab-a'b': In a-a', what happens (a) when the Spirit is given to the believers (a') is provided. When Jesus said about the Spirit (b), the Spirit was not yet given, for he was not yet glorified (b'). II33. Chiastic, ab-b'a': In b-b', the Spirit whom the believers were to receive but which was not yet given is the focus, while, a-a', Jesus who speaks about the Spirit (a) was not yet glorified (a').

In II28–29, believing in him and receiving the Spirit are the focus. In II30, coming and drinking are arranged in a pair. II31 focuses on the inseparable relation between believers and the Spirit. In II32, it is highlighted that the Spirit will be received by believers. II33 focuses on the relation between Jesus and the Spirit.

A'. The Jews: The Prophet from Galilee? (7:40–52)

There is one comprehensive, chiastic structure leading the text into a unity (II34). Apart from this, there are thirteen smaller parallels: eight chiasms (35, 38–39, 41–43, 45, and 47), three parallelisms (II36–37 and 44), and two duals (II40 and 46). The complex, parallel relations (II36–39) occur in A of II34. II35 shows the cohesiveness of the first part of this unit (40–44; AB), while II41 and 43 support that of the last part (45–52; B'A'). II40 and 42 reflect their own cohesions of B and B' of II34, respectively. II44–47 belong to A' of II34, partially and limitedly. II38 reflect the connection between A and A' of II34.

II34. Chiastic, AB-B'A': In A, the multitude becomes divided into two groups in conflict: confessors and deniers. In the final part, A', a dialogue in conflict between the Pharisees and a Pharisee, Nicodemus, is introduced. In B-B', some of the multitude want to seize Jesus but fail (B), and the officers who were sent to arrest him return in failure back to the leaders of the Jews (B'). **II35**. Chiastic, ab-x-b'a': In a-a', there is the contrast between some of the multitude who thought Jesus was the prophet (a) and some of them who wanted to seize him (a'). It is a contrast of responses: positive vs. negative. In b-b', we can see the division in argument among the multitude. In the center x, they refer to the origin of Christ regarding the Scripture.

II36. Parallel, ab-a'b': In a-a', some say (a) and others say (a'). They say, "This is really the prophet" (b); "This is the Christ" (b'). Two kinds of confession are made.

---

2. Cf. Ridderbos introduces a different chiasm referring to NRSV: a ("If anyone thirst"); b ("let him come to him"); b' ("and let him drink"); a' ("who believes in me"). Ridderbos, *Gospel according to John*, 272–73.

II37. Parallel, ab-a'b': In a-a', others say (a) and some say (a'). But they say differently in contrast: "This is the Christ" (b, confession); "The Christ does not come from Galilee, does he?" (b', denial). II38. Chiastic, ab-b'a': In a-a', regarding the prophet issue, confession (a) and denial (a') are contrasted: "This is really the prophet" (a) versus "that no prophet arises out of Galilee" (a'). In b-b', regarding the Christ issue, confession (b) and denial (b') are also contrasted: "This is the Christ" (b) versus "The Christ does not come from Galilee, does he?" (b'). As far as the format is concerned, a and b are similar, while b' and a' are also similar, both indicated his origin as Galilee.

II39. Chiastic, a-x-a': In the center x, the saying of the Scripture is focused. In a-a', they claim that the Christ does not come from Galilee (a), and they quote the Scripture for a proof of their assertion, that the Christ comes from the offspring of David (a'). II40. Dual, a-a': Some wanted to seize him (a) but they could not do it (a'). Two sentences are combined. II41. Chiastic, a-x-a': In the center, there is the defensive response of the officers, while, in a-a', the Pharisees rebuke and blame those who did not bring Jesus in.

II42. Chiastic, a-x-a': In a-a', the officers went back to the leaders (a) and they made excuses for not having arrested him (a'). In the middle x, the leaders ask them why they did not bring him. In the meanwhile, a is the background and x is the question and a' is its answer. II43. Chiastic, a-x-a': In the middle x, Nicodemus expresses his opinion to support Jesus, while, in a-a', the Pharisees show their enmity against Jesus and his followers.

II44. Parallel, ab-a'b': The Pharisees assert that none of them believes in Jesus (a), but Nicodemus, one of them, appears seemingly to take the side of Jesus, arguing for their law (a'), which they referred to as they talked to the officers (b). They keep insulting those who are positive toward Jesus: the multitude (b) and Nicodemus (b'). II45. Chiastic, a-x-a': In a-a', the Pharisees attack any positive response toward Jesus (a) and even regard the mob as accursed, who follow him, condemning them as those who do not know the law (a'). Those who show any positive response to Jesus are regarded as being deceived (a) and being accursed (a'). In the center x, they are convinced that none of them believes in Jesus.

II46. Dual, a-a': Two ways of fair process before judgement are suggested by Nicodemus: first hearing from him (a); then knowing what he does (a'). II47. Chiastic, a-x-a': In the center x, the expression "Search and see" is focused, while, in a-a', the Galilee issue is highlighted: "You are not from Galilee, are you?" (a); "that no prophet arises out of Galilee" (a').

Who Is He and Where Is He From?

V	34	35	36			Phrases	Translation
40	A	a	a		38	Ἐκ τοῦ ὄχλου οὖν ἀκούσαντες τῶν λόγων τούτων ἔλεγον·	Some of the multitude therefore, when they heard these words, said,
	-	-	b	37	a	οὗτός ἐστιν ἀληθῶς ὁ προφήτης·	"This is really the prophet."
41	-	b	a'	a		ἄλλοι ἔλεγον·	Others said,
	-	-	b'	b	b	οὗτός ἐστιν ὁ χριστός,	"This is the Christ."
	-	-		a'	39	οἱ δὲ ἔλεγον·	But some said,
	-	-		b'	b' a	μὴ γὰρ ἐκ τῆς Γαλιλαίας ὁ χριστὸς ἔρχεται;	"The Christ does not come from Galilee, does he?
42	-	x			x	οὐχ ἡ γραφὴ εἶπεν	Does not the Scripture say
	-	-			a'	ὅτι ἐκ τοῦ σπέρματος Δαυὶδ καὶ ἀπὸ Βηθλέεμ τῆς κώμης ὅπου ἦν Δαυὶδ ἔρχεται ὁ χριστός;	that the Christ comes from the offspring of David, and from Bethlehem, the town where David was?"
43	-	b'		40		σχίσμα οὖν ἐγένετο ἐν τῷ ὄχλῳ δι' αὐτόν·	Thus there was a division in the multitude because of him.
44	B	a'		a		τινὲς δὲ ἤθελον ἐξ αὐτῶν πιάσαι αὐτόν,	And some of them wanted to seize him,
	-	-	41	a'	42	ἀλλ' οὐδεὶς ἐπέβαλεν ἐπ' αὐτὸν τὰς χεῖρας.	but no one laid hands on him.
45	B'		a		a	Ἦλθον οὖν οἱ ὑπηρέται πρὸς τοὺς ἀρχιερεῖς καὶ Φαρισαίους,	The officers then went back to the chief priests and Pharisees,
	-	-			x	καὶ εἶπον αὐτοῖς ἐκεῖνοι·	and they said to them,
	-	-			-	διὰ τί οὐκ ἠγάγετε αὐτόν;	"Why didn't you bring him?"
46	-	x			a'	ἀπεκρίθησαν οἱ ὑπηρέται·	The officers answered,
	-	43	-		-	οὐδέποτε ἐλάλησεν οὕτως ἄνθρωπος.	"No man ever spoke like this man."
47	A'	a	a'		45	ἀπεκρίθησαν οὖν αὐτοῖς οἱ Φαρισαῖοι·	The Pharisees answered them,
	-	-	-	44	a	μὴ καὶ ὑμεῖς πεπλάνησθε;	"You have also been deceived, haven't you?
48	-	-	a		x	μή τις ἐκ τῶν ἀρχόντων ἐπίστευσεν εἰς αὐτὸν ἢ ἐκ τῶν Φαρισαίων;	Have any of the rulers or Pharisees believed in him?
49	-	-	b		a'	ἀλλ' ὁ ὄχλος οὗτος ὁ μὴ γινώσκων τὸν νόμον ἐπάρατοί εἰσιν.	But this multitude which does not know the law is accursed."
50	-	x			a'	λέγει Νικόδημος πρὸς αὐτούς, ὁ ἐλθὼν πρὸς αὐτὸν [τὸ] πρότερον, εἷς ὢν ἐξ αὐτῶν·	Nicodemus, who had gone to him before, and who was one of them, said to them,
51	-	-	-	46		μὴ ὁ νόμος ἡμῶν κρίνει τὸν ἄνθρωπον	"Our law does not condemn a man,
	-	-	-		a	ἐὰν μὴ ἀκούσῃ πρῶτον παρ' αὐτοῦ	unless it first hears from him
	-	-	47	-	a'	καὶ γνῷ τί ποιεῖ;	and knows what he does, does it?"
52	-	a'	a	b'		ἀπεκρίθησαν καὶ εἶπαν αὐτῷ· μὴ καὶ σὺ ἐκ τῆς Γαλιλαίας εἶ;	They answered him, "You are not from Galilee, are you?
	-	-	x	-	38	ἐραύνησον καὶ ἴδε	Search and see
	-	-	a'	-	a'	ὅτι ἐκ τῆς Γαλιλαίας προφήτης οὐκ ἐγείρεται.	that no prophet arises out of Galilee."

In II34, there are two groups in conflict: negative vs. positive responses to Jesus. II35 highlights the division among the multitude regarding the origin of Christ. In II36, the focus is on the witness to Jesus as the Christ. II37 contrasts confessors with deniers. In II38, the Christ and the prophet issues are repeated. In II39, the negative insistence that the Christ does not come from Galilee is emphasized. II40 focuses on their failure to seize Jesus. II41 focuses on the contrast between the officers and the Pharisees regarding the arrest of Jesus. In II42, there is the excuse of the officers for not bringing Jesus in. In II43, the positive expression of Nicodemus vs. the negative reaction of the Pharisees are contrasted. In II44, the Pharisees keep insulting those who support Jesus in some ways. In II45, those who show any positive response to Jesus are regarded as being deceived and being accursed. II46 focuses on two ways of fair judgement by Nicodemus. In II47, it is highlighted that no prophet can come from Galilee.

Reading in Structure-Style

1. Based on II1, we may read vv. 10-52, interactively, considering the relations of matched clusters as pairs: First, in A (10-15) and A' (40-52), there are some inter-related connections such as those who are in fear of the Jews (A) and those who scare people with questioning, curse, and condemnation (A'). The people are wondering about the learnedness of Jesus regarding his sayings (A) and the officers confess that no man ever spoke like this man (A'). At first, there is a controversy whether he is a good man or a deceiver (A), and, at last, they argue about whether he is the prophet or not regarding his origin (A'). At first, the people are seeking Jesus where he is (A), and, at last, the Jewish leaders are catching him (A').

Second, in B (16-24) and B' (37-39), there are the Jesus' sayings that are related to each other. In B, Jesus defends himself and rebukes the Jews who do not believe and are going to kill him. The tone is negative throughout B, where a serious conflict exists between Jesus and the Jews. In B', the tone is reversed: positive. Jesus invites the people to believe in him and makes the promise of the Spirit. Those who are stubborn and not ready to listen to Jesus and do not believe in him and those are ready to listen to him and do believe are in contrast.

Third, in C (25-27) and C' (35-36), we can see the similar, inter-connected issues in a negative tone. In C, the Jews insist that they know where he is from, supposing that they would not know where the Christ is from. But in C', it is proved that they do not know anything about what Jesus says regarding where he is going or where he is originally from. Thus, it is read that they have not known anything about where Jesus is from and where he is going to.

Fourth, in D (28-29) and D' (33-34), Jesus says that they do not know anything about where he is from and who sent him (D), and that they never come to him because they know nothing (D'). Although they insist that they do know something about Jesus, they cannot do anything to come to him, if they do not believe in him regarding where he is from and where he is returning.

Fifth, in X (30–32), his time issue comes to the fore again, that is connected to the previous passage, particularly vv. 6 and 8. Additionally, the signs that he has done are referred to by those who believe in him. This scene includes also a negative reaction from the Jewish leaders.

Sixth, the Jews struggle with arguments regarding who Jesus is and where he is from (A-A', C-C'). Most of them are reluctant to believe in Jesus because they are afraid of the threats and condemnations of the Jewish leaders (A-A'). But many of them have believed in him (X). There are also unknown, secret kinds of believer such as the officers who did not arrest Jesus and Nicodemus (A').

Seventh, Jesus who came from the Father speaks the words from the Father and does his signs (B). He invites all the people who are willing to listen to him and he makes the promise of the Spirit (B'). In the middle of the text, Jesus says he is going back to where he belongs (D-D').

2. Considering II9, vv. 18–24, where Jesus defends himself and rebukes the Jews, are all about what he has said (a) and what he has done (a'). He claims that he speaks with truthfulness and righteousness to the people (a) and his work amazes them (a').

Verse 19 (bcd of II9) seems to make an illogical jump in what Jesus says. He says first that Moses has given them the law and then rebukes them for not keeping it. But he seems not to provide any ground for this rebuke. On what grounds is it claimed they do not keep the law? Because they seek to kill him? It can be said so. But, why does their killing him become not keeping the law? We may not find any answer here.

The answer is provided in vv. 22–23 (b'c'd' of II9, counterparts of bcd), particularly v. 23. As Moses has given the Jews circumcision and thus they circumcise a child on the Sabbath, Jesus made a man's whole body well on the Sabbath (see ch. 5). Jesus rebukes them for becoming angry regarding this healing ministry on the Sabbath. (Their first amazement is altered finally to their anger. See II11.)

Their anger (d') is deepened to the point of killing Jesus (d). Anger comes first and killing second. However, their anger and hatred to death are not grounded in the law, because Jesus healed a man just as they circumcise a child on the Sabbath (c'). Thus, they are contradicting themselves, not keeping the law (c). The answer to the question raised in v. 19 is found in vv. 22–23.

How about v. 24? Verse 24 is definitely based on the logic of v. 23, where Jesus confirms that he was right in healing a man on the Sabbath. But what does it mean, "Do not judge by appearance, but judge with righteous judgment"? We may interpret it as Jesus rebuking them regarding that they see the surface level of the healing event ("by appearance") and they become angry and want to kill him without any righteous judgment. It can be interpreted thus, if we consider the text, sequentially.

The second alternative interpretation appears in connection to the counterpart (e) in parallelism. In v. 20, the Jews misjudge Jesus about two things: (1) he has a demon; (2) no one is seeking to kill him. Either in this verse or in the following ones, the direct answer of Jesus to correct their misjudgment cannot be found until v. 24 where two things are pointed out: (1) do not judge by appearances; (2) judge with righteous judgment.

If we consider these verses (20 and 24) as complementary to each other, we may grasp the ideas that: (1) They will know that he has no connection to a demon if they try to see beyond the surface appearance; (2) If they try to judge with righteous judgment, they will come to know who are the men who seek to kill Jesus. The answer of Jesus to their words in v. 20 (e) is finally achieved in v. 24 (e').

Which is proper: the sequential interpretation or the interactive one? Both can be considered interactively and without exclusion.

Interrelations in parallelism

18	His words: true and righteous	a	a'	His deed: they are amazed	21
19	Moses has given them the law.	b	b'	Moses has given them circumcision.	22
	They do not keep the law.	c	c'	They circumcise a child on the Sabbath in order not to break the law.	23
	They seek to kill Jesus.	d	d'	They are angry with Jesus because of the Sabbath ministry of healing.	
20	"You have a demon; Who is seeking to kill you?"	e	e'	"Do not judge by appearance, but judge with righteous judgment."	24

Issues in Structure-Style

1. The Structure of vv. 1–9

Talbert sees in vv. 1–9 a chiastic structure:[3] A. v. 1: Jesus went about in Galilee, because the Jews sought to kill him; B. vv. 2–4: His brothers say to Jesus: Go to Judea, because no one works in secret if he seeks to be known; B'. vv. 6–8a: Jesus says to his brothers: Go yourselves, because although my time has not come, your time is always here; A'. vv. 8b–9: Because his time had not fully come, Jesus remained in Galilee.

---

3. Talbert, *Reading John*, 144.

First, we can say that there is certainly a chiastic structure, an AB-B'A' type, in vv. 1–9. His division needs to be revised, though. Compare it with I1 (A, 1–2; B, 3–5; B', 6–7; A', 8–9).

Second, vv. 1–2 are not to be divided because of the existence of I2 (ab-b'a'). We have to also consider I3 (a-b1b2-c-c'-b'2b'1-a') in vv. 3–5. It means that both vv. 1–2 and 3–5 are kinds of entities within themselves.

Third, vv. 1–2 are in a pair with vv. 8–9 as A and A': (1) they share the "feast" issue (2 and 8); (2) Jesus does not go up to Jerusalem and stays in Galilee (1 and 8–9).

Fourth, without v. 5, the cohesion of vv. 3–5 cannot be built (see I3). And vv. 3–5 (the saying of his brothers and a comment of the author) match vv. 6–7 (part of the saying of Jesus) that show I5 (ab-b'a') regarding their own internal cohesion.

Fifth, v. 8 cannot be separated into v. 8a and 8b, for vv. 8–9 are an entity with I7 (ab-x-b'a') as well as these verses being related to vv. 1–2. Although there is I4 which comprises vv. 6–8 (all the saying of Jesus), excluding v. 9, we cannot separate v. 8 into v. 8a and 8b because of another unity between vv. 8–9 (I7). It is assumed that Talbert also sees the connection between vv. 2 and 8a and thus places these parts in his B and B'. However, his division disregards the cohesions among vv. 1–2, 3–5, 6–7 and 8–9 as they appear with their own constructions in parallel.

Sixth, the reason why Talbert removes v. 5 from his structure is probably caused by the fact that he tries to highlight the comparison between the saying of the brothers (3–4) with that of Jesus (6–8). If anyone wants to include v. 8 or a part of v. 8 such as v. 8a in vv. 6–8(8a), he/she has to include v. 2 in the group of cluster vv. 2–4 because of the manifest connection between vv. 2 and 8a regarding the feast issue. We can presume that Talbert does so, but has to separate v. 8b (another part of the saying of Jesus) from v. 8a, attaching it to v. 9, for vv. 8b–9 show their connection to v. 1.

2. The Relations among vv. 10–14

Talbert also suggests a chiastic pattern in vv. 10–14:[4] A. v. 10: Jesus went up (ἀνέβησαν), not publicly but privately; (a) The Jews were looking for him at the feast (11); B. vv. 11–13: (b) People mutter, "He is a good man," or "He is leading the people astray" (12); (a') For fear of the Jews (9:22; 12:42; 19:12–13, 38; 20:19) no one spoke openly of him (13); A'. v. 14: Jesus went up (ἀνέβη), publicly.

First, we can say that his division of structure is so insightful that the relation between vv. 10 and 14 is clearly noticed. And it may be possible to see the relation between vv. 11 and 13 as a pair.

Second, the counterpart of v. 11 is not v. 13 but v. 15, as seen in II2. In vv. 11 and 15, we find two related questions: "Where is that man?"; "How did this man get such learning . . . ?" Verses 12 and 13 are in a pair: whispering in controversy (12) and not speaking in public (13). Definitely, vv. 10 and 14 are in a pair.

4. Ibid.

Third, the reasons why v. 15 should be included in this cluster (10–15) are as follows: (1) This verse is a part of the combined, chiastic structure, II2; (2) Verse 15 has not any connection in parallel with the following verse(s); (3) Verses 16–17 show their own chiasm (II6, ab-x-b'a'), unrelated to v. 15.

Fourth, if we consider any possibility of attaching vv. 14–15 to the following verses, it would be advisable that the two verses and vv. 16–17 may be regarded as a group, for vv. 18–24 are in themselves an entity as a whole, as seen in II9 (abcde-a'b'c'd'e'). But when we do that, it will be difficult to discern the functions of vv. 10–13 and 14–17 in relation to the rest of the chapter. It is hardly thought that it was designed in that way. Verses 10–15 are an entity describing the arguments among the Jews with two questions (11 and 15) regarding Jesus who went up to Jerusalem and taught in the temple (10 and 14).

3. The Relations between vv. 14, 25–30, and 37–44 and between vv. 31–36 and 45–52

Transposing vv. 15–24 to ch. 5 because of their Sabbath healing issue, Bultmann divided the rest of the chapter into two parts, each of which has two subsections: vv. 14, 15–20 and 31–36; 37–44 and 45–52. He also regarded that the first two subsections (14, 25–30 and 37–44) correspond to each other in theme: the question of Jesus' origin; the second two (31–36 and 45–52) also are related to each other: the attempt of the authorities to have Jesus arrested by sending their servants.[5]

Additionally, Bultmann pointed out that vv. 31–36 and 45–52 must take place on the same day; v. 31 is awkward after v. 30, but fits after v. 44; vv. 37–44 came after v. 30. After all, Bultmann rearranged the original order of the chapter: vv. 1–3; 14, 25–30; 37–44; 31–36; 45–52.[6]

On the contrary, Moloney categorizes chs. 7 and 8 into four units according to the time-difference:[7] A. 7:1–9: Before the feast. A schism (*schisma*) arises between Jesus and his brothers about going to the feast; B. 7:10–13: At the feast. In Jerusalem there is a schism about Jesus: is he a good man, or does he lead the people astray?; C. 7:14–36: About the middle of the feast. i. Verses 14–24: Jesus teaches in the temple and conflict emerges. ii. Verses 25–31: The question of Jesus' messiahship and his origins create schism. iii. Verses 32–36: A conflict arises over the destiny of Jesus; D. 7:37—8:59: On the last day of the feast. i. 7:37–52: Jesus' self-revelation as giver of

---

5. Bultmann, *Gospel of John*, 287. Compare with the three recurring cycles of Köstenberger: 7:10–24, 37–39; 7:25–31, 40–44; 7:32–36, 45–52. Köstenberger, *John*, 226.
6. Bultmann, *Gospel of John*, 287–88. According to Bultmann, Schneider who took ch. 7 as a single unit excluded vv. 33–36, regarding them as an insertion and replaced v. 32 between vv. 44 and 45. Schneider, "Zur Komposition von Joh 7," 108–19.
7. Moloney, *Gospel of John*, 236.

the living water leads to schism. ii. 8:12–30: Jesus reveals himself as "the light of the world." iii. 8:31–59: Jesus and "the Jews" in conflict over their respective origins.

First, for Bultmann to exclude vv. 15–24 and transpose them to ch. 5, only because they contain the issue of the Sabbath healing ministry, has been critically disproved. As for the relations between his four subsections: that between vv. 14, 15–20 and 31–36; that between vv. 37–44 and 45–52, it is said that he might have found the AB-A'B' system where A and A' (the origin of Jesus); B and B' (the Jewish authorities attempting to arrest Jesus) correspond to each other. Unfortunately, he relocated them as A-A'-B-B'.

Second, even his division of four clusters may not be correct because of his overlooking some significant facts: (1) There are five passages regarding arguments among the Jews: vv. 10–15, 25–27, 30–32, 35–36, and 40–52, among which the first and the last are related in a positive-negative tone and the second and the fourth are related but mostly in negativity, while vv. 30–32 are located in the middle (in a positive-negative tone); (2) Verses 28–29 and 33–34 are very similar both in size and style, and they contain in common a similar pattern of parallels with six clauses: II17 (28b–29; a1a2-b-b'-a'1a'2) and II23 (33b–34; a1a2-b-b'-a'2a'1). Even in theme, these verses match each other: where Jesus is from (28–29) and where he is going (33–34).

Third, the origin issue does come up not only in vv. 25–29 and 40–44 but also in vv. 15 and 52. And the "where he is going" issue also is deeply related to it, appearing in vv. 33–36. Moreover, as far as the origin issue is concerned, vv. 37–39 (the discourse of Jesus regarding the Holy Spirit) are not relevant to the issue, if vv. 15–24 are excluded because of their difference of theme, as Bultmann concluded.

Fourth, although we may not exclude the possibility that vv. 31–36 and 45–52 happened on one day, we may also not exclude another possibility that the officers sent by the Jewish leaders did not go back to their leaders immediately during the Feast. Moreover, we have to first think over the reason why the text is arranged in this way. If vv. 45–52 are located after v. 32 or 36, as Bultmann did, the chiastic structure (II1) that is designed so beautifully would be totally broken and become no longer a Johannine text written in his unique style. Verses 45–52 follow vv. 40–44 because they both share the positive-negative arguments among the Jews that continue naturally from the latter (between lay people) to the former (between the authorities).

Fifth, the structure of Moloney who divides the text according to the time factor and then regards vv. 1, 10, 14, 37 as demarcation markers cannot be ignored as an alternative to the structure issue. However, we have to respect that time is not the single factor for demarcation in this chapter. Verses 1 and 10 can be the starters of vv. 1–9 and 10–15, but v. 14 cannot. As we have discussed, v. 14 belongs to the cluster vv. 10–15 and cannot be separated from vv. 10–13, even though the time is changed in v. 14. Additionally, his model does not reflect any interactive relation among the passages such as that between vv. 37–52 and 10–24 and those among vv. 25–36 owing to his considering solely the time factor.

4. The Relations between vv. 14-24 and 37-39 and between vv. 25-36 and 40-52

Brown regarded vv. 1-13 as an introduction and then divided vv. 14-52 into two scenes according to the time difference:[8] Scene one in the middle of the feast: (a) Jesus' right to teach; resumption of the Sabbath question (14-24) and (b) The origins of Jesus; his return to the Father (25-36); Scene two on the last day of the feast: (a) Jesus, the source of living water (37-39) and (b) Reactions to Jesus' statement (40-52).

As distant from Bultmann who rearranged the text as he wished, Brown tried to treat the material "as we find it in the Gospel," even if he thought that the themes in this chapter are arranged in "rambling unity" as "a polemic collection of what Jesus said in reply to attacks"[9]

Regarding the relation between vv. 25-36 (particularly 25-32) and 40-52, Brown suggested five duplications: A. Jesus' statements cause some of the people or crowd to pass judgment on him (25, 40); B. The question of whether he is the Messiah and an objection (26-27, 41-42); C. A poorly defined group want to arrest him but no one can lay a finger or hand on him (30, 44); D. His works or his words impress some greatly (31, 46); E. The beginning and conclusion of the attempt of the temple police to arrest him (32, 45-49).[10]

Talbert, depending on Lindars, regards vv. 14-52 as a loose, parallel structure:[11] A. vv. 14-24: Jesus teaches in the temple in the middle of the feast; B. vv. 25-29, 31: Speculation among the people – Can this be the Christ?; C. vv. 30, 32-36: Abortive attempt to arrest Jesus; A'. vv. 37-39: Jesus' teaching in the temple on the last day of the feast; B'. vv. 40-43: Speculation among the people – is this the prophet/Christ? ; C'. vv. 44-52: Attempt to arrest Jesus aborted.

First, the structure of Brown who also considered the time factor as a priority advanced beyond that of Moloney in that he tried to systematize the structure a little more, seeing the connection between the two discourses in vv. 14-24 and 37-39.

But, second, he ignored the interactive relations among the passages in vv. 25-36 as others do, simply saying that there is a "rambling unity." We can admit that these relations are complex but exist in a Johannine style (BC-X-C'B'), quite different from any "rambling" way of writing or sort of "collection."

Third, his finding regarding the duplications between vv. 25-36(32) and 40-52 is valuable. However, it does not mean that vv. 25-36 and 50-52 are in a pair. (1) The arguments among the Jews in vv. 25-27, 30-32, and 35-36 are, of course, related to

---

8. Brown, *Gospel according to John I-XII*, 202; for more details see 305-31.
9. Ibid., 315.
10. Brown, *Gospel according to John I-XII*, 330-31.
11. Talbert, *Reading John*, 145; Lindars, *Gospel of John*, 286. Cf. Barrett, who introduced the Schneider parallel in vv. 15-52: (1) Jesus teaches (15-24); 37-39); (2) His teaching evokes speculation among the people (25-31; 40-44); (3) Mission of the Jewish officials and its consequences (32-36; 45-52). Barrett, *Gospel according to St. John*, 316.

vv. 40-52 and thus duplications are found among them. But we should not exclude vv. 10-15 when we consider these relations or duplications among the verses in relation to the arguments of the Jews. (2) There are in all four discourses of Jesus in vv. 10-52: vv. 16-24, 28-29, 33-34, and 37-39. If we consider the relation between the first (16-24) and the last (37-39), we also have to note the connection that between the second (28-29) and the third (33-34) in terms of their interrelation. The second-third relation shows similarity of size and style, and is regarded as complementary in theme: where Jesus is and where he is going, while the first and the last are in contrast of theme: his rebuke of their rejection and his promise of the Spirit.

Fourth, we may further think that vv. 10-15 (the introductory section) consist of two parts: vv. 10-13 and 14-15, although they cannot be separated from each other. We may compare this with the two parts of vv. 40-52 (40-44 and 45-52; the concluding one). The problem is that they are not similar in size: the former is smaller, while the latter is larger. However, if we continue the pairing between vv. 16-24 and vv. 37-39, two discourses of Jesus, we cannot help finding a certain balance in size between vv. 10-24 (arguments of the Jews, 10-15; discourse of Jesus, 16-24) and 37-52 (discourse of Jesus, 37-39; arguments of the Jews, 40-52).

We can say that two kinds of discourse (16-24 and 37-39) are presented to the Jews at the Feast in a pair, and the first response of the Jews (10-15) and the last one (40-52) are found in a pair. Meanwhile, we can also see that there are some related discourses of Jesus (28-29 and 33-34), particularly in theme (where he is from and where he is going), and the related responses of the Jews mostly in negativity (25-27, 30-32, and 35-36).

Fifth, we can say the same things regarding the model of Talbert-Lindars: (1) the relations among the five arguments of the Jews (10-15, 25-27, 30-32, 35-36, and 40-52); (2) the relation between the two similar discourses of Jesus (28-29 and 33-34); the relation between vv. 10-15 and 40-52. Additionally, it is unnatural to remove v. 30 or 31 from its location.

5. The Relation between vv. 1-13 and 45-52

Bultmann wrote, "The original intention must then have been that 7:1-13 and 7:45-52 provide the introduction and conclusion for Jesus' appearance in Jerusalem, the account of which falls into two scenes, 7:14, 25-30 and 7:37-44, 31-36."[12]

First, we have discussed that vv. 10-15 are in a pair with vv. 40-52 as vv. 16-24 and 37-39 are. Nevertheless, we may consider the possibility of the relation between vv. 1-9 (not including 10-13) and 45-52 as that of the introduction and the conclusion. This theory provides the similarity regarding that the contrast between Jesus and

---

12. Bultmann, *Gospel of John*, 288.

his brothers in vv. 1–9 is compared with that between the officers-Nicodemus and the Jewish authorities.

Second, in that case, we also continue to consider the relation between vv. 10–15 and 40–44, which is certain. We can move further on considering the relation between vv. 16–24 and 37–39, which is also manifest. In this way, we can draw the whole chapter as a single chiastic structure: A (1–9); B (10–15); C (16–24); D (25–27); E (28–29); X (30–32); E' (33–34); D' (35–36); C' (37–39); B' (40–43); A' (45–52).

Third, a few troubles still remain in this theory: (1) The relation between vv. 16–24 and 37–39 is found but cannot be explained in terms of their size difference; (2) The similarity between vv. 10–15 and 45–52 cannot be explained in terms of the positive-negative arguments among the Jews in response to Jesus, which motif cannot be found in vv. 1–9. It means that vv. 10–15 are not only related to vv. 40–45 but also vv. 45–52, which are not closer to vv. 1–9 than to 10–15; (3) It is unnatural that this chapter which belongs to the group of chapters (5–10) does not follow the dual mode in structure which appears as their characteristic in these chapters. Thus, this theory is not preferred here.

8 "I Am the Light of the World," I

"Importantly, although the text's relationship to Johannine tradition is debated, the consensus is that the story does indeed preserve a primitive piece of Jesus tradition. That is, John 7:53—8:11 could be as old as most any pronouncement story in the Jesus tradition. Claims for or against the historicity of the text play no role in resolving the mixed testimony of the manuscript evidence."[1]

"Yet, if the Gospel of John shows a significant interest in the fulfillment of the Passover, then John 8:31–47 provides a significant element. In these verses, Jesus defines the problem, slavery to sin and the devil, and the solution, freedom through the truth and the Son."[2]

Dual Mode in Structure

Between John 7 and 8, there is the story of the adulteress (7:53—8:11), which has been doubted as being a genuine passage of the original John. (We will discuss later its structure-style as well as its theme regarding whether it is suitable to the rest of the chapter or not.) Whether considering it as a part of the chapter or not, John 8 may be regarded as in dual mode.

If we consider this episode as a part of this chapter, John 8 can be categorized into two units: (1) the story of the adulteress (1–11); (2) the dialogue in argument between Jesus and the Jews regarding his witness and judgment (12–59). Even if we exclude the woman story, vv. 12–59 are in a dual, divided into two groups: (1) the witness and judgment of Jesus regarding sin and freedom (12–36); (2) who the father is indeed (37–59).

The reason why vv. 12–59 can be categorized into two clusters is: First, the theme is moved from the freedom and sin issue (12–36) to the father argument: who their

---

1. O'Day, "John 7:53—8:11," 639.
2. Attridge, "Thematic Development," 160. Hoskins, "Freedom from Slavery," 62-63.

father is: Abraham or the devil (37–59). Second, vv. 12–36 and 37–59 are supported by their own parallel structures: II2 (ABCD-A'B'C'D') and II48 (AB-A'B'). It means that this section is made up of two distinguishable groups of cluster.

Thus, we may depict the outline as follows:

I.	The story of the adulteress (7:53-8:11)
II.	The dialogue in argument regarding the witness and judgment (8:12-59)
	IIA. The witness and judgment regarding sin and freedom (8:12-36)
	IIA'. Who is their father? (8:37-59)

Is the Story of the Adulteress Suitable to Its Location?

This story has been well-known for its textual problem.[3] Many scholars have not dealt with it significantly and primarily, being doubtful of its genuineness as an episode suitable to where it is in the chapter.[4] Considering the nature of the story, specifically regarding its structure-style, we may make some points as follows:

First, the Johannine style of writing is found throughout the episode, particularly in vv. 6b–11 as seen in I9–10 and 12. There are the phenomena of the repetitive expressions, such as "Jesus bent down and wrote . . ." (6b, 8), "he stood up and said to . . ." (7b, 10a), the structural cycle, for example, abc-a'b'c' in I9, and the parallel pattern in comparison such as I14 (a [οὐδείς, no one], b [σε, you], c [κατέκρινεν;, has ~ condemned?]; a' [οὐδὲ ἐγώ, Neither do I], b [σε, you], c [κατακρίνω, condemn]).

Second, I6 (3–6a), a chiastic parallel, can be regarded as one of Johannine style in structure. But it seems to be difficult to point out apparently how the Johannine styles are manifested in 7:53—8:6a, though, if we exclude I2 in 7:53—8:1.

Third, considering the whole structure (I1), the former part (AB, 7:53—8:6a) is indispensable in existence of the latter (B'A', 6b–11) in creating a type of Johannine structure.

Fourth, moreover, the theme of this episode is perfectly matched with the theme of the chapter, the light/sin issue. Jesus is indeed the light of the world which purifies the darkness or the sins of the people. He is the solution to sin and the Savior from death in sin. The woman, a sinner in public, is compared with the Jews who insist that they are not slaves to sin. Who is the sinner after all?

---

3. Regarding the internal and external problems of the story, see Köstenberger, *John*, 245–49; Bridges, "Canonical Status of the *Pericope Adulterae*," 213–21; Burge, "Specific Problem," 141–48.

4. According to Moloney, it is generally accepted that the *palin* of 8:12 is a continuation of 7:52. Moloney, *Signs and Shadows*, 66. Cf. Borchert, *John 1–11*, 369–70; Brown, *Gospel according to John 1–XII*, 332–38.

Fifth, the episode is suitable to the chapter,[5] not only because of its theme in relation to its compatibility with the rest of the chapter and its micro-structure-style similarly presented here with the Johannine one, but also because of its location in the front of the chapter, consisting of dual mode in structure: story (event) and dialogue (discourse), similar to the previous chs. 5–6.

In conclusion, we assume the possibility that the original episode was first located but later lost. It would have been restored by the group (or the man) which remembered the original story. They would re-write it and put it there as much as they could remember, totally depending on their memory. In this process, the structure-style of this episode was similarly restored, but probably not in detail nor in the original vocabulary.

I. The Story of the Adulteress (7:53—8:11)

Chiastic, I1 (AB-B'A')[6]

In A, the background of the story begins: Jesus is teaching in the temple. In A', this story ends with the final dialogue between Jesus and the woman: "Do not sin anymore." In the middle of the story, two scenes are shown: the Jews brought a woman caught in adultery to test Jesus (B); Jesus says something and they are removed from the situation (B').

In 7:53—8:11, there are sixteen parallels: one overarching chiastic structure (I1) with nine parallelisms (I3–5, 8–12, and 14), two chiasms (I6 and 13), two duals (I15–16), and two combined parallelisms (I2 and 7). Besides I1, 6 and 13 which are chiastic, all the other relations are parallel-oriented. In 7:53—8:6a, II2 and 6 can be regarded as the main parallel pillars. II6 supports the cohesion of B of I1. The role of the others are partial. In vv. 6b–11, the predominant structure is I9, including the latter part of the episode. B' of I1 shows its strong cohesion with the help of I10–11 and 13. I12 reflects the connection between B' and A' of I1.

I2. Combined parallel, a1a2-b-a'2a'1-b': Two sentences are arranged in comparison: Καὶ ἐπορεύθησαν (And ~ went, a1) and ἐπορεύθη (went, a'1); ἕκαστος (each, a2) and Ἰησοῦς δὲ (But Jesus, a'2); εἰς τὸν οἶκον αὐτοῦ (to his own home, b) and εἰς τὸ ὄρος τῶν ἐλαιῶν (to the Mount of Olives, b'). We may read that they went their own ways, but Jesus went to another ministry (or to prepare for it). **I3.** Parallel, ab-a'b': Jesus came

---

5. See the interesting suggestion of Johnson, who asserts the invalidity of the statistical method and also that v. 6 is in typical Johannine style. Johnson, "Stylistic Trait of the Fourth Gospel," 91–96; also Trites, "Woman Taken in Adultery," 137–46. Cf. Keith, "Initial Location of the *Pericope Adulterae*," 209–31.

6. Moloney sees rightly the interaction among the characters: (a) Introduction (7:53—8:2); (b) The Scribes and Pharisees and Jesus (8:3–6a); (c) Jesus and the Scribes and Pharisees (8:6b–9); (d) Jesus and the woman (8:10–11). Moloney, *Gospel of John*, 260.

again (a) to the temple (b), and all the people came (a') to him (b'). Because of a, Jesus came, a' happens.

V	1	2				Phrases	Translation
53	A	a1				[Καὶ ἐπορεύθησαν	[And ~ went ~
-	-	a2				ἕκαστος	each ~
-	-	b				εἰς τὸν οἶκον αὐτοῦ,	~ to his own home.
1	-	a'2				Ἰησοῦς δὲ	But Jesus
-	-	a'1				ἐπορεύθη	went
-	-	b'	3			εἰς τὸ ὄρος τῶν ἐλαιῶν.	to the Mount of Olives.
2	-		a			Ὄρθρου δὲ πάλιν παρεγένετο	Early in the morning he came again
-	-		b	4		εἰς τὸ ἱερὸν	to the temple.
-	-		a'	a		καὶ πᾶς ὁ λαὸς ἤρχετο	All the people came
-	-		b'	b	5	πρὸς αὐτόν,	to him,
-	-			a'	a	καὶ καθίσας ἐδίδασκεν	and he sat down to teach
-	6			b'	b	αὐτούς.	them.
3	B	a			a'	Ἄγουσιν δὲ οἱ γραμματεῖς καὶ οἱ Φαρισαῖοι	And the scribes and the Pharisees brought
-	-	-	7		b'	γυναῖκα	a woman
-	-	-	a			ἐπὶ μοιχείᾳ	~ in adultery.
-	-	-	b1			κατειλημμένην	caught ~
-	-	-	b2			καὶ στήσαντες αὐτὴν ἐν μέσῳ	They made her stand in the midst,
4	-	b				λέγουσιν αὐτῷ· διδάσκαλε,	they said to him, "Teacher,
-	-	-	a'			αὕτη ἡ γυνὴ	this woman
-	-	-	b'2			κατείληπται	was caught
-	-	-	b'1			ἐπ' αὐτοφώρῳ μοιχευομένη·	in the act of adultery.
5	-	b'	8			ἐν δὲ τῷ νόμῳ ἡμῖν	In the law ~ us ~
-	-	-	a			Μωϋσῆς	Moses
-	-	-	b			ἐνετείλατο τὰς τοιαύτας λιθάζειν.	commanded ~ to stone such women.
-	-	-	a'			σὺ οὖν	~ then do you ~
-	-	-	b'			τί λέγεις;	What ~ say?"
6a	-	a'				τοῦτο δὲ ἔλεγον πειράζοντες αὐτόν, ἵνα ἔχωσιν κατηγορεῖν αὐτοῦ.	They said this to test him, that they might have a basis for accusing him.

I4. Parallel, ab-a'b': All the people came (a) to him (b) and Jesus sat down to teach (a') them (b'). This parallelism seems to be in rhyme: 1st line (a), 8 syllables; 2nd line (b), 3 syllables; 3rd line (a'), 8 syllables; last (b'), 2 syllables. **I5**. Parallel, ab-a'b': Jesus sits down to teach (a), but the Jews brought a woman caught in adultery (a'). They are contrasted. Jesus who helps is contrasted to the Jews who came to condemn and test. Those who are taught (b) and the woman who is caught in adultery (b') are seemingly compared.

I6. Chiastic, ab-b'a': The reason that the Jews brought a woman caught in adultery (a) is that they test Jesus (a'). They speak about the woman in adultery (b) and about

"I Am the Light of the World," I

the law of Moses (b'). **I7**. Combined parallel, a-b1b2-a'-b'2b'1: A repetition of similar expression with exchange of order describing the woman caught in adultery appears: γυναῖκα (a woman, a) ἐπὶ μοιχείᾳ (in adultery, b1) κατειλημμένην (caught, b2); αὕτη ἡ γυνὴ (this woman, a') κατείληπται (was caught, b'2) ἐπ' αὐτοφώρῳ μοιχευομένη (in the act of adultery, b'1). **I8**. Parallel, ab-a'b': Moses (a) and Jesus (a') are compared. Moses is described as the one who condemns this kind of sinner (b). They ask what Jesus would be (b'): a follower of Moses or his refuter.

In I2, it compares that they went at home but Jesus went to the mountain. In I3, Jesus and the people came together. In I4, two things are focused: what the people do and what Jesus does. I5 contrasts Jesus who teaches the Jews who bring a woman. In I6, the reason why they brought her to Jesus is shown. In I7, there is a repetitive introduction to the woman in adultery. I8 contrasts Jesus with Moses in dealing with this type of woman.

V	1	9	10	11		Phrases	Translation
6b	B'	a	a	a		ὁ δὲ Ἰησοῦς κάτω κύψας	But Jesus bent down
-	-	-	-	b		τῷ δακτύλῳ κατέγραφεν εἰς τὴν γῆν.	and wrote with his finger on the ground.
7	-	b	b		12	ὡς δὲ ἐπέμενον ἐρωτῶντες αὐτόν,	But when they continued to ask him,
-	-	c	-	a		ἀνέκυψεν καὶ εἶπεν αὐτοῖς·	he stood up and said to them,
-	-	-	-	b		ὁ ἀναμάρτητος ὑμῶν πρῶτος ἐπ' αὐτὴν βαλέτω λίθον.	"He who is without sin among you, let him be the first to throw a stone at here.
8	-	a'	a'	a'		καὶ πάλιν κατακύψας	And again he bent down
-	-	-	-	b'	13	ἔγραφεν εἰς τὴν γῆν.	and wrote with his finger on the ground.
9	-	b'	b'		a	οἱ δὲ ἀκούσαντες	But those who heard
-	-	-	-		b	ἐξήρχοντο εἷς καθ' εἷς ἀρξάμενοι ἀπὸ τῶν πρεσβυτέρων	began to go away one by one, beginning with the older ones,
-	-	-	-		b'	καὶ κατελείφθη μόνος	and only he was left,
-	-	-	-		a'	καὶ ἡ γυνὴ ἐν μέσῳ οὖσα.	and the woman, where she was, there.
10	A'	c'		a'		ἀνακύψας δὲ ὁ Ἰησοῦς εἶπεν αὐτῇ·	And Jesus stood up and said to her,
-	-	-	14	b'		γύναι, ποῦ εἰσιν;	"Woman, where are they?
-	-	-	a	-		οὐδείς	~ no one ~
-	-	-	b	-		σε	~ you?"
-	-	-	c	-		κατέκρινεν;	Has ~ condemned ~
11	-	-			15	ἡ δὲ εἶπεν· οὐδείς, κύριε. εἶπεν δὲ ὁ Ἰησοῦς·	She said, "No one, sir." And Jesus said,
-	-	-	a'	a		οὐδὲ ἐγώ	"Neither do I
-	-	-	b'	-		σε	~ you.
-	-	-	c'	-	16	κατακρίνω·	condemn ~
-	-	-	a'	a		πορεύου,	Go,
-	-	-	-	a'		[καὶ] ἀπὸ τοῦ νῦν μηκέτι ἁμάρτανε.]	and from now on do not sin anymore."

I9. Parallel, abc-a'b'c': Both in a-a', Jesus bends down and writes with his finger on the ground. Both in c-c', Jesus stands up and says something to them (c) and to her (c').[7] In b-b', they continue to ask Jesus (b) and eventually they leave the scene one by one (b'). Three divided parts recur in similarity. I10. Parallel, ab-a'b': In a-a', Jesus bends down and writes with his finger, while, in b-b', Jesus says something to those who continue to ask him (b), and then they leave the situation one by one but for the woman (b').

I11. Parallel, ab-a'b': Two actions of Jesus are presented in repetition and in relation: Jesus bent down (a-a'); he wrote with his finger on the ground (b-b'). I12. Parallel, ab-a'b': Both in a-a', the expression, "Jesus stood up and said" is repeated. The contents of b are that which Jesus says to them, while those of b' are that which he says to her. I13. Chiastic, ab-x-b'a': In a-a', those who heard (a) and the woman who stayed there (a') are compared, and, similarly, in b-b', those who went away one by one (b) and Jesus who is left (b') are compared. They go away and he is left.

I14. Parallel, abc-a'b'c': Two sentences are composed of three divisions in similarity: οὐδείς (no one, a) and οὐδὲ ἐγώ (Neither do I, a'); σε (you, b) and σε (you, b'); κατέκρινεν (has condemned, c) and κατακρίνω (condemn, c'). I15. Dual, a-a': Two sayings are given to the woman: "Neither do I condemn you" (a); "Go and from now on do not sin anymore" (a'). I16. Dual, a-a': Two imperatives are presented: "Go" (a) and "do not sin" (a').

I9 contains two types of Jesus' words (to the Jews and to her) as well as what happens to those who brought her. In I10, there are what Jesus does and says, and what the Jews do after hearing him. I11 contains a repetitive action of Jesus. In I12, there are two similar acts and sayings of Jesus. In I13, there is a contrast between those who heard and left and the woman who stayed. I14 emphasizes that no one including Jesus condemns her. In I15, there are two types of Jesus' saying: no condemnation; to go and not to sin. In I16, there are two commands of Jesus: go and do not sin.

II. THE DIALOGUE IN ARGUMENT REGARDING THE WITNESS AND JUDGMENT (8:12–59)

Dual, II1 (A-A')

As discussed earlier, each of these two sections (12–36 and 37–59) contains its own distinguishable parallel structure: ABCD-A'B'C'D' (12–36, II2) and AB-A'B' (37–59, II48). As a whole, they share the light/sin issue. In the first one (12–36), the freedom and sin issue is primary, while, in the latter one (37–59), their seeking to kill Jesus is

---

7. Compare the triple parallels of O'Day: Jesus bends down and writes on the ground (6b and 8); Jesus stands up to address his conversation partners (7b and 10a); Jesus speaks (7c and 11b). O'Day, "John 7:53—8:11," 633.

predominant in theme. Both are related to each other in terms of the light-life and the sin-death.

| A. | The witness and judgment regarding sin and freedom (12-36) | ABCD-A'B'C'D' |
| A'. | Who is the father? (37-59) | AB-A'B' |

IIA. The Witness and Judgment regarding Sin and Freedom (8:12-36)

PARALLEL, II2 (ABCD-A'B'C'D')

The section (12–36) consists of eight clusters in division, designed as an overall parallel structure. First, as a whole, the section can be categorized into two groups: vv. 12–24 and 25–36. The themes in the former group (12–24) are similarly repeated in the latter one (25–36).

Second, each group contains four subunits: two smaller and two larger ones. In the former group, v. 12 declares that Jesus is the light of the world, but, in vv. 13–19, the theme shifts to the witness of truthfulness as well as his judgment. Verse 20 is the response of the Jews. The saying of Jesus restarts at v. 21 and continues up to v. 24. In vv. 21–24, we read a different issue from the previous verses (specifically vv. 13–20), dying in sin and different origins.

Third, in v. 25, the first verse of the latter group (25–36), we meet the same issue (who he is), certainly declared in v. 12 ("the light of the world"). The Jews ask him "who are you?" (σὺ τίς εἶ;). Responding to this, Jesus answers, "Even what I have told you from the start, haven't I" (τὴν ἀρχὴν ὅ τι καὶ λαλῶ ὑμῖν;). We may translate literally this sentence, "From the beginning, what I am, even I have told you." Both the relative pronoun (neuter accusative) ὅ and the indefinite pronoun (neuter accusative) τι indicate what he earlier mentioned regarding who he is. He claims to be (ἐγώ εἰμι, I am) the light (τὸ φῶς, the light; neuter) of the world in v. 12. There is no other verse revealing who Jesus is in the previous verses of this chapter. Moreover, this declaration of his identity as the light is the overarching theme of the whole chapter.

Fourth, the latter group of clusters (25–36) can also be divided into four subunits. Except for v. 25, Jesus seems not to mention directly about who he is in the proximate following verses, not until v. 36 where he mentions the Son who makes them free. Verses 26–29 deal with the issue of the intimate relationship between Jesus and the Father, particularly regarding his word and deeds with the Father. In v. 30, there is the response of the people, believing in him. In vv. 31–36, the main issue is free-from-sin vs. slave-to-sin. (From v. 37, another theme, seeking to kill him, is presented.)

Fifth, the four subunits of the former and those of the latter are arranged in a pair. We may name them as ABCD-A'B'C'D'.

Sixth, we have already discussed how A (12) and A' (25) are in a pair. Both in B-B', we can see the Father-Son relationship. In B (13–19), the focus is on the witness of Jesus with the Father including his judgment. And in B' (26–29), Jesus emphasizes that the Father is always with him when he speaks. Both mean that whatever he says and acts he does do with and from the Father.

Seventh, C (20) and C' (30) are related to each other, both describing the responses of the Jews to the sayings of Jesus: one is negative (C) and the other is positive (C').

Eighth, D (21–24) and D (31–36) share the theme, the sin issue, distinguished from that of C-C'. In D, Jesus refers to dying in sin in emphasis. They will die in sin because they belong to the world, unless they believe in him. In D', for this time, Jesus focuses on free-from-sin. If they believe in him, they will be free from sin by the truth in the Son, not staying in slavery to sin. In this way, D and D' are in a pair.

We may draw out the points in a pair as follows:

A. 12	Who Jesus is 1: "I am the light of the world."		
	B. 13-19	The Father-Son relationship 1: His true testimony and judgment with the Father 1. Declaring his testimony's truthfulness (13-14, 16a) 2. The reason of truthfulness of his own testimony: being with the Father (two witnesses, 16b-18) 3. The inseparability of Jesus and his Father (19)	
		C. 20	Jesus' saying and their response 1: His hour had not yet come.
		D. 21-24	Dying in sin and different origins 1. Dying in sin (21c, 24ac) 2. Believing 'me' (24b) 3. Difference of status between Jesus and them (21d, 23)
A'. 25	Who Jesus is 2: "Who are you?"		
	B'. 26-29	The Father-Son relationship 2: The Father is with the Son, who speaks. 1. The Father's truthfulness (26b) 2. He speaks from his Father who is with him (26c, 28b, and 29a). 3. The inseparability of Jesus and his Father (29b)	
		C'. 30	Jesus' saying and their response 2: Many believed in him.
		D'. 31-36	Free from sin vs. slave to sin 1. Free from sin (32b, 33b, and 36) 2. "The Son makes you free" (36; cf. 31b) 3. Contrast between the son in freedom and the slave in bondage (34-35)

"I Am the Light of the World," I

A. "I am the light of the world" (8:12)

Verse 12 contains two parallelisms (II3–4) without having any connective, parallel relation outside the verse. It means that it is independent.

V			Phrases	Translation
12	3		Πάλιν οὖν αὐτοῖς ἐλάλησεν ὁ Ἰησοῦς λέγων·	Again therefore Jesus spoke to them, saying,
	a		ἐγώ	"I
	b		εἰμι τὸ φῶς τοῦ κόσμου·	am the light of the world.
	a'	4	ὁ ἀκολουθῶν ἐμοὶ	He who follows me
	b'	a	οὐ μὴ περιπατήσῃ	will not walk
	-	b	ἐν τῇ σκοτίᾳ,	in the darkness,
	-	a'	ἀλλ' ἕξει	but will have
	-	b'	τὸ φῶς τῆς ζωῆς.	the light of life."

II3. Parallel, ab-a'b': The subjects, "I" (a) and his follower (a') that come first in both sentences, and verb phrases, b and b', are interrelated in terms of "light": being the light to the world (b); not walking in the darkness but having the light of life (b'). **II4.** Parallel, ab-a'b': In a-a', two actions are contrasted: a ("will not walk") and a' ("but will have"). And, in b-b', two contrasted concepts appear: b ("in the darkness) and b' ("the light of life"). A similar idea is duplicated in two sentences. In II3, there is the relation between Jesus and his followers regarding the light. In II4, not to walk in darkness is namely to have the light of life.

B. His True Testimony and Judgment with the Father (8:13–19)

In vv. 13–19, there are fifteen parallels including a comprehensive chiastic structure II5 with embedded parallels: seven parallelisms (II6, 10, 12, 15, and 17–19), four chiasms (II8, 11, 13, and 16), two combined chiasms (II9 and 14), and one combined parallelism (II7). In A of II5 (13–14), II6–8 and 10 are supporting the cohesion of the cluster, overlapping each other. II9 is even extended to X (15–16). II11–12 are for cohesion in X. II13 seems to exist to connect X (16) and A' (17–19). And, in A', we cannot see any larger parallel including all of vv. 17–19. II14–18 are partial in role. II19 builds the connection between A and A', specifically v. 14 and v. 18.

II5. Chiastic, A-X-A': In A, there are two foci: (1) the truthfulness of his testimony; (2) the contrast between the knowledge of Jesus and their ignorance regarding whence he came and where he is going. In A', there are also two foci: (1) the truthfulness of his testimony with his Father; (2) the emphasis on their ignorance regarding the Father and the Son. And, in X, the truthfulness of his judgment is focused, compared with A-A' where the witness is the main issue.

V	5	6				Phrases	Translation
13	A	a	7			Εἶπον οὖν αὐτῷ οἱ Φαρισαῖοι·	The Pharisees therefore said to him,
-	b	a				σὺ	"You,
-	-	b1				περὶ σεαυτοῦ	to yourself,
-	-	b2	8			μαρτυρεῖς·	are bearing witness;
-	c	a				ἡ μαρτυρία σου	your witness
-	-	b				οὐκ ἔστιν	is not
-	-	c				ἀληθής.	true."
14	-	a'		9		19 ἀπεκρίθη Ἰησοῦς καὶ εἶπεν αὐτοῖς·	Jesus answered and said to them,
-	b'	a'	a1		a	κἂν ἐγὼ	"Even if I
-	-	b'2	-		b	μαρτυρῶ	bear witness
-	-	b'1	-		c	περὶ ἐμαυτοῦ,	to myself,
-	c'	c'	-			ἀληθής	true
-	-	b'	-			ἐστιν	is
-	-	a'	-	10		ἡ μαρτυρία μου,	my witness.
-			a2	a		ὅτι οἶδα	for I know
-			-	b		πόθεν ἦλθον	whence I came
-			-	c		καὶ ποῦ ὑπάγω·	and whither I am going,
-			-	a'		ὑμεῖς δὲ οὐκ οἴδατε	but you do not know
-			-	b'		πόθεν ἔρχομαι	whence I come
-	11	12	-	c'		ἢ ποῦ ὑπάγω.	or whither I am going.
15	X	a	a	x		ὑμεῖς	You
-	-	-	b	-		κατὰ τὴν σάρκα κρίνετε,	judge according to the flesh,
-	-	b	a'	-		ἐγὼ	I
-	13	-	b'	-		οὐ κρίνω οὐδένα.	judge no one *likewise*.
16	-	a	b'	a'1		καὶ ἐὰν κρίνω δὲ ἐγώ,	But even if I judge
-	-	-	a'	-		ἡ κρίσις ἡ ἐμὴ ἀληθινή ἐστιν,	my judgment is true,
-	-	-		a'2		ὅτι μόνος οὐκ εἰμί, ἀλλ' ἐγὼ καὶ ὁ πέμψας με πατήρ.	for I am not alone, but I and the Father that sent me.
17	A'	x				καὶ ἐν τῷ νόμῳ δὲ τῷ ὑμετέρῳ γέγραπται ὅτι δύο ἀνθρώπων ἡ μαρτυρία ἀληθής ἐστιν.	Even in your law it is written that the testimony of two men is true.
		14					
18	-	a'	a		a'	ἐγώ	I
-	-	-	b1		b'	εἰμι ὁ μαρτυρῶν	am he who bears witness
-	-	-	b2		c'	περὶ ἐμαυτοῦ	to myself,
-	-	-	b'1			καὶ μαρτυρεῖ	and ~ bears witness
-	-	-	b'2			περὶ ἐμοῦ	to me
-	-	-	a'	15		ὁ πέμψας με πατήρ.	the Father who sent me ~."
19	-		a			Ἔλεγον οὖν αὐτῷ·	Then said they to him,
-			b			ποῦ ἐστιν ὁ πατήρ σου;	"Where is your Father?"
-			a'	16	17	ἀπεκρίθη Ἰησοῦς·	Jesus answered,
-			b'	a	a	οὔτε ἐμὲ	"~ neither me,
-			-	x	-	οἴδατε	"You know ~,
-	18		-	a'	b	οὔτε τὸν πατέρα μου·	nor my Father;
-			a	-	a'	εἰ ἐμὲ	if ~ me
-			b	-	-	ᾔδειτε,	you knew ~,
-			a'	-	b'	καὶ τὸν πατέρα μου	~ my Father also
-			b'	-	-	ἂν ᾔδειτε.	you would know ~."

II6. Parallel, abc-a'b'c': The Pharisees' denial of the witness of Jesus, a-b-c, is refuted by Jesus himself in similar order, a'-b'-c': the Pharisees say (a) and Jesus says (a'); "you are bearing witness to yourself" (b) and "Even if I bear witness to myself" (b'); "your witness is not true" (c) and "my witness is true" (c'). **II7**. Combined parallel, a-b1b2-a'-b'1b'2: The sequential order of syntax, a-b1-b2 (σὺ - περὶ σεαυτοῦ - μαρτυρεῖς), is changed into a'-b'2-b'1 (κἂν ἐγὼ - μαρτυρῶ - περὶ ἐμαυτοῦ). Both sentences indicate Jesus' witness to himself. **II8**. Chiastic, abc-c'b'a': The contrastive contents are reversed in syntactical order: ἡ μαρτυρία σου (your witness, a) and ἡ μαρτυρία μου (my witness, a'); οὐκ ἔστιν (is not, b) and ἔστιν (is, b'); ἀληθής (true, c) and ἀληθής (true, c').

II9. Combined chiastic: a1a2-x-a'1a'2: The format of a1a2 and a'1a'2 is similar because both contain ἐάν -clause as well as ὅτι-clause. See the parallels in form: "even if I bear witness to myself, my witness is true" (a1) and "But even if I judge, my judgment is true" (a'1); "for I know...but you do not know..." (a2) and "for I am not alone, but I..." (a'2). Here, a2-a'2 are the grounds to support the insistence of Jesus in a1-a'1. In x, "you" who does wrongly and "I" who judge no one *likewise* are in contrast. **II10**. Parallel. abc-a'b'c': This parallel clearly contrasts Jesus' knowledge with their ignorance of the issue of the place he came from or he is going to: ὅτι οἶδα (for I know, a) and ὑμεῖς δὲ οὐκ οἴδατε (but you do not know, a'); πόθεν ἦλθον (whence I came, b) and πόθεν ἔρχομαι (whence I come, b'); καὶ ποῦ ὑπάγω (and whither I am going, c) and ἢ ποῦ ὑπάγω (or whither I am going, c').

II11. Chiastic, ab-b'a': In this, a ("your judgement") and a' ("my judgement") are contrasted to each other in terms of the truthfulness of their judgements, while both b and b', in common, describe "I judge." **II12**. Parallel, ab-a'b': The pronouns, "you" and "I" are emphatically contrasted in a (ὑμεῖς) and a' (ἐγώ). Two sentences are antithetical in meaning: "you judge according to the flesh" (ab) vs. "I judge no one *likewise*" (a'b'). **II13**. Chiastic, a-x-a': In a and a', Jesus asserts that he is not alone both in judgment (a) and in witnessing to himself (a'), mentioning the Father as his other witness. In x, the center of the chiasm, a quotation, regarding how the testimony is proved true, is emphasized.

II14. Mixed Chiastic, a-b1b2-b'1b'2-a': "I" in a and "the Father who sent me" in a' are the common witnesses who bear witness (b1 and b'1) to Jesus (b2 and b'2). The two-witnesses theory is completed in this verse. **II15**. Parallel, ab-a'b': They asked (a) and Jesus answered (a') regarding where "your/my Father" is (b and b'). **II16**. Chiastic, a-x-a': The center x shows what they know or do not know about both "me" (a) and "my Father" (a').

II17. Parallel, ab-a'b': Both a and a' regard knowing (or unknowing) "me", while b and b' deal with knowing (or unknowing) "my Father." **II18**. Parallel, ab-a'b': In a-a', "me" (ἐμέ) and "my Father" (τὸν πατέρα μου) are compared, while, in b-b', a concept of knowing is repeated: ᾔδειτε (you know, b) and ἂν ᾔδειτε (you would know, b'). **II19**. Parallel, abc-a'b'c': It is the similar pattern in repetition. In a-a', "I" is repeated:

κἂν ἐγώ (Even if I, a) and ἐγώ (I, a') and, in b-b', the witness of Jesus is emphasized: μαρτυρῶ (bear witness, b) and εἰμι ὁ μαρτυρῶν (am he who bears witness, b'). And in c-c', περὶ ἐμαυτοῦ (to myself) is repeated.

In II6, the defense of Jesus is made against the Pharisees who deny the truthfulness of his testimony. II7 focuses on Jesus' witness to himself. In II8, there is an argument about the truthfulness of his witness to himself. In II9, the truthfulness of Jesus' witness and his judgment are backed up regarding his knowledge and two witnesses. II10 contrasts what Jesus knows with what they do not know. II11–12 contrast "your" judgment with "my" judgment. II13–14 focus on the truthfulness of two witnesses: the Son and the Father. In II15, they know neither the Father nor the Son. II16 and 18 present twofold ignorance, of both the Father and the Son. In II17 shows the connection between knowing the Father and knowing the Son. In II19, the witness of Jesus to himself is repeated.

C. His Hour Had Not Yet Come (8:20).

In v. 20 (C of II2), there is just one parallelism, II20, while II21 extends its parallel connection to v. 30 (C' of II2), thereby pairing two verses to each other.

V	21		Phrases	Translation
20	20	a	Ταῦτα τὰ ῥήματα	~ these words
		a	ἐλάλησεν	He spoke ~
		b	ἐν τῷ γαζοφυλακίῳ	in the treasury,
		a'	διδάσκων	as he taught
		b'	ἐν τῷ ἱερῷ·	in the temple;
		b	καὶ οὐδεὶς ἐπίασεν αὐτόν,	but no one seized him,
			ὅτι οὔπω ἐληλύθει ἡ ὥρα αὐτοῦ.	because his hour had not yet come.

II20. Parallel, ab-a'b': In a and a', Jesus "spoke" (a) or "taught" (a') in specific places: in the treasury (b) and in the temple (b'). Two clauses show a similar pattern. **II21.** Parallel, ab-a'b': In a and a', we can read Jesus "speaking these things (or words)," while, in b and b', their contrastive responses to him are shown: "no one seized him" (b); "many believed in him" (b'). This parallelism is made between v. 20 and 30.

In II20, where he spoke and taught is focused. In II21, two reactions of the people after hearing the words of Jesus are in contrast: negative and positive.

D. Dying in Sin and Different Origins (8:21–24)

In vv. 21–24, there are eight parallels: four chiasms (II22–24 and 29), three parallelisms (II25–27), and one combined parallelism (II28). Among them, II22 is the

"I Am the Light of the World," I

comprehensive one. II23–25 support the cohesion of A (of II22), and II26–28 that of X, and II29 that of A'.

V	22			Phrases	Translation
21	A	23	24	Εἶπεν οὖν πάλιν αὐτοῖς·	He said therefore again to them,
-	-	a	a	ἐγὼ	"I
-	-	-	b	ὑπάγω	go away,
-	-	b	b'	καὶ ζητήσετέ	and you will seek
-	-	-	a'	25 με,	me,
-	-	b'	a	καὶ ἐν τῇ ἁμαρτίᾳ ὑμῶν ἀποθανεῖσθε·	and die in your sin;
-	-	a'	b	ὅπου ἐγὼ ὑπάγω	where I go,
-	-	-	c	ὑμεῖς οὐ δύνασθε ἐλθεῖν.	you cannot come."
22	-			ἔλεγον οὖν οἱ Ἰουδαῖοι·	Then said the Jews,
-	-		a'	μήτι ἀποκτενεῖ ἑαυτόν,	"Will he kill himself,
-	-		b'	ὅτι λέγει· ὅπου ἐγὼ ὑπάγω	because he said: 'where I go,
-	-		c'	ὑμεῖς οὐ δύνασθε ἐλθεῖν;	you cannot come'?"
23	X	26	27	καὶ ἔλεγεν αὐτοῖς·	And he said to them,
-	-	a	a	ὑμεῖς	"You
-	-	-	b	ἐκ τῶν κάτω	~ from below
-	-	-	c	ἐστέ,	are ~,
-	-	b	a'	ἐγὼ	I
-	-	-	b'	ἐκ τῶν ἄνω	~ from above
-	-	-	c'	28 εἰμί·	am ~.
-	-	a'	a	ὑμεῖς	You
-	-	-	b1	ἐκ τούτου τοῦ κόσμου	~ of this world
-	-	-	b2	ἐστέ,	are ~.
-	-	b'	a'	ἐγὼ	I
-	-	-	b'2	οὐκ εἰμὶ	am not
-	-	-	b'1	ἐκ τοῦ κόσμου τούτου.	of this world.
24	A'		29	εἶπον οὖν ὑμῖν	I said therefore to you,
-	-		a	ὅτι ἀποθανεῖσθε ἐν ταῖς ἁμαρτίαις ὑμῶν·	that you will die in your sins
-	-		x	ἐὰν γὰρ μὴ πιστεύσητε ὅτι ἐγώ εἰμι,	unless you believe that I am he,
-	-		a'	ἀποθανεῖσθε ἐν ταῖς ἁμαρτίαις ὑμῶν.	you will die in your sins."

II22. Chiastic, A-X-A': Both A and A' contain the same issue of "dying in sin," while, in X, the contrast between Jesus and the Jews in origin and belonging. In A-A', dying in sin is repeatedly emphasized. They will die in their sins because they cannot come where Jesus goes (A). They will die in their sins because of their unbelief (A').

II23. Chiastic, ab-b'a': In a and a', "I go (away)" is repeatedly shown, while b and b' are related to what "they" are going to do: seeking Jesus (b); dying in their sins (b'). "Seeking him" means actually their effort to kill him (cf. v. 37). **II24**. Chiastic, ab-b'a': Both a and a' indicate Jesus ("I" and "me"), and b and b' refer to contrastive deeds by "I" and "you": going away (b) and seeking him (b'). **II25**. Parallel, abc-a'b'c': The meaning of his words in a ("and die in your sin") is misunderstood by them in a' ("will he kill himself"), although both a and a' deal with the same issue of "dying." Two pairs, b ("where I go") and b' ("because he said, "where I go"), c ("you cannot come") and c' ("you cannot come") are duplicated.

II26. Parallel, ab-a'b': In this, a and b are in contrast as a' and b' are; a (ὑμεῖς ἐκ τῶν κάτω ἐστέ, you are from below) and a' (ὑμεῖς ἐκ τούτου τοῦ κόσμου ἐστέ, you are of this world) refer to "you", while b (ἐγὼ ἐκ τῶν ἄνω εἰμί, I am from above) and b' (ἐγὼ οὐκ εἰμὶ ἐκ τοῦ κόσμου τούτου, I am not of this world) deal with "I." **II27**. Parallel, abc-a'b'c': The parallel, same order in syntax appear both in a-b-c and a'-b'-c', which are antithetical in meaning: ὑμεῖς (you, a) and ἐγώ (I, a'); ἐκ τῶν κάτω (from below, b) and ἐκ τῶν ἄνω (from above, b'); ἐστέ (are, c) and εἰμί (am, c').

II28. Combined parallel, a-b1b2-a'-b'2b'1: The parallel but mixed way of syntactical arrangement is shown, differing from II27. Two sentences are contrasted in meaning: ὑμεῖς (you, a) and ἐγώ (I, a'); ἐκ τούτου τοῦ κόσμου (of this world, b1) and ἐκ τοῦ κόσμου τούτου (of this world, b'1); ἐστέ (are, b2) and οὐκ εἰμί (am not, b'2). **II29**. Chiastic, a-x-a': The idea of "dying in your sins" in a is repeated in a', while x focuses on the issue of "believing" ("unless you believe that I am he").

In II22, two issues, dying in sin and different origins, are revealed. II23 compares that Jesus will go and they will die. In II24, Jesus who goes and the Jews who seek him are compared. II25 focuses on their misunderstanding of Jesus' words regarding dying in sin. II26–27 contrast Jesus from above with those from below. II28 contrasts Jesus as not of the world with those of the world. In II29, dying in sin due to their unbelief is the focus.

A'. "Who are you?" (8:25)

Verse 25 has one parallelism, II30, which covers the verse.

V	30	Phrases	Translation
25	a	Ἔλεγον οὖν αὐτῷ·	Then said they to him,
	b	σὺ τίς εἶ;	"Who are you?"
	a'	εἶπεν αὐτοῖς ὁ Ἰησοῦς·	Jesus said to them,
	b'	τὴν ἀρχὴν ὅ τι καὶ λαλῶ ὑμῖν;	"Even what I have told you from the start.

"I Am the Light of the World," I

II30. Parallel, ab-a'b': They asked (a) and Jesus answered (a') regarding who he is: "who are you?" (b) and "Even what I have told you from the start." (b'). In II30, the identity of Jesus is re-emphasized.

B'. THE FATHER IS WITH THE SON, WHO SPEAKS (8:26–29).

In vv. 26–29, there are seven parallels: one comprehensive chiasm (II31) with four parallelisms (II32 and 34–36) and two chiasms (II33 and 37). II35–36 support the connections between B and B' and between D and D' of II31, respectively. II32 reflects the relation among the first part of II31 (ABCD), while II34 is for connection within its latter part (D'C'B'A').

V	31	32	33		Phrases	Translation
26	A	a	a	35	πολλὰ ἔχω περὶ ὑμῶν λαλεῖν καὶ κρίνειν,	I have much to say and to judge;
	B	b	x	a	ἀλλ' ὁ πέμψας με	but He who sent me
	-	-	-	b	ἀληθής ἐστιν,	is true,
	C	a'	a'		κἀγὼ ἃ ἤκουσα παρ' αὐτοῦ ταῦτα λαλῶ	and the things I have heard from him I
				36	εἰς τὸν κόσμον.	speak to the world."
27	D	b'		a	οὐκ ἔγνωσαν	They did not understand
	-	-		b	ὅτι τὸν πατέρα αὐτοῖς ἔλεγεν.	that he spoke to them of the Father.
28	X				εἶπεν οὖν [αὐτοῖς] ὁ Ἰησοῦς·	Jesus therefore said,
	-	34			ὅταν ὑψώσητε τὸν υἱὸν τοῦ ἀνθρώπου,	"When you lift up the son of man,
	D'	a		a'	τότε γνώσεσθε	then you will know
	-	-		b'	ὅτι ἐγώ εἰμι,	that I am he,
	-	-		-	καὶ ἀπ' ἐμαυτοῦ ποιῶ οὐδέν,	and that ~ of myself
	-	-		-	ἀλλὰ καθὼς ἐδίδαξέν με ὁ πατὴρ	I do nothing ~,
	C'	b			ταῦτα λαλῶ.	but ~ as the Father taught me.
	-	-	37		καὶ ὁ πέμψας με	I speak these things ~.
29	B'	a'	a	a'	μετ' ἐμοῦ ἐστιν·	And He who sent me
	-	-	b	b'	οὐκ ἀφῆκέν με μόνον,	is with me;
	A'	b'	b'		ὅτι ἐγὼ τὰ ἀρεστὰ αὐτῷ ποιῶ πάντοτε.	he has not left me alone,
	-	-	a'		πολλὰ ἔχω περὶ ὑμῶν λαλεῖν καὶ κρίνειν,	for I always do what pleases him."

II31. Chiastic, ABCD-X-D'C'B'A': B and B' have a similar pattern: "He who sent me is . . .", regarding "the Father." In C and C', Jesus discloses that he does speak "the things he has heard from him" (C) or "these things as the Father taught him" (C'). D and D' are in common in terms that both imply the relationship of Jesus-the Father. X may be located as the center because of its significant issue, his lifting-up, implying crucifixion. Thus, A and A' become related to each other, implying that his deeds of saying and judging (A) would be the action that pleases his Father (A').

II32. Parallel, ab-a'b': In a-a', Jesus is the man who says something: "I have much to say and to judge" (a); "and the things I have heard from him I speak to the world" (a'). Both b and b' refer to the Father: "but he who sent me is true" (b); "and the things I have heard from him I speak to the world" (b'). II33. Chiastic, a-x-a': His saying and judging (a) come from his hearing from the Father (a'). And the sender, who told (and sent) his son to speak, is true (x).

II34. Parallel, ab-a'b': In a-a', the emphasis is on that Jesus is always with the Father (a') and does not do anything without the Father (a). In b-b', what the Father does and what the Son does, responding to his Father, are emphasized: "but I speak these things as the Father taught me" (b); "he has not left me alone for I always do what pleases him" (b').

II35. Parallel, ab-a'b': As described in the notes on II31, both sentences have the same syntactical pattern, regarding the same subject, the Father, "He who sent me." Each phrase contains the same numbers in syllable: 5 (a) + 5 (b) = 5 (a') + 5 (b'). It says that the Father who sent the Son is true and also with him. II36. Parallel: ab-a'b': They "did not understand" in a, but they "will understand" in a', regarding the relationship between "I" and "the Father," in b and b'. II37. Chiastic, ab-b'a': The pair, b and b', deals with the issue of "the Father with the Son," while, in a, the Father did to "me," and, in a', "I" do to him.

In II31, it is emphasized that the Father is true and with the Son, who speaks from the Father. II32–33 focus on the fact that Jesus always speaks from his Father. In II34, the Father is always with Jesus, never leaving him alone. In II35, "He who sent me" is in repetition. In II36, what they did not know and what they will know are compared. In II37, the Son does what pleases his Father who is with him.

C'. Many Believed in Him (8:30)

Verse 30 does not have its own parallel but it is connected to other verses such as v. 31 and v. 20, as seen in II38 and 21. Here the role of II21 is primary in that it links the previous verses (25–29) to the following ones (31–36) in the middle, as v. 20 does in between vv. 13–19 and 21–24.

V	38	21	Phrases	Translation
30	a	a'	Ταῦτα αὐτοῦ λαλοῦντος	As he spoke these things,
	b	b'	πολλοὶ ἐπίστευσαν εἰς αὐτόν.	many believed in him.

II38. Parallel, ab-a'b': Both a and a' deal with Jesus' saying: "As he spoke these things" (a) and "Jesus then said" (a'). And b ("many believed in him") and b' ("to the Jews who had believed in him") refer to their believing in him. II38 repeats two things: Jesus speaks and the people believe in him.

D'. Free from Sin vs. Slave to Sin (8:32–36)

In vv. 31–36, there is an overarching structure of combined chiasm (II39) with eight embedded parallels: four chiasms (II42–43, 45 and 47) and four parallelisms (II40–41, 44, and 46). Among them, II40 and 42 support the cohesion of A (of II39) and II46 does that for B'1. Including II41 and 43, most of those parallels are for combining all the verses in this cluster in unity. But II47 seems to be connected with v. 37 for keeping the continuity between vv. 32–36 and vv. 37–41.

II39. Combined chiastic, A-B1B2-B'2B'1-A':[8] In A and A', the issue of "being free" recurs: by the truth in A; by the Son in A'. B1 and B'1 deal with the similar issue in contrast: "descendants"/the son versus slaves. In B2, they asked Jesus regarding "being free," and in B'2, Jesus answered that they are not free but rather, slaves to sin.

V	39		38					Phrases	Translation
31	A		a'					Ἔλεγεν οὖν ὁ Ἰησοῦς	Jesus then said
-			b'					πρὸς τοὺς πεπιστευκότας αὐτῷ Ἰουδαίους·	to the Jews who had believed in him,
-		40	a					ἐὰν ὑμεῖς μείνητε	"If you abide
-			-					ἐν τῷ λόγῳ τῷ ἐμῷ,	in my word,
-			b	41	42	43	44	47	ἀληθῶς μαθηταί μού ἐστε	you are truly my disciples,
32	-		a'	a	a	a	a	a	καὶ γνώσεσθε	and you will know
-	-		-	-	b	-	-	-	τὴν ἀλήθειαν,	the truth,
-	-		b'	-	b'	-	b	-	καὶ ἡ ἀλήθεια	and the truth
-	-		-	`	a'	-	-	-	ἐλευθερώσει ὑμᾶς.	will make you free."
33	B1		b		b			b	ἀπεκρίθησαν πρὸς αὐτόν· σπέρμα Ἀβραάμ ἐσμεν	They answered him, "We are descendants of Abraham,
-	-		-		b'			-	καὶ οὐδενὶ δεδουλεύκαμεν πώποτε·	and have never been slaves to anyone.
-	B2		a		a'			-	πῶς σὺ λέγεις ὅτι ἐλεύθεροι γενήσεσθε;	How do you say that 'you will be made free'?"
-				45						
34	B'2		b	a					ἀπεκρίθη αὐτοῖς ὁ Ἰησοῦς·	Jesus answered them,
-	-		-	-					ἀμὴν ἀμὴν λέγω ὑμῖν	"Truly, truly, I say to you,
-	-		-	-					ὅτι πᾶς ὁ ποιῶν τὴν ἁμαρτίαν	everyone who commits sin is a
-	-		-	-		46			δοῦλός ἐστιν τῆς ἁμαρτίας.	slave to sin.
35	B'1			b	a				ὁ δὲ δοῦλος	And the slave
-	-			-	b				οὐ μένει ἐν τῇ οἰκίᾳ	does not remain in the house
-	-			-	c				εἰς τὸν αἰῶνα,	forever;
-	-			b'	a'				ὁ υἱὸς	the son
-	-			-	b'				μένει	remains
-	-			-	c'				εἰς τὸν αἰῶνα.	forever.
36	A'		a'	a'					ἐὰν οὖν ὁ υἱὸς ὑμᾶς ἐλευθερώσῃ,	So if the Son makes you free,
-			-	b'					ὄντως ἐλεύθεροι ἔσεσθε.	you will be free indeed.

---

8. Compare the chiasm of Ellis in vv. 31–36: A (31); B (33a); C (33b); B' (34); A' (35–36). Ellis, "Inclusion, Chiasm, and the Division," 278.

II40. Parallel, ab-a'b': In this, a and a' describe the same connotation of "my word" or "the truth": "If you abide in my word" (a) and "and you will know the truth" (a'). It means that "being my disciples" (b) and "being free by the truth" (b') are interrelated in semantic category. II41. Parallel, ab-a'b': In a-a', Jesus tells them of the truth that will make them free (a), but the Jews misunderstand "being made free" (a'). In b-b', they insist that they are descendants of Abraham, who have never been slaves to anyone (b), but Jesus responds that they are slaves because of their committing sin (b').

II42. Chiastic, ab-b'a': Knowing (a) the truth (b) is the same as "being free" (a') by the truth (b'). II43. Chiastic, ab-b'a': In this, a and a' deal in common with "making/being free," while b and b' regard their national pride as free men or descendants of Abraham. II44. Parallel, ab-a'b': Two sentences show how they become free in a similar way. It is emphasized that "being free" by the truth (His words) is, in other words, by the Son.

II45. Chiastic, ab-b'a': In a and a', "slave to sin" and "being free" are in contrast, as in b and b', "the slave" and "the son" are in contrast regarding "remaining." II46. Parallel, abc-a'b'c': The former, a-b-c, are contrasted to the latter, a'-b'-c', both in syntax and in meaning ὁ δὲ δοῦλος (And the slave, a) and ὁ υἱὸς (the son, a'); οὐ μένει ἐν τῇ οἰκίᾳ (does not remain in the house, b) and μένει (remains, b'); εἰς τὸν αἰῶνα (forever, c) and εἰς τὸν αἰῶνα (forever, c').

II47. Parallel, ab-a'b': In b-b', the Jews proudly emphasize that they are descendants of Abraham (b), and Jesus agrees with them in this regard (b'): "I know that you are descendants of Abraham." Nevertheless, in a-a', it is proved that they are not free but slaves to sin, for they seek to kill him because they do not have his word in them (a'), namely the truth that makes them free (a).

In II39, being freed by the truth vs. being slaves to sin are in contrast. II40 highlights how to be free and his disciples. In II41, there is a contrast between those who are slaves and those who are not. II42 focuses on the relation between knowing the truth and being free. II43 focuses on those who are free. In II44, freedom by the truth and that by the Son are in parallel. II45 contrasts the slave to sin with the son in freedom. In II46, the slave who does not remains forever and the son who remains forever are in contrast. II47 highlights both how to be free and why they are not free.

IIA'. Who Is the Father? (8:37–59)

Parallel, II48 (AB-A'B')

This section is made up of four clusters, creating a comprehensive, parallel structure. In A, the descendants of Abraham issue is the main one regarding whether they are his children or not. The Jews insist that they are but Jesus refutes it, for they do not do the works of God and instead act in opposition to it. In A', Jesus discloses who

"I Am the Light of the World," I

their father is indeed, the devil, because they act like him, the father of lies and also a murderer. In A-A', there are at least four shared ideas: (1) the father-children issue; (2) Jesus' saying from the Father; (3) his words are not in them; (4) their attempt to kill him or unbelief.

B and B' focus mostly on the issues of Jesus himself regarding who he is and where he is from. In B, the Jews declare that they were not born of fornication. It seems to imply the controversial issue of the origin of Jesus regarding his physical father. Jesus replies affirmatively that he came from God. In B', they still raise the issue of his origin, saying that he is a Samaritan and has a demon (being sent from the devil but not from God). In replying to this, Jesus reveals his relation with the Father regarding who he is and when he was. In B-B', we read what they share: (1) the origin of Jesus; (2) his relation with the Father.

We may draw out the points of shared ideas within the pairs in the structure:

A. 37-41a	The descendants of Abraham controversy	A'. 43-47	"The devil is your Father."
	1. The father-children controversy (37-39, 41a)		1. "The devil is your father" (44a)
	2. "I speak from the Father" (38, 40b).		2. His word, the truth, from the Father (43b, 45a, 46b, 47a)
	3. "My word has no place to you" (37).		3. "You cannot hear (do not understand) my word" (43b, 47b).
	4. "You seek to kill me" (37b, 40a).		4. "You do not believe in me" (45, 46b).
B. 41b-42	Origin of Jesus	B'. 48-59	Identity of Jesus
	1. "We were not born of fornication" (41b).		1. "You are a Samaritan and have a demon" (48b, 52b; cf. 53b, "Who do you claim to be?")
	2. "I came from God" (42b).		2a. "Your God is my Father" (54b; 55a, "I know Him").
			2b. "Before Abraham was, I am" (58).

A. Jesus Acts from the Father and They Act from Their Father (8:37–41A).

In vv. 37–41a, II49 is the comprehensive, parallel structure which has nine embedded parallels: five parallelisms (II50–51 and 53–55), three chiasms (II52 and 57–58), and one combined chiasm (II56). II50–52 seem to be built up to connect the first part of II49 (ABCD) and its last one (A'B'C'D'). All of II54–58 are to combine the last part of II49, while, in the first one, there is only one parallel (II53) to play this role.

II49. Parallel, ABCD-A'B'C'D': In A-A', the phrase, descendants of Abraham, is repeated in Jesus' saying (A) and the Jews' saying (A'): "I know that you are descendants of Abraham" (A) and "Abraham is our father" (A'). In B-B', Jesus discloses repeatedly that they seek to kill him: because of their lack of his word (B); because they are not in fact Abraham's children (B'). In C, Jesus speaks the things which he has seen from the Father and, in C', he has spoken the truth which he heard from God. After seeing and hearing from God the Father, the Son speaks. D and D' share in what they do, following their real father, supposedly the devil.

II50. Parallel, ab-a'b': In a, Jesus says that they are the descendants of Abraham and, in a', they say that Abraham is their father. In both b and b', it is repeatedly indicated that they seek to kill Jesus. II51. Parallel, ab-a'b': In a-a', it is disclosed that they seek to kill Jesus. Both b and b' indicate the reasons why they are going to kill him: because his word is not in them (b); because Jesus told them the truth (b'). These two are related to each other in terms of Jesus' word.

V	49				47	Phrases	Translation
37	A	50			b'	Οἶδα	I know
-	a				-	ὅτι σπέρμα Ἀβραάμ ἐστε·	that you are descendants of Abraham.
			51				
	B	b	a		a'	ἀλλὰ ζητεῖτέ με ἀποκτεῖναι,	But you seek to kill me,
-		b			-	ὅτι ὁ λόγος ὁ ἐμὸς	because my word
-		-	52	53	-	οὐ χωρεῖ ἐν ὑμῖν.	has no place in you.
38	C		a	a		ἃ ἐγὼ ἑώρακα	~ the things which I have seen
-			-	b		παρὰ τῷ πατρὶ	from the Father
-			b	c		λαλῶ·	I speak ~,
	D			a'		καὶ ὑμεῖς οὖν ἃ ἠκούσατε	and you ~ the things which you heard
-				b'		παρὰ τοῦ πατρὸς	from the father
-				c'	54	ποιεῖτε.	do ~."
39	A'				a	Ἀπεκρίθησαν καὶ εἶπαν αὐτῷ·	They answered and said him,
-	a'				b	ὁ πατὴρ ἡμῶν Ἀβραάμ ἐστιν.	"Abraham is our father."
	B'			55	a'	λέγει αὐτοῖς ὁ Ἰησοῦς·	Jesus said to them,
-			a		b'	εἰ τέκνα τοῦ Ἀβραάμ	"If you ~ Abraham's children
-			b	-	56	ἐστε,	were ~,
'-			a'	-	a1	τὰ ἔργα τοῦ Ἀβραάμ	~ the things Abraham did
-			b'	-	-	57	ἐποιεῖτε·	you would do ~.
40	-	b'	a'		58	a2	a	νῦν δὲ ζητεῖτέ με ἀποκτεῖναι ἄνθρωπον	But now you seek to kill me, a man
	C'		b'		a	x	b	ὃς τὴν ἀλήθειαν	who ~ the truth,
-		-	b'	x	-	-	ὑμῖν λελάληκα	~ has told you ~,
-			a'	a'	-	b'	ἣν ἤκουσα παρὰ τοῦ θεοῦ·	which I heard from God;
	D'				a'1	a'	τοῦτο Ἀβραὰμ οὐκ ἐποίησεν.	Abraham did not do this.
41a	-				a'2		ὑμεῖς ποιεῖτε τὰ ἔργα τοῦ πατρὸς ὑμῶν.	You do the deeds of your father."

II52. Chiastic, ab-b'a': In ab, Jesus speaks the things which he has seen from the Father and, in a'b', he has told the truth which he heard from God. Without seeing and

hearing from the Father, the Son never speaks. **II53**. Parallel, abc-a'b'c': In this, three constituents are arranged in syntax but with a contrast in meaning: ἃ ἐγὼ ἑώρακα (the things which I have seen, a) and καὶ ὑμεῖς οὖν ἃ ἠκούσατε (and you ~ the things which you heard, a'); παρὰ τῷ πατρὶ (from the Father, b) and παρὰ τοῦ πατρός (from the father, b'); λαλῶ (I speak, c) and ποιεῖτε ([you] do, c').

II54. Parallel, ab-a'b': They said (a) and Jesus said (a'). In b-b', the relation between Abraham and the Jews is duplicated: "Abraham is our father" (b) and "If you were Abraham's children" (b'). **II55**. Parallel, ab-a'b': If they belong (b) to Abraham as his children (a), they will do (b') what he did (a'). Their relationship with Abraham needs to be matched to their behavior in following him.

II56. Combined chiastic, a1a2-x-a'1a'2: In a1-a'1, the Jews are proved not to follow the model of Abraham. In x, the focus is on the telling-hearing of Jesus issue. In a2, their seeking to kill Jesus is disclosed. In a'2, it is finally divulged that their deed of seeking to kill is following their real father, supposedly the devil. **II57**. Chiastic, ab-b'a': Seeking to kill the Son (a) is not like the work of Abraham (a'). In b-b', Jesus' telling the truth (b) and hearing it from God (b') are connected. **II58**. Chiastic, a-x-a': The truth (a) is nothing but what Jesus has heard from God (a'). It is he who has told the people (x).

In II49, the issue, whose descendants they are, is highlighted. In II50, the Jews as the descendants of Abraham are divulged as those who seek to kill Jesus. II51 discloses the reason why they seek to kill Jesus, their lack of Jesus' word. II52 emphasizes his seeing and hearing from the Father in order to say his word. In II53, the contrast between Jesus and the Jews regarding whom to follow is focused. II54 focuses on the relation between Abraham and the Jews. In II55, their relationship with Abraham is connected to their behavior. In II56–57, they are proved that they do not follow Abraham but instead do the works of the devil. II58 focuses on the quality of the truth.

B. God Is Their Father? (8:41b–42)

In vv. 41b–42, II59 is to connect these verses with vv. 48–49 (the front part of B' of II48), while II71 seems to connect v. 41 to v. 44. II60–61 are the parallels within these verses.

V	59	60		Phrases	Translation
41b	A	a	71	Εἶπαν [οὖν] αὐτῷ·	They [therefore] said to him,
-		b1	a	ἡμεῖς	"We
-		-	b	ἐκ πορνείας	~ of fornication;
-		-	c	οὐ γεγεννήμεθα,	were not born ~;
-		b2		ἕνα πατέρα ἔχομεν τὸν θεόν.	we have one Father God."
42	B	a'		εἶπεν αὐτοῖς ὁ Ἰησοῦς·	Jesus said to them,
-		b'2		εἰ ὁ θεὸς πατὴρ ὑμῶν ἦν	"If God were your Father,
-		b'1	61	ἠγαπᾶτε ἂν ἐμέ,	you would love me,
-			a	ἐγὼ γὰρ ἐκ τοῦ θεοῦ ἐξῆλθον	for I came from God
-			b	καὶ ἥκω·	and now am here.
-			a'	οὐδὲ γὰρ ἀπ' ἐμαυτοῦ ἐλήλυθα,	I have not come on my own;
-			b'	ἀλλ' ἐκεῖνός με ἀπέστειλεν.	but he sent me.

II59. AB-A'B': vv. 41b–42 and 48–49 form a parallel with the pattern of the Jews' attack and Jesus' defense. In A, the Jews seem to allude to the rumor of the origin of Jesus regarding his father by insisting that they were not born of fornication. They also emphasize their relation with one God. In A', they attack him for his origin (a Samaritan) and relation (having a demon). Both in A and A', the readers see their misjudgment of Jesus regarding his origin and relationship with the Father. In B, Jesus defends himself against them, saying that he came from God who sent him. Here his origin and relation are explained. In B', Jesus denies the relation with the demon and instead emphasizes his relation with the Father.

II60. Combined parallel, a-b1b2-a'-b'2b'1: In a-b1b2, they raise the issues, attacking Jesus, while, in a'-b'2b'1, Jesus defends himself, responding to them. b2 and b'2 highlight whether God is their father or not. In b1, by the words from their mouth, they show how they misjudge and even disparage Jesus. In b'1, Jesus says that they do not love him. **II61.** Parallel, ab-a'b': Both a and a' contain the similar syntax with related meaning: ἐγὼ γὰρ ἐκ τοῦ θεοῦ ἐξῆλθον (for I came from God, a, 10 syllables) and οὐδὲ γὰρ ἀπ' ἐμαυτοῦ ἐλήλυθα (I have not come on my own, a', 11 syllables). And in b-b', we may see a relation between them, cause and effect: I am now here (effect, b) because he sent me (cause, b').

In II59, the primary focus is on the origin and relation of Jesus in relation to the Father. In II60, it is proved that they do not have God as their Father. II61 focuses on the relationship between Jesus and the Father regarding his origin.

A'. The Devil Is Their Father (8:43–47)

Verses 43–47 have one overarching, combined chiastic structure, II62, with eight smaller parallels: five chiasms (II64, 66–67, and 69–70), two parallelisms (II63 and

65), and one combined chiasm (8:68). 8:63 is designed to combine mostly B1B2-B'1B'2 of 8:62. 8:64, 65, 67, 69, and 70 are made up to support each constituent of 8:62 such as A1-A2, B1, B2, B'1, and A'2, respectively. 8:68 connects B'1B'2 to A'1.

8:62. Combined chiastic: A1A2-B1B2-B'1B'2-A'1A'2: In A1-A'1, they do not understand what Jesus says (A1) and they do not believe him who tells the truth (A'1). The reasons are suggested in A2 and A'2: because they cannot hear his word (A2); because they are not of God (A'2). Here, A2 occurs because of A'2, as explained in A'2 itself. In B1, the relationship between "you" and the devil is emphasized: they belong to the devil and want to do his desires. In B'1, the relation between Jesus and them appears: he tells the truth but they do not believe him. In this way, B1 and B'1 are in contrast. In B2, the devil is demonstrated as a murderer and a liar, while, in B'2, Jesus declares that no one can convict him of sin. In B2 and B'2, the devil and Jesus are in contrast regarding sin. Although the whole structure is chiastic, the relations between A1A2 and A'1A'2 and between B1B2 and B'1B'2 are in parallel.

8:63. Parallel, ab-a'b'-a''b'': The triangular relations are suggested between "you" (a, the Jews), "he" (a', the devil), and "I" (a'', Jesus). In each of b-b'-b'', two points are presented. In b, (1) they belong to the devil; (2) they want to do the desires of the devil. In b', (1) the devil is a murderer; (2) he is a liar. In b'', (1) Jesus tells the truth but they do not believe him; (2) no one can convict him of sin. Here, "you" and the devil are in intimacy, while Jesus and the devil are in contrast, and Jesus and the Jews are detached.

8:64. Chiastic, ab-b'a': In both b and b', the similar expression is repeated: "you do not understand" (b) and "you cannot hear" (b'). Both a and a' describe the word of Jesus: "what I say" (a) and "my word" (a'). **8:65.** Parallel: ab-a'b': Jesus points out that they belong to (a) their father, the devil (b) and they want to do (a') the desires of their father (b'). Their belonging (a) and their desires (a') are from their father, the devil (b-b').

V	62		64			Phrases	Translation
43	A1		a			διὰ τί τὴν λαλιὰν τὴν ἐμὴν	Why ~ what I say?
-	-		b			οὐ γινώσκετε;	do you not understand
-	A2		b'			ὅτι οὐ δύνασθε ἀκούειν	It is because you cannot hear ~
-	-		63	a'		71 τὸν λόγον τὸν ἐμόν.	~ my word.
44	B1	a		65	a'	ὑμεῖς	You
-	-	b		a	b'	ἐκ τοῦ πατρὸς τοῦ διαβόλου	~ of your father the devil,
-	-	-		b	c'	ἐστὲ	are ~,
-	-	-		a'		καὶ τὰς ἐπιθυμίας τοῦ πατρὸς ὑμῶν	and ~ the desires of your father
-	-	-		66	b'	θέλετε ποιεῖν.	you want to do ~.
-	B2	a'	a			ἐκεῖνος	He
-	-	b'	-			ἀνθρωποκτόνος ἦν ἀπ' ἀρχῆς	was a murderer from the beginning,
-	-	-	b	67		καὶ ἐν τῇ ἀληθείᾳ οὐκ ἔστηκεν, ὅτι οὐκ ἔστιν ἀλήθεια ἐν αὐτῷ.	and does not stand in the truth, because there is no truth in him.
-	-	-	b'	a		ὅταν λαλῇ	When he tells
-	-	-	-	b		τὸ ψεῦδος,	the lie,
-	-	-	-	b'		ἐκ τῶν ἰδίων	~ of his own,
-	-	-	-	a'		λαλεῖ,	he speaks ~,
-	-	-	a'	68	69	ὅτι ψεύστης ἐστὶν καὶ ὁ πατὴρ αὐτοῦ.	for he is a liar and the father of lies.
45	B'1	a''	a1		a	ἐγὼ δὲ	But because I
-	-	b''	-		b	ὅτι τὴν ἀλήθειαν λέγω,	tell the truth,
-	-	-	a2		b'	οὐ πιστεύετέ	you do not believe
-	-	-	-		a'	μοι.	me.
46	B'2	-	x			τίς ἐξ ὑμῶν ἐλέγχει με περὶ ἁμαρτίας;	Which one of you convicts me of sin?
-	A'1	-	a'1			εἰ ἀλήθειαν λέγω,	If I tell the truth,
-	-	70	a'2			διὰ τί ὑμεῖς οὐ πιστεύετέ μοι;	why do you not believe me?
47	A'2		a			ὁ ὢν ἐκ τοῦ θεοῦ	He who is of God
-	-		b			τὰ ῥήματα τοῦ θεοῦ ἀκούει·	hears the words of God;
-	-		b'			διὰ τοῦτο ὑμεῖς οὐκ ἀκούετε,	for this reason you do not hear *them*,
-	-		a'			ὅτι ἐκ τοῦ θεοῦ οὐκ ἐστέ.	because you are not of God."

II66. Chiastic, ab-b'a': In a-a', the devil is described as a murderer (a) and also a liar (a'). In b-b', the devil has no relation to the truth, neither standing in it (b) nor telling it (b'), because there is no truth inside him. II67. Chiastic: ab-b'a': In a-a', what he speaks is duplicated: "when he tells" (ὅταν λαλῇ, a) and "he speaks" (λαλεῖ, a'). In b-b', what he speaks is the lie (b, τὸ ψεῦδος) and from which he speaks (b', of his own, ἐκ τῶν ἰδίων) are described. The reason why he tells the lie is that there is nothing but lies coming from him.

II68. Combined chiastic: a1a2-x-a'1a'2: In a1-a'1, "telling the truth" is duplicated and, in a2-a'2, "not believing him" is repeated: "you do not believe me" (a2); "why do you not believe me?" (a'2). In the center, x, the question of Jesus, "Which one of you convicts me of sin?," is located. Jesus reveals himself as the one who tells the truth and has no sin, while they are the unbelievers. **II69**. Chiastic, ab-b'a': Both a and a' indicate Jesus himself. In b-b', "I" who tell the truth and "you" who do not believe are in contrast. **II70**. Chiastic, ab-b'a':[9] In a-a', he who is of God and "you" who are not of God are contrasted to each other. And, in b-b', hearing the words of God and not hearing them are in contrast. In this way, it is emphasized that hearing the words of God is the key if anyone belongs to God.

II71. Parallel, abc-a'b'c': The contrasts are made among the pairs: ἡμεῖς (We, a) and ὑμεῖς (You, a'); ἐκ πορνείας (of fornication, b) and ἐκ τοῦ πατρὸς τοῦ διαβόλου (of your father the devil, b'); οὐ γεγεννήμεθα (were not born, c) and ἐστε (are, c'). In this way, the Jews' own confidence regarding their pride of origin is disregarded by Jesus' conviction regarding their belonging to the devil.

In II62, it is emphasized that the Jews who belong to the devil do not accept what Jesus says, who tells the truth in opposition to the devil. II63 demonstrates the triangular relations: Jesus, the Jews, and the devil. II64 focuses on the fact that they do not understand the word of Jesus. II65 emphasizes their close relationship with the devil. In II66, the devil appears as a murderer and a liar. II67 discloses that he is the liar of liars. In II68, Jesus is presented as the one of the truth without sin. In II69, the truth-teller and unbelievers are in contrast. In II70, the relation between hearing the words of God and being of God is highlighted. In II71, the contrast between what they assert to be and what they really are is presented.

B'. "I am before Abraham was" (8:48–59)

In vv. 48–59, there are fifteen parallels: six chiasms (II76, 78, 80–81, 83, and 86), five parallelisms (II75, 77, 82, and 84–85), two combined parallelisms (II73 and 79), one dual (II74), and one combined chiasm (II72). Among them, the main pillars in structure would be II72–73 and 80 that together penetrate throughout this section, overlapping in some verses (52–54), though. In this sense, II72 and 80 are arranged in complexity in parallel construction. II75–76 support the cohesion of B1 of II72. II77, 79, and 81 are for B2. II84–85 are built up to keep the cohesion within B'1 of II72. II82 shows a connection between B1 and B'1. II73 seems to play a role of sustaining the unity of II72, while II83 is to cohere the latter parts of II80, c'b'a'.

---

9. Bullinger, *Figures of Speech*, 302.

Sourcebook of the Structures and Styles in John 1–10

V	59	72	73				Phrases	Translation
48	A'	A	a				Ἀπεκρίθησαν οἱ Ἰουδαῖοι καὶ εἶπαν αὐτῷ· οὐ καλῶς λέγομεν ἡμεῖς	The Jews answered and said to him, "Do we not say rightly
	-	-	-		74	a	ὅτι Σαμαρίτης εἶ σὺ	that you are a Samaritan
	-	-	-		78	a'	καὶ δαιμόνιον ἔχεις;	and have a demon?"
49	B'	B1	b1	75		a	ἀπεκρίθη Ἰησοῦς·	Jesus answered,
	-	-	-	a	76	-	ἐγὼ	"I
	-	-	-	a		-	δαιμόνιον	~ a demon
	-	-	-	b		-	οὐκ ἔχω,	do not have ~;
	-	-	-	b	b'	-	ἀλλὰ τιμῶ	but I honor
	-	-	-	c	a'	-	τὸν πατέρα μου,	my Father
	-	-	-	a'		-	καὶ ὑμεῖς	and you
	-	-	-	b'		-	ἀτιμάζετέ	dishonor
	-	-	-	c'		82	με.	me.
50		-	-	b		a	ἐγὼ δὲ οὐ ζητῶ τὴν δόξαν μου·	Yet I do not seek my glory;
		-	-	-		b	ἔστιν ὁ ζητῶν καὶ κρίνων.	there is One who seeks and judges.
			77		79			
51		B2	b2	a		a	ἀμὴν ἀμὴν λέγω ὑμῖν,	Truly, truly, I say to you,
		-	-	-		b1	ἐάν τις τὸν ἐμὸν λόγον τηρήσῃ,	if anyone keeps my word,
		-	-	-		b2	θάνατον οὐ μὴ θεωρήσῃ εἰς τὸν αἰῶνα.	he will never see death."
	80							
52	a	-	a'	b	81		Εἶπον [οὖν] αὐτῷ οἱ Ἰουδαῖοι·	The Jews said to him,
	-	-	-	-		a	νῦν ἐγνώκαμεν ὅτι δαιμόνιον ἔχεις.	"Now we know that you have a demon.
	-	-	-	-		b	Ἀβραὰμ ἀπέθανεν καὶ οἱ προφῆται,	Abraham died, and the prophets *also*;
	-	-	b'2	a'	c	a'	καὶ σὺ λέγεις·	and you say,
	-	-	-	-	-	b'1	ἐάν τις τὸν λόγον μου τηρήσῃ,	'If any one keeps my word,
	-	-	-	-	-	b'2	οὐ μὴ γεύσηται θανάτου εἰς τὸν αἰῶνα.	he will not taste death forever.
53	b	-	b'1	b'	c'		μὴ σὺ μείζων εἶ τοῦ πατρὸς ἡμῶν Ἀβραάμ,	Are you greater than our father Abraham,
	-	-	-	-	b'		ὅστις ἀπέθανεν; καὶ οἱ προφῆται ἀπέθανον.	who died? and the prophets died.
	-	-	-	-	a'		τίνα σεαυτὸν ποιεῖς;	Who do you claim to be?"
54	c	B'1	-	b'			ἀπεκρίθη Ἰησοῦς·	Jesus answered,
	-	-	-	-	a'		ἐὰν ἐγὼ δοξάσω ἐμαυτόν, ἡ δόξα μου οὐδέν ἐστιν·	"If I glorify myself, my glory is nothing;
	-	-	-	-	b'		ἔστιν ὁ πατήρ μου ὁ δοξάζων με, ὃν ὑμεῖς λέγετε ὅτι θεὸς ἡμῶν ἐστιν,	it is my Father who glorifies me, of whom you say, 'He is our God'.
			83		84			
55	c'	-	a	a'	a		καὶ οὐκ ἐγνώκατε	And you have not known
	-	-	-	-	b		αὐτόν,	Him;

"I Am the Light of the World," I

-	-	-	-	a'		ἐγὼ δὲ οἶδα		but I know
-	-	-	85	-	b'	αὐτόν.		Him;
-	-	-	-	a	-	κἂν εἴπω ὅτι οὐκ οἶδα αὐτόν,		and if I said I do not know Him,
-	-	-	-	b	-	ἔσομαι ὅμοιος ὑμῖν ψεύστης·		I would be a liar like you,
-	-	-	-	a'	-	ἀλλ' οἶδα αὐτὸν		but I do know Him,
-	-	-	-	b'	-	86	καὶ τὸν λόγον αὐτοῦ τηρῶ.	and keep His word.
56	b'	B'2	b			a	Ἀβραὰμ ὁ πατὴρ ὑμῶν ἠγαλλιάσατο	Your father Abraham rejoiced
-	-	-				b	ἵνα ἴδῃ τὴν ἡμέραν τὴν ἐμήν,	to see my day,
-	-	-				b'	καὶ εἶδεν	and he saw *it*
-	-	-				a'	καὶ ἐχάρη.	and was glad."
57	-	-	x				εἶπον οὖν οἱ Ἰουδαῖοι πρὸς αὐτόν· πεντήκοντα ἔτη οὔπω ἔχεις καὶ Ἀβραὰμ ἑώρακας;	The Jews then said to him, "You are not yet fifty years old, and you have seen Abraham?"
58	-	-	b'				εἶπεν αὐτοῖς Ἰησοῦς· ἀμὴν ἀμὴν λέγω ὑμῖν, πρὶν Ἀβραὰμ γενέσθαι ἐγὼ εἰμί.	Jesus said to them, "Truly, truly, I say to you, I am before Abraham was."
59	a'	A'	a'				Ἦραν οὖν λίθους ἵνα βάλωσιν ἐπ' αὐτόν. Ἰησοῦς δὲ ἐκρύβη καὶ ἐξῆλθεν ἐκ τοῦ ἱεροῦ.	Therefore they picked up stones to throw at him; but Jesus hid himself, and went out of the temple.

II72. Combined chiastic: A-B1B2-B'1B'2-A': This narrative is made up of six subunits, arranged in chiastic structure. In the first part of the narrative (A), the Jews blaspheme against Jesus regarding what kind of person he is, insisting that he is a Samaritan and has a demon. At the end of the episode (A'), they are going to kill him by stoning and Jesus hides himself. Both in B1 and B'1, the relationship between the Father and the Son, specifically regarding honor and glory, is presented in duplication. Both in B2-B'2, the contrast between Jesus and Moses is presented: who is the greater. **II73.** Combined parallel: a-b1b2-a'-b'2b'1: In a-a', the Jews deprecate Jesus, mentioning him as the man with a demon. In b1-b'1, some issues seem to be shared: calling God his Father ("my Father") and honoring him but not seeking his own glory (b1); he who is greater than Abraham and who calls him his Father ("my Father") who glorifies him (b'1). In b2-b'2, the expression, anyone who keeps his word will not see death, is duplicated.

II74. Dual, a-a': Two issues are raised by the Jews against Jesus: "you are a Samaritan" (a) and "you have a demon" (a'). **II75.** Parallel, abc-a'b'c': Two contrastive sentences are arranged in syntax: ἐγώ (I, a) and καὶ ὑμεῖς (and you, a'); ἀλλὰ τιμῶ ([but] honor, b) and ἀτιμάζετέ (dishonor, b'); τὸν πατέρα μου (my Father, c) and με (me, c'). This contrastive parallel implies that they have to honor him as he does the Father. **II76.** Chiastic, ab-b'a': What Jesus does not have (b) is a demon (a') and what he does to his Father (b') is honoring him (a'). Honoring his Father (b'a') is the proof that he does not have a demon (ab). **II77.** Parallel, ab-a'b': In a-a', it is repeated that keeping his words means never-seeing-death: by Jesus (a) and by the Jews (a'). In b-b', first, Abraham and the prophets, who both died, are referred to. Second, what kind of person he is is stated: "you have a demon" (b); "Are you greater than our father Abraham?... Who do you claim to be?" (b').

II78. Chiastic: ab-b'a': Both in a and a', the relationship between Jesus and the Father is emphasized: "honoring my Father" (a) and "knowing him and keeping his word" (a'). They also share the "you" parts: "you dishonor me" (a, implying that "you" dishonor the Father unlike "me"); "you have not known Him" (a', in contrast to "I" who know Him). In b-b', first, Jesus repeats his words regarding seeking not his own glory: "I do not seek my glory" (b); "If I glorify myself, my glory is nothing" (b'). Second, he discloses instead that Father is the One who glorifies him: "there is One who seeks..." (b) and "it is my Father who glorifies me" (b'). Third, Jesus refers to the problem of the Jews: "... judges" (b, implying that they will be eventually judged by the Father); "of whom you say, 'He is our God'" (b', probably questioning if he is really their God).

II79. Combined parallel: a-b1b2-a'-b'1b'2: it is seen of "I say" (a) and "you say" (a'). Keeping-his-word (b1-b'1) and never-seeing-death (b2-b'2) are repeated. **II80**. Chiastic: abc-c'b'a': In b-b', there is the argument about who is greater, Jesus or Abraham. Jesus claims that he is before Abraham was. In c-c', the intimate relationship between Jesus and the Father is emphasized: The Father glorifies the Son (c); the Son knows him and keeps his word (c'). In a, the Jews misjudge and misunderstand Jesus, and finally, in a', they are going to kill him by stoning. Jesus hides himself. **II81**. Chiastic, abc-c'b'a': In b-b', the Jews refer repeatedly to Abraham who died and the prophets who died. Jesus' word about keeping his word and not-tasting death (c) lets them regard it as an implication that he is greater than Abraham (c'). In a', they question him about who he is, but, in a, they misjudge him as having a demon.

II82. Parallel, ab-a'b': In a-a', Jesus repeatedly expresses that he does not glorify himself: "Yet I do not seek my glory" (a); "If I glorify myself, my glory is nothing" (a'). In b-b', Jesus declares instead that his Father is the One who glorifies him: "there is One who seeks and judges" (b); "it is my Father who glorifies me, of whom you say, 'He is our God'" (b'). **II83**. Chiastic, ab-x-b'a': Both in b-b', Jesus declares his relationship with Abraham, who rejoiced to see his day and saw it (b) and before whom he is (b'). In a, we can see his emphasis on the exceptional relationship with the Father: knowing him and keeping his word, in contrast to the Jews who have not known Him. In a', the Jews are going to kill him with stones because of his words about his relationship with the Father as well as that with Abraham. In x, the Jews do not understand any word of Jesus about Abraham.

II84. Parallel, ab-a'b': In b-b', the same word, αὐτόν (Him), recurs, while, in a-a', the contrast between "you" who do not know and "I" who know is presented: "And you have not known" (a) and "but I know" (a'). **II85**. Parallel, ab-a'b': In this, not only a ("and if I said I do not know Him") and a' ("but I do know Him") are in contrast, but also b ("I would be a liar like you") and b' ("and keep his word") are. **II86**. Chiastic, ab-b'a': In a-a', Abraham rejoiced (a) or was glad (a'). In b-b', it is duplicated that Abraham saw the day of Jesus: he tried to see (b) and he actually saw (b').

In II72, what kind of person Jesus is, particularly in relation to the Father and Abraham is the focus. In II73, Jesus' defense against their deprecation in relation to the Father is the focus. In II74, two issues against Jesus are presented. In II75, there is the contrast between "I" who honor the Father and "you" who do not honor Jesus. In II76, the relation between honoring the Father and not having a demon is focused. In II77, misjudgment and misunderstanding of the Jews are focused. II78 highlights the close relationship between the Father and the Son. In II79, the relation between keeping-his-word and never-seeing-death is focused. In II80, the focus is on what kind of person Jesus is, compared with Abraham. II80, the contrast between Jesus and Abraham and the relationship between Jesus and the Father are emphasized. In II82, the Father who glorifies his Son is highlighted. In II83, the relations of Jesus with the Father and with Abraham are in focus. II84 contrasts "you" who do not know him with "I" who know Him. In II85, knowing him and not-knowing him as well as being a liar and keeping his word are contrasted to each other. II86 emphasizes the joy of Abraham who saw the day of Jesus.

READING IN STRUCTURE-STYLE

1. According to II2, v. 12 and v. 25 are in a pair, A and A'. Thus, the answer of Jesus in v. 25 to the question of the Jews ("who are you?") needs to be interpreted in the context of v. 12. Jesus refers to what he has before revealed himself to be ("the light of the world") when they ask him here.[10] Thus, he is reminding them of what he has told them about who he is.

2. Verses 13–19 (B) are complemented by vv. 26–29 (B'). Both describe the Father-Son relationship. In B, the focus is on the truthfulness of the witness and judgment of Jesus being with the Father, while, in B', it is emphasized that Jesus does not speak anything, whether it is to witness or to judge, of himself but from the true Father who always is with him. In short, B focuses on the genuineness of the witnesses for Jesus, and B' rather on the inseparability between Jesus and the Father when he speaks.

3. Verses 21–24 (D) also need to be complemented by vv. 31–36 (D'). In D, the tone is mostly negative: they will die in their sin unless they believe in him because they are from below, belonging to the world. But in D', the tone becomes rather positive as a whole: they will be free if they know the truth (or if the Son makes them so), although they are negatively disclosed as the slaves to sin. In short, the foci shifts: to die in sin (D) and to be free from sin (D').

---

10. See the comment of Talbert regarding how the light issue is significant at the Feast of Tabernacles. Talbert, *Reading John*, 152–53. See also Hughes, *John*, 255–56.

4. According to II48, vv. 37–41a (A) and vv. 43–47 (A') are in a pair to be complemented in reading. First, their father is not Abraham (A) but the devil (A'). That they seek to kill him is not to follow the model of Abraham (A) but is because they are of the devil their father, a murderer from the beginning (A'). Second, Jesus speaks from the Father what he has seen and what he has heard (A) but they cannot hear and do not understand and do not believe in him (A'). Third, they are sinners who seek to kill Jesus (A). It is proved that they are on the side of the devil who is a murderer as well as a liar, the sinner of sinners, in contrast to Jesus whom no one convicts of sin (A'). The ideas are developed from A to A'.

5. Verses 41b–42 (B) and vv. 48–59 (B') complement each other. Both in B and B', we have information regarding the Jews' prejudice against Jesus based on their ignorance. They misjudge him regarding his birth (B) as well as the originality and source of the power (B'). Both in B and B', we may read that the Jews show their extreme hatred for Jesus, going as far as stoning him (B'). Jesus points out the reason: God is not their father (B). Additionally, Jesus claims that he came from God the Father who sent him (B). Thus, Jesus honors the Father and he seeks the glory of Jesus and judges those who ignore him (B').

Issues in Structure-Style

1. The Structure of vv. 12–59

Talbert suggests five smaller thought units in vv. 12–59 with similar patterns: (1) A provocative statement by Jesus appears first; (2) A Jewish response follows; (3) Jesus gives a reply to it: monologue or dialogue (12–20; 21–30; 31–40; 41–50; 51–59).[11]

Brown regarded vv. 12–59 as miscellaneous discourses which are categorized into three units:[12] (1) A discourse at the temple treasury: Jesus the light of the world and his witness to himself (12–20); (2) An attack on the unbelieving Jews and the question of who Jesus is (21–30); (3) Jesus and Abraham (31–59). And he divided again vv. 31–59 into three subunits: Abraham and the Jews (31–41a); The real father of the Jews (41b–47); The claims of Jesus; comparison with Abraham (48–59).[13] He saw a break at vv. 21 and 31 but had to acknowledge that the sequence is far from simple and there are doublets of other discourses. Thus, he admitted the difficulty in analyzing the structure of vv. 12–59 more than that of any other chapter.[14]

---

11. Talbert, *Reading John*, 152.
12. Brown, *Gospel according to John 1–XII*, 202.
13. But Moloney regards vv. 31–59 as the most difficult section in John where a unifying narrative effect is created by the increase in hostility between Jesus and the Jews, grouping them into three parts: vv. 31–38; 39–47; 48–59. Moloney, *Gospel of John*, 274.
14. Brown, *Gospel according to John 1–XII*, 342.

First, as seen in II2 (ABCD-A'B'C'D', 12–36), vv. 12 (A) and 25 (A'), vv. 13–19 (B) and 26–29 (B'), vv. 20 (C) and 30 (C'), and vv. 21–24 (D) and 31–36 (D') are connected in pairs. It means that these pairs are to be read considering their interrelations. Two pairs (A-A' and C-C') are shorter and two other pairs (B-B' and D-D') are larger. In the two shorter pairs, A and A' deal with the identity of Jesus (who he is), C and C' indicate the responses of the people: negative (C) and positive (C'). In the two larger pairs (B-B' and D-D'), which are considered as the discourse of Jesus or his dialogue with the Jews, there are in all four return responses or questions of the Jews to Jesus, which appear once in each passage (13, 22, 27, and 33). Among them, two responsive questions are raised only in D-D' (22, "Will he kill himself . . . ?"; 33, "How do you say that 'you will be made free'?"). The other two (13 and 27 in B-B') are not a type of question but of evaluation (13, "your witness is not true") or of commentary (27, "They did not understand that he spoke to them of the Father").

Second, as discussed earlier in II48, the structure of vv. 37–59 is chiastic: AB-A'B'. Verses 37–41a (A) and 43–47 (A'), and vv. 41b–42 (B) and 48–59 (B') are in a pair in the system of structure. A and A' are presented with the same issue (the descendants of Abraham), as B and B' are (the origin of Jesus). In A-A', there are at least four issues to be shared, and in B-B' there are two.[15] It is absolutely necessary to find the relations among them.

However, third, there is one problem that still needs to be solved. The relation between B (41b–42) and B' (48–59) is not simple because they show a big difference to each other in size. They are definitely connected though, specifically vv. 41b–42 and 48–49 (see II59, AB-A'B'). However, we cannot separate vv. 48–49 and 50–59 from each other, for they are deeply inter-connected in structure (see II72, A-B1B2-B'1B'2-A').

Fourth, vv. 49–50 and 54–55 are in a pair of duplication and reversely presented (II78, ab-b'a'). Verses 51–53 are cohesive inside (see II77, ab-a'b') and simultaneously related to vv. 56–58 regarding the Abraham controversy. If we see only the relation in structure of vv. 49–58 except for vv. 48 and 59, it is in parallel: AB-A'B' (or B1B2-B'1B'2). After including vv. 48 and 59, which are the responses of the Jews (condemnation in word and enmity in action), we can find a complex chiasm in the structure as a whole: A-B1B2-B'1B'2-A' (II72).

Fifth, there is a possibility that the last part of this chapter (48–59) was intended to be related to its first part, the episode of the adulteress (1–11), on condition that this story was originally placed as it is. They could become an *inclusio*. In this *inclusio*, the two parts share a few interesting points: the condemnation by the Jews (committing the sin of adultery or having a demon); the enmity of the Jews, killing by stoning; the death-and-life issue. Thus, we may say that vv. 48–59 were possibly designed to be not only the counterpart of vv. 41b–42 but also that of vv. 1–11 for an *inclusio* at the same time. It could be the reason why this passage is so long, much longer than its

---

15. For the details, see the diagram in relation to II48.

counterpart in a pair (41b–42) that its function is to be paired also to the episode of the woman in sin. However, we have to admit that it is just a possibility.

Sixth, the division of Talbert cannot be agreed with, if we see the two parallel structures of vv. 12–36 and of vv. 37–59, although his outline is neatly presented. The provocative statement of Jesus appears not only vv. 12, 21, 31, 41, and 51 but also everywhere as in vv. 19, 23–24, 38, 46–47, and 56, where another Jewish response follows. Most of all, his division does not reflect any connection in theme between the passages. Thus, there is, for example, no explanation of why the issue of judgment appears both in vv. 15–16 and 26 and why vv. 21–24 share the sin issue with vv. 31–36.

Seventh, similarly, we cannot divide vv. 12–59 into three units as Brown did. We have to consider the similarity both in function and in size, even in contents between vv. 12 and 25; between 20 and 30. The relations between vv. 13–19 and 26–29; between vv. 21–24 and 31–36 cannot be ignored, as discussed previously, because this passage is not arranged simply in sequence but is done interactively.

2. The Functions of vv. 13–20 and 21–29

Separating from the previous verse (12) and the following ones (21–30), Bultmann relocated vv. 13–20 into a place after 5:30–47 and 7:15–24, because he thought vv. 13–20 was the original conclusion regarding the witness and judgment issue. All three passages also contain the appeal to the law of Moses: 5:45–47; 7:19–23; 8:17–18.[16] And Bultmann concluded that 9:1–41; 8:12; 12:44–50; 8:21–29; 12:34–36 belong to the same "complex" and 10:19–21 are their conclusion.[17]

But as for Brown, it is a literary concern to see vv. 12–20 as a structural unit, because he observed that v. 20 is the ending and v. 21 starts another issue and also that there is an *inclusio* between vv. 12 and 20 by the repetition of "spoke," although the thought skips and jumps within vv. 12–20, for example, vv. 14c,d and 15–16 which interrupt the sequence between vv. 14b and 17.[18] Brown also indicated that vv. 21–30 are bound by the same type of inclusion of vv. 12–20.[19]

First, as far as Brown's perspective is concerned, vv. 14c,d and 15–16 could be regarded as the interruption of the sequence between vv. 14b and 17, for these verses describe the judgment issue, seemingly different from the witness one. However, if we see the Johannine way of construction, these verses (particularly vv. 15–16) are located in the center of vv. 13–19 and function as X of II5 complementing the issue of witness in A-A'. It means that the two issues: witness and judgment are combined in these verses, intentionally and in a system of chiasm. Thus, there is no interruption.

16. Bultmann, *Gospel of John*, 238.
17. Ibid., 313–14, 342.
18. Brown, *Gospel according to John 1–XII*, 342–43.
19. Ibid., 342. Moloney highlights the significance of "again" which begins at vv. 12 and 21. Moloney, *Gospel of John*, 270.

This issue (judgment) is further used as material connecting this cluster (13–19) to vv. 26–29 (particularly 26).

Second, neither vv. 12–20 and 21–30 (Brown) nor 13–20 and 21–29 (Bultmann) can be regarded as units. We have to consider the system in structure in vv. 12–36 (II2). If we want to specify smaller units, it would be better to categorize the verses into vv. 12–24 (ABCD) and 25–36 (A'B'C'D') or, if smaller than them, 12–19 (AB) and 20–24 (CD); 25–29 (A'B') and 30–36 (C'D').

Third, Bultmann thought that vv. 13–20 need to be placed after 5:30–47 and 7:15–24 because of their connection in theme (judge). However, the main issue in these verses is that of witness rather than that of judge, probably similar with 5:30–47 but not with 7:15–24. The latter two share the Sabbath issue as well as that of judgment, but hardly that of witness.[20] In vv. 13–20, there is no concept in relation to the Sabbath controversy. Although there is some similarity and duplication in theme among them, we have to consider their differences in function in the places where they are located. In vv. 12–19, the issue of witness-judgment is related to that of the light which is highlighted regarding the matter of sin-death throughout the chapter. But in 5:30–47 this issue is not presented in this context but instead regarding the matter of life-giver and judge for salvation. Thus, if we detach the passage from the place as it is, its function is lost.

Fourth, the *inclusio* of Brown seeing "to say" at vv. 12 and 20 as well as vv. 21 and 30 seems to be plausible but not crucial in division, for there is no reason to exclude this phenomenon of "to say" particularly in vv. 25b, and 28. Verses 12 and 20 can be interrelated (as A and C, smaller units of II2) but vv. 21 and 30 are not; instead are vv. 25 (or 25b) and 30 similarly (as A' and C', smaller units). Thus, he overlooked the relation between vv. 31–36 and 21–24 as similar to that between vv. 13–19 and 26–29.

3. The Division of vv. 30–47

Bultmann regarded vv. 30–47 as two fragments: vv. 30–40 (the Jews appeal to be children of Abraham but Jesus contests it) and 41–47 (they appeal that they are children of God but Jesus rebukes them as children of the Devil).[21] He did not admit that the two themes are specifically related, even though they seem to be, because, in vv. 41–47, the freedom issue is missing and the contrast between the free man and the slave is no longer sustained. Although there seems to be a connection between freedom and truth as in v. 32, Bultmann insisted, even this is "not adequate proof of an original literary relationship." Moreover, he thought that vv. 30–40 are addressed to believers, while vv. 41–47 are to those who are not. In relation to it, he recommended that vv. 41–47 are to be placed before vv. 51–53 and 56–59, while vv. 30–40 are to be taken with 6:60–71 to the end of ch. 12.[22]

---

20. In this sense, we can also see the connection between 5:19–30 and 7:15–24.
21. Bultmann, *Gospel of John*, 314.
22. Bultmann, *Gospel of John*, 315.

According to Brown,[23] the themes of freedom and slavery and of being true descendants of Abraham also run through vv. 31–41 which are directed at Jewish Christians. But the desire of these Jews in v. 37 to kill Jesus does not fit in with this idea.

First, it is understandable that many, including Bultmann and Brown, link vv. 31–36 with the rest of the chapter, because there seems to be. (1) The issue of the descendants of Abraham flows from these verses to the following ones. (2) There is no manifest marker of demarcation in v. 37 to separate these verses from the rest.

Second, there are some reasons to separate vv. 31–36 from 37–59, even though both share the issue of Abraham: (1) These verses are suitable as part of the comprehensive, parallel structure of vv. 12–36 (II2), without which the structure cannot stand completely as typical Johannine style. In particular, these verses are the concluding part of vv. 21–24 in terms of freedom from sin which results in death. (2) Although there are in common the descendants of Abraham issue both in vv. 31–36 and 37–59, their foci are different from each other: the focus of the former is primarily on the slave in sin and the son in freedom, regardless of whether they are the descendants of Abraham or not, while the focus of the latter is on their authenticity as descendants of Abraham, whether they are qualified as his descendants and also on that they are in fact children of the Devil. It means that the issue of Abraham is not significant in the former, while it is highlighted in the latter. In other words, in the former, freedom from sin is the key in theme, while, in the latter, it is "who their father is."

Third, nevertheless, for it is undeniable that there is a connection between vv. 31–36 and 37–59, it can be said that vv. 31–36 play two roles in this chapter: (1) The last and concluding unit matching vv. vv. 21–24 regarding the whole structure in vv. 12–36; (2) The link connects the previous verses (12–30) to the following ones (37–59) in issue, although these verses are not directly included in vv. 37–59 in terms of construction of structure in parallel. It means that vv. 37–59 come forward owing to the existence of vv. 31–36.

Fourth, the problem of Brown regarding the awkwardness of the killing motif in v. 37 may be solved, if vv. 31–36 and 37–59 are separated from each other as we do. The tone along with the theme drastically shifts at v. 37 and becomes more intensified in conflict.

4. The Relations among vv. 48–59

Bultmann recognized two themes in vv. 48–59 which alternate with each other but are not related to: (1) the glory of Jesus (48–50 and 54–55); (2) Jesus and Abraham (51–53 and 56–59), finding that vv. 54 and 50 are connected, as are vv. 56 and 53.[24]

---

23. Brown, *Gospel according to John 1–XII*, 362.
24. Bultmann, *Gospel of John*, 314, 325.

He regarded vv. 51–53 and 56–59 as the conclusion of the preceding passage but vv. 48–50 and 54–55 were inserted later, which should be located after 7:29.

First, as Bultmann observed, there are certainly connected units in a themed pair such as vv. 49–50 (except 48) and 54–55; 51–53 and 56–58 (except 59). These pairs of units are created to construct a parallelism (AB-AB, or B1B2-B1B2 of II72), a Johannine style of structure. Thus, they should not be relocated or rearranged far from their locations where they are, as Bultmann did. They are presented as perfectly suitable to the style of John, creating the combined, chiastic structure of II72 with the help of vv. 48 and 59, which share the enmity of the Jews toward Jesus.

Second, the relations among the four units (49–50, 51–53, 54–55, and 56–58) are to be given attention. Verses 49–50 and 54–55 are complementary by each other regarding the issues of honor and glory which reveal the close relation between the Father and the Son, while vv. 51–53 and 56–58 regard the identity of Jesus who existed before Abraham. These two issues are deeply interrelated in terms of the divinity of Jesus as the Son of God (*contra* Bultmann), finally resulting in stoning by the Jews regarding blasphemy.

5. The Function of v. 25

According to Bultmann, the question of the Jews about the identity of Jesus, "Who are you?," in v. 25 reflects that they have failed to understand who Jesus is. And the answer of Jesus responding to it is connected with difficulty to v. 12, which is too far away, while it indicates that "he is everything which he has claimed to be" and also the title, the Son of Man in v. 28 is presented in relation to ἐγώ εἰμι.[25]

Brown introduced various possible translations (or attempts) of the words of Jesus in v. 25:[26] (1) "What I have been telling you from the beginning" (Brown's); (2) "Primarily [I am] what I say to you" (as an affirmation); (3) "First of all [I am] what I say to you" (as an affirmation); (4) "[I am] from the beginning what I say to you" (as an affirmation); (5) "How is it that I speak to you at all?" (as a question); (6) "That I seak to you at all" (as an exclamation); (7) "[I am] the beginning who also speaks to you" (Latin translators); (8) "I told you at the beginning what I am also telling you [now]" (Funk and Smothers).

First, as Brown indicated, this sentence (or phrase) is "a famous difficulty" to be interpreted.[27] There have been several versions in translation. Regardless of which version we choose or how we translate it, we may point out three things in this sentence: (1) It is the issue of who Jesus is (ὅ τι); (2) He said (or has said) previously about it (τὴν ἀρχὴν); (3) He is still saying and referring to it (καὶ λαλῶ ὑμῖν).

---

25. Ibid., 348.
26. Brown, *Gospel according to John 1–XII*, 347–48.
27. Ibid.

Second, where did Jesus say about who he is with an emphatic expression of ἐγώ εἰμι? We can find it in v. 12. There are some reasons why we recall this verse as a reference to Jesus in v. 25 regarding the issue of his identity: (1) There are five places where ἐγώ εἰμι is used in this chapter (12, 18, 24, 28, and 58); (2) Among them, the titles in relation to uses of ἐγώ εἰμι appear in vv. 12 (the light of the world), 18 (the testifier), and 28 (the Son of Man). But either "the testifier" (ὁ μαρτυρῶν) or "the Son of Man" (τὸν υἱὸν τοῦ ἀνθρώπου) are not relevant to this case, because they are masculine. When Jesus refers to his title regarding his identity by using a combination of relative pronoun (ὅ) and indefinite pronoun (τι), these are all neuters; (3) The title in v. 12, the Light (τὸ φῶς), is neuter and matches this case; (4) Moreover, the parallel structure in vv. 12–36 (II2) shows that vv. 12 (A) and 25 (A') are in a pair and connected to each other, deeply and inseparably, revealing who Jesus is, the Light of the world. This theme is one of the primary keys to understand this chapter where the sin issue predominates.

9 "I Am the Light of the World," II

"As we return to the enigmatic 'expulsion from the synagogue' passages in the Fourth Gospel, we approach them with a refreshed paradigm for understanding the Jewish-Christian conflict in the first century as an intra-Jewish conflict in existence well before AD 70. And the immediate result of the above discussion is that the term ἀποσυνάγωγος, which according to Martyn reflects a tension that could not have occurred before the late first century, can no longer qualify as an anachronism."[1]

COMBINED CHIASTIC STRUCTURE[2]

1. As far as characters are concerned, the scenes are divided into eight groups in a cluster. In vv. 1–3(5), there are Jesus and the disciples in dialogue and, in vv. 4(6)-7, Jesus and the man who was blind come up in the healing process. In vv. 8–12, the man who was healed and the people are the characters in conversation and, in vv. 13–17, the Pharisees and the healed man are in interrogation. And in vv. 18–23, the figures shift to the Jews (probably the Pharisees) and the parents of the healed man. But in vv. 24–34, the Jews and the man are the main figures again. In the next scene, vv. 35–38, Jesus and the man are the focus again, while, in vv. 39–41, Jesus and the Pharisees are.

2. Among these divisions, the first and the second parts need to be re-examined. The division between vv. 1–3 and 4–7 does not depend on the characters but instead

---

1. Klink III, "Expulsion from the Synagogue?," 111–12.

2. The structure of this chapter is not dual unlike most other chs. 1–10, but instead is chiastic (A-X-A'). The effect of the chiastic structure in John 9 may be similar to the dual mode in structure in that it presents two kinds of scene as a whole: (1) the scenes where Jesus is the main figure (A-A', 1–7 and 35–41); (2) the scenes in interrogation (X, 8–34). This phenomenon was observed in the case of the prologue which contains two witnesses: the Baptist and the author group, "we," in its chiastic structure. As far as the witness is concerned, there are two kinds of witness in John 9: (1) Jesus himself speaks and acts regarding the witness to himself (1–7 and 35–41); (2) The man who was blind becomes the witness to Jesus (8–34).

on the switch of theme, or the issue: from "whose sin?" (1–3) to "the work of God" (4–7). Moreover, the parallel features observed here are the supporters of this division. (Verses 4–7 keep an overarching, chiastic structure, I6, A-X-A', as their cohesive unity.) As Jesus says about the works of God (4, A), he is carrying out one of the works of God, healing the man of blindness (6–7, A'), because he is the light of the world, enlightening the people (5, X).

3. Thus, we may present these eight scenes as follows:

Scenes	Verses	Characters	Contents/ Foci, Considering the Relations of Scenes
Scene 1	1-3	Jesus & the disciples	They discuss the question of sin: who the sinners are.
Scene 2	4-7	Jesus & the man	Jesus physically opens the eyes of the blind man: beginning His work.
Scene 3	8-12	The man & the people	The neighbours question the man regarding the identity of the man and how he is healed.
Scene 4	13-17	The Pharisees & the man	The Pharisees first interrogate the man regarding two issues: 'from God,' and 'sinner.'
Scene 5	18-23	The Jews & the parents	The Jews interrogate the parent of the man regarding the identity of the man and how he is healed.
Scene 6	24-34	The Jews & the man	The Jews interrogate the man again regarding two issues: 'sinner' and 'from God,' and cast him out.
Scene 7	35-38	Jesus & the man	Jesus finally opens the spiritual eyes of the man: finishing His work.
Scene 8	39-41	Jesus & the Pharisees	Jesus condemns them regarding their blindness, revealing that they are indeed the sinners.

4. A firm relation exists between scene 4, the first interrogation of the man by the Pharisees, and scene 6, the last interrogation of the man by the Jews. In these two scenes, two main issues, "from God" and "sinner," are manifestly seen to regard the identity of Jesus and his origin.

5. There seems to be a similarity between scene 3 and scene 5 in that, in these two scenes, questioning regarding the identity of the man who was blind and how he is healed is primarily the issue. Even the "not-knowing" concept is presented in both scenes, specifically vv. 12 and 21.

6. If scene 2 describes that Jesus physically heals the blind man, beginning the work of the Father as the light of the world, in scene 7, we can see that Jesus meets him again to have him receive the spiritual brightness, finalizing the work of the Father for this man. In this sense, the two scenes are deeply connected.

7. How about the relation between scene 1 and scene 8? In scene 1, Jesus and the disciples discuss the issue of sin or blindness regarding who the sinner is. In the last

scene, scene 8, Jesus reprimands the Pharisees for their spiritual blindness or sins. It means that they are indeed sinners to be finally judged.

8. If scene 1 is related to scene 8 and scene 2 is related to scene 7, we may say that these four scenes are interrelated to create a chiastic parallel such as AB-B'A' (or A1A2-A'2A'1). Considering the relations between scene 3 and scene 5 and between scene 4 and scene 6, these four scenes are designed to create a parallelism in structure such as AB-A'B' (or B1B2-B'1B'2). It means that eight scenes are combined in two ways: chiastic and parallel. We may say that it is a "complex-parallel structure," one of the Johannine type of structures.

9. Considering the close connection between scenes 1–2 and 7–8 and among scenes 4–6, we may classify them into three categories at large: I. 1–7 (A); II. 8–34 (X); III. 35–41 (A'). More specifically, if we regard all the eight units, we may draw their relations in complex parallelism as follows:[3]

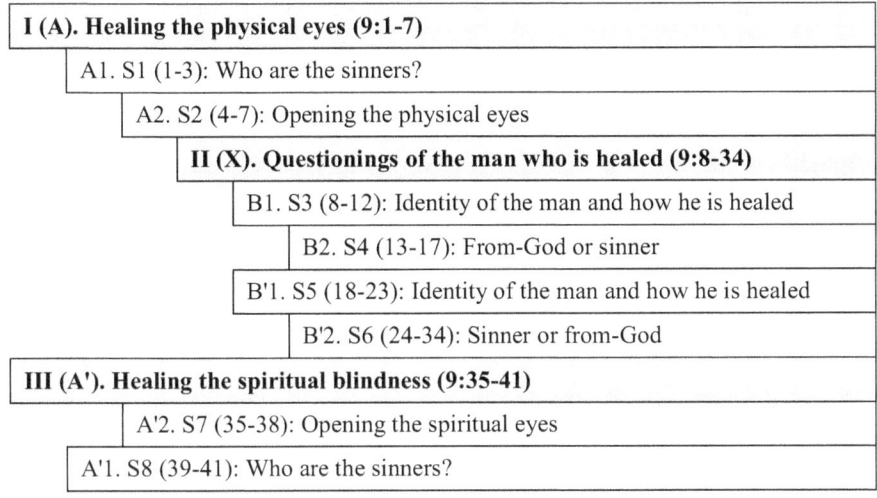

---

3. Painter also divides the chapter into eight sections: "*First Encounters*: 1. The problem of sin and suffering (vv. 2–5); 2. The account of the miracle (vv. 6–7); 3. The proof of the miracle (vv. 8–12); 4. The controversy over the Law (vv. 13–17); 5. The threat of excommunication (vv. 18–23); *Reprise (partial)*: 6. Faith overcomes fear of excommunication (vv. 24–34); 7. Jesus reveals himself as the heavenly Son of Man (vv. 35–38[39]). Verse 39 is both the conclusion of this dialogue and the bridge to the one that follows; *New Encounter*: 8. Unbelief is condemned (vv. 39–41)." But his division differs from mine and Lee's in that he does not consider any parallel relation among the scenes. Painter, *Quest for the Messiah*, 313. Compare also the structure of Asiedu-Peprah regarding his judicial and narrative theory: Healing account and its immediate aftermath (9:1–15); Resumption of controversy (re-instatement of accusations, 9:16); Search for witnesses (9:17–27); Defence controversy and its aftermath (9:28–38); Juridical parable and its application (9:39–10:18); Conclusion of the Sabbath juridical controversy (10:19–21). Asiedu-Peprah, *Johannine Sabbath*, 120

An Alternative in Structure

If anyone regards vv. 1–12 as a chiastic structure such as AB-X-B'A', thus paying attention to the cohesiveness of these verses, it would be recommended that the whole structure be grouped into three divisions like: A (1–12); X (13–34); A' (35–41).

First, it is probable that there is a comprehensive chiasm in vv. 1–12: A (1–3, a question of his disciples, who the sinner is regarding the blindness); B (4, we have to work the works of God); X (5, I am the light of the world); B' (6–7, Jesus works the work of God); A' (8–12, many questions regarding who he is, how the eyes are opened, and where he is). In this structure, A and A' are compared in terms of the interests or concerns of the people in contrast to those of Jesus, besides the relation among B-X-B', which was also explained in the previous structure (A1A2-B1B2-B'1B'2-A'2A'1), specifically A2 (4–7).

Second, this alternative seems to be also supported by the intensive connection between vv. 13–34 such as A (13–17, the first interrogation, to the man); X (18–23, the second interrogation, of the parents); A' (24–34, the last interrogation, of the man).

Third, however, we have to point out some weakness in this structure: (1) We cannot ignore the connectivity between scene 3 (8–12) and scene 5 (18–23) in terms of shared themes: the identity of the healed man and how he is healed. It means that the connection between vv. 8–12 and 13–34 is more intensified than that between vv. 1–7 and 8–12. (2) As vv. 1–3 and 39–41 are in a pair, so vv. 4–7 and 35–38 are. Thus, vv. 8–12 may not be a part of vv. 1–12.

Therefore, it is better and safer for us to keep to the first suggestion of the structure.

I (A). Healing the Physical Eyes (9:1–7)

A1. Who Are the Sinners? (9:1–3)

In vv. 1–3, there are three parallels and two connecting ones with the following verses: three chiasms (I1 and 3–4) and two duals (I2 and 5). I1 seems to be comprehensive, but the role of combining the cluster lies in I3.

I1. Chiastic, A-X-A': In both A and A', Jesus acts and speaks: passing by and seeing a blind man (A); saying something regarding the blind man (A'). In X, there are his disciples who ask him about the man. I2. Dual, a-a': His disciples' question (who sinned?, a) and Jesus' answer (no one sinned, a') are provided in a and a'. **I3**. Chiastic, ab-x-b'a': In b-b', "this man" and "his parents" are referred to. In the center x, the fact that he was born blind is located. In a-a', the question, "who sinned?" (a) is switched in focus to Jesus' statement, "we must the works of him who sent me" (a').

"I Am the Light of the World," II

V	1				Phrases	Translation
1	A				Καὶ παράγων εἶδεν ἄνθρωπον τυφλὸν ἐκ γενετῆς.	And as he passed by, he saw a man blind from his birth.
		2				
2	X	a			καὶ ἠρώτησαν αὐτὸν οἱ μαθηταὶ αὐτοῦ λέγοντες·	And his disciples asked him,
			3	4		
-	-	a	a		ῥαββί, τίς ἥμαρτεν,	"Rabbi, who sinned,
-	-	b	-		οὗτος ἢ οἱ γονεῖς αὐτοῦ,	this man or his parents,
-	-	x	-		ἵνα τυφλὸς γεννηθῇ;	that he was born blind?"
3	A'	a'			ἀπεκρίθη Ἰησοῦς·	Jesus answered,
-	-	b'	b	5	οὔτε οὗτος ἥμαρτεν οὔτε οἱ γονεῖς αὐτοῦ,	"Neither this man or his parents sinned,
-	-	a'	b'	a	ἀλλ' ἵνα φανερωθῇ τὰ ἔργα τοῦ θεοῦ ἐν αὐτῷ.	but that the works of God might be made manifest in him.

I4. Chiastic, ab-b'a': In a, his disciples ask Jesus regarding who sinned that he was born blind. In b-b', he answers two things: (1) no one is responsible for his blindness (b); it is for the works of God to be manifested in him (b'). In a', Jesus says to his disciples, "We must work the works of him," thus switching their concern from responsibility for blindness (a) to the works of God (a'). **I5.** Dual, a-a': Both in a-a', the works of God are focused in common. We may read them together: the works of God need to be manifested in him (a); but Jesus and his disciples, "we," have to do these works (a').

In I1, the dialogue between Jesus and his disciples is introduced. I2 focuses on the sin issue. In I3–4, Jesus switches the issue of sin to that of the works of God. I5 focuses on doing the works of God.

A2. Opening the Physical Eyes (9:4–7)

Here we have six parallels: one overarching chiasm (I6) with one chiasm (I7), a combined chiasm (I10), a triple (I9), a dual (I8), and a parallelism (I11) which extends its connection with the following verses, specifically v. 11. I7 appears in v. 4 (A of I6), while I8–10 are related to force the cohesion of vv. 6–7 (A' of I6).

I6. Chiastic, A-X-A': In A, Jesus regards working the works of the Father while it is day. In A', Jesus heals the man, doing the work of God. What he said in A is accomplished in A'. In the center X, Jesus declares that he is the light of the world, assuredly lightening their darkness and restoring their sights to see the light. **I7.** Chiastic, ab-b'a': In b-b', it is contrasted that day is in the presence and night is in the future. In a-a', "we must work the works of him" (a) is also contrasted to ". . . no one can work" (a'). **I8.** Dual, a-a': In a, after saying something, Jesus does a work of God in healing him; in a', he says something about doing the work of God regarding healing him.

273

V	6	7		4	5	Phrases	Translation
4	A	a		a'	a'	ἡμᾶς δεῖ ἐργάζεσθαι τὰ ἔργα τοῦ πέμψαντός με	We must work the works of him who sent me,
-	-	b		-	-	ἕως ἡμέρα ἐστίν·	while it is day.
-	-	b'		-	-	ἔρχεται νὺξ	Night comes,
-	-	a'		-	-	ὅτε οὐδεὶς δύναται ἐργάζεσθαι.	when no one can work.
5	X 8					ὅταν ἐν τῷ κόσμῳ ὦ, φῶς εἰμι τοῦ κόσμου.	While as I am in the world, I am the light of the world."
6	A'	a	9	10		Ταῦτα εἰπὼν	Having said this,
-	-	-	a	a	11	ἔπτυσεν χαμαὶ	he spat on the ground
-	-	-	a'	-	a	καὶ ἐποίησεν πηλὸν ἐκ τοῦ πτύσματος	and made clay of the spittle
-	-	-	a"	-	b	καὶ ἐπέχρισεν αὐτοῦ τὸν πηλὸν ἐπὶ τοὺς ὀφθαλμοὺς	and spread the clay on his eyes,
7	-	a'			c	καὶ εἶπεν αὐτῷ·	and said to him,
-	-	-		b1	-	ὕπαγε	"Go,
-	-	-		b2	-	νίψαι	wash
-	-	-		-		εἰς τὴν κολυμβήθραν τοῦ Σιλωάμ (ὃ ἑρμηνεύεται ἀπεσταλμένος).	in the pool of Siloam" (which is translated, Sent).
-	-	-		b'1	d	ἀπῆλθεν οὖν	And so he went
-	-	-		b'2	-	καὶ ἐνίψατο	and washed,
-	-	-		a'	-	καὶ ἦλθεν βλέπων.	and came back seeing.

I9. Triple, a-a'-a": Regarding his healing ministry for the man blind, three actions are presented in parallel: spitting on the ground (a); making clay of the spittle (a'); spreading the clay on his eyes (a"). **I10**. Combined chiastic, a-b1b2-b'1b'2-a': In b1-b1', as Jesus says to him, "Go" (b1), he goes (b'1). In b2-b2, he says to him, "wash" (b2), so he washes (b'2). Based on Jesus' action in a, he came finally seeing in a'. **I11**. Parallel, abcd-a'b'c'd': The similar process of being healed is described twice: making clay in a-a'; spreading it on the eyes in b-b'; saying, "Go and wash," in c-c'; obeying, "went and washed" in d-d'. In abcd, the healing occurs, while, in a'b'c'd', this healing scene is retold by the man who is cured. There is just one action of Jesus, spitting on the ground (6), which is missed in the latter part (11).

In I6, we see that Jesus works the Father's work, enlightening the blind. In I7, the time of doing the work and that of not doing it are in contrast. I8 describes the healing ministry of Jesus as a work of God. In I9, three actions for healing are arranged. In I10, the work of healing is realized in detail. I11 repeats the healing process of Jesus.

"I Am the Light of the World," II

II (X). Questioning the Man Who Is Healed (9:8–34)

B1. Identity of the Man and How to Be Healed (9:8–12)

In vv. 8–12, there are six parallels: four parallelisms (II1 and 3–5), one chiasm (II2), and one combined chiasm (II6). Among them, II1 is comprehensive, unifying the cluster and repeating the pattern thrice. II2–5 combine vv. 8–9 (AB of II1). II6 is similar to I10.

V	1	2	3			Phrases	Translation
8	A	a	a			Οἱ οὖν γείτονες καὶ οἱ θεωροῦντες αὐτὸν τὸ πρότερον ὅτι προσαίτης ἦν	The neighbors and those who previously saw him as a beggar,
	-	-	b	4		ἔλεγον· οὐχ οὗτός ἐστιν ὁ καθήμενος καὶ προσαιτῶν;	said, "Is not this the man who sits and begs?"
9	B	b	a'	a		ἄλλοι ἔλεγον	Some said,
	-	-	b'	b	5	ὅτι οὗτός ἐστιν,	"It is he,"
	-	b'	a'	a		ἄλλοι ἔλεγον·	others said,
	-	-	b'	b		οὐχί, ἀλλ᾽ ὅμοιος αὐτῷ ἐστιν.	"No, he only looks like him."
	-	a'		a'		ἐκεῖνος ἔλεγεν	He himself said,
	-	-		b'		ὅτι ἐγώ εἰμι.	"I am the man."
10	A'					ἔλεγον οὖν αὐτῷ·	Therefore they said to him,
	-					πῶς [οὖν] ἠνεῴχθησάν σου οἱ ὀφθαλμοί;	"Then how were your eyes opened?"
11	B'	6			I11	ἀπεκρίθη ἐκεῖνος·	He answered,
	-	a			a'	ὁ ἄνθρωπος ὁ λεγόμενος Ἰησοῦς πηλὸν ἐποίησεν	"The man called Jesus made clay
	-	-			b'	καὶ ἐπέχρισέν μου τοὺς ὀφθαλμοὺς	and spread it on my eyes,
	-	-			c'	καὶ εἶπέν μοι	and said to me,
	-	b1			-	ὅτι ὕπαγε εἰς τὸν Σιλωὰμ	'Go to Siloam
	-	b2			-	καὶ νίψαι·	and wash.
	-	b'1			d'	ἀπελθὼν οὖν	So I went
	-	b'2			-	καὶ νιψάμενος	and washed
	-	a'			-	ἀνέβλεψα.	and received my sight."
12	A"					καὶ εἶπαν αὐτῷ·	They said to him,
	-					ποῦ ἐστιν ἐκεῖνος;	"Where is he?"
	B"					λέγει·	He said,
	-					οὐκ οἶδα.	"I do not know."

II1. Parallel, AB-A'B'-A"B": There are three questions, A-A'-A", and three answers, B-B'-B". The answers are "Is not this the man who sits and begs?" (A); "Then how were your eyes opened?" (A'); "Where is he?" (A"). The answers are: "... I am the man" (B); "the man called Jesus ... and received my sight" (B'); "I do not know" (B").
II2. Chiastic, ab-b'a': In the middle, b-b', some who speak positively and others who speak negatively are contrasted: "It is he" (b) and "No, he only looks like him" (b'). The

275

question raised in a is answered directly by the man who is cured in a': "is not this the man who sits and begs?" (a) and "I am the man" (a').

II3. Parallel, ab-a'b': A question (b) is raised by the neighbors and others (a), while its answer (b') is made by some (a'). **II4**. Parallel, ab-a'b': There are two contrastive groups: positive groups (ab) and negative ones (a'b'). Both in a-a', the same expression occurs: ἄλλοι ἔλεγον (some/others said). In b-b', the sayings of two groups are differentiated. **II5**. Parallel, ab-a'b': Others say (a) and the man who is cured says (a'). Their answers are contrasted: "No, he only looks like him" (b) and "I am the man" (b'). **II6**. Combined chiastic, a-b1b2-b'1b'2-a': In b1-b1', as Jesus says to him, "Go" (b1), he went (b'1). In b2-b'2, he says to him, "wash" (b2), so he washed (b'2). Based on Jesus' action in a, the result of receiving his sight is done in a'.

In II1, triple questions and answers appear. II2–5 highlight the argument on whether he is the man who was blind or not. In II6, the healing ministry of Jesus and its miraculous result are retold.

B2. From God, or a Sinner? (9:13–17)

In vv. 13–17, there are two chiasms (II9, and 12) and four parallelisms (II7–8 and 10–11). The comprehensive structure is II7. The former part of II7 (AB, 13–15), includes two combined parallel features, II8–9. And A' (16) contains one parallel (II10), while B' (17) has two combined parallel ones, II11–12. Each part of II7 demonstrates its own cohesion.

II7. Parallel, AB-A'B': In A-A', the Sabbath issue is predominant in relation to the healing ministry of Jesus. In both B and B', their questioning of the man who was blind is described in relation with the Jesus' healing miracle, concluding that Jesus is a prophet. **II8**. Parallel, ab-a'b': They brought to the Pharisees the man who was blind (a, what they did), while the Pharisees asked him regarding his recovery of sight (a', what the Pharisees did). Both b and b' deal in common with the issues of how Jesus opened his eyes. **II9**. Chiastic, a-x-a': Questioning of the Pharisees lies in the center, x, while in both a and a', the issue of how the former blind man was healed.

II10. Parallel, ab-a'b': Some (τινές) said in a, while others (ἄλλοι) said in a'. In b and b', controversial arguments in division are introduced regarding the identity of Jesus: "from God" (b) or "a sinner" (b'). **II11**. Parallel, ab-a'b': They said to the blind man (a) and he said to them (a'), while the question (b, who he is) and its answer (b', "He is a prophet") are provided. **II12**. Chiastic, a-x-a': The center x indicates the very act of his healing, while a is a question of who Jesus is and a' is its answer.

"I Am the Light of the World," II

V	7	8		Text	Translation
13	A	a		Ἄγουσιν αὐτὸν πρὸς τοὺς Φαρισαίους τόν ποτε τυφλόν.	They brought to the Pharisees the man who was formerly blind.
14	-	b	9 a	ἦν δὲ σάββατον ἐν ᾗ ἡμέρᾳ τὸν πηλὸν ἐποίησεν ὁ Ἰησοῦς καὶ ἀνέῳξεν αὐτοῦ τοὺς ὀφθαλμούς.	And it was a Sabbath on the day when Jesus made the clay and opened his eyes.
15	B	a'	x	πάλιν οὖν ἠρώτων αὐτὸν καὶ οἱ Φαρισαῖοι πῶς ἀνέβλεψεν.	Therefore the Pharisees again asked him how he had received his sight.
-	-	b'	a' 10	ὁ δὲ εἶπεν αὐτοῖς· πηλὸν ἐπέθηκέν μου ἐπὶ τοὺς ὀφθαλμοὺς καὶ ἐνιψάμην καὶ βλέπω.	And he said to them, "He put clay on my eyes, and I washed, and I see."
16	A'		a	ἔλεγον οὖν ἐκ τῶν Φαρισαίων τινές·	Therefore some of the Pharisees said,
-	-		b	οὐκ ἔστιν οὗτος παρὰ θεοῦ ὁ ἄνθρωπος, ὅτι τὸ σάββατον οὐ τηρεῖ.	"This man is not from God, for he does not keep the Sabbath."
-	-		a'	ἄλλοι [δὲ] ἔλεγον·	But others said,
-	-		b'	πῶς δύναται ἄνθρωπος ἁμαρτωλὸς τοιαῦτα σημεῖα ποιεῖν;	"How can a man who is a sinner do such signs?"
-	-	11		καὶ σχίσμα ἦν ἐν αὐτοῖς.	And there was a division among them.
17	B'	a	12	λέγουσιν οὖν τῷ τυφλῷ πάλιν·	So they said to the blind man again,
-	-	b	a	τί σὺ λέγεις περὶ αὐτοῦ,	"What do you say about him,
-	-	-	x	ὅτι ἠνέῳξέν σου τοὺς ὀφθαλμούς;	since he opened your eyes?"
-	-	a		ὁ δὲ εἶπεν·	And he said,
-	-	b	a'	ὅτι προφήτης ἐστίν.	"He is a prophet."

II7 focuses on the Jews' controversy, while they are questioning the man in relation to the Sabbath issue along with the Jesus' origin. In II8, it is focused on how Jesus performs the miracle. II8–9 focus on the interrogation of how he was healed on the Sabbath. In II10, there is the controversial argument about the identity of Jesus. II11–12 emphasize the man's confession regarding who Jesus is, a prophet.

B'1. Identity of the Man and How to Be Healed (9:18–23)

In vv. 18–23, there are nine parallels: four chiasms (II13, 16, and 18–19) and three parallelisms (II14–15 and 17). Among them, II13 is comprehensive, binding the cluster. Verse 18, the first part of II13, seems not to have any parallel in it, while vv. 19–21, the center of II13, contains three parallelisms (II14–15 and 17) and one chiasm (II16) altogether, demonstrating tight cohesive relations among those verses, while two chiastic relations (II18–19) are found in relation to vv. 21b–23.

II13. Chiastic, AB-B'A': A and A' are commentaries by the evangelist, each of which demonstrates the doubt of the Jews (A) and the fear of the parents (A'). In B-B', the Jews question (B) and the parents answer (B') regarding two issues: "Is this your son?"; "How then does he now see?" **II14**. Parallel, ab-a'b': two groups of questions (a and b) and their related answers (a' and b') are presented in pairs: regarding who the blind man is (a and a') and regarding how he is healed (b and b'). His parents reply positively to the first question and negatively to the second one. **II15**. Parallel, ab-a'b': regarding the blind man's identity, two types of questions (a and b) and answers (a' and b') are shown, whether or not that he was their son (a and a') and also that he was born blind (b and b').

II16. Chiastic, ab-b'a': their attitudes of answering in a ("We know") and a' ("we don't know") are contrasted, while b (who the blind man is) and b' ("how he now sees") are two issues raised by the Jews. **II17**. Parallel, ab-a'b': in both a and a' ("we don't know"),[4] the parents emphasize their ignorance on two issues in a ("how he now sees") and a' ("who opened his eyes"). **II18**. Chiastic, a-x-a': the parents' request that they should ask his son directly appear both in a and a', while, in x, their inner motive for making this request, the fear of the Jews, is explained. **II19**. Chiastic, ab-b'a': the same expressions are duplicated: a and a' (αὐτὸν ἐρωτήσατε), and b and b' (ἡλικίαν ἔχει).

II13 compares his parents who fear the Jews with the Jews who disregard the facts. In II14, two questions, who he is and how he is healed, are in focus. The focus of II15 is limited to the first question regarding who he is, while that of II17 is to the second one regarding how he is healed. In I16, two answers are given by his parents. II18 discloses the real motive of the parents who answer the questions. II19 emphasizes that their son is grown up.

---

4. According to Keener, "That their words in 9:20 begin with οἴδαμεν and end with οἴδαμεν in 9:21 suggests deliberate wording...; the repetition of the term at the end of two successive clauses in 9:21 also suggests *antistrophe*, also called *epiphora*." Keener, *Gospel of John*, 788.

"I Am the Light of the World," II

V	13						Text	Translation
18	A						Οὐκ ἐπίστευσαν οὖν οἱ Ἰουδαῖοι περὶ αὐτοῦ ὅτι ἦν τυφλὸς καὶ ἀνέβλεψεν ἕως ὅτου ἐφώνησαν τοὺς γονεῖς αὐτοῦ τοῦ ἀναβλέψαντος	But the Jews did not believe that he had been blind and had received his sight, until they called the parents of the man who had received his sight,
			14					
19	B	a	15				καὶ ἠρώτησαν αὐτοὺς λέγοντες·	and asked them, saying,
-	-	-	a				οὗτός ἐστιν ὁ υἱὸς ὑμῶν,	"Is this your son,
-	-	-	b				ὃν ὑμεῖς λέγετε ὅτι τυφλὸς ἐγεννήθη;	who you say was born blind?
-	-	b					πῶς οὖν βλέπει ἄρτι;	How then does he now see?"
20	B'	a'					ἀπεκρίθησαν οὖν οἱ γονεῖς αὐτοῦ καὶ εἶπαν·	His parents answered them and said,
			16					
-	-	-	a				οἴδαμεν	"We know
-	-	-	a'	b			ὅτι οὗτός ἐστιν ὁ υἱὸς ἡμῶν,	that this is our son,
-	-	-	b'	-	17		καὶ ὅτι τυφλὸς ἐγεννήθη·	and that he was born blind.
21	-	b'		b'		a	πῶς δὲ νῦν βλέπει	But how he now sees,
-	-	-		a'		b	οὐκ οἴδαμεν,	we don't know,
-	-	-		a'			ἢ τίς ἤνοιξεν αὐτοῦ τοὺς ὀφθαλμοὺς	or who opened his eyes,
-	-	-	18	19		b'	ἡμεῖς οὐκ οἴδαμεν·	we don't know.
-	-	a		a			αὐτὸν ἐρωτήσατε,	Ask him;
-	-	-		b			ἡλικίαν ἔχει,	he is of age,
-	-	-					αὐτὸς περὶ ἑαυτοῦ λαλήσει.	he will speak for himself."
22	A'	x					ταῦτα εἶπαν οἱ γονεῖς αὐτοῦ ὅτι ἐφοβοῦντο τοὺς Ἰουδαίους· ἤδη γὰρ συνετέθειντο οἱ Ἰουδαῖοι ἵνα ἐάν τις αὐτὸν ὁμολογήσῃ χριστόν, ἀποσυνάγωγος γένηται.	His parents said this because they feared the Jews, for the Jews had already agreed that if anyone should confess him to be Christ, he was to be put out of the synagogue.
23	-	a'					διὰ τοῦτο οἱ γονεῖς αὐτοῦ εἶπαν	For this reason his parents said,
-	-	-	b'				ὅτι ἡλικίαν ἔχει,	"He is of age,
-	-	-	a'				αὐτὸν ἐπερωτήσατε.	ask him."

B'2. A Sinner, or From God? (9:24–34)

In vv. 24–34, we can see one comprehensive chiastic structure (II20) with seventeen parallels: seven parallelisms (II21–22, 27, 30–31, 33, and 35), six chiasms (II23, 28–29, 34, and 36–37), and four duals (II24–26 and 32). B-B' of II20 (24b–33) contain the story of interrogation in well-designed parallelism, II21. The former parts of II21, A-B-C (24b–28), demonstrate their own parallels such as II22–23 in A, II24–25 in B, II26–27 in C. II24–26 are the three consecutive dual type of expressions. On the other hand, the latter parts of II21, A'-B'-C' (29–33), show a different phenomenon in providing parallels. There are some interrelated, mixed parallels between constituents such as II33–34, particularly between A' and B'. And there are also some parallels such

Sourcebook of the Structures and Styles in John 1–10

as II29–30 in A', II35–36 in B'. The reason for this phenomenon is probably caused by the intense cohesion among A'-B'-C', as appearing clearly in II28.

II20. Chiastic, AB-B'A': In A (24a), the man who had been blind is called again and the second questioning begins, while in A' (34), matching A, the Jews make a final judgment, casting him out, that all the questionings may be completed. (They said, "Give glory to God" in A, but ironically they themselves refute his glory by choosing the evil side, casting-him-out, in A'.) In the B-B' (24b–33), interrogation and disputation between the Jews and the man are written mostly regarding the identity of Jesus. See II21.

V	20				Text	Translation
24	A				Ἐφώνησαν οὖν τὸν ἄνθρωπον ἐκ δευτέρου ὃς ἦν τυφλὸς καὶ εἶπαν αὐτῷ· δὸς δόξαν τῷ θεῷ·	So a second time they called the man who had been blind, and said to him, "Give glory to God.
		21	22			
	B	A	a		ἡμεῖς οἴδαμεν	We know
	-	-	b	23	ὅτι οὗτος ὁ ἄνθρωπος ἁμαρτωλός ἐστιν.	that this man is a sinner."
25	-	-	a		ἀπεκρίθη οὖν ἐκεῖνος· εἰ ἁμαρτωλός ἐστιν	He answered, "Whether He is a sinner or not,
	-	-	b		οὐκ οἶδα·	I don't know;
	-	-	a'	b'	ἓν οἶδα	one thing I know,
	-	-	b'	a'	ὅτι τυφλὸς ὢν ἄρτι βλέπω.	that, whereas I was blind, now I see."
26	-	B		24	εἶπον οὖν αὐτῷ·	Then they said him,
	-	-	a		τί ἐποίησέν σοι;	"What did he do to you?
	-	-	a'		πῶς ἤνοιξέν σου τοὺς ὀφθαλμούς;	How did he open your eyes?"
27	-	-	25		ἀπεκρίθη αὐτοῖς·	He answered them,
	-	-	a		εἶπον ὑμῖν ἤδη	"I have told you already,
	-	-	a'	26	καὶ οὐκ ἠκούσατε·	and you did not listen.
	-	C	a		τί πάλιν θέλετε ἀκούειν;	Why do you want to hear it again?
	-	-	a'		μὴ καὶ ὑμεῖς θέλετε αὐτοῦ μαθηταὶ γενέσθαι;	You don't want to be his disciples, do you?"
28	-	-		27	καὶ ἐλοιδόρησαν αὐτὸν καὶ εἶπον·	And they reviled him, and said,
	-	-		a	σὺ	"You
	-	-		b	μαθητὴς εἶ ἐκείνου,	are his disciple,
	-	-		a'	ἡμεῖς δὲ	but we
	-	-		b'	τοῦ Μωϋσέως ἐσμὲν μαθηταί·	are disciples of Moses.

II21. Parallel, ABC-A'B'C': Both A (24b–25) and A' (29–30) focus on certain knowledge in relation to the identity of Jesus, namely whether he is a sinner (A) and where he is from (A'). A and A' share the personal testimony of the man who was blind about healing: "… now I see" (A), "… yet he opened my eyes" (A'). In B (26–27a) and B' (31–32), their dialogue is finished about the issue of what happened, particularly how he did it (B) and how he could do it (B'). These B and B' contain the same "hearing/listening" motif. In C (27b–28) and C' (33), the controversy and conflict between the

Jews and the man is raised highly regarding the issues: "whose disciples are we?" (C); "Jesus is certainly from God." (C'), showing their inner, hidden testimony, actually and finally. The man discloses himself as a genuine disciple of Jesus by this testimony.

II22. Parallel, ab-a'b': Both the Jews and the formerly blind man claim their knowledge (a, "We know"; a', "one thing I know") regarding who Jesus is (b, "a sinner") and what happened to the man (b', "now I see"), respectively, indeed contrasting their knowledge, namely true or false, regarding what really happened to the man. **II23**. Chiastic, ab-b'a': The man admits one thing (a, regarding "being a sinner") he does not know (b) but he insists the other thing (a', regarding "now seeing") he does know (b'). **II24**. Dual, a-a': The Jews questioned the man with two (dual) questions (a and a') in relation to the healing miracle of Jesus on the Sabbath: what he did (a) and how he opened the eyes (a').

II25. Dual, a-a': The man who was blind also replies with two (dual) answers (a and a'), reminding them of what he had already said to them (a) but they did not listen (a'). **II26**. Dual, a-a': The man raises conversely two (dual) questions with the Jews (a and a'), criticizing them for their wrong attitude regarding the questioning. **II27**. Parallel, ab-a'b': This discloses whose disciples "you" (a) or "we" (a') are in contrast: the disciple of Jesus (b) or disciples of Moses (b').

II20–21 focus mainly on two issues: whether Jesus is from God or a sinner, contrasting the man who is healed and knows something and the Jews in ignorance. II22 divulges the contrast between what they know vs. what the man knows. In II23, what he does not know and what he does know are compared. II24 focuses on what he did and how he did it. II25 focuses on telling and not-listening in contrast. II26 focuses on two reactive criticisms by the man. In II27, there is the contrast between "you" and "we" regarding of whom they are disciples.

II28. Chiastic, a-x-a': Both a (29–30) and a' (33) focus on the same issue of where Jesus is from, while the center x focuses on the issue regarding to whom God listens and how Jesus did such a miracle. **II29**. Chiastic, a-x-a': "we" claims that "we" know much (a), but they are actually criticized due to their ignorance (a'), and in the center x ("this is marvellous"), the man doubts their claim regarding their knowledge. **II30**. Parallel, ab-a'b': The Jews in boastfulness contrast their "knowing" (a) regarding Moses (b) to their "unknowing" (a') regarding Jesus (b'). **II31**. Parallel, ab-a'b': The Jews admit their ignorance (a, "we don't know") of the origin of Jesus (b, "where he is from") and also the man who was blind identically indicates their ignorance (a', "for you don't know") on the origin of Jesus (b', "where he is from").

Sourcebook of the Structures and Styles in John 1–10

V	20	21	28	29	30			Text	Translation
29	B'	A'	a	a	a			ἡμεῖς οἴδαμεν	We know
	-	-	-	-	b			ὅτι Μωϋσεῖ λελάληκεν ὁ θεός,	that God spoke to Moses,
	-	-	-	-	31			τοῦτον δὲ	but as for this man,
	-	-	-	-	a'	a		οὐκ οἴδαμεν	we don't know
	-	-	-	-	b'	b		πόθεν ἐστίν.	where he is from."
30	-	-	-	x				ἀπεκρίθη ὁ ἄνθρωπος καὶ εἶπεν αὐτοῖς· ἐν τούτῳ γὰρ τὸ θαυμαστόν ἐστιν,	The man answered and said to them, "This is marvelous,
						32	33		
	-	-	-	a'	a'	a	a	ὅτι ὑμεῖς οὐκ οἴδατε	for you don't know
	-	-	-	-	34	b'	-	b	πόθεν ἐστίν,	where he is from,
	-	-	-	-	a	a'	-	καὶ ἤνοιξέν μου τοὺς ὀφθαλμούς.	and yet he opened my eyes.
31	-	B'	x	b	35		a'	οἴδαμεν	We know
	-	-	-	-	a		b'	ὅτι ἁμαρτωλῶν	that ~ to sinners,
	-	-	-	-	b	36	-	ὁ θεὸς οὐκ ἀκούει,	God does not listen ~
	-	-	-	-	a'	a		ἀλλ' ἐάν τις θεοσεβὴς ᾖ καὶ τὸ θέλημα αὐτοῦ ποιῇ	but if anyone is a God-fearer and does his will,
	-	-	-	-	-	b		τούτου	~ to him.
	-	-	-	-	b'	-		ἀκούει.	He listens ~
32	-	-	-	x		b'		ἐκ τοῦ αἰῶνος οὐκ ἠκούσθη	Never since the beginning of time has it been heard
	-	-	-	-		a'		ὅτι ἠνέῳξέν τις ὀφθαλμοὺς τυφλοῦ γεγεννημένου·	that anyone opened the eyes of a person born blind.
33	-	C'	a	b'				εἰ μὴ ἦν οὗτος παρὰ θεοῦ,	If this man were not from God,
	-	-	-	a'				οὐκ ἠδύνατο ποιεῖν οὐδέν.	he could do nothing."
34	A'		37					ἀπεκρίθησαν καὶ εἶπαν αὐτῷ·	They answered and said to him,
	-		a					ἐν ἁμαρτίαις σὺ ἐγεννήθης ὅλος	"You were born entirely in sins,
	-		x					καὶ σὺ διδάσκεις ἡμᾶς;	and are you teaching us?"
	-		a'					καὶ ἐξέβαλον αὐτὸν ἔξω.	And they cast him out.

II32. Dual, a-a': The formerly blind man indicates two facts regarding their ignorance (a) and the fact that had happened indeed to him (a'). **II33**. Parallel, ab-a'b': The man contrasts two different facts: their ignorance (a) and his knowledge (a') regarding who really could do this healing miracle in intimacy with God (b and b'). **II34**. Chiastic, ab-x-b'a': Both a ("and yet he opened my eyes") and a' ("he could do nothing") are related in terms of the healing miracle of Jesus, while both b (God listens to the God-fearer who does his will), regarding to whom God listens, and b' ("If this man were not from God") show the intimate relationship between God and Jesus, the man to whom God listens, while x emphatically indicates the fact that no one has heard of a miracle like this since the beginning of the world. The pair a-b is positively described, while the pair a'-b' is negatively done.

II35. Parallel, ab-a'b': In this parallel, those whom God does not listen to (a-b, sinners) and those whom God does listen to (a'-b', a God-fearer and doer of his will) are contrasted. II36. Chiastic, ab-b'a': In this, a ("but if anyone is a God-fearer and does his will)" is related to a' that describes the miracle of opening the eyes, while both b ("He listens to him") and b' ("Never since the beginning of time has it been heard") are in common dealing with the "hearing" issue (ἀκούει - ἠκούσθη). II37. Chiastic, a-x-a': In a-a', the Jews' determined condemnation and judgment on the man who is healed and defends Jesus are introduced: "You were born entirely in sins" (a, condemnation) and "And they cast him out" (a', judgment). In x, they reject any testimony from him: "and are you teaching us?"

Their foci are: where Jesus is from and to whom God listens (II28); their claim of knowledge vs. the lack of knowledge (II29); their ignorance of the origin of Jesus (II30–31); their ignorance vs. what really happened (II32); their ignorance vs. his knowledge (II33); Jesus to whom God listens and who does his will (II34); to whom God listens (II35); who the person to whom God listens is and who can perform the miracle from God (II36); their condemnation of the man who is healed (II37).

III (A'). Healing the Spiritual Blindness (9:35–41)

A'2. Opening the Spiritual Eyes (9:35–38)

In vv. 35–38, there are four parallels: one overarching chiasm (III1) with one chiasm (III2), one parallelism (III3), and one dual (III4). III3 functions to sustain the interconnection among the constituents of III1, while III2 and 4 belong to the parts.

V	1	2		Phrases	Translation
35	A	a		Ἤκουσεν Ἰησοῦς	Jesus heard
-		b		ὅτι ἐξέβαλον αὐτὸν ἔξω	that they had cast him out,
-		b'		καὶ εὑρὼν αὐτὸν	and having found him,
-		a'	3	εἶπεν·	he said,
-		-	a	σὺ πιστεύεις εἰς τὸν υἱὸν τοῦ ἀνθρώπου;	"Do you believe in the Son of man?"
36	B			ἀπεκρίθη ἐκεῖνος καὶ εἶπεν·	He answered,
-		b		καὶ τίς ἐστιν, κύριε,	"And who is he, sir,
-		a'		ἵνα πιστεύσω εἰς αὐτόν;	that I may believe in him?"
37	B'		4	εἶπεν αὐτῷ ὁ Ἰησοῦς·	Jesus said to him,
-		b'	a	καὶ ἑώρακας αὐτὸν	"You have seen him,
-		-	a'	καὶ ὁ λαλῶν μετὰ σοῦ ἐκεῖνός ἐστιν.	and he is the one speaking with you."
38	A'			ὁ δὲ ἔφη·	And he said,
-		a''		πιστεύω, κύριε·	"Lord, I believe,"
-		b''		καὶ προσεκύνησεν αὐτῷ.	and he worshiped him.

III1. Chiastic, AB-B'A': In A-A', Jesus says, "Do you believe in the Son of man?" (A), and he finally responds, "Lord, I believe, and he worshiped him" (A'). In the middle of dialogue, B-B', the identity of Jesus as the object of belief is highlighted: "who is he?" (B) and "he is the one speaking with you" (B'). **III2**. Parallel, ab-a'b': In b-b', the Jews cast him out (b) but Jesus finds him (b'). Their actions are contrasted. In a-a', Jesus heard about him (a) and says to him (a').

III3. Parallel, ab-a'b'-a"b": All the a-a'-a" are related, focusing on the issue of belief: "Do you believe in the Son of Man?" (a); "that I may believe in him?" (a'); "Lord, I believe" (a"). All the b-b'-b" are related to the issue of identity of Jesus: "who is he, sir" (b); "... he is the one speaking with you" (b'); "he worshiped him" (b"). **III4**. Dual, a-a': Jesus says to the man about himself in a duplicated way: "You have seen him" (a); "he is the one speaking with you" (a').

In III1, the focus is on his belief in Jesus responding to Jesus' word. III2 contrasts the Jews who cast him out to Jesus who finds him and says something. In III3, there is the man's belief and the identity of Jesus. III4 focuses on Jesus in front of the man.

A'1. Who Are the Sinners? (9:39–41)

In vv. 39–41, there are one chiasm (III5), two parallelisms (III7–8), and one dual (III6), among which III5 is comprehensive, while II6–8 are partial in function, belonging to parts of III5.

V	5			Phrases	Translation
39	A	6		Καὶ εἶπεν ὁ Ἰησοῦς·	And Jesus said,
-		a	7	εἰς κρίμα ἐγὼ εἰς τὸν κόσμον τοῦτον ἦλθον,	"For judgment I came into this world,
-		a'	a	ἵνα οἱ μὴ βλέποντες	that those who do not see
-		-	b	βλέπωσιν	may see,
-		-	a'	καὶ οἱ βλέποντες	and that those who see
-		-	b'	τυφλοὶ γένωνται.	may become blind."
40	X			ἤκουσαν ἐκ τῶν Φαρισαίων ταῦτα οἱ μετ' αὐτοῦ ὄντες καὶ εἶπον αὐτῷ·	Some of Pharisees who were with him heard these things, and said to him,
-				μὴ καὶ ἡμεῖς τυφλοί ἐσμεν;	"We are not blind too, are we?"
41	A'		8	εἶπεν αὐτοῖς ὁ Ἰησοῦς·	Jesus said to them,
-			a	εἰ τυφλοὶ ἦτε,	"If you were blind,
-			b	οὐκ ἂν εἴχετε ἁμαρτίαν·	you would have no sin,
-			a'	νῦν δὲ λέγετε ὅτι βλέπομεν,	but now because you say, 'We see,'
-			b'	ἡ ἁμαρτία ὑμῶν μένει.	your sin remains."

III5. Chiastic, A-X-A': In A-A', two contrastive pairs with similar contents are presented: "that those who do not see may see and that those who see may become blind" (A); "If you were blind, you would have no sin, but now because you say, 'We

see,' your sin remains." (A'). In these sentences, those who are blind are blessed but those who believe that they see are miserable. In the center X, some Pharisees respond to Jesus, whether they are blind or not. III6. Dual, a-a': In a, there is Jesus' declaration of judgement as his purpose in coming, and, in a', the content of judgment is present.

III7. Parallel, ab-a'b': Syntactically, contrasted phrases are presented: ἵνα οἱ μὴ βλέποντες (that those who do not see, a) and καὶ οἱ βλέποντες (and that those who see, a'); βλέπωσιν (may see, b) and τυφλοὶ γένωνται (may become blind, b'). **III8**. Parallel, ab-a'b': Similarly in pattern, but contrasted in contents, two sentences are provided: εἰ τυφλοὶ ἦτε (If you were blind, a) and νῦν δὲ λέγετε ὅτι βλέπομεν (but now because you say, "We see," a'); οὐκ ἂν εἴχετε ἁμαρτίαν (you would have no sin, b) and ἡ ἁμαρτία ὑμῶν μένει (your sin remains, b').

III5 and 7 contrast those who do not see with those who do see. In III6, two things regarding judgment are suggested: his purpose in coming and the content of judgment. III8 focuses on the relation between seeing and having sin.

Reading in Structure-Style[5]

1. Considering vv. 1–3 (A1) and 4–7 (A2), we can deduce the contrast between Jesus and his disciples in relation to their interests. Jesus is concerned for the man and the work of God but they show their interest in the sin, whose sin is the cause of his blindness.

2. Comparing the original scene of healing (6–7) with the verbal description of the man who is healed (11; see I11), it is observed that one (or two) actions of Jesus, spitting on the ground, is not referred to in the latter. The man who was healed does not refer to this action of Jesus, spitting and making clay of the spittle, probably due to two reasons: (1) because he did not see this action before he came back seeing; (2) because he intentionally skipped this so as not to let Jesus be disturbed by referring to this action, prohibited on the Sabbath at that time.

3. The first interrogation section (13–17, B2) focuses on four issues: (1) the controversy over the identity of Jesus whether he is "a sinner" who broke the Sabbath; (2) the controversy over the origin of Jesus whether he is "from God" regarding his miracle of healing; (3) the unbelief of the Jews; (4) the confession by the man of Jesus as a prophet.

The last interrogation section (24–34, B'2) is deeply connected to the first one as follows: (1) the controversy over the identity of Jesus if he is "a sinner"; (2) the controversy

---

5. Any literary or linguistic style can affect its textual meaning, because meanings are generated both in contents (thematic messages) and form (stylistic expression). Kim, "1 John 2:29—3:10," 114. See Lee regarding "the form-content dynamic." She focuses on "literary form as both the conveyer and the expression of meaning." Lee, *Symbolic Narratives of the Fourth Gospel*, 33–34.

over the origin of Jesus whether he is "from God"; (3) the stubborn unbelief of the Jews; (4) the contrast between the disciple of Jesus versus the disciples of Moses.

4. In vv. 13–17, specifically in v. 16 (A' of II7), two antithetical issues regarding Jesus are raised: "Is he from God?," "Is he a sinner?" Interestingly, each issue is denied as follows: "he is not from God" and "he is not a sinner." These two issues, the origin of Jesus and the issue whether he is a sinner, recur in the last interrogation (24–34), more in detail, such as the sinner issue (24b–25; A of II21) and the origin one (29–30; A' of II21). But, this time, the sinner issue comes first and the origin one follows. The order of appearance is reversed, comparing them with those in v. 16 in which these two issues are initially raised.

5. The question raised by the Jews in vv. 26–27a (B of II21), "How did he do this to you? How did he open your eyes?" is replied in its parallel verses, vv. 31–32 (B' of II21), by the man who was healed, who implies, by saying, that Jesus could open the eyes because God listens to him who does his will.

6. Considering the connection between vv. 27b–28 (C of II21) and 33 (C'), we may read the contrast between, in vv. 27b–28, the Jews boast of being the disciples of Moses and, in v. 33, the man who is healed confesses that Jesus is from God, declaring indeed that he is a disciple of Jesus. Whose disciples should we be? It is a contrast.

7. In vv. 24b–28 (A-B-C of II21), the Jews seem to have won over the man who was blind, while, in vv. 29–33 (A'-B'-C'), the man takes the lead in the dialogue between the Jews and himself. In the latter (29–33), not only the origin issue but also the issue of whether Jesus is a sinner or not are clearly answered by the man who was once blind: Jesus cannot be a sinner to whom God does not listen but is instead the one from God, to whom God listen.

8. The attitude of the Jews in v. 24a (A of II20), speaking of the glory of God, is in contrast with their stubborn action casting the man of confession in v. 34 (A' of II20), out of their community.

9. Two questions raised by the Jews in v. 18, "Had he been really blind?" "How did he receive his sight?" The following verses, vv. 19–23, responses to these two questions are provided regarding these two issues, sequentially or one by one: "this is our son . . . he was born blind" and "how he now sees, we don't know . . . ask him".

In particular, if we consider the parallel relation between v. 18 (A of II13) and vv. 22–23 (A' of II13), the similarity in character between the Jews regarding their unbelief and the parents regarding their fear or cowardice[6] is observed here.

---

6. The issue of exclusion from the synagogue in vv. 22, 34 is not considered here. For a discussion of this matter, see Talbert, *Reading John*, 161–62.

10. As a whole, the Jews are contrasted with the man who was blind in B2 (13–17) and B'2 (24–34). The Jews boasting in their status as the disciples of Moses show their strong unbelief of Jesus and their disregard of the miracle of healing, while the man who was blind demonstrates his simple belief in Jesus, publicly confessing himself as an authentic disciple of Jesus.[7]

The parents are also compared with their son regarding of whom they are afraid: the Jews or God. Although the parents seem to be unlike the Jews who show their radical unbelief of Jesus, it is true that they stand on the opposite side to the truth.

In other words, while the Jews and the parents are compared in similarity, the man and the Jews or the man and the parents are contrasted in dissimilarity. The passage highlights the stubborn unbelief of the Jews, the cowardice of the parents, and the bold confession of the man who was blind, as a real disciple of Jesus, respectively.

11. Considering the pair of A2 (4–7) and A'2 (35–38), we come to know the deep concern of Jesus for the man, both physically and spiritually. The Jews including those who had seen him before and even his parents do not show their concern for him enough to be healed and helped. Their interests lie in their tradition, regulations, curiosities, fear of the Jews, and so on. But Jesus initiates his love toward the man who was blind by granting him sight and also finalizes it by enlightening his spiritual sight and thus providing his salvation at last. This is the work of God which Jesus performed as the light of the world.

12. Considering the pair of A1 (1–3) and A'1 (39–41), we may see the sin issue shared in these units. In A1, the issue, whose sin is the cause of the blindness, is focused on, but, in A'1, we can see who the sinner is indeed in relation to this blindness issue. The focus of issue shifts: from "who sinned regarding the physical blindness" to "who the sinner is, regardless of physical eyes."

Issues in Structure-Style

1. The Source Theory

Bultmann insists that this chapter was written with numerous embellishments by the evangelist in vv. 4–5, 22–23, 29–30, and vv. 39–41, and also that "additional later editorial indications" exist in vv. 16–18 and vv. 35–38.[8]

Modifying Bultmann's source theory, Haenchen simply thinks that "an artfully constructed source is reproduced virtually without editorial insertion; only verses

---

7. The article of Parsons is interesting in that it discloses the man born blind to be "a Johannine Model Disciple," highlighting *ego eimi* in 9:9. Parsons, "Neglected *EGO EIMI* Saying," 145–80.

8. Bultmann, *Gospel of John*, 329; Borchert, *John 1–11*, 310. Regarding Bultmann's contribution to the study of John, see Macrae, "Theology and Irony," 103.

4f. stem from the Evangelist, and he has probably added verses 39–41."[9] Although Haenchen does not determine a specific range of sources in the story, differing from Bultmann, we may say that he assumes the source theory that the evangelist took over a detailed written source, entirely depending on it in the process of writing the story of John 9.

Brown insisted that some significant features in John, that reflect "the Johannine theological interests" are hard to find in the Synoptic Gospels, such as "blind from birth; use of mud; healing through the water of Siloam; interrogation about the miracle; questioning of parents."[10] And then he moves to conclude that "therefore one is hard put to prove scientifically that they were not invented for the sake of pedagogy."[11]

First, Borchert critically evaluates this source theory, sternly considering it as a theory based on "extremely subjective presuppositions," and believing that this theory "reduces the unique skills of the great evangelist to the role of a mere editor."[12] Barrett also points out[13] that "The cure of the blind man has no precise parallel in the Synoptic Gospels. . . . There is no need to suppose it was invented as a whole; it was probably drawn from the still-flowing stream of tradition."

Second, considering II18, the chiastic relation between vv. 21b–23 (a-x-a'), we cannot find any reason that vv. 22–23 differ from other passages in John, against the Bultmann who claimed that only these verses, like few other verses such as vv. 4–5, 29–30, and 39–41, are genuinely from the evangelist.

Third, in vv. 29–30, we can also see a Johannine pattern of chiasm, II29 (a-x-a'), that coherently matches the other parts. II30–31 in these two verses are typical of Johannine styles in parallelism. In particular, vv. 29–30 are one essential part consisting of II21 (ABC-A'B'C'), inseparable from the cluster of vv. 24b–33.

Fourth, in relation to vv. 4–5,[14] we may detect a Johannine chiasm (I6): A (4, Jesus says that we have to do the work of God); X (5, Jesus says that I am the light of

---

9. Haenchen, *John 2*, 41. Differently, Painter regards v. 39 as "a summary conclusion following the dialogues," while vv. 40–41 are considered as a later addition of the evangelist. Painter, *Quest for the Messiah*, 317. But we may say that he does not succeed in properly seeing the Johannine parallel way of writing that combines vv. 39–41 as a unit. See the following paragraphs of mine, specifically no. 4.

10. Brown, *Gospel according to John I–XII*, 378.

11. Ibid., 378–79.

12. Borchert, *John 1–11*, 311. See also Carson, *Gospel according to John*, 360–61; Bauckham, "Audience of the Fourth Gospel," 103–6; cited in Köstenberger, *John*, 277.

13. Barrett, *Gospel according to St. John*, 354. He adds, "To say that vv. 8–41 must be a dramatic expansion because miracle stories are interested only in the healer and not in the healed (Martyn, 5) overstates the matter," and also, "John's insight into the theological significance of the earlier tradition is the most important single factor in the shaping of this chapter, and, unlike other kinds of analysis, hardly a matter of conjecture." Barrett, *Gospel according to St. John*, 355. See also Carson's criticism of Martyn and Haenchen. Carson, *Gospel according to St. John*, 359–61.

14. See also a smaller chiasm within v. 4 (I7, ab-b'a').

the world); A' (6–7, Jesus does the work of God, healing the blind man). Moreover, as previously observed, scene 2 including vv. 4–5 is matched to scene 7 as a parallel.

Fifth, vv. 39–41, a counterpart in the chiasm of scene 1, vv. 1–3, show their Johannine way of arrangement, namely a chiasm (III5): A (39, Jesus says that I came into the world to judge); X (40, Some Pharisees say "Are we also blind?"); A' (41, Jesus says that your sin remains regarding their blindness). In A (39) and A' (41), the issue of seeing and not-seeing is shared in contrast. These styles[15] reflect a typical Johannine phenomenon of parallelism or chiasm as do any other passages in John 9.

Sixth, for what proof can be given to regard vv. 16–18 and vv. 35–38 as the verses in which the later additional indications exist, as Bultmann insists[16]? We can prove that these verses also reflect typical Johannine styles within and in relation to them: see II7, 10–13, and III1–4.

Seventh, observing the consistency in presenting Johannine parallel styles throughout John 9, particularly in relation to the sampling data from the analysis of details in vv. 13–34, we may conclude that the healing story was written by one author, the evangelist, consistently and coherently. We cannot arbitrarily determine which part is from the source and which one belongs to the evangelist. Of course, we may not prove at all that the story was not invented by the evangelist, but we can also say that no one can prove that the story was invented by him, entirely or partially. The story of John 9 can only show that it was written in typical Johannine ways of style and structures.

2. The Structure of the Chapter

Painter describes that "only two characters/groups appear on "the state" at any given time, heightening the dramatic effect and, in these dialogues, emphasizing the force of the conflicts."[17] Resseguie moves one step further: "The imagery, the structure, the movement of the plot, and the characterisation work together to form a unified whole."[18] In the literary sense, making an attempt to show how the form and content of John 9 form a unity, he suggests seven scenes: scene 1 (vv. 1–7), scene 2 (vv. 8–12), scene 3 (vv. 13–17), scene 4 (vv. 18–23), scene 5 (vv. 24–34), scene 6 (vv. 35–38), and scene 7 (vv. 39–41).[19]

---

15. Two more, but smaller parallelisms are found within v. 39 (III7, ab-a'b') and v. 41 (III8, ab-a'b').
16. Bultmann, *Gospel of John*, 329.
17. Painter, *Quest for the Messiah*, 313.
18. Resseguie, "John 9," 120.
19. Ibid., 115–22. See also Resseguie, *Strange Gospel*, 139–44. Depending on Martyn, who saw the chapter as a drama, Beasley-Murray also divides the chapter into seven sections: vv. 1–7, 8–12, 13–17, 18–23, 24–34, 35–38, and 39–41, but under a different category or name. Beasley-Murray, *John*, 152. See also Martyn, *History and Theology*, 30–36. Martyn here divides the chapter into the miracle story (vv. 1–7) and its expansion (vv. 8–41). Sloyan relies heavily on Martyn. Sloyan, *John*, 112–14.

Lee categorizes the healing story, somehow differing from Resseguie who simply arranges the scenes sequentially or linearly, into three acts and seven scenes:[20]

Act 1	*Healing of the Man and the Question of Judgment (9:1-7)*	
Scene 1:	Jesus and the disciples discuss the question of sin and judgment, introducing the basic polarities of the narrative: blindness/sight, darkness/light, vv. 1-5	a
Scene 2:	Jesus heals the blind man's sight, vv. 6-7	b
Act 2	*Interrogations and Escalating conflict (9:8-34)*	
Scene 1:	Questioning of the man by his neighbours, vv. 8-12	
Scene 2:	Questioning of the man by the Pharisees and the beginning of conflict, vv. 13-17	
Scene 3:	Hostile interrogation of the man's parents by the 'Jews', vv. 18-23	
Scene 4:	Hostile interrogation of the man by the Pharisees and rejection of him, vv. 24-34	
Act 3	*Illumination of the Man and Judgment on the 'Jews' (9:35-41)*	
Scene 1:	The man is given 'sight' by Jesus, vv. 35-38	b'
Scene 2:	Jesus and the Pharisees discuss sin and judgment, using the polarites of blindness/sight, darkness/light; they are condemned by Jesus and accused of sin, vv. 39-41	a'

First, it is great that Lee categorizes eight such scenes in detail and observes certain relations among the specific scenes. For example, she interrelatedly compares scene 1 (a, Jesus and the disciples discuss the question of sin and judgement, introducing the basic polarities of the narrative: blindness/sight, darkness/light) of act 1 with scene 2 (a', Jesus and the Pharisees discuss sin and judgment, using the polarities of blindness/sight, darkness/light . . .) of act 3; and scene 2 (b, Jesus heals the blind man's sight) of act 2 with scene 1 (b', The man is given "sight" by Jesus) of act 3. Her concern with their chiastic relations of those scenes is marvellous.

Second, however, what is missed in her model is that any specific relation among the four scenes in act 2 is not found, for her concern is put mostly on the "symbols" appearing in this chapter. In other words, we have to move beyond the linear sequence of scenes, searching for the interactive, parallel relations among the seven scenes and also among the three acts, particularly regarding the macro, overarching structure of scenes.

Third, if we find the relation between the first two scenes (1–3[5] and 4[6]–7) and the last ones (35–38 and 39–41), why can we not observe the relation among the four scenes (8–12; 13–17; 18–23; 24–34)? The former relation is chiastic (AB-B'A' or A1A2-A'2A'1), the latter is parallel (AB-A'B' or B1B2-B'1B'2). It is in a complex parallelism that two different types of parallels, such as parallelism and chiasm, appear

---

20. Lee, *Symbolic Narratives*, 165.

together, simultaneously and adroitly, that is, one typical Johannine type in the construction of sentences (including phrases) and paragraphs.

Fourth, as a whole, for the first two scenes match the last ones, they become A and A' (like an *inclusio*) and the four in the middle become X in the middle. Thus, the overall structure of this chapter is chiastic: A (1–7) – X (8–34) – A' (35–41). In A-A', the main figure is Jesus who converses with his disciples, the man who was blind, and the Jews, while, in X, the Jewish authorities are prioritized in figure in contrast to the man who was blind and also in comparison with his parents.

10 The Shepherd and the Sheep

"There is a voluminous scholarly literature of attempts to solve this Johannine mystery. This is perhaps why Raymond E. Brown once remarked that Johannine scholars often enjoy detective stories in their leisure time."[1]

"Lindars agrees with the analysis of J. A. T. Robinson that in verses 1–5 two originally distinct parables have been meshed (Lindars, 1972:354–355; Robinson, 1962:69). Barrett suggests that the passage contains numerous pieces which have been reworked by the evangelist (368). Dodd (1963:383) immortalized his analysis of the passage when he described it as 'the wreckage of two parables fused into one, the fusion having partly destroyed the original form of both.'"[2]

Chiastic Structure

AT A GLIMPSE, JOHN 10 may be divided into two sections: vv. 1–21 and 22–42, if we primarily consider the time and the place factors in v. 22, regarding vv. 19–21 as the concluding part of the previous discourse (1–18). However, there are other variants that we need to consider.

First, vv. 1–16 are made up of one united entity by itself as shown in I1 (ABCD-A'B'C'D'), although vv. 17–18 share the idea of laying down his life with the previous verses, particularly in vv. 11 and 15.

Second, rather, vv. 17–18 are regarded as an additional passage complementing the previous verses with a particular function such as a linker. The difference between vv. 1–16 and 17–18 is that the former focuses on the relationship between the shepherd, the sheep, thieves and robbers, the hireling, etc., while the latter mainly highlights that between the Father and the Son. Even though there is, in vv. 1–16, an implication regarding the relationship between the Father and the Son only in v. 15

---

1. Burge, *Interpreting the Gospel of John*, 58.
2. Kysar, "Johannine Metaphor," 84.

("as the Father knows me and I know the Father"), the focus in this verse and its aim is different from that in vv. 17–18, where Jesus says that his voluntary laying down his life leads into the love of the Father for the Son because of his obedience to his commandment.

Third, the theme in vv. 17–18 (laying down his life in relation to the Father) is connected to the next scene regarding the stoning issue (22–42), specifically v. 31, and also in predicting his suffering to come on the cross, which is expected to appear in the following chapters.

Fourth, in vv. 19–21, the controversy regarding the word and the act of Jesus is not only a direct result of the previous discourse of Jesus (1–18), but is also deeply connected to the following scene at the Feast of Dedication (22–42), where two contrastive responses toward Jesus are shown. Moreover, this type of conflict among the Jews may be regarded as a sort of summary in terms of the continuous response of the Jews in the previous chapters.

Fifth, thus, these two short clusters, vv. 17–18 and 19–21, play the role of linker in this chapter, as stepping stones, connecting the previous verses (1–16) and the following verses (22–42), that cannot stand alone by themselves, different from vv. 1–16 and 22–42 which are entities of clusters.

Sixth, vv. 22–42 need to be regarded as one united section, producing the combined chiastic structure, III1 (A1A2-B-B'-A'1A'2) as a whole. In this section, the shepherd theme in vv. 1–16 is still significant as in vv. 26–28.

Seventh, therefore, we may grasp the structure of John 10 as a chiastic one: A (1–16); B (17–18); B' (19–21); A' (22–42).

I.	The gate-shepherd discourse (10:1-16)		A
II.	Two linkers (10:17-21)		
	IIA.	The Father's commandment: Jesus' laying down his life (10:17-18)	B
	IIA'.	Two contradicting responses to Jesus (10:19-21)	B'
III.	At the Feast of Dedication (10:22-42)		A'

I. The Gate-Shepherd Discourse (10:1–16)

Parallel, I1 (ABCD-A'B'C'D')

First, vv. 1–16 consists of two clusters in the gate-shepherd cycle: vv. 1–6 and 7–16. The first signal to indicate the cycle is the well-known, emphatic sentence of Jesus ("Truly, truly, I say to you") in vv. 1a (A) and 7a (A').

Second, after this statement, the gate and the shepherd in theme are followed as in vv. 1b–5 and 7b–15. More specifically speaking, the gate issue appears first in vv. 1a–2 (B) and reappears in vv. 7–10 (B'). Similarly to this, the shepherd issue is first described in vv. 3–5 (C) and reissued in vv. 11–15 (C').

293

Third, each cluster is supported by its own cohesive structure generated for one entity: the first gate issue (1b–2, I3); the first shepherd issue (3–5, I4); the second gate issue (7b–10, I12); the second shepherd issue (11–15, I18).

Fourth, in the second part of the gate-shepherd cycle (11–15), each issue produces a twofold way of presentation regarding the identity of Jesus with ἐγώ εἰμι . . . (I am . . .) such as in vv. 7b and 9a; 11 and 14.

Fifth, in both last parts in cycle, vv. 6 and 16, the theme regarding misunderstanding is primary. In v. 6, his disciples do not understand what Jesus says. In v. 16, it would be difficult for the readers to understand what he is really talking about here, referring to "other sheep that he must bring" and "one flock and shepherd." In this sense, both verses describe misunderstanding.

Therefore, we may draw the parallel structure as follows:

A	Truly, truly, I say to you (10:1a)			
	B	The first gate issue (10:1b-2)		
		C	The first shepherd issue (10:3-5)	
			D	Misunderstanding 1 (10:6)
A'	Truly, truly, I say to you (10:7a)			
	B'	The second gate issue (10:7b-10)		
		C'	The second shepherd issue (10:11-15)	
			D'	Misunderstanding 2 (10:16)

ABCD. The First Cycle of the Gate-Shepherd Discourse (10:1–6)

Besides I1 that connects vv. 1–6 and 7–16, in vv. 1–6, there are ten parallels: four chiasms (I6–7 and 10–11), four parallels (I3–4 and 8–9), one dual (I2), and one combined parallelism (I5). Verses 1–2 have their inter-connection with vv. 7–10 as in I1 and 2. I3, a parallelism, shows the cohesion of B of I1, while I4 ties up the whole C (3–5) of I1. I4 contains at least six parallels (I5–10) as its embedded ones. Verse 6 (D of I1) contains its own chiasm, I11.

V	1	2		Phrases	Translations
1	A	a	3	Ἀμὴν ἀμὴν λέγω ὑμῖν,	Truly, truly, I say to you,
	B		a	ὁ μὴ εἰσερχόμενος διὰ τῆς θύρας εἰς τὴν αὐλὴν τῶν προβάτων ἀλλ' ἀναβαίνων ἀλλαχόθεν	he who does not enter the sheep pen by the gate but climbs in by another way,
	-		b	ἐκεῖνος κλέπτης ἐστὶν καὶ λῃστής·	that man is a thief and a robber.
2	-		a'	ὁ δὲ εἰσερχόμενος διὰ τῆς θύρας	But he who enters by the gate
	-		b'	ποιμήν ἐστιν τῶν προβάτων.	is the shepherd of the sheep.

I2. Dual, a-a': The same, emphatic pattern of Jesus ("Truly, truly, I say to you") is repeated, emphasizing the truthfulness and sincerity of Jesus' words, probably signalling the recurrence of the interrelated contents that follows. **I3. Parallel, ab-a'b':** Each of a and a', b and b' are contrasted to each other, demonstrating the identity of two different kinds of men: he who does not enter by the gate (a) and he who enters by the gate (a'); a thief and a robber (b) and the shepherd (b').

V	1	4	5			Phrases	Translations
3	C	a	a1			τούτῳ	To him
-	-	-	a2			ὁ θυρωρὸς	the gatekeeper
-	-	-	b	7		ἀνοίγει	opens;
-	-	b	a'2		a	καὶ τὰ πρόβατα	and the sheep
-	-	-	a'1	-		τῆς φωνῆς αὐτοῦ	his voice
-	-	-	b'	6	-	ἀκούει	hear;
-	-	a'		a	b	καὶ τὰ ἴδια πρόβατα	and ~ his own sheep
-	-	-		b	-	φωνεῖ	~ he calls ~
-	-	-		x	-	κατ' ὄνομα	by name;
-	-	-		b'	c	καὶ ἐξάγει	and he leads ~ out.
-	-	-	8	a'	-	αὐτά.	~ them ~
4	-	-		a	c'	ὅταν τὰ ἴδια πάντα	When ~ all his own
-	-	-		b	-	ἐκβάλῃ,	~ he has brought out ~,
-	-	-		a'	b'	ἔμπροσθεν αὐτῶν	~ before them
-	-	-		b'	9	-	πορεύεται	he goes ~,
-	-	b'		a	a'	καὶ τὰ πρόβατα αὐτῷ ἀκολουθεῖ,	and the sheep follow him,
-	-	-		b	10	ὅτι οἴδασιν τὴν φωνὴν αὐτοῦ·	because they know his voice.
5	-	-		a'	a	ἀλλοτρίῳ δὲ	Then, a stranger
-	-	-		-	b	οὐ μὴ ἀκολουθήσουσιν,	they will not follow,
-	-	-		-	b'	ἀλλὰ φεύξονται	but will flee
-	-	-		-	a'	ἀπ' αὐτοῦ,	from them,
-	-	-		b'		ὅτι οὐκ οἴδασιν τῶν ἀλλοτρίων τὴν	because they do not know their voices.
-	-	-	11			φωνήν.	
6	D	a				Ταύτην τὴν παροιμίαν εἶπεν αὐτοῖς ὁ Ἰησοῦς,	Jesus used this figure of speech with them,
-	-	x				ἐκεῖνοι δὲ οὐκ ἔγνωσαν τίνα ἦν	but they did not understand what they are,
-	-	a'				ἃ ἐλάλει αὐτοῖς.	that he was saying to them.

I4. Parallel, ab-a'b': In this, a, which regards "the gatekeeper," is not exactly contrasted to a', that deals with the shepherd, but a and a' are, in a sense, compared with each other: the gatekeeper is not like the shepherd. Both of b and b' focus on the intimacy between the shepherd and the sheep. **I5. Combined parallel, a1a2-b-a'2a'1-b':** As a whole, this structure shows a parallel feature: a1a2 ("the gatekeeper ~ to him") and a'2a'1 ("and the sheep ~ his voice"); b ("opens") and b' ("hear"). But there are also chiastic elements between a1-a2-a'2-a'1: a1 ("To him") and a'1 ("his voice"); "a2 ("the gatekeeper") and a'2 ("and the sheep").

I6. Chiastic, ab-x-b'c': The chiastic connection among constituents is typical, showing the shepherd's personal intimacy and his affection for the sheep. Both a and a' refer to the sheep: "his own sheep" (a) and "them" (a'). Both b and b' indicate what the shepherd does to the sheep: "he calls" (b) and "he leads out" (b'). In the center (x), "by name" exists. **I7**. Chiastic, abc-c'b'a': In this, a (hearing) and a' (following) indicate the sheep's reactions responding to their shepherd's guidance in b (calling by name) and b' (going before them), respectively. In this, c and c' describe the shepherd's taking them out from the pen: leading them out (c, ἐξάγει) and bringing them out (c', ἐκβάλῃ).

I8. Parallel, ab-a'b': This simple parallelism rhythmically shows the shepherd's double action toward his sheep: ". . . all his own" (a) and "before them" (a'); "he has brought out" (b) and "he goes" (b'). **I9**. Parallel, ab-a'b': The contrasts between a (following) and a' (not following), b (knowing) and b' (not knowing) are clearly shown. **I10**. Chiastic, ab-b'a': In this, a (". . . a stranger") and a' ("from them") tell about the stranger, while b ("they will not follow") and b' ("but will flee") describe the similar actions of the sheep against him/them. **I11**. Chiastic, a-x-a': In this, a ("Jesus used this figure of speech with them) is similarly repeated in a' ("that he was saying to them"), while x ("but they did not understand what they are") indicates how they feel.

In I2, the word of Jesus (ἀμὴν ἀμὴν λέγω ὑμῖν) is repeated for emphasis. I3 contrasts the shepherd and thief-robbers regarding the gate. In I4, the comparison between the gatekeeper and the shepherd and the contrast between the shepherd and the stranger are shown. I5 focuses on the comparison between the gatekeeper and the shepherd. In I6, two actions of the shepherd are focused. In I7, what the shepherd does to his sheep and how they respond to the shepherd are emphasized. In I8 also like I6, two actions of the shepherd appear. I9 contrasts between following-knowing and not-following-not-knowing. I10 shows the actions of the sheep against the stranger. I11 focuses on the fact that they do not understand what Jesus is saying.

A'B'C'D'. The Second Cycle of the Gate-Shepherd Discourse (10:7–16)

In vv. 7–16, there are at least thirteen parallels: ten parallelisms (I12–13, 15–17, 19–23), two chiasms (I14, 24), and one combined parallelism (I18). It is interesting that most of them are parallelisms. I12, 18, and 24 are the main pillars that build up the structure of this cluster. I13–17 establish the cohesion of I12 as much as I19–23 do for I18.

The Shepherd and the Sheep

V	1	2				Phrases	Translations
7	A'	a'				Εἶπεν οὖν πάλιν ὁ Ἰησοῦς· ἀμὴν ἀμὴν λέγω ὑμῖν	Therefore Jesus said again, truly, truly, I say to you,
		12	13				
	B'	a	a			ὅτι ἐγώ εἰμι ἡ θύρα	I am the gate
	-	-	b	14		τῶν προβάτων.	of the sheep.
8	-	b	a			πάντες ὅσοι ἦλθον [πρὸ ἐμοῦ]	All who came [before me]
	-	-	b			κλέπται εἰσὶν καὶ λῃσταί,	are thieves and robbers;
	-	-	b'			ἀλλ' οὐκ ἤκουσαν αὐτῶν	but ~ did not listen to him.
	-	-	a'			τὰ πρόβατα.	~ the sheep ~
9	-	a'	a'	15		ἐγώ εἰμι ἡ θύρα·	I am the gate;
	-	-	b'	a	17	δι' ἐμοῦ ἐάν τις εἰσέλθῃ	if anyone enters through me,
	-	-	-	b	a	σωθήσεται	he will be saved,
	-	-	-	a'		καὶ εἰσελεύσεται καὶ ἐξελεύσεται	and will come in and go out,
	-	-	-	16	b'	b	καὶ νομὴν εὑρήσει.	and find pasture.
10	-	b'	a			ὁ κλέπτης οὐκ ἔρχεται	The thief comes
	-	-	b			εἰ μὴ ἵνα κλέψῃ καὶ θύσῃ καὶ ἀπολέσῃ·	only to steal and kill and destroy;
	-	-	a'			ἐγὼ ἦλθον	I have come
	-	-	b'	a'		ἵνα ζωὴν ἔχωσιν	that they may have life,
	-	-	-	b'		καὶ περισσὸν ἔχωσιν.	and have it abundantly.

I12. Parallel, ab-a'b': In this, a, the concept of the gate of the sheep ("the gate" plus "of the sheep"), is repeated in a' with some expanded explanation ("the gate" plus the reason why he is the gate of the sheep). Both b and b' deal with the "thief" theme: who thieves and robbers are (b) and what they do (b'). **I13.** Parallel, ab-a'b': In a-b, it is seen that a simple repetitive parallelism, emphasizing Christ's being the gate, or the gate of the sheep: "I am the gate." The phrase "of the sheep" (b) is expanded in explanation in terms of how he is the shepherd of the sheep regarding salvation and giving life in b'. **I14.** Chiastic, ab-b'a': Both a and a' are subjects (a, "all who came before me"; a', "the sheep"), while b and b' are verbal phrases, contrasted to each other, disclosing who they are.

I15. Parallel, ab-a'b': Both a and a' focus on coming-in and going-out through the gate, Christ, while b and b' indicate two results of those deeds: salvation (b) and finding pasture (b'). **I16.** Parallel, ab-a'b': Typical contrastive parallelism, emphasizing two different purposes of the comings of the thief and of Jesus Christ: to steal and kill and destroy (b) vs. to let them have life and have it abundantly (b'). **I17.** Parallel, ab-a'b': Both a and a' tell about salvation, while b and b' identically indicate certain abundant life after salvation: finding pasture (b) and having abundantly (b').

V	1	18				Phrases	Translations
11	C'	a				Ἐγώ εἰμι	I am
-	-	-	20		22	ὁ ποιμὴν ὁ καλός.	the good shepherd.
-	-	b1	19	a	a	ὁ ποιμὴν ὁ καλός	The good shepherd
-	-	-	a	b	-	τὴν ψυχὴν αὐτοῦ	~ his life
-	-	-	b	-	-	τίθησιν	lays down ~
-	-	-	c	-	21	ὑπὲρ τῶν προβάτων·	for the sheep.
12	-	b2	a'	a	b	ὁ μισθωτὸς καὶ οὐκ ὢν ποιμήν, οὗ οὐκ ἔστιν τὰ πρόβατα ἴδια,	The hireling is not the shepherd, and the sheep are not his possession.
-	-	-	b'	b	-	θεωρεῖ τὸν λύκον ἐρχόμενον καὶ ἀφίησιν τὰ πρόβατα καὶ φεύγει-	So when he sees the wolf coming, he leaves the sheep and flees;
-	-	-	a''		a'	καὶ ὁ λύκος	and the wolf
-	-	-	b''		-	ἁρπάζει αὐτὰ καὶ σκορπίζει-	snatches them and scatters them,
13	-	-		a'	b'	ὅτι μισθωτός ἐστιν	because he is a hireling
-	-	-		b'	-	καὶ οὐ μέλει αὐτῷ περὶ τῶν προβάτων.	and cares nothing for the sheep.
14	-	a'				Ἐγώ εἰμι	I am
-	-	-		23		ὁ ποιμὴν ὁ καλός	the good shepherd;
-	-	b'2		a		καὶ γινώσκω τὰ ἐμὰ	I know my own
-	-	-		b		καὶ γινώσκουσίν με τὰ ἐμά,	and my own know me,
15	-	-		a'		καθὼς γινώσκει με ὁ πατὴρ	as the Father knows me
-	-	-		b'		κἀγὼ γινώσκω τὸν πατέρα,	and I know the Father;
-	-	b'1	a'			καὶ τὴν ψυχήν μου	and ~ my life
-	-	-	b'			τίθημι	~ I lay down ~
-	-	-	c'	24		ὑπὲρ τῶν προβάτων.	for the sheep.
16	D'			a		καὶ ἄλλα πρόβατα ἔχω ἃ οὐκ ἔστιν ἐκ τῆς αὐλῆς ταύτης·	And I have other sheep that are not of this sheep pen;
-	-			b		κἀκεῖνα δεῖ με ἀγαγεῖν	I must bring them also,
-	-			b'		καὶ τῆς φωνῆς μου ἀκούσουσιν,	and they too will listen to my voice;
-	-			a'		καὶ γενήσονται μία ποίμνη, εἷς ποιμήν.	and there shall be one flock and shepherd.

I18. Combined parallel, a-b1b2-a'-b'2b'1: His being the good shepherd in a is duplicated in a'. Both b1 and b'1 contain the same content: his sacrificial spirit. And b2 and b'2 are contrasted: b2 shows the distant relationship between the hireling and the sheep, while b'2 shows the intimate relationship between the shepherd and his sheep. As a whole, it is a parallelism, but b1-b2-b2'-b1 is a chiasm.

I19. Parallel, abc-a'b'c': The similar, repetitive pattern in the same order is used, deliberately and intentionally: τὴν ψυχὴν αὐτοῦ (his life, a) and καὶ τὴν ψυχήν μου (and ~ my life, a'); τίθησιν (lays down, b) and τίθημι (I lay down, b'); ὑπὲρ τῶν προβάτων (for the sheep, c) and ὑπὲρ τῶν προβάτων (for the sheep, c'). I20. Parallel, ab-a'b'-a"b":

All as (a, a', and a") indicate three types of sheep-related beings in contrast: the good shepherd, the hireling, and the wolf. Bs (b, b', and b") reveal their deeds toward the sheep, also in contrast. **I21**. Parallel, ab-a'b': Both a and a' tell about the identity of the hireling, while b and b' indicate his careless, irresponsible actions to the sheep. Thus, a-a' is the reason for the actions of b-b'.

I22. Parallel, ab-a'b': In this, a and a' are contrasted: a demonstrates the sacrifice of the good shepherd, while a' shows the wolf's cruelty. Both b and b' deal with the hireling who is somehow contrasted to both the shepherd and the wolf. **I23**. Parallel, ab-a'b': The relationship between the shepherd and the sheep (knowing each other), a-b, is emphatically described, the same as the relationship between the Father and his Son (knowing each other), a'-b'. **I24**. Chiastic, ab-b'a': Both a and a' indicate other sheep that are not here but somewhere else. In b and b', Jesus, as their shepherd, tells of his relationship with that flock: Jesus brings them (b) and they listen to him (b').

Their foci are as follows: the gate of sheep vs. thieves-robbers (I12); Jesus is the gate of the sheep (I13); distant relationship between thieves-robbers and the sheep (I14); what are given through the gate of the sheep (I15); two contrastive results between the coming of the thief and that of Jesus (I16); salvation and abundant life (I17); two relationships between the hireling and the sheep and between the shepherd and his sheep (I18); double emphasis of laying down his life (I19); triple contrast among the shepherd, the hireling, and the wolf (I20 and 22); the irresponsibility of the hireling (I21); similarity of two relationships between the Father and the Son and between the shepherd and the sheep (I23); Jesus and other sheep that are not known (I24).

II. Two Linkers (10:17–21)

II1. Dual, A-A': As discussed earlier, vv. 17–18 and 19–21 share in their role as the link between the previous verses (1–16) and the following verses (22–42). In this sense, we may call them A (17–18) and A' (19–21). In A (17–18), the theme of laying down his life, which appeared already in vv. 11, 15, is re-instated in different way, particularly emphasizing the relation between the Father and the Son: the Father loves him and gives him the commandment to lay down his life. In A' (19–21), the controversy regarding the word and the act of Jesus comes as the direct result of the discourse of Jesus (1–18) and also reappears in the following scene at the Feast of Dedication (22–42).

| A. | The Father's commandment: Jesus' laying down his life (17-18) | ab-x-b'a' |
| A'. | Two contradicting responses to Jesus (19-21) | abc-a'b'c' |

IIA. The Father's Commandment: Jesus' Laying Down His Life (10:17–18)

In vv. 17–18, II2 is comprehensive and two chiasms (II3–4) are partial, signifying their cohesiveness.

V	2			Phrases	Translation
17	a	3		Διὰ τοῦτό με ὁ πατὴρ ἀγαπᾷ	For this reason the Father loves me,
	b	a		ὅτι ἐγὼ τίθημι τὴν ψυχήν μου,	because I lay down my life,
	-	b	4	ἵνα πάλιν λάβω αὐτήν.	that I may take it again.
18	x	b'	a	οὐδεὶς αἴρει αὐτὴν ἀπ' ἐμοῦ,	No one takes it from me,
	-	a'	b	ἀλλ' ἐγὼ τίθημι αὐτὴν ἀπ' ἐμαυτοῦ.	but I lay it down of my own accord.
	b'		b'	ἐξουσίαν ἔχω θεῖναι αὐτήν,	I have power to lay it down,
	-		a'	καὶ ἐξουσίαν ἔχω πάλιν λαβεῖν αὐτήν·	and I have power to take it again.
	a'			ταύτην τὴν ἐντολὴν ἔλαβον παρὰ τοῦ πατρός μου.	This commandment I received from my Father."

II2. Chiastic, ab-x-b'a': In b-b', similar, twofold statements are repeatedly expressed: "because I lay down my life, that I may take it again" (b); "I have power to lay it down, and I have power to take it again" (b'). In the center x, the third party, "no one" appears in this issue: "No one takes it from me, but I lay it down of my own accord." Both in a-a', the relation between the Father and the Son is focused: ". . . the Father loves me" (a); "The commandment I received from my Father" (a'). It says that the Father loves the Son, because he does as in b-x-b', according to the commandment of his Father (a').

II3. Chiastic, ab-b'a': In a-a', ἐγὼ τίθημι (I lay down) is duplicated regarding his life, while b and b' are compared: "that I may take (grasp, λάβω) it again" (b) and "No one takes (removes, αἴρει) it from me" (b'). **II4.** Chiastic, ab-b'a': In b-b', ἐγὼ τίθημι αὐτὴν ἀπ' ἐμαυτοῦ (I lay it down of my own accord, b) and ἐξουσίαν ἔχω θεῖναι αὐτήν (I have power to lay it down, b') are actually duplicated in concept. In a-a', a (No one takes [removes, αἴρει] it from me) is compared with a' (I have power to take [to grasp, λαβεῖν] it again).

In II2, the emphatic repetition regarding laying down his life and taking it back as well as the relation between the Father and Jesus are focused together. Both II3 and 4 contrast "I" who lay down "my" life and take it again vs. "no one" who takes it from "me."

IIA'. Two Contradicting Responses to Jesus (10:19–21)

Verses 19–21 contain three parallels: one overarching parallelism (II5) and two duals (II6–7). II6–7 support the cohesion of II5, specifically the relation between c and c' of II5.

V	5		Phrases	Translation
19	a		Σχίσμα πάλιν ἐγένετο ἐν τοῖς Ἰουδαίοις διὰ τοὺς λόγους τούτους.	There arose a division again among the Jews because of these words.
20	b	6	ἔλεγον δὲ πολλοὶ ἐξ αὐτῶν·	Many of them said,
	c	a	δαιμόνιον ἔχει	"He has a demon
	-	a'	καὶ μαίνεται·	and is mad.
	a'		τί αὐτοῦ ἀκούετε;	Why do you listen to him?"
21	b'	7	ἄλλοι ἔλεγον·	Others said,
	c'	a	ταῦτα τὰ ῥήματα οὐκ ἔστιν δαιμονιζομένου·	"These are not the sayings of a man possessed by a demon.
	-	a'	μὴ δαιμόνιον δύναται τυφλῶν ὀφθαλμοὺς ἀνοῖξαι;	Can a demon open the eyes of the blind?"

II5. Parallel, abc-a'b'c': Two groups are differentiated: subjects, many (b) and others (b'); contents, negative- "He has a demon and is mad" (c) and positive- "These are not the sayings of a man possessed by a demon. Can a demon open the eyes of the blind?" (c'). In a-a', the focus is on the sayings of Jesus. **II6.** Dual, a-a': Two clauses are in fact similar in meaning: having a demon (a) and being mad (a'). **II7.** Dual, a-a': Two sentences are different in meaning, but similar in approving Jesus: regarding his saying (a) and his doing (a'). In II5, two contrastive responses toward the discourse of Jesus are focused. In II6, a negative response and, in II7, a positive one are shown.

III. At the Feast of Dedication (10:22–42)

Combined Chiastic, III1 (A1A2-B-B'-A'1A'2)

In A1 (22–24a), the time (the Feast of Dedication, winter) and the place (the portico of Solomon, temple) are introduced. There are Jesus and the Jews who want to know something from him. In A2 (24b), the question of the Jews is regarding whether Jesus is the Christ or not. In the final stage, in A'1 (39–40), there are again Jesus and the Jews who, this time, seek to seize him. The place (beyond the Jordan, the place where John was first baptizing) is referred. In A'2 (41–42), many came to him and believed in him at last, certainly receiving him as the Christ.

In B-B', Jesus testifies to himself with two clusters of words, dual witnesses to himself: B ("The works testify about me; You do not believe me; I give my sheep eternal life," 25–29), B' ("I and the Father are one; Believe the works; the Father is in me and I am in the Father," 30–38).

A	A1	The Jews who come to Jesus at the Feast of Dedication (10:22-24a)	a
	A2	Asking, "If you are the Christ, tell us plainly" (10:24b)	b
B		B	Belief as his sheep and having eternal life (10:25-29)
B'		B'	The Son of God controversy (10:30-38)
A'	A'1	The Jews who seek to seize him (10:39-40)	a'
	A'2	Those who believe in him (10:41-42)	b'

A1A2. "If you are the Christ, tell us plainly" (10:22-24)

In vv. 22-24, there are two chiasms (III2 and 4) and one combined chiasm (III3). There is no overarching structure besides III1.

V	1	2		Phrases	Translation
22	A1	a		Ἐγένετο τότε τὰ ἐγκαίνια	At that time the Feast of Dedication took place
-		x		ἐν τοῖς Ἱεροσολύμοις,	at Jerusalem.
-		a'	3	χειμὼν ἦν,	It was winter,
23	-		a1	καὶ περιεπάτει	and ~ was walking
-			a2	ὁ Ἰησοῦς	Jesus
-			x	ἐν τῷ ἱερῷ ἐν τῇ στοᾷ τοῦ Σολομῶνος.	in the portico of Solomon.
24	-		a'1	ἐκύκλωσαν οὖν αὐτὸν	So ~ gathered around him
-			a'2	οἱ Ἰουδαῖοι	the Jews
-			4	καὶ ἔλεγον αὐτῷ·	and said to him,
-	A2		a	ἕως πότε τὴν ψυχὴν ἡμῶν αἴρεις;	"How long will you keep us in suspense?
-			b	εἰ σὺ εἶ ὁ χριστός, εἰπὲ ἡμῖν παρρησίᾳ.	If you are the Christ, tell us plainly."

III2. Chiastic, a-x-a': Two parts are related in the sense of the time: the Feast of Dedication (a); winter (a'). In the middle, the place ("at Jerusalem") is located. III3. Combined chiastic, a1a2-x-a'1a'2: Jesus (a2) walks (a1) and the Jews (a'2) gather around him (a'1). In the middle, there is the place ("in the portico of Solomon"). III4. Chiastic, ab-b'a': As the Jews ask him to tell them if he is the Christ (b), he answers, "I told you" (b'). They complain that Jesus keeps them in suspense so long (a), but rather he says that they do not believe (a'). In III2, the place and the time are introduced. III3 compares what Jesus does with what the Jews do. III4 reflects the contradiction of the Jews who continue to ask him to tell them, although he has already told them.

B. Belief as His Sheep and Having Eternal Life (10:25-29)

In vv. 25-29, there are ten parallels: four chiasms (III6-7 and 10-11), three parallelisms (III8-9 and 12), and two duals (III5 and 13). As a whole, II5 as a dual is comprehensive. The phenomenon of parallel combination is so extraordinary that several parallels are interrelated in complex such as III7-12. We call them complex parallelisms (including chiasms), a typical phenomenon of Johannine parallels. III6 and 7, and again III7 and 8, and again III8 and 9, and again III9 and 10, and again III10 and 11 overlap each other, simultaneously and sequentially.

The reason why v. 30 is recommended as located in the following unit (30–38), although there is III14 that seems to bind vv. 25b–30 into one entity. First, we respect the chain of complex parallelisms, III6–11, which combine all the verses in vv. 25–29 but excluding v. 30. Second, we need to consider III16 as a cohesive entity binding vv. 30–33. Third, the primary theme of vv. 25–29 (B) and that of vv. 30–38 (B') are different to each other: "belief and eternal life" (B) and "the relationship between the Father and the Son" (B'), even though two clusters share some ideas such as belief, witness, and the works.

V	5					Phrases	Translation
25	A	6	4			ἀπεκρίθη αὐτοῖς ὁ Ἰησοῦς·	Jesus answered them,
-	a	b'				εἶπον ὑμῖν	"I told you,
-	b	a'		14		καὶ οὐ πιστεύετε·	and you do not believe.
-	c				a	τὰ ἔργα ἃ ἐγὼ ποιῶ ἐν τῷ ὀνόματι τοῦ πατρός μου	The works that I do in my Father's name,
-	c'	7			-	ταῦτα μαρτυρεῖ περὶ ἐμοῦ·	they testify about me.
26	-	b'	a		b	ἀλλ' ὑμεῖς οὐ πιστεύετε,	But you do not believe,
-	a'	b	8		-	ὅτι οὐκ ἐστὲ ἐκ τῶν προβάτων τῶν ἐμῶν.	because you are not of my sheep.
27	A'	b'	a		-	τὰ πρόβατα τὰ ἐμὰ	My sheep
		a'	-	9		τῆς φωνῆς μου ἀκούουσιν,	hear my voice,
-		b	a	10	-	κἀγὼ γινώσκω αὐτὰ	and I know them,
-		12	a'	b	a	καὶ ἀκολουθοῦσίν μοι,	and they follow me.
28	-	a	b'	a'	b	b'	κἀγὼ δίδωμι αὐτοῖς ζωὴν αἰώνιον	And I give them eternal life,
-	-	11	b'	b'		καὶ οὐ μὴ ἀπόλωνται εἰς τὸν αἰῶνα	and they will never perish,
-	b	a	a'	-	13	καὶ οὐχ ἁρπάσει τις αὐτὰ ἐκ τῆς χειρός μου.	and no one will snatch them out of my hand.
29	-	a	a'	b		-	ὁ πατήρ μου ὃ δέδωκέν μοι	My Father, who has given them to me,
-	-	-	b'		-	πάντων μεῖζόν ἐστιν,	is greater than all,
-	a'	b'	a'		-	καὶ οὐδεὶς δύναται ἁρπάζειν ἐκ τῆς χειρὸς τοῦ πατρός.	and no one can snatch them out of my Father's hand.

III5. Dual, A-A': In A, the focus is on those who do not believe him. Jesus says that they do not believe him because they are not of his sheep, although his works testify to him. In A', the focus is on those who follow him. Jesus calls them "my sheep" and promises to give them eternal life. **III6.** Chiastic, abc-c'b'a': In b-b', their unbelief is highlighted. In c-c', the witness of the works that he does in his Father's name (c) and their testimony about Jesus (c') are focused. Jesus does the work and the work testifies

about him. In a-a', Jesus says that "I told you" (a), but they did not listen and do not believe him (b-b'), because they are not his sheep (a').

III7. Chiastic, ab-b'a': In b-b', those who are not of his sheep (b) and his sheep (b') are contrasted. The former do not believe in him (a), while the latter hear his voice (a'). Two groups are in contrast. **III8.** Parallel, ab-a'b': Both a and a' describe his sheep: they hear his voice (a) and they follow him (a'). In b-b', Jesus does something for them: he knows them (b) and he gives them eternal life (b'). **III9.** Parallel, ab-a'b': Both a-a' describe the acts of Jesus: knowing them (a) and giving them eternal life (a'). Both b-b' describe his sheep: they follow him (b) and they will never perish (b'). As they follow Jesus they will never perish because Jesus knows them and gives them eternal life.

III10. Chiastic, ab-b'a': In b-b', the cause ("I give them eternal life") and its effect ("they will never perish") are shown. In fact, having-eternal-life (b) leads to never-perishing (b'). The relation of a and a' is also a causal relationship. When they follow him (cause, a), no one will snatch them out of the hand of the Son (effect, a'). **III11.** Chiastic, ab-b'a': In a-a', we can see a similar expression of the same meaning: "and no one will snatch them out of my hand" (a) and "and no one can snatch them out of my Father's hand" (a'). "My hand" (a) is switched to "my Father's hand" (a'), thereby causing a double emphasis for safety of salvation. In b-b', the Father is described in two ways: the Father who has given them to the Son (b) and the Father who is greater than all (b').

III12. Parallel, ab-a'b': In b-b', Jesus says that no one will (or can) snatch his sheep out of his hand (b) and out of the Father's hand (b'). In a', his Father is the one who has given them to him and is greater than all, while, in a, Jesus is the one who gives them eternal life. The Father and the Son are connected to each other and share their roles in providing them eternal life. III13. Dual, a-a': Two sentences are connected in meaning: "My Father . . . is greater than all" (a) and "no one can snatch them out of my Father's hand" (a').

III14. Chiastic, ab-b'a': In a, Jesus says that the works of the Father testify about him, while, in a', he himself testifies, "I and the Father are one." In b-b', Jesus says that they are not his sheep to follow him (b) and that no one can snatch his sheep from the Father and the Son (b'). The relationship between his sheep and Jesus as the Shepherd is shared in b and b'.

Their foci are: those who do not believe him vs. those who follow him (III5); the testimony of his works and their unbelief (III6); the contrast between his sheep and those who are not his sheep (III7); what Jesus does for them and how his sheep respond (III8); what Jesus does for them and what his sheep who follow him become (III9); his followers and their eternal life (III10); no one can ever snatch believers from the hands of God (III11); the cooperation between the Father and the Son in giving eternal life (III12); The power of the Father who gives the people to the Son (III13); Two testimonies, his works and himself, and two kinds of people, those who do not believe vs. those who follow him (III14).

B'. The Son of God Controversy (10:30–38)

In vv. 30–38, there are thirteen parallels: six chiasms (III15–16, 18, and 20–22), three parallelisms (III17 and 24–25), and three duals (III19, 23, and 26–27). III15 is the comprehensive structure in chiasm that are firmly sustained by three significant chiasms: III16, 18, and 21. III17 supports the connection between c and c' of III16. III20 is for III18 and III22–27 are for III21, while III19 seems to connect III18 and the first part of III21.

III15. Chiastic, A-X-A': In the opening A (30–33), Jesus claims that he and the Father are one and the Jews are going to stone him, and, in the final A' (36–38), Jesus reaffirms that he is the Son of God, explaining the inseparable relationship between him and the Father and rebuking them for their assertion of blasphemy. In the center (X, 34–35), the Scripture is quoted and emphasized to defend his claim of divinity.

III16. Chiastic, abc-c'b'a': In a-a', Jesus' claim, "I and the Father are one" (a), is rejected by the Jews as "you . . . make yourself God" (a'). In b, the Jews are to stone him and, in b', their reason for going to stone him is explained ("for blasphemy"). In c, Jesus raises a question of why they are going to stone him in spite of his good works, and, in c', they reply that they do not stone him because of a good work. **III17**. Parallel, ab-a'b': In a-a', Jesus' good work(s) is repeated. Jesus says that he has shown them many "good works" (ἔργα καλὰ, plural, a) from the Father, while they say just one "good work" (καλοῦ ἔργου, singular, a'). In b-b', the issue of stoning is shared: "For which of these do you stone me?" (b); "we do not stone you" (b').

III18. Chiastic, ab-b'a': In a-a', the Scripture or the law written is similarly focused: "Is it not written in your law" (a) and "and Scripture cannot be broken" (a'). In b-b', the plural "gods" are repeated: "I said, you are gods" (b) and "If he called them gods to whom the word of God came" (b'). **III19**. Dual, a-a': In a, Jesus quotes the Scripture (esp. Psalm 82:6) that indicates that "you are gods," and suggests it is an unbreakable scriptural foundation to call those who receive the word of God gods. In a', he defends himself regarding his assertion that he is the Son of God based on the scriptural ground to which he refers. **III20**. Chiastic, ab-b'a': "I said" (a) is related to "to whom the word of God came" (a') in terms of the word of God. In b-b', the concept of "gods" is shared: "you are gods" (b) and "If he called them gods" (b').

III21. Chiastic, ab-b'a': In a-a', the intimate relationship of the Father and the Son is accentuated in similarity: the Father sanctified and sent the Son in the world (a); the mutual abode between the Father and the Son (a'). In b-b', Jesus says that they are blaspheming him because of his words (b), but that instead they have to believe his works because he does the works of his Father (b'). **III22**. Chiastic, a-x-a': In a, Jesus says that he is the one whom the Father sanctified and sent into the world, and in a', he says that he is the Son of God. Both a and a' deal with the divine identity of Jesus. In the center x, he says, "you said, 'You are blaspheming.'" II23. Dual, a-a': Two actions of the Father regarding his Son are introduced: sanctifying (a) and sending (a').

V	15	16			14	Phrases	Translation
30	A	a			a'	ἐγὼ καὶ ὁ πατὴρ ἕν ἐσμεν.	I and the Father are one."
31	-	b				Ἐβάστασαν πάλιν λίθους οἱ Ἰουδαῖοι ἵνα λιθάσωσιν αὐτόν.	The Jews picked up stones again to stone him,
32	-	c	17			ἀπεκρίθη αὐτοῖς ὁ Ἰησοῦς·	Jesus answered them,
	-	-	a			πολλὰ ἔργα καλὰ ἔδειξα ὑμῖν ἐκ τοῦ πατρός·	"I have shown you many good works from the Father.
	-	-	b			διὰ ποῖον αὐτῶν ἔργον ἐμὲ λιθάζετε;	For which of these do you stone me?"
33	-	c'				ἀπεκρίθησαν αὐτῷ οἱ Ἰουδαῖοι·	The Jews answered him,
	-	-	a'			περὶ καλοῦ ἔργου	"For a good work
	-	-	b'			οὐ λιθάζομέν σε	we do not stone you,
	-	b'				ἀλλὰ περὶ βλασφημίας,	but for blasphemy,
	-	a'				καὶ ὅτι σὺ ἄνθρωπος ὢν ποιεῖς σεαυτὸν θεόν.	and because you, being a man, make yourself God."
34	X		18	19		ἀπεκρίθη αὐτοῖς [ὁ] Ἰησοῦς·	Jesus answered them,
	-	a		a		οὐκ ἔστιν γεγραμμένον ἐν τῷ νόμῳ ὑμῶν	"Is it not written in your law,
					20		
	-	b		-	a	ὅτι ἐγὼ εἶπα·	'I said,
	-	-		-	b	θεοί ἐστε;	you are gods'?
35	-	b'		-	b'	εἰ ἐκείνους εἶπεν θεοὺς	If he called them gods
	-	-		-	a'	πρὸς οὓς ὁ λόγος τοῦ θεοῦ ἐγένετο,	to whom the word of God came
	-	21	a'	-	22	23 καὶ οὐ δύναται λυθῆναι ἡ γραφή,	and Scripture cannot be broken,
36	A'	a		a'	a	a ὃν ὁ πατὴρ ἡγίασεν	to the one whom the Father sanctified
	-	-		-	-	a' καὶ ἀπέστειλεν εἰς τὸν κόσμον	and sent into the world,
	-	b		-	x	ὑμεῖς λέγετε ὅτι βλασφημεῖς,	you said, 'You are blaspheming,'
	-	-		-	a'	ὅτι εἶπον· υἱὸς τοῦ θεοῦ εἰμι;	because I said, 'I am the Son of God'?
					24		
37	-	b'			a	εἰ οὐ ποιῶ τὰ ἔργα τοῦ πατρός μου,	If I do not do the works of my Father,
	-	-			b	μὴ πιστεύετέ μοι·	do not believe me.
38	-	-	25		a'	εἰ δὲ ποιῶ,	But if I do them,
	-	-	a		b'	κἂν ἐμοὶ	even though ~ me,
	-	-	b		-	μὴ πιστεύητε,	~ you do not believe ~
	-	-	a'		-	τοῖς ἔργοις	~ the works,
	-	-	b'	26		πιστεύετε,	believe ~
	-	a'		a		ἵνα γνῶτε	that you may know
	-	-		a'	27	καὶ γινώσκητε	and understand
	-	-		a		ὅτι ἐν ἐμοὶ ὁ πατὴρ	that the Father is in me
	-	-		a'		κἀγὼ ἐν τῷ πατρί.	and I am in the Father."

The Shepherd and the Sheep

III24. Parallel, ab-a'b': In a-a', doing the works of the Father is focused in contrast: "If I do not do the works of my Father" (a) and "If I do them" (a'). In b-b', the belief issue is shared: "do not believe me" (b); "even though you do not believe me, believe the works" (b'). **III25**. Parallel, ab-a'b': Two contrasted sentences are arranged in parallel: κἂν ἐμοί (even though ~ me, a) and τοῖς ἔργοις (the works, a'); μὴ πιστεύητε (you do not believe, b) and πιστεύετε (believe, b'). III26. Dual, a-a': γνῶτε (get to know, subj. aorist) and γινώσκητε (keep knowing, subj. present) are used for double emphasis regarding knowing. III27. Dual, a-a': Both "the Father is in me" (a) and "I am in the Father" (a') demonstrate the intimate relationship between the Father and the Son.

Their foci are as follows: Jesus' claim about his divinity in relation to the Father and the Jews who are to stone him (III15); The claim of Jesus about his divinity and its consequence (being accused of blasphemy (III16); his good works vs. their stoning (III17); the scriptural ground that the people can be called gods (III18); Scriptural grounds of his assertion of being the Son of God (III19); The word of God and those who are called gods (III20); the close relationship between the Father and the Son in relation to the works of God (III21); His divinity as the Son of God vs. their accusation of blasphemy (III22); sanctifying and sending as God's actions for his Son (III23); the works of the Father and belief (III24); believing the works despite not believing in him (III25); getting to know and keeping knowing (III26); the mutual abode of the Father and the Son (III27).

A'1A'2. Those Who Seek to Seize Him and Those Who Believe in Him (10:39–42)

In vv. 39–42, there are three parallels: two chiasms (III29–30) and one dual (III28). There is no overarching structure besides III1.

V	1	28		Phrases	Translation
39	A'1	a		Ἐζήτουν [οὖν] αὐτὸν πάλιν	Again they were seeking
-	-			πιάσαι,	to seize him,
-		a'	29	καὶ ἐξῆλθεν ἐκ τῆς χειρὸς αὐτῶν.	but he escaped from their hands.
40	-		a	Καὶ ἀπῆλθεν πάλιν	And he went again
-			b	πέραν τοῦ Ἰορδάνου	beyond the Jordan
-			b'	εἰς τὸν τόπον ὅπου ἦν Ἰωάννης τὸ πρῶτον βαπτίζων	to the place where John was first baptizing,
-			a'	30 καὶ ἔμεινεν ἐκεῖ.	and he remained there.
41	A'2		a	καὶ πολλοὶ ἦλθον πρὸς αὐτὸν καὶ ἔλεγον	And many came to him, and they said,
-			b	ὅτι Ἰωάννης μὲν σημεῖον ἐποίησεν οὐδέν,	"John performed no sign,
-			b'	πάντα δὲ ὅσα εἶπεν Ἰωάννης περὶ τούτου ἀληθῆ ἦν.	but everything that John said about this man was true."
42	-		a'	καὶ πολλοὶ ἐπίστευσαν εἰς αὐτὸν ἐκεῖ.	And many believed in him there.

III28. Dual, a-a': They seek to seize him (a) but fail, for Jesus escaped from their hands (a'). It says that they fail and he succeeds. **III29**. Chiastic, ab-b'a': In b-b', information about the place is introduced: "beyond the Jordan" (b); "to the place where John was first baptizing" (b'). In a-a', his actions in relation to this place appear: "he went again" (a); "he remained there" (a'). **III30**. Chiastic, ab-b'a': In a-a', many came to him (a) and they believed in him (a'). In b-b', they said two things regarding John: "John performed no sign" (b); "but everything that John said about this man was true" (b'). The first one, b, is to compare John with Jesus and the second one is to regard John as the testifier to Jesus. In III28, there is the contrast between their seeking to seize him and his escape. III29 focuses on the place where he went and stayed. In III30, there are those who came to him and believed in him.

Reading in Structure-Style

1. Considering the first gate issue (1b–2, B of I1) and the second one (7b–10, B'), it is observed that the first one focuses on the contrast between the one who does not enter through the gate and the one who enters through the gate, while the second one shows the benefits of the gate and the purposes of the two opposite comings: Jesus vs. the thief. The second gate cluster consists of a twofold content (issued in dual): vv. 7b–8 and 9–10, initiated by recurrence of ἐγώ εἰμι ἡ θύρα (I am the gate; 7b and 9a). Interestingly, these two subunits (7b–8 and 9–10) reflect vv. 1b–2, both containing two contrastive characters: thieves-robbers vs. the shepherd of the sheep (Jesus). In vv. 7b–8, the thieves-robbers are implied in contrast to Jesus who came to his sheep after them. In vv. 9–10, the thief who does evil to the sheep and Jesus who does good to them are in contrast.

In other words, in the first part of the gate cycle, the focus is on the issue of qualification in terms of who the good shepherd is regarding the gate. In the second one, the focus switches to the relation between the sheep and the thieves-robbers as well as the contrast between the good shepherd (Jesus) and them regarding their purpose in coming, but still keeping the continuity from the first one in terms of the contrast between Jesus vs. the thief.

The gate in cycle: 1st (1b-2)	The gate in cycle: 2nd (7b-10)		
1. Implying that he is the gate of the sheep (ab and a'b')	**A**	a	"I am the gate"
		b	"of the sheep"
		c	The contrast between the thieves-robbers and Jesus (or the sheep)
2. The contrast between the thieves-robbers and the shepherd regarding the gate (c and c')	**A'**	a'	"I am the gate"
		b'	The reason why he is the gate of the sheep
		c'	The contrast between the thief vs. Jesus regarding the purpose in coming

2. Considering the first shepherd issue (3–5, C of I1) and the second one (11–15, C'), we can find that both demonstrate the intimate relationship between the shepherd and the sheep. The characters in vv. 3–5 in comparison with the shepherd are the gatekeeper and the stranger, while, in vv. 11–15, the hireling and the wolf appear as contrastive characters to the shepherd. Additionally, the latter (11–15) emphasizes the sacrifice of the shepherd with a double repetition. In this second part of the shepherd cycle, twofold contents (issued in dual), vv. 11–13 and 14–15 are presented with the same initiative sentence of Ἐγώ εἰμι ὁ ποιμὴν ὁ καλός (I am a good shepherd; 11a and 14a), similar as in the gate cycle.

In vv. 11–13, there are two contrasts between the good shepherd and the hireling and between the good shepherd and the wolf regarding how much to take care of the sheep. In vv. 14–15, the intimate relationship between Jesus as the good shepherd and his sheep is intensified again, this time using the analogy of the relationship between the Father and the Son.

The shepherd in cycle: 1st (3-5)	The shepherd in cycle: 2nd (11-15)		
1. Implying that he is the good shepherd (a and a')	**A**	a	"I am the good shepherd."
2. The intimate relationship between the shepherd and the sheep (b')		b	The contrasts between the shepherd and the hireling; between the shepherd and the wolf
3. The contrasts between the shepherd and the gatekeeper; between the shepherd and the stranger (b)	**A'**	a'	"I am the good shepherd."
		b'	The intimate relationship between the shepherd and the sheep

3. Considering I17, the issue of being saved and finding pasture in v. 9 is reiterated as that of having life and having it abundantly in v. 10. It means that being saved is the same as having life and finding pasture as having it abundantly.

4. Considering the chain-linking, complex parallel pattern in vv. 25–28 (III6–11), the reading in these verses warrants careful attention to understand this type of connection in terms of how they are interwoven with each other, although as a whole the verses can be divided into two subunits: those who do not believe him (25–26, A of III5) and those who follow him (27–29, A').

We may read them one by one: (1) You do not believe me as well as my works that testify of me, because you are not my sheep (III6); (2) You do not believe because you are not of my sheep, but my sheep hear my voice (III7); (3) My sheep hear my voice and follow me, and I know them and give them eternal life (III8); (4) I know them and give them eternal life and they follow me and will never perish (III9); (5) I give them eternal life and they who follow me will never perish so that no one may snatch them out of my hand (III10); (6) No one can snatch them out of my hand as well as of my Father's hand (III11).

In this way, the ideas of Jesus regarding belief, his works, his sheep, and eternal life are inter-connected to each other.

Issues in Structure-Style

1. The Original Order of Arrangement

Bultmann rearranged John 10 as follows: 22–26, 11–13, 1–10, 14–18, 27–30, 31–39, which he thought was the original order, and relocated vv. 19–21 after 9:39–41, regarding some verses as the source: vv. 11–13, 1–5, 8, 10, 14–15a, and 27–30.[3] He could not assume that the order of vv. 1–18 and 22–39 is possible, because, he thought, vv. 22–26 are the beginning of the new scene and the discourse of vv. 1–18 cannot possibly be connected to the healing episode in John 9.[4] Additionally, he believed that vv. 27–30 form "a closely knit" unit and functions as the conclusion of the discourse.[5]

First, Brown criticized Bultmann for subjectivity which is a drawback in that he violated the deliberate plan of vv. 1–21, "a purposeful arrangement and not a product of accident of confusion."[6] In particular, he regarded the function of vv. 1–21 as a bridge between Tabernacles (ch. 9) and Dedication (vv. 22ff.),[7] refuting any attempt to

---

3. Bultmann, *Gospel of John*, 360. Compare with the order of Turner: vv. 9–30; 1–18; 31–42. Turner, "History of Religions Background," 33–52.

4. Bultmann, *Gospel of John*, 312.

5. Ibid., 358.

6. Brown, *Gospel according to John I–XII*, 390.

7. Talbert also demonstrates how Tabernacles and Dedication were deeply interrelated at that time. Talbert, *Reading John*, 164–71. See also Carson, *Gospel according to John*, 379–80.

connect this discourse only to what preceded (the blind man episode) excluding the connection to what followed, seeing that there is an abrupt change of topic in vv. 1–18 from the previous chapter and the manifest relation between vv. 1–21 and 22–42, such as the connection of vv. 3–5 and vv. 26–27 regarding the shepherd-sheep relationship.[8]

Second, vv. 1–16 are exceptionally adroit in design (see I1, ABCD-A'B'C'D'), reflecting a typical Johannine style. Thus, any of these verses cannot be separated from its location, arbitrarily and subjectively. Each four parts of I1 recur in a cycle, systematically. In A and A', the expression, "Truly, truly, I say to you," is duplicated, while, in D and D', there is a sort of misunderstanding. B-B' and C-C' are two main bodies where the gate and the shepherd issues are shared, respectively and interactively (see the diagram of I1).

Third, that vv. 1–16 are an inseparable unit may mean that vv. 17–18 are the verses which are added for a complementary purpose. Verses 17–18 do not have any parallel connection in form with the previous discourse but have only a thematic relation (the sacrifice of the shepherd) with it, which first appears in vv. 11 and 15. Then we may ask that why these two verses are located there? Is it only for the complementation to the previous discourse (1–16)? Why are they so short?

Fourth, vv. 19–21 are a kind of conclusion to the whole discourse (1–18), existing as an entity in independence having no parallel connection to either the previous or following verses. As far as the theme (division in argument regarding the sayings of Jesus) is concerned, these verses are not separated from the following passages where two opposite responses to the sayings of Jesus appear, such as vv. 31 (stoning to kill him), 39 (attempting to arrest him), and 42 (believing in him).

Fifth, fascinatingly, vv. 22–42 are a large cluster which cannot be broken in pieces, generating a combined chiastic structure, III1 (A1A2-B-B'-A'1A'2), which is also arranged deliberately, suitable to a type of Johannine pattern. A1A2 and A'1A'2 (or A and A') are in parallel and also become an *inclusio*. There are two main clusters in the middle, B (25–29) and B' (30–38), each of which comprises several parallels including III5 (A-A', 25–29) and III15 (A-X-A', 30–38). The various parallels existing in them denote that they are cohesive within them.

Sixth, if we set aside the two passages (17–18 and 19–21) which are located at the middle, we can see that there are two main larger sections in John 10 (1–16 and 22–42), which are inseparable, particularly in theme. We can understand that the two shorter units function as links between the two larger ones, complementing them as well in issue. All the units exist where they are, playing their specific roles as drawers, in a kind of chest of drawers, which contain their own issues and are interactively connected to each other.

---

8. Brown, *Gospel according to John I–XII*, 391.

2. The Structure of vv. 1–16 and the Function of vv. 1–5

Bultmann did not consider vv. 1–18 as an ordered whole, because he thought they are not closely related to each other but instead hung together very loosely, even though they comprise separate units, which share the image of the shepherd and the sheep. And he insisted that vv. 7 and 9 are the evangelist's glosses.[9] Unlike him, Brown introduced the finding of Schneider who saw that the three themes in the parable of vv. 1–5 are explained in the following verses: (1) the gate (7–10); (2) the shepherd (11–18); (3) the sheep (26–30).[10]

Talbert also signifies three themes but different from those of Brown and Schneider:[11] (1) as a good shepherd, I lay down my life for the sheep (11, 15); (2) My sheep hear my voice; I give them eternal life; they shall never perish (27–28); and (3) I bring my other sheep into the one flock (16). For this reason, he classifies John 10 into two parts: vv. 1–6 (a figure) and 7–42 (its explanation).[12] And he divides vv. 1–6 into two: vv. 1–3a (access to the sheepfold); 3b–5 (the mutual confidence between sheep and shepherd). According to him, part two (7–42) is divided into three: (1) vv. 7–10 (a meditation on the figure of 1–5 by means of a double explanation of "gate" with "thief"); (2) vv. 11–18 (a meditation on the figure of 1–5 by means of double explanation of "shepherd" with "know" and "voice"); (3) vv. 22–42 (a controversy section focused on Jesus' works, in the middle of which is an explanation of "sheep" with "voice").[13]

First, we have discussed how vv. 1–16 are designed, deliberately and adroitly:[14] a four part cycle with two central issues (gate and shepherd) which are highlighted by four ἐγώ εἰμι.

Second, vv. 1–5 are not categorized into vv. 1–3a and 3b–5,[15] but instead into vv. 1–2 and 3–5, thus should be carefully treated as two figures (gate and shepherd) in terms of how they are combined sequentially. The gate figure contains two points: (1) implying that Jesus is the gate of the sheep; (2) the contrast between the thieves-robbers and the shepherd. These two points recur in vv. 1–2 and 7–10. The shepherd figure contains three points: (1) implying that Jesus is the good shepherd; (2) the inti-

---

9. Bultmann, *Gospel of John*, 358.

10. Brown, *Gospel according to John I–XII*, 391; Cf. Schneider, "Zur Komposition von Joh. 10," 108–19.

11. Talbert, *Reading John*, 164.

12. Ibid., 165.

13. Ibid., 166.

14. See Second-Third of the number 1; also the note of I1; the number 1 of "Reading in Structure-Style."

15. Robinson highlights the door-keeper in vv. 1–3a, the shepherd in vv. 3b–5, the hired man in vv. 12f as main characters who are mostly focused, because he misreads the two essential motifs in vv. 1–5 and 7–15: the gate (1–2; 7–10) and the shepherd (3–5; 11–15) and their cyclical structure. Robinson, *Priority of John*, 320; Robinson, *Twelve New Testament Studies*, 67–75; Cf. Painter, "Tradition, History and," 57.

The Shepherd and the Sheep

mate relationship between the shepherd and the sheep; (3) two contrasts between the shepherd and the gatekeeper (or hireling) and between the shepherd and the stranger (or wolf). We can see all three factors both in vv. 3–5 and 11–15.[16]

Third, the reasons why v. 3a is not included to the first cluster (1–2) are as follows: (1) existence of parallels with the following verses (I4–5); (2) that all the contents of vv. 1–2 are repeated in vv. 7–10 and complemented by them; (3) similarity of the gatekeeper and the hireling in their roles in contrast to the shepherd; (4) that, thus, the gatekeeper is not the primary character here unlike Robinson's giving priority to the gatekeeper.[17]

Fourth, there are four ἐγώ εἰμι (7, 9, 11, and 14), disclosing who/what Jesus is: twice, "the gate of the sheep" (7 and 9); twice, "the good shepherd" (11 and 14).[18] In the motif of the gate of the sheep, there is only one contrast: between shepherd vs. thief/robber (1–2 and 8–10), while in the motif of the shepherd, there are in all four contrast-comparisons: between shepherd and gatekeeper (3); between shepherd and stranger (4–5); between shepherd and hireling (11–13); between shepherd and wolf (11–12).

It means that the contrastive idea in the gate motif continues flowing from vv. 1–2 to vv. 7–10, consistently, and that the two contrasts in vv. 3–5 are kept but there is a shift of characters in vv. 11–15. The contrast of shepherd and gatekeeper is similar to that of shepherd and hireling in that both are not so antithetical and reflect the shepherd as the main figure in role. The second contrast, namely that of shepherd and stranger, is similar to that of shepherd and wolf, for both demonstrate opposite results regarding the sheep: their following and escaping from (shepherd vs. stranger); taking care of the sheep vs. hurting them (shepherd vs. wolf).

Fifth, besides those contrasts, the intimate relationship between shepherd and sheep recurs in vv. 3–4 and 14–15, which issue is definitely related to the closeness between the Father and the Son (15) that flourishes later in vv. 22–42 as a major theme.

Sixth, thus, two motifs in vv. 1–5 (the gate and the shepherd) are the firm ground for the recurrence of these issues and for expanding them in vv. 7–15 with two categories at issue (7–10 and 11–15).

For vv. 17–18 are not directly from vv. 1–5, they need to be dealt with separately as vv. 7–15 are treated. These two verses are deeply related to vv. 11, 14–15 where the sacrifice of the shepherd is issued. We may say that they do not belong directly to vv. 7–16 but play a complementary role to the previous discourse.

---

16. If anyone does not recognize the beautiful cycle of the gate-shepherd issues in vv. 1–16, he/she could not help believing that vv. 1–6 were a first stratum and vv. 7–18 were added later, as Painter did. Painter, *Quest for the Messiah*, 346–49.

17. See Robinson, *Twelve New Testament Studies*, 67–75; see also Carson, *Gospel according to John*, 380.

18. Busse asserts that v. 7 needs to be read as "I am the Shepherd," matching the textual variant of P^{75}. Busse, "Open Questions on John 10," 10. However, the four *ego eimi* system in vv. 7, 9, 11, and 14 does not allow that reading.

Seventh, another discourse regarding the relation between shepherd and sheep (26–29) needs also to be regarded as the additional part of the previous discourse of the shepherd-sheep relation, particularly in relation to the response of the sheep to their shepherd, which appears not only in vv. 3–4 (leading and following) but also in v. 14 (knowing each other), expanded and explained in more detail.

Eighth, in other words, the prime issues in vv. 1–5 are not the three which are suggested by Talbert but the two (the gate and the shepherd) where the first contrast between shepherd and thief-robber and the second two between shepherd and gate-keeper; shepherd and stranger are demonstrated, respectively. In addition to them, the closeness between shepherd and sheep is associated in the shepherd motif, recalling an analogy of the relationship between the Father and the Son. And vv. 17–18 complement vv. 11, 14–15,[19] while vv. 26–29 do vv. 3–4 and 14.

Ninth, the theme in vv. 22–42 regarding the relationship between the Father and the Son should not be regarded as what is totally disconnected or new to the previous shepherd discourse. Instead, it is inseparable to the discourse where the ἐγώ εἰμι are repeated four times (7, 9, 11, and 14) so as to reveal who Jesus is regarding his identity. Moreover, we can even see the direct reference to the close relationship between the Father and the Son in v. 15. Additionally, the sacrifice issue in vv. 11, 15, and 17–18 is also related to the relationship between the Father and the Son (specifically 15 and 17) and demonstrates his genuine, divine authority over death (specifically 18).

3. The Structure of vv. 22–42

When Brown divided vv. 22–39 into vv. 22–31 (Jesus as the Messiah) and 32–39 (Jesus as the Son of God), he saw that there are two basic questions in vv. 22–39: Is Jesus the Messiah? (24); Does he make himself God? (33), and each receives an answer of approximately the same length (25–30 and 34–38), which ends on the theme of Jesus' unity with his Father and to each of which the Jews react with hostility: first with an attempt to stone him (31); then with an attempt to arrest him (39).[20] According to him, vv. 40–42 are a conclusion to chs. 5–10 because they seem to bring to an end the public ministry of Jesus. Moreover, these verses function as a part of an *inclusio* with 1:19–28 because they remind the readers of the scene where the Baptist was baptizing and testifying to Jesus.[21]

Carson who regards vv. 22–39 as Christological claims and open opposition divides them into two: (1) Jesus the messiah (22–30); (2) Jesus the Son of God (31–39). And he names vv. 40–42 as strategic retreat, continued advance.[22] Similarly, Beasley-

---

19. Kysar asserts that vv. 17–18 constitute a new subunit in terms of the shift of language and its own integrity as a pericope. Kysar, "Johannine Metaphor," 91.
20. Brown, *Gospel according to John I-XII*, 404–8.
21. Ibid., 412–13.
22. Carson, *Gospel according to John*, 390–401.

Murray classifies these verses into three: (1) Jesus the Messiah (22–30); Jesus the Son of God (31–39); (3) Jesus' withdrawal to Transjordan (40–42).[23]

First, vv. 22–39 are not divided into two units (22–31 and 32–39) as Brown suggested but instead into three (22–24a, 24b–29, and 30–38) or four (if including 39–42), which are constructed as chiastic but complex in parallel, as discussed previously (see Fifth-Sixth of the above number 1).

Second, more specifically speaking, vv. 25–29 are made up of at least ten parallels (III5–14), among which III6, 7, 8, 9, 10, and 11 are sequentially chained to each other, particularly to the next one. It is the chain of complex parallelisms, one of typical Johannine style. Verses 30–38 contain three significant chiasms (30–33, II16, abc-c'b'a'; 34–35, II18, ab-b'a'; 36–38, II21, ab-b'a') which support the comprehensive one (II15, A-X-A' in 30–38). It means that vv. 30–38 are categorized into three parts which are related to each other in chiasm, existing as an inseparable entity.

Third, if we consider only the parallel relation of v. 30 with other verses, v. 30 shows both connections with the previous verses (25b–30, III14, ab-b'a') and the following ones (30–33, III16, abc-c'b'a'). It may mean that it is possible for this verse to connect to either the previous verses or the following ones. However, as far as the theme is concerned, v. 30 is preferred as belonging to the following paragraph (30–38) where the issue of the divine relationship between the Father and the Son is dominant.

Fourth, vv. 22–24 and 39–42 share two points: (1) There is time (Dedication, winter) and space (the portico of Solomon, temple; beyond the Jordan, the place where John was first baptizing) factors; (2) There are the Jews who ask in suspense who Jesus is or who finally believe in him. It means that they are in a pair and an *inclusio*. Thus, we can say that there are four parts in vv. 22–42, creating a chiastic structure (AB-B'A', III1).

Fifth, Brown's observation that vv. 40–42 and 1:19–28 become an *inclusio* which are related to the Baptist issue is probable. We may also consider a possibility that 13:1 which describes two issues (his loving of the disciples to the end and his departure) could be related to the last scene of Jesus with Peter (21:15–23) which focuses on the love of Peter for Jesus (or Jesus' final care for Peter to the end) with the background of the departure of Jesus, creating an *inclusio*.

---

23. Beasley-Murray, *John*, 167.

Bibliography

Anderson, Paul N. "From One Dialogue to Another: Johannine Polyvalence from Origins to Receptions." In Thatcher and Moore, *Anatomies of Narrative Criticism*, 93–119.

———. "The *Sitz im Leben* of the Johannine Bread of Life Discourse and Its Evolving Context." In Culpepper, *Critical Readings of John 6*, 1–59.

Ashton, John, ed. *The Interpretation of John*. 2nd ed. Edinburgh: T. & T. Clark, 1997.

———. "Second Thoughts on the Fourth Gospel." In Thatcher, *What We Have Heard from the Beginning*, 1–18.

———. *Understanding the Fourth Gospel*. Oxford: Clarendon, 1991.

Asiedu-Peprah, Martin. *Johannine Sabbath Conflicts as Juridical Controversy*. Tübingen: Mohr Siebeck, 2001.

Attridge, Harold W. "Thematic Development and Source Elaboration in John 7:1–36." *CBQ* 42 (1980) 160–70.

Avishur, Yitzhak. *Stylistic Studies of Word-Pairs in Biblical and Ancient Semitic Literatures*. Kevelaer, Germany: Butzon & Bercker, 1984.

Bailey, Kenneth E. *Poet and Peasant: A Literary Cultural Approach to the Parables in Luke*. Grand Rapids: Eerdmans, 1976.

Bailey, Raymond. "John 6." *RE* 85 (1988) 95–98.

Barrett, C. K. *The Gospel according to St. John: An Introduction with Commentary and Notes on the Greek Text*. Philadelphia: Westminster, 1978.

Bauckham, Richard. "The Audience of the Fourth Gospel." In Fortna and Thatcher, *Jesus in Johannine Tradition*, 101–11. Louisville: Westminster John Knox, 2001.

Beasley-Murray, George Raymond. *John*. WBC 36. Waco, TX: Word, 1987.

Berlin, Adele. *The Dynamics of Biblical Parallelism*. Bloomington: Indiana University Press, 1985.

Beutler, Johannes. "In Search of a New Synthesis." In Thatcher, *What We Have Heard from the Beginning*, 23–34.

———. "The Structure of John 6." In Culpepper, *Critical Readings of John 6*, 115–27.

Beutler, Johannes, and Robert T. Fortna, eds. *The Shepherd Discourse of John 10 and Its Context: Studies by Members of the Johannine Writings Seminar*. Cambridge: Cambridge University Press, 1991.

Black, David Alan, ed. *Linguistics and New Testament Interpretation: Essays on Discourse Analysis*. Nashville: Broadman, 1992.

Bligh, John. "Jesus in Samaria." *HeyJ* 3 (1964) 329–46.

Blomberg, Craig "The Structure of 2 Corinthians 1–7." *CTR* 4 (1989) 3–20.

Boismard, M.-E. "Les traditions johanniques concernant le Baptiste." *RB* 70 (1963) 5–42.

Bondi, Richard A. "John 8:39–47: Children of Abraham or of the Devil?" *JES* 34 (1997) 473–98.

Borchert, Gerald L. *John 1–11*. NAC. Broadman & Holman, 1996.

Bibliography

———. "The Passover and the Narrative Cycles in John." In Sloan and Parsons, *Perspectives on John*, 303–16.

Borgen, Peter. *Bread from Heaven: An Exegetical Study of the Conception of Manna in the Gospel of John and the Writings of Philo*. NovTSS 10. Leiden: Brill, 1965.

———. "John 6: Tradition, Interpretation and Composition." In *From Jesus to John: Essays on Jesus and New Testament Christology in Honour of Marinus de Jonge*, edited by Martinus C. de Boer, 268–91. JSNTSS 84. Sheffield: JSOT, 1993.

———. "Logos Was the True Light: Contributions to the Interpretation of the Interpretation of the Prologue of John." In Orton, *The Composition of John's Gospel*, 107–22.

Botha, Eugene. "John 4.16: A Difficult Text Speech Act Theoretically Revisited." In Stibbe, *The Gospel of John as Literature*, 183–92.

Boyd, W. J. Peter. "The Ascension according to St John: Chapters 14–17 Not Pre-passion but Post-resurrection." *Theology* 70 (1967) 207–11.

Boys, Thomas. *Tactica Sacra*. London: Hamilton, 1824.

Breck, John. "Chiasmus as a Key to Biblical Interpretation." *SVTQ* 43 (1999) 249–67.

———. *The Shape of Biblical Language: Chiasmus in the Scriptures and Beyond*. Crestwood, NY: St. Vladimir's Seminary Press, 1994.

Bridges, Carl B. "The Canonical Status of the *Pericope Adulterae* (John 7:53—8:11)." *SCJ* 11 (2008) 213–21.

Brodie, Thomas L. *The Gospel according to John: A Literary and Theological Commentary*. New York: Oxford University Press, 1993.

Brouwer, Wayne. *The Literary Development of John 13–17: A Chiastic Reading*. Atlanta: SBL, 2000.

Brown, Raymond E. *The Gospel according to John I–XII*. Anchor Bible 29. New York: Doubleday, 1966.

———. *The Gospel according to John XIII–XXI*. Anchor Bible 29a. New York: Doubleday, 1970.

———. "The Prologue of the Gospel of John: John 1:1–18." *RE* 62 (1965) 429–39.

Bryan, Steven M. "Power in the Pool: The Healing of the Man at Bethesda and Jesus' Violation of the Sabbath (Jn. 5:1–18)." *TB* 54 (2003) 7–22.

Bulembat, Jean-Bosco Matand. "Head-Waiter and Bridegroom of the Wedding at Cana: Structure and Meaning of John 2.1–12." *JSNT* 30 (2007) 55–73.

Bullinger, E. W. *The Companion Bible*. London: Oxford University Press, 1922.

———. *Figures of Speech Used in the Bible: Explained and Illustrated*. Grand Rapids: Baker, 1968.

Bultmann, Rudolf. *The Gospel of John: A Commentary*. Philadelphia: Westminster, 1971.

———. "The History of Religions Background of the Prologue to the Gospel of John." In Ashton, *The Interpretation of John*, 27–46.

———. *History of the Synoptic Tradition*. Oxford: Blackwell, 1963.

Burge, Gary M. *Interpreting the Gospel of John*. Guides to New Testament Exegesis 5. Grand Rapids: Baker, 1992.

———. *John: From Biblical Text . . . to Contemporary Life*. NIV Application Commentary. Grand Rapids: Zondervan, 2000.

———. "A Specific Problem in the New Testament Text and Canon: The Woman Caught in Adultery (John 7:53–8:11)." *JETS* 27 (1984) 141–48.

Busse, Ulrich. "Open Questions on John 10." In Beutler and Fortna, *The Shepherd Discourse of John 10 and Its Context*, 6–17.

Carson, D. A. *The Gospel according to John*. Pillar New Testament Commentary. Grand Rapids: Eerdmans, 1991.

———. "Reflections upon a Johannine Pilgrimage." In Thatcher, *What We Have Heard from the Beginning*, 87–107.

Carter, Warren. "The Prologue and John's Gospel: Function, Symbol and the Definitive Word." *JSNT* 39 (1990) 35–58.

Cassidy, Richard J. *John's Gospel in New Perspective: Christology and the Realities of Roman Power*. Maryknoll: Orbis, 1992.

Charlesworth, James H. "The Dead Sea Scrolls and the Gospel according to John." In Culpepper and Black, *Exploring the Gospel of John*, 65–97.

Clark, David J. "Criteria for Identifying Chiasm." *LB* 5 (1975) 63–72.

Coloe, Mary L. *God Dwells with Us: Temple Symbolism in the Fourth Gospel*. Collegeville: Liturgical, 2001.

———. "Temple Imagery in John." *Int* 63 (2009) 368–81.

———. "Witness and Friend: Symbolism Associated with John the Baptiser." In Frey et al., *Imagery in the Gospel of John*, 319–32.

Coloe, Mary L., and Tom Thatcher, eds. *John, Qumran, and the Dead Sea Scrolls: Sixty Years of Discovery and Debate*. Atlanta: SBL, 2011.

Conway, Colleen M. "There and Back Again: Johannine History on the Other Side of Literary Criticism." In Thatcher and Moore, *Anatomies of Narrative Criticism*, 77–91.

Cotterell, Peter, and Max Turner. *Linguistics and Biblical Interpretation*. Downers Grove, IL: InterVarsity, 1989.

Crossan, J. D. "It Is Written: A Structuralist Analysis of John 6." In Stibbe, *The Gospel of John as Literature*, 145–64.

Culpepper, R. Alan "The Amen, Amen Sayings in the Gospel of John." In Sloan and Parsons, *Perspectives on John*, 57–101.

———. *Anatomy of the Fourth Gospel: A Study in Literary Design*. Philadelphia: Fortress, 1983.

———, ed. *Critical Readings of John 6*. Leiden: Brill, 1997.

———. "Design for the Church in the Imagery of John 21:1–14." In Frey et al., *Imagery in the Gospel of John*, 369–402.

———. Introduction to *The Johannine Literature*, edited by Barnabas Lindars et al., 9–27. Sheffield, UK: Sheffield Academic, 2000.

———. "John 5:1–18—A Sample of Narrative Critical Commentary." In Stibbe, *The Gospel of John as Literature*, 193–207.

———. "The Pivot of John's Prologue." *NTS* 27 (1980/81) 1–31.

Culpepper, R. Alan, and C. Clifton Black, eds. *Exploring the Gospel of John: In Honor of D. Moody Smith*. Louisville: Westminster John Knox, 1996.

Davies, Margaret. *Rhetoric and Reference in the Fourth Gospel*. JSNTSS 69. Sheffied: Sheffied Academic, 1992.

Davies, W. D. "Reflections on Aspects of the Jewish Background of the Gospel of John." In Culpepper and Black, *Exploring the Gospel of John*, 43–64.

De Boer, M. C. "Narrative Criticism, Historical Criticism, and the Gospel of John." In Ashton, *The Interpretation of John*, 301–14.

———. "Narrative Criticism, Historical Criticism, and the Gospel of John." In *The Johannine Writings*, edited by Stanley E. Porter and Craig A. Evans, 95–108. Sheffield: Sheffield Academic, 1995.

Bibliography

De Jonge, Marinus. "The Gospel and the Epistles of John Read against the Background of the History of the Johannine Community." In Thatcher, *What We Have Heard from the Beginning*, 127–44.

Deeks, David, "The Structure of the Fourth Gospel." In Stibbe, *The Gospel of John as Literature*, 77–101.

Derickson, Gary W. "Matthew's Chiastic Structure and Its Dispensational Implications." *BSac* 163 (2006) 423–37.

Dockery, David S. "Reading John 4:1–15: Some Diverse Hermeneutical Perspectives." *CTR* 3 (1988) 127–40.

Dodd, C. H. *The Interpretation of the Fourth Gospel*. Cambridge: Cambridge University Press, 1953.

Dorsey, David. *The Literary Structure of the Old Testament: A Commentary on Genesis–Malachi*. Grand Rapids: Baker, 1999.

Du Rand, Jan A. "A Syntactical and Narratological Reading of John 10 in Coherence with Chapter 9." In Beutler and Fortna, *The Shepherd Discourse of John 10 and Its Context*, 94–115.

Ellis, Peter F. *The Genius of John: A Composition-Critical Commentary on the Fourth Gospel*. Collegeville: Liturgical, 1984.

———. "Inclusion, Chiasm, and the Division of the Fourth Gospel." *SVTQ* 43 (1999) 269–338.

———. "Understanding the Concentric Structure of the Fourth Gospel." *SVTQ* 47 (2003) 131–54.

Eltester, Walther. "Der Logos und sein Prophet." In *Apophoreta: Festschrift für Ernst Haenchen*, edited by Ernst Haenchen, 109–34. Berlin: Töpelmann, 1964.

Eslinger, Lyle. "The Wooing of the Woman at the Well." In Stibbe, *The Gospel of John as Literature*, 165–82.

Evans, Craig A. *Word and Glory: On the Exegetical and Theological Background of John's Prologue*. JSNTSS 89. Sheffield: JSOT, 1993.

Farelly, Nicolas. "John 2:23–25: What Kind of Faith Is This?" *Presbyterion* 30 (2004) 37–45.

Fee, Gordon D. *New Testament Exegesis: A Handbook for Students and Pastors*. Louisville: Westminster John Knox, 1993.

Fortna, Robert Tomson. *The Fourth Gospel and Its Predecessor: From Narrative Source to Present Gospel*. Philadelphia: Fortress, 1988.

———. *The Gospel of Signs: A Reconstruction of the Narrative Source Underlying the Fourth Gospel*. Cambridge: Cambridge University Press, 1970.

Fortna, Robert Tomson, and Tom Thatcher. *Jesus in Johannine Tradition*. Louisville: Westminster John Knox, 2001.

Frey, Jörg, et al., eds. *Imagery in the Gospel of John: Terms, Forms, Themes, and Theology of Johannine Figurative Language*. Tübingen: Mohr Siebeck, 2006.

Garland, David E. "The Fulfillment Quotations in John's Account of the Crucifixion." In Sloan and Parsons, *Perspectives on John*, 230–50.

Gaventa, Beverly Roberts. "The Archive of Excess: John 21 and the Problem of Narrative Closure." In Culpepper and Black, *Exploring the Gospel of John*, 240–52.

Geller, Stephen A. *Parallelism in Early Hebrew Poetry*. Missoula: Scholars, 1979.

———, ed. *A Sense of Text: The Art of Language in the Study of Biblical Literature*. Winona Lake, IN: Dropsie College / Eisenbrauns, 1983.

———. "Through Windows and Mirrors into the Bible: History, Literature and Language in the Study of Text." In Geller, *A Sense of Text*, 3–40.

George, Larry Darnell. *Reading the Tapestry: A Literary-Rhetorical Analysis of the Johannine Resurrection Narrative (John 20–21)*. SBL 14. New York: Lang, 2000.

Gerhard, John J. "The Literary Unity and Compositional Methods of the Gospel of John." PhD diss., Catholic University of America, 1975.

Giblin, Charles H. "Two Complementary Literary Structures in John 1:1–18." *JBL* 104 (1985) 87–103.

Godet, Frederic Louis. *Commentary on John's Gospel*. Grand Rapids: Kregel, 1978.

Gooding, D. W. "The Composition of the Book of Judges." *Eretz-Israel* 16 (1982) 70–79.

Gordley, Matthew. "The Johannine Prologue and Jewish Didactic Hymn Traditions: A New Case for Reading the Prologue as a Hymn." *JBL* 128 (2009) 781–802.

Grassi, Joseph A. "The Role of Jesus' Mother in John's Gospel : A Reappraisal." *CBQ* 48 (1986) 67–80.

———. "The Wedding at Cana (John II 1–11): A Pentecostal Meditation?" *NovT* 16 (1972) 131–36.

Gray, Bennison. "Repetition in Oral Literature." *JAF* 84 (1971) 289–303.

Gray, Gary B. *The Forms of Hebrew Poetry*. London: Ktav, 1972. First published in 1915.

Greenstein, Edward L. "How Does Parallelism Mean?" In Geller, *A Sense of Text*, 41–70.

Grigsby, Bruce. "Washing in the Pool of Siloam." In Orton, *The Composition of John's Gospel*, 251–59.

Guthrie, George H., and J. Scott Duvall. *Biblical Greek Exegesis: A Graded Approach to Learning Intermediate and Advanced Greek*. Grand Rapids: Zondervan, 1998.

Haenchen, Ernst. *John 1: A Commentary on the Gospel of John Chapters 1–6*. Edited by Ulrich Busse. Translated by Robert Walter Funk. Hermeneia. Philadelphia: Fortress, 1984.

———. *John 2: A Commentary on the Gospel of John Chapters 7–21*. Edited by Ulrich Busse. Translated by Robert Walter Funk. Hermeneia. Philadelphia: Fortress Press, 1984.

Harner, Philip B. *Relation Analysis of the Fourth Gospel: A Study in Reader-Response Criticism*. Lewiston, NY: Mellen, 1993.

Harvey, John D. *Listening to the Text: Oral Patterning in Paul's Letters*. Grand Rapids: Baker, 1998.

Hendricksen, William. *Exposition of the Gospel according to John*. Vol. 1. Grand Rapids: Baker, 1953.

Hitchcock, F. R. M. "Is the Fourth Gospel a Drama?" In Stibbe, *The Gospel of John as Literature*, 15–24.

Howard-Brook, Wes. *Becoming Children of God: John's Gospel and Radical Discipleship*. Maryknoll: Orbis, 1994.

Hughes, R. Kent. *John: That You May Believe*. Wheaton: Crossway, 1999.

Jensen, Alexander S. *John's Gospel as Witness: The Development of the Early Christian Language of Faith*. Burlington, VT: Ashgate, 2004.

Jeremias, Joachim. "Chiasmus in den Paulusbriefen." *ZNW* 49 (1958) 145–56.

Johanson, Bruce C. *To All the Brethren: A Text-Linguistic and Rhetorical Approach to 1 Thessalonians*. Coniectanea Biblica 16. Stockholm: Almqvist & Wiksell, 1987.

Johnson, Alan F. "A Stylistic Trait of the Fourth Gospel in the *Pericope Adulterae*?" *BETS* 9 (1966) 91–96.

Kaiser, Walter. *Toward an Exegetical Theology*. Grand Rapids: Baker, 1981.

Keener, Craig S. *The Gospel of John: A Commentary*. Vol. 1. Peabody: Hendrickson, 2003.

Keith, Chris "The Initial Location of the *Pericope Adulterae* in Fourfold Tradition." *NovT* 51 (2009) 209–31.

Bibliography

Kim, Sang-Hoon. "A Comparative Study on the Prologue of John and the Preface of 1 John in Terms of Their Parallel Features." *KENTS* 9 (2010) 369–408.

———. "A Discussion of the Structure and Styles of John 6." *ShinhakJinam* 313 (2012) 14–37.

———. *Interaction between Koinonia and Zoe in 1 John: A Relational Reading.* Unpublished DTh diss., University of Stellenbosch, 1998.

———. "Johannine Complex Structures in John 9." *CTJ* 20 (2012) 3–30.

———. "A New Way of Analytic Methods of the NT Greek Text." *KENTS* 6 (2007) 181–202.

———. "A Study on the Chiastic Structure and the Styles of John 5:19–30 (Jesus Discourse)." *KENTS* 10 (2011) 479–511.

Kim, Sang-Hoon, and Byung-Chan Go. "A New Approach on the Structure of John." *KENTS* 9 (2010) 97–131.

Kim, Stephen S. "The Significance of Jesus' First Sign-Miracle in John." *BSac* 167 (2010) 201–15.

———. "The Significance of Jesus' Healing the Blind Man in John 9." *BSac* 167 (2010) 307–18.

Klink, Edward W., III. "Expulsion from the Synagogue? Rethinking a Johannine Anachronism." *TB* 59 (2008) 99–118.

Koester, Craig R. "'The Savior of the World' (John 4:42)." *JBL* 109 (1990) 665–80.

Köstenberger, Andreas J. *John.* Grand Rapids: Baker Academic, 2004.

Kysar, Robert. "Johannine Metaphor—Meaning and Function : A Literary Case Study of John 10:1–18." *Semeia* 53 (1991) 81–111.

———. "The Source Analysis of the Fourth Gospel: A Growing Consensus?" In Orton, *The Composition of John's Gospel,* 127–47.

———. *Voyages with John: Charting the Fourth Gospel.* Waco, TX: Baylor University Press, 2005.

Lamarche, Paul. "The Prologue of John." In Ashton, *The Interpretation of John,* 47–65.

Lee, Dorothy A. *The Symbolic Narratives of the Fourth Gospel: The Interplay of Form and Meaning.* Sheffield, UK: Sheffield Academic, 1994.

Léon-Dufour, X. "Le mystère du pain de vie (Jean VI)." *Recherches de Science Religieuse* 46 (1958) 481–523.

———. "Trois chiasmes johanniques." *NTS* 7 (1960–61) 249–55.

Lewis, Jack P. "The Semitic Background of the Gospel of John." In *Johannine Studies: Essays in Honor of Frank Pack,* edited by James E. Priest, 97–110. Malibu, CA: Pepperdine University Press, 1989.

Lindars, Barnabas. *The Gospel of John.* NCBC. Greenwood, SC: Attic, 1972.

Louw, Johannes P. *Semantics of New Testament Greek.* Philadelphia: Fortress, 1982.

Lowth, Robert. *Isaiah: A New Translation with a Preliminary Dissertation and Notes.* London, 1868.

———. *Lectures on the Sacred Poetry of the Hebrews.* London, 1753.

Lund, Nils Wilhelm. *Chiasmus in the New Testament: A Study in the Form and Function of Chiastic Structures.* Peabody, MA: Hendrickson, 1970.

———. "The Influence of Chiasmus upon the Structure of the Gospel according to Matthew." *ATR* 13 (1931) 405–33.

———. "The Influence of Chiasmus upon the Structure of the Gospels." *ATR* 13 (1931) 27–48.

———. "The Literary Structure of Paul's Hymn to Love." *JBL* 50 (1931) 266–76.

———. "The Presence of Chiasmus in the New Testament." *JR* 10 (1930) 74–93.

Luter, A. Boyd, and Michelle V. Lee. "Philippians as Chiasmus: Key to the Structure, Unity and Theme Questions." *NTS* 41 (1995) 89–101.
MacRae, George W. "Theology and Irony in the Fourth Gospel." In Stibbe, *The Gospel of John as Literature*, 103–14.
Malina, Bruce J., and Richard L. Rohrbaugh. *Social-Science Commentary on the Gospel of John*. Minneapolis: Fortress, 1998.
Man, Ronald E. "The Value of Chiasm for New Testament Interpretation." *BSac* 141 (1984) 146–54.
Maritz, Petrus, and Gilbert van Belle. "The Imagery of Eating and Drinking in John 6:35." In Frey et al., *Imagery in the Gospel of John*, 333–52.
Martyn, J. Louis. *History and Theology of the Fourth Gospel*. Nashville: Abingdon, 1979.
———. "The Johannine Community among Jewish and Other Early Christian Communities." In Thatcher, *What We Have Heard from the Beginning*, 183–90.
Mead, A. H. "The βασιλικός in John 4:46–53." *JSNT* 23 (1985) 69–72.
Meynet, Roland. *Rhetorical Analysis: An Introduction to Biblical Rhetoric*. JSOTSS 256. Sheffield, UK: Sheffield Academic, 1998.
Mlakuzhyil, George. *The Christocentric Literary Structure of the Fourth Gospel*. Rome: Editrice Pontificio Istituto Biblico, 1987.
Moloney, Francis J. *Belief in the Word: Reading the Fourth Gospel; John 1–4*. Minneapolis: Fortress, 1993.
———. "The Function of John 13–17 within the Johannine Narrative." In Segovia, *What Is John?*, 43–66.
———. "The Function of Prolepsis." In Culpepper, *Critical Readings of John 6*, 129–48.
———. *Glory Not Dishonor: Reading John 13–21*. Minneapolis: Fortress, 1998.
———. *The Gospel of John*. Sacra Pagina 4. Collegeville: Liturgical, 1998.
———. "Into Narrative and Beyond." In Thatcher, *What We Have Heard from the Beginning*, 195–210.
———. "John 21 and the Johannine Story." In Thatcher and Moore, *Anatomies of Narrative Criticism*, 237–51.
———. *Signs and Shadows: Reading John 5–12*. Minneapolis: Fortress, 1996.
Morris, Leon. *The Gospel according to John*. Grand Rapids: Eerdmans, 1971.
———. *Jesus Is the Christ: Studies in the Theology of John*. Leicester, UK: InterVarsity, 1989.
———. *Studies in the Fourth Gospel*. Grand Rapids: Eerdmans, 1969.
Mounce, William D. *A Graded Reader of Biblical Greek*. Grand Rapids: Zondervan, 1996.
Muilenburg, James. "For Criticism and Beyond." *JBL* 88 (1969) 1–18.
———. "A Study in Hebrew Rhetoric: Repetition and Style." *SVTQ* 1 (1953) 97–111.
Müller, D. H. *Die Propheten in ihrer ursprünglichen Form*. Vienna: Hölder, 1896.
Neill, Stephen, and N. T. Wright. *The Interpretation of the New Testament, 1861–1986*. 2nd ed. New York: Oxford University Press, 1988.
Nida, Eugene A. *Signs, Sense, Translation*. Cape Town: Bible Society of South Africa, 1984.
Niditch, Susan. *Oral World and Written Word: Ancient Israelite Literature*. Louisville: Westminster John Knox, 1996.
Nissen, Johannes, and Sigfred Pedersen, ed. *New Readings in John: Literary and Theological Perspectives; Essays from the Scandinavian Conference on the Fourth Gospel*. JSNTSS 182. Sheffield, UK: Sheffield Academic, 1999.
O'Day, Gail R. "John 7:53—8:11: A Study in Misreading." *JBL* 111 (1992) 631–40.
———. "Spirituality and Community in the Fourth Gospel." *W&W* 8 (1988) 53–61.

Bibliography

———. "The Word Become Flesh: Story and Theology in the Gospel of John." In Segovia, *What Is John?*, 67–76.

O'Grady, John F. *According to John: The Witness of the Beloved Disciples.* New York: Paulist, 1999.

Olsson, Birger. *Structure and Meaning in the Fourth Gospel: A Text-Linguistic Analysis of John 2:1–11 and 4:1–42.* Lund: CWK, 1974.

Orton, David E., ed. *The Composition of John's Gospel.* Leiden: Brill, 1999.

Painter, John. *John: Witness and Theologian.* London: SPCK, 1975.

———. *The Quest for the Messiah: The History, Literature, and Theology of the Johannine Community.* Nashville: Abingdon, 1993.

———. "Tradition, History and Interpretation in John 10." In Beutler and Fortna, *The Shepherd Discourse of John 10 and Its Context*, 53–74.

Parsons, Mikeal C. "A Neglected *EGO EIMI* Saying in the Fourth Gospel? Another Look at John 9:9." In Sloan and Parsons, *Perspectives on John*, 145–80.

Parunak, H. Van Dyke. *Structural Studies in Ezekiel.* PhD diss., Harvard University, 1978.

Porter, Stanley E. *Verbal Aspect in the Greek of the New Testament, With Reference to Tense and Mood.* New York: Peter Lang, 1989.

Porter, Stanley E., and Jeffrey T. Reed. "Philippians as a Macro-Chiasm and Its Exegetical Significance." *NTS* 44 (1998) 213–31.

Purvis, James D. "The Fourth Gospel and the Samaritans." In Orton, *The Composition of John's Gospel*, 148–85.

Radday, Yehuda T. "Chiasmus in Hebrew Biblical Narrative." In Welch, *Chiasmus in Antiquity*, 50–117.

———. "On Chiasm in Biblical Narrative." *BM* 20–21 (1964) 48–72.

Reese, James M. "Literary Structure of Jn 13:31—14:31; 16:5-6, 16–33." *CBQ* 34 (1972) 321–31.

Reinhartz, Adele. "Building Skyscrapers on Toothpicks: The Literary-Critical Challenge to Historical Criticism." In Thatcher and Moore, *Anatomies of Narrative Criticism*, 55–76.

Resseguie, James. "John 9: A Literary-Critical Analysis." In Stibbe, *The Gospel of John as Literature*, 115–22.

———. *The Strange Gospel: Narrative Design and Point of View in John.* Leiden: Brill, 2001.

Ridderbos, Herman N. *The Gospel according to John: A Theological Commentary.* Grand Rapids: Eerdmans, 1997.

———. "The Structure and Scope of the Prologue to the Gospel of John." In Orton, *The Composition of John's Gospel*, 41–62.

Robinson, J. A. T. *The Priority of John.* London: SCM, 1985.

———. "The Relation of the Prologue to the Gospel of St. John." *NTS* 9 (1962–1963) 120–29.

———. *Twelve New Testament Studies.* London: SCM, 1962.

Rohrbaugh, Richard L. "The Gospel of John in the Twenty-First Century." In Segovia, *What Is John?*, 257–63.

Ruckstuhl, Eugen. *Die literarische Einheit des Johannesevangeliums.* Fribourg, Switzerland: Paulusverlag, 1951.

———. "Johannine Language and Style: The Question of Their Unity." In *L'Evangile de Jean: Sources, rédaction, théologie*, edited by Marinus de Jonge et al., 125–47. Leuven: Leuven University Press, 1977.

Schnackenburg, Rudolf. *The Gospel according to St. John.* Vol. 1. New York: Seabury, 1980.

Schneider, J. "Zur Komposition von Joh 7." *ZNW* 45 (1954) 108–19.

Schuchard, Bruce G. *Scripture within Scripture: The Interrelationship of Form and Function in the Explicit Old Testament Citations in the Gospel of John.* SBLDS 133. Atlanta: Scholars, 1992.
Scott, M. Philip "Chiastic Structure: A Key to the Interpretation of Mark's Gospel." *BTB* 15 (1985) 17–26.
Scott, Steven Richard. "Chapter Six as the Centre of John." Paper presented at ISBL, London, July 2011.
Segovia, Fernando F. *The Farewell of the Word: The Johannine Call to Abide.* Minneapolis: Fortress, 1991.
———. "The Structure, Tendenz, and Sitz im Leben of John 13:31—14:31." *JBL* 104 (1985) 471–93.
———. "Toward a New Direction in Johannine Scholarship: The Fourth Gospel from a Literary Perspective." *Semeia* 53 (1991) 1–22.
———, ed. *What Is John?* Vol. 2, *Literary and Social Readings of the Fourth Gospel.* Atlanta: Scholars, 1998.
Shea, William H. "The Qinah Structure of the Book of Lamentations." *Biblical* 60 (1979) 103–7.
Sheeley, Steven M. "Lift Up Your Eyes: John 4:4–42." *RE* 92 (1995) 81–87.
Sloan, Robert B., and Mikeal C. Parsons, eds. *Perspectives on John: Methods and Interpretation in the Fourth Gospel.* NABPRS 11. Lewiston: Mellen, 1993.
Sloyan, Gerard S. *John.* Interpretation. Atlanta: John Knox, 1988.
Smith, D. Moody. *The Composition and Order of the Fourth Gospel: Bultmann's Literary Theory.* New Haven: Yale University Press, 1965.
Snodgrass, Klyne R. "That Which Is Born from *PNEUMA* Is *PNEUMA*: Rebirth and Spirit in John 3:5–6." In Sloan and Parsons, *Perspectives on John*, 181–205.
Spencer, Patrick E. "Narrative Echoes in John 21: Intertextual Interpretation and Intratextual Connection." *JSNT* 75 (1999) 49–68.
Stagg, Frank. "The Farewell Discourses: John 13–17." *RE* 62 (1965) 459–72.
Staley, Jeffrey Lloyd. *The Print's First Kiss: A Rhetorical Investigation of the Implied Reader in the Fourth Gospel.* SBLDS 82. Atlanta: SBL, 1988.
———. *Reading with a Passion: Rhetoric, Autobiography, and the American West in the Gospel of John.* New York: Continuum, 1995.
———. "The Structure of John's Prologues: Its Implications for the Gospel's Narrative Structure." *CBQ* 48 (1986) 241–64.
Sternberg, Meir. *The Poetics of Biblical Narrative.* Bloomington: Indiana University Press, 1985.
Stibbe, Mark W. G., ed. *The Gospel of John as Literature: An Anthology of Twentieth-Century Perspectives.* Leiden: Brill, 1993.
———. *John as Storyteller: Narrative Criticism and the Fourth Gospel.* SNTSMS 73. Cambridge: Cambridge University Press, 1992.
———. "Magnificent but Flawed: The Breaking of Form in the Fourth Gospel." In Thatcher and Moore, *Anatomies of Narrative Criticism*, 149–65.
Stramara, Daniel F., Jr. "The Chiastic Key to the Identity of the Beloved Disciple." *SVTQ* 53 (2009) 5–27.
Stuart, Douglas K. *Old Testament Exegesis: An Handbook for Student and Pastors.* Philadelphia: Westminster John Knox, 2001.

Bibliography

Talbert, Charles H. "Artistry and Theology: An Analysis of the Architecture of Jn 1:19—5:47." *CBQ* 32 (1970) 341–66.

———. *Reading John: A Literary and Theological Commentary on the Fourth Gospel and the Johannine Epistles*. London: SPCK, 1992.

Teeple, Howard M. *The Literary Origin of the Gospel of John*. Evanston, IL: Religion and Ethics Institute, 1974.

Temple, Sydney. *The Core of the Fourth Gospel*. London: Mowbrays, 1975.

———. "The Two Signs in the Fourth Gospel." *JBL* 81 (1962) 169–74.

Thatcher, Tom. "Anatomies of the Fourth Gospel: Past, Present, and Future Probes." In Thatcher and Moore, *Anatomies of Narrative Criticism*, 1–35.

———. *The Riddles of Jesus in John: A Study in Tradition and Folklore*. Atlanta: SBL, 2000.

———, ed. *What We Have Heard from the Beginning: The Past, Present, and Future of Johannine Studies*. Waco, TX: Baylor University Press, 2007.

Thatcher, Tom, and Stephen D. Moore, eds. *Anatomies of Narrative Criticism: The Past, Present, and Futures of the Fourth Gospel as Literature*. Atlanta: SBL, 2008.

Thomson, Ian H. *Chiasmus in the Pauline Letters*. Sheffield, UK: Sheffield Academic, 1995.

Thyen, Hartwig. "Aus der Literatur zum Johannesevangelium." *TR* 44 (1979) 97–134.

Tolmie, D. F. *Jesus' Farewell to the Disciples: John 13:1—17:26 in Narratological Perspective*. Leiden: Brill, 1995.

Topel, L. John. "A Note on the Methodology of Structural Analysis in Jn 2:23—3:21." *CBQ* 33 (1971) 212–20.

Tovey, Derek. *Narrative Art and Act in the Fourth Gospel*. JSNTSS 151. Sheffield, UK: Sheffield Academic, 1997.

Trites, Allison A. "Woman Taken in Adultery." *BSac* 131 (1974) 137–46.

Turner, John D. "The History of Religions Background of John 10." In Beutler and Fortna, *The Shepherd Discourse of John 10 and Its Context*, 33–52.

Van Belle, Gilbert. "Repetitions and Variations in Johannine Research: A General Historical Survey." In van Belle et al., *Repetitions and Variations in the Fourth Gospel*, 33–85.

———. *The Signs Source in the Fourth Gospel: Historical Survey and Critical Evaluation of the Semeia Hypothesis*. Leuven: Leuven University Press, 1994.

———. "Theory of Repetitions and Variations in the Fourth Gospel: A Neglected Field of Research?" In van Belle et al., *Repetitions and Variations in the Fourth Gospel*, 13–32.

———. "Tradition, Exegetical Formation, and the Leuven Hypothesis." In Thatcher, *What We Have Heard from the Beginning*, 325–42.

Van Belle, Gilbert, et al., eds. *Repetitions and Variations in the Fourth Gospel: Style, Text, Interpretation*. Leuven: Peeters, 2009.

———. *The Signs Source in the Fourth Gospel: Historical Survey and Critical Evaluation of the Semeia Hypothesis*. Leuven: Leuven University Press, 1994.

Van der Watt, Jan G. "The Composition of the Prologue of John's Gospel: The Historical Jesus Introducing Divine Grace." *WTJ* 57 (1995) 311–32.

———. "Repetition and Functionality in the Gospel according to John: Some Initial Explorations." In van Belle et al., *Repetitions and Variations in the Fourth Gospel*, 87–108.

———. "Riddles, Repetitions, and the Literary Unity of the Johannine Discourses." In van Belle et al., *Repetitions and Variations in the Fourth Gospel*, 357–77.

Von Wahlde, Urban C. *The Gospel and Letters of John*. Vol. 2, *Commentary on the Gospel of John*. Grand Rapids: Eerdmans, 2010.

Voorwinde, Stephen. "John's Prologue beyond Some Impasses of Twentieth-Century Scholarship." *WTJ* 63 (2002) 15–44.

Watson, Wilfred G. E. *Traditional Techniques in Classical Hebrew Verse.* Sheffield, UK: Sheffield Academic, 1994.

Welch, John W. "Chiasmus in Ancient Greek and Latin Literatures." In Welch, *Chiasmus in Antiquity*, 250–68.

———, ed. *Chiasmus in Antiquity: Structures, Analyses, Exegesis.* Provo, UT: Research, 1999.

———. "Chiasmus in the New Testament." In *Chiasmus in Antiquity*, 211–49.

Wellhausen, Julius. *Das Evangelium Johannis.* Berlin: Reimer, 1994.

Whitacre, Rodney A. *John.* IVP New Testament Commentary 4. Downers Grove: InterVarsity, 1999.

Wilson, Jeffrey. "The Integrity of John 3:22–36." *JSNT* 10 (1981) 34–41.

Witherington, Ben, III. *John's Wisdom: A Commentary on the Fourth Gospel.* Louisville: Westminster John Knox, 1995.

Wolfe, K. R. "The Chiastic Structure of Luke-Acts and Some Implications for Worship." *SJT* 22 (1980) 60–71.

www.ingramcontent.com/pod-product-compliance
Lightning Source LLC
Chambersburg PA
CBHW080934300426
44115CB00017B/2816